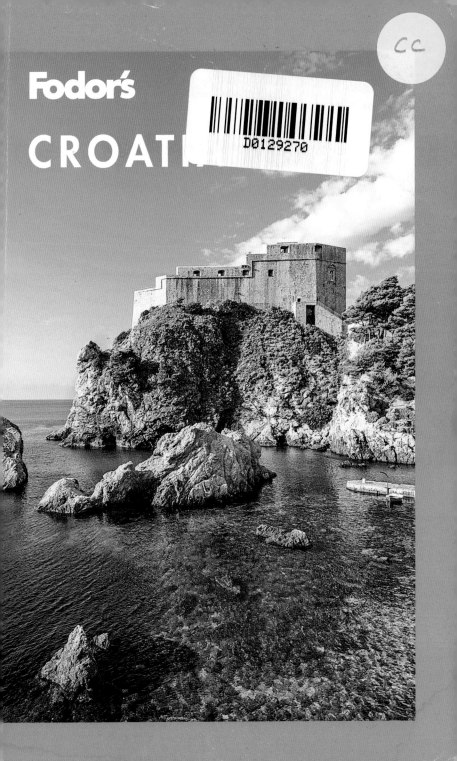

CC

Fodor's

CROATI

WELCOME TO CROATIA

Croatia's splendors extend from the deep-blue waters of the Adriatic coastline to the waterfall-laced mountains of the Dinaric Alps and throughout its medieval towns. From Dubrovnik's walled city where baroque buildings are surrounded by centuries-old forts to the lively islands of Brač and Hvar, this Central European country is an exciting blend of glamour and tradition. Croatia's vibrant, historic cities, sprawling vineyards, gorgeous beaches, and thousand-plus islands give travelers plenty of places to dance, sip wine, sail, and soak up the sunshine.

TOP REASONS TO GO

★ **History:** Dubrovnik's walled Old Town, Split's Diocletian palace.

★ **Cool Cities:** Zagreb's museums and café culture, Rovinj's old city charm.

★ **Beaches:** From secluded hideaways to oceanside party spots, each beach is unique.

★ **Natural Parks:** Plitvice Lakes, Brijuni Islands, Mljet.

★ **Wine:** From Istria to Korčula, vineyards and wineries abound.

★ **Sailing:** Southern Dalmatia's dramatic coastline is paradise for boating enthusiasts.

12

TOP EXPERIENCES

Croatia offers terrific experiences that should be on every traveler's list. Here are Fodor's top picks for a memorable trip.

1 Dubrovnik

Few sights in Croatia are as impressive or popular as this medieval wonder of a city. With its ancient walls and bell towers set high above the blue waters of the Adriatic, Dubrovnik commands a spectacular location. *(Ch. 8)*

2 Sailing

A coastline studded with stunning islands, emerald inlets, unspoiled beaches, and lively towns makes the country a paradise for avid boating enthusiasts. *(Ch. 1)*

3 Diocletian's Palace, Split

The city's main attraction, the Roman emperor Diocletian's summer palace, dates to the 3rd century AD. The walls of this spectacular site surround the old town. *(Ch. 7)*

4 Hvar Town

The seaside town of Hvar is the country's nightlife capital and a favorite destination of yachting revelers and nature enthusiasts alike. *(Ch. 7)*

5 Seafood

Croatians believe in simple yet high-quality cooking. Many restaurants serve delicious fresh seafood, and sometimes you can pick a fish to be cooked right off the platter. *(Ch. 7)*

6 National Parks

Parks protect some of Croatia's abundant natural wonders. Plitvice National Park, one of the most spectacular, has 16 magnificent lakes connected by cascades. *(Ch. 2)*

7 Museums in Zagreb

Two of the country's best museums are in Zagreb, the charming capital set in the interior: the Museum of Contemporary Art and the Museum of Broken Relationships. *(Ch. 2)*

8 Wine

Vineyards produce excellent wines, many from Istrian villages like Motovun. Sometimes touted as "the new Tuscany," Istria is known for its white Malvazija and red Teran. *(Ch. 4)*

9 Café Culture

Coffee drinking is a favorite national pastime. Do it the local way: linger at a café, unwind, and make that cappuccino or espresso last for at least an hour. *(Ch. 2)*

10 Beaches

Lovely beaches abound in Croatia, but Zlatni Rat, a spit of land on Brač Island, is particularly stunning with its white sand, lush pine groves, and intensely blue water. *(Ch. 7)*

11 Biking

Exploring towns and the countryside by bike is both fun and smart. Village streets aren't always easy to navigate on foot, and rural roads have scenic views. *(Ch. 4)*

12 Picturesque towns

It's hard to imagine a city with a more romantic and relaxing setting than quaint Rovinj, with its gentle sea breezes, limestone alleys, and colorful architecture. *(Ch. 4)*

CONTENTS

1 **EXPERIENCE CROATIA** 13
   What's Where 14
   Croatia Today 16
   Quintessential Croatia 18
   When to Go 20
   If You Like. 21
   Great Itineraries. 24
   On The Calendar 28
   Kids And Families 30
   Top 10 Croatian Foods to Try 31
   Wine in Croatia 33
   Sailing and Cruising in Croatia. . . .37

2 **ZAGREB AND ENVIRONS** 41
   Orientation and Planning 42
   Zagreb. 49
   Excursions North of Zagreb 68
   Excursions South of Zagreb 81
   Excursions in Lonjsko Polje 87

3 **SLAVONIA**. 89
   Orientation and Planning 91
   Osijek 94
   Kopački Rit Nature Park 103
   Vukovar 106
   Ilok 110
   Đakovo 112
   Požega 114

4 **ISTRIA**. 119
   Orientation and Planning 121
   Pula 128
   Vodnjan 135
   Nacionalni Park Brijuni. 136
   Rovinj 138
   Poreč. 145
   Novigrad 150
   Umag 153
   Motovun. 155

   Grožnjan. 157
   Eastern Istria: Labin and Rabac. . .158

5 **KVARNER** 161
   Rijeka 168
   Risnjak National Park. 177
   Opatija. 177
   Cres 181
   Lošinj 184
   Krk 189
   Delnice 195
   Rab. 196

6 **ZADAR AND NORTHERN
   DALMATIA**. 201
   Orientation and Planning 203
   Zadar. 208
   Nin 218
   Sali and Telaščica Nature Park . . .221
   Murter and the Kornati Islands. . .223
   Paklenica National Park 226
   Pag Island 228

7 **SPLIT AND CENTRAL
   DALMATIA**. 233
   Orientation and Planning 235
   Split 242
   Šibenik. 256
   Prvić 257
   Krka National Park 258
   Trogir. 261
   Omiš and the Cetina Valley. 263
   Brač 265
   Hvar 269
   Vis 276
   Makarska 278
   Lastovo 281

8 **DUBROVNIK AND SOUTHERN
   DALMATIA**. 283

CONTENTS

Orientation and Planning 285
Dubrovnik. 290
Lopud 308
Cavtat 309
Trsteno. 312
Ston 313
Orebić 314
Korčula 317
Mljet 322
9 MONTENEGRO 325
Orientation and Planning 327
Kotor. 331
Perast 338
Sveti Stefan. 341

UNDERSTANDING CROATIA . 343
A Short History of Croatia. 344
Croatian Vocabulary 350

TRAVEL SMART CROATIA. . . . 353

INDEX. 370

ABOUT OUR WRITERS. 384

MAPS

Zagreb. 52–53
Excursions from Zagreb 69
Slavonia. 95
Osijek 97
Istria 124
Pula 129
Rovinj 139
Kvarner 168
Rijeka 170
Krk 190
Rab. 197
Northern Dalmatia 205
Zadar. 210
Split and Central Dalmatia 236
Split 244
Hvar 271
Dubrovnik and Southern
Dalmatia 285
Dubrovnik. 294–295
Korcula 317
Montenegro. 328
Kotor Old Town 333

ABOUT THIS GUIDE

Fodor's Recommendations

Everything in this guide is worth doing—we don't cover what isn't—but exceptional sights, hotels, and restaurants are recognized with additional accolades. Fodor'sChoice★ indicates our top recommendations. Care to nominate a new place? Visit Fodors.com/contact-us.

Trip Costs

We list prices wherever possible to help you budget well. Hotel and restaurant price categories from $ to $$$$ are noted alongside each recommendation. For hotels, we include the lowest cost of a standard double room in high season. For restaurants, we cite the average price of a main course at dinner or, if dinner isn't served, at lunch. For attractions, we always list adult admission fees; discounts are usually available for children, students, and senior citizens.

Hotels

Our local writers vet every hotel to recommend the best overnights in each price category, from budget to expensive. Unless otherwise specified, you can expect private bath, phone, and TV in your room. Hotel reviews have been shortened. For full information, visit Fodors.com.

Top Picks	Hotels & Restaurants
★ Fodor'sChoice	🏨 Hotel
Listings	⇥ Number of rooms
✉ Address	¶◯¶ Meal plans
✉ Branch address	✗ Restaurant
☎ Telephone	⚓ Reservations
🖶 Fax	🏛 Dress code
⊕ Website	▭ No credit cards
✎ E-mail	$ Price
🎫 Admission fee	**Other**
⊙ Open/closed times	⇨ See also
Ⓜ Subway	☞ Take note
⊹ Directions or Map coordinates	🏌 Golf facilities

Restaurants

Unless we state otherwise, restaurants are open for lunch and dinner daily. We mention dress code only when there's a specific requirement and reservations only when they're essential or not accepted. To make restaurant reservations, visit Fodors.com.

Credit Cards

The hotels and restaurants in this guide typically accept credit cards. If not, we'll say so.

EUGENE FODOR

Hungarian-born Eugene Fodor (1905–91) began his travel career as an interpreter on a French cruise ship. The experience inspired him to write *On the Continent* (1936), the first guidebook to receive annual updates and discuss a country's way of life as well as its sights. Fodor later joined the U.S. Army and worked for the OSS in World War II. After the war, he kept up his intelligence work while expanding his guidebook series. During the Cold War, many guides were written by fellow agents who understood the value of insider information. Today's guides continue Fodor's legacy by providing travelers with timely coverage, insider tips, and cultural context.

EXPERIENCE
CROATIA

WHAT'S WHERE

The following numbers refer to chapters.

2 Zagreb. Croatia's interior capital is a charming, well-kept city that evokes a distant Habsburg past and features a pretty Upper Town. That said, Zagreb falls significantly short of Vienna or Prague in terms of stature and architecture. Good roads lead to the coast: Plitvice National Park—a spectacular series of 16 cascading lakes nestled in a wild forest—is about halfway to Zadar.

3 Slavonia. The least-visited part of Croatia offers charming villages and quiet rural life. Come if you want to get away from the hordes of tourists and experience the road less traveled.

4 Istria. The distinct Roman and Venetian influences blend into a vibrant café scene and authentic culinary delights. Croatia's western peninsula is well situated, with the western coast as the highlight and beautiful hilltops and vineyards inland.

5 Kvarner. Protected by mountain ranges on three sides, Kvarner enjoys a particularly mild climate. Opatija, the best-known destination, offers a whiff of the faded aristocratic grandeur of the Habsburgs and acts as a portal to the postindustrial

Rijeka and the green Kvarner islands.

6 Northern Dalmatia.
Zadar doesn't rival Split or Dubrovnik for ancient ruins, but it is surrounded by interesting places to see and offers good museums and the impressive Church of St. Donatus to boot.

7 Split and Central Dalmatia. Split boasts good transport connections and its main attraction: the Diocletian's palace, which dominates the Old Town. You're also in a great position to set out island-hopping, be it to Vis, Brač, or Hvar, a haven for partiers and yachting revelers.

8 Southern Dalmatia. Few cities in the world impress as Dubrovnik does, with its ancient walls and towers perched above the deep blue waters of the Adriatic. If you need to escape, strike out for Korčula, Marco Polo's birthplace, or the quiet Mljet Island.

9 Montenegro. An independent country since 2006, tiny Montenegro lies on the Adriatic coast and is bordered by Croatia, Bosnia-Herzegovina, Serbia, Kosovo, and Albania. Although its name means "black mountain," the main draw is its beautiful coastline.

CROATIA TODAY

As little as 20 years ago, it was not uncommon to hear the newly independent republic of Croatia mistaken for other formerly socialist republics, its position on the map by and large unknown to most people. Having been a part of two Yugoslav federations and the Austro-Hungarian Empire before that, Croatia had to start from scratch in terms of international recognition as a tourist destination.

The road that Croatia has traveled in two decades is remarkable. Today, at the mention of Croatia, people from California to New Zealand readily respond with the line "I hear it's beautiful there." And it is. Hands-down, of all countries on the European side of the Mediterranean, Croatia offers the most wonderful nature with the least amount of tourist fanfare and, arguably, with the lowest price tags. Apart from central Europeans, who have known about the beauties of Croatia for many years and even kept visiting during the civil war of the 1990s, the country is now on the radar of North Americans, South Americans, Asians, and even Australians as the must-see European destination.

From Communism to Elitism

The stunning coast was always there. Different rulers treated it differently, and to this date it is clearly visible on the architecture, ranging from Roman, via Venetian and Napoleonic, to Habsburg and finally communist. The last era left the biggest impression, embodied in big cement squares on the coast—the numerous hotels built in the 1960s and '70s for the rest and recuperation of the Yugoslav working class. Yugoslavia came to its end, but the buildings remained. In the 1990s many of them housed refuges from the war, which dilapidated hotels and, in addition to tarnishing Croatia's image, pushed its tourism decades back.

It really took surprisingly little for the country to rebound, attract investors, and completely remodel the old-style hotels, which still may be a bit of an eyesore on the outside, but offer all of the amenities one can look for in travel destinations. The older hotels, most of them from the Habsburg times, as well as the ones built after Croatia's independence, generally verge on high-end tourist offers, which hardly fall short of their Italian and Greek counterparts. In a short time, Croatia has stepped up and entered the ring with the European tourism heavyweights.

EU and Economic Woes

Unlike tourism, which has been on the steady rise, the rest of the country's economy has had two very rough decades and looks toward the future with an uncertain eye. The transition period from communism to capitalism was marked by nontransparency and controversy on the highest levels, leaving the young country industrially handicapped as it entered the third millennium. Consequently, more focus was placed on developing tourism as an industry, a move that has proven successful, particularly in the stunning coastal region, but still not satisfying the question of long-term economic stability.

The long-awaited accession into the European Union on July 1, 2013, was not welcomed without cynicism considering the multitude of problems the EU had been facing. Still, some optimism reigned regarding the easier movement of capital and resources, but not much seems to have changed for the better, financially or socially, at this writing.

Safe and Sporty

Despite its standards not being on par with Western Europe, Croatia is still a remarkably safe country with one of the lowest violent crime rates in Europe. The social frustration is much more felt on the roads, with some Croatian drivers choosing to obey few rules or even common sense. Even experienced drivers should be cautious while navigating the narrow local roads as many local drivers always seem to be in a hurry and angry about something.

The one place where there is little anger, however, is undoubtedly in the domain of sports. Croatians are very passionate about sports and, for a country of 4.8 million, extremely successful, too. If visiting during a major international competition like the Olympic Games or the World Cup, you will have a chance to spend your evening at one of the many cafés where locals and tourists gather to watch games and share in the excitement. The game, mind you, is just the beginning of the night: a fruitful platform for recollections of times and successes past.

In Tune

If there is one thing that a visitor to Croatia should not miss in the summer months, that would be a concert or a music festival. From house to Wagner, from pop to jazz, Zagreb and the coast have it all covered. There are big music festivals and concerts that attract thousands of Croatians and foreigners alike, but there are also countless small-scale gigs and concertos that resound with the Croatians' appreciation of eclectic music, as well as its commercial value.

The thriving music scene partly compensates for the mostly uninspiring theatrical events and fine arts exhibitions, of which there is ample quantity but considerably less quality. Bigger cities like Zagreb, Split, or Dubrovnik will occasionally host memorable international events, but do not expect to just walk into one. On the other hand, visitors will find a satisfactory number of film festivals in Croatia, most of them carrying an interesting blend of nonmainstream international films.

The New Generation

Few differences are as apparent as the schism in customer service and attitude between the generation that grew up under communist Yugoslavia and the younger generation that has been much more exposed to western influences and education. Perhaps the most pragmatic difference is of linguistic nature: older people will be more likely to speak German, Italian, or even Russian, while younger ones inexorably lean toward English, which they speak very well. The former group will also be more prone to lament about the way things used to be, whereas the latter group has their eye on the ball and will go out of their way to help.

Having said that, it must be added that customer service is not universally understood around Croatia and that there are still places, especially in Dalmatia, where you will wait for 10 or more minutes before the waiter walks over or where your hosts will feel inclined to share their views of U.S. politics without having been asked to do so. Thankfully, such instances are few and far between, but if they do occur, try to smile and not let the unpleasantness affect the amazing holiday that Croatia can offer.

QUINTESSENTIAL CROATIA

Dalmatian Summer

Although most Zagreb residents go to Kvarner, for many Croatians summer holidays mean Dalmatia. Every family has its favorite spot on the coast and people remember their blissful childhood holidays in Dalmatia with the most detailed accuracy. Tales of Dingač or Plavac wine, *paski sir* (sheep cheese from the island of Pag), and fresh sea bass enjoyed in a simple seaside restaurant feature heavily in the national memory. Whether a holiday means a wooded campsite in a national park, a sandy beach on Brač, or a small pension on Losinj, summer holidays begin and end for Croatians on their own splendid coast. Roads, accommodations, and ferry travel along the coast have improved over the years, turning Dalmatia into an international tourist destination. After you've relaxed for a week or more, soaking up the sun Dalmatian-style, you'll ask the same question the Croatians do: Why go anywhere else?

Rakija

Get one or two Croatians together, and somebody's bound to introduce rakija, a distilled herbal or fruit spirit that makes up an important part of Croatian culture. All across the country business deals are sealed, friendships are cemented, and journeys are begun to the clink of a few shot glasses of the fiery schnapps. Croatians often brew rakija themselves at home, using everything from plums and pears to herbs and juniper berries. In the countryside you can often find roadside stands selling the family blend with pride. Rakija is also enjoyed in Slovenia, where it often begins a meal as an aperitif. If you're game to order one on your travels in the region, start first with the sweeter, fruitier brews (blueberry is a good choice), and then work your way up to the somewhat digestive herbals.

If you want to get a sense of contemporary Croatian culture, and indulge in some of its pleasures, start by familiarizing yourself with the rituals of daily life. These are a few highlights—things you can take part in with relative ease.

Naturism

Like it or not, there's a long history of naturism in Croatia, and this country has been one of the most progressive in pioneering the nude resort. Naturist campsites, beaches, and even sailing charters abound in certain parts of the coast (mainly Istria), and hundreds of thousands flock here each year to enjoy some fun in the sun *au naturel*. Naturism in Croatia goes back before World War II, when a leading Viennese naturist developed a beach on the island of Rab. Since then, a thriving culture of naturism has taken root, mainly among European enthusiasts. A glossy brochure published by the Croatian National Tourist Board lists 14 naturist "camps" and "villages" and about as many officially designated "free naturist beaches" on the country's Adriatic coast. Croatians themselves don't seem to make up the bulk of the clientele at naturist resorts, but they graciously make visitors welcome.

Face to face

Generally speaking, Croatians make for good hosts that are eager to help and show you around. In fact, this might hold particularly true of those people who do not actively work in tourism, but are happy to be asked a question, dust off their English and share their opinions of the places you should see (many of which aren't listed in any guide book). Therefore, feel free to give your smartphone a day off and ask for directions the old fashioned way. There is just one thing, though: much like cars, streets and houses, personal space is significantly smaller in Croatia than it is the United States. Croatian collocutors will stand a mere foot from each other as they communicate, often giving out the impression that they are all discussing matters of utmost delicacy. Therefore, it may seem like passers-by crave a little too much intimacy, but do not be taken aback - it's merely the local communication culture.

WHEN TO GO

The tourist season in Croatia generally runs from April through October, peaking in July and August. The Dalmatian coast is busy all summer long. Early booking is essential in July and August, when most of the summer festivals take place. Roads back from the coast are clogged with returning European tourists on late summer weekends. Spring and fall can be the best times to visit, when the heat has abated somewhat at the coast and the days are long.

Climate

Croatia enjoys a long, hot summer that's usually dry. Southern Dalmatia can still be mild in October, when the first cold snap has already hit in the interior, although swimming then may be only for the brave. Wet winters are the norm for most of the country, making a trip here in January or February somewhat rainy and cold. Winters on the coast are milder but still wet. Kvarner, sheltered on three sides by mountain ranges, has a short, temperate winter and an early spring. It remains mild throughout the summer.

The following graphs show the average daily maximum and minimum temperatures for major cities in the region.

IF YOU LIKE

Pleasures at Sea

Croatia offers prime opportunities to spend time by the clear blue waters of the Adriatic. Each of these unique pleasures is designed to highlight the mysteries of life by the sea. This list of favorites makes for unforgettable vacation memories.

Hvar Town, Central Dalmatia. A favorite destination among the yachting fraternity, Hvar remains completely at ease with its age-old beauty: medieval stone houses are built around a natural harbor and backed by a hilltop fortress. Hvar is also renowned as the nightlife capital of Southern Dalmatia.

Strolling around Rovinj's old city, Istria. It's hard to imagine a more romantic and relaxed setting: the warm sea breezes invigorate as you tread the limestone alleys surrounded by the captivating Venetian architecture.

Zlatni Rat, Bol, Central Dalmatia. The spectacular beach on the island of Brač is the jewel of the Adriatic: white, with very fine pebbles, and lapped on three sides by the gentle blue sea.

A walk on the Lungomare in Opatija, Kvarner. Built in 1889, this 12-km (7½-mile) promenade along the sea leads from the quaint, artsy borough of Volosko, through Opatija—passing in front of old hotels, parks, marinas, and sumptuous villas—and all the way past the villages of Ičići and Ika to Lovran in the south.

An excursion to Mljet, Southern Dalmatia. A long, thin island of steep, rocky slopes and dense pine forests, Mljet is one of Croatia's most beautiful islands. One of Croatia's few sand beaches, Saplunara, is at its southeastern tip, which remains relatively wild and untended.

Soft Adventure

National parks abound in Croatia, with surefire opportunities to commune with the great outdoors. In every season there are peaks to climb, seas to dive in, and white-water rivers to conquer. Here are some of our favorite spots for those seeking a bit of soft adventure.

Rafting on the Neretva River, Southern Dalmatia. A rush of adrenaline strikes you as you make your way through the lush valley in a raft or a on a paddleboard.

Diving in Kvarner Bay. Diving in the crystal clear waters of Kvarner Bay—particularly near the islands of Cres and Losinj—is an eye-opening experience. Just remember that the most thrilling sights below the waves are usually wrecks.

Cliff Climbing at Paklenica National Park, Northern Dalmatia. Velebit Mountain, Croatia's largest massif, yields the way to the Adriatic swiftly and steeply at Paklenica, creating a cliff-climbing paradise that attracts thousands of Europeans every year.

Roman History

The cultural and historical richness of Croatia make it a destination that satisfies even the most well-traveled visitor. All over the country there are ruins of former civilizations and empires that give you a glimpse of the country's past. A trip to this list of favorites will enrich any vacation to Croatia.

Diocletian's Palace, Split. Roman Emperor Diocletian's summer palace, built in the 3rd century AD, is one of the most spectacular sites in all of Croatia. It's unmissable.

The Arena, Pula. Designed to accommodate 22,000 spectators, the Arena is the sixth-largest amphitheater in the world

(after the Colosseum in Rome and similar arenas in Verona, Catania, Capua, and Arles), and one of the best preserved.

Crkva sv Donata, Zadar. Zadar's star attraction, this huge, cylindrical structure is the most monumental early Byzantine church in Croatia.

Eufrazijeva Basilica (St. Euphrasius Basilica), Poreč. This is among the most perfectly preserved Christian churches in Europe, and one of the most important monuments of Byzantine art on the Adriatic.

Katedrala Sveti Lovrijenac (Cathedral of St. Lawrence), Trogir. A perfect example of the massiveness and power of Romanesque architecture, the most striking detail is the main portal, decorated with minutely carved stonework during the 13th century.

Summer Nightlife

Seaside nightlife in Croatia generally doesn't disappoint. All over the coast people are enjoying themselves outside most evenings, sipping trendy cocktails, listening to music, or tasting the local wine. Even the smallest village on the coast is littered with outdoor cafés and bars in the summertime. If you find yourself near any of these, join in the fun!

Dubrovnik Summer Festival, Southern Dalmatia. The world-renowned summer festival in Dubrovnik offers quality theatrical performances and classical-music concerts with international performers, all set against the backdrop of the azure Adriatic.

Aquarius, Zagreb. Having climbed out of its postwar depression, Zagreb is once again alive at night. Aquarius is the top spot for dancing until dawn—in the summer and all year-round.

Carpe Diem, Hvar, Central Dalmatia. A harbor-side cocktail bar with a summer terrace is where Hvar's richest and most glamorous visitors come to see and be seen.

Byblos, Poreč, Istria. Situated in a former factory near the sea, Byblos has successfully attracted a blend of young and trendy partygoers for a decade. Many Italians flock over the border for a night here and tourists from all over join in.

Imperium, Split, Central Dalmatia. With the opening of Imperium located near the ferry harbor, Split valiantly returned to the nightlife map of Croatia. The place is packed during the summer and often stays open until 7 am.

Going Native

You can find gustatory pleasures at every level in Croatia. Sometimes the ones to seek out are the favorites of the locals, who don't allow restaurants to rest on their laurels. Whether it's a snack at a market stall or a simple seaside restaurant, one of the great pleasures of travel is finding these popular spots. All of these are favorites for their commitment to local, seasonal food.

Slavonska Kuća, Osijek, Slavonia. This small, local restaurant is about as atmospheric as can be. If you stick to the local specialties, you'll enjoy a fine introduction to Slavonian cuisine.

Konoba kod Sipe, Sali, Northern Dalmatia. This rustic favorite is known for serving some of the freshest fish dishes in town. Fishnets hanging from the ceiling's wooden beams plus an outdoor terrace shaded by grapevines add to the homey atmosphere.

Sirius, Losinj, Kvarner. The national press claim that this would be a top contender for best restaurant in the country if it were

open year-round, so deserved is its reputation for fresh seafood.

Vodnjanka Restaurant, Vodnjan, Istria. This is the place to go for the most mouthwatering homemade pasta dishes you can imagine, not least *fuži* with wild arugula and prosciutto in cream sauce—delicious.

Wining and Dining

A vacation wouldn't be a vacation if you didn't seek out some of the country's finest dining. All of the following have built their reputation on first-rate cuisine and an impressive wine list to match.

Adio Mare, Korčula, Southern Dalmatia. The menu at this renowned eatery hasn't changed since it opened in 1974: traditional Dalmatian seafood and Balkan meat specialties, prepared over burning coals. Dinner here is unforgettable.

Monte, Rovinj, Istria. An elegant Italian restaurant just below St. Euphemia's offers an excellent repast and quiet surroundings in which to enjoy a long afternoon's lunch.

Katunar, Krk Town, Vrbnik, Kvarner. The wines produced on Krk Island are among the best in Croatia. The torch-lit grill is the place for dinner, but the experience is all about the wine.

Valsabbion, Pula, Istria. This superb restaurant was one of the first in Croatia to specialize in what has come to be known as "slow food," and has been voted the best restaurant in Istria as well as Croatia several times. The menu changes regularly, but you can expect such delights as frogfish in vine leaves or tagliatelle with aromatic herbs and pine nuts.

Agava, Zagreb. The Italian-inspired menu of this central, swanky restaurant includes dishes such as tagliatelle with prosciutto and asparagus, crispy roast duck on red cabbage with figs, and oven-roasted monkfish with bread crumbs, pine nuts, and thyme.

Natural Wonders

Croatia is not short on natural wonders. The unusual karst terrain of its western region has created caves and waterfalls and made a home for many species of wildlife. Many of the region's best natural areas are now protected as national parks that are accessible throughout the year.

Nacionalni Park Plitvička Jezera, Zagreb and Environs. One of the first-class natural areas in Croatia, this national park has 16 cascading lakes nestled in a protected forest.

Kornati National Park, Zadar, Northern Dalmatia. More than 100 remote islands here are privately owned. Although anything but lush today, their almost mythical beauty is ironically synonymous with their barrenness: the bone-white-to-ochre colors present a striking contrast to the azure sea.

Brijuni Archipelago, Istria. Designated a national park in 1983, this group of 14 islands north of Pula has been a vacation retreat par excellence for almost 2,000 years. Yugoslav leader Marshal Josip Broz Tito brought famous guests here from the world over. Today, you can come, too.

GREAT ITINERARIES

ZAGREB, ISTRIA, AND KVARNER

Zagreb makes an excellent starting point if your trip is meant to cover western Croatia in a week. You'll get the mountains and the seaside, city and countryside, and a first-class Roman ruin. This itinerary is best done by car, but it can be done (perhaps a bit more slowly) by train and bus.

Day 1: Zagreb

Zagreb can best be explored on foot. Begin at the massive Trg Bana Jelačića and check out the statue of Ban Josip Jelačić, hero of Croatian resistance to the Austro-Hungarian empire. It's an imposing figure on an imposing square. From here walk to the funicular and head to the Gornji Grad (Upper Town). Stroll around the castle area and visit the Croatian Historical Museum. You'll get a glimpse of Croatia's recent history, including the controversial nationalism of the 1990s. From here, head back down to the Lower Town and check out Ilica, Zagreb's modern high street. Spend the night here.

Day 2: Plitvice Lakes

The next morning head south toward the coast, getting off the highway in Karlovac in the direction of Plitvice National Park. Plitvice is a naturally occurring water world, with cascading pools and waterfalls connecting each other. This is one of Croatia's biggest tourist sites and has been for years, so the park is well protected and organized. Consider getting a map and exploring the lakes, which cover about 300 square km (186½ square miles) on your own. The park is well marked, but the guided tours only take you to the highlights. Relax in the evening when the tour buses have gone home and spend the night here at a nearby hotel.

TIPS

■ This itinerary is well served by bus, although that may take more time than driving yourself.

■ The main highway connecting Zagreb to Istria, the A6, is well-maintained and offers beautiful views of Gorski Kotar. Toll can be paid in cash or by card.

■ Since Plitvice is on the main highway from Zagreb to Zadar, consider seeing the park on a weekday, when traffic is lighter.

■ The closest ferry crossing from Opatija to Cres and Lošinj is at Brestova in Istria. If you plan to take your car in the height of summer, count on a wait. In winter it is much less crowded.

Day 3: Rab Island

Drive to Rab Island from Plitvice, descending down the Velebit Mountain to the eastern Kvarner coast and catching a ferry to Rab, one of the bay's most beautiful islands. Once there, take in the sights of the medieval stone town of Rab, renowned for its history, coast, and Mediterranean herbs. Also take the opportunity to visit one of Croatia's top wineries, where you can also spend the night. If you still have the energy, take a ferry from Rab to the island of Krk and enjoy the cliff-top town of Valbiska, home of the *žlahtina* white wine.

Day 4: Rijeka and Opatija

Take the ferry from Rab or the bridge from Krk and head out to Opatija, briefly stopping in the city of Rijeka for a stroll down the pedestrian zone Korzo. Once you see the palm trees lining the streets of Opatija, you'll see this is a place for winding down, Habsburg-style. Choose one of the atmospheric, turn-of-the-century hotels for a little slice of nostalgia and settle in with a good book. Should you visit in winter, you'll find the weather downright Mediterranean. Take time to stroll along a part of the 12-km-long (7½-mile-long) promenade that zigzags along the sea. If you get antsy for more seaside diversity, plan instead to leave Opatija and catch the Istrian side ferry to the islands of Cres of Lošinj. The islands—with their attractive Venetian town squares—have a different character altogether.

Day 5: Pula

From Opatija or Lošinj head south or west, respectively, to Pula and spend a part of the day exploring the incredible Roman amphitheater. This is one of the best-preserved sites in the Roman world. After walking about the Roman forum and amphitheater, as well as Napoleon's fortress on the top of the hill, take a boat to the Brijuni Islands for the afternoon and see the zoo and tropical gardens that Tito designed. Drive the short distance to Rovinj for the night.

Day 6: Rovinj and Poreč

Wake up to the beautiful limestone architecture of Rovinj before exploring the Venetian houses and Church of St. Euphemia in the morning. From there, stop off at one of the many fine wineries en route to Poreč, another Roman-meets-Venetian-meets-Habsburg seaside gem. Check out the St. Euphrasius basilica, one of the most important remnants of Byzantine art on the Adriatic. Spend the night at one of the many fine hotels.

Day 7: Motovun and Zagreb

Head back to Zagreb via the Istrian interior. Drive east toward Pazin, stopping in the medieval hill towns of Motovun or Grožnjan for lunch and breathtaking views. These medieval villages are in the heart of truffle country, so keep your eyes open for some fresh goods to bring home. Continue northeast toward Zagreb on A6, possibly stopping at the mountain town of Fužine for the famous cherry strudel with views of Lake Bajer.

CENTRAL AND NORTHERN DALMATIA

Well-connected to the rest of the country, Central and Northern Dalmatia have a lot to offer, even beyond the staple cities of Split and Zadar. Plan for a combination of car and boat travel, and try to schedule the car trips on weekdays. The roads can get busy during weekends, peaking on Saturdays, especially if you get on the A1 highway. Avoid taking the car to the islands to circumvent both intimidating ferry lines and scarily narrow island roads. Both Split and Zadar have international airports, so you can start this itinerary from either one.

Day 1: Split

Arrive in Split and head to a hotel (which you booked months ago) or take one of the many private rooms available around town. Spend this first day getting your bearings and exploring the Meštrović Gallery and the Archaeological Museum, two of the city's best museums, before dedicating at least half a day to the Diocletian's Palace. Sit in the open peristyle and admire the imperial quarters, the Cathedral of St. Domnius, and the Egyptian black sphinx before supper and a good night's sleep.

Days 2 and 3: Island Hopping

Take one of the ferries or catamarans from Split to Brač, Hvar, or Vis, and spend the night in an island paradise. This is the heart of Dalmatia, after all, and these islands are the stuff of glossy tourist brochures. Book your accommodations in advance, or try to book a private room through an agency in Split. In summer, ferries, hydrofoils, and catamarans operate regularly to the islands. Rent a bike or scooter once you've landed and tour the back roads where you can find uncrowded coves and beaches. Remember, Hvar also boasts some of the finest Dalmatian wineries, not to mention the glitzy nightlife.

Day 4: Kornati National Park

Take a ferry back to Split and from there make your way down the stunning coastline to Vodice, stopping off at Primošten and Šibenik for sights and food along the way. At Vodice, board one of the many boats heading out for day trips to Kornati islands, a bare and beautiful archipelago that has been attracting mariners for centuries. If possible, take a boat that will drop you off at Zadar on the way back. Alternatively, drive from Vodice to Zadar to spend the night.

Days 5 and 6: Zadar and Paklenica National Park

Zadar has fast emerged into one of the top Croatian tourist destinations and not without a reason. The beautiful peninsula on which the medieval city center was built hides many remarkable architectural, cultural, and gastronomic feats. Be sure to visit the St. Donatus church and check out the sea organ and the Greeting to Sun. Take a drive or a bus to neighboring Nin and see the former seat of the Dalmatian royal family as well as a quaint little salt museum.

TIPS

■ Don't take a car to the islands. Ferry reservations for cars must be made well in advance, and you won't need one once you arrive.

■ As you get closer to Velebit Mountain, expect the chances of summer showers to grow, so bring an umbrella or, better, a waterproof jacket.

■ When going to Paklenica NP, it is a good idea to have an umbrella or, better yet, a waterproof jacket.

The following day, adventure out to NP Paklenica, an imposing canyon in Velebit Mountain. This rugged limestone offers some great hiking and the ultimate challenge for cliff climbers. Also check-out the old A-bomb shelter that Marshal Tito had built in the 1950s in case Stalin got a little too aggressive.

Day 7: Krka National Park, Trogir, and Split

Head back toward Split and stop along the way at Krka NP. This river's estuary challenges Plitvice Lakes for cascading water and amazing turquoise waterfalls. Be sure to wear at least sneakers and, in the summer months, a bathing suit as it is hard to say no to the lure of this pristine river. From there it is an easy drive to Split via Trogir and its UNESCO heritage cathedral.

DUBROVNIK, SOUTHERN DALMATIA, AND MONTENEGRO

Dubrovnik has an international airport that is well-connected to all European hubs during the summer season. It is extremely popular in the summer, so be warned: you won't be sightseeing by yourself in August. Try to start your weeklong trip on a weekday (Monday to Monday, for example) instead of the weekend, so that your weekends are spent on a quiet island instead of in bustling Budva or Dubrovnik.

Days 1 and 2: Dubrovnik

If arriving by sea or air, you'll see one of the prettiest fortified cities in the world and you are very likely to immediately fall in love with it. From this view, you can tell why Dubrovnik (formerly Ragusa) was once master of all of Dalmatia. Choose a hotel slightly outside the city walls, as the crowds flock there daily in high season. Have lunch in one of the many fish restaurants near the fish market and enjoy some Dalmatian wine. Save the sightseeing for the late afternoon, when the cruise-ship day-trippers have departed. Stroll along the *placa* in the early evening with the locals, stopping along the way for some Italian-style ice cream.

Day 3: Pelješac and Korčula

Pelješac peninsula is home to Croatia's best red wine growing region, Dingač. Do not miss the opportunity to travel down the windy roads via Mali Ston (renowned for its oysters) and stopping off at the family-owned wineries producing varietals like Plavac Mali or Pošip. At the town of Orebić catch a short ferry ride to Korčula, another jaw-droppingly gorgeous town fortified with bright limestone city walls. Check out the local dance Moreška and have fish overlooking hundreds of windsurfers taking advantage of the *maestral* wind in the Pelješki channel. Either spend a night at a local hotel or apartment or head back to Dubrovnik to your hotel.

TIPS

■ Don't take a car to Korčula. Ferry reservations for cars must be made well in advance. Once you're there, it's easy enough to get around by bus or rented scooter.

■ Be wary of *soba* (room) offers. Although many are legitimate, there are unscrupulous vendors out there hard at work in high season. And always have a map ready to mark the location to make sure you aren't out in the sticks.

Days 4, 5, and 6: Montenegro

Travel by bus or hire a car from Dubrovnik down the coast to the sparkling Bay of Kotor. See the Roman mosaics at Risan and the tiny islands of Perast, and stay at a boutique hotel in one of the charming fishing villages on the bay such as Perast or Dobrota. Continue to the UNESCO World Heritage Site town of Kotor and explore its churches, markets, and city walls, then have lunch in one of the marble piazzas. Take the road heading inland that emerges at the sea's edge not far from Budva and a stretch of coast where you can treat yourself to some excellent seafood and a day on the beach. Make sure to see the stunning yet exclusive Sveti Stefan hotel, the jewel of the Montenegrin coastline.

Day 7: Cavtat

Day 7 will most likely be a travel day, no matter if you travel by car, plane, or ferry. Have one last seafood lunch at the town Cavtat, taking the time to visit the mausoleum by Croatia's prime sculptor Ivan Meštović, buy a bottle of Dalmatian wine to take home, and vow to come back next year.

ON THE
CALENDAR

	For exact dates and further information about events in Croatia, check the Croatian National Tourist Board website (⇨ *www.croatia.hr*).
WINTER	
February	Rijeka stages its own **Karneval,** giving Croatia the second-biggest Carnival celebration in Europe after Venice. It also provides Croatia some fiery action in the otherwise bleak and rainy month of February.
SPRING	
April	In alternate years Zagreb, Croatia's capital, hosts a **Biennale,** an international festival of contemporary music. It's attended by the heavy hitters of the classical world as well as groundbreaking pioneers.
SUMMER	
June	**Lavender Festival** on the island of Hvar takes place toward the end of June and features the best that this polyvalent herb has to offer. From oils and ornaments to cakes and lavender bread, this is a sure shot for lovers of Mediterranean herbs.
July	The Roman Arena in Pula makes Istria a stunning venue for the five-day **Pula Film Festival.** Around the same time, the five-day **International Folklore Festival** in Zagreb attracts folklore groups from Eastern Europe and beyond, staging music and dance in traditional costume.
July and August	Practically every island and city up and down the Dalmatian coast has some kind of music festival in July and August, most taking place in a pretty church or palazzo on the Old Town square. Check with local tourist offices once you arrive for what's going on that week. Croatia's largest and most prestigious cultural event, the **Dubrovnik Summer Festival** (⊕ *www.dubrovnik-festival.hr*), draws international artists and musicians and features drama, ballet, concerts, and opera, all performed on open-air stages within the city fortifications. Similarly, the **Split Summer Festival** hosts opera, theater, and dance events at open-air venues within the walls of Diocletian's Palace. The **Motovun Film Festival** (⊕ *www.*

	motovunfilmfestival.com) highlights international independent films in a rustic medieval setting.
July–September	
	In Porec, Croatia, the **Concert Season** in the Basilica of St. Euphrasius features eminent musicians from Croatia and abroad, with sacral and secular music from all periods played inside the magnificent 6th-century basilica.
FALL	
September	The **Epidaurus Festival** brings a variety of concerts, mostly classical and jazz, as well as an excellent selection of hands-on workshops to the town of Cavtat, just south of Dubrovnik toward the Montenegrin border.
September and October	The **Varaždin Baroque Evenings** see eminent soloists and orchestras from Croatia and abroad perform baroque-music recitals in the city's most beautiful churches.
November	In Zagorje, Croatia, **Martinje (St Martin's Day)**, which is November 11, sees the blessing of the season's new wine, accompanied by a hearty goose feast and endless toasts. Nearby Slovenia, too, celebrates **St. Martin's Day** on November 11, which sees festivities throughout the country, culminating with the traditional blessing of the season's young wine.

KIDS AND FAMILIES

Croatia could very well be the most kid-friendly country on the Mediterranean. It is not so much the programs that make it suitable to bring the little ones along, but the sheer unspoiled beauty of nature. Whether you are pursuing history, nature, food, or sports, the kids can be easily incorporated into the trip and, what is more, have a fun and learning experience.

Where to Stay. Resorts are not to be found everywhere in Croatia. Western Istria, island Krk, Zadar, and Dubrovnik offer the most options, luring travelers with great deals for kids staying in the same room. Always be sure to ask for children's discounts, which will typically vary according to your children's age. Private accommodation, or self-catering apartments, is on the rise in Croatia both in terms of quantity and quality. These are ideally suited for families as they can fit the whole entourage at only a fraction of what the hotel would cost and you are also free to cook your own food (and, regrettably, do your own dishes). If booking online, make sure to read the reviews of previous guests as pictures can often be deceiving and descriptions incomplete. Finally, Croatia is also dotted with very attractive campsites along the Adriatic, which is certainly a tempting fact for those parents who don't mind their children getting a little dusty every now and again. Campsite accommodations range from tents to elitist bungalows with all modern amenities.

Outdoor Activities. Croatia was not designed for staying indoors, especially in the eyes of children. The crystal clear Adriatic is an instant magnet for almost any little one, but make sure to pack a pair of rubber sandals for them—most of the coast is rocky and sea urchins, too,

enjoy the clear shallow waters. There are a number of sailing schools along the coast and snorkeling is never bad due to the water's clarity. Most of the coast immediately transforms into mountains, particularly lush toward the west, which offers great hiking opportunities. All Croatian national parks are also great places to spend a day with the offspring, and they do offer discounts for families. Most importantly, Croatia is very safe and it is not at all uncommon to see children playing by themselves at playgrounds while the parents catch a breath of sea air or a glass of cool wine. Do be aware, however, that kids' clubs or cafés are in short supply, so make sure to have a plan of action for the occasional rainy day.

Sports Camps. It is well known that, when it comes to sports, Croatia punches above its weight. All those accolades have to come from somewhere and there are indeed many sports camps for children and youth that visitors can join into, providing that you plan and research in advance. From the national flagpoles like soccer, basketball, and water polo to individual sports like tennis, cliff-climbing, and sailing, there are many options that will occupy (and exhaust) the energy bombs while the parents take a breather.

Culture and History. Over the past years, there has been a strong push toward making museums and historic buildings, well, less boring for the children. In addition to free or symbolic entrance, many museums now offer interactive programs in which the younger visitors get to participate as opposed to just observing. The trick, if it is a trick, has worked quite well thus far.

TOP 10 CROATIAN FOODS TO TRY

Throughout history, Croatia has served as the crossroads between Western Europe and the Orient, and this shows in a number of cultural facets, not least the food. While gathering the best from a wide array of Italian, Hungarian, and Turkish culinary influences, it is not uncommon for Croatians to seek inspiration from the one side of the country not surrounded by land and fish out their dinner straight from the Adriatic. The food served in front of you will mostly depend on your whereabouts. Try to keep your orders local, too: a sea bass in Slavonia is never a good idea, just like a Dalmatian chef probably won't know how to make those stuffed peppers just right. Also, try to pair local food with local wines for a true experience, although *dingač* red will be great with the Continental meat dishes and *graševina* white, albeit from the north, has no problem sharing stomach space with Adriatic fish. If the bottle is right, be unafraid to drink outside the box.

Dalmatian Prosciutto and Pag Island Cheese

Most dinners on the Dalmatian coast begin with this delectably comestible tandem. The *pršut,* as it's known locally, is made from Dalmatian pigs and contains several ingredients specific to the region: Adriatic salt, ground spicy paprika, and the key ingredient—the *bura* wind as the drying mechanism. The end result is seemingly simple yet hard to stop eating, especially when paired with sheep cheese from the island of Pag. The island offers limited pasture areas mostly by the sea and the grass receives a liberal salty sprinkling carried by the bura wind. Saltier grass makes saltier milk and this, in turn, provides gourmets with an excellent, inherently salty cheese.

Fuži Pasta and Truffles

The rolling hills of inland Istria are home to a highly sought-after culinary delight—the truffle. The black truffle season conveniently peaks at the same time as the tourist season, from May until October, and it is therefore relatively easy, if not inexpensive, to find this rare mushroom on the menus of Istrian restaurants. The white truffle, on the other hand, grows in the winter months and may be harder to locate. The secretive, flavorful truffles are found in forests by specially trained dogs or pigs and can be incorporated into a number of dishes. To keep the experience truly Istrian though, order truffle sauce on homemade *fuži* or *pljukanci* pasta and wash it down with a glass of malvasia.

Purica i Mlinci

Roasted turkey with *mlinci* dumplings has long been a favorite of the Zagreb area and northern Croatia. Croatians like their birds roasted and they do a great job with it. In this case, the turkey is typically prepared with ample garlic, bacon, and rosemary, and then traditionally served with mlinci, simple but tasty dumplings made of flour, water, salt, and oil that are then covered with the succulent bird to infuse its juices. Second helpings are often in order.

Grilled Adriatic Squid and Blitva Chard

When it comes to squid, size does not matter. You won't find a better example of this outside of Croatia, where the squid is small but delicious! A typical serving will include between 8 and 10 squid and will be more than enough to satiate and delight. Pair the squid (when grilled, it retains more flavor than fried) with Dalmatian-style *blitva,* a chard-family green prepared with cooked potatoes and local olive oil. If in need of spicing it up, ask for the Trieste sauce, a garlic, parsley, and olive oil bomb that will make the dish explode in your mouth.

Fish Paprikash

For once, a delicious Croatian fish dish that does not come from the Adriatic. The fish paprikash is the pride of the region around Osijek city in Slavonia, which joins the best of the Hungarian cuisine and Danube tributaries' fish. The meal can be cooked using trout, pike, catfish—or all of the above—together with onions, paprika, peppers, and white wine. The result is quite a holiday for the palate, best served and consumed with hearty homemade bread and a glass of Slavonian Riesling.

Veal or Lamb under the "Peka"

Meat lovers will love this one. The *peka* is a heavy iron bell specially made to fit into an open-fire grill. The veal or lamb, depending on the day and restaurant, will be placed onto the lower part of the bell along with rosemary-seasoned potatoes before the large lid is lowered onto it and covered with coal and ash. The meat and potato cook in their own juice for just over an hour becoming as tender as they'll ever be, certainly tender enough for your plate. This meal is very popular with restaurants along the old Lika magistrala road connecting Zagreb to Zadar via Plitvice lakes, but it can also be found in most of Dalmatia. The *plavac mali* is an excellent wine to accompany the meat and locals will also keep *šljivovica*, the plum-based rakija, on the table.

Tuna Steaks

Up until recently, Croatia exported almost all of its tuna to Japan and it was very hard to find on local menus. Much to the delight of local and visiting gourmets, the export contract was not renewed and you are now likely to find fresh tuna fish steaks on menus along the coast. The tuna is crisp and tasty, and exceptionally well complemented with asparagus risotto in the spring months.

Pašticada

This beef dish has been the pride of Dalmatia for centuries. The beef is adorned with pancetta, garlic, onion, celery, laurel, and other Mediterranean herbs, and the ineludible red wine. It is left to soak in this mouthwatering sauce overnight and then slowly cooked (often with dried figs added into the mix) until tender and served with gnocchi or mashed potatoes.

Istrian Minestrone Stew

The *manestra* stew is the quintessential Istrian dish and it will be found, in different variations, on the tables of most restaurants, *konobas,* and homes of Croatia's largest peninsula. The ingredients will greatly depend on the season and availability, but beans, corn, and olive oil are the backbone of this hearty dish that can be a meal in itself, especially when served with homemade bread. The stew will also typically include potatoes, sausages, and sauerkraut during the winter, displaying the Austro-Hungarian culinary legacy.

Štrukli

Štrukli is the most famous hors d'oeuvre from the Zagreb and Zagorje region, and it is not uncommon to also see it served as the main course or even a dessert. This baked cheese, cream, eggs, and butter combo will not make you your physician's favorite patient, but it tastes great and leaves none hungry.

WINE IN CROATIA

A wine renaissance is occurring in Croatia today. The early 20th century was bad for the wine business—phylloxera, war, crippling economic policies, all of which ravaged wineries here and led to the mass emigration of many vintners who fled to the United States, New Zealand, Australia, South Africa, and South America. Bringing their knowledge of vine cultivation and wine production with them, they left Croatia's vineyards virtually deserted.

More recently, the 1990–95 war for Croatian independence, which cast a global spotlight on the tiny country, nearly wiped out a viticulture two millennia in the making. It appears, however, that the land itself cannot forget its heritage. Blessed with unique geography, so crucially ideal for wine, Croatia currently hosts more than 100 indigenous grapes—second only to Italy. The country's wines are once again finding a special place in the hearts of oenophiles everywhere. The Mediterranean landscape is particularly suited to *Vitus vinifera L* (the cultivated grapevine), a hearty and prolific, yet temperamental plant that requires precise combinations of climate, geography, and soil to flourish. In Croatia, with her numerous, diverse microclimates, the grape has had the necessary conditions to proliferate.

Wine-Making and Its Deep Roots

The Delmati, an Illyrian tribe, were the first to cultivate the vine in modern-day Croatia, as early as the 11th century BC. When the Romans invaded the Dalmatian Coast in the 3rd century BC, they discovered that wine production had preceded them; they found, in fact, an entire wine industry. The Greeks, who'd been sharing the region with the Illyrians, had not failed to exploit *Vitus sylvestris* (the wild grapevine), which was plentiful there,

merging it with the strains of the cultivated vines they brought from their own country. The conquering Roman soldiers also brought new varietals with them as a way of expanding their culture; the vine itself was a symbol of their power.

By the 9th century, Croatian princes had a cup bearer as part of their court staff. When Venice subjugated much of Dalmatia and Istria in the 14th century, the planting of new vineyards was restricted to the areas around Split. It was in this period that noble families, after building their vineyards, built fortresses in the middle of their estates for protection, perhaps anticipating the destruction of the coming Venetian-Turkish wars. By the time the Habsburgs had ousted the Ottomans, the Austrians were already well on their way to introducing new varietals to the area, capitalizing on the superior wine-producing capacity of their newly acquired resources.

Modern developments in cloning techniques and the use of industrial machinery brought wine-making in Croatia to the economic position it occupies today, where 10% of the population derives income from the industry.

The Napa Valley Connection

Croatia has had some world-class help in reestablishing its wine-making industry. Miljenko "Mike" Grgić of Napa Valley fame is at the forefront of the race to expand and realize the potential of Croatia's indigenous varietals. Grgić left Croatia in 1954, feeling stifled by the communist government. In California, he became renowned as a winemaker when his 1973 Chateau Montelena Chardonnay won a blind tasting in Paris. Afterward, the top-quality wine market opened its mind and wallet to wines from the world over. Mr. Grgić then established Grgich Hills Cellar in Napa Valley, and it is now one of California's most respected producers.

Grgić Vina. When Croatia won its independence in 1995, Croatian-born Mike Grgić came back from Napa Valley to establish Grgić Vina in a tiny town of some 100 residents on the Pelješac Peninsula in Southern Dalmatia, the home of the Dingač terroir. Croatia's first international winery surprised everyone by turning a profit within two years (5 to 10 years is typical). The winery produces high-end boutique wines: a flavorful, fruity white from the indigenous pošip; and a ruby-red, from the hearty plavac mali, the "little blue" grape that is widely considered the highest-quality Croatian varietal, closely related to the zinfandel vine. These bottles range between $20 and $50 a bottle. Grgić hopes to support the local wine communes by using their grapes as well. ⊠ *Trstenik 78, Trstenik* ☏ *020/748–090 from Croatia* ⊕ *www.grgich.com.*

Regions and Wineries

Croatia is split into two main wine-growing regions: the arid continental part and the coastal region, much of which shares the same latitude as Bordeaux, Provence, Tuscany, and Oregon. The continental region produces 90% of the country's whites, the coastal almost 70% of the reds. There are 12 subregions in Croatia, the most important of which are: **Central and Southern Dalmatia**, where the hearty *plavac mali* flourishes on the Pelješac Peninsula; **Middle Dalmatia**, where the famous *babić* grape is grown near Primošten; and the **Northern Coastal Belt**, which includes the islands of Cres, Lošinj, Rab, Pag, and Krk. These are breathtaking regions, as is **Istria**, known for its *malvasia Istriana*

(white) and *teran* (red). The region of **Međimurje**, situated in continental Croatia along the Slovenian and Hungarian border, also has some fine wineries specializing in white wines made from *graševina* grapes, better known as Welschriesling, as well as tramina, chardonnay, and sauvignon blanc.

Istrian Wineries

AgroLaguna Winery. At AgroLaguna Winery it is possible to taste a number of high-quality Istrian wines. One white varietal, malvasia, is well known throughout the Adriatic, dating back to the days of the Venetian city-states. Muškat ottonal is another high-quality native variety. Small, lovingly produced batches of barrique provide high-quality (red) wine. ⊠ *Vukovarska 19, Poreč* ☏ *052/453–179* ⊕ *www.agrolaguna.hr.*

Matošević. Matošević Winery, with vineyards in the northeast, welcomes visitors at their top-notch cellars in Krunčići, not far from Rovinj. Their *malvasia rubina* bears international renown. ⊠ *Krunčići* ⊕ *www.matosevic.com.*

Moreno Coronica. Moreno Coronica, in the northeast corner of the peninsula, produces the gran teran, a local variety of red wine, that has been a gold-medal winner at international wine competitions. ⊠ *Koreniki 86, Koreniki* ☏ *052/730–196* ⊕ *www.coronica.eu.*

Northern Coastal Belt Wineries

Katunar Winery. At Katunar Winery on the island of Krk you can sample the žlatina varietal, which is indigenous to the island. Individual visits and group tours can be arranged to sample the dry white *žlahtina Katunar* or the *černo Katunar* (a dry red), or the "pearl wine" *biser mora,* a dessert wine produced from 100% zlahtina grapes. This dry white wine is famous among Croatians around the world. ⊠ *Sv. Nedilija, Krk Town* ☎ *051/857–393* ⊕ *www.katunar.hr.*

Central and Southern Dalmatian Wineries

The *plavac mali* grapes grown on the steep hillsides of Dingač produce a full-bodied, slightly dry wine. These particular 168 acres, along with some areas of Hvar, have the highest average temperatures in Croatia, the reason why Dingač's alcohol content may reach as high as 17.6%. The seaside slopes on which the grapes are grown are so steep that donkeys are the only possible helpmates (machine harvesting is impossible). The donkey found on some bottles of Dingač is a symbol of the hearty, stubborn vine that reaches its full potential in this very limited region.

Frano Miloš Winery. Frano Miloš Winery is north of Dubrovnik. Visitors may have the opportunity to sample obscure small-batch wines of unique geographic origins. Be ready to try such wines as plavac ponikve, nadahnuće, and stagnum. The stagnum here is of a particularly high quality. ⊠ *Ponikve 15, Ston* ☎ *020/753–098* ⊕ *www.milos.hr.*

Plančić Winery. On the beautiful lavender-scented island of Hvar you can visit Plančić Winery, where Antun Plančić has been producing a variety of top-quality wines, including rosé and dessert wines, as well as some local rakija since 1919. Look out for *bogdanuša* (dry white wine) or *Ivan Dolač* (a select red). ⊠ *21462 Vrbanj Svirče* ☎ *021/768–030* ⊕ *www. plancic.com.*

The Plenković Winery. The Plenković Winery on the island of Hvar, along with its restaurant and hotel, are also well worth a visit. In fact, in the past few years the zlatan plavac (a dry red) made by Zlatan Plenković has continually won prestigious awards at local and international wine fairs. Plenković is the largest single-family producer in Croatia. ⊠ *Sveta Nedjelja, Hvar* ☎ *021/745–703* ⊕ *www. zlatanotok.hr.*

Vinarija Dingač Cooperative (*P.Z. Dingač*). At one of Croatia's best-known wineries, Vinarija Dingač Cooperative, it is possible to sample several excellent wines. Each year, Vinarija Dingač produces 12,500 cases of a deep-red wine that is fruity without being sweet. In a market flooded with low-priced good-quality wines from South Africa and Australia, many in the Croatian wine industry believe that the future of Croatian wine depends on these superior products. This boutique-style varietal is widely available abroad. ⊠ *Potomje* ☎ *020/742–010.*

Vinarija Ivo Skaramuča. In Southern Dalmatia's Pelješac Peninsula, visitors are welcome at Vinarija Ivo Skaramuča to sample the indigenous plavac mali varietals. ⊠ *Pijavičino, Potomje* ☎ *020/742– 211* ⊕ *www.dingac-skaramuca.hr.*

Northern Dalmatia Wineries

The vineyards that surround Primošten Bay have been compared to a honeycomb, and are an impressive sight to behold. A photograph of the region even hangs in the lobby of the United Nations building in New York. The stone walls, so carefully built by human hands centuries ago, have the UN-administered status of a monument to human effort. The fields of babić grapes surrounding Primošten Bay were built on layers of rock—an unlikely success story—but the vines adapted to the karst landscape, their roots going deep into the soil.

Bibich Winery. The Bibich Winery, which operates a wine boutique in Zadar, produces wine both from native Dalmatian varieties, including babić, plavina, lašina, and debit, and non-native grapes, including grenache and shiraz. The winery is just outside of Skradin. ⊠ *Plastovo* ☎ *023/329–260.*

Vinoplod-Vinarija. Vinoplod-Vinarija, the award-winning makers of primoštenski babić, can be contacted for tours and tastings. ⊠ *Velimira Škorpika 2, Šibenik* ☎ *022/333–671, 022/334–011* ⊕ *www.vinoplod-vinarija.hr.*

Continental Wineries

Jakopić Winery. Jakopić Winery, near the spa town of Sveti Martin in the Varaždin region, is operated by brothers Martin and Branimir Jakopić, who offer superb dining as well as scenic tours of the lush vineyards situated on the borders of Slovenia, Hungary, and Austria. ⊠ *Železna Gora 92, Orehovčak Štrigova* ☎ *040/851–300* ⊕ *www.vina-jakopic.hr.*

The Zinquest: Finding Zinfandel in Croatia

Much excitement has been generated around California's ubiquitous zinfandel grape, whose origin had long been guessed at, but that remained shrouded in mystery. In 1998 Professor Carole Meredith of the University of California at Davis, a renowned grapevine geneticist who had previously uncovered the origins of chardonnay, cabernet sauvignon, and petit syrah, began a similar search for zinfandel's origin. The exciting four-year project, which entailed the collection of leaf samples from indigenous varieties of southern Dalmatia, DNA fingerprinting analyses of samples cultivars, and comparisons with zinfandel cuttings from California, shed new light on the origins of the state's most popular grape.

In the spring of 1998, Professor Meredith collected leaf samples from 148 individual plavac mali vines in Southern Dalmatia, including Hvar, Pelješac, and Korčula. Although the initial search in 1998 gave no positive matches with zinfandel, the expeditions that followed led the team of scientists to an old vineyard in Kaštel Novi, where a few additional "suspects" were discovered. The DNA analyses performed at Davis confirmed that a wine locally known as *crljenak kaštelanski*—completely forgotten and virtually eradicated from Dalmatian vineyards—is the long-sought Croatian corollary of zinfandel.

Jasenka Piljač's book, *Zinfandel: A Croatian-American Wine Story* (⊕ *www.crozinfandel.com*) chronicles her work as a part of the Meredith Zinquest team and includes in-depth information about Croatia's viticultural past, present, and future.

SAILING AND CRUISING IN CROATIA

The Croatian Adriatic has more than 2,000 km (1,242 miles) of mainland coast, with more than 1,000 islands and islets (67 of which are inhabited). Unlike Greece, where the islands are dispersed, the Croatian islands run parallel to and close to the mainland coast, which, for the most part, means easy island-hopping in protected waters.

Besides the picturesque coastal towns, Croatia has three national parks on the sea: Brijuni National Park (a cluster of 14 small green islands just off Istria), Kornati National Park (an archipelago of 89 arid, rocky islands, islets, and reefs off North Dalmatia), and Mljet National Park (a large, fertile island, one-third of which is covered with coniferous forest, in South Dalmatia). In addition, Krka National Park (a spectacular series of waterfalls in a canyon in Central Dalmatia), can even be approached by sailboat, if you sail up the Šibenik Channel as far as Skradin.

Sailing

Often considered a glamorous and expensive way to travel, a holiday aboard a sailboat is now an affordable alternative to a land-bound vacation. In fact, it is the ultimate way to explore Croatia's stunningly beautiful mainland coast and islands. No other form of transport gives you such flexibility and such close contact with the sea: aboard a yacht you can sunbathe on the deck, put down anchor and swim wherever you choose, and discover isolated coves accessible only from the water, some of which have idyllic beaches and informal restaurants serving the very freshest seafood. And, surprisingly, a week aboard a sailing boat can be cheaper than staying in a mid-range hotel.

If you are already an experienced sailor, you can charter a so-called bareboat yacht, meaning that you rent just the boat and sail independently. By Croatian law, at least one of the crew needs to have an internationally recognized sailing license, plus a radio certificate (available from all port authorities).

If you have never sailed before, or have little experience, then you will need a skipper. Generally skippers do more than just guide the boat: most are from the region and, therefore, know the local waters and weather conditions, the history and culture, the protected coves for putting down anchor, the local gastronomic hideouts, and the best diving spots.

The third option is sailing in a flotilla. A flotilla is a group of yachts (typically between 5 and 10), with people of mixed levels of sailing experience, led by a qualified expert. You gain the privacy of your own sailboat but also the security of knowing that help is always close at hand should you need it. Of course, you also get to meet new people.

A typical one-week sailing itinerary in Central Dalmatia could run as follows. Day 1: Set sail from Split to Maslinica on the island of Šolta. Day 2: Maslinica to Vis Town on the island of Vis. Day 3: Sail round the island, from Vis Town to Komiža, calling at Biševo en route. Day 4: Komiža to Hvar Town on the island of Hvar. Day 5: Hvar Town to Bol on the island of Brač. Day 6: Bol to Milna on the island of Brač. Day 7: Early morning departure from Milna to Split. The Croatian Adriatic has 50 well-equipped marinas providing 13,500 sea berths and 4,500 dry berths. All berths are equipped with water and power supplies, and most marinas also have at least one restaurant, a grocery store, a nautical-gear store, a repair shop, a gas station, and toilets and

showers. Some, but not all, have laundry facilities. The leading nautical-tourism company, Adriatic Croatian International (known as ACI, pronounced "Atsi"), runs 21 marinas. Twenty Croatian marinas have been awarded the European "Blue Flag" for safety, cleanliness, and respect for the environment. Most marinas stay open all year.

Last but not least, remember that Croatia recently introduced a law declaring zero-alcohol tolerance for those in charge of a boat. If you are caught sailing in a state of inebriation you could face steep fines.

Charter Companies

On the Croatian Adriatic there are more than 140 charter companies operating tens of thousands of boats of all sizes, making this one of the busiest charter areas in Europe. As a rough guide to prices, in summer 2014 high season, Sail Croatia offered an eight-berth Beneteau Cyclades 43 sailing boat for €3,200 per week, though this price does not include food, fuel, or mooring fees.

The most popular way to research and book charter yachts is via the Internet. Most sites include photos and layout schemes of the boats, lists of onboard equipment, and even sample itineraries. Once you have selected your boat, all you need to do is confirm the availability of the date with the charter company and pay a nonrefundable deposit equal to 30% to 50% of the charter price. The remaining 50% to 70% of the charter fee is usually paid four weeks before the commencement of the charter.

The season runs from May through October, with the best winds for sailing in May and June. Demand and prices peak in July and August, when you can expect calmer sea and less wind, making conditions ideal for motorboats but less fun for true sailors. During peak season, charter rentals generally begin at 5 pm Saturday and end at 9 am the following Saturday.

Some companies offer extra activities, which can be combined with sailing, such as scuba diving, kayaking, surfing, hiking, mountain biking, or vineyard tours. Another popular option is "sail and stay," which gives you a week aboard a yacht followed by a week in a hotel or villa. There are even special sailing packages for weddings and honeymoons. As tourism is developing rapidly in Croatia, you should check with individual companies to see what the new season has to offer.

International Companies

Most of the international companies are headquartered in the United Kingdom, but there are a couple of worldwide operations that have offices in the United States as well.

Activity Yachting. Activity Yachting offers sailing programs that operate along the 161 km (100-mile) stretch of coastline between Split and Zadar. Flotilla holidays (with or without tuition) are available, sharing a five-berth boat. Bareboat rental can also be arranged, or you can take a tailor-made program combining a week's sailing with a week in a villa or hotel. ☎ 1243/641–304 from U.K. ⊕ www. activityyachting.com.

Dalmatian Destinations. Dalmatian Destinations is an upmarket travel company out of the United Kingdom that provides fully crewed sailing boats, motorboats, and gulets in Croatia. Their itineraries include an "Organic Route" tracking down Dalmatia's best seasonal and regional cuisine and a "Cultural Route" taking in architecture, art, and music

along the coast. ☎*+44 333/700–8007* ⊕*www.dalmatiandestinations.com.*

LateSail. LateSail acts as a clearinghouse for the world's leading charter operators and offers a wide range of yachts and speedboats at cut-rate prices in more than 50 destinations, including Croatia. ☎*+44 1227/479–900* ⊕*www.latesail.com.*

The Moorings. The Moorings is an international sailing specialist based out of Kremik (Primošten, near Šibenik) in Croatia. The company offers bareboat, skippered, and flotilla sailing in yachts and catamarans with anything from two to five double cabins. ☎*+33 15/300–3030* ⊕*www.moorings.com.*

Nautilus. Nautilus keeps yachts, catamarans, and motorboats at bases in Pula, Zadar, Biograd, Murter (close to Kornati National Park), Split, and Dubrovnik. Flotilla sailing is also available. ☎*1732/867–445* ⊕*www.nautilus-yachting.com.*

Sail Croatia. Sail Croatia offers a fleet of 15 yachts of various sizes up to 56 feet, sleeping between 2 and 10 people; or you can book one of a couple of larger crewed yachts measuring up to 100 feet with 12 berths. Boats can be chartered on a bareboat basis or with a skipper who will provide guidance and tuition. Itineraries are flexible, but departures are generally from Split. It's also possible to opt for sail-and-stay, including time on land. ✉*Split* ☎*+385 21/494–885* ⊕*www.sail croatia.net.*

Croatian Companies

ACI. Adriatic Croatia International is the country's largest marine management company. It runs charters from its multiple bases, either bareboat or with a skipper. ☎*51/271–288* ⊕*www.aci.hr.*

Adriatic Skipper Association. If you want to simply rent a boat and choose your own skipper, you can contact the Adriatic Skipper Association. Expect to pay €100–€150 per day for his or her services, and remember that you are also responsible for the skipper's food. ⊕*www.usj.hr.*

Club Adriatic. Club Adriatic is an online charter service with more than 1,500 bareboat, crewed, and luxury yachts along the coast. The site is particularly recommended when you are searching for special low-season offers and last-minute discounts. ☎*01/467–7395 in Croatia, +44 560/156–7088 in U.K.* ⊕*www. charter.hr.*

Croatian National Tourist Board. For a full list of charter companies, the Croatian National Tourist Board publishes a list on its website. Go to "Activities and Attractions" then "Nautics," where you will find region-by-region listings. ⊕*www. croatia.hr.*

Euromarine. Euromarine has bases in Pula, Biograd, Split, and Dubrovnik, chartering more than 100 sailing boats, motorboats, and catamarans. ☎*01/555–2222 in Croatia* ⊕*www.euromarine.com.hr.*

Sailing Schools

Adriatic Nautical Academy (*ANA*). Adriatic Nautical Academy is an annual sailing school held at Jezera on the island of Murter in Central Dalmatia, offering one-week courses (late March to early November). The school also has a summer base in Cavtat, near Dubrovnik in Southern Dalmatia (late April to late October). In 2014 a one-week Level 1 Beginner's Course at Jezera costs €550. ⊕*www.anasail.com.*

Ultra Sailing. Ultra Sailing was founded by former members of the Croatian Olympic Team who now work as instructors,

offering one-week courses (March through October) in Split and Milna on the island of Brač (in Central Dalmatia). In 2014 the one-week Basic Course cost €795. ✉ *Split* ☎ *021/398–980* ⊕ *www. ultra-sailing.hr.*

Cruising

A visitor with limited time in Croatia will find that traveling down the Adriatic aboard a cruise ship is an ideal way to see the country's mainland ports and islands. Although it is tempting to try using the Jadrolinija coastal ferry, which runs from Rijeka to Dubrovnik with several stops en route, it's not really an ideal solution. The timetable is complicated, running only twice a week in each direction and selling all the cabins out very quickly. At best, the ferry makes a fine way to travel overnight from Rijeka to Split, or through the day from Split to Korčula or Dubrovnik. Many of the well-known international cruise lines (notably Carnival, Celebrity, Costa, Crystal, Cunard, Holland America, Norwegian, Oceania, Princess, Seabourn, Silversea, Star Clippers, and Windstar) now include Croatia (Dubrovnik and sometimes Korčula) on their Mediterranean itineraries, mainly en route from Venice to the Greek islands. Croatia is also included in some "Eastern Mediterranean" cruises, which might include Greece, Turkey, North Africa, and the Middle East. The favorite port of call is undoubtedly Dubrovnik, but Korčula Town, Hvar Town, Split, Šibenik, Rab Town, Opatija, Pula, and Rovinj also show up on some itineraries. An alternative to cruising on a large ship is traveling aboard a medium-size old-timer. Several Croatian companies now offer informal one-week cruises on beautifully restored wooden gulets, generally taking between 12 to 40 passengers.

Cruises Croatia. Cruises Croatia, aka Adria Travel, runs three cruise ships that call at the top Dalmatian destinations. ☎ *212/845–9604 from U.S.* ⊕ *www. cruises-croatia.com.*

Elite Travel. Elite Travel offers one-week motor-sail cruises aboard old-timers running Saturday to Saturday. The "Dalmatian Highlights Cruise," for up to 26 passengers, starts and ends in Dubrovnik, visiting the Elafiti, Mljet, Vela Luka (Korčula), and Hvar islands. Alternatively, the "Adriatic Paradise Cruise" has a capacity of 40 passengers, beginning and ending in Trogir, taking in Split, Vis, Korčula, Dubrovnik, Mljet, and Hvar. In 2014, the cruises cost €740 per person. ☎ *020/358–200 in Croatia* ⊕ *www.elite.hr.*

Katarina Line. Katarina Line offers one-week cruises aboard 21 vintage sailing ships from mid-May to mid-October, for groups of between 22 and 40 passengers. Departures are from Opatija (covering Kvarner and North Dalmatia) and Split and Dubrovnik (covering Central and South Dalmatia). Itineraries are variable but include visits to the islands and plenty of time for swimming. ☎ *051/603–400* ⊕ *www.katarina-line.com.*

ZAGREB AND ENVIRONS

By Jadranka
Vuković
Rodríguez and
A. Chapin
Rodríguez

Zagreb has emerged as a tourist destination in recent years, and much of its success has to do with the country's spectacular Adriatic coast—beautiful medieval towns, crystal clear azure waters, and, of course, well-developed tourist resorts. It's all too easy, however, to overlook the fact that much of the country's natural beauty and cultural heritage is rooted in places well inland from the sea. Unless you arrive overland from Slovenia, by boat from Italy, or by one of the few air routes that deliver you straight to the coast, chances are that your first encounter with Croatia will be Zagreb, an eminently strollable capital city of attractive parks, squares, and museums.

Instead of hightailing it to Dalmatia or Istria, stay a few days to explore the capital's historic center and pastoral environs. You'll be in for a pleasant surprise and will go home with a fuller, more satisfying appreciation of what this alluring country is all about. With its historic center on the northern bank of the Sava River, Zagreb has the walkability of Prague, with the added bonus that the streetcars have to yield to pedestrians. Spacious, inviting public spaces, grand Austro-Hungarian architecture, and a rich array of churches and museums will lure you down small side streets.

ORIENTATION AND PLANNING

GETTING ORIENTED

With the exception of the vast plains of Slavonia that stretch to the east (⇨ *Chapter 3*), the rest of the inland region, with Zagreb as its approximate center, can be divided into two parts, north and south. To the north is the hilly, castle-rich Zagorje region; the smaller, often-overlooked and yet likewise appealing Međimurje region; and, just a tram and bus ride from the city center, the hiking trails and ski slopes of Sljeme. To the south is the relatively busy route to the coast that includes Karlovac, an important regional center, as well as Croatia's most visited national park, Plitvice Lakes; and a second route along the less traveled banks of the Sava River to Lonjsko Polje, known for its natural beauty, a 16th-century fortress, and historical reminders of Croatia's role in World War II.

GREAT ITINERARIES

To explore Croatia's interior, begin with Zagreb and work your way outward from there. If you have just a day or two, stick to the capital, but the more time you have beyond that, the more you will want to explore. If you're headed to the coast anyway, you'll pass by Plitvice Lakes National Park; keep that natural wonder on your radar screen for a daytime visit at the very least.

IF YOU HAVE 3 DAYS

Stick to **Zagreb,** with a side trip to its immediate environs. As compact as it is compared to other regional capitals such as Budapest, Croatia's capital nonetheless invites long strolls and more than a fleeting look into at least a few of its museums and parks. This alone can take three days; but you can probably cover most key sights without feeling rushed in two days, leaving a bit of time to spare for a half-day excursion to the charming village of **Samobor,** for example, or to the scenic hills of Sljeme north of the capital. Renting a car will allow you to cover more of the castles and

towns of the **Medvednica hills** and the Zagorje region, but even if you have only one full day at your disposal, you can take in a couple of these nearby sites by bus.

IF YOU HAVE 5 DAYS

Start as above, devoting at least two or, better yet, two-and-a-half days to Zagreb, with a half-day excursion to the Medvednica hills on the third day. Visit a castle or two in the Zagorje, such as the recently renovated **Veliki Tabor,** on the fourth day, and spend the night either in the nearby countryside or else in the ancient town of **Varaždin** before making your way back for a fond farewell to Zagreb on the fifth.

IF YOU HAVE 7 DAYS

Do all of the above, but take in both a castle in the Zagorje and an afternoon and evening in Varaždin; throw in a one-night visit to **Plitvice Lakes National Park,** with a daytime stopover to visit the old town center of Karlovac on the way. This one-week option will work well if, for example, you wish to spend the second (or first) week on the Adriatic coast.

PLANNING

WHEN TO GO

Although Zagreb and environs are well worth a visit at any time of year, the capital really comes alive in spring and summer, which essentially means anytime between April and late September. Since summer is coastal vacation time for so many, July and August are considered low season in the capital, meaning that the city is much less crowded and more economical than the coast.

GETTING HERE AND AROUND
AIR TRAVEL
Zagreb International Airport (ZAG) is actually located in the city of Velika Gorica, 17 km (10 miles) southeast of Zagreb.

There are no direct flights between the United States and Zagreb, but Croatia Airlines and several major European carriers fly to Zagreb from Amsterdam, Brussels, Frankfurt, Munich, London, Paris, Vienna,

TOP REASONS TO GO TO ZAGREB

■ With lovely parks, squares, museums, and churches, hoofing it in Croatia's compact capital is an unforgettable experience. If your feet fail, you can always jump on a convenient tram.

■ Plitvice Lakes National Park, a UNESCO World Heritage site, is Croatia's most-visited park, with 16 crystal clear turquoise lakes connected by waterfalls and cascades.

■ Zagorje's forested hills north of Zagreb are ornamented with some

lovely fortresses, built to ward off centuries of onslaughts by various foes.

■ Varaždin is the most harmonious and beautifully preserved baroque town in this corner of the continent.

■ Here you get the best of both worlds: top-notch seafood *and* Central European meaty, spicy fare. And best of all, prices are fairly reasonable even at the top restaurants.

Moscow, Rome, and other cities. Croatia Airlines operates at least two flights daily to Split (45 minutes) and three flights daily to Dubrovnik (55 minutes). In summertime there are also flights to Lisbon (2 hours, 25 minutes), Barcelona (2 hours, 10 minutes), Tel Aviv (3 hours, 15 minutes), and other cities.

A regular shuttle bus runs from the airport to the main bus station every 30 minutes from 7 am to 8 pm and from the main bus station to the airport from 4:30 am to 8:30 pm. A one-way ticket costs 30 Kn, and daily return ticket costs 40 Kn. The trip takes 30 minutes. By taxi, expect to pay 150 Kn to 200 Kn to make the same journey; the trip will be slightly faster, about 20 minutes.

Airline Contacts Aeroflot ⊠ *Andrije Hebranga 4* ☎ *01/487–2055, 01/487–2076, 01/456–2258 Zagreb International Airport* ⊕ *www. aeroflot.ru*. **Air France/KLM** ⊠ *Krsnjavoga 1, Zagreb* ☎ *01/489–0800 reservations* ⊕ *www.airfrance.hr* ☉ *Weekdays 9–5*. **Austrian Airlines** ⊠ *Ulica Rudolfa Fizira 1, Velika Gorica* ☎ *01/626–5900* ⊕ *www.aua. com*. **British Airways** ⊠ *Zagreb International Airport, Ulica Rudolfa Fizira 1* ☎ *01/456–2506* ☉ *Mon.–Sun. 10–1*.**Croatia Airlines** ⊠ *Zrinjevac 17, Donji Grad, Zagreb* ☎ *01/481–9633 Information, 01/616–4581 Zagreb airport* ⊕ *www.croatiaairlines.hr*. **Lufthansa** ⊠ *Ilica 191, Zagreb* ☎ *01/390–7284 Zagreb city center office, 072/220–220 Lufthansa Call Centar* ⊕ *www.lufthansa.com*. **Qatar Airways** ⊠ *Trg Nikole Šubića Zrinskog 14* ☎ *01/496–1111, 01/456–2267 Zagreb Internatioanl Airport, 01/456–2368 Zagreb International Airport* ⊕ *www.qatarairways. com*. **TAP** ☎ *01/487–8774, 01/487–8776* ⊕ *www.flytap.com*. **Turkish Airlines** ⊠ *Trg bana Josipa Jelačića 4/1* ☎ *01/492–1854, 01/492–1855, 01/492–1856, 01/626–5158 Zagreb International Airport, 01/456–2008 Zagreb International Airport* ⊕ *www.turkishairlines.com*.

Airport Contacts Zagreb International Airport (*Zagreb Pleso Airport*). ⊠ *Rudolfa Fizira 1, Velika Gorica* ☎ *01/4562-222 general information,*

01/456–2229 lost and found, 060/320-320 within Croatia, +38 51/4562–170 outside Croatia ⊕ www.zagreb-airport.hr.

Airport Transfer Contacts Airport bus (*Pleso prijevoz*). ✉ *Pleso prijevoz, Avenija Marina Držića 4, Zagreb* ☎ *01/633–1982* ⊕ *www.plesoprijevoz.hr.*

BUS TRAVEL

Frequent regular coach service to destinations all over mainland Croatia departs from the capital. The traveling time is 6 hours from Zagreb to Split and 10½ hours from Zagreb to Dubrovnik. There are also daily international bus lines to Slovenia (Ljubljana), Hungary (Barcs and Nagykanisza), Serbia (Belgrade), Austria (Graz), Germany (Munich, Stuttgart, Frankfurt, Dortmund, Cologne, and Düsseldorf), and Switzerland (Zurich). Timetable information is available from the main bus station, a 20-minute walk from the center.

About 30 buses run daily between Zagreb and Karlovac in just under an hour and for a one-way fare of around 45 Kn.

Samobor is a 50-minute bus ride from Zagreb; buses between Zagreb and Samobor run every 30 minutes or so weekdays, roughly every hour on weekends; the fare is around 30 Kn each way, and Samobor's small bus station is about 100 yards north of the main square.

There are daily direct buses to Plitvice Lakes National Park. Some buses between Zagreb and Split will stop at both entrances to Plitvice Lakes National Park; the fare is around 95 Kn one-way between Zagreb and Plitvice.

A small handful of buses go daily from Zagreb to Sisak and then continue on narrow, two-lane roads to the charming village of Čigoć.

Contacts Varaždin Bus Station ✉ *Zrinskih i Frankopana BB, Varaždin* ☎ *042/407–888.* **Zagreb Bus Station** ✉ *Av. Marina Držića 4, Zagreb* ☎ *060/313–333* ⊕ *www.akz.hr.*

BUS AND TRAM TRAVEL WITHIN ZAGREB

An extensive network of city buses and trams—almost exclusively trams within the town center—runs 24 hours a day, with less frequent night service starting at approximately 11:30 pm and lasting until 4 am. Tickets cost 10 Kn for a day-service ride and 15 Kn for a night-service ride. A full-day ticket (30 Kn), available at some kiosks, is valid until 4 am the next morning. As an alternative, you can buy the Zagreb Card for 90 Kn; this covers public transport within the city limits for three days and offers substantial discounts at various museums and other cultural venues. After you board the bus or tram, you must validate your ticket with a time stamp (little yellow machines located only in the first and last cars of each tram); tickets are good for 1½ hours and are transferable in the same direction. If you are caught without a valid ticket, you will be fined 250 Kn, payable on the spot.

Contact ZET (*Zagreb Transport Authority*). ✉ *Ozaljska 105* ☎ *060/100–001* ⊕ *www.zet.hr.*

CAR TRAVEL

Prices vary, and you will probably pay less if you rent from a local company that's not part of an international chain; it's best to shop around. You can find economy cars (e.g., Seat Ibiza or Volkswagen Polo) from 350 Kn per day, compact cars (e.g., Volkswagen Golf or Hyundai) from 450 Kn per day, intermediate cars (e.g., Skoda Octavia) from 720 Kn per day, or standard cars (e.g., Audi A4) from 850 Kn per day. If you can't drive a stick shift, beware: automatic transmission is rarely available on smaller cars. These prices include unlimited mileage, CDW (collision damage waiver) and TP (theft protection), but not PAI (personal accident insurance). If you drive one-way (say, from Zagreb to Dubrovnik), there is an additional drop-off charge, but it depends on the type of car and the number of days you are renting. While staying in the capital you are better off without a car, but if you wish to visit the nearby hills of Zagorje, or go farther afield to the Međimurje region, a vehicle is helpful unless you want to take a bus to a different attraction each day.

Contacts **Avis** ⊠ *Oreškovićeva 21, Donji Grad, Zagreb* ☎ *01/467–6111* ⊕ *www.avis.com.hr* ⊠ *Zagreb International Airport, Velika Gorica* ☎ *01/626–5190* ⊕ *www.avis.com.hr.* **Budget** ⊠ *Oreškovićeva 21, Donji Grad, Zagreb* ☎ *01/615–8858* ⊕ *www.budget.hr* ⊠ *Zagreb International Airport, Velika Gorica* ☎ *01/626–5193* ⊕ *www.budget.hr.* **Hertz** ⊠ *Ulica Grada Vukovara 274, Donji Grad, Zagreb* ☎ *01/484–6777, 0900–1300* ⊕ *www.hertz.hr* ⊠ *Zagreb International Airport, Velika Gorica* ☎ *01/456–2635, 0800–2100* ⊕ *www.hertz.hr.* **Sixt** ⊠ *Trg sportova 9, Donji Grad, Zagreb* ⊕ *hr.sixt.com.*

TAXI TRAVEL

You can find taxi ranks in front of the bus and train stations, near the main square of Ban Jelačić, and in front of the larger hotels. Several companies are now available: Radio Taxi Zagreb, Taxi Zagreb 3628, Ekotaxi and Taxi Cammeo. It is also possible to order a taxi. All drivers are bound by law to run a meter—but this doesn't necessarily mean they will unless you ask—and the price can vary from 8.80 Kn for flagfall and from 4.90 Kn per km. Most companies have the same prices for day and night riding, as well as for rides on Sundays and holidays. Most companies do not charge for luggage.

Contacts **Eko Taxi** ⊠ *Vodovodna 20a, Zagreb* ☎ *01/889–2012* ⊕ *www.ekotaxi.hr.* **Radio Taxi** ⊠ *Ulica Božidara Magovca 55* ☎ *600/800–800* ⊕ *www.radio-taksi-zagreb.hr.* **Taxi Cammeo** ⊠ *Radnička cesta 27, Zagreb* ☎ *01/1212* ⊕ *www.taxi-cammeo.hr.*

TRAIN TRAVEL

Zagreb's main train station lies in Donji Grad, a 10-minute walk south from the main square of Ban Jelačić. There are daily international trains to and from Budapest (Hungary), Belgrade (Serbia), Munich (Germany), Vienna (Austria), and Venice (Italy). From Zagreb there are six trains daily to Split in Dalmatia (6–8 hours) and three trains daily to Rijeka in Kvarner (3½–4½ hours). The easiest way to get to Varaždin from Zagreb is by rail, with some 15 trains daily. Travel time is about 2½ hours and costs 65 Kn each way. About 15 trains run daily between Zagreb and Karlovac (with a similar number of buses), in just under an hour for a one-way fare of 36 Kn. If you don't have wheels, your best bet to reach Sisak is by rail for 34 Kn, with 15 trains daily from Zagreb that take about an hour.

Contacts Hrvatske željeznice (*Croatia Railways*). ⊠ *Trg kralja Tomislava 12, Donji Grad, Zagreb* ☎ *060/333–444 information* ⊕ *www.hzpp. hr.* **Karlovac Train Station** ⊠ *Vilima Reinera 3, Kalovac* ☎ *060/333–444 Information, 060/646–244 information.* **Varaždin Train Station** ⊠ *Kolodvorska 17, Varaždin* ☎ *060/333–444.* **Zagreb Train Station** ⊠ *Trg kralja Tomislava 12, Donji Grad, Zagreb* ☎ *060/333–444* ⊕ *www.hznet.hr.*

TOURS

The tourist information centers inside the Zagreb train station and on the main square (Trg bana Jelačića 11) organize amusing and informative guided tours of the city.

Hop on hop off Zagreb. Zagreb's tourists have an opportunity to see the city from attractive open-top buses, which operate along two routes (red and green routes) throughout the city. Tickets are valid for an entire day, which is plenty of time to see most of Zagreb's most famous landmarks. This service is provided by the Zagreb Electric Tram Company (ZET) in cooperation with the Zagreb Tourist Board. The red line (1-hour tour) operates within the narrow city center with six stops along the route. The green line (1.5-hour tour) includes the best known green oases of Zagreb with seven stops along the route. The departure point is from Bakačeva Street on Kaptol. The red line departs at 10 am, noon, 6 pm, and 8 pm; the green line departs at 2 pm and 4 pm. The price for a one-day ticket is 70 kuna, while children between the ages of 7 and 18 pay half price. You can purchase tickets from the driver or at the ZET office, Petrićeva 4, from 8 am to 9 pm weekdays and from 8 am to 3:50 pm on Saturday. ⊠ *Zagreb* ☎ *060/100–001* ⊕ *zet.hr.*

Ibus. Every day of the week the Ibus travel agency offers combination bus-and-walking guided tours of the city center for 165 Kn a person (minimum four people); call a day in advance to reserve. It also provides tours of attractions farther afield, including Veliki Tabor, Trakošćan, and Varaždin, and Plitvice Lakes National Park. ⊠ *Tkalčićeva 7/1, Gornji Grad, Zagreb* ☎ *01/369–4333, 01/364–8633* ⊕ *www.ibus.hr.*

Segway CityTour. For a state-of-the-art experience, you can try the Segway CityTour from mid-April through mid-October. The 50-minute "Basic Ride" takes place daily at 9 am and costs 250 Kn per person; the 130-minute "All Around Tour" takes place daily at 9 am and costs 495 Kn per person. They offer also themed tours such as Sensual Zagreb, Zagreb Talks, ZagrebByBike, Secret Zagreb Walks, and a Night Tour of Gornji Grad called the "Secret of Grič." ☎ *01/456–6055* ⊕ *www. segway.hr.*

RESTAURANTS

Although there are seafood restaurants in Zagreb and large towns like Varaždin, this inland region is better known for roasted meats accompanied by heavy side dishes such as *zagorski štrukli* (baked cheese dumplings). For dessert, walnut-, jam-, and sweet curd-cheese–filled *palačinke* (crepes) are on nearly every menu. Balkan-style grilled meats such as *ćevapčići* (well-seasoned sausage links, often served with raw onions) are popular, and lower in price than more elaborate main courses. The influence of Slavonia to the east and Hungary to the north is evident in the form of paprika-rich dishes, whether *fiš paprikaš* (made from fish and also called *riblji paprikaš*) or various goulashes. Some restaurants, particularly in Zagreb, and especially those owned and operated by folks from Dalmatia, do excel in fresh seafood straight from the Adriatic. But when it comes to fish, you are likely to find more freshwater options such as carp, pike, and pike-perch. Many restaurants serve pasta and pizza as budget alternatives, but there is not as much Italian-style fare here as there is on the coast. If you head to Varaždin or a smaller town, prices will drop somewhat, though not dramatically. Last but not least, note that some restaurants close for two to four weeks between late July and August 20, when everybody heads to the coast.

HOTELS

It's a fact of life that Zagreb doesn't get the same sort of tourist traffic as the coast, so the region's major hotels have gone to great lengths since the end of the Yugoslav war to cater to business travelers. Although this trend has yielded a spate of impressive renovations (some still ongoing or planned as of this writing), it has also driven prices up considerably. Rates of €100 or (much) more for a double room are not uncommon in central Zagreb's largest hotels, though a 10- to 20-minute walk or short tram ride from downtown will bring you to comfortable, modern pensions for considerably less. You have to go to smaller towns or to the countryside to get cheaper options, though some private rooms and agritourism-style accommodations are quite affordable.

Hotel reviews have been shortened. For full information, visit Fodors.com.

WHAT IT COSTS IN EUROS (€) AND CROATIAN KUNA (KN)			
$	**$$**	**$$$**	**$$$$**
Restaurants under 35 Kn	35 Kn–60 Kn	61 Kn–80 Kn	over 80 Kn
under €5	€5–€8	€9–€10	over €10
Hotels under 925 Kn	925 Kn–1,300 Kn	1,301 Kn–1,650 Kn	over 1,650 Kn
under €121	€121–€170	€171–€216	over €216

Restaurant prices are the average cost of a main course at dinner or, if dinner is not served, at lunch. Hotel prices are the lowest cost of a standard double room in high season.

VISITOR INFORMATION

Zagreb's main tourist information center is right on the main square, Trg bana Jelačića. It's open weekdays 8:30 am to 9 pm, weekends 9 to 6 (summer working hours). A smaller office is within the train station and open weekdays 9–9 and weekends noon–8:30.

Contacts Croatian National Tourist Board ⊠ *Iblerov trg 10/IV, Zagreb* ☎ *01/469–9300* ⊕ *croatia.hr.* **Plitvice Lakes National Park Tourist Information** ⊠ *Entrance No. 1 to NP Plitvička Jezera, Velika Poljana* ☎ *053/776–798 tourist board office* ⊕ *www.tzplitvice.hr* ☉ *Daily 8–8.* **Samobor**

Tourist Information ✉ *Trg Krajla Tomislava 5, Samobor* ☎ *01/336–004* ⊕ *www.tz-samobor.hr* ⊙ *Weekdays 8–5, Sat. 9–5, Sun. 10–5.* **Varaždin Tourist Information** ✉ *Ivana Padovca 3, Varaždin* ☎ *042/210–987* ⊕ *www. tourism-varazdin.hr.***Zagreb Tourist Information** ✉ *Trg bana J. Jelačića, Donji Grad, Zagreb* ☎ *01/481–4051, 01/481–4052, 01/481–4054* ⊕ *www.zagreb-touristinfo.hr* ⊙ *Summer: weekdays 8:30–9, weekends 9–6; Winter: weekdays 8:30-8, Sat. 9–6, Sun. 10–4.*

2

ZAGREB

The capital of Croatia, Zagreb has a population of roughly 1 million and is situated at the extreme edge of the Pannonian Plain, between the north bank of the Sava River and the southern slopes of Mt. Medvednica. Its early years are shrouded in mystery, though there are indications of a Neolithic settlement on this site. The Romans are said to have established a municipality of sorts that was destroyed around AD 600, when Croatian tribes moved in.

Like so many other notable European cities, Zagreb started out as a strategic crossroads along an international river route, which was followed much later by north–south and east–west passages by road and rail. For much of its history the city also served as a bastion on a defensive frontier, pounded for half a millennium by thundering hordes of invaders, among them Hungarians, Mongols, and Turks.

From the late Middle Ages until the 19th century, Zagreb was composed of two adjoining but separate towns on the high ground (Gornji Grad): one town was secular, the other expressly religious. In 1242 the secular town, named Gradec (Fortress), was burned to the ground in a wave of destruction by the Tartars, after which it locked itself up behind protective walls and towers. It is from this time that the real Zagreb (meaning Behind the Hill) began to evolve; it was accorded the status of a free royal city in the same year by the Hungarian-Croatian king Bela IV. In the 15th century the ecclesiastical center, named Kaptol (Chapter House), also enclosed itself in defensive walls in response to the threat of a Turkish invasion.

When Zagreb became the capital of Croatia in 1557, the country's parliament began meeting alternately in Gradec and at the Bishop's Palace in Kaptol. When Kaptol and Gradec were finally put under a single city administration in 1850, urban development accelerated. The railway reached Zagreb in 1862, linking the city to Vienna, Trieste, and the Adriatic. It was at this time that Donji grad (Lower Town) came into being. Lying between Gornji grad and the main train station, it was designed to accommodate new public buildings—the National Theater, the university, and various museums. Built in grandiose style and interspersed by wide, tree-lined boulevards, parks, and gardens, it makes a fitting monument to the Habsburg era.

The Tito years brought a period of increasing industrialization coupled with urban expansion, as the new high-rise residential suburb of Novi Zagreb was constructed south of the Sava. In 1991 the city escaped the war of independence relatively unscathed, except for an attempted rocket attack on the Croatian Parliament building in Gradec. Zagreb did, however, suffer severe economic hardship as the country's industries collapsed, post-Communist corruption set in, and an influx of refugees—mainly from Bosnia and Herzegovina—arrived in search of a better life.

Since 2000 public morale has picked up considerably: trendy street cafés are thriving, numerous smart new stores have opened, and the public gardens are once again carefully tended. However, underlying this apparent affluence, unemployment remains a lingering problem. That said, unlike in Budapest, the much larger capital of neighboring Hungary, obvious signs of economic distress—such as panhandlers and homeless people—are relatively rare, and the casual observer will probably notice a general atmosphere of prosperity (fueled in part by coastal tourism). Croatia's accession to the European Union in July 2013 holds the promise of continued economic vitality.

GETTING HERE AND AROUND

After arriving in this regional hub city by any one of numerous flights from Germany (Frankfurt, Munich), United Kingdom (London), France (Paris), Austria (Vienna), Hungary (Budapest), or elsewhere, the best way to get into the city is by taxi or the economical airport shuttle. The best way to get around the city is by the efficient tram system, for which you can buy multiuse and all-day tourist cards online and at many hotels and hostels.

EXPLORING

The city is clearly divided into two distinct districts: **Gornji grad** (Upper Town) and **Donji grad** (Lower Town). While hilltop Gornji grad is made up of winding cobbled streets and terra-cotta rooftops sheltering beneath the cathedral and the Croatian Parliament building, Donji grad is where you'll find the city's most important 19th-century cultural institutions, including the National Theater, the university, and a number of museums, all in an organized grid.

GORNJI GRAD (UPPER TOWN)

The romantic hilltop area of Gornji grad dates back to medieval times, and is undoubtedly the loveliest part of Zagreb.

TOP ATTRACTIONS

Fodor's Choice **Crkva svetog Marka** (*St. Mark's Church*). The original building was ★ erected in the 13th century, and was once the parish church of Gradec. The baroque bell tower was added in the 17th century, while the steeply pitched roof—decorated in brilliant, multicolor tiles arranged to depict the coats of arms of Zagreb on the right and the Kingdom of Croatia, Dalmatia, and Slavonia on the left—was added during reconstruction in the 19th century. It underwent another reconstruction in the first half of the 20th century. At that time, renowned painter Jozo Kljakovic painted its walls, while the altar was decorated with works of famous sculptor Ivan Mestrovic. ✉ *Trg Svetog Marka 5, Gornji Grad, Zagreb* 🕾 *01/485–1611* 💲 *Free* ☉ *Open for mass only, July and Aug: weekdays 6 pm, Sat. 7:30 am, Sun. 11 am, and 6 pm; during rest of day, only church lobby is open to public.*

Dolac (*Market*). Farmers from the surrounding countryside set up their stalls here daily, though the market is at its busiest on Friday and Saturday mornings. On the upper level, fresh fruit and vegetables are displayed on an open-air piazza under the protective shade of oversize umbrellas with a distinctive red color, known as Sestinski kisobrani because much smaller versions form part of the traditional garb of Sestine, a village just north of Zagreb. Dairy products and meats are sold in an indoor market below. ⊠ *Tržnica, Dolac 9, Gornji Grad, Zagreb* ⊕ *www.trznice-zg.hr* ⊙ *Weekdays 6:30–3, Sat. 6:30–2, Sun. 6:30–1.*

Fodor's Choice
★

Museum of Broken Relationships. Opened in 2010, this museum displays objects connected to love stories that didn't work out. The entire exhibition is made up of personal belongings donated by people from around the world who endured a failed relationship, and each exhibit is accompanied by a brief text, explaining the connection between the object and the relationship. Subtly illustrating the tragicomedy that is love, it is now one of Zagreb's most visited museums and its collection has toured numerous locations in Asia, Africa, the United States, and Europe. ⊠ *Ćirilometodska 2, Gornji Grad, Zagreb* ☎ *01/485–1021* ⊕ *www.brokenships.com* ▣ *25 Kn* ⊙ *June–Sept., daily 9 am–10:30 pm; Oct.–May, daily 9–9.*

Museum of Contemporary Art (*Muzej suvremene umjetnosti*). Opened in 2009, this long-awaited museum displays works created since 1950 by Croatian and foreign artists. It's well worth a visit for anyone interested in modern art—the vast collection includes paintings, sculptures, graphic design, films, and videos. It lies outside the city center. To get here, take Tram 6 from the Trg bana Jelačića (east direction); journey time is approximately 30 minutes. ⊠ *Avenija Dubrovnik 17, Novi Zagreb, Zagreb* ☎ *01/605–2700* ⊕ *www.msu.hr* ▣ *30 Kn* ⊙ *Tues.–Fri. and Sun. 11–6, Sat. 11–8.*

Muzej grada Zagreba (*Zagreb City Museum*). Well worth a visit for anyone interested in urban design, this museum traces the city's most important historical, economic, political, social, and cultural events from medieval times to the present day. Exhibits include detailed scale models of how the city has evolved, as well as sections devoted to the old trade guilds, domestic life, and sacred art. ⊠ *Opatička 20, Gornji Grad, Zagreb* ☎ *01/485–1361, 01/485–1362* ⊕ *www.mgz.hr* ▣ *30 Kn* ⊙ *Tues.–Fri. 10–6, Sat. 11–7, Sun. 10–2* ⊙ *Closed public holidays.*

WORTH NOTING

Crkva svete Katarine (*St. Catherine's Church*). Built for the Jesuit order between 1620 and 1632, this church is the most beautiful baroque church in Zagreb. It is a one-nave church with six side chapels and a shrine. The vaults and the walls are decorated with pink and white stucco from 1732 as well as 18th-century illusionist paintings. The altars are the work of Francesco Robba and 17th-century Croatian artists. The church was thoroughly reconstructed after the 1880 earthquake, based on the design of Hermann Bolle. ⊠ *Katarinin trg BB, Gornji Grad, Zagreb* ☎ *01/485–1950* ▣ *Free* ⊙ *Mass: weekdays 6 pm, Sun. 11 am.*

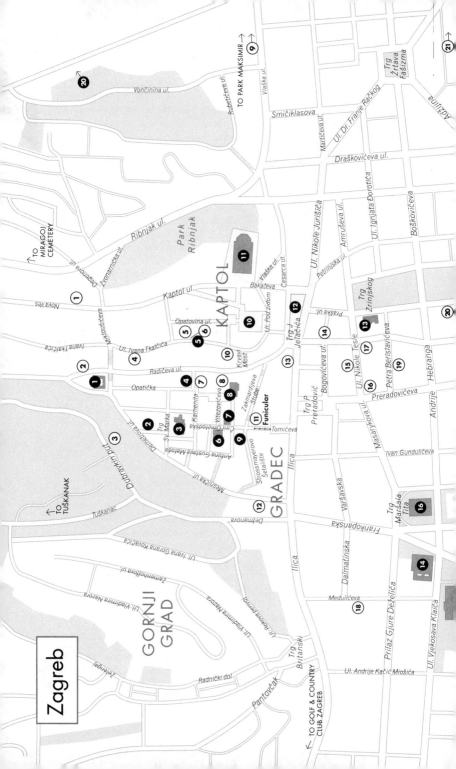

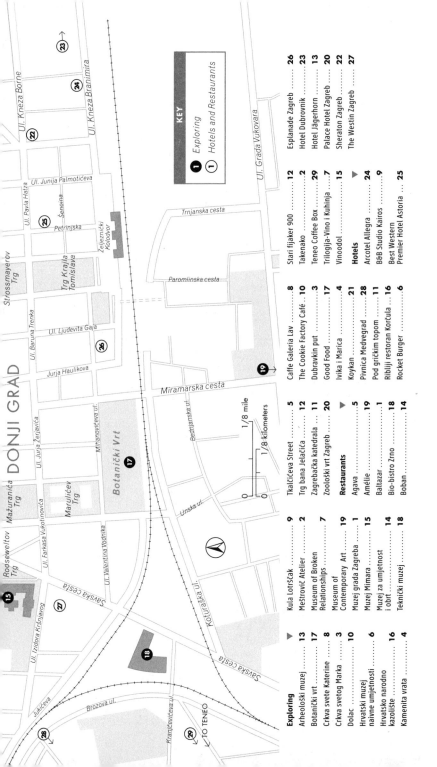

DONJI GRAD

Mažuranića Trg

Rooseweltov Trg

Botanički Vrt

KEY

1 Exploring

1 Hotels and Restaurants

Exploring

Arheološki muzej	**13**
Botanički vrt	**17**
Crkva svete Katerine	**8**
Crkva svetog Marka	**3**
Dolac	**10**
Hrvatski muzej naivne umjetnosti	**6**
Hrvatsko narodno kazalište	**16**
Kamenita vrata	**4**
Kula Lotrščak	**9**
Meštrović Atelier	**2**
Museum of Broken Relationships	**7**
Museum of Contemporary Art	**19**
Muzej grada Zagreba	**1**
Muzej Mimara	**15**
Muzej za umjetnost i obrt	**14**
Tehnički muzej	**18**
Tkalčićeva Street	**5**
Trg bana Jelačića	**12**
Zagrebačka katedrala	**11**
Zoološki vrt Zagreb	**20**

Restaurants

Agava	**5**
Amélie	**19**
Baltazar	**1**
Bio-bistro Zrno	**18**
Boban	**14**
Caffe Galeria Lav	**8**
The Cookie Factory Café	**10**
Dubravkin put	**3**
Good Food	**17**
Ivika i Marica	**4**
Koykan	**21**
Pivnica Medvegrad	**28**
Pod griškim topom	**11**
Ribiljii restoran Korčula	**16**
Rocket Burger	**6**
Stari fijaker 900	**12**
Takenako	**2**
Teneo Coffee Box	**29**
Trilogija-Vino i Kuhinja	**7**
Vinoodol	**15**

Hotels

Arcotel Allegra	**24**
B&B Studio Kairos	**9**
Best Western Premier Hotel Astoria	**25**
Esplanade Zagreb	**26**
Hotel Dubrovnik	**23**
Hotel Jägerhorn	**13**
Palace Hotel Zagreb	**20**
Sheraton Zagreb	**22**
The Westin Zagreb	**27**

1/8 mile

1/8 kilometers

Hrvatski muzej naivne umjetnosti (*Croatian Museum of Native Art*). This unusual school of painting dates back to the 1930s and features more than 1,600 works of untutored peasant artists, primarily from the village of Hlebine in Koprivnica Križevci County. Canvases by the highly esteemed Ivan Generalić dominate here, though there are also paintings, drawings, sculptures, and prints by other noted members of the movement,

> **FUEL UP**
>
> If you're out and about exploring and your belly starts grumbling, the simplest solution, as elsewhere in Croatia, is to pick up a *burek* (a meat-filled pastry) or a *pita sa sirom* (a cheese-filled pastry) at a *pekarna* (bakery) for a quick, greasy, decidedly budget (10 Kn or less) snack.

plus a section devoted to foreigners working along similar lines. ⊠ *Sv. Ćirila i Metoda 3, Gornji Grad, Zagreb* ☎ *01/485–1911* ⊕ *www.hmnu. org* ☜ *20 Kn* ☉ *Tues.–Fri. 10–6, weekends 10–1* ☉ *Closed Mon. and national holidays* .

Kamenita vrata (*Stone Gate*). The original 13th-century city walls had four gates, of which only Kamenita Vrata remains. Deep inside the dark passageway, locals stop to pray before a small shrine adorned with flickering candles. In 1731 a devastating fire consumed all the wooden elements of the gate, except for a painting of the Virgin and Child, which was found in the ashes, remarkably undamaged. Kamenita Vrata has since become a pilgrimage site, as can be seen from the numerous stone plaques saying *Hvala Majko Bozja* (Thank you, Mother of God). ⊠ *Kamenita vrata, Gornji Grad, Zagreb* ⊕ *www.zagreb-touristinfo.hr.*

OFF THE BEATEN PATH

Mirogoj Cemetery. A satisfying if somber little outing can be had by catching Bus 106 or 226 on Kaptol, in front of the Zagreb Cathedral, and riding it about 10 minutes to the fifth stop, Arkade. Designed by architect Herman Bollé and opened in 1872, Zagreb's most celebrated cemetery is set on a hillside north of downtown and features an imposing entrance: a long, massive brick wall topped by a row of striking green cupolas. Just behind this is the black-marble grave of Franjo Tudjman, the man who served as Croatia's first president after the nation declared its independence from the former Yugoslavia. This lovely parklike cemetery, marked by paths lined with towering horse chestnut trees and by more black marble graves than you can count, is the final resting place for those of many creeds, from Roman Catholic and Serbian Orthodox to Jewish and Muslim. ⊠ *Aleja Hermanna Bollea 27* ⊕ *www.gradskagroblja.hr* ☉ *Apr.–Sept., 6 am–8 pm; Oct.–Mar., 7:30 am–6 pm.*

Kula Lotršćak (*Lotršćak Tower*). Formerly the entrance to the fortified medieval Gradec, Kula Lotršćak now houses a multilevel gallery with occasional exhibits of contemporary art. Each day at noon a small cannon is fired from the top of the tower in memory of the times when it was used to warn of the possibility of an Ottoman attack. You can climb the tower partway, via a spiral wooden staircase, for a look into the gallery rooms (which occupy several floors), or you can ascend all the way to the observation deck for splendid views of Zagreb and environs. ⊠ *Strossmayerovo šetalište, Gornji Grad, Zagreb* ☎ *01/485–1926*

⊕ *www.galerijaklovic.hr* 📷 *Obser-vation deck 20 Kn; gallery free* ☉ *Weekdays 9–9, weekends 10–9.*

Meštrović Atelier. This 17th-century building, with its interior court-yard, served as home and studio to Ivan Meštrović from 1922 until his emigration to the United States in 1942. The building was exten-sively remodeled according to plans devised by the artist and was turned into a memorial museum with a permanent exhibition of his sculp-tures and drawings after his death in 1962. (There is a larger collec-tion of his works in the Meštrović Gallery in Split.) ✉ *Mletačka 8, Gornji Grad, Zagreb* ☎ *01/485–1123, 01/485–1124* ⊕ *www.mdc.hr* 📷 *20 Kn* ☉ *Tues.–Fri. 10–6, weekends 10–2* ☉ *Closed Mon., public holidays.*

> ### CITY VIEWS
>
> For sublime views east toward the Old Town, with its three prominent church steeples and many red-tile rooftops (including more than a few satellite dishes), stroll through the open wrought-iron gate just to the right of St. Catherine's Church. You'll find yourself on a spacious concrete plaza where you can take in the scene and then catch a flight of steps down past a lively café-bar toward Ilica.

Fodor's Choice ★ **Tkalčićeva Street.** This street was once a channel forming the boundary between Kaptol and Gradec, then known as Potok (the brook). Today, it is a charming, well-maintained pedestrian zone lined with 19th-century town houses, many of which have been converted into popular café-bars at street level—attracting a huge cross section of Croatian and international youth from morning until late at night. ✉ *Tkalčićeva, Gornji Grad, Zagreb.*

Trg bana Jelačića (*Ban Jelačić Square; Trg*). Buildings lining the square date from 1827 onward and include several fine examples of Viennese Secessionist architecture. The centerpiece is an equestrian statue of Ban Jelačić, the first Croatian viceroy, erected in 1866. Originally facing north toward Hungary, against which Jelacic waged war as a com-mander in the Austrian Imperial Army, the statue was dismantled after World War II by the Communist government, only to be reinstalled in 1990, this time facing south. The square features the Manduševac fountain located to the east. ✉ *Between Ilica to west, Praška to south, and Jurišićeva to east, Donji Grad, Zagreb.*

Fodor's Choice ★ **Zagrebačka katedrala** (*The Cathedral of Assumption of the Blessed Vir-gin Mary and Saint Stephen and Saint Ladislaus*). Dedicated to the Assumption of Mary and to the kings Saint Stephen and Saint Ladis-laus, the Zagreb Cathedral was built on the site of a former 12th-cen-tury cathedral destroyed by the Tartars in 1242. The present structure was constructed between the 13th and 16th centuries. The striking neo-Gothic facade was added by architect Herman Bollé following the earthquake of 1880, its twin steeples being the identifying feature of the city's skyline. Behind the impressive main altar are crypts of Zagreb's archbishops and of Croatian national heroes. The interior is imposing and inspires silent reflection. Don't neglect the north wall, which bears an inscription of the Ten Commandments in 12th-century Glagolithic script. ✉ *Kaptol 31, Gornji Grad, Zagreb* ☎ *01/481–4727* ⊕ *www.*

zg-nadbiskupija.hr ✉ *Free* ☉ *Daily 7–7. Masses held Mon.–Sat. 7 am, 8 am, 9 am, 6 pm, Sun. and church holidays masses at 7 am, 8 am, 9 am, 10 am, 11:30 am, 6 pm.*

Pingvin Sandwich Bar. If you are looking for a quick and inexpensive lunch, consider the Pingvin Sandwich Bar, groundbreaking for being the first in the city. This popular stand just a few minutes' walk from Trg Bana Jelačića offers things like grilled chicken sandwiches or soy-patty-equipped veggie burgers. Ordering is simple: not only do most clerks speak English, but there are also user-friendly pictures and English translations. ✉ *Nikole Tesle 7, Donji Grad, Zagreb* ☎ *01/481–1446* ☉ *Mon.–Sat. 9 am–4 am, Sun. 7 pm–2 am.*

WHY HIKE WHEN YOU CAN RIDE?

If you're walking along Ilica from the main square, you might wonder about the best route up the hill to Lotrščak Tower and beyond to St. Mark's Church. Well, you can save yourself the steep hike up by catching the funicular, which runs six times an hour, 6:30 am to 10 pm, from short Tomićeva ulica (just off Ilica) just a few hundred yards up the hillside. The cost is 4 Kn; you can buy the ticket when you board.

DONJI GRAD (LOWER TOWN)

Donji grad came into being during the late 19th century. The urban plan, which follows a grid pattern, was drawn up by Milan Lenuci and combines a succession of squares and parks laid out in a "U" shape (known as the Green Horseshoe), all overlooked by the city's main public buildings and cultural institutions.

TOP ATTRACTIONS

Arheološki muzej (*Archaeological Museum*). Museum exhibits focus on prehistoric times to the Tartar invasion. Pride of place is given to the Vučedol Dove, a three-legged ceramic vessel in the form of a bird, dating back to the 4th millennium BC, and a piece of linen bearing the longest known text in ancient Etruscan writing. The courtyard features a collection of stone relics from Roman times. ✉ *Trg Nikole Šubića Zrinskog 19, Donji Grad, Zagreb* ☎ *01/487–3000, 01/487–3101* ⊕ *www.amz.hr* ✉ *30 Kn* ☉ *Tues., Wed., Fri., and Sat 10–6, Thurs. 10–8, Sun. 10–1* ☉ *Closed Mon. and public holidays.*

Botanički vrt (*Botanical Garden*). Founded in 1889 as research grounds for the Faculty of Biology at Zagreb University, the garden includes an arboretum with English-style landscaping, a small artificial lake, and an ornamental Japanese bridge. ✉ *Marulićev trg 9a, Donji Grad, Zagreb* ☎ *01/489–8060* ⊕ *hirc.botanic.hr/vrt/home.htm* ✉ *Free* ☉ *Apr.–Nov., Mon., Tues. 9–2:30, Wed.–Sun. 9–7.*

FAMILY   **Tehnički muzej** (*Technical Museum*). It may be in a drab box of a building, but this museum is guaranteed to appeal to children and civil engineers alike; try to see it in the afternoon on a weekday or in the late morning on the weekend, when a series of guided visits are offered. The highlight here is the demonstration of some of Nikola Tesla's inventions, which takes place weekdays at 3:30 and weekends at 11:30, but there's also

2

the tour of a lifelike reconstruction of a coal mine at 3 on weekdays and 11 on weekends, and a planetarium visit at 4 on weekdays, noon on weekends. That's not to mention all the various engines on display, as well as a fascinating historical exhibit of firefighting equipment including trucks, ladders, and hoses aplenty. ⊠ *Savska cesta 18, Donji Grad, Zagreb* ☎ *01/484–4050* ⊕ *tehnicki-muzej.hr/* ⊠ *Museum 20 Kn, planetarium 15 Kn extra* ☉ *Tues.–Fri. 9–5, weekends 9–1.*

WORTH NOTING

Hrvatsko narodno kazalište (*Croatian National Theater*). The building dates from 1895, designed by the Viennese firm Hellmer and Fellner as part of the preparations for a state visit by Emperor Franz Josef. In front of the theater, set deep in a round concrete basin, is Meštrović's little, eerily lifelike sculpture *Zdenac Života* (*Fountain of Life*), from 1912, which depicts four naked couples writhing uncomfortably in each other's arms around a small pool of water while one lone, likewise naked gentleman stares meditatively into the pool. The only way to see the impressive, stately interior of the theater is to attend a performance. ⊠ *Trg maršala Tita 15, Donji Grad, Zagreb* ☎ *01/488–8418* ⊕ *www. hnk.hr.*

Muzej Mimara (*Mimara Museum*). In a huge gray building that's dull compared to some of those nearby, this vast private collection, including paintings, sculptures, ceramics, textiles, and rugs, was donated by Ante Topić Mimara (1898–1987), a Croatian who spent many years abroad where he made his fortune, supposedly as a merchant. On display are canvases attributed to such old masters as Raphael, Rembrandt, and Rubens, as well as more modern works by the likes of Manet, Degas, and Renoir, and ancient artifacts including Egyptian glassware and Chinese porcelain. ⊠ *Rooseveltov trg 5, Donji Grad, Zagreb* ☎ *01/482– 8100, 01/482–6079* ⊕ *www.mimara.hr* ⊠ *40 Kn* ☉ *Oct.–June, Tues., Wed., Fri., and Sat. 10–5, Thurs. 10–7, Sun. 10–2; July–Sept., Tues.–Fri. 10–7, Sat. 10–5, Sun. 10–2.*

Muzej za umjetnost i obrt (*Museum of Arts and Crafts*). Designed in 1888 by Herman Bollé, the architect responsible for the Zagreb Cathedral facade, this pleasant museum traces the development of the applied arts from the baroque period to the 20th century. Exhibits are displayed in chronological order, and although furniture design predominates, there are also sections devoted to sacred art, clocks, and clothing. ⊠ *Trg maršala Tita 10, Donji Grad, Zagreb* ☎ *01/488–2111* ⊕ *www.muo.hr* ⊠ *30 Kn* ☉ *Tues.–Sat. 10–7, Sun. 10–2.*

OFF THE BEATEN PATH

Maksimir Park. For a peaceful stroll in southeastern Europe's oldest landscaped, English-style park, hop on a tram and go visit Maksimir Park. A short ride east of the center of Zagreb (10 minutes on Tram 11 or 12 from Trg bana Jelačića or 15 minutes on Tram 4 or 7 from the train station), this 44½-acre expanse of vine-covered forests and several artificial lakes was a groundbreaker when it opened back in 1794. After getting off the tram, you walk forward a bit and enter on the left, through a prominent gate opposite the city's main soccer stadium, aptly named Stadion Maksimir. A long, wide promenade flanked by benches leads from here to Bellevue Pavilion (1843), perched atop a small hill and featuring a café. Be sure to check out the Echo Pavilion (Paviljon jeka), built in the late 19th century in honor of the Greek nymph Echo. Stand in the middle and you can hear the whispers of anyone standing within the pavilion, as if they were right next to you.

Zoološki vrt Zagreb. To your right along the way are some small lakes

> **SUMMER BREAK**
>
> If you're in town between late July and the third week of August, don't be surprised to find many restaurants closed for two to four weeks while the staff are off at the coast, as is much of Zagreb.

and, beyond, the city's modest zoo, where admission is 30 Kn; it's open daily from 9 am to 8 pm (last tickets sold at 6:30). To your left is a playground.

WHERE TO EAT

For budget fare, leave the main square, Trg bana Jelačića, and go up the steps towards Dolac (the main market). Halfway up the steps on your right is a row of bistros where you can get everything from *bureks* (a savory cheese- or meat-filled pastry) to simple pizzas to Balkan-style grilled meats for around half what you'd pay at a modestly priced restaurant. And do remember, though Zagreb is not exactly overflowing with budget sandwich shops, traditional bakeries have long fulfilled that role for locals; at such places, which are on practically every street corner, you can pick up a burek for as little as 10 Kn a piece.

GORNJI GRAD (UPPER TOWN)

$$$$ ✕ **Agava.** This is the only one among the many dining and drinking
MEDITERRANEAN   venues along bustling Tkalčićeva to require a steep walk up a flight of steps—but it's worth it. In warm weather you can enjoy your meal sitting on a wooden terrace overlooking the street, or else bask in the homey elegance of the inside space, with its wood-beamed ceiling, parquet floor, and rattan furnishings. Large windows let you gaze out onto the pedestrian thoroughfare below. So sit back, relax, and enjoy *hvarska pogača*, pasta, seafood or interesting desserts. $ *Average main: 110 Kn* ✉ *Tkalčićeva 39, Gornji Grad, Zagreb* ☎ *01/482–9826* ⊕ *www.restaurant-agava.hr* ⌦ *Reservations essential.*

$$ ✕ **Baltazar.** Nestled in a courtyard lying 10 minutes' walk uphill beyond
MEDITERRANEAN   the cathedral, just beyond Pizzeria 2, Baltazar is best known for classic Balkan dishes such as *ražnjići* (pork on the spit), *čevapčići* (spiced, ground-meat kebabs), and *zapečeni grah* (oven-baked beans). The interior is elegant, albeit slightly smoky, and the spacious courtyard has leaf-shaded seating. Complementing the main restaurant Baltazar at the same location are the fish restaurant Gašpar and the wine bar Melcior offering fresh fish and the best of local and international wines. $ *Average main: 300 Kn* ✉ *Nova ves 4, Gornji Grad, Zagreb* ☎ *01/466–6999, 01/466–6824* ⊕ *www.restoran-baltazar.hr* ⌦ *Reservations essential* ⊗ *Closed Sun. in July and Aug.*

$ CAFÉ Fodor's Choice ★ 🍴 **Caffe Galerija Lav.** Don't let the casual café fare fool you; this place is anything but standard. Located just up the hill (first right) from Kamenita Vrata, it is a perfect place to take a load off after the alpine climb into Gornji Grad, before heading on to seeing the Parliament, Museum of Broken Relationships and Crkva Svetog Marka. In Caffe Lav, you'll feel as if you were sitting in an art gallery, or perhaps the living room of a wealthy, art-collecting uncle. If you're lucky, the weather will be fine and you'll find a seat on the charming outside terrace, perched atop the passage leading down to the Kamenita Vrata. [$] *Average main: 30 Kn* ✉ *Opaticka 2, Gornji Grad, Zagreb* ☎ *01/492–2108* 💳 *No credit cards.*

$$$ MEDITERRANEAN Fodor's Choice ★ 🍴 **Pod gričkim topom.** This cozy, endearingly rustic yet elegant restaurant, built into a stone wall on the hillside up a modest flight of steps from the Hotel Jagerhorn, on Ilica, and close to the funicular station in Gornji grad, affords stunning views over the city rooftops. Dalmatian cooking predominates, with dishes such as *Jadranske lignje na žaru* (grilled Adriatic squid) and *crni rižoto od sipe* (cuttlefish-ink risotto), appreciated by locals and visitors alike. [$] *Average main: 110 Kn* ✉ *Zakmardijeve stube 5, Gornji Grad, Zagreb* ☎ *01/483–3607* 🌐 *www.restoran-pod-grickim-topom.hr* ✍ *Reservations essential* 🕓 *Closed Sun.*

$$$$ JAPANESE 🍴 **Takenoko.** Don't be deterred by the tiny English-language translations on the menu outside; inside, the menu of this utterly chic, sparkling restaurant is completely readable. You can choose between sushi, both traditional Japanese rolls and American-style varieties; teriyaki; wok dishes; and specialties such as carrot and tofu soup or sea bass in jalapeno-wasabi sauce. Manned by head chefs Moto Mochizuki and Nenad Stošić, the Takenoko gives meaning to the word "fusion," merging Asian and European cuisine. Black chairs, black place mats, and cherry-toned wood floors set the scene in one of the glittery, glass-walled spaces on the ground floor of the Kaptol Centar facing Tkalćićeva. The drinks menu—including sake, of course—is extensive. [$] *Average main: 90 Kn* ✉ *Nova Ves 17, Gornji Grad, Zagreb* ☎ *01/486–0530* 🌐 *www.takenoko.hr.*

$$$$ MEDITERRANEAN 🍴 **Trilogija-Vino i kuhinja.** In Gornji grad close to Kamenita vrata, this quaint unpretentious restaurant offers superb food, an excellent wine list, and friendly professional staff. The menu changes frequently depending on the seasons and what's fresh at the morning market, but you can expect creative dishes such as shrimp risotto with wild asparagus, tuna steak with green polenta, as well as a hearty steak sandwich. [$] *Average main: 100 Kn* ✉ *Kamenita 5, Gornji Grad, Zagreb* ☎ *01/485–1394* 🌐 *www.trilogija.com* 🕓 *Closed Sun.*

DONJI GRAD (LOWER TOWN)

$ CAFÉ Fodor's Choice ★ 🍴 **Amélie.** For a cake and coffee experience that the French namesake of this cute little café would be proud of, pop into Amélie just down the hill from the Zagreb Cathedral. The wooden tables and cozy white interior give the place a charming, even slightly rustic feel, and the surprisingly varied selection of delectable cakes and pies will release all your caloric inhibitions. This unique gem among Zagreb watering holes offers unique sweets you won't find anywhere else, and they've recently begun offering ice creams. [$] *Average main: 30 Kn* ✉ *Vlaska ulica, Donji Grad, Zagreb* ☎ *01/558–3360* 🌐 *www.slasticeamelie.com.*

$$ ✕ **Bio-bistro Zrno.** If you want to strengthen the body and nourish the
VEGETARIAN spirit with seasonal, organic fresh fruits and vegetables, walk a few
blocks west from the main square to Bio-bistro Zrno, which offers fresh
vegetables, tofu, seitan, warm sourdough bread, organic coffee, wine,
tea, juice, smoothies, and shakes. All ingredients are delivered each day
directly from Croatia's first organic farm of the same name. Ⓢ *Average
main: 60 Kn* ✉ *Medulićeva 2, Donji Grad, Zagreb* ☎ *01/484–7540*
⊕ *www.zrnobiobistro.hr* ☾ *Mon.–Sat. noon–9:30.*

$$ ✕ **Boban.** Just down the street from the Hotel Dubrovnik, Boban is not
ITALIAN only a street-level bar but also a restaurant in the large vaulted cellar
space below. There is also a stylish dining room at street level, as well
as several tables outside for dining, chilling with a glass of white wine
and people-watching. Specializing in pasta dishes, it is extremely popular with locals, so be prepared to line up for a table, because reservations are not accepted. The owner, Zvonimir Boban, was captain of the
Croatian national football team during the 1998 World Cup. Ⓢ *Average
main: 75 Kn* ✉ *Gajeva 9, Donji Grad, Zagreb* ☎ *01/481–1549* ⊕ *www.
boban.hr.*

$ ✕ **The Cookie Factory Café.** Think of your favorite bakery, ice-cream par-
CAFÉ lor, and basic café rolled into one, and that's the Cookie Factory. With
Fodor's Choice its bright white interior, its walls gaily decorated with quirky graffiti,
★ and its extensive selection of cookies, brownies, and cakes hard to find
on this side of the Atlantic, you'll simply have to stop and relax for a
little while. Some of the tables have bench seating, so if you're just a
few people, you may end up making some fast friends. Try the mint
fudge brownie, because you're unlikely to find a version this authentic
anywhere else in this part of the world. The owners of this café also
run a smoothie, shake, and coffee bar farther up Tkalčićeva between
Nos. 30 and 32. Ⓢ *Average main: 30 Kn* ✉ *Tkalčićeva 21, Donji Grad,
Zagreb* ☎ *099/494–9400* ⊕ *www.cookiefactory.hr* ▭ *No credit cards.*

$$$$ ✕ **Dubravkin put.** Nestled in a verdant dale in Tuškanac Park, a 15-min-
SEAFOOD ute walk from the center in a low-rise building that might be mistaken
Fodor's Choice for a ranch-style house, this prestigious fish restaurant specializes in
★ creative Mediterranean fare, with the house favorites including *buzara*
(stew prepared with shellfish and scampi and/or fish) and sea bass fil-
lets in saffron and scampi sauce, as well as appetizers like avocado
with scampi, not to mention a few meat delicacies. The dining room
is light and airy, with candlelit tables, a wooden floor, palmlike little
trees, and colorful abstract art. There's also an adjoining wine bar.
In warm weather there's outdoor seating on a spacious, leafy terrace,
and a playground just outside invites children to scamper about while
parents rest on benches. Reservations are recommended, but only on
weekdays, as the Dubravkin put is a popular venue for business dinners.
Ⓢ *Average main: 120 Kn* ✉ *Dubravkin put 2, Zagreb* ☎ *01/483–4975*
⊕ *www.dubravkin-put.com* ⚐ *Reservations essential* ☾ *Closed Sun.,
2 wks in Aug.*

$ ✕ **Good Food.** One of the few fast-food places in the city where you can
FAST FOOD select from a range of decent salads, which they prepare right in front
of you, as well as other light, refreshing fare, including ciabatta sandwiches and vegetarian tortillas. Of course, they also serve the fast-food

standbys of burgers and fries, in case you're hungering for more carbs and protein. Try one of their in-house desserts, such as tiramisu. $ *Average main: 25 Kn* ✉ *Teslina 7, Donji Grad, Zagreb* 🕾 *No phone* ⊕ *www. goodfood.hr* ▭ *No credit cards* ⊘ *Mon.–Thurs. 11 am–1 am, Fri. 11 am–2 am, Sat. 10 am–2 am, Sun. 11 am–midnight.*

$$$ ✕ **Ivica i Marica.** Celebrated for its delectable cakes made with whole wheat and unrefined brown sugar, Ivica i Marica also serves traditional Croatian pastas, likewise using whole wheat, as well as hearty meat dishes. Try the tofu-stuffed pepper, homemade ravioli stuffed with spinach and cheese, or Zagorje specialties including *štrukli* (baked pastry filled with cheese). This being in Zagreb, you can also choose grilled seafood or, say, begin with an octopus salad. Waitstaff are decked out in folk costume, and an earnest attempt is made to evoke a folksy atmosphere, with carriage wheels and farm implements hanging from the ceiling. It's a tad touristy, but this charming restaurant, with white tablecloths, sparkling wine glasses, and an upbeat sound track, is still a great place to dine. $ *Average main: 85 Kn* ✉ *Tkalčićeva 70, Zagreb* 🕾 *01/481–7321* ⊕ *www.ivicaimarica.com.*

EASTERN EUROPEAN

$ ✕ **Koykan.** One of the few true meccas for vegetarians in the city, albeit a fast-food one. You can spend at least 15 minutes working your way through the menu, loaded with options for breads and fillings, with everything assembled to order. Piadinas, wraps, quesadillas, burritos, *somuni* (pita), and gyros can be filled with vegetarian, fish, and meat options. You can then spend another 10 minutes placing your order as you indicate your preference for sauce and toppings. Round out your meal with bubble tea or one of the numerous mochi flavors. $ *Average main: 25 Kn* ✉ *Gajeva 8, Donji Grad, Zagreb* 🕾 *01/482–7223* ▭ *No credit cards.*

FAST FOOD

$$ ✕ **Pivnica Medvedgrad.** Best known for its excellent beers brewed on the premises, the Pivnica Medvedgrad also serves up generous portions of roast meats, goulash, and beans and sausage, accompanied by a range of salads. One cavernous beer hall—replete with long wooden tables, high leather-backed chairs, and wood-beamed ceilings—is about a 10-minute walk west from the main square. The second, Little Medo, is somewhat smaller and is located in Tkalčićeva catering for younger audiences. $ *Average main: 60 Kn* ✉ *Ilica 49, Donji Grad, Zagreb* 🕾 *01/484–6922* ⊕ *pivnica-medvedgrad.hr.*

EASTERN EUROPEAN

$$$ ✕ **Ribliji restoran Korčula.** As suggested by the *ribliji* (fish) in its full name, the Korčula is a reliable choice for fresh seafood, including Dalmatian-style cod and tuna with mangold (i.e., Swiss chard). The menu also has a sprinkling of meat dishes, such as stewed beef in wine sauce with dumplings. A five-minute walk from the main square and popular with locals, this cozy restaurant is a moderately appealing place to sit back and fuel up for an hour or two, adorned as it is with black-and-white photos and fishnets hanging from the ceiling. $ *Average main: 110 Kn* ✉ *Nikole Tesle 17, Donji Grad, Zagreb* 🕾 *01/487–2159* ⊕ *www. restoran-korcula.hr* ⊘ *Closed Sun.*

SEAFOOD

$$ ✕ **Rocket Burger.** This recent addition to the range of dining and imbibing options along Tkalciceva doubled the neighborhood's "street cred" as a cosmopolitan quartier because it is the first truly American-style

AMERICAN

diner in this neck of the global woods. It may also well be the only place in Zagreb, if not the entire country, where you can get a relatively authentic American breakfast. Though the establishment itself projects a limited diner vibe, as it is forced to occupy a small closet space offering no room for a proper spread of wire-rimmed tables and squat bar stools, the menu does the job quite nicely. Cheeseburgers, bacon cheeseburgers, a monster called the "Double Double," and the Cheddar Bacon Supreme start off the menu. Then come other American classics like pulled pork, grilled cheese sandwiches, and chicken wings. For breakfast, enjoy the American pancakes (with syrup that tastes natural, believe it or not), a bacon omelet, or French toast. $ *Average main: 60 Kn* ✉ *Tkalčićeva 44, Donji Grad, Zagreb.*

$$ ✕ **Stari fijaker 900.** This old-fashioned restaurant with vaulted ceilings,
EASTERN wood-paneled walls, and crisp, white table linens is the first one in Cro-
EUROPEAN atia with the certificate of Croatian Authentic Cuisine. The restaurant is just off Ilica, a five-minute walk from the main square on a cobblestone side street. The menu features carefully presented traditional Croatian dishes such as *zagorska juha* (Zagorje-style potato soup with ham and mushrooms), *pečena teletina* (roast veal), *punjene paprike* (stuffed peppers), and even ostrich steak. $ *Average main: 70 Kn* ✉ *Mesnička 6, Donji Grad, Zagreb* ☎ *01/483–3829* ⊕ *www.starifijaker.hr* ⌖ *Reservations essential.*

$ ✕ **Teneo Coffee Box.** Teneo Coffee Box, situated in a quiet, residential
CAFÉ area of Zagreb, just three steps from the "Tresnjevacki trg" stop on tram line 12 and less than 10 minutes' walk from the Hotel Panorama, is a 129-square-foot café full of hot, cold, and iced coffee and tea options that make most other Zagreb cafés seem truly bland by comparison. Caramel Latte, White Chocolate Mocha, and dozens of other concoctions are on offer; be sure to try the aptly named Tiger Chai, whose delicate spices will tingle your palate. They also offer their own home roast, which they brew freshly on the premises. Check out their assortment of coffee packages, which make great souvenirs and gifts for people back home. If you have time, why not attend one of their workshops on preparing traditional Croatian coffee? Don't be put off by the small size: the café has several tables and chairs outside where you can soak in the sun and watch the shoppers. There's even a well-stocked play area for the kids. $ *Average main: 15 Kn* ✉ *Trešnjevački Trg 2, Donji Grad, Zagreb* ☎ *095/868–0604* ⊕ *www.facebook.com/teneocoffee* ⊟ *No credit cards.*

$$$ ✕ **Vinodol.** A few blocks southwest of the main square, the Vinodol is an
EASTERN elegant spot locals flock to when they hanker for traditional meaty fare
EUROPEAN such as veal and lamb, pork with plum sauce, or, for starters, *zagorska*
Fodor's Choice *juha* (Zagorje-style potato soup with ham and mushrooms). Enjoy all
★ this in a spacious, shaded courtyard or inside under brick-vaulted ceilings and amid low lighting that contrive to give you an elegant, wine-cellar sensation even though you're not in a cellar at all. $ *Average main: 80 Kn* ✉ *Nikole Tesle 10, Donji Grad, Zagreb* ☎ *01/481–1427* ⊕ *www.vinodol-zg.hr* ⌖ *Reservations essential.*

WHERE TO STAY

Zagreb offers a good choice of large, expensive hotels well geared to the needs of business travelers. This may be in part because tourists tend to frequent the coast, whereas the corporate crowd sticks to the city. However, for summertime vacationers who choose to check out the capital, this is good news: since so much of the country and indeed Europe are on the

> ### DOUBLY SWEET DREAMS
>
> Regardless of the price range, Croatian hotels often count two single beds pushed together as a double bed. If it's important to you, be sure to ask if they have rooms with a double mattress.

coast, Zagreb's "low season," when rates are lowest at many hotels, is from early July through late August. Since 2000 several of the capital's major hotels have come under new ownership and been given complete makeovers, guaranteed to appeal to those seeking mid- to upper-range accommodations.

DONJI GRAD (LOWER TOWN)

$ **Arcotel Allegra.** Design is the word in this trendy boutique hotel in
HOTEL the same building as the Branimir Center, a bustling little shopping mall. **Pros:** near train station; easy access to shops and restaurants; contemporary and artsy decor. **Cons:** majority of guests are business travelers; no pool. *$ Rooms from: €90 ⊠ Branimirova 29, Donji Grad, Zagreb ☎ 01/469–6000 ⊕ www.arcotelhotels.com ⤢ 147 rooms, 4 suites ❍| Breakfast.*

$ **B&B Studio Kairos.** If you are looking for something more intimate,
B&B/INN you can choose family-run B&B Studio Kairos. **Pros:** close to the center; reasonable price; laundry service; bike rental; an experience off the beaten track. **Cons:** small number of rooms; no credit cards. *$ Rooms from: €78 ⊠ Vlaška 92, Donji Grad, Zagreb ☎ 01/464–0680 ⊕ www. studio-kairos.com ⤢ 4 rooms ▭ No credit cards ❍| Breakfast.*

$$ **Best Western Premier Hotel Astoria.** Less than five minutes by foot from
HOTEL the train station and 10 minutes from downtown, the hotel offers bright, modern rooms with the silky bedspreads and partly marble bathrooms that meet the requirements of its Premier category. **Pros:** good location on a quiet side street midway between the train station and the main square; luxurious bathrooms with excellent amenities; top-notch 24-hour business center; free parking for guests. **Cons:** smallish rooms; no health facilities or pool. *$ Rooms from: €130 ⊠ Petrinjska 71, Zagreb ☎ 01/480–8900 ⊕ www.hotelastoria.hr ⤢ 98 rooms, 2 suites ❍| Breakfast.*

$$$ **Esplanade Zagreb.** This beautiful hotel, diagonally across from the
HOTEL train station, was built in 1925 for travelers on the original *Orient*
Fodor's Choice *Express*. **Pros:** unmitigated luxury; right by the train station; great fit-
★ ness center. **Cons:** pricey and formal (i.e., not a place to shuffle around in your cut-offs); smallish lobby. *$ Rooms from: €190 ⊠ Mihanovićeva 1, Donji Grad, Zagreb ☎ 01/456–6666 ⊕ www.esplanade.hr ⤢ 194 rooms, 14 suites.*

$$ 🏨 **Hotel Dubrovnik.** Claiming the most central location in the city, just
HOTEL off Trg bana Jelačića, Hotel Dubrovnik has been popular with business travelers and tourists alike since opening back in 1929. **Pros:** right off the main square; near shops and restaurants; numerous amenities; recently renovated. **Cons:** low on historic grandeur. $ *Rooms from:* €130 ✉ *Gajeva 1, Donji Grad, Zagreb* 🕾 *01/486–3555* ⊕ *www.hotel-dubrovnik.hr* ↪ *214 rooms, 8 suites* 🍽 *Breakfast.*

$$ 🏨 **Hotel Jägerhorn.** Completely renovated in 2013, this friendly hotel
HOTEL (formerly classed as a pension but since upgraded) occupies the building where Zagreb's first restaurant opened back in 1827. **Pros:** central location; big cozy rooms; excellent breakfast. **Cons:** small, so often fully booked. $ *Rooms from:* €130 ✉ *Ilica 14, Donji Grad, Zagreb* 🕾 *01/483–3877* ⊕ *www.hotel-jagerhorn.hr* ↪ *16 rooms, 2 suites* 🍽 *Breakfast.*

$ 🏨 **Palace Hotel Zagreb.** Built in 1891 as the Schlessinger Palace and con-
HOTEL verted in 1907 to become the city's first hotel, the Palace Hotel offers romantic, old-fashioned comfort. **Pros:** great location across from park-like Strossmayerov trg and close to Trg bana J. Jelačića; historical ambience; excellent café; Tao wellness center offering massage, sauna, and gym. **Cons:** although there is an elevator some rooms require walking up an extra flight of stairs; no pool. $ *Rooms from:* €100 ✉ *Strossmayerov trg 10, Donji Grad, Zagreb* 🕾 *01/489–9600* 🖶 *01/481–1357* ⊕ *www.palace.hr* ↪ *118 rooms, 5 suites* 🍽 *Breakfast.*

$$$$ 🏨 **Sheraton Zagreb.** High standards make this modern, six-story hotel
HOTEL a relative bargain. **Pros:** top-notch facilities and services; indoor pool; superb dining options. **Cons:** 20-minute walk from the main square; pricey; not exactly cozy. $ *Rooms from:* €270 ✉ *Kneza Borne 2, Donji Grad, Zagreb* 🕾 *01/455–9107* 🖶 *01/455–3035* ⊕ *www.hotel-sheratonzagreb.com/* ↪ *306 rooms, 29 suites* 🍽 *Breakfast.*

$$$$ 🏨 **The Westin Zagreb.** After a complete renovation in 2005, this colos-
HOTEL sal 17-story modern structure between the Mimara Museum and the
Fodor's Choice Botanical Garden—previously the Opera Zagreb—still looks homely
★ on the outside, but on the inside it's a sparkling, five-star affair. **Pros:** big, comfy rooms; top-notch luxury; excellent amenities and services; superb dining options. **Cons:** 15-minutes from the main square. $ *Rooms from:* €280 ✉ *Izidora Kršnjavoga 1, Donji Grad, Zagreb* 🕾 *01/489–2000* ⊕ *www.hotelwestinzagreb.com/hr* ↪ *305 rooms, 44 suites* 🍽 *Breakfast.*

NIGHTLIFE AND PERFORMING ARTS

Climbing full-steam ahead out of the economic depression caused by the war, Zagreb now has a lively entertainment scene. Bars, clubs, and cinemas are predominantly frequented by the city's student population, whereas the concert hall and theater remain the domain of the older generation. For information about what's on, pick up a free copy of the monthly *Events and Performances,* published by the city tourist board.

GORNJI GRAD (UPPER TOWN)

BARS AND NIGHTCLUBS

Oliver Twist Pub. This is definitely not a bleak house. This is one of *the* places to be after dark on Tkalčićeva. Although in good weather practically all the (mostly young) patrons are seated out front, inside is an immaculate English-style pub whose walls, on the upper floor, are decorated with memorabilia associated with different Dickens novels. ⊠ *Tkalčićeva 60, Gornji Grad, Zagreb* ☎ *01/481–2206.*

DONJI GRAD (LOWER TOWN)

BARS AND NIGHTCLUBS

Bulldog. Bulldog is a popular split-level café-cum-wine-bar and bistro with summer terrace. At night it becomes a club where you can enjoy soul, rock, blues and jazz performers. ⊠ *Bogovićeva 6, Donji Grad, Zagreb* ☎ *01/400–2072* ⊕ *www.bulldog-pub-zagreb.com/.*

Old Pharmacy Pub. A peaceful pub with CNN on the television and a selection of English-language newspapers. A mirror behind the brass bar, pharmacy-related sepia photographs and vintage adverts crowding the walls, and dark wood everywhere. A no-smoking section in the back is full of leather armchairs and cozy corners, perfect for an intimate chinwag. ⊠ *Andrije Hebranga 11a, Donji Grad, Zagreb* ☎ *01/492–1912* ⊕ *www.mojestranice.com* ☉ *Closed Sun.*

JARUN

DISCOS

Aquarius Club. Aquarius is Zagreb's top club for dancing, especially for disco and techno music. It overlooks the beach at Malo jezero, the smaller of the two interconnected lakes comprising Lake Jarun, 4 km (2½ miles) from the city center. ⊠ *Aleja Mateja Ljubeka BB, Jarun, Zagreb* ☎ *01/364–0231* ⊕ *www.aquarius.hr.*

PERFORMING ARTS

ARTS FESTIVALS

Promenade Concerts. For the best of concerts in the park, keep your eye out for the free Promenade Concerts by Croatian chamber orchestras, brass bands, and choirs, held every Saturday from 11 am to 1 pm from around mid-June to mid-August at the music pavilion set amid the lovely plane trees and fountains of Zrinjevac Park, on trg Nikole Šubića Zrinskog. Adding color to this series are 19th-century-costume contests and displays, an antiques market, a play area and programs for children, rides in horse-drawn carriages, and even souvenir stands. Sunday from 11 to noon is reserved for the legendary Wing Orchestra of Zagreb Electric Tram, which performs waltzes, marches, evergreens, and patriotic songs. If you are in the Upper Town on Saturday or Sunday between 10 and noon you will enjoy the streets filled with the romantic sound of street musicians. If you want to visit Maksimir Park, Sunday would be the perfect day; waltzes, polkas, chansons, and arias from operettas fill the air there between 10:30 and 12:30. ⊕ *www.zagreb-touristinfo.hr.*

Fodor'sChoice ★ **Summer on Stross - Strossmartre.** Embark on a journey toward the Strossmayer Promenade, next to the Lotrščak Tower and you will see one of the best Zagreb entertainment projects. Strossmartre brings you a bit of the Parisian spirit—lots of concerts, exhibitions, art workshops, and great wine and beer offers for more than 100 days, from the end of May until the beginning of September. And don't forget to come to the Half New Year's Party on June 30. ⊠ *Strossmayerovo šetalište* ⊕ *www. ljetonastrosu.com* ⊘ *May–Sept.*

World Theatre Festival. For one week in mid-September, the World Theatre Festival brings to Zagreb theater companies from all over Europe—if not exactly the world—for one or more performances each evening at various theatrical venues about town. ☎ *01/487–4562* ⊕ *www.zagrebtheatrefestival.hr.*

FILM

Cineplexx. Cineplexx is Croatia's first multiplex cinema, in the Centar Kaptol shopping complex, wedged in a serene, parklike atmosphere a 10-minute walk north of the main cathedral. Head first along Kaptol and then along Nova Ves. Most foreign films (including those from the United States) are shown in their original language with Croatian subtitles. ⊠ *Nova Ves 17, Gornji Grad, Zagreb* ☎ *01/563–3888* ⊕ *www.cineplexx.hr.*

> ### GET THE CARD
>
> At 26 venues about town—including several major hotels—you can pick up one of the best deals in town. The Zagreb Card is valid for 72 or 24 hours from the date and time stamped on the card and costs 90 or 60 Kn. It provides not only unlimited travel on public transport in Zagreb but also discounts of up to 50% at more than 30 museums and galleries as well as discounts at the zoo, on parking and car rental, and 20% discounts at many shops, restaurants, theaters, and concert halls. Considering the cost of similar cards in other European capitals, this is truly a bargain.

SHOPPING

Although Zagreb may not be a shopping mecca, a walk down the bustling Ilica or other nearby streets will take you past plenty of stores brimming with the latest fashions. Frankopanska particularly is turning into something of a fashion avenue, with labels like Lacoste, Cacharel, and others. Don't pass up the chance to stroll through the beautiful Oktogon shopping arcade, with its long, spacious yellow hall, elaborate wrought-iron gates at each end and lovely glass ceilings from 1901. The arcade connects Ilica 5 with Trg Petra Preradovića and offers more than a few high-class shops along the way. In the center of the arcade you'll find the elegant Croata, with its wide selection of silk scarves, men's dress shirts and, suitably for the birthplace of the cravat, countless variations on the classical necktie.

GORNJI GRAD (UPPER TOWN)
SHOPPING CENTERS AND MARKETS

Fodor's Choice
★

Dolac open-air market. For an authentic Croatian shopping experience, visit the Dolac open-air market, where besides fresh fruit and vegetables there are also a number of arts-and-crafts stalls. It's open weekdays 7 to 3 and weekends until 2. ⊠ *Tržnica Dolac, Dolac 9, Zagreb* ⊕ *www. trznice-zg.hr/.*

Importanne Centar. It's easy to miss downtown's largest shopping mall, the Importanne Centar, since it's completely underground and not well marked on the street level. Look for the escalators leading down, and once you're inside, good luck finding your way back out. ■**TIP→** There's a **24-hour parking garage here as well.** ⊠ *Trg Ante Starčevića 7, Zagreb* ☎ *01/467–7076* ⊕ *www.importanne.hr* ☾ *Mon.–Sat. 9–9.*

WINE

Fodor's Choice **Vinoteka Bornstein.** Housed in a tastefully arranged, vaulted brick cellar,
★ Vinoteka Bornstein stocks a wide range of quality Croatian wines, olive oils, and truffle products. ⊠ *Kaptol 19, Gornji Grad, Zagreb* ☎ *01/481–2361* ⊕ *www.bornstein.hr.*

DONJI GRAD (LOWER TOWN)

BOOKS

Algoritam. Algoritam has a huge selection of English-language books, including plenty of guides and coffee-table books on Croatia. ⊠ *Gajeva 1, Donji Grad, Zagreb* ☎ *01/488–1555* ⊕ *www.algoritam.hr* ☾ *Weekdays 8:30 am–9 pm, Sat. 9–5.*

CLOTHING

Croata. Ties may not be the most original of gifts, but they are uniquely Croatian. During the 17th century, Croatian mercenaries who fought in France sported narrow, silk neck scarves, which soon became known to the French as *cravat* (from the Croatian *hrvat*). At Croata you can buy "original Croatian ties" in presentation boxes, accompanied by a brief history of the tie. There, you can also find tasteful gifts for ladies, including scarves, shawls and accessories. ⊠ *Ilica 5, within Oktogon arcade, Donji Grad, Zagreb* ☎ *01/481–2726* ⊕ *www.croata.hr.*

FOODSTUFFS

Natura Croatica. All manner of Croatian delicacies that use only natural ingredients are offered here from brandies and liqueurs to jams, olive oils, cheeses, truffles, soaps, wild-game jerkies, and pâtés. ⊠ *Preradovićeva 8, Donji Grad, Zagreb* ☎ *01/485–5076* ⊕ *www.naturacroatica.com.*

Story of Salt. In search of a gift that will capture the pure sun and breeze of the Adriatic? Try visiting this brand-new gift shop–museum run by the Solana Nin Saltworks, a major sea salt manufacturer based near Zadar on the coast. Here you can buy the "Salt flower" (*cvjet soli*), affectionately called the "caviar of salt" for its unique flavor and composition. Spend several minutes taking in the images and implements that pay tribute to the sea salt industry; the mini-museum features several implements from traditional (and modern) salt manufacturing, including salt rakes, transport wagons, and a wooden packing unit. ⊠ *Gajeva 8, Donji Grad, Zagreb* ☎ *01/487–6765* ⊕ *www.solananin.hr.*

SPORTS AND THE OUTDOORS

GOLF

Golf & Country Club Zagreb. There's nothing like some swinging and putting to work off the tension of traveling. You can do it (alongside some of the many business travelers the capital has been drawing in recent years) at the Golf & Country Club Zagreb, which opened as the capital's first golf course in 1995. In addition to the gently challenging

9-hole course (green fees 130 Kn, aditional 50 Kn for daily ticket), there is also a driving range with 40 grass bays and a 12-bay covered area in the event of bad weather (30 Kn for 50 balls), fitness facilities, and a restaurant. To get there, drive to the roundabout near the Zagrebački Velesajam (Zagreb Fair) and follow the sign for Karlovac. Turn right at the second light and pass the hospital on your left. Continue for about 1 km (½ mile) until you see the Golf & Country Club Zagreb on your left. ⊠ *Jadranska avenija 6, Zagreb* ☎ *01/653–1177* ⊕ *www.gcczagreb.hr/*.

WATER SPORTS

You don't have to go all the way to the Adriatic to find a beach. Zagreb's pride and joy, Lake Jarun, is not terribly natural-looking but is apparently a quite clean body of water in the middle of an urban oasis located 4 km (2½ mile) from the center. Here you will find beaches (equipped with showers, sanitary facilities, and changing stalls); a children's pool; canoe, paddle-boat, bicycle, and rollerblade rentals; a jogging track; mini-golf and table tennis; restaurants, cafés, bars, and dance clubs including the ultrahip Aquarius (*see Nightlife and the Arts*). A long peninsula actually creates two lakes: *malo jezero* (small lake) and *veliko jezero* (large lake). The clear, spring-fed water is carefully regulated to maintain its quality. Though you can walk here from the train station in less than an hour, you can also take Tram 17 from Trg bana Jelačića 15 stops east (direction: Prečko) or Tram 5 from the bus station 17 stops (likewise in the Prečko-bound direction). After 11 pm there's service every 40 minutes.

EXCURSIONS NORTH OF ZAGREB

A favorite excursion to the outskirts of Zagreb is to the heights of Sljeme and its observatory. And then there is the peaceful spa town of Stubičke Toplice and, a bit farther to the northeast, the Catholic pilgrimage site of Marija Bistrica. Farther to the north, beyond the Medvednica Hills, lies a pastoral region known as Zagorje. The scenery is calm and enchanting: redbrick villages, such as Kumrovec, are animated with ducks and chickens, and the hillsides are inlaid with vineyards and orchards. Medieval hilltop castles, including Veliki Tabor and Dvor Trakošćan, survey the surrounding valleys. To the northeast of Zagreb is the charming baroque town of Varaždin. Although Sljeme and Stubičke Toplice are reasonably easy to get to from the capital by bus, having a car at your disposal for a day or two will give you a chance to cover more ground efficiently (e.g., without having to return to Zagreb to board yet another bus).

SLJEME

5 km (3 miles) north of Zagreb by tram and bus.

A favorite excursion on the outskirts of Zagreb is to the heights of Sljeme, the peak of Mt. Medvednica, at 3,363 feet.

Excursions from Zagreb

HUNGARY

Štrigova

Mursko
Središće

Međimurje

Ormož

Čakovec

Mura

Varaždin

Drava

Trakošćan

Koprivnica

Krapina

41

Veliki
Tabor

Bilo

SLOVENIA

A2

gora

Kumrovec

Tuheljske
Toplice

Marija Bistrica

Križevci

A4

Stubičke
Toplice

Vrbovec

Bjelovar

Medvednica
Nature Park

Sljeme

28

Zaprešić

Sesvete

Samobor

ZAGREB

Dugo Selo

Žumberak-
Samoborko
Nature Park

Ivanić-Grad

26

Velika
Gorića

A1

E71

31

Lonjsko polje
Nature Park

36

Kupa

36

Sisak

Loma

Karlovac

Petrinja

Sava

Čigoč

Duga Resa

A6

Glina

30

Vrbovsko

Dobra

Korana

Vojnić

Topusko

Hrvatska
Kostajnica

Jasenovac

Ogulin

6

Dubica

Slunj

Plaški

9

Dvor

A1

Una

BOSNIA-
HERZEGOVINA

Brinje

43

Nacionalni park
Plitvička jezera

Plitvice

Otočac

Plitvička
Ljeskovac

Korenica

20 miles

A1

20 kilometers

GETTING HERE AND AROUND

You can reach Sljeme by taking Tram 14 (direction Mihaljevac) all the way to the terminal stop, where you should change to the bus, which goes to Sljeme (Tomislavov dom).

EXPLORING

Fodor's Choice ★ **Sljeme.** Sljeme is an ideal place for picnicking, but you may wish to save your appetite for dinner at one of the excellent restaurants on the road home. On the southwest flank of the summit of Mt. Medvednica is a reconstructed fortress called **Medvedgrad.** The original was built in the 13th century by Bishop Filip of Zagreb, and after a succession of distinguished owners over the next two centuries it was destroyed in an earthquake in 1590. You can wander around the outside (for free), and take in great views of Zagreb. It's a one-hour trek to the fortress from the cable car, or you can reach it more directly by taking Bus 102 from Britanski trg in central Zagreb (just off Ilica, a 20-minute walk west of Trg bana Josipa Jelačića) to the "Blue Church" in Šestine, and then hiking some 40 minutes uphill from there. Take trail No. 12, which is off the paved road past the church cemetery. ✉ *Sljeme* 🌐 *www.sljeme.hr.*

WHERE TO EAT

$$$ EASTERN EUROPEAN 🍴 **Stari Puntijar.** On the road between Zagreb and Sljeme, Stari Puntijar is renowned for game and traditional 19th-century Zagreb dishes such as *podolac* (ox medallions in cream and saffron), *orehnjača* (walnut loaf), and *makovnjača* (poppy-seed cake). The wine list is excellent, and the interior design is marked by trophies, hunting weapons, old paintings, and big chandeliers. [$] *Average main: 80 Kn* ✉ *Gračanska cesta 65, Medveščak, Zagreb* ☎ *01/467–5600* 🌐 *www.hotelpuntijar.com.*

STUBIČKE TOPLICE

37 km (23 miles) north of Zagreb.

Established in 1805 on the foundations of a Roman-era thermal bath and expanded into a full-fledged complex in 1930, this peaceful spa at the northern edge of the Medvednica hills is where the capital's residents go to soak away those nerves and ailments in temperatures ranging from 45°C to 65°C (113°F to 149°F).

MARIJA BISTRICA

17 km (11 miles) east of Stubičke Toplice, 40 km (25 miles) northeast of Zagreb.

Other than its famous pilgrimage site, there's not much of interest in Marija Bistrica. Definitely do this as a day trip, unless you want to spend a night in nearby Stubičke Toplice.

Hodočasnička Crkva Majke Božje Bistričke (*Pilgrimage Church of St. Mary of Bistrica*). Croatia's preeminent religious pilgrimage site, the Crkva Majke Božije Bistričke is home to the Blessed Virgin of Bistrica, a black wooden, 15th-century Gothic statue of the Holy Mother associated with miraculous powers (having survived not only the Turkish invasion but a subsequent fire) and set in the main altar. The church, which was proclaimed a Croatian shrine by the nation's parliament in 1715, was rebuilt in neo-Renaissance style in the late 19th century by Hermann Bollé, who also designed the Zagreb Cathedral; the shrine complex adjacent to the church was enlarged in time for a 1998 visit by Pope John Paul II, who was in town to beatify Alojzije Stepinac, who became Archbishop of Zagreb in 1937 but was jailed and later placed under house arrest in postwar, Tito-led Yugoslavia. Behind the church is a huge amphitheater that was built for the pope's visit, and from there you can climb up Kalvarija (Calvary Hill) to the stations of the cross, ornamented with sculptures by Croatian artists. ✉ *Župni ured, Trg pape Ivana Pavla II. 32, Marija Bistrica* ☎ *049/469–156* ⊕ *www. svetiste-mbb.hr* 💲 *Free* ☉ *Masses Mon.–Sat. 10:30 am and 6 pm, Sun. 7:30 am, 9 am, 11 am, and 6 pm.*

KUMROVEC

40 km (25 miles) northwest of Zagreb.

The former Yugoslavia's late president Josip Broz Tito was born here in 1892, and his childhood home has been turned into a small memorial museum. In the courtyard of his birthplace stands an imposing bronze likeness of him by Antun Augustinčić.

FAMILY
Fodor's Choice
★

Kumrovec Staro selo (*Kumrovec Old Village*). The old quarter of Kumrovec, known as Kumrovec Staro selo, is an open-air museum with beautifully restored thatched cottages and wooden farm buildings, orchards, and a stream giving a lifelike reconstruction of 19th-century rural life. On weekends craftspeople, including a blacksmith, a candle maker, and others, demonstrate their skills. ✉ *Kumrovec BB, Kumrovec* ☎ *049/225–830* ⊕ *www.mdc.hr* 💲 *20 Kn* ☉ *Apr.–Sept., daily 9–7; Oct.–Mar., daily 9–4.*

VELIKI TABOR

15 km (9 miles) north of Kumrovec.

On a lofty hilltop stands the massive fortress of Veliki Tabor. The main pentagonal core of the building dates back to the 12th century, whereas the side towers were added in the 15th century as protection against the Turks.

GETTING HERE AND AROUND

Nine buses daily will get you here from Zagreb's main bus station in 2½ hours for 69 Kn one-way; but after getting off you have a 3-km (2-mile) walk still ahead of you. Hence, as is true more generally of site-hopping in the Zagorje region, a rental car may come in handy.

Fodor's Choice
★

Veliki Tabor. On a lofty hilltop stands the massive fortress of Veliki Tabor. The main pentagonal core of the building dates back to the 12th century, whereas the side towers were added in the 15th century as protection against the Turks. The colonnaded galleries of the interior cast sublime shadows in moonlight. To reach it, you really need to rent a car, and make it part of a half-day tour of rural Zagorje. ✉ *Košnički Hum 1, Desinić* ☎ *049/374–970* ⊕ *www.velikitabor.com* 💲 *20 Kn* ☉ *Apr.– Sept., Tues.–Fri. 9–5, weekends 9–7; Oct. and Mar., Tues.–Fri. 9–4, weekends 9–5; Nov.–Feb., Tues.–Sun., 9–4.*

WHERE TO EAT

$$$ EASTERN EUROPEAN 🍴 **Grešna Gorica.** Visiting this rustic tavern is like stepping into a friend's home. That said, your friend's home is unlikely to have a stuffed fawn and a pair of *kuna* (martens), the national currency's namesake, on the wall. (The use of kuna dates back from when the fur of this large, weasel-like creature was in fact a currency.) All produce used here is supplied by local farmers, and the menu features typical Zagorje dishes, including *zagorski štrukli* (baked pastry filled with cheese) and *pura s mlincima* (turkey with savory pastries). The garden affords sublime views down onto Veliki Tabor fortress. [$] *Average main: 70 Kn* ✉ *Veliki Tabor, Desinić* ☎ *049/343–001* 🌐 *www.gresna-gorica.com* 💳 *No credit cards.*

WHERE TO STAY

$ HOTEL Fodor's Choice ★ 🏨 **Dvorac Bežanec.** There's a lovely old manor house waiting for you—a 15-minute drive east of Veliki Tabor—where you can have your spacious room with period furniture and breakfast, too, for under €100 a night. **Pros:** historical ambience; spacious rooms; reasonable rate. **Cons:** far from major tourist areas and towns, restaurants, and shopping. [$] *Rooms from: 700 Kn* ✉ *Valentinovo 55, Pregrada* ☎ *049/376–800, 098/230–343* 🌐 *www.hotel-dvorac-bezanec.hr* 🛏 *20 rooms, 5 suites* 🍽 *No meals.*

KRAPINA

20 km (12½ miles) east of Veliki Tabor, 66 km (41 miles) north of Zagreb.

FAMILY Zagorje's quaint administrative and cultural center is on the tourism radar screen primarily as the home of *krapinski pračovjek* (Krapina Neanderthal)—no, not the town's one male inhabitant but a Neanderthal of a sort, whose bones were discovered on a hillside a short walk from the town center in 1899, in what was a settlement of these early humanlike creatures 30,000 to 40,000 years ago. Indeed, this may be one of the few places in the world today where you can meet up with a family of such hominids and even a fearsome bear in the woods—that is, with life-size statues of Neanderthals going about their daily business (wielding clubs, throwing rocks, tending fire), at the spot where the discovery was made.

Fodor's Choice ★ **Kraneamus Krapina Neanderthal Museum** (*Muzej krapinskih neandertalaca*). The new Krapina Neanderthal Museum is near the world-famous site of the Krapina Neanderthals "Hušnjakovo," and its architecture evokes the habitat of the prehistoric man. Displays at the Museum provide insight into who these early Neanderthals were and how they lived, and more broadly into the region's geology and history. ✉ *Šetalište Vilibalda Sluge BB, Krapina* ☎ *049/371–491* 🌐 *www.mkn.mhz.hr* 🎟 *Adults 50 Kn, students/seniors 25 Kn, families 100 Kn* 🕒 *Apr.–June and Sept. 9–7; July and Aug., Tues.–Fri. 9–6, weekends 9–5; Nov.–Feb., Tues.–Fri. 9–4, weekends 9–5; Mar. and Oct. 9–6.*

TRAKOŠĆAN

41 km (25½ miles) west of Varaždin, 36 km (22½ miles) northeast of Veliki Tabor.

Perched resplendently several hundred feet above the parking lot where the tour buses come and go, the romantic white hilltop Dvor Trakošćan is set amid beautifully landscaped grounds, overlooking a lovely lake circled by a hiking trail.

Fodor's Choice ★ **Dvor Trakošćan** (*Trakošćan Castle*). Croatia's most-visited castle took on its present neo-Gothic appearance during the mid-19th century, compliments of Juraj VI Drašković, whose family had already owned the castle for some 300 years and would go on to live there until 1944 (there has been a building here since the 14th century). The inside is as spectacular as the outside, with the wood-paneled rooms—a baroque room, a rococo room, a neoclassical room, and so on—filled with period furnishings and family portraits, giving you some idea of how the wealthy local aristocracy once lived. A restaurant, café, and souvenir shop occupy an uninspiring, Ministry of Culture–owned building at the foot of the hill. ⊠ *3 miles northwest of village of Bednja, Trakošćan 1, Bednja* ☎ *042/796–281, 042/796–422* ⊕ *www.trakoscan.hr* 🎟 *30 Kn* ☉ *Apr.–Oct., daily 9–6; Nov.–Mar., daily 9–4.*

VARAŽDIN

70 km (48 miles) northeast of Zagreb.

Situated on a plain just south of the River Drava, Varaždin (pop. 50,000) is the most beautifully preserved baroque town in this corner of the continent. A vibrant commercial and cultural center, still basking in the glow of its heyday in the 18th century, Varaždin is richly adorned by extraordinary churches and the palaces of the aristocratic families that once lived here. It was Croatia's capital from 1756 until a devastating fire in 1776 prompted a move to Zagreb. First mentioned under the name Garestin in a document by the Hungarian-Croatian king Bela III from 1181, it was declared a free royal town by King Andrew II of Hungary's Arpad dynasty in 1209 and went on to become an important economic, social, administrative, and military center. Near the heart of the city, in a park surrounded by grassy ramparts, the well-preserved castle is the main attraction. A short walk from the castle, on the outskirts of town, is one of Europe's loveliest cemeteries, with immense hedges trimmed and shaped around ornate memorials. Note that Varaždin's main churches are open only around an hour before and after mass, which is generally held several times daily, more often on weekends; the tourist information office can help you contact individual churches to arrange a look inside at other times.

GETTING HERE AND AROUND

After arriving in this charming city by bus from Zagreb, the best thing to do is to walk straight to the historical downtown, which will serve as your base for sightseeing and café-visiting.

CLOSE UP

Varaždin's Guitar Great

Although the global economic crisis forced Vladimir Šimunov Proskurnjak, Varaždin's most famous string instrument maker, to close his workshop on Krančevićeva 5, his legacy lives on. It's not by chance that he specialized in guitars. This particular instrument holds a special place in the hearts of the classical-music lovers of Varaždin. Indeed, there was a time when the guitar was among the most popular instruments in Croatia and elsewhere in Europe and earned the respect of the great music critics of the day. That time, in Croatia, peaked in the first half of the 19th century. The nation's greatest guitarist of the era, and one of the continent's best, was Varaždin's own Ivan Padovec. Born in 1800, Ivan was often ill as a child and extremely nearsighted. To make matters worse, at the age of 10 he was left half blind when a stone thrown at him by another boy hit his left eye. Since his physical limitations meant he could not become a priest, as his parents had hoped, Padovec trained to become a teacher. However, he chose quite another path.

By the age of 19 Ivan Padovec had not only taught himself to play the guitar, he was able to support himself by giving lessons to friends. Before

long he decided to devote his life to music. Within five years, Padovec had a reputation not only as a virtuoso guitarist but also as a talented composer. By 1827 he was giving concerts from Zagreb and Varaždin to Zadar, Rijeka, and Trieste, and before long he'd earned the respect of even the court in Vienna. While living in the Austrian capital from 1829 to 1837, Padovec gave concerts throughout Europe, though weakening eyesight eventually forced a return to his native Varaždin. After a concert in Zagreb in 1840, one critic wrote, "[Padovec] showed that even on such an instrument it was possible to play tenderly and skillfully, thus surpassing everyone else." In addition to writing more than 200 compositions, he authored an influential book on guitar instruction and invented a 10-string guitar. Completely blind by 1848, Padovec retreated to his sister's house in Varaždin, unable to compose or teach. In 1871 he gave his final performance at the city theater. A life of music reaped little financial compensation for Padovec, and he died in poverty on November 4, 1873. Appropriately, Varaždin's tourist office is located in the house where he was born, at Ivana Padovca 3.

EXPLORING
TOP ATTRACTIONS
Franjevačka crkva (*Franciscan Church*). Consecrated in 1650 on the site of a medieval predecessor, the pale yellow Franjevačka crkva has the highest tower in Varaždin, at almost 180 feet. In front is a statue of 10th-century Croatian bishop Grgur Ninski, a replica of the original which is in Split; another such replica can be seen in Nin. ⊠ *Franjevački trg 8, Varaždin* ☎ *042/213–166* ⊗ *Masses: Oct.–June, Mon.–Sat. 7, 8, 6:30, Sun. 6, 7, 8, 9, 11, 6:30; July and Aug., Mon.–Sat. 7, 8, 6:30, Sun. 7, 9, 11, 6:30.*

Gradska vijećnica (*City Hall*). Gradska vijećnica, one of Europe's oldest city halls, is still in use. This imposing landmark has been the seat of

Varaždin's public administration since December 14, 1523. Restored after the great fire of 1776, it received a thorough external makeover in 1793. From May through October you can stop by on a Saturday morning between 11 and noon to watch the changing of the guard called Purgari, a 250-year-old tradition that lives on. ⊠ *Trg kralja Tomislava 1, Varaždin* ⊕ *www.varazdin.hr.*

Gradsko groblje (*Town Cemetery*). Built in 1773 and thoroughly relandscaped in 1905 by Hermann Haller, a self-taught landscape architect who revolutionized traditional notions of what graveyards should look like, Varaždin's Gradsko groblje is as pleasant a place for a restful stroll as it may be, when the time comes, to be laid to rest in. Replete with flower beds and rows of tall cedars and linden trees flanking ornate memorials and laid out in geometric patterns, the cemetery sublimely manifests Haller's conviction that each plot should be a "serene, hidden place only hinting at its true purpose, with no clue as to whether its occupant is rich or poor, since all are tended equally, surrounded by every kind of flower . . . producing perfect harmony for the visitor." Haller himself, who ran the cemetery from 1905 to 1946, is buried here in a rather conspicuous mausoleum. You can reach the cemetery by walking about 10 minutes east of the castle along Hallerova aleja. ⊠ *Hallerova aleja, Varaždin* ⊕ *www.parkovi.com* ☉ *May–Sept., daily 7 am–9 pm; Oct., Mar., and Apr., daily 7 am–8 pm; Nov.–Feb., daily 7 am–5 pm.*

Palača Varaždinske županije (*Varaždin County Hall*). Palača Varaždinske županije rivals City Hall (on nearby Trg kralja Tomislava) in terms of sheer visual appeal, even if it is more than two centuries younger, what with its flamingo-pink facade and its location right across from the Franciscan Church. Opened in 1772, it boasted a late-baroque pediment for four years only, until the fire of 1776 did away with that, and saw it bestowed with a triangular, neoclassical one. ⊠ *Franjevački trg, Varaždin* ⊕ *www.varazdinska-zupanija.hr.*

Stari grad (*Castle*). Today a historical museum, Varaždin's main attraction is the massive Stari grad, which assumed its present form in the 16th century as a state-of-the-art defense fortification against the Turks, complete with moats, dikes, and bastions with low, round defense towers connected by galleries with openings for firearms. In the ensuing centuries it was often reconstructed by the families that owned it; for more than three centuries, until its 1925 purchase by the city, it belonged to the Erdödy clan. From the 12th century up until 1925, the castle served as the seat of the county prefect. You enter through the 16th-century tower gatehouse, which has a wooden drawbridge, to arrive in the internal courtyard with three levels of arcaded galleries. Indoors, there's an extensive display of antique furniture, with pieces laid out in chronological order and each room representing a specific period. Even if you don't go inside, do take a stroll around the perimeter, along a path that takes you between the outer wall and a ditch that used to be the moat. ⊠ *Strossmayerovo Šetalište 7, Varaždin* ☎ *042/658–773* ⊕ *www.gmv.hr* 🎫 *12 Kn* ☉ *Tues.–Fri. 9–5, weekends 9–1.*

WORTH NOTING

Food market. For a bite of Varaždin's specialty bakery product, a *klipić* (a salted, finger-shape bread), stop by one of the bakeries at the city's open-air food market, which is open Monday through Saturday from 7 am to 2 pm. ⊠ *Gradska tržnica, Augusta Šenoe 12, Varaždin* ☎ *042/320–956* ⊕ *www.varazdinskiplac.hr.*

FAMILY **Entomološka zbirka** (*Entomological Collection*). Housed in the Herzer Palace, the Entomološka zbirka museum has a fascinating presentation of some 50,000 different insect specimens. ⊠ *Franjevački trg 6/I, Varaždin* ☎ *042/658–754* ⊕ *www.gmv.hr* 🎫 *20 Kn* ⊙ *Tues.–Fri. 9–5, weekends 9–1.*

Galerija starih i novih majstora (*Gallery of Old and Modern Masters*). The Galerija starih i novih majstora is housed in the striking, 18th-century rococo Palača Sermage (Sermage Palace)—characterized by cinnamon-color, black-framed geometric medallions decorating its facade and an impressive wrought-iron terrace. The museum has a rich array of traditional paintings by Croatian and other European artists. ⊠ *Trg Miljenka Stančića 3, Varaždin* ☎ *042/658–754* ⊕ *www.gmv.hr* 🎫 *25 Kn* ⊙ *Tues.–Fri. 9–5, weekends 9–1.*

Lisakova kula (*Lisak Tower*). The 16th-century Lisakova kula is the only part of Varaždin's northern town wall that has been preserved. The wall formed part of the onetime city fortress, but most of it was razed in the early 19th century. Unfortunately, you can't enter the tower. ⊠ *Trg bana Jelačića, Varaždin* ⊕ *www.varazdin-online.com.*

Uršulinska crkva Rođenja Isusovog (*Ursuline Church of the Birth of Christ*). The Uršulinska crkva Rođenja Isusovog, a single-nave, pale-pink baroque church with a particularly colorful, late-baroque altar, was consecrated in 1712 by the Ursuline sisters, who came to Varaždin from Bratislava nine years earlier at the invitation of the Drašković family. Its charming, strikingly slender tower was added in 1726. ⊠ *Uršulinska 3, Varaždin* ⊕ *www.ursulinke.hr* ⊙ *Masses: weekdays: 7 am, Sun., and holidays: 8 am, Thurs. 7:30 pm adorations, the 8th of every month 6 pm.*

Župna crkva sv. Nikole (*Parish Church of St. Nicholas*). Consecrated to Varaždin's patron saint in 1761 on the site of an older church, the Župna crkva sv. Nikole is a baroque structure that is more attractive on the outside than the inside. Note the false yet imposing white columns in the facade; the red-tiled, conical steeple; and the sculpture at the foot of the steeple of a firefighting St. Florian pouring a bucket of water onto a church, presumably an allusion to the fire that devastated Varaždin in 1776. ⊠ *Trg slobode 11, Varaždin* ⊕ *www.zupa-sv-nikole-varazdin. hr* ⊙ *Masses: Mon.–Sat. 8, 7, Sun. 8, 10, 11:30, 7.*

WHERE TO EAT

$ ✕ **Pizzeria Domenico.** This little gem of a place is hidden away at the end
ITALIAN of a cobblestone alleyway off one of Varaždin's main squares. With red-checkered tablecloths and a spacious, airy inner room—with little windows that look out onto a peaceful courtyard on the other side—it's

a justifiably popular place for pizza. $ *Average main: 30 Kn ⊠ Trg slobode 7, Varaždin* ☎ *042/212–017* ⊟ *No credit cards.*

$$$ ✕**Restoran Angelus.** Whether Varaždin's best pizza is here or at the more
ITALIAN   laid-back and affordable Domenico is debatable, but here you can have
FAMILY   your pie by candlelight, with soothing background music under brick-arched ceilings to boot. Across the street from a peaceful shaded park, a five-minute walk from the center of town, the Angelus has a huge menu that also includes plenty of pastas and other, meatier (and more pricey) fare, not to mention a half dozen creative salads and lots of beer (including Guinness and Kilkeny). Be sure to save room for dessert. Don't be fooled by the plural in peaches capelleti: it's actually a single peach—bathed in cherry sauce, sweet curd, and ice cream—sliced in half. $ *Average main: 70 Kn ⊠ Alojzija Stepinca 3, Varaždin* ☎ *042/303–868* ⊕ *angelus.com.hr* ⚲ *Reservations essential* ☾ *Mon.–Thurs. 10 am–11 pm, Fri. and Sat. 10 am–midnight, Sun. and holidays noon–10.*

WHERE TO STAY
Hotel options were limited in Varaždin until 2006—with just one large hotel, the characterless Hotel Turist, and a couple of pension-style accommodations. But that changed in 2007 with the opening of the Hotel Varaždin and the Hotel Istra. Prices even at the newer Varaždin hotels are refreshingly lower than in Zagreb.

$ 🏨**Hotel Istra.** Varaždin's one and only centrally located accommodation,
HOTEL   the Istra has 11 simply furnished but sleek, pricey rooms with small windows that don't offer much of a view. **Pros:** near attractions, shops, and restaurants; all rooms have bathtubs. **Cons:** pricey; hallways are hot in warm weather; small windows; few frills. $ *Rooms from: €120* ⊠ *Ivana Kukuljevića 6, Varaždin* ☎ *042/659–659* ⊕ *www.istra-hotel. hr/* ⬏ *11 rooms* ⊚| *Breakfast.*

$ 🏨**Hotel Varaždin.** This hotel is in an early-20th-century building across
HOTEL   the street from the train station and a 15-minute walk from downtown. **Pros:** convenient if you come by train; attractive breakfast room; all rooms are no-smoking. **Cons:** a hefty walk from the town center; small bathrooms; few frills. $ *Rooms from: €77 ⊠ Kolodvorska 19, Varaždin* ☎ *042/290–720* ⊕ *www.hotelvarazdin.com* ⬏ *27 rooms* ⊚| *Breakfast.*

$ 🏨**Pansion Garestin.** A few hundred yards down the road from the Pen-
B&B/INN   sion Maltar and a bit farther from the town center, this small hotel occupies an elegant, erstwhile single-family house. **Pros:** reasonably priced; comfy basic rooms; pleasant outdoor dining terrace. **Cons:** small bathrooms; small windows; no Internet access; few frills. $ *Rooms from: €55 ⊠ Zagrebačka 34, Varaždin* ☎ *042/214–314* ⊕ *gastrocom-ugostiteljstvo.com* ⬏ *13 rooms* ⊚| *Breakfast.*

$ 🏨**Pansion Maltar.** A short walk from the town center, this small pension
B&B/INN   has clean, no-frills, but spacious rooms that are quite acceptable for a short stay. **Pros:** good price; friendly service; a five-minute walk to the town center. **Cons:** smoky café; modest decor $ *Rooms from: €65* ⊠ *Franca preserna 1, Varaždin* ☎ *042/311–100, 042/311–521* ⊕ *www. maltar.hr* ⬏ *25 rooms, 3 suites* ⊚| *Breakfast.*

NIGHTLIFE AND PERFORMING ARTS

Advent in Varaždin. Throughout the month of December, the town celebrates Advent in Varaždin, when the streets and squares come alive with the Christmas spirit. Ornaments and sweets are on sale, there's outdoor skating, and, yes, Santa Claus wanders about handing out gifts to kids. ⊕ *www.tourism-varazdin.hr.*

> **DON'T BRING MOM**
>
> For your fill of martial arts, horror, and sci-fi flicks, check out the **Trash Film Festival,** a three-day event Varaždin hosts annually in various locations in mid-September.

Aquamarin. Aquamarin is one of several bustling cafés on or near Trg kralja Tomislava, the site of City Hall. Trg Miljenka Stančića, by the tourist office, is another good place to sit back at one of the cafés and enjoy some drinks. ⊠ *Gajeva 1, Varaždin* ☎ *042/311–868.*

Rock Art Café. For a beer or two between walls adorned with pictures of famous revolutionaries from Elvis to Che Guevara, not to mention glass-encased electric guitars, stop by the Rock Art Café, which has frequent live-music evenings September through April. ⊠ *Petra Preradovića 24, Varaždin* ☎ *042/321–123* ⊕ *www.rock-art.hr.*

Špancirfest. For 10 days from late August to early September, the Špancirfest (translated in tourist brochures as "Street Walkers' Festival") occupies various squares in the center of town. It features a colorful array of free, open-air theatrical and acrobatic performances, live music from classical to rock, traditional and modern dance, arts-and-crafts exhibits, and more. ⊕ *www.spancirfest.com.*

Fodor's Choice ★ **Varaždin Baroque Evenings.** For three weeks from mid-September to early October, the Varaždin Baroque Evenings take the form of classical-music concerts in various churches, palaces, and other venues throughout town. This is one of the most important cultural events in northern Croatia. ⊠ *A. Cesarca 1, Varaždin* ☎ *042/212–907* ⊕ *www.vbv.hr.*

ČAKOVEC AND THE MEĐIMURJE

15 km (9½ miles) northeast of Varaždin.

At the northernmost tip of Croatia, between the Drava River to the south and the Mura River to the north, the Međimurje region looks small on the map, but it possesses a distinctive character that makes it ripe for at least a day's worth of exploration. Long off the radar screens of Croatia-bound visitors, the Međimurje is also one of the country's newest up-and-coming inland tourist destinations: its largest town, Čakovec, is the most important cultural center between Varaždin and Hungary and Slovenia to the north (many Zagreb–Budapest trains stop there). Its many small villages are the home of rich wine-making and embroidery traditions, and there is even a locally cherished spa town, Toplice Sveti Martin, to the very north close to the Mura River. Back in the 13th century, Count Dimitrius Chaky, court magistrate of the Croatian-Hungarian king Bela IV, had a wooden defense tower erected in the central part of the Međimurje that eventually became known as Chaktornya (Chak's Tower). It was around this tower and other nearby fortifications that Čakovec saw a period of intense economic and cultural development under the influential Zrinski family, from the mid-16th century to the late 17th century. After a failed rebellion by the Zrinskis and the Frankopans against the Viennese court, the Viennese imperial army plundered the tower for building materials, and the last Zrinski died in 1691. A disastrous earthquake in 1738 saw the old, Gothic architecture give way to the baroque. Međimurje's last feudal proprietors were the Feštetić counts, who lived here from 1791 to 1923—a period during which the region came under the administrative control of Hungary, then Croatia, then Hungary once again (until 1918). Toward the close of the 19th century the region was linked inextricably to the railroad network of the Austro-Hungarian Empire, setting the stage for intense economic development.

GETTING HERE AND AROUND

After arriving by bus from Zagreb, walk directly to the city center and begin experiencing the history all around you.

EXPLORING

TOP ATTRACTIONS

Župna crkva sv. Nikole Biskupa i franjevački samostan (*Parish Church of St. Nicolas Bishop and the Franciscan Monastery*). Čakovec's key ecclesiastical landmark was built between 1707 and 1728 on the site of a wooden monastery that burned down in 1699. The bell tower was added in the 1750s. Inside is a late-baroque altar decorated with elaborate statues; on the outside is a facade from the turn of the 20th century (when Hungary ruled the region), with reliefs of several great Hungarian kings from ages past. ⊠ *Franjevački trg 1, Čakovec* ☎ *040/312–806* ⊕ *www.ofm.hr/zupa_cakovec* ☉ *Masses: Mon.–Sat. 7, 6:30, Sun. 7, 9, 11, 6:30.*

WORTH NOTING

Stari grad Zrinskih (*Zrinski Castle*). Set in the middle of a large shaded park right beside the main square is Čakovec's key landmark, the massive four-story Stari grad Zrinskih. Built over the course of a century from around 1550 by Nikola Šubic Zrinski, in an Italian-Renaissance style, it was the Zrinski family nest until the late 17th century. The fortress's foremost present-day attraction, the **Muzej Međimurja** (Museum of Međimurje), can be reached through the courtyard. Though it receives too few visitors to have regular opening hours, a staff member will be happy to let you in. Just climb the steps to the hallway of offices on the second floor to find someone. If you kindly overlook the lack of English-language text, you will be treated on this floor to an intriguing, life-size look at a year in the life of a peasant family, from season to season as you proceed through the rooms. Move up a floor for a chronological display of the region's history, from the Stone Age to the recent past. Also on this floor are individual rooms dedicated to the Zrinski family (this one does have English text); lovely, period furniture; displays of printing machinery; an old pharmacy; a fascinating collection of 19th- and 20th-century bric-a-brac; and, last but not least, a three-room gallery of impressive modern art by various painters.

✉ *Trg Republike 5, Čakovec* ☎ *01/313–499* ⊕ *www.muzej-medjimurja. hr* 🎟 *Adults 20 Kn* ⊙ *Weekdays 8–3, weekends 10–1.*

Trgovački Kasino (*Commercial Casino*). Čakovec's main square, Trg Republike, is a mostly bland, modern affair—with the striking exception of Trgovački Kasino. Odd that the key gathering place of the town's early-20th-century rising bourgeois class should have survived the communist era intact, but here it has stood since 1903, wearing its Hungarian art nouveau style very much on its sleeve: redbrick interspersed with a white stucco background, squares and circles across the bottom, curved lines formed by the brickwork working their way to the top. Back in its heyday, this was much more than a casino in the gambling sense of the word: in addition to a card room and a game parlor, it housed a ladies' salon, a reading room, and a dance hall. It was mostly a trade-union headquarters in the post–World War II era—and so it is today, rendering the inside off-limits to the public. Just off the main square, by the way, is Trg kralja Tomislava, the town's one and only major pedestrian shopping street. ✉ *Trg Republike, Čakovec* ⊕ *www. tourism-cakovec.hr.*

OFF THE
BEATEN
PATH

Štrigova. Please don't take literally the unfortunately translated sign outside one of Međimurje's most important ecclesiastical landmarks: "Saint Jerome's Church is a zero category monument of culture." Of course, in this case the "zero" means "top," for this church (plus a well-developed local wine industry) is what guarantees the otherwise sleepy, out-of-the-way village of Štrigova a place on the tourism map. In a bucolic hilly setting near the Slovenian border, 15 km (9½ miles) northwest of Čakovec, Štrigova is indeed best known for **Crkva sv. Jeronima** and as the largest producer of Međimurje wines. Whether you arrive by bus (45-minute runs from Čakovec daily) or car, the first thing you are likely to notice is the striking yellow-and-white double steeple of the church, which is perched sublimely on a hillside just above the village center. Completed in 1749 on the site of a 15th-century chapel that was destroyed in the region's 1738 earthquake, the church is dedicated to the village's most famous son: St. Jerome (340–420), known for translating the Bible from Greek and Hebrew into Latin. Note the painting of a bearded St. Jerome on the facade, framed by two little windows made to look like red hearts. The church is most famous, actually, for its lovely wall and ceiling frescoes by the famous baroque artist, Ivan Ranger the Baptist (1700–53). The main steeple was completed only in 1761, and the church also has two smaller steeples. The church is usually closed, but you can call the local parish to arrange a look inside. While you can get to Štrigova easily enough by one of several daily buses from Čakovec, it's good to have a car if you want to drop by the smaller village of Železna Gora, some 5 km (3 miles) south of Štrigova, along a country road to Čakovec. Travel just 2½ km (1½ miles) south of the center of Železna Gora, and you will find the best restaurant in these parts, **Restoran Dvorac Terbotz.** ✉ *Štrigova* ☎ *040/851–325* ⊕ *strigova.info.*

WHERE TO EAT

$$$ EASTERN EUROPEAN 🍴 **Restoran Dvorac Terbotz.** In the village of Železna Gora some 5 km (3 miles) south of Štrigova, along a country road to Čakovec, stands the best restaurant in these parts. At the Dvorac Terbotz you can dine on everything from poultry to pork to wild game to seafood, in a lovely country house with wood-beamed ceilings. A spacious terrace overlooks the area's sweeping vineyards, and on a breezy day you'll hear the clackety-clack of the windmill just outside. [$] *Average main: 70 Kn* ✉ *Železna Gora 113, Železna Gora* ☎ *040/857–444* 🌐 *www.terbotz.hr* 🕓 *Closed Mon.*

$$$ EASTERN EUROPEAN 🍴 **Restoran Katarina.** You needn't venture far from Čakovec's main square, Trg Republike, for some fairly fine dining—on foot it's just a minute to this comely cellar restaurant in an antique building that now functions mostly as a shopping center. Replete with brick-arched ceilings, pink cloth napkins, an extensive wine list, and pop music that mars the elegance, the Katarina has a big menu, but specializes in pork, poultry, and beef dishes. The popular Katarina Platter, for example, is a sizeable two-person affair including pork stuffed with tomatoes and Gorgonzola cheese, turkey stuffed with cranberries and walnuts, and mixed veggies on the side. And then there's beef with truffles or, say, the goose liver pâté with mushroom sauce. [$] *Average main: 80 Kn* ✉ *Matice hrvatske 6, Čakovec* ☎ *01/311–990* 🌐 *www.restoran-katarina.com/.*

WHERE TO STAY

You can stay in Varaždin and venture into Međimurje for a day trip, but Čakovec does have a couple of decent lodging options, one of which is a short walk from the main square.

$ HOTEL 🏨 **Rooms Aurora.** A short walk from both the bus station and the main square, this uninspiring modern building has a chic, light-filled interior whose simple furnished rooms have dark blue carpeting, pinkish walls, and a sofa and coffee table in each. **Pros:** close to the bus station and the main square; large common areas and breakfast room; reasonable rate. **Cons:** small, hard-to-reach windows; along a bland, busy road; few frills. [$] *Rooms from: 480 Kn* ✉ *Franje Punčeca 2, Čakovec* ☎ *040/310–700* 🌐 *roomsaurora.freshcreator.com/* 🛏 *9 rooms* 🍽 *Breakfast.*

EXCURSIONS SOUTH OF ZAGREB

SAMOBOR

20 km (12½ miles) west of Zagreb.

That Samobor has been one of the capital's top weekend haunts since before the turn of the 20th century without really being on the way to anything else in Croatia testifies to its abundant cultural and natural charms. Close to the Slovenian border, this picturesque medieval town on the eastern slopes of the lushly forested Samoborsko gorje was chartered by the Hungarian-Croatian king Bela IV in 1242. The town and environs are popular with hikers, with trails leading into the hillside right from the center of town. Perched in those hills, just 30 minutes from town on foot, are the ruins of a 13th-century castle, which ennoble the main square from their sublime heights. And what would a visit to Samobor be without a stroll along Gradna, the peaceful stream that runs through town?

After an energetic hike, you may wish to fortify yourself with a glass of locally made *bermet,* a vermouth-like drink whose secret recipe was apparently brought here by French forces during their occupation from 1809 to 1813.

GETTING HERE AND AROUND

Take a 45-minute bus ride from the central bus station in Zagreb or travel for about 30 minutes by rental car to this charming getaway town where you can while away half a day leisurely strolling along the river and cobblestone streets and soak in the atmosphere from yesteryear.

EXPLORING

WORTH NOTING

Museum Marton. May 2003 saw Croatia's first private museum open in a quiet street just above Trg kralja Tomislava. Museum Marton was created to house a private collection of furniture, paintings, glass- and metalware, porcelain, and clocks previously on loan to the Zagreb Museum of Arts & Crafts. ⊠ *Jurjevska 7, Samobor* ☎ *01/336–4160, 01/483–8700* ⊕ *www.muzej-marton.hr* ▱ *10 Kn* ⊙ *Weekends 10–1 and by appointment.*

Samoborski fašnik. By far, Samobor's most famous event is its carnival, the *Samoborski fašnik,* which draws many thousands of visitors to town for several days beginning the weekend before Lent to catch the dazzling sight of its parades, featuring floats and masked revelers. ⊠ *Trg kralja Tomislava 5, Samobor* ☎ *01/336–0044* ⊕ *www.fasnik.com.*

Samobor Museum. Located in a lovely streamside park by the square, the Samobor Museum tells the story of the town's past. ⊠ *Livadićeva 7, Samobor* ☎ *01/336–1014* ⊕ *www.samoborskimuzej.hr* ▱ *8 Kn* ⊙ *Tues.–Fri. 9–3, Sat. 9–1, Sun. 10–4.*

Trg kralja Tomislava. The rectangular main square is called Trg kralja Tomislava. Its largely baroque look is positively lovely, all the more so because some building facades show art nouveau influences. In particular, the pharmacy building at No. 11 has two angels presiding, appropriately, on top. Also overlooking the square is a 17th-century parish church. ⊠ *Samobor* ⊕ *www.samobor.hr.*

NEED A BREAK?

U prolazu. If you need a dose of sugar to perk you up, try some *samoborska kremšnita,* a mouthwatering block of vanilla custard between layers of flaky pastry that, served warm, can be tasted at its best at the otherwise small and smoky café U prolazu. ⊠ *Trg kralja Tomislava 5, Samobor* ☎ *01/336-6420* ⊕ *www.tz-samobor.hr* ⊙ *Mon.–Sun. 7–11.*

WHERE TO EAT

$$$

EASTERN EUROPEAN

✕ **Pri staroj vuri.** Small yet ever so cozy, its walls decorated with old clocks (as per its name in Croatian) and paintings by noted Croatian artists, this lovely old villa a few minutes' walk from the main square is the best place in town to try such meaty fare as *teleća koljenica* (knuckle of veal) and *češnjovke* (smoked sausage cooked in sour cabbage). Unfortunately, the latter is available only late in the year, after the hogs are butchered and the sausage smoked. Round off with a glass of bermet, served with lemon and ice. $ *Average main: 70 Kn* ⊠ *Giznik 2, Samobor* ☎ *01/336–0548* ⊕ *www.staravura.pondi.hr* ☾ *Mon.–Sat. noon–11.*

WHERE TO STAY

$ ☷ **Hotel Livadic.** If you want to spend more than a half-day in Samobor,
HOTEL   you could do much worse than this elegant and pleasant hotel right on the main square. **Pros:** centrally located; redolent of history. **Cons:** rooms vary in size; downstairs café is smoky; few frills. $ *Rooms from: €62* ⊠ *Trg kralja Tomislava 1, Samobor* ☎ *01/336–5850* ⊕ *www.hotel-livadic.hr* ⤶ *21 rooms* ◉ *Breakfast.*

KARLOVAC

40 km (25 miles) south of Zagreb.

Many tourists taste the beer, but few stop by for a taste of the city. Karlovac is much more than home to one of Croatia's most popular brews, Karlovačko. Founded by the Austrians in 1579 as a fortress intended to ward off the Turks, Karlovac is today that big dot on the map between Zagreb and the coast that visitors to the country, more often than not, simply pass by. Anyone intrigued by the question of how a onetime fortress—still much in evidence—can develop into an urban center will want to stop here for at least a half-day and, perhaps, spend a night on the way to or from the coast. Once you pass through the city's industrial-looking suburbs, there is an inviting historical center awaiting you, one rendered more romantic because it is wedged between two of Croatia's most important rivers, the Kupa and the Korana. The city's Renaissance-era urban nucleus is popularly known as the Zvijezda (Star), since its military planners were moved to shape it as a six-pointed star—evidenced in the surrounding moat, which is today a pleasant, if sunken, green space that is even home to a basketball court. Eventually, this center's military nature gave way to civilian life, and it took on the baroque look more visible today. Though the town walls were razed in the 19th century, their shape is still discernible.

GETTING HERE AND AROUND

By far the best way to come here is by bus from Zagreb; it is along the route of countless buses from the capital. Once there, the best thing is to make a pedestrian beeline to the historical center.

EXPLORING

Trg bana Josipa Jelačića. At the center of this old part of town, which you access over any of several bridges over the moat, is the main square, Trg bana Josipa Jelačića, one side of which, alas, features a great big empty building with some missing windows. At the center of this otherwise largely barren square is an old well dating to 1869; long filled in, it is ornamented with allegorical imagery. ⊠ *Karlovac* ⊕ *karlovac-touristinfo.hr.*

WHERE TO EAT

$$$ ✕ **Ribarska kuća Mirna.** Off on its own, overlooking the quietly flowing
SEAFOOD Korana River on the edge of the town center, this restaurant, which
has a terrace for outdoor dining, makes the best of the view. The sea-
food here—whether squid, octopus, sea bass, or freshwater variet-
ies such as carp, pike-perch, catfish, pike, or trout—is abundant and
excellent. Round off your meal with a jam- or walnut-filled palačinke
and reflect on what went through the mind of whoever designed the
funky, hectagonal tubing of the ceiling lights. $ *Average main: 75 Kn*
✉ *Rakovačko šetalište BB, Karlovac* ☎ *047/654–172* ⊕ *www.ribarska-
kuca-mirna.com.*

WHERE TO STAY

$$ ⊞ **Hotel Korana Srakovčić.** Deep within a tree-shaded park a few min-
HOTEL utes' walk from the Old Town, this luxury hotel overlooks a peaceful
stretch of its namesake, the Korana River. **Pros:** luxurious; spacious
rooms; in a tranquil park; two restaurants; indoor pool; excellent
business facilities. **Cons:** pricey; 25-minute walk from the town center. $ *Rooms from: €130* ✉ *Perivoj Josipa Vrbanića 8, Karlovac*
☎ *047/609–090* 🖷 *047/609–091* ⊕ *www.hotelkorana.hr* ⤴ *16 rooms,
3 suites* |○| *Breakfast.*

$ ⊞ **Hotel Carlstadt.** At the center of Karlovac's business district, a cou-
HOTEL ple of minutes' walk from the Old Town, the Carlstadt—the town's
original name under Austrian rule—offers simply furnished, modern
rooms. **Pros:** centrally located; modest prices. **Cons:** some rooms get
street noise; few frills. $ *Rooms from: €60* ✉ *Ambroza Vraniczanya
2, Karlovac* ☎ *047/611–111* ⊕ *www.carlstadt.hr* ⤴ *37 rooms, 3 suites*
|○| *Breakfast.*

NACIONALNI PARK PLITVIČKA JEZERA

135 km (84 miles) southwest of Zagreb.

Triple America's five Great Lakes, shrink them each to manageable size
(i.e., 536 acres in all), give them a good cleaning until they look virtually
blue, envelop them in lush green forest with steep hillsides and cliffs all
around, and link not just two but all of them with a pint-sized Niagara
Falls. The result? Nacionalni park Plitvička jezera, a UNESCO World
Heritage Site and Croatia's top inland natural wonder.

GETTING HERE AND AROUND

The park is on the route of numerous cross-country buses starting from
the coast (Zadar, Dubrovnik, Split) or from the capital, Zagreb. After
arriving at the park, your feet are the only things you need to work
your way around the wonders of this natural miracle.

Fodor'sChoice **Nacionalni park Plitvička jezera** (*Plitvice Lakes National Park*). The park
★ is right on the main highway (E71) from Zagreb to Split, and it's cer-
tainly worth the three-hour trip from the capital. This 8,000-acre park
is home to 16 beautiful, emerald lakes connected by a series of cascading
waterfalls, stretching 8 km (5 miles) through a valley flanked by high,
forested hills home to deer, bears, wolves, and wild boar. Thousands
of years of sedimentation of calcium, magnesium carbonate, algae, and

Bloody Easter

It's called "Bloody Easter" for a good reason. Sunday, April 2, 1991, has gone down in Croatian history as the day Croatia suffered its first casualties—and its first fatality—in its war of independence from the former Yugoslavia. And the unlikely setting was none other than one of Europe's most visited natural wonders, Plitvice Lakes National Park.

Two days earlier, Croatian Ministry of Interior commando units—under the direction of General Josip Lucić, later to become head of the Croatian Armed Forces—were dispatched to Plitvice to restore order after the region had been occupied by Serbs led by Milan Martić, who aimed to annex the park to Serbian Krajina. The commandos were ambushed en route, near the group of hotels at Entrance 2. One member of the team, Josip Jović, was killed and seven of his comrades were wounded. As recorded in the annals of Croatian history, nine of the "terrorists" were arrested, and order was restored. For a time.

The region, which had long been home to many Serbs, was occupied by Serb forces for the next four years. The national park became a military encampment, and soldiers threatened to blow up the fragile travertine dams separating the lakes. UNESCO sent missions to prevent war from wreaking such havoc on a natural wonder. In the end, with the exception of the park's red-deer population, which fell dramatically during the occupation—the park's natural beauty pulled through intact. Only the human infrastructure was damaged, including the hotels. By 1999, four years after Croatian forces reoccupied the park and painstakingly cleared the area of mines, the last of the three hotels reopened, and the park was back in business.

Today a memorial in the park—behind the bus stop at Entrance 2 on the southbound side of the road—marks the life and death of Josip Jović, the first fatality in what was to be a long and bloody war.

---

moss have yielded the natural barriers between the lakes, and since the process is ongoing, new barriers, curtains, stalactites, channels, and cascades are constantly forming and the existing ones changing. The deposited sedimentation, or tufa, also coats the beds and edges of the lakes, creating their sparkling, azure look. Today a series of wooden bridges and waterside paths leads through the park. The only downside: as lovely as it is, all of Europe and a lot of Asia want to see it, so the trails can get crowded from June through September. That said, there's not a bit of litter along the way—a testament either to respectful visitors or to a conscientious park staff, or both. No camping, no bushwhacking, no picking plants. And no swimming! This is a place to visit, for a day or two, but not to touch. It is, however, well worth the 180 Kn summertime entrance fee. There are three entrances just off the main road about an hour's walk apart, creatively named Entrance 1, Entrance 2, and auxiliary Entrance Flora. The park's pricey hotels are near Entrance 2, the first entrance you'll encounter if arriving by bus from the coast. However, Entrance 1—the first entrance if you arrive from Zagreb—is typically the start of most one-day excursions, if only because it's within a 20-minute walk of Veliki slap, the 256-foot-high waterfall. Hiking the entire loop that winds its way around the lakes takes six to eight hours, but there are other hikes, ranging from two to four hours. All involve a combination of hiking and being ferried across the larger of the park's lakes by national park service boats.

There are cafés near both entrances, but avoid them for anything but coffee, as the sandwiches and strudels leave much to be desired. Instead, buy some of the huge, heavenly strudels sold by locals at nearby stands, where great big blocks of cheese are also on sale. At the boat landing near Entrance 2, by the way, you can rent gorgeous wooden rowboats for 50 Kn per hour. ⊠ *Plitvicka Jezera* ☎ *053/751–014, 053/751–015* ⊕ *www.np-plitvicka-jezera.hr* ▤ *July and Aug. 180 Kn; Apr.–June, Sept., and Oct. 110 Kn; Nov.–Mar. 55 Kn* ⊙ *Daily 7 am–8 pm.*

WHERE TO EAT

Although there's a restaurant near the hotels at Entrance 2, it has the same uninspiring look and feel as the hotels, and few people flock to it. You're much better off heading over to the excellent restaurant at Entrance 1—unless of course the food store near Entrance 2 provides you enough in the way of staples for all the hiking you'll be up to.

WHERE TO STAY

None of the park's state-run, communist-era hotels is much to write home about—and they were damaged extensively by Serb forces during the early 1990s. However, the main advantage of staying in a park hotel is that you'll be right in the center of all the hiking action. The hotels are particularly convenient if you arrive without your own car.

As an alternative, there are lots of private rooms in the immediate vicinity, where doubles go for around 240 Kn, a bargain compared to the hotels. We recommend checking out the tiny village of Mukinje, about a 15-minute hike south of Entrance 2. A bit farther south is the village of Jezerce, which also has rooms. (Note that the bus does not stop at either Mukinje or Jezerce, but it's a pleasant walk to both.) You can also get a private room in the rather faceless, one-road village of Rastovača, just off the main road a few hundred yards north of Entrance 1 (where the bus stops). Practically every one of the village's newish-looking houses has rooms for rent, and they're generally bright, clean, and modern.

A bit farther afield, the village of Rakovica, 12 km (7½ miles) north of the park, usually has more vacancies in high season and is a good option if you have a car. The tourist office in Rakovica (☎ *047/784–450*) can help with bookings. Last but not least, bear in mind that there's no place to store your bags in the park during the day if you arrive by bus and plan to head on to the coast or to Zagreb later in the day—so unless you're ready to cart your bags for hours along the park's steep trails or are traveling light, plan on an overnight stay.

$ ▦ **Hotel Jezero.** Yards away from two other, lower priced, fewer-frills
HOTEL   hotels (the Plitvice and the Bellevue), this long, three-story, wood-paneled building looks almost like a U.S.–style motel. **Pros:** centrally located (near trails, gift shops, and so on); the best of the park's three hotel options; a decent array of services and amenities. **Cons:** pricey; slightly worn rooms; the hotel bustles with so many tourists that you

can forget you're in the midst of stunning nature. $\boxed{\$}$ *Rooms from: €115* ✉ *Nacionalni park Plitvička jezera, near Entrance 2, Plitvicka Jezera* ☎ *053/751–500* ⊕ *www.np-plitvicka-jezera.hr* 🛏 *222 rooms, 7 suites* ⊙⃝ *Breakfast.*

2

EXCURSIONS IN LONJSKO POLJE

An excursion southeast of Zagreb to the Lonjsko polje region along the Sava River will bring you to an area that is rarely seen by most visitors. Along Croatia's extensive border with Bosnia and Herzegovina are two sights of pronounced historical interest, and one—Lonjsko polje Nature Park—holds special appeal to lovers of big birds, along with plenty of pretty wooden architecture in and around the sleepy villages along the way.

SISAK

75 km (47 miles) southeast of Zagreb via the Autocesta Expressway.

The unassuming little town of Sisak was the site of one of the more important battles in Croatia's history.

Knightly Tournament. On a weekend in early June, the locals celebrate victory over the Turks with their annual Knightly Tournament. A whole lot of folks in medieval garb will entertain you with archery and equestrian contests, not to mention balloon rides, souvenirs, and plenty of food and drink. Check with the Sisak tourist-information office for details on this free event. ⊕ *www.sisakturist.com.*

Sisak Fortress. A bit to the south of the town center—3 km (2 miles) to be exact, where the rivers Kupa and Sava meet—stands the once-mighty Sisak Fortress (built 1544–50), with one prominent bastion at each point of its famously triangular form and a hugely significant past. It was here, on June 22, 1593, that the Habsburgs, in the company of Croats and Slovenes, pulled off a monumental victory over the fearsome Ottoman Turks, a triumph that figured prominently in halting the Turks' advance toward Zagreb and farther into Western Europe. ⊕ *www.sisakturist.com/.*

ČIGOĆ

28 km (17½ miles) southeast of Sisak.

The charming village of Čigoć is officially known as the "European Village of Storks" because it draws so many of the migrating birds each spring, and a testament is its annual Stork Festival in late June. Several hundred of the birds while away much of the summer here before embarking on their long journey to southern Africa. That said, people live here, too, evidenced by the wooden, thatched-roof houses that are likewise a sight to behold.

Fodor'sChoice ★ **Čigoč and Lonjsko polje Nature Park.** The Čigoč Information Center, in a traditional house of Posavina oak, is on the main road that runs through the village center. It is the top regional source for all you need to know about storks, the Stork Festival, and last but not least, Lonjsko polje Nature Park. It's open daily 8–4, and park maps are available for purchase. The admission in the Nature Park is 40 Kn. Be sure to find out about the Park's educational programs or attractive boat trips, in case you're interested. ⊠ *Čigoč 26, Čigoč* ☎ *044/715–115, 098/222–085 ask for Davor Anzil* ⊕ *www.pp-lonjsko-polje.hr.*

JASENOVAC

35 km (22 miles) southeast of Čigoć.

Located where the Sava takes on the task of tracing Croatia's long east-west border with Bosnia and Herzegovina until taking a turn into Serbia more than 150 km (94 miles) away, Jasenovac is the site of Croatia's most notorious World War II labor camps. Current estimates are that somewhere between 56,000 and 97,000 people—mostly Serbs, it is believed, along with Jews, Gypsies, and Croatian antifascists—perished at this string of five camps on the banks of the Sava River between 1941 and 1945 from exhaustion, illness, cold weather, and murder.

Fodor's Choice   **Lonjsko polje Nature Park.** As a happier contrast to its labor-camp memo-
★   rial, Jasenovac is home to the headquarters of Lonjsko Polje Nature Park. ⊠ *Krapje 16, Krapje* ☎ *044/672–080, 044/611-190* ⊕ *www. pp-lonjsko-polje.hr* ⊠ *Adults 40 Kn; students, 30 Kn.*

Memorial Museum Jasenovac. Though the camp was razed after the war, a memorial park was eventually established at the site, along with a museum featuring photographs and other documentation of what happened. ⊠ *Braće Radić 147, Jasenovac* ☎ *044/672–319* ⊕ *www.jusp-jasenovac.hr* ⊠ *Free* ☉ *Mar.–Nov., weekdays 9–5, weekends 10–4; Dec.–Feb., weekdays 9–4.*

As a contrast to the labor-camp memorial, Jasenovac is also home to the headquarters of the beautiful Lonjsko Polje Nature Park. One of the largest floodplains in the Danubian basin, this unique ecological and cultural landscape of 20,506 acres along the Sava River was accorded park status in 1990 and is included on UNESCO's roster of World Heritage sites. It has numerous rare and endangered plant and animal species, from white-tailed eagles and saker falcons to otters and the Danube salmon—as well as storks, which are as easy to come by as in Čigoć. Its 4,858 acres of pastureland is also home to Croatia's highest concentration of indigenous breeds of livestock. Traditional village architecture—in particular, houses made of posavina oak—further contributes to the region's appeal. The park office provides park maps and other information on where to go and what to see; and, yes, it issues park entrance passes (40 Kn). The easiest way to access the park is by car: while driving from Zagreb, exit the motorway at Popovača and take the road to the right through the villages of Potok and Stružec toward Sisak.

SLAVONIA

By Andrea
MacDonald

Let's be clear: Slavonia is not the part of Croatia most people visit. There is no sea here, which has always meant fewer tourists. What it offers instead is something increasingly rare: unspoiled culture and undiscovered treasures. There are art galleries in Osijek, centuries-old wine cellars in Ilok, baroque towns, natural parks, hot springs and rural festivals. As the breadbasket of Croatia, it has miles of cornfields, vineyards, and, in the right season, towering sunflowers in bloom. There are even sandy beaches along the Danube. One thing is certain: Slavonia will not stay undiscovered for long. But for now, it's all yours. Welcome to the green heart of Croatia.

The sweeping agricultural plain of eastern Croatia shares a border with Hungary to the north, Serbia to the east, and Bosnia and Herzegovina to the south. Long a vital transport route, particularly between Zagreb and Belgrade, Slavonia today is still recovering from the aftermath of the Yugoslav war of the early 1990s. Most infamously, the baroque town of Vukovar, whose siege and utter destruction in 1991 was viewed on televisions around the world. Despite some remaining hurdles and the unalterable fact that the coast is far away (along with most tourists), much of Slavonia today looks and feels almost as rejuvenated as the rest of Croatia. The region's sleepy towns and rural surroundings—from cornfields to forest-covered hills—have a distinctive low-key charm that can only be called Slavonian.

Slavonia has been inhabited since ancient times, and the Romans had a settlement called Mursa on the outskirts of present-day Osijek. Though its flatness is broken in places—by the Papuk Hills in the center and around the celebrated wine region of Ilok in the east—the region's largely lowland terrain has been inhabited and traversed through the ages by more ethnicities than practically any other region of Croatia: Croats, Serbs, Hungarians, Germans, Ottomans, and others. First settled by Slavic tribes in the 7th century and later an integral part of the Hungarian-Croat kingdom, Slavonia experienced a major change of culture with Sultan Suleiman the Magnificent's march toward Hungary and Austria in 1526. For almost 150 years much of the region became an Ottoman stronghold. Osijek and Požega flourished not as part of Christian Europe, but rather as full-fledged, mosque-filled Turkish towns. The Turkish retreat in the late 17th century ushered in an era of Austrian influence, with Osijek, now with a vastly different look, the region's economic, administrative, and cultural capital. North of Osijek is the Baranja, a marshy, particularly fertile corner of northeastern Slavonia that straddles the gentle, vineyard-rich hills of southern Hungary to the north.

ORIENTATION AND PLANNING

GETTING ORIENTED

Slavonia has been inhabited and traversed through the ages by more ethnicities than practically any other region in Croatia, thanks mainly to its location. Occupying the northeastern section of Croatia, it is wedged in between Serbia to the east, Hungary to the north, and Bosnia to the south. It has been home to Romans, Turks, Austrians, Hungarians, Serbs, and Croats, and each has left its mark on the culture.

PLANNING

WHEN TO GO

Slavonia can be sweleringly hot in summer, with no sea for cooling off, so you may want to save this region for spring, late summer, or early fall, which are conveniently the same months when hundreds of thousands of birds gather at the Kopački Rit Nature Park. On the other hand, because everyone heads to the coast from June to August, summertime is actually considered the low season in Slavonia, when prices drop and hotels have plenty of availability. August and September are harvest season, a nice time to visit a winery or farmhouse and maybe lend a hand. It gets cold and snowy in Slavonia in winter, but there are traditional Christmas markets, winter festivals, and local mulled wine to keep you warm.

GETTING HERE AND AROUND

BUS TRAVEL

Public transport in Slavonia is, to put it mildly, difficult. It is infrequent, particularly on weekends and holidays. Come summer, when kids aren't traveling to school, many routes are cancelled entirely. You can trust neither online schedules, nor what the people working at the stations tell you. If possible, rent a car; however, if you must use public transport, the bus is more reliable than the train. The Osijek bus station is quite modern, with around six buses daily making the 45-minute trip to Vukovar for 35 Kn one way, or to Đakovo an hour away for around 30 Kn. Remember that it is often cheaper to buy a return ticket than two separate one-ways.

Contacts Osijek Bus Station ⊠ *Bartula Kašića 70, Osijek* ☎ *060/353–353.* **Požega Bus Station** ⊠ *Industrijska 14, Požega* ☎ *034/273–133.* **Vukovar Bus Station** ⊠ *Olajnica, Vukovar* ☎ *060/337–799.*

CAR RENTALS

Having wheels will make your life a whole lot easier, particularly if you want to travel on weekends, or visit wineries, parks or small towns that are not served by public transport. You might consider taking a train or bus to Osijek and then renting a car here for a day or two; small

TOP REASONS TO GO TO SLAVONIA

■ Strolling around Osijek, Slavonia's largest town, packs a lot of charm into a compact space, from attractive churches and parks to Tvrđa, the Old Town redolent of ages past.

■ Head out with your binoculars to serenely beautiful Kopački Rit Nature Park, one of the last great wetlands on the continent, for excellent bird-watching.

■ Discover Slavonia's rich ecclesiastical heritage at Đakovo's

magnificent cathedral, and if you're lucky you might catch a show by the city's famous white Lipizzaner horses.

■ The baroque town of Vukovar is a testament to the destruction wrought by the Yugoslav war and to the quiet strength of Croatia's rejuvenation.

■ Cruise the wine roads of Slavonia, visiting 600-year-old cellars in Ilok, or the region around Požega that the Romans nicknamed "Golden Valley."

cars go for around 400 Kn per day, including taxes, insurance, and unlimited mileage.

Contacts Hertz ✉ *Gundulićeva 32, Osijek* ☎ *031/200–422* ⊕ *www.hertz.hr.* **Uni-Rent** ✉ *Osijek Airport, Osijek* ☎ *031/205–058* ⊕ *www.uni-rent.net.* **Uni-Rent** ✉ *Reisnerova 70, Osijek* ☎ *031/205–058* ⊕ *www.uni-rent.net.*

TRAIN TRAVEL

Due to funding cuts, train services have been reduced in recent years and many stations have fallen into disrepair. Traveling between Zagreb and Osijek is quick and comfortable; venturing further afield is a different story. Fortunately, the train and bus stations are usually next to each other, so you can easily figure out which option best suits your schedule (or use a combination of the two). The most reliable source for train scheduling information is, strangely enough, the German website ⊕ *bahn.de*. Once you actually get onto the train, the experience is quite whimsical; it cuts right through the heart of Slavonia, giving you a real sense of the sweeping vistas of Croatia's breadbasket. Six trains run daily between Zagreb and Osijek (around 110 Kn one-way), one of these being an express, three-hour run; most take four to five hours.

Contacts Osijek Train Station ✉ *Trg L. Ružičke, Trg L. Ružičke 2, Osijek* ☎ *060/333–444.* **Požega Train Station** ✉ *Franje Cirakija 5, Požega* ☎ *034/273–911.*

RESTAURANTS

The first thing you might notice about Slavonian restaurants is that there aren't many of them. Locals generally prefer to eat dinner at home, then go out for coffee or ice cream, which explains the abundance of trendy caffe-bars. Apart from Osijek, where you'll be spoiled for choice, your best bet is often hotels or wineries, where you can sample hearty, spicy and delicious Slavonian cuisine. Cabbage and cottage cheese are common side dishes, and with parika-rich Hungary not far away, you'll often see dishes characterized by an unmistakable, bright-red zest. Meat is a key part of the dining picture; regular menu staples include *čobanac,* a stew made with game meat, bathed in paprika sauce and usually served with spaetzle; chicken paprikash; *sarma* (pork-stuffed cabbage leaves); and, last but not least, *kulen* (spicy, air-dried sausage). Slavonia also counts river fish among its staples—namely, carp, pike, catfish, and pike-perch. One of the must-try menu items is the spicy-hot, paprika-flavored fish stew known as *riblji paprikaš* or *fiš paprikaš*, usually served in a bowl big enough for two. Slavonian wines are cheap, local, and wonderful, particularly the whites: look for varieties such as *graševina*, Riesling, and *Traminac* (a type of Gewürztraminer). Red wine lovers should try the delicious *frankovka*. And, of course, this would not be Croatia without *rakija* (fruit brandy). Hearty meals, delicious wine and extremely affordable prices all add up to one certainty: you are going to eat and drink far too much in Slavonia, and you'll love it.

HOTELS

In most Slavonian towns—apart from Osijek, which offers a nice selection of hotels plus a few smaller, pension-style accommodations—your sleeping choices are quite limited. The few luxury hotels are expensive by Slavonian standards, and throughout the region there are practically no private rooms or apartments. But fear not: rural tourism is blossoming. If you're happy to stay slightly out of the center, there is a wealth of wonderful accommodations options, from converted farmhouses to horse stables to wineries, where you can enjoy the countryside, taste homemade products, and even get your hands dirty helping out at harvest time. *Hotel reviews have been shortened. For full information, visit Fodors.com.*

WHAT IT COSTS IN EUROS (€) AND CROATIAN KUNA (KN)			
	$	$$	$$$	$$$$
Restaurants	under 35 Kn	35 Kn–60 Kn	61 Kn–80 Kn	over 80 Kn
	under €5	€5–€8	€9–€10	over €10
Hotels	under 925 Kn	925 Kn–1,300 Kn	1,301 Kn–1,650 Kn	over 1,650 Kn
	under €121	€121–€170	€171–€216	over €216

Restaurant prices are the average cost of a main course at dinner or, if dinner is not served, at lunch. Hotel prices are the lowest cost of a standard double room in high season.

VISITOR INFORMATION

The websites of the tourist boards responsible for **Osijek-Baranja County** (⊕ *www.tzosbarzup.hr*) and **Vukovar-Srijem County** (⊕ *www.tzvsz.hr*) have information on towns within their purview without individual sites.

Contacts Đakovo Tourist Information ⊠ *Kralja Tomislava 3, Đakovo* 🕾 *031/812–319* ⊕ *tzdjakovo.eu.* **Daruvar Tourist Information** ⊠ *King Tomislav square 12, Daruvar* 🕾 *043/331–382.* **Ilok Tourist Information** ⊠ *Trg Nikole Iločkog 2, Ilok* 🕾 *032/590–020, 032/592–966* ⊕ *www. turizamilok.hr.* **Osijek Tourist Information** ⊠ *Županijska 2, Osijek* 🕾 *031/203–755* ⊕ *www.tzosijek.hr.* **Požega Tourist Information** ⊠ *Antuna*

Kanižlića 3, Požega ☎ *034/274–900.* **Vukovar Tourist Information** ✉ *J. J. Strossmayera 15, Vukovar* ☎ *032/442–889* ⊕ *turizamvukovar.hr.*

OSIJEK

280 km (175 miles) east of Zagreb.

Far from where sea-spirited tourists typically tread—and surrounded on all sides by cornfields—Osijek is an often overlooked treasure trove of cultural and architectural attractions. Croatia's fourth-largest city (pop. 108,000) and the economic, administrative, and cultural capital of Slavonia, it rests on the south bank of the Drava River, 22 km (14 miles) west of that river's confluence with the Danube, a short drive from the Hungarian border to the north and Serbia to the east.

GETTING HERE AND AROUND

Although it is certainly possible to walk everywhere in Osijek, hopping aboard one of the trams that wind their way around the city will save you time. To get between Gornji Grad and Tvrđa, take Tram No. 1; to get between the train station and Gornji Grad, it's Tram No. 2. Fares are 10 Kn for a one-way ticket, or you can buy a reusable electronic ticket from Tisak newsstands around town. An even better option is to take advantage of Osijek's miles of bus lanes; bikes can be rented from Guesthouse Maksimilian.

EXPLORING

By the mid-12th century, Osijek was a prosperous market town in the Hungarian-Croatian kingdom, occupying the area of present-day **Tvrđa** ("citadel"). After more than 150 years of Ottoman occupation in the 16th and 17th centuries, it was a flowering Turkish town, mosques and all. At 11 am on September 26, 1687, that era ended, with the flight of the last Turkish soldier. (As a continuing legacy of this watershed event, the church bells of Osijek undertake a celebratory ringing every Friday at 11 am.) Osijek henceforth became a military garrison under the Austrians, who turned it into a walled fortress in the late 17th century. Tvrđa, a somewhat sleepy historical and cultural old town today, has one of the best-preserved ensembles of Baroque buildings in Croatia, with old barracks, churches, and monasteries. The **Gornji Grad** (Upper Town) was developed by the Austrians during this period; today it's the city's commercial and administrative center. You can see beautiful baroque architecture along Europska Avenija, which stretches between the two parts of the city. With kilometers of tree-lined streets and bike lanes, plus 17 parks, including the King Tomislav Gardens, Osijek has an outdoorsy feel in nice weather. The Drava river runs the length of the city and is the favorite recreational area for locals; you'll see them biking, rollerblading, walking dogs, or sitting at one of the many riverside terraces for a coffee.

Slavonia

SLOVENIA

HUNGARY

SERBIA

BOSNIA-HERZEGOVINA

Mursko Središće
Čakovec
Varaždin
Krapina
Samobor
Žumberak-Samoborsko Nature Park
Zábok
Tepoglava
Medvednica Nature Park
ZAGREB
Velika Gorica
Karlovac
Duga Resa
Samobor
Koprivnica
Križevci
Vrbovec
Ivanić-Grad
Bjelovar
Bilo gora
Čazma
Garešnica
Kutina
Sisak
Petrinja
Glina
Dvor
Hrvatska Kostajnica
Dubica
Okučani
Novska
Lipik
Pakrac
Nova Gradiška
Daruvar
Virovitica
Slatina
Požega
Papuk Nature Park
Donji Miholjac
Našice
Beliśće
Valpovo
Bizovac
Čepin
Đakovo
Slavonski Brod
Donji Miholjac
Beli Manastir
Dvorac Tikveš
Kopački Rit Nature Park
Osijek see detail map
Tenja
Borovo
Vukovar
Vinkovci
Županja
Ilok
Brod

Drava
Mura
Sava
Kupa
Korana
Danube
Vuka
Česma
Lonjsko polje
Plitvice Lakes National Park

A1 A2 A3 A4 A5

0 20 miles
0 20 kilometers

GREAT ITINERARIES

IF YOU HAVE 3 DAYS

Spend two days in **Osijek**, with either a short visit to nearby **Kopački Rit Nature Park** or a daytrip to Vukovar. On the third day, drive to **Đakovo**, whose cathedral is well worth a look; and if you're heading back toward Zagreb, do stop for a glass of wine in lovely little **Požega**.

IF YOU HAVE 5 DAYS

Start in Osijek for your first two days, with an afternoon at **Kopački**

Rit Nature Park. On the third day, head to Vukovar to visit its stirring museums and memorials. Spend the night there, or visit the Ovčara Memorial en route to **Ilok**, where you will spend the night among the medieval history and world-class wines. On your fourth day, check out the Municipal Museum of Ilok before making your way to **Đakovo**, then pass through **Požega** on your fifth and final afternoon.

TOP ATTRACTIONS

Fodor's Choice
★
Erdutski Vinogradi. If you've got extra time in Osijek, take a day trip to one of the most renowned wine-producing areas in Slavonia. The lovely village of Erdut, with a medieval castle overlooking the Danube, is just 37 km (23 miles) east, and along with Baranja was the first area to become part of the Vintour, the European Union wine roads. There are several wineries to visit around the village, including Erdutski Vinogradi, where you can see one of the quirkiest sights in the Croatian wine world: a barrel made of 150-year-old Slavonian oak that holds 75,000 liters of wine. An interesting stopover along the way to Erdut is the tiny village of Aljmaš; every August 15, tens of thousands of people from nearby villages, even as far as Serbia, make their way on foot to a shrine in this typically sleepy town to celebrate the Feast Day of the Assumption of Mary. ⊠ *Trg Branka Hercega 1, Erdut* ☎ *031/596–555* ⊕ *erdutski-vinogradi.hr.*

Fodor's Choice
★
Josić. North of Osijek you'll find the unspoiled Baranja region, whose name itself means "Mother of Wine" in Hungarian. You can visit traditional villages, take part in folk festivals, and make a stop at the progressive Josić winery in the settlement of Zmajevac. There is an excellent on-site restaurant, which mixes traditional Slavonian dishes with a few twists, such as smoked freshwater fish and goose liver in cognac. Those craving a glass of red wine will be happy to learn that Josić is known for its experimental blends of merlot, cabernet sauvignon and Shiraz. ⊠ *Planina 194, Zmajevac* ☎ *031/734–410* ⊕ *josic.hr.*

Fodor's Choice
★
Konkatedrala Sv. Petra i Pavla (*Co-cathedral of Saints Peter and Paul*). This majestic, single-naved church is the highlight of Osijek's downtown skyline. At 292 feet, its redbrick, neo-Gothic steeple is the second highest structure in Croatia. Built between 1894 and 1898 on the site of a former church of the same name by the architects Franz Langenberg of Germany and Robert Jordan of Austria, and on the initiative of the famous Đakovo-based bishop Josip Juraj Strossmayer, it has no less than five altars, an unusually frescoed ceiling replete with individual

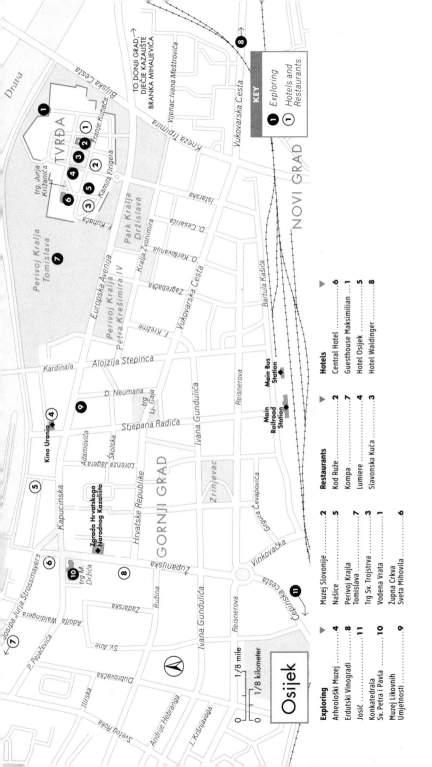

Osijek

0 ——— 1/8 mile
0 ——— 1/8 kilometer

Exploring ▶

Arheološki Muzej **4**
Erdutski Vinogradi **8**
Josić **11**
Konkatedrala
Sv. Petra i Pavla **10**
Muzej Likovnih
Umjetnosti **9**

Muzej Slovonije **2**
Našice **5**
Perivoj Kralja
Tomislava **7**
Trg Sv. Trojstrva **3**
Vodena Vrata **1**
Župna Crkva
Sveta Mihovila **6**

Restaurants ▶

Kod Ruže **2**
Kompa **7**
Lumiere **4**
Slavonska Kuća **3**

Hotels ▶

Central Hotel **6**
Guesthouse Maksimilian **1**
Hotel Osijek **5**
Hotel Waldinger **8**

KEY

●1 Exploring
① Hotels and Restaurants

Drava

TVRĐA

TO DONJI GRAD;
DJEČJE KAZALIŠTE
BRANKA MIHALJEVIĆA

Perivoj Kralja Tomislava

Park Kralja Držislava

NOVI GRAD

GORNJI GRAD

Zrinjevac

Main Railroad Station

Main Bus Station

Kino Uranja

Zgrada Hrvatskoga
Narodnog Kazališta

praying figures human and divine, and stained-glass windows. The walls are painted with colourful frescoes. ⊠ *Trg Ante Starčevića, Pavla Pejačevića 1, Gornji Grad* ☎ *031/310-020* ⊕ *www.svpetaripavao.hr* ⊙ *Daily 6:30–7.*

Fodor'sChoice **Muzej Likovnih Umjetnosti** (*Museum of Fine Arts*). Europska Avenija is
★ the broad avenue that connects the new and old towns in Osijek. It is lined with late 19th-early 20th century neoclassical and art nouveau houses, built as private residences, complete with gardens and cast-iron railings. One of those mansions, formerly belonging to a prominent attorney, is now the home of the Museum of Fine Arts, with a focus on Croatian and Slavonian artists and a permanent collection of paintings, sculpture, and graphic arts from the 18th century to now. It is well worth a visit, particularly to check out its temporary exhibitions on the ground floor. ⊠ *Europska avenija 9, Gornji Grad* ☎ *031/251–280* ⊕ *www.gluo.hr* ⊠ *15 Kn.*

FAMILY **Perivoj Krajla Tomislava** (*King Tomislav Gardens*). One of Osijek's most soothing spots, the King Tomislav Gardens is a spacious, forested oạsis that was laid out in the 18th century. It separates historic Tvrđa from Gornji Grad, the more bustling, commercial heart of town. The park is home to playgrounds and a tennis club. ⊠ *2 Europska avenija.*

Trg Sv. Trojstva (*Holy Trinity Square*). Chief among the architectural highlights on Tvrđa's main square is the plague pillar at its center. The Votive Pillar of the Holy Trinity is one of Osijek's finest baroque monuments. Erected in 1729–30 by the widow of General Maksimilijan Petraš, who died of the plague in 1728, it has an elaborate pinnacle and four pedestals at its base bearing the statues of various saints, including St. Sebastian. Overlooking the northwest side of the square is the yellow Zgrada Glavne straže (Building of the Main Guard), built in 1729 with the observation post jutting out of its roof and capped by a Venetian-Moorish dome. ⊠ *Trg Svetog Trojstva, Tvrđa.*

WORTH NOTING

Arheološki Muzej (*Archeological Museum*). Diagonally across Tvrđa's main square from the Museum of Slavonia, you'll find the spacious Archeological Museum, opened in 2007 in the renovated City Guard-house. It has an impressive range of artifacts from Slavonia through the ages, from the Neolithic Starčevo culture through to Celtic and Roman times. The building itself is modern and airy, with a glass dome over the arcaded courtyard, and the exhibitions are well laid out across several rooms. ⊠ *Trg. Sv. Trojstva 6, Tvrđa* ☎ *031/250–730.*

Muzej Slavonije (*Museum of Slavonia*). Slavonia's oldest museum was established in 1877 and moved to this location on the eastern side of Trg Svetog Trojstrva in 1946. The myriad objects on display give a lasting impression of the region's folklore, culture, and natural history; everything from stuffed animals to old coins, pottery to swords, a collection of 16th- to 19th-century locks and keys, timepieces and typewriters. A key attraction is in the courtyard: a sarcophagus and other sculptural fragments from Mursa, the Roman settlement that was situated in present-day Donji Grad. If the front door is locked during open hours, press the buzzer to be let in. ⊠ *Trg Sv. Trojstva 6,*

Tvrđa ☎ *031/250–730* ⊕ *www.mso.hr* 🖼 *15 Kn* ☉ *Tues., Wed., Fri. 9–7, Thurs. 9–10, weekends 10–2.*

Vodena Vrata (*Water Gate*). Facing the Drava River, the Water Gate, which was once known by the Latin appellation Porta Aquatica, is the only remaining gate in the original fortress wall, most of which was razed in the 1920s. Flanked by columns, this arched entrance to the fortress was built as part of a major construction project that also included several bastions and was completed by 1715. ⊠ *Vodena Vrata, Tvrđa.*

NEED A BREAK? **Kavana Waldinger.** Offering old-world Viennese-style elegance, the Kavana Waldinger is Osijek's finest café. Locals flock here all day until closing time at 11 pm to indulge in coffee, beer, and other drinks, plus exquisite pralines and heavenly cakes. After extensive renovations in 2014 see it merge with the Restaurant Waldinger, it will also feature healthy, light lunches and smoothies. Try the favorite *Esterházy cake*, named after an 18th-century Hungarian Prince who had a castle in nearby Darda. ⊠ *Hotel Waldinger, Županijska 8, Gornji Grad* ☎ *031/250–470* ⊕ *waldinger. hr/gastronomija/kavana-waldinger.*

Župna Crkva Sveta Mihovila (*St. Michael's Parish Church*). On the site of the onetime Kasim-Pasha Mosque, this mustard-yellow church was built over three decades by Jesuits, beginning in 1725 after all remaining Turks were expelled from Osijek. It has a single nave with two bulb-topped bell towers on each side of its facade. In accord with the late-baroque style in fashion in continental Croatia at the time, the interior displays a conspicuous absence of paintings. It's closed except during services or by appointment. ⊠ *Trg Jurja Križanića 2, Tvrđa* ☎ *031/208–990* ☉ *Mass held daily at 6:30 pm, Sat. 7:30 am, and Sun. 8:30 am, 10:30 am, and 6:30 pm. Closed Mon.*

NEED A BREAK? **Copacabana Rekreacijski Centar** (*Copacabana Recreation Center*). A 20-minute walk across Osijek's pedestrian bridge over the Drava, and across from Trvđa, is Copacabana, a pleasant and spacious aquatic-recreation complex that includes pools, a waterslide, a restaurant, and plenty of willow trees. In August it hosts the popular five-day Pannonian Challenge, an extreme sport and music festival. Impossible to miss if you stroll along this section of the river, it operates from mid-June through mid-September, daily from 10 to 8 pm (weekends from 9 to 8) ⊠ *Along Drava River, Lijeva obala Drave* 🖼 *7 Kn adults, under 12 free.*

OFF THE BEATEN PATH **Našice.** On the northern slopes of the Krndija hills, the sleepy town of Našice makes a lovely day trip from Osijek. It is a popular hunting and fishing ground, home to a Gothic-Baroque Franciscan Monastery and a medieval church built by the Knights Templar. It's also where you'll find the most beautiful manor in Slavonia, the Dvorac Pejačević (Pejačević Palace), once owned by the noble, powerful Pejačević family, who were given ownership of the town by the Habsburgs as thanks for their support during the Ottoman wars. The massive baroque building, which dates to 1812 and is surrounded by a lovely and spacious English-style

WAR-WEARY FACADES

While strolling around Osijek, you might start to notice unusual sculptures on roundabouts, in the middle of gardens and fields, possibly even hanging out at your hotel. They might be in the shape of a bird, a bike, maybe even a high-heeled shoe, and they all have one thing in common: they're made of straw. One of the most original rural festivals in the country is Slama, a multi-day "Land Art" festival held every summer in a field somewhere in Slavonia. It began in 2006, when seven local artists set out to explore the possibilities of their region's most abundant natural material, the way coastal Croatians use their famous white stone. An ancient harvest ritual in the area involved building monuments out of straw and setting them on fire, believing it would grant fertility to the soil for the following year, so they gave it a try. Since then, the sculptures have grown bigger and more complex, and the festival itself has grown to attract artists from around Croatia and beyond, plus thousands of festivalgoers who come to enjoy the traditional food, music, even sports competitions such as bale-throwing. And like any good party in a field, it all ends with a bonfire, as the sculptures are burned to the ground (🌐 *www.slama.hr*).

garden, is now the site of the Našice Regional Museum, which has impressive exhibits on the history of the surrounding area from ancient times to World War II. The collection includes everything from displays of ancient archaeological fragments and 16th-century coins, to the bygone equipment of the local fire brigade, to an ethnographic exhibit of a typical room from a turn-of-the-20th-century peasant home. There are four attractive memorial rooms dedicated to distinguished Croatian artists, including Dora Pejačević, Croatia's first female composer. There are several trains each day to Našice from Osijek (45–60 minutes). ✉ *Trg dr. Franje Tuđmana 5, Našice* ✣ *51 km (32 miles) southwest of Osijek* ☎ *031/613–414* 🌐 *www.tznasice.hr.*

WHERE TO EAT

$$$ EASTERN EUROPEAN Fodor's Choice ★

🍴 **Kod Ruže.** Kod Ruže seems to have all the trappings you'd expect from a typical Slavonian restaurant—heavy furniture, faded old photos, embroidered hand towels, river fish, and stews. But look closer and you'll realize something special is happening here: the seats are leather, the decor is antique-chic, the pike-perch is on skewers, and the stew is made with frog. It's traditional-meets-designer, and on weekends, it's all accompanied by a live Gypsy band! More fun than you ever thought you could have while wearing a fish paprikaš bib. [$] *Average main: 50 Kn* ✉ *Kuhačeva 25a, Tvrđa* ☎ *031/206–066* 🌐 *omnia-osijek.hr/ruza.php.*

$ EASTERN EUROPEAN Fodor's Choice ★

🍴 **Kompa.** On the bank of the Drava, just across the river from the Osijek zoo, you'll find Kompa Restaurant. In a city full of variations on the same theme, Kompa takes traditional dishes to another level. Their homemade sausages are perfectly spicy, and the *koljenica* (pig's knuckle) is a firm favorite. If you are around on a Sunday or holiday, join the locals for a big feast of *teleće pečenje* (roast veal). The service is friendly and attentive, the ambience is peaceful. It's a shame about the mosquitoes but it's to be expected from a riverside restaurant and they have bug spray on hand if needed. And Kompa offers a bonus that you wouldn't normally expect from a Slavonian restaurant: an excellent sunset view. ⓢ *Average main: 50 Kn* ✉ *Splavarska 1, Gornji Grad* ☎ *031/375–755* ⊕ *www.restorankompa.hr.*

$$
ITALIAN
✕ **Lumiere.** Under the glow of the Kino Urania sits Lumiere restaurant, a bright new light in a city full of traditional restaurants. The menu is Italian-inspired, with homemade pasta, sundried tomatoes, rocket salad, and seafood delivered straight from the Adriatic. The large interior is decorated with cream colors, soft cushions, and light wood furnishings. Two oversize stills from Casablanca—a nod to the classic cinema next door—hang on the wall. Locals love it because it's modern and different, you'll love it when you're ready for something that doesn't involve paprika. ⓢ *Average main: 60 Kn* ✉ *Šetaliste Kardinala Franje Šepera 8, Gornji Grad* ☎ *031/201–088.*

$$
EASTERN
EUROPEAN
✕ **Slavonska Kuća.** Just a couple of blocks from Tvrđa's main square, this small one-room eatery is about as atmospheric as can be, with rustic wooden benches, walls adorned with bric-a-brac, including a fishing net, and folksy background music. Choose between regional fare like *fiš paprikaš* and *od divljači* (venison stew). ⓢ *Average main: 45 Kn* ✉ *Kamila Firingera 26, Tvrđa* ☎ *031/369–955* ⊕ *www.slavonskakuca.com.*

WHERE TO STAY

$
HOTEL
🏨 **Central Hotel.** It could use some sprucing up, but Osijek's oldest continuously operated hotel, opened in 1889, is somehow romantic in its decay. **Pros:** old-world elegance at a decent price; splendid views of main square from many rooms; elegant bathrooms. **Cons:** some rooms are noisy; few frills. ⓢ *Rooms from: 534 Kn* ✉ *Trg Ante Starčevića 6, Gornji Grad* ☎ *031/283–399* ⊕ *www.hotel-central-os.hr* ⤏ *39 rooms* ❝❞ *Breakfast.*

$
B&B/INN
Fodor'sChoice
★
🏨 **Guesthouse Maksimilian.** Art, history, culture, and comfort come together in this 14-room guesthouse in Tvrđa, a one-of-a-kind accommodation option in Osijek. **Pros:** beautifully decorated guest rooms; friendly and personal service; location in Tvrđa. **Cons:** rooms can be noisy; distant from center of town. ⓢ *Rooms from: 344 Kn* ✉ *Franjevačka 12, Tvrđa* ☎ *031/497–567* ⊕ *maksimilian.hr* ⤏ *14 rooms* ❝❞ *Breakfast.*

$$
HOTEL
🏨 **Hotel Osijek.** This skyline-dominating, steel-and-glass edifice is the city's only luxury hotel. **Pros:** great views; centrally located; excellent services and amenities; fine in-house dining; a lovely, light-filled café. **Cons:** impersonal; many rooms smallish. ⓢ *Rooms from: 856 Kn* ✉ *Šamačka 4, Gornji Grad* ☎ *031/230–333* ⊕ *www.hotelosijek.hr* ⤏ *140 rooms, 7 suites* ❝❞ *Breakfast.*

$$$
HOTEL
Fodor'sChoice
★
🏨 **Hotel Waldinger.** Opened in 2004 in a 19th-century art nouveau building on one of central Osijek's main thoroughfares, the Waldinger—named after famous local painter Adolf Waldinger—offers luxury on a par with the Hotel Osijek, but on a cozier scale and with a period look and feel. **Pros:** superior in-house restaurant; lavish breakfast friendly

service. **Cons:** pricey (for Slavonia); rooms on top floor have smallish windows. [$] *Rooms from: 950 Kn* ✉ *Županijska 8, Gornji Grad* ☎ *031/250–450* 🌐 *www.waldinger.hr* 🛏 *15 rooms, 1 suite* 🍴 *Breakfast.*

NIGHTLIFE AND PERFORMING ARTS

NIGHTLIFE

Osijek has a large student population, which lends a youthful atmosphere to the entire city, particularly its bars and cafés, which are full day and night with people drinking coffee, eating ice cream, or enjoying a local Osječko, the oldest beer in Croatia.

The Kavana. A great place for your afternoon coffee break is on the terrace of the Kavana, right on the square beside the redbrick church. It's a stylish café with wall clocks made from twigs, designer furniture from Istanbul, and original paintings from local artists. ✉ *Županijska 2, Gornji Grad* ☎ *091/752–5523.*

St. Patrick's Pub. If you get thirsty while sightseeing in Tvrđa, there are five café-bars with terraces on the main square, distinguishable only by their different-color umbrellas. St. Patrick's Pub, a paean to all things English, was the pioneer, and still one of the most popular. ✉ *South side of Trg Svetog Trojstva, Franje Kuhača 15, Tvrđa* ☎ *031/205–202* 🌐 *www.st-patricks-pub.hr.*

Fodor's Choice ★ **Trica.** The promenade along the city harbor (Zimska Luka) is lined with inviting caffe-bars, and really comes alive on summer weekends with live music across the outdoor terraces. A great option is Trica, a popular student hangout on a side street beside Hotel Osijek. It has a lively soundtrack and quirky decor, and stretches over three rooms on split-levels, with leather chairs, couches and pillows for lounging, and a few tables in the lovely garden out back. ✉ *Lučki prilaz 2, Gornji Grad* ☎ *031/211–333.*

PERFORMING ARTS

FAMILY **Dječje Kazalište Branka Mihaljevića** (*Children's Theatre*). The Children's Theater is the place to go for a good puppet show. ✉ *Trg bana J. Jelačića 19, Gornji Grad* ☎ *031/501–485* 🌐 *www.djecje-kazaliste.hr.*

Hrvatsko Narodno Kazalište (*Croatian National Theater*). The Hrvatsko Narodno Kazalište is Osijek's venue for a broad array of Croatian and international plays. The building that has housed the theater since 1907 is an imposing ochre structure whose Venetian-Moorish style renders it the most striking of a string of classical facades along Županijska ulica. ✉ *Županijska 9, Gornji Grad* ☎ *031/220–700* 🌐 *www.hnk-osijek.hr.*

Kino Urania (*Urania Cinema*). This one-of-a-kind historic cinema, based on drawings by famed Osijek architect Viktor Axmann, looks a tad like a church, displaying a heady mix of art nouveau and modernist influences. Movie fans will love the old-school charm, particularly the vintage posters on the walls. Films are in English with subtitles. ✉ *V. Hengla 1, Gornji Grad* ☎ *031/205–507.*

SHOPPING

There are two big shopping malls in Osijek; a free bus runs from the center to both of them. Bustling Županijska, leading up to Trg Ante Starčevića, is the best stretch of street in the center to see what's for sale.

Lega-Lega. For a cool Slavonian souvenir, visit Lega-Lega. Their colorful, quirky prints, featuring characters such as owls, bicycles and foxes, are created in-house by Osijek designers, printed on garments made in akovo, and sold in milk carton–inspired boxes. They also do a range of notebooks, coasters, posters, and drawing pads. ⊠ *Županijska 25, Gornji Grad* ☎ *031/494–104* ⊕ *lega-lega.com.*

Fodor'sChoice
★ **Osijek Antiques Market.** If you're lucky enough to visit Osijek on the first Saturday of the month, head to the Osijek Antiques Market in Tvrđa's main square, where more than 100 antiques dealers from Croatia and beyond sell everything from porcelains to furniture to weapons. ⊠ *Trg. Svetog Trojstva, Tvrđa* ☎ *031/203–755.*

Rukotvorine. Rukotvorine has a rich array of top-notch Slavonian embroidery and handicrafts in its small store across the street from the Hotel Waldinger. ⊠ *Županijska 15, Gornji Grad* ☎ *031/212–217.*

KOPAČKI RIT NATURE PARK

10 km (6 miles) northeast of Osijek.

More than 80% of the historical wetlands along the Danube has been lost since the late 19th century. One of the largest remaining areas is now preserved in Kopački Rit Nature Park, a place of serene beauty that makes for a deeply satisfying visit whether or not you're partial to birds.

Fodor'sChoice
★ **Kopački Rit Nature Park.** Embracing more than 74,100 acres immediately north of the Drava, where the fast river flows eastward into the Danube, the park is covered with immense reed beds as well as willow, poplar, and oak forests and crisscrossed by ridges, ponds, shallow lakes, and marshes. Its exact aquatic contours vary a tad each year, depending on the degree to which the Danube backs up under pressure from the Drava and floods over the area. More than 293 bird species, hundreds of varieties of plants, and dozens of species of butterflies, mammals, and fish live in Kopački Rit. A vital spawning ground for Danube river fish, the park is also a breeding area for numerous endangered species— including the white-tailed sea eagle, the black stork, and the European otter. Egrets, herons, and cormorants are abundant, as are red deer, roe deer, and wild boar. In winter, Kopački Rit plays host to thousands of migrating geese and ducks. Although efforts have been underway since 1999 to make Kopački Rit a full-fledged national park, the going has been slow on this front—in no small part because the necessary restrictions on hunting in such a game-rich area make the issue politically sensitive. The best times of year to visit are during spring and autumn bird migrations, when there are often several hundred thousand birds in the park. Should you come in warm weather, be prepared to be feasted on by mosquitoes. Although the park administration building is in Bilje, the information office at the park entrance in Kopač serves

CLOSE UP

Slavonian Wine

Locals will tell you the only difference between Croatian wine and its more famous European counterparts is centuries of marketing. But that is quickly changing, particularly in Slavonia, which shares the 45th parallel—recognized as the ideal latitude for wine-growing—with the most renowned vineyards in France and Italy. *The vineyards of the Baranja County (north of Osijek), Đakovo, and Erdut (east of Osijek)* have become part of the EU-designated Vintour, which also includes wine roads in Italy, Spain, and Hungary.

Wine-making is a crucial part of Slavonian history; you can visit lands cultivated by Romans and subsequently owned by Ottomans, try wines favored by the Austrian Empire, or a Traminac (a type of Gewürztraminer) that was served at the coronation of Queen Elizabeth II.

A wine-based itinerary will take you to all corners of Slavonia, allowing you to tap into the local way of life, particularly as an increasing number of vineyards add accommodation.

Bjelovar is the first Slavonian town you hit when leaving Zagreb, where you'll find the small, beautifully restored farmhouse and winery Vinarija Vinia. Any wine tour must include a stop in tiny Kutjevo, near Požega. Even the main square is named Trg Graševine, after Slavonia's signature white wine, Graševina (known elsewhere as Welschriesling).

The largest and most historical winery is Kutjevačko Vinogorje, but be sure to visit the lovely Krauthaker winery as well.

As you move east, spend the night 20 km (12½ miles) away at Vinarija Zdjelarević, Croatia's original wine hotel, and one of the first private wineries to emerge from under communist control. It combines a stunning restaurant with 15 private rooms on beautifully landscaped vineyards.

The easternmost point of Slavonia is Ilok, where you can stay in historical Stari Podrum for the evening. Their Traminac, produced here since the 18th century, is renowned.

As you reach Osijek, one of the most prominent wine-producing areas is only a day trip away. The lovely village of Erdut, just 37 km (23 miles) east, is best known for its 14th-century castle and for its vineyards. Check out the famous barrel at Erdutski Vinogradi, made of 150-year-old Slavonian oak, which holds 75,000 liters of wine.

Finish your tour in the unspoiled Baranja region, whose name itself means "Mother of Wine" in Hungarian. You can visit traditional villages, take part in folk festivals, and make a stop at the progressive Josić winery in the settlement of Zmajevac where there is an excellent on-site restaurant. Tours of Slavonian wineries, including several tastings and a bread and cheese platter, generally cost between 40–75 Kn, while overnight stays start at 400 Kn.

visitors. A short nature trail leads to the landing where boat excursions set out daily into the marshy heart of the park along a channel to Kopačevo Jezero, the largest lake. It is also possible to bring a bicycle into the park and ride on the bike lanes. In 2014, plans were underway to install a tourist train for winter excursions. In 1991, Kopački Rit became a no-man's-land along the front line of the Yugoslav war. For the next six years the natural area and the human communities around it were ravaged, not least by thousands of land mines, which have not only brought great danger to humans but have drastically reduced populations of large mammals such as deer and wild boar. Getting to Kopački Rit from Osijek is simple if you have a car—just follow the signs once you're in Bilje. If you go by bus, get off in Bilje and follow the signs on foot for some 4 km (2½ miles) along rural roads to the entrance of the park. Better yet, ride a bike to Kopački Rit from Osijek (Guesthouse Maksimilian rents bikes) or from Bilje (rent a bike at Agrotourism Crvendač). ✉ *Information Center near Kopačevo, Kopacevo* ☎ *031/752–320* 🌐 *www.kopacki-rit.hr.*

3

Dvorac Tikveš (*Castle Tikveš*). A prized hunting and fishing area for centuries—and in particular during the Austro-Hungarian Empire—Kopački Rit also has a rich cultural-historical heritage. Dvorac Tikveš, a historic villa with a rich history dating back to the Austro-Hungarian monarchy, also served as a hunting lodge for Yugoslav leader Josep Broz Tito. The complex includes a restaurant and research laboratories for visiting scientists. ✉ *15 km (9 miles) north of Bilje* ☎ *031/285–394* 🌐 *www.kopacki-rit.hr.*

WHERE TO EAT AND STAY

$ EASTERN EUROPEAN

🍴 **Restoran Kod Varge.** On Bilje's main road a few hundred yards before the major intersection (if you're coming from Osijek and going toward Kopački Rit), this charming restaurant, with a dark, woodsy interior and a large covered terrace, offers such hearty regional fare as *ribli paprikaš, čobanac,* and fish *perkelt* (fish stew with pasta and cottage cheese). [$] *Average main: 60 Kn* ✉ *Ul Kralja Zvonimira 37a, Bilje* ☎ *031/750–031.*

$$ EASTERN EUROPEAN FAMILY Fodor's Choice ★

🍴 **Zelena Žaba.** Also known locally by its Hungarian name, Zöld Béka, the Green Frog restaurant is an absolutely delightful village restaurant, with a quiet, willow-fringed marsh behind the building that you can look out upon from the back room. Its hunting-cum-fishing theme is expressed in the form of rifles, antlers, an oar, and fishnets on the walls. Try house specialties such as *žabliji kraci* (frogs' legs) and *riblji perkelt* (fish in a thick paprika sauce), plus other favorites such as roast pike. For dessert, there's nothing like *palačinke* filled with walnuts or jam. [$] *Average main: 70 Kn* ✉ *Ribarska ul 3, Kopacevo* ☎ *031/752–212.*

$ B&B/INN

🏨 **Crvendać.** If you want to stay a little closer to Kopački Rit, an option is to stay in Bilje, located about halfway between Osijek and the park entrance. **Pros:** friendly owner; location near Kopački Rit; rental bikes on-site. **Cons:** basic rooms; not much to do around Bilje. [$] *Rooms from: 310 Kn* ✉ *Biljske satnije, ZNG RH 5, Bilje* ☎ *031/750–264* 🌐 *www.crvendac.com* 🛏 *3 rooms* 💳 *No credit cards* 🍽 *Breakfast.*

VUKOVAR

35 km (22 miles) southeast of Osijek.

There's no doubt that a visit to Vukovar hurts. As you visit the sights, the story of what happened here will slowly unfold, made even sadder by the glimpses of what a beautiful, cultural city this once was. It's a place that holds a tender spot in the hearts of most Croatians, and it will earn a spot in yours, too. But today, it is as much the scene of urban renewal as it is of destruction, and this is a perfect time to visit, as Vukovar begins to recover from its painful past and strives to regain its former vitality.

In 1991, Vukovar was a prosperous city. Located at the confluence of the Danube and Vuka rivers, it had a lovely ensemble of Baroque architecture, fine museums and many restaurants. It was named after the ancient Vučedol culture that inhabited a site 5 km (3 miles) downstream from the present-day city some 5,000 years ago. The area was later the site of a Roman settlement, and by the 11th century a community existed at the town's present location; this settlement became the seat of Vukovo County in the 13th century. After Turkish rule (1526–1687), almost all of Vukovar and environs was bought by the counts of Eltz, a German family that strongly influenced the development of the town for the next two centuries and whose palace is home to the town museum.

When Yugoslavia started to break apart in 1991 and Croatia declared independence, the JNA (Yugoslav People's Army) and Serb militias began seizing control of areas with a large Serbian population. Vukovar, which at the time had a mixed population of 47% Croatians and 37% Serbians, was steadfastly claimed by both sides. A battle for the city ensued; it was up to lightly armed soldiers of the newly created Croatian National Guard, as well as 1,100 civilian volunteers, to defend it. During the 87-day siege, 12,000 shells and rockets were launched daily in the fiercest European battle since World War II. Those who had not fled Vukovar in the beginning became trapped inside, taking refuge in Cold War–era bomb shelters. On the 18th of November, the defenders of the city, running out of ammunition, numbers and strength, could hold on no longer, and Vukovar fell. The once-lovely city was reduced to rubble. More than 30,000 Croatian residents were deported, thousands were killed, and thousands more are still reported as missing. Several military and political officials have since been indicted and jailed for war crimes, including those involved in the notorious Vukovar hospital massacre.

In 1998, Vukovar was peacefully reintegrated into Croatia. The population is now half of what it was prewar, and although it is mixed, the two ethnic communities remain divided. In a poignant reminder of what happened here not long ago, the visitor cannot help but notice a steady, somber stream of pedestrian traffic to one of Vukovar's most conspicuous sites: a tall, simple concrete cross situated at the tip of a narrow causeway overlooking the Danube, with inscriptions in both Cyrillic and Roman letters, honoring all victims on both sides. Today, Vukovar is recovering. New houses and ongoing construction are much in evidence, there are modern shopping malls, the Eltz Castle and the Franciscan Monastery have been rebuilt, and the center is once again

Young Love

The Baranja region, north of Osijek reaching up to the Hungarian border, is the most traditional, untouched part of Slavonia. It is full of quaint villages with only a few thousand residents at most, where life is lived around the Danube, on vineyards and fertile fields, and near the swamps of Kopački Rit. There are fish-stew cook-offs, harvest festivals, labyrinths of flowers, wine, goulash, and everything is sprinkled with paprika. You can visit the wineries in Zmajevac, an impressive monument to the Red Army in Batina, or the region's biggest town, Beli Manastir. The best village to spend the evening is Karanac, just 30 km (18 miles) from Osijek, where you'll find the popular Baranjska Kuća: a traditional Slavonian restaurant which doubles as an impressive

outdoor ethnological museum, complete with a model street and houses showing what life in rural Baranja was once like (⊕ *baranjska-kuca.com*). Stay overnight at the beautifully-restored Ivica I Marica ("Hansel and Gretel") estate, where you can go horseback riding, fishing, or just hang out in the big backyard with the very welcoming hosts (⊕ *www.ivica-marica.com*). The entire region is quite compact, but it is tricky to get around Baranja by public transport; if you have your own wheels, you'll be able to cover a lot of ground. If you would like a guided tour to a couple of villages, departing from Osijek, contact the very friendly, enthusiastic Mislav Pavosevic at Putovanja Slavonijom (☎ *031/740–091*).

full of busy cafés and bustling markets. Vukovar is a stop along the Danube bike path network, attracting cycling groups each summer, and its proximity to Ilok has made it a stop on many wine tours. There is even a six-day Vukovar Film Festival in August, featuring films also shown at the Cannes or Berlin Film Festival.

Yet the memories are never far away. Next to brand-new structures are the burnt-out frames of old buildings. Walls are still pockmarked, houses are empty, and many of the city's main sights take on deeper significance due to the destruction wrought upon them. There is hope in the air, but it's usually not long before a conversation with a local will, inevitably, turn to the past.

Vukovar is a living war museum.

GETTING HERE AND AROUND
Around five trains and buses make the daily 45-minute journey from Osijek to Vukovar, several of them continuing onward to Ilok further south. Regular buses and trains also travel between Zagreb and Vukovar, stopping in Vinkovci along the way.

EXPLORING

TOP ATTRACTIONS

Fodor's Choice ★ **Gradski Muzej Vukovar** (*Vukovar Town Museum*). In the 18th-century palace Dvorac Eltz, which was severely damaged in the siege of Vukovar, the Gradski Muzej Vukovar is back in business. After decades of reconstruction, the entire museum is once again open for viewing. It has an excellent range of archaeological artifacts from all eras of Vukovar history, from the Vučedol culture that flourished in the region from around 3000 BC, right up to the siege of Vukovar in 1991. If you don't know much about the city before you arrive, make this museum your first stop: you will learn a lot about Vukovar in a broader context than just the war, and the rest of your time there will be much more meaningful. ⊠ *Županijska 2* ☎ *032/441–271* 🖃 *25 Kn* ⊘ *Tues.–Fri. 10–6, weekends 10–1.*

Mjesto Sjećanja - Vukovar Bolnica (*Place of Memory - Vukovar Hospital*). You'll want to bring a steady set of nerves with you to this site. During the siege of Vukovar, the top four floors of the hospital were destroyed by consistent bombing, despite being designated an official safe zone; still, staff continued to work in the basement and bomb shelter, helping civilians and soldiers, operating even without running water. After Vukovar fell in 1991, and despite an agreement that the hospital must be safely evacuated, more than 200 people were removed from the hospital by a Serbian militia and brought to Ovčara farm, where they were beaten, tortured, and eventually executed. Others were sent to prisons or to refugee camps. Today, the structure has been rebuilt and functions as a regular hospital again, but the areas used during that time have been left as they were, and are now a chilling multimedia museum/memorial. You can drop by on your own and ask the guards at the gate how to find the museum; the entrance is marked by a giant red cross, full of holes. Or visit the tourist information center to arrange a guided tour. ⊠ *Županijska 35* ⊕ *www.ob-vukovar.hr* ⊘ *Daily 8–3.*

Spomen Dom Ovčara (*Ovčara Memorial*). On November 20–21, 1991, more than 200 soldiers and civilians were brought from the hospital to this former agricultural hangar, 4 km (2½ miles) outside the city and surrounded by fields of crops, by a Serbian militia. They were beaten, tortured, and eventually executed at another site 1 km away. The mass grave was exhumed in 1996, and 194 bodies were identified; among the dead were men ranging from 16 to 77 years old, one woman, a prominent radio journalist, and a French volunteer. Ovčara Memorial is a somber, powerful site; it respectfully pays homage to the victims as well as conveys the horror that took place here. To get to the site, follow signs along the road to Ilok for 6 km (4 miles) past the Memorial Cemetery of Homeland War Victims, the largest mass grave in Europe since WWII—eventually turning right and driving another 4 km (2½ miles) down a country road. If you don't have wheels, check with the tourist information center about your transportation options. ⊠ *Ovčara* ☎ *032/512–345* ⊘ *Daily 10–5.*

WORTH NOTING

FAMILY   **Ada.** Vukovar locals live their lives on the banks of the Danube, and when it gets hot outside, they hop right into it! Ada is the name of a sandy beach on Vukovar Island, in the middle of the river where locals go to swim, play volleyball and suntan. There is a café on the island, but not many other facilities. It is a fun retreat, 10 minutes from the city, and can be reached by boats that leave regularly from near the

Hotel Lav and Vrske restaurant. A return ticket costs 10 Kn. ✉ *Island of Vukovar* ⊘ *Boat runs in summer, weekdays 11–8, weekends 10–8.*

Franjevački Samostan i Župa sv. Filipa i Jakova (*Franciscan Monastery & Church of Sts. Philip and James*). High on a hill southeast of the town center you'll find Vukovar's main ecclesiastical attraction, and one of the largest in Croatia: the Franciscan Monastery and Church of Sts. Philip and James. Construction on the Baroque monastery began in 1723, and it held one of the richest and most valuable libraries in the country, as well as prominent paintings and gold and silver vessels. Both have been restored to their former glory after being ravaged in the war. ✉ *Samostanska 5* ☎ *032/441–381* ⊘ *Weekdays 8–3, Sat. 8–noon.*

NEED A BREAK?

Caffe El Maritimo. Yards away from the pedestrian bridge you'll find the hip little café bar Caffe El Maritimo. With bohemian decorations indoors and plenty of inviting seats outside, it's a great place for an afternoon coffee or an evening beer. ✉ *Josipa Jurja Strossmayera 6.*

Water Tower. Visible from everywhere in Vukovar is its most famous symbol: the water tower. Rising 150 feet into the air, the imposing, red-brick structure once had a restaurant at the top with lovely views over the river and surrounding vineyards. Its sheer size made it a frequent target during the siege; it was hit with artillery more than 600 times. But it is still standing, with gaping holes on all sides, and will remain that way as a constant reminder, and a testament to the strength of the city. ✉ *1 Ulica Velika Skela, Vukovar.*

WHERE TO EAT

$$ ╳**Dunavska Golubica.** With a sprawling terrace overlooking the Danube and views of the monastery spires and the water tower, this large, restored restaurant has an old-fashioned fireplace as its centerpiece and pictures of old Vukovar on the walls. It specializes in grilled fish, such as perch and carp, but does a nice, abundant meat platter and a delicious venison *čobanac* with homemade spaetzle. Beside the restaurant there is a playground; look closer to see a thought-provoking monument of houses falling like dominoes. Ⓢ *Average main: 50 Kn* ✉ *Dunavska šetnica 1* ☎ *032/445–434.*
EASTERN EUROPEAN

$$ ╳**Vrške.** This apricot-color restaurant with a charming farmhouse look rests on an islet reached by a pedestrian bridge behind the Hotel Lav. Its spacious, thatched-roof terrace overlooks the Danube; the interior features reed walls and wood-beamed ceilings. Carp, catfish, pike-perch, and other freshwater fish are the favorites here, whether grilled, fried, or in a thick, vegetable-rich sauce; they are typically complemented by French fries. You can get a huge, four-person bowl of paprika-rich *riblji paprikaš* (fish stew). Combine this with some Ilok wine and a *palačinke s marmeladom* (jam-filled crepe). Ⓢ *Average main: 60 Kn* ✉ *Parobrodarska 3* ☎ *032/441–788* ⊕ *www.restoran-vrske.hr.*
EASTERN EUROPEAN

WHERE TO STAY

$$$ 🏨 **Hotel Lav.** Hotel Lav—a sparkling white building with a glass front—
HOTEL   is the only luxury hotel in Vukovar. **Pros:** the only luxury hotel in town;
centrally located; excellent restaurant. **Cons:** pricey; no pool. $ *Rooms
from: 1014 Kn* ✉ *J. J. Strossmayera 18* ☎ *032/445–100* ⊕ *www.hotel-
lav.hr* ↪ *39 rooms, 4 suites* ❍❙ *Breakfast.*

$ 🏨 **Rooms Biser Dunava.** This newly opened property, halfway between
HOTEL   a boutique hotel and private apartments, is run by a friendly young
local named Davor in the family home that he renovated himself. **Pros:**
small, intimate hotel; best budget option in Vukovar. **Cons:** rooms can
be noisy; far distance from the center of Vukovar; breakfast costs extra.
$ *Rooms from: 250 Kn* ✉ *Osječka 11* ☎ *092/271–7082* ⊕ *www.biser-
dunava.com* ↪ *6 rooms.*

$ 🏨 **Vila Vanda.** Built as an addition to the popular Konoba Megaron,
HOTEL   these 13 rooms offer a nice, midrange accommodation choice, 10 min-
utes walk from the center. **Pros:** spacious rooms with nice balconies;
located in a quiet neighborhood; friendly staff. **Cons:** slightly far from
the center of town; breakfast is very basic. $ *Rooms from: 435 Kn*
✉ *Dalmatinska 3* ☎ *032/414–410* ⊕ *konoba-megaron.hr* ↪ *13 rooms*
❍❙ *Breakfast.*

ILOK

*37 km (22 miles) southeast of Vukovar, 74 km (45 miles) southeast
of Osijek*

Perched high on the western slopes of the Fruška Gora hills above the
Danube and built around a medieval fortress, Ilok, Croatia's eastern-
most town, affords resplendent views of the gently rolling, vineyard-
draped hills, the Danube, and the Vojvodina plain on the Serbian side
of the river. On a clear day, you can see all the way to Novi Sad.

Ilok has been inhabited since the Neolithic era, but its golden age came
in the 15th century under the Iločki family, particularly Nicholas of
Ilok, the Ban of Croatia and King of Bosnia. He built a fortification on
a plateau overlooking the river and a castle within, turning Ilok into
a fortified royal residence, and began the first construction of wine
cellars. The last member of the Iločki family died in 1524; two years
later, Ilok was occupied by the Ottomans, under whose rule it remained
until 1697. There are still the remains of a hammam and a Turkish
grave in the Old Town from this period. After defeating the Turks, the
Habsburgs gave Ilok to the aristocratic Odescalchi family from Italy
as thanks for their assistance in the Ottoman wars, and they quickly
set about rebuilding the town, particularly the castle, in baroque style.
They developed the wine cellars below the castle, and began produc-
tion of the celebrated Traminac wine. Besides Stari Podrum ("Old Cel-
lar"), there are now a dozen other vineyards around town producing
many varieties of wine, particularly Graševina and Traminac. All can
be visited by appointment.

Ilok became part of Yugoslavia in 1918. At the beginning of the war in
1991, it was rapidly surrounded and occupied by Serb forces, sparing

it the drawn-out devastation suffered by nearby Vukovar. Ilok was integrated into the Republic of Serb Krajina, and not re-integrated into Croatia until 1998.

Ilok is comprised of two parts: the upper half is where the feudal families lived and where today you'll find the cities' historical sights, while the lower half has traditionally been where the townsfolk lived and worked, and where you'll find sandy beaches along the Danube.

GETTING HERE AND AROUND

There are frequent buses between Vukovar and Ilok (45 minutes, 35 Kn), many of which start or finish in Osijek; the bus will let you off in the center of the lower town. The tourist information center is located in the Upper Town.

3

EXPLORING

TOP ATTRACTIONS

Fodor'sChoice **Muzej Grada Iloka** (*Town Museum of Ilok*). From the very first arti-
★ fact—the fossils of a wooly mammoth—you will be impressed by this museum. It contains pottery from the Neolithic Vučedol culture that flourished between Ilok and Vukovar, one of the world's best-preserved antiquity-era Roman swords, and takes you through the ages of Ilok, from the Ottoman era to the Austrian Empire, from the wars of the 20th century right up to a modern art gallery. There are particularly interesting exhibits on the area's Jewish population pre-1945, relics from a 19th-century pharmacy, and an ethnological section on the top floor, focusing on traditional clothing, folk art, and household items, with a concentration on Ilok's large Slovak population. The museum is housed in the Odescalchi Castle, an imposing fortified structure overlooking the Danube, which was built on the foundations of the 15th-century castle of Nicholas of Ilok, the Ban of Croatia. Legend says that even Suleiman the Magnificent once slept in this castle. The rooms themselves are exquisitely designed with period pieces, even mood music, in keeping with their original function, such as the hunting room and the drawing room. ⊠ *Šetalište oca Mladena Barbarića 5, Ilok* ☎ *032/827–410* ⊕ *www.mgi.hr* 🖅 *20 Kn, call ahead to arrange guided tour* ☉ *Tues.– Thurs. 9–3, Fri. 9–6, Sat. 11–6, Sun. open only for arranged visits. Closed Mon.*

Fodor'sChoice **Stari Podrum** (*Old Cellars*). A wine cellar, restaurant, hotel, and history
★ lesson all rolled into one, Stari Podrum is a must-see when visiting Ilok. It is located next door to the Odescalchi Castle; in fact, the incredibly atmospheric cellars, stretching 100 meters long, stretch underneath it. The Odescalchi family began producing high-class wines here in the 18th century, including the celebrated Traminac, which was served at the coronation of Queen Elizabeth II. A guided tour will take you through the cool cellars, past Slavonian oak barrels, to the prestigious archive wines that were once exported by the Austrian Empire, and the old bottles, full of dust and cobwebs that were buried in sand for protection during the Homeland War. You can try all of the wines produced here, and buy souvenir bottles at very reasonable prices (a bottle of Traminac costs 35 Kn). The on-site restaurant serves delicious Slavonian

dishes, including freshwater fish paprikash with homemade noodles; you can eat inside surrounded by traditional embroidery and heavy wooden furniture, or outdoors in the sunny central courtyard. Accommodation can be arranged in one of 18 nicely decorated rooms; a double room costs 500 Kn, with major discounts in July and August. ✉ *Dr. Franje Tuđmana 72, Ilok* ☎ *032/590–088* 🌐 *www.ilocki-podrumi.hr.*

WORTH NOTING

Župa Sv. Ivana Kapistrana (*Church of St. John of Capistrano*). This Franciscan church and monastery overlooking the Danube, first constructed in 1349, holds the remains of St. John of Capistrano, a Franciscan friar and Catholic priest. In 1456, at age 70, he led a successful battle against the Ottomans, which earned him the nickname "Soldier Priest." He died three months later in Ilok of the Bubonic Plague but was said to have performed miracles even on his deathbed. The church—which also holds the remains of Nicholas and Lawrence of Ilok, both of whom made expansions to the monastery complex during their reign—was given a 20th-century neo-Gothic face-lift by Herman Bollé, the same architect who helped design the Cathedrals in Đakovo and Zagreb, as well as Zagreb's Mirogoj Cemetery. Mass is held daily at 7 am and 6:30 pm—call the church directly or tourist information to arrange a visit. ✉ *Trg Sv. Ivana Kapistrana 3, Ilok* ☎ *032/592–860.*

WHERE TO STAY

$$ HOTEL 🏨 **Principovac Country Estate.** For those looking for an extraordinarily romantic escape, Principovac is your place. **Pros:** classy, beautifully designed premises; excellent restaurant; lots of land for walking, biking, or playing sports. **Cons:** distant from civilization; no public transport. [$] *Rooms from: 800 Kn* ✉ *Principovac 1, Ilok* ☎ *032/593–114* 🛏 *6 rooms* 🍴 *Breakfast.*

$ HOTEL 🏨 **Villa Iva.** This peaceful boutique hotel and restaurant is in the lower part of Ilok, at the base of the steps leading up to the Old Town. **Pros:** nicely decorated rooms; proximity to bus stop from Vukovar; on-site wine cellar and restaurant. **Cons:** distance from the Old Town and main Ilok sights. [$] *Rooms from: 300 Kn* ✉ *S. Radića 23, Ilok* ☎ *032/591–011* 🌐 *villa-iva-ilok.biz* 🛏 *13 rooms* 🍴 *Breakfast.*

ĐAKOVO

38 km (24 miles) southeast of Osijek.

Đakovo is a peaceful little town, where the din of bicycles and the dribbling of basketballs on a Sunday afternoon outdo the roar of cars. The relatively bustling pedestrian main street is Ivana Pavla II, whose far end has a little parish church that was built rather cleverly from a former 16th-century mosque, one of the few remaining structures left in Slavonia from 150 years of Ottoman rule. The best time to be in town—though a difficult time to book a room on short notice—is the last weekend in September, during the annual Đakovački Vezovi (Đakovo Embroidery Festival), which sees a folklore show replete with traditional embroidered costumes, folk dancing, and folk singing, an array of song-and-dance performances, and an all-around party atmosphere—even a show by the famous Lipizzaner horses, who train in town.

GETTING HERE AND AROUND

You can get to Đakovo from Osijek in about 40 minutes by one of several daily trains for roughly 35 Kn one-way. The Đakovo train station is 1 km (½ mile) east of the center, at the opposite end of Kralja Tomislava.

EXPLORING

TOP ATTRACTIONS

Fodor'sChoice ★ **Đakovačka Katedrala** (*Đakovo Cathedral*). Đakovo's centerpiece is its majestic redbrick, neo-Gothic cathedral, which towers above the city and is a stunning first sight as you arrive into town. Commissioned by the Bishop of Đakovo, Josip Juraj Strossmayer (1815–1905), and designed by architect Frederick Schmidt, the cathedral was called the "most beautiful church between Venice and Constantinople" by Pope John XXIII. Consecrated in 1882 after two decades of construction—7 million bricks were reportedly used in the building—the three-nave structure is distinguished by two steeples towering to 274 feet, beehivelike cones on either side of the entrance, and a pinnacled cupola. The interior features colorful biblical scenes, some representing the life of the cathedral's patron saint, St. Peter, which were painted on the walls over 12 years by father-and-son team Alexander and Ljudevit Seitz. The striking blue ceiling is dotted with gold stars and the floor is paved with red, yellow, and black checkered tile. ⊠ *Trg Strossmayera* ☎ *031/811–784* ⊘ *Daily 8–noon and 3–6.*

FAMILY

Fodor'sChoice ★ **Lipizzan State Stud Farm.** The history of the Đakovo stud farm dates back to 1506, when one of the bishops kept 90 Arabic horses there. But perhaps the year that really put it on the map was 1972, when Queen Elizabeth II saw the famous Đakovo four-horse team perform at the opening ceremony of the Olympics and insisted on paying them a visit. The story goes that there was no paved road outside the stud farm at the time; by the time the Queen arrived to take a carriage ride, one had been built. There are two locations in Đakovo where the prized white Lipizzaners are trained and bred; the Stallion Stable in the center of Đakovo, where a musical show is also held twice per month and plans are in place to build a museum; and Ivandvor, 6 km (4 miles) away, a pasture where the mares and offspring are kept in a peaceful, rural setting. It is possible to visit both farms to catch a glimpse of the horses and their stables, and a carriage ride through town can also be arranged. ⊠ *Augusta Šenoe 45* ☎ *031/822–535* ⊕ *www.ergela-djakovo.hr* ✉ *Ticket for 2 locations, 50 Kn; ticket for 2 locations and horse show, 60 Kn.*

WORTH NOTING

Spomen-muzej Biskupa Josipa Jurja Strossmayera (*Strossmayer Museum*). Just north of the cathedral is the Spomen-muzej Biskupa Josipa Jurja Strossmayera, which presents the life of the influential bishop by displaying some of his effects and writings. ⊠ *Luke Botića 2* ☎ *031/813–698* ✉ *5 Kn* ⊘ *Weekdays 8–6, Sat. 8–7.*

WHERE TO EAT

$$ PIZZA 🍴 **Mon Ami.** This pizzeria is in a big, redbrick building around the corner from the Cathedral. The interior is dark and publike, you probably won't find anyone who speaks English inside, and the service is as gruff and indifferent as can be. It's fantastic! [$] *Average main: 50 Kn* ✉ *L. Botića 12* ☎ *031/821–477.*

$$$ EASTERN EUROPEAN Fodor's Choice ★ 🍴 **Sokak.** One of the best places to find traditional Slavonian food in akovo, Sokak not only offers the chance to try local specialties such as Slavonian soup veal *peka* (cooked under the bell—order in advance), it also gives you a glimpse at what a traditional Slavonian neighborhood used to look like. The restaurant was built to resemble the two sides of a street, one half symbolizing the side where the wealthy people owned houses, the other half where the rural workers lived. The authentic furniture and decorations around the restaurant, especially in the atmospheric wine cellar, are particularly lovely. [$] *Average main: 70 Kn* ✉ *Augusta Šenoe 40* ☎ *031/820–332.*

WHERE TO STAY

$ HOTEL 🏨 **Croatia-Tourist.** Accommodation is scarce in the city center, but this homey hotel, just down the road from the Cathedral, will do. **Pros:** good price; near the cathedral. **Cons:** 25-minute walk from train station. [$] *Rooms from: 322 Kn* ✉ *P. Preradovića 25* ☎ *031/813–391* 🌐 *www.croatiaturist.hr* 🛏 *11 rooms* 🍽 *Breakfast.*

$ HOTEL 🏨 **Hotel Đakovo.** With cheerful rooms, a big restaurant specializing in Slavonian food and wine, a games room perfect for kids young and old (chessboard, pool table, and even a Nintendo Wii!). **Pros:** friendly service; on-site restaurant; spacious rooms. **Cons:** distance from town and train/bus stations. [$] *Rooms from: 470 Kn* ✉ *N.Tesle 52* ☎ *031/840–570* 🌐 *www.hotel-djakovo.hr* 🛏 *23 rooms, 2 suites* 🕒 *Open year-round* 🍽 *Breakfast.*

$ HOTEL Fodor's Choice ★ 🏨 **Vinarija Zdjelarević.** Fifty kilometers southwest of Đakovo lies Slavonski Brod, Slavonia's second-largest city. [$] *Rooms from: 300 Kn* ✉ *Vinogradska 65, Brodski Stupnik* ☎ *035/427–775* 🌐 *zdjelarevic.hr* 🛏 *15 rooms* 🍽 *Breakfast.*

POŽEGA

66 km (41 miles) southeast of Bjelovar, 150 km (94 miles) southeast of Zagreb, 96 km (60 miles) southwest of Osijek.

In the center of a fertile, vineyard-rich valley, which the ancient Romans knew as "Vallis Aurea," or Golden Valley, lies Požega (pop. 21,000), the prettiest city in central Slavonia. Požega was first mentioned in historical documents in 1227, but not much remains on the ground of that early era of local history. Stari Grad, a 13th-century fortress, today exists only as a small, thickly wooded hilltop park right beside the town center. During the 150-year-long period of Ottoman rule that began in 1537, Požega become central Slavonia's most important administrative and military center. With the expulsion of the Turks in 1688, a new era of Habsburg control ensued. In 1739 the town was ravaged by a plague that killed 798 citizens, but by the mid-18th century it had become a vibrant university center, and the town core was fast on its way to assuming its present appearance. By the 19th century Požega's cultural dynamism had earned it a reputation as the "Athens of Slavonia." In 1847 it became the first city to officially adopt the Croatian language. The construction of the central Slavonian railway, which began in 1894, was vital to the local economy as the 20th century arrived. Today it is a quiet city, surrounded by forests, with cute, colorful houses and wonderfully fresh air. It makes a lovely place for a day trip, or as a base while you explore nearby Papuk Nature Park.

GETTING HERE AND AROUND
As with much of Slavonia's interior, reaching Požega is easiest by car. By train, it takes about three hours to get here from Osijek (100 Kn), with two stops en route.

EXPLORING

TOP ATTRACTIONS

Fodor's Choice ★ **Gradski muzej** (*City Museum*). Tucked away in the corner of the main square is the Gradski muzej, whose collection of some 30,000 items comprises almost 20 display rooms on three floors covering regional archaeology, history, art, and ethnography from prehistoric times to the present day. You'll find paintings by regional artists, including family portraits by the renowned 19th-century painter Gustav Poša, and early-20th-century work by Miroslav Kraljević. There are also regional folk costumes and embroidery, ancient pottery and jewelry, and artifacts from the Roman occupation of the region. From time to time, they host an exhibition called Museum in a Pot, which explores the gastronomic heritage of Slavonia (the best part: you can eat the exhibits at the end!). ⊠ *Matice Hrvatske 1* ☎ *034/272–130* 🖾 *10 Kn* ☽ *Weekdays 9–2, weekends by appointment.*

Fodor's Choice ★ **Kutjevo.** Just 23 km (14 miles) northeast of Požega is a small town called Kutjevo. It sits in the middle of the Golden Valley, with hills draped with vineyards on either side. If there is any town where all of life is dedicated to viticulture, it is here. Nearly all 2,500 residents make a living from wine, and even the main square is named Trg Graševine, after Slavonia's signature white wine, Graševina (known elsewhere as Welschriesling); indeed, this is an excellent place to try it, as 80% of total Graševina production is made here. ⊠ *Kutjevo.*

Fodor's Choice ★ **Kutjevačko Vinogorje.** There are 20 different wineries to choose from around the town: the biggest, and oldest, is **Kutjevačko Vinogorje.** The story of this winery is the story of the Kutjevo itself; its cellars date back to 1232 (though the guides will tell you Romans were producing wine here long before that), when the town was founded by Cistercian Monks from Hungary. Over the years, it passed into the hands of Ottomans, Jesuits, Habsburgs, and private families, and the stories of each of these eras and the influence they left on Kutjevo are etched chronologically onto the Slavonian oak barrels in the cellar. A tour of the winery and cellars, plus a sampling of five wines and a souvenir glass, costs 75 Kn. In 2014, plans were in place to open a hotel and restaurant in the adjacent 18th-century Jesuit monastery. ⊠ *Kralja Tomislava 1, Kutjevo* ☎ *034/255–019* ⊕ *www.kutjevo.com.*

Fodor's Choice **Krauthaker.** Another smaller winery you won't want to miss is **Krau-**
★ **thaker,** one of the first private wine producers to emerge after the fall of communism. It only dates back to 1992, but it produces 24 different varieties, including an award-winning chardonnay, in case you're looking to change things up from graševina for a while. The location is lovely, with a terrace overlooking the town, a small pond and quaint bridge, and colorfully painted wine barrels scattered around the premises. A tour of the cellars, plus a cheese and bread platter and three tastings (which usually turns into six tastings) costs 40 Kn. Call ahead to both wineries to make appointments. There is an infrequent public bus to Kutjevo: check at the tourist information or bus station in Požega for times. ⊠ *Ivana Jambrovića 6, Kutjevo* ☎ *034/315–000* ⊕ *krauthaker.com.*

Crkva Sv. Lovre (*Church of St. Lawrence*). The town's main ecclesiastical attraction, the Gothic Crkva Sv. Lovre, was built in the 14th century on the foundations of an even older church; until the Jesuits arrived in town in the late 17th century, it was dedicated to St. Mary. Impressive medieval frescoes adorn on its south wall, and in the sanctuary you can see a Renaissance tabernacle. It is beside the imposing Bishop's Palace. ⊠ *Trg Sv. Trojstva 18* ☎ *034/294–300* ☉ *Daily 1–7.*

Franjevački Samostan i Crkva Duha Svetoga (*Franciscan Monastery and Church of the Holy Spirit*). Opposite the votive pillar, the Franjevački Samostan i Crkva Duha Svetoga was built in the late 19th century on the foundations of a 13th-century Gothic church ravaged by the Turks. Inside are impressive baroque altars and paintings, and a crypt (under the sanctuary) where a number of prominent local citizens—judges, political leaders, and nobility—are buried, including friar Luka Ibrišimović, credited with liberating the Požega area from the Turks. The monastery has a library of some 15,000 books, many of them rare historic volumes. ⊠ *Trg Sv. Trojstva* ☉ *Weekdays 9:30–11:30 and 4–6, Sat. 9–11:30.*

Katedrala Sv. Terezije Avilske (*Cathedral of St. Theresa of Avila*). At the foot of a hill where once there was a medieval fortress now stands one of Slavonia's loveliest baroque cathedrals. Completed in 1763, and endorsed by Empress Maria Theresa, it is marked by a single nave and two side chapels and has double volutes (spirals) on each side of its yellow facade. The interior is dominated by a grand altar blending playful baroque and rococo elements, and rococo pews carved from oak. The impressive wall and ceiling frescoes were made in 1898 and 1899 by the famous Croatian painters Celestin Medović and Oton Iveković—including Medović's striking scene on the sanctuary ceiling of St. Theresa ascending to heaven. The six stained-glass windows were added in the late 19th century. ⊠ *Trg Sv. Terezije 13.*

Trg Sv. Trojstva (*Holy Trinity Square*). Though not exactly square-shaped, Požega's main square is one of the most striking in Croatia, with baroque archways, the Franciscan Monastery to one side and the massive Bishop's Palace at the other end. There is a plague column in the middle of the square, built in memory of 798 local residents who perished a decade earlier; an inscription explains that the pillar was sculpted by one Gabriel Granici at a cost of 2,000 eggs and 300 forints. He didn't eat the eggs or give them to his relatives, though: he used them to cement the pillar's marble sand. ⊠ *Trg Svetog Trojstvra.*

WHERE TO EAT

$$ ✕ **Aureus.** There are many caffe-bars in the center of Požega, but your
PIZZA restaurant choices are very limited. Aureus is a simple pizzeria, but it will tick two boxes: you can sit and people-watch with the locals, while also getting a bite to eat. There are more than 30 varieties of pizzas, available in small and jumbo-size, and a variety of pasta dishes. ⓢ *Average main: 30 Kn* ⊠ *Kamenita Vrata 2* ☎ *034/274–931* ▭ *No credit cards.*

$ ✕ **Restoran Obrtnički Dom.** Just down the road from the Vila Stanišic,
EASTERN the Obrtnički Dom gives you a choice between a somewhat spuriously
EUROPEAN elegant interior with folksy Croatian tunes for background music or, in fair weather, outdoor seating in wicker chairs facing a shaded park. The simple fare ranges from grilled meats to grilled carp. ⓢ *Average main: 60 Kn* ⊠ *Dr. Franje Tuđmana 9* ☎ *034/313–125* ▭ *No credit cards.*

WHERE TO STAY

$ 🏨 **Vila Stanišic.** The simple rooms in this hotel are smallish, but other-
HOTEL wise have what it takes for a good night's sleep: pleasant peach-hued walls; either a king-size bed (half the rooms) or two twin beds; and extra furniture including a desk and at least one armchair. **Pros:** between the train station and the town center; on-site dining. **Cons:** smallish rooms; few frills. ⓢ *Rooms from: 390 Kn* ⊠ *Dr. F. Tuđmana 10* ☎ *034/312–168* ⊕ *vila-stanisic.hr* ⤳ *18 rooms, 3 dormitories* ⦿ *Breakfast.*

█████
█ OFF THE
█ BEATEN
█ PATH

Daruvar. The ancient Romans called the town of Daruvar (pop. 9,815) Aquae Balissae—and they knew a good spa site when they saw one. On the forested slopes of the Papuk Hills, 68 km (42 miles) northwest of Požega and just west of Papuk National Park, Daruvar is Slavonia's prettiest place to sit and soak. The present-day face of Daruvar's center—including an imposing two-story baroque manor house—took shape from 1760 to 1777 within the estate of Count Antun Janković. Beyond having two 18th-century baroque churches also worth a look, Daruvar and some nearby villages carry the unusual distinction of being home to Croatia's largest population of ethnic Czechs—many of whom still speak their native tongue and observe Czech customs. In this light, it is not surprising that Daruvar is also the home of a major brewery that produces Staročeško pivo Old Bohemian Beer—based on an old Czech recipe, of course. You can reach Daruvar by train or bus from Požega, but if you have a car available, that is by far the more convenient option. ⊠ *Daruvar* ☎ *043/623–623.*

Daruvarske Toplice. Among other buildings with which the family endowed Daruvar are the key structures of its spa, Daruvarske Toplice, which they built between 1810 and 1818 on the foundations of the very baths the Romans once enjoyed. Celebrated for its mildly alkaline water, which is said to be good for treating various ailments, the bath complex also includes a large park full of rare old trees. You can stay on-site at one of their two accommodations, seek a variety of health and wellness treatments, or just spend a couple of hours relaxing in the Finnish and Turkish saunas and three thermal pools. ⊠ *Julijev park, Daruvar* ☎ *043/623–623* ⊕ *www.daruvarske-toplice.hr* ✉ *29 Kn for entrance to pools* ☾ *Baths open 8 am–9 pm.*

ISTRIA

Updated
by Vera
and Frank
Galparsoro

Explore a remarkable 1,900-year-old Roman amphitheater in Pula. Visit Poreč and Rovinj, Croatia's two most popular seaside resorts, with Venetian-style campanili, loggias, and reliefs. Discover a thousand years of rich Istrian history in hilltop fortresses, early Christian churches, Byzantine mosaics, and baroque palaces, and treat your taste buds to two local specialties: white and black truffles—a series of festivals is dedicated to them—and wine: crisp and fruity white Istarska Malvazija and light and harmonious red Teran.

The word conjures something magical as it rolls off the tongue: *Istria.* Beyond sounding poetic, however, the name of this region of Croatia is derived from the name of the Illyrian people who occupied the area well before the Romans first arrived in the 3rd century BC—namely, the Histrians, whose chief architectural legacy comprised numerous hilltop fortresses. In the northwest corner of Croatia bordering Slovenia, the triangular-shape Istrian peninsula looks rather like a bunch of grapes—and, given its strong viticultural heritage, some might say this is not a coincidence.

Much of Europe's history has passed through Istria for more than a thousand years, not least the history associated with three great civilizations—the Roman, the Germanic, and the Slavic. Centuries of Venetian rule later reinforced by years of Italian occupation between the world wars have left a sizable Italian minority here, and Italian influence is apparent in the architecture, the cuisine, and the local dialect. Here, even the effects of the concrete-box style of communist-era architecture seem relatively minimal compared to the overall sense of a much deeper past suggested by the rich mix of architectural styles—from a whole array of well-preserved Roman ruins to Romanesque basilicas; from breathtakingly well-preserved medieval towns, towers, and town walls to baroque palaces and Austro-Hungarian fortifications.

The region's principal city and port, Pula, is on the tip of the peninsula and is best known for its remarkably preserved 1,900-year-old Roman amphitheater and Forum as well as the Triumphal Arch of the Sergians. Close by, the beautifully nurtured island retreat of Brijuni National Park can be visited in a day. Towns along the west coast have an unmistakable Venetian flavor left by more than 500 years of Venetian occupation (1238–1797). Poreč and Rovinj, Croatia's two most popular seaside resorts, are both endowed with graceful campanili, loggias, and reliefs of the winged lion of St. Mark, patron saint of Venice. The effects of package tourism have long encroached—to varying degrees—on the outskirts of various towns, most notably Poreč among Istria's largest coastal destinations. Rovinj, though likewise brimming with tourists in high season, retains more of its ravishing historic beauty and redolence than almost any other town on the Adriatic. A side trip to the romantic hill towns of Motovun and Grožnjan will prove unforgettable, whether as a brief excursion from the sea in the warmer months or as a more substantial autumn journey. This inland area is particularly rich in truffles and mushrooms, and from mid-September to late October these local delicacies are celebrated with a series of gastronomic festivals.

ORIENTATION AND PLANNING

GETTING ORIENTED

Istria is the Northern Adriatic region of Croatia and the country's largest peninsula, facing Venician lagoon to the west and Kvarner Bay to the southeast. Reaching Istria is easy: many large European cities are less than a five-hour drive away. Pula is a seasonal airport, and airports in Venice, Trieste, and Zagreb are all within a three-hour drive.

PLANNING

WHEN TO GO

If you are partial to sun and the idea of swimming in the warm, blue-green waters of the Adriatic, and you don't mind crowds and a bit of extra expense, by all means visit Istria in summer. Otherwise, this tourism-trampled region might be best saved for spring or fall (the water stays warm well into September), when you might save as much as 15% to 20% on lodging. The season in Istria for many restaurants and bars is Easter through the first week in November. You won't find much going on at all in January.

GETTING HERE AND AROUND

AIR TRAVEL

Croatia Airlines operates flights to Pula from Zagreb. Ryanair has service from London Stansted two times a week to Pula and daily from to Trieste, Italy. Jet2.com flies from Leeds, Manchester, and Newcastle to Pula from May until mid-September.

Contacts Croatia Airlines ⊠ *Pula Airport, Valtursko polje 210, Ližnjan* ☎ *052/218–909* ⊕ *www.croatiaairlines.com.* **Jet2.com** ⊕ *www.jet2.com.* **Ryanair** ⊕ *www.ryanair.com.*

BOAT AND FERRY TRAVEL

In summer Venezia Lines runs a catamaran service from Venice to Rovinj, Pula, and Poreč. Tickets are available online.

Contacts Venezia Lines ⊠ *Trg Matije Gupca 11, Poreč* ☎ *052/422–896* ⊕ *www.venezialines.com.*

BUS TRAVEL

There are domestic connections all over mainland Croatia to and from Pula, Poreč, and Rovinj, and local services between these towns and smaller inland destinations such as Motovun and Vodnjan. International buses offer daily connections to Italy (Trieste) and Slovenia (Ljubljana, Koper, Piran, and Portorož). Timetables are available at all bus

GREAT ITINERARIES

IF YOU HAVE 3 DAYS

There is so much to see in Istria that three days is a must, though it may seem like a rush if that's all the time you have. Start in Pula, as suggested below, if you are coming from Zagreb; if from the north (from Slovenia or Italy), start with Rovinj instead. Either way, do visit Rovinj. If you are interested in Istria's ecclesiastical heritage, you may want to prioritize Poreč over Pula; if Roman ruins are more your thing, by all means focus on Pula, whose architecture also gives you more of a sense of Istria's Austro-Hungarian past. On the first day, start off in **Pula.** Visit the Arena and at least take a stroll to the Forum. By all means spend the night here. A short drive or bus ride toward the Verudela or Stoja resort area gets you to eminently swimmable, if rocky, stretches of shoreline. The next morning, head off to **Rovinj.** Visit the 18th-century baroque Crkva Sv Eufemije, and just revel in strolling about the most beautiful town on the Istrian coast. On the third day, spend some more time in or around Rovinj, whether strolling the Old Town or taking a dip in the sea. If you're up to it, particularly if you have a car, move on to **Poreč** to see the Eufrazijeva Basilica.

IF YOU HAVE 5 DAYS

Spend your first day as above, but consider adding an excursion from Pula to **Vodnjan** or **Brijuni National Park,** depending on whether you're more interested in Vodnjan's countryside, medieval atmosphere, mummies, and food, or in Brijuni's natural splendors and luxurious, seaside ambience. Move on to **Rovinj** by the evening of Day

2 or the morning of Day 3, spending at least a full day or more there. On Day 4, it's on to **Poreč.** Perhaps go inland and spend the night in **Motovun.** On Day 5, if you're driving, take a look at **Grožnjan** as well before heading back. If you're getting around by bus, it's time to head back to a major town on the coast. Indeed, why not spend a few more hours in Rovinj or Pula before bidding adieu to Istria?

IF YOU HAVE 7 DAYS

Spend your first five days as above, but be sure to supplement your time in Rovinj, Pula, and Poreč with a lunch in **Labin,** on the east coast of Istria. If you're driving from Zagreb do it on the way to the more important towns; if you're driving through the countryside that takes you through both **Motovun** and **Grožnjan,** spend a night in or near Motovun. Before going inland, you may want to pay a visit to Vrsar and the Limski kanal or, instead, Baredine Cave. If you have a car, you can do so as you go inland or on your way back to the coast; if traveling by bus, you can get to these places most easily on a group excursion from Poreč or Rovinj. You may want to visit **Novigrad,** too, especially if you're driving, but save Umag for a 10-day trip. Spend Day 6 in Grožnjan then go back to Poreč or, better yet, Rovinj for the night. On Day 7, proceed to **Pula,** with a stop in **Labin** if you haven't been there yet and will be going farther east. Perhaps spend your final night in Labin as well.

TOP REASONS TO GO TO ISTRIA

■ Take a walk through the Roman area in Pula, where you will find one of the world's biggest and best-preserved amphitheaters (in fact, the sixth-largest in the world).

■ Have dinner at one of Rovinj's elegant seaside restaurants (Bluand Monte are among the city's finest dining establishments).

■ A scenic drive through the medieval towns of Grožnjan and Motovun in the hilly interior is not to be missed; these are villages that time seems to have forgotten. Indulge in a wine or olive-oil tasting at Kabola, Cuj, or Chiavalon estates.

■ Enjoy a tour of the amazing 6th-century Byzantine mosaics at St. Euphrasius Basilica in Poreč; St. Euphrasius is one of the best-preserved early Christian churches in Europe.

■ As in Italy, gelato is available everywhere in dozens of flavors all over Istria. Grab a cone and enjoy the early evening passeggiata, a stroll through any town square in the evening, just like a local.

stations. However, as elsewhere in Croatia, the sheer number of different companies offering bus service out of each station can be confusing; it's best to confirm at the information window what you might find posted on the wall.

Information Poreč Bus Station ⊠ *Rade Končara 1, Poreč* ☎ *060/333–111.*
Pula Bus Station ⊠ *Trg I. Istarske brigade BB, Pula.* **Rovinj Bus Station** ⊠ *Trg na Lokvi 6, Rovinj* ☎ *060/333–111.*

CAR TRAVEL

While visiting Pula, Rovinj, and Poreč a car may be more of a hindrance than an asset: all three towns are served by good bus connections, and having your own vehicle only causes parking problems. The best way to see the Istrian interior, however, is by car. The "sight" to see is the countryside itself and the small villages that dot it, so renting a car even for a day will give you much more satisfaction than trying to arrange a bus trip to one or another hill town. (And bus connections to the interior are infrequent.) If you are traveling from Zagreb, you can, of course, rent there, but major agencies have offices in Pula, and other towns along the coast all have one or more local agencies that generally offer better rates than the major chains without sacrificing quality of service; however, they may be less equipped than the major chains to take reservations by phone. (Some, such as Vetura and Lucky Way, also rent bicycles and scooters [i.e., mopeds].) Lastly, bear in mind that finding an available car on short notice in midsummer can be tricky regardless of the agency involved.

Novigrad GoAdria Agency ⊠ *Mirna 2, Novigrad* ☎ *052/555–555.*

Poreč Oryx Poreč ⊠ *Aldo Negri 1, Poreč* ☎ *052/423–300* ⊕ *www.oryx-rent. hr.* **Vetura** ⊠ *Trg Joakima Rakovca 2, Poreč* ☎ *052/434–700* ⊕ *www.vetura-rentacar.com* ⊠ *Zelena Laguna, Info Centar, Poreč* ☎ *052/451–391* ⊕ *www. vetura-rentacar.com.*

Pula Europcar ✉ *Pula Airport, Valtursko polje 210, Pula* ☎ *098/475–346, 052/550–971* ⊕ *www.europcar.com*. **Hertz** ✉ *Verudela BB, Pula* ☎ *052/210–868, 091/310–8681* ⊕ *www.hertz.com* ✉ *Pula Airport, Valtursko polje 210, Pula* ☎ *091/310–8681*. **Oryx Pula** ✉ *Scalierova 1, Pula* ☎ *052/522–176* ⊕ *www.oryx-rent.hr* ✉ *Airport Pula, Valtursko polje 210, Pula* ☎ *052/522–176* ⊕ *www.oryx-rent.hr*.**Vetura** ✉ *TN Punta Verudela, Pula* ☎ *052/210–294, 091/494–9627* ⊕ *www.vetura-rentacar.com*.

Rabac Vetura ✉ *Hotel Allegro, Rabac* ☎ *052/872–129, 091/557–5113* ⊕ *www. vetura-rentacar.com*.

Rovinj Oryx Rovinj ✉ *Šetalište Vjeća Europe BB, Rovinj* ☎ *052/814–259* ⊕ *www.oryx-rent.hr*. **Vetura** ✉ *Šetalište Vjeća Europe, Rovinj* ☎ *052/815–209, 091/730–4408* ⊕ *www.vetura-rentacar.com*.

Umag Interauto ✉ *Trgovačka 19, Umag* ☎ *052/741–483* ⊕ *www.inter-auto.hr*.

TRAIN TRAVEL

Istria is not well connected to the rest of Croatia by rail. To get to Zagreb or Split you need to transit through Rijeka.

Contact Pula Train Station ✉ *Kolodvorska 5, Pula* ☎ *052/541–982, 060/333–444 calls from Croatia*.

TOUR COMPANIES

Self-guided cycling tours of Istria can be arranged by Saddle Skedaddle, a U.K.-based cycling outfit. Gourmet tours, including wine-tasting tours of Istria, can be arranged through Winerist.

Information Saddle Skeddadle. This U.K.-based agency specializing in cycling tourism offers self-guided cycling holidays to Istria. The eight-day tour starts high above the Lim Fjord in the village of Klostar and leads you through the Istrian countryside. With daily distances set between 48 and 60 km (30 to 37 miles), this tour is suitable for regular cyclists. Saddle Skeddadle arranges all accommodation, luggage transfers, and provides you with an itinerary. ☎ *191/265–1110 in U.K.* ⊕ *www.skedaddle.co.uk* ✉ *From £655.*

TRAVEL AGENCIES

Kompas Travel can arrange daily excursions to Venice or Plitvice, as well as tours to the Limski kanal from either Poreč or Rovinj. Excursions Delfin also arranges tours to the Limski kanal, as do several other local companies and independent operators who happen to own boats and post flyers about their towns. Activa Travel Istria arranges boat tours.

Information Activa Travel Istra. This agency arranges panoramic boat tours from Pula to Rovinj or the Brijuni archipelago with a swim stop on the Red Island or the village of Barbariga. The agency is conveniently located at Scalierova ulica, right next to the amphiteater, and also sells tickets for Pula's many concerts and festivals. ✉ *Scalierova 1, Pula* ☎ *052/215–497* ⊕ *www.activa-istra.com* ✉ *From 240 Kn.*

Excursions Delfin. This local operator out of Rovinj offers daily boat tours to Lim Fjord (half- and full-day tours), panoramic boat tours of Rovinj and its archipelago, and boat excursions from Rovinj to Poreč and Vrsar. They also provide free transfers between all tourist resorts and campsites in Rovinj and the boat. ✉ *Zagrebačka 5, Rovinj* ☎ *052/848–265, 091/514–2169* ⊕ *www.excursion-delfin.com* ✉ *From 75 Kn.*

Winerist. This online company connects local experts and wineries with tourists in search of wine holidays. Wineriest offers four-, five-, and seven-day group wine and gourmet tours of Istria, which include accommodation, airport transfers (Trieste or Pula), simple culinary classes, all meals, and wine tastings. ☎ *020/7096–1006* ⊕ *www.winerist.com* ✉ *From €570.*

ESSENTIALS

INTERNET

Many hotels and rentals in Istria offer complimentary Wi-Fi, and lots of seaside towns provide Wi-Fi hot spots within the downtown area, though the connection isn't always stable. Most cafés and bars have free Wi-Fi, too. All the major hotels in Istria have an Internet center. Expect to pay at least 30 Kn for 30 minutes, or 40 Kn per hour. The Tourist Information Office in Poreč offers 15 minutes of free Internet use, more if no one is waiting in line (*see Visitor Information, below*).

RESTAURANTS

Food in Istria is more sophisticated and varied than in the rest of Croatia. Culinary tourism is one of the region's biggest draws, and you will get (for a price) a markedly better meal here than elsewhere in the country. The quaysides and old town squares have a plethora of touristy restaurants, and many new exceptional places have opened in recent years, helping to set the standard for the country's gastronomical identity. Istrian food today means fresh and simple seafood dishes, locally made *fuži* (egg noodles), elegant truffle sauces and flavors, and earthy *pršut* (air-dried local ham), alongside the familiar Italian staples of pizza and pasta. Seafood is usually grilled, baked in sea salt, or served *crudo* (raw) with a dash of local olive oil. Truffles are the superstars of the interior villages and work their way onto autumn menus in pastas, game dishes, and on beds of homemade polenta. Keep your eyes peeled for traditional favorites like *supa,* a brew of red wine, sugar, olive oil, pepper, and warm, toasted bread; and *meneštra,* an Istrian bean soup, both popular in winter. All these gourmet aspirations mean that dining in Istria can be costly relative to much of inland Croatia. Average prices for main courses start at 40 Kn for pasta and pizza, and move up to 80 Kn, or even twice that, for seafood (much of which is priced by the kilogram) and certain beef dishes. For a quick and cheap, albeit greasy, lunch, you can buy a *burek* (a curd-cheese or meat-filled pastry) in a bakery for around 12 Kn apiece.

HOTELS

In Istria, as in most other reaches of the Croatian coast, it's basically a question of whether to stay at the big, impersonal resorts on the beach, with a full range of services and activities available, or at smaller, boutique, sometimes family-run hotels. Either way it's imperative to book ahead, as most places—big and small—book up fast for the summer months. Bear in mind that some hotels and pensions impose a surcharge—usually 20%—for stays of fewer than three nights in high season, since they cater primarily to tourists who stay a week or two. Hotels listed here are geared toward the traveler who is looking to stay fewer than seven nights in the same city. *Hotel reviews have been shortened. For full information, visit Fodors.com.*

VILLA RENTALS

Villa rentals are popular in Istria, where many properties—from one-bedroom apartments to houses for 16—have been brought up to a high standard in recent years. The medieval villages of the hilly interior are scenic and offer sweeping (and almost uninterrupted) views of vineyards and olive groves. Hunkering down in a stone farmhouse and exploring the rest of the peninsula from there is certainly a leisurely way to appreciate Istria. Sadly, the region's been a bit oversold as "the new Tuscany" by tourism specialists, and while comfortable villas with pools are available, often they're as expensive as their equivalent in France or Italy but not quite as well appointed or charming. On the upside though, Istria is still not nearly as crowded as other parts of Europe, so you won't have to share your view with the hordes. The following companies specialize in villa rentals in Istria.

Information HomeAway. One of the most popular vacation-rentals sites, HomeAway lists many properties in Istria. ☎ *+44 20/8827–1971 in U.K.* ⊕ *www.homeaway.co.uk.*

Novasol. This Danish travel agency specializes in apartments and villa rentals in Europe and offers a good selection in Istria. All villas are bookable through their website. ☎ *0845/680–5856 in U.K.* ⊕ *www. novasol.co.uk.*

Thomson. This agency arranges excellent half- or full-board packages to Istria with airfare from the United Kingdom for the best per-night rates available. ☎ *0871/231–4691* ⊕ *www.thomson.co.uk.*

Villas.com. A subsidiary of Booking.com dedicated solely to apartment and villa rentals, this website has by far the largest choice of vacation rentals in Istria available for instant online booking. ✉ *Zagreb* ☎ *+44 20/3320–2609* ⊕ *www.villas.com.*

WHAT IT COSTS IN EUROS (€) AND CROATIAN KUNA (KN)				
	$	$$	$$$	$$$$
Restaurants	under 35 Kn	35 Kn–60 Kn	61 Kn–80 Kn	over 80 Kn
	under €5	€5–€8	€9–€10	over €10
Hotels	under 925 Kn	925 Kn–1,300 Kn	1,301 Kn–1,650 Kn	over 1,650 Kn
	under €121	€121–€170	€171–€216	over €216

Restaurant prices are the average cost of a main course at dinner or, if dinner is not served, at lunch. Hotel prices are the lowest cost of a standard double room in high season.

VISITOR INFORMATION

Although the official tourist offices listed here can provide you with every bit of information imaginable, they generally leave the booking of rooms and excursions to private tourist agencies.

Contacts Fažana Tourist Information ✉ *Titova riva 2, Fažana* ☎ *052/383–727* ⊕ *www.infofazana.hr.* **Grožnjan Tourist Information** ✉ *Umberta Gorjana 3, Grožnjan* ☎ *052/776–131, 052/776–064* ⊕ *www.tz-groznjan.hr.* **Istria Tourist Board** ☎ *052/880–088* ⊕ *www.istra.hr.* **Labin & Rabac Tourist Information** ✉ *A. Negri 20, Labin* ☎ *052/855–560, 052/852–399* ⊕ *www.rabac-labin.com.* **Novigrad Tourist Information** ✉ *Mandrač 29a, Novigrad* ☎ *052/757–075* ⊕ *www.novigrad-cittanova.hr.* **Poreč Tourist Information** ✉ *Zagrebačka 9, Poreč* ☎ *052/451–293* ⊕ *www.to-porec.com.* **Pula Tourist Information** ✉ *Forum 3, Pula* ☎ *052/219–197* ⊕ *www.pulainfo.hr.* **Rovinj Tourist Information** ✉ *Obala Pina Budičina 12, Rovinj* ☎ *052/811–566* ⊕ *www.tzgrovinj.hr.* **Umag Tourist Information** ✉ *Trgovačka 6, Umag* ☎ *052/741–363* ⊕ *www. coloursofistria.com.* **Vodnjan Tourist Information** ✉ *Narodni trg 3, Vodnjan* ☎ *052/511–700* ⊕ *www.istria-vodnjan.com.*

PULA

270 km (168 miles) southwest of Zagreb.

Today an industrial port town and Istria's chief administrative center (pop. 58,000), as well as a major tourist destination, Pula became a Roman colony in the 1st century BC. This came about a century after the decisive defeat by the Romans, in 177 BC, of the nearby Histrian stronghold of Nesactium, prompting the Histrian king Epulon to plunge a sword into his chest lest he fall into the hands of the victors, who indeed conquered all of Istria. Remains from Pula's ancient past have survived up to the present day: as you drive in on the coastal route toward its choice setting on a bay near the southern tip of the Istrian peninsula, the monumental Roman amphitheater blocks out the sky on your left. Under Venetian rule (1331–1797), Pula was architecturally neglected, even substantially dismantled. Many structures from the Roman era were pulled down, and stones and columns were carted off across the sea to Italy to be used for new buildings there. Pula's second great period of development took place in the late 19th century, under the Habsburgs, when it served as the chief base for the Imperial Austro-Hungarian Navy. Today it's as much working city as tourist town, where Roman ruins and Austro-Hungarian architecture serve as backdrop for the bustle of everyday life amid a bit of communist-era soot and socialist realism, too. James Joyce lived here for a short time, in 1904–05, before fleeing what he dismissed as a cultural backwater for Trieste. What's more, there are some outstanding restaurants and a number of pleasant family-run hotels, not to mention the nearby resort area of Verudela, where seaside tourism thrives in all its soothing, sunny sameness.

GETTING HERE AND AROUND

Pula is Istria's main entry point, home to the only regional airport for commercial flights located 9 km (5½ miles) from the town center. There is a shuttle bus from the airport to Pula's main bus station (located downtown), but also to the resort areas of Verudela, Medulin, and Puntižela. The best way to get around Pula is on foot. However, buses run every 20 minutes to half an hour depending on the line.

EXPLORING

Pula's compact commercial and administrative center is on a small, semicircular protrusion of land in the Puljski Zaljev (Bay of Pula), which faces west into the Adriatic. Several ringlike streets radiate inward from the port, culminating in the small, fortress-capped hill at the center of this semicircle. Most of the cultural and historical sites are along this web of streets to the south, west, and north of the hill, with the huge Roman amphitheater on the northeastern fringes of this zone (accessible via Giardini and then Istarska ulica, on the landward side of the hill, a couple of blocks in from the bay); the bus station is another few minutes' walk from there. Meanwhile, a long walk (or a short drive) south of the city center are suburbs that culminate with the Verudela

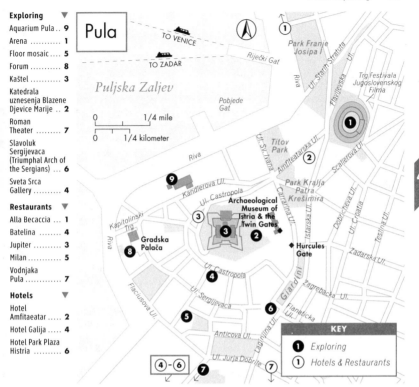

Exploring ▼

Aquarium Pula .. **9**
Arena **1**
Floor mosaic **5**
Forum **8**
Kaštel **3**
Katedrala uznesenja Blazene Djevice Marije .. **2**
Roman Theater **7**
Slavoluk Sergijevaca (Triumphal Arch of the Sergians) ... **6**
Sveta Srca Gallery **4**

Restaurants ▼

Alla Becaccia ... **1**
Batelina **4**
Jupiter **3**
Milan **5**
Vodnjaka Pula **7**

Hotels ▼

Hotel Amfitaeatar **2**
Hotel Galija **4**
Hotel Park Plaza Histria **6**

and Stoja peninsulas, home to bustling tourist resorts, beaches, and some excellent restaurants.

TOP ATTRACTIONS

Fodor'sChoice ★ **Arena** (*Roman Amphitheater*). Designed to accommodate 23,000 spectators, Pula's arena is the sixth-largest building of its type in the world (after the Colosseum in Rome and similar arenas in Verona, Catania, Capua, and Arles). Construction was completed in the 1st century AD under the reign of Emperor Vespasian, and the Romans staged gladiator games here until such bloodthirsty sports were forbidden during the 5th century. During the 16th century, the Venetians planned to move the Arena stone by stone to Venice, where it was to be reconstructed in its original form. The plan failed, and it has remained more or less intact, except for the original tiers of stone seats and numerous columns that were hauled away for other buildings. Today it is used for summer concerts (by musicians including Sting, James Brown, and Jose Carreras), opera performances, and the annual film festival in late July. The underground halls house a museum with large wooden oil presses and amphorae. ⊠ *Scalierova ulica 30* ☎ *052/219–028* ⊕ *www.ami-pula.hr* ▦ *40 Kn* ☉ *Jan.–Mar. and Oct.–Dec., daily 9–5; Apr., daily 8–8; May–June and Sept., daily 8 am–9 pm; July and Aug., daily 8 am–midnight.*

Forum. Still Pula's most important public meeting place after 2,000 years, the ancient Roman forum is today a spacious paved piazza ringed with cafés. There were once three temples here, of which only one remains. Next to it stands the **Gradska Palača** (Town Hall), which was erected during the 13th century using part of the Roman Temple of Diana as the back wall. The Renaissance arcade was added later. The perfectly preserved Augustov Hram (Temple of Augustus), the Forum's only remaining temple, was built between 2 BC and 14 AD on the north side of the square. ⊠ *Forum* ⊕ *www.ami-pula.hr* ⌂ *Forum free, Augustus Hram 10 Kn* ⊙ *Mid-May–June, weekdays 9–9; July and Aug., weekdays 9 am–10 pm; Sept., weekdays 9–8; Oct.–mid-Oct., weekdays 9–7, weekends 9–3*

NEED A BREAK?

Café Galerija Cvajner. Stop at the chic but unpretentious Café Galerija Cvajner for morning coffee or an evening aperitif. Inside, contemporary art and minimalist furniture play off frescoes uncovered during restoration, and outdoor tables offer great views onto the Forum square. There's also free Wi-Fi. ⊠ *Forum 2* ☎ *052/216–502.*

Kaštel (*Fortress*). Whether from the cathedral or elsewhere along Kandlerova ulica, a walk up the hill will lead you within minutes to the 17th-century Venetian fortress, the Kaštel, that towers over Pula's city center and houses the **Historical and Maritime Museum of Istria.** Though the museum has a somewhat lackluster collection, including scale-model ships as well as Habsburg-era relics, it does carry the value-added benefit of allowing you to wander around its ramparts. ■TIP➜ But simply walking around its perimeter also ensures fine views of the city's shipyard below and, if you look to the north, the steeple of Vodnjan's church 12 km (7½ miles) away. ⊠ *Gradinski uspon 6* ☎ *052/211–566* ⊕ *www.ppmi.hr* ⌂ *20 Kn* ⊙ *Apr.–Sept., daily 8 am–9 pm; Oct.–Mar., daily 9–5.*

Slavoluk Sergijevaca (*Triumphal Arch of the Sergians*). Built by the Sergi family in 29 BC as a monument to three relatives who were great warriors, this striking monument features elaborate reliefs that inspired even Michelangelo to draw the arch during a 16th-century visit to Pula. The surrounding city gate and walls were removed in the 19th century to allow the city's expansion beyond the Old Town. Locals call it *Zlatna vrata,* "the golden gate." ⊠ *Between Giardini and Sergijevaca ulica.*

WORTH NOTING

FAMILY **Aquarium Pula.** On the ground floor of the onetime Austro-Hungarian fortress in the resort complex of Verudela, a few kilometers from the city center, the aquarium also serves as a sea-turtle rescue center. Its five rooms offer a colorful look at hundreds of sea creatures from the Adriatic's underwater world, and include a touch pool with sea stars, sea urchin, crab, and sea squirt. ■TIP➜ Climb to the roof of the fort for great vistas over Pula. ⊠ *Verudela BB* ☎ *052/381–402, 091/138–1415* ⊕ *www.aquarium.hr* ⌂ *60 Kn* ⊙ *Apr., May, and Sept., daily 10–6; June–Aug., daily 9 am–10 pm; Oct.–Mar., daily 10–4.*

Floor mosaic. The central scene of this large and lovely mosaic—which otherwise features geometric patterns and plants aplenty—is of the punishment of Dirce, who, according to Greek legend, lies under the enraged bull to whose horns she is about to be fastened. Once part of a Roman house, it was unearthed after World War II bombing. ■ TIP→ **The mosaic can be viewed for free by looking down through a grate beside an uninspiring apartment building a stone's throw from the Crkva Sv.Marije od Trstika (Chapel of St. Mary of Formosa).** ⊠ *Between Sergijevaca ulica and Flaciusova ulica, left off Sergijevaca ulica, 2 blocks before Forum.*

Katedrala uznesenja Blazene Djevice Marije (*Cathedral of the Assumption of the Blessed Virgin Mary*). Built originally in the 4th century by the town's defense walls and facing the sea, Pula's star ecclesiastical attraction—more often called simply St. Mary's Cathedral—was transformed in the second half of the 5th century into a three-nave basilica. Extensive reconstruction began in the 16th century, with the adjacent campanile constructed in the late 17th century from stones taken from the Arena. Note that the Roman-era mosaic on the floor of the central nave bears a 5th-century donor's inscription. ⊠ *Kandlerova ulica 27* ☉ *May–Sept., daily 10–6.*

Roman Theater. If you make your way down from the Fortress along the eastern slope of the hill, toward the Archaeological Museum (closed for renovation) and the Twin Gates, you will pass right through the ruins of the 2nd-century Roman Theater, a quiet, sublime spot to rest and reflect. ⊠ *Malo rimsko kazalište, Kastel, Fortress Hill.*

Sveta Srca Gallery (*Sacred Hearts Gallery*). This small gallery, located in a deconsecrated church built in 1908, is the off-site exhibition space of Pula's Archaeological Museum. One of the most renowned of Pula's artistic venues, the Sveta Srca Gallery has had exhibitions of abstract landscapes, modern art, light installations, and the Istrian diet through time. ⊠ *De Villeov uspon 8* ☎ *052/353–185* ⊕ *www.ami-pula.hr* ✉ *20 Kn* ☉ *July and Aug., 9 am–11 pm; Sept.–June, 9–9.*

NEED A BREAK?

Narodni trg. For a lively and aromatic atmosphere in which to have a shot of espresso, buy a banana, or just wander about gazing at food stands, check out Pula's market square, Narodni trg. On one side of its stately, two-story market building—whose iron-and-glass construction was state-of-the-art when it opened to great fanfare in 1903—you'll find fruit and vegetable stands, and on the other side, cafés; inside are a fish market (downstairs) and fast-food eateries (second floor). ⊠ *Narodni trg 9.*

WHERE TO EAT

$$$$

EUROPEAN

✕ **Alla Becaccia.** Located in the village of Valbandon, close to Fažana, the restaurant of the guesthouse Alla Becaccia offers hearty meat dishes with an emphasis on game—the owner is a hunter. Snipe, venison, and wild boar are often on the menu, and regulars rave about the homemade sausages. Other dishes include T-bone steak from Istrian ox, various risottos, and excellent Istrian prosciutto. A huge fireplace dominates the dining room in the simple but tasteful interior, and the kitchen door is always open. There is a covered terrace for dining alfresco and a nice garden and play area for kids. $ *Average main: 150 Kn* ✉ *Pineta 25, Fažana* ☎ *052/520–753* ⊕ *www.beccaccia.hr* ☉ *Closed Nov.*

$$$$
SEAFOOD
Fodor's Choice
★

✕ **Batelina.** This quirky, innovative restaurant is considered by many locals—and foodies around the world—to be the best seafood restaurant in Croatia. Run by a family of fishermen, Batelina is popular for its delicious appetizers, often created from what Anthony Bourdain, on his visit here, described as "trash fish"; specialties include tripe stew, shark liver pâté, bonito tartare, cuttlefish stew, and fish carpaccio. The best way to experience Batelina's cuisine is to sample many of their unique dishes. ■ **TIP**➜ **Don't go by the menu: just ask for a little bit of everything.** $ *Average main: 100 Kn* ✉ *Čimulje 25* ☎ *052/573–767* ⚠ *Reservations essential* ▭ *No credit cards* ☉ *Closed Aug. and Dec.–mid-Jan. Closed Sun. No lunch.*

$$
ITALIAN

✕ **Jupiter.** In a quiet street a couple of blocks' walk above the Forum, this is Pula's premier place for budget, Italian-style fare. Try any of its 20 types of pizza, grilled meat, or a plate of pasta as you sip a glass of house red wine at one of the rustic wooden tables on the rear terrace. There's a cozy little table in a nook on your way up the stairs. $ *Average main: 60 Kn* ✉ *Castropola 42* ☎ *052/214–333* ⊕ *pizzeriajupiter.com.*

$$$$
SEAFOOD

✕ **Milan.** This family-run restaurant in the Stoja neighborhood has been serving fresh local seafood along with steaks since 1967. Upscale but casual and relaxed, Mila's service is impeccable, the olive oil is homemade, and the wine list is extensive, with many Croatian wines and a good choice of international labels. Regulars rave about the selection of amuse-bouches, such as marinated sardines served with fresh cheese, or marinated black olives. Other selections include langoustine risotto, scallops, and Adriatic fish like monkfish and sea bass. $ *Average main: 140 Kn* ✉ *Stoja 4* ☎ *052/300–200* ⊕ *www.milan1967.hr.*

$$
VENETIAN

✕ **Vodnjanka Pula.** One of the few restaurants in downtown Pula offering honest and authentic Croatian dishes, no-frills Vodnjanka is a short walk from the farmers market. Lunch is the best time to enjoy its flavorful, unpretentious home-cooked dishes—a truly local experience that brings back the forgotten flavors of old times. Depending on the season, dishes may include homemade gnocchi, meatballs, cod in tomato sauce, roasted veal, dandelion with hard-boiled eggs, grilled sardines—the dishes Istrian grannies make. $ *Average main: 60 Kn* ✉ *D. Vitezića 4* ☎ *052/210–655* ▭ *No credit cards* ☉ *Closed Sun.*

WHERE TO STAY

$$
HOTEL

🛏 **Hotel Amfiteatar.** Opened in 2011, this hotel in a converted three-story town house close to the Arena and just one block from the seafront has 18 rooms with smart minimalist furniture, free Wi-Fi, and spacious bathrooms. **Pros:** central location; good restaurant with open-air terrace. **Cons:** "sea views" are disappointing; only one room has a balcony; top-floor rooms only have skylights (no windows). $ *Rooms from:* €*125* ✉ *Amfiteatarska 6* ☎ *052/375–600* ⊕ *www.hotelamfiteatar.com* 🛏 *18 rooms* ¶⚪∣ *Breakfast.*

$
HOTEL

🛏 **Hotel Galija.** This family-run establishment centrally located in a bright yellow building on a quiet street just two blocks from Giardini and the Sergian Gate has bright, spacious, and clean rooms, some in the main building and others in a building right across the street. **Pros:** prime downtown location; secured parking nearby. **Cons:** no elevator; some rooms rather small. $ *Rooms from: 760 Kn* ⊠ *Epulonova 3* ☎ *052/383–802* ⊕ *www.hotelgalija.hr* ↝ *27 rooms, 2 suites* |O| *Breakfast.*

$$$ 🏨 **Hotel Park Plaza Histria.** With its superb location at the tip of the VerHOTEL udela peninsula overlooking both the marina and the sea, this hotel has stylish, modern rooms that are comfortable and well appointed with comfy beds, flat-screen TVs, Wi-Fi, and balconies. **Pros:** quiet seaside location; all rooms and suites have a balcony; panoramic views from some rooms; good in-room and on-site facilities. **Cons:** large hotel can feel overcrowded in summer; a bit of a hike from town; not enough loungers by the outdoor pool. $ *Rooms from: 1500 Kn* ⊠ *Verudella 17* ☎ *052/590–000* ⊕ *www.arenaturist.hr* ↝ *355 rooms, 13 suites* |O| *Multiple meal plans.*

NIGHTLIFE AND PERFORMING ARTS

BARS AND CLUBS

Club life in Pula tends to begin in early April and continue through late October or early November. Pubs are open year-round.

Club Uljanik. Conveniently located in the city center, with posters announcing its various musical events ubiquitous about town, Club Uljanik is an exceedingly popular counterculture haven with "DJ nights" all year and live music on its spacious terrace. ⊠ *Jurja Dobrile 2* ☎ *092/236–8289* ⊕ *www.clubuljanik.hr.*

E&D Lounge Bar. Set in a landscaped garden with a small swimming pool surrounded by lounge chairs, E&D Lounge Bar is the perfect place to laze during the day with a coffee or a beer and views over the sea; dance the night away with DJ parties. During the summer the bar also serves light Mediterranean dishes. ⊠ *Verudela 22* ☎ *052/213–404* ⊕ *www. eanddlounge.com.*

Pietas Julia. This large, seafront dance club also features a coffee bar and pizzeria. This is the place to dance a night away in Pula, with DJs playing electronic, house, techno, and R&B music. A great choice of cocktails makes this popular among Pula's hip crowd. ⊠ *Riva 20* ☎ *091/181–1811, 052/811–811* ⊕ *www.pietasjulia.com.*

PERFORMING ARTS FESTIVALS

Being the most prominent place in town, the Arena hosts a fair share of the city's core art events.

Outlook Festival. Celebrating sound-system culture with the latest dance music from house to dubstep, the Outlook Festival takes place in the first week of September at the 19th-century Punta Christo Fort and the surrounding area. Four days of music and parties—including infamous boat and beach parties—make Outlook one of the most popular summer festivals in Istria. Previous lineups have included Busta Rhymes, Lauryn Hill, Barrington Levy, DJ Premier, DJ EZ, and many others. ⊠ *Fort Punta Christo, Stinjan* ⊕ *www.outlookfestival.com.*

Pula Film Festival. The decades-old annual festival occurs around the third week of July, before the Motovun Film Festival (⇨ *See Nightlife and the Arts in Motovun*). It features both Croatian and, in recent years, an increasing number of international works. ⊕ *www.pulafilmfestival.hr.*

SPORTS AND THE OUTDOORS

Unlike some smaller towns farther up the coast, such as Rovinj, downtown Pula is a bit too much of a port and industrial center to allow for a dip in the sea in between visits to cultural attractions. Now for the good news: the **beaches** aren't far away. A short drive or bus ride to the Verudela or Stoja resort areas, each around 4 km (2½ miles) south of downtown along the coast, will provide the clear water (and rocky shores) Croatia has in no short supply. You might also try the long stretch of relatively isolated beach between the two, on the Lungomare. If you have a car or a bicycle, this lovely little stretch of undeveloped coast is close to town and popular with locals as well as tourists. Head south about 2 km (1½ miles) along the main road out of Pula and follow the signs to the right toward Stoja, a resort-cum-camping area. Once there, proceed left and then back north along the pine-fringed coastal road Lungomare as it makes its way to the Verudela resort area.

If you have a car at your disposal, drive 10 km (6¼ miles) southwest of central Pula to the Premantura peninsula. The relatively remote shoreline there, at the very southern tip of Istria, is even more scenic, punctuated by cliffs and caves, and the crowds are mercifully thinner.

SHOPPING

Pula is no shopping mecca, but it does have a handful of stores with quality goods from Istria and Croatian delicacies, wines, crafts, and more. On Monday and Wednesday evenings in July and August (from 8 to 11) the Forum hosts an open-air fair of Istrian handicrafts. A walk through the Triumphal Gate of the Sergians onto bustling Sergijevaca ulica will show you much of what the city has available, shopping-wise; the stores listed here are on the fringe of this central business zone.

Merlin souvenirs. Look for original handmade souvenirs, such as masks made of clay and painted with Istrian soil, inspired by Pula's historical and cultural heritage. Sold at small stands near the amphitheater, these crafts are made by Merlin Association, a nonprofit dedicated to improving the local community through creative and educational workshops. ⊠ *Gajeva 3, Rojc Center* ☎ *091/789–4481, 052/387–515* ⊕ *www.merlinpula.hr/en.*

Pula Green Market. Join locals stocking up on fresh and seasonal products early in the morning. The **Jelenic charcuterie** offers homemade, traditional Istrian cured meat like cooked ham, prosciutto, and homemade sausages. Taste an award-winning sheep's milk cheese from **Gligora Dairy** on the first floor of the market. **Kumparicka Dairy** produces unpasteurized, fresh, and aged (up to 30 months) goat cheeses. ⊠ *Narodni trg 9* ☎ *052/218–122.*

VODNJAN

12 km (7½ miles) north of Pula.

Vodnjan may look a bit run-down at first glance, but there are three good reasons to come here: its saintly mummies; its quiet, narrow, centuries-old streets populated by a higher percentage of Italian speakers than you'll find almost anywhere else in Istria; and the Vodnjanka restaurant's scrumptious fare.

GETTING HERE AND AROUND

There are 10 buses daily between Pula and Vodnjan, at 12 Kn each way, payable directly to the driver.

EXPLORING

Chiavalon Olive Oil Tasting Room. Sandi Chivalon was barely 13 years old when he planted his first olive trees and decided to become an olive oil producer. Less than two decades later, Chiavalon's extra virgin olive oil was chosen among the 15 best olive oils in the world by the prestigious Flos Olei. A visit to the Chiavalon tasting room is well worth a detour, just call in advance to arrange the tasting, some of which are accompanied by delicious Istrian fare like cheese, prosciutto, and sausages. ⊠ *Vladimira Nazora 16* ☎ *098/441–561, 052/511–906* ⊕ *www. chiavalon.hr* ⚑ *Reservations essential* ⊗ *Daily 10–8.*

FAMILY   **Crkva svetog Blaža** (*St. Blaise's Church*). From the tourist office on the main square, stroll down ulica Castello to Crkva svetog Blaža, an 18th-century structure built in the style of architect Palladio that not only has the highest campanile in all of Istria but is also the unlikely home of the mummies or mummified body parts of six saints impressively preserved without embalming. Though some see divine intervention behind their state of preservation, the degree to which these saints are really intact—they are definitely chipping away at the edges, it must be said—is open to question. Among the best-preserved of the saints are St. Nicolosa Bursa and Leon Bembo the Blessed. Nicolosa, whose relatively elastic skin and overall postmortem presentableness have given her the distinction of being among the best-preserved human bodies in Europe, was born in Koper (Istria) in the 15th century and developed a reputation for holiness as a nun in Venice and elsewhere; she's the one with the garland of flowers still on her head. Leon Bembo the Blessed was a 12th-century Venetian priest who was tortured to the point of disfigurement in religious riots while ambassador to Syria, and spent his final years back in Venice in monastic contemplation. And then there is St. Sebastian, a Roman officer-turned-Christian who was whipped and strangled around AD 288 in Rome after initially surviving torture by arrows. The head, spinal column, neck muscles, and related parts of this very famous saint are on display here. As for St. Barbara, from 3rd-century Nicomeda (in present-day Turkey), only her leg remains; she so disagreed with her father's pagan, slave-keeping lifestyle that he personally killed her with a sword, though legend has it that he was then promptly struck by lightning and turned to ashes. Admittance to the mummy room, behind the main altar, includes an English-language recording that sums up the saints' lives and roads to mummihood. ✉ *Župni ured Sv. Blaža, Sv. Roka 4* ☎ *052/511–420* 🌐 *www.zupavodnjan.com* 🎫 *35 Kn* 🕑 *June–Sept., daily 9:30–1 and 2:30–6:30.*

WHERE TO EAT

$$$$ VENETIAN Fodor's Choice ★ 🍴 **Vodnjanka.** This restaurant is the place to go for the most mouthwatering homemade pasta dishes you can imagine, not least *fuži* with wild asparagus and prosciutto in cream sauce, which is simply unforgettable. The outer of two small rooms features bizarre but fantastic wall art by sculptor/painter Lilia Batel: 3-D reliefs with sponge-based puppets caricaturing real locals as they gaze out their windows, sit at the bar, and so on. The inner room, with its six tables and framed family-style photographs, is positively homey. Staff, including the owner, Svjetlana Celija, is very friendly and can help you navigate through the menu. In summer, be sure to make a reservation for dinner. [$] *Average main: 100 Kn* ✉ *Istarska 22* ☎ *052/511–435* 🕑 *Closed Sun.*

WHERE TO STAY

$$ B&B/INN 🏨 **La Casa di Matiki.** Located in the countryside near the village of Žminj, La Casa di Matiki may not be a fully working farm, but you'll find donkeys, sheep, chickens, and two dogs here, and you can opt to sleep on hay in the converted barn. **Pros:** peaceful location far from the crowds; excellent breakfast with homemade and homegrown products. **Cons:** remote location means a car is essential. [$] *Rooms from: 550 Kn* ✉ *Matiki 14, Žminj* ☎ *052/846–297* 🌐 *www.matiki.com* 🛏 *4 studio apartments, 3 apartments* 💳 *No credit cards.*

NACIONALNI PARK BRIJUNI

Ferry from Fažana, which is 15 km (9 miles) northwest of Pula.

When Austrian industrialist Paul Kupelwieser set off for Brijuni by boat from Fažana in 1885 with a bottle of wine, roast chicken, bread, and peaches (and a couple of brawny locals to row him and his son there), the archipelago had long been a haven for the Austro-Hungarian military and for malaria. Kupelwieser was to change all that. In 1893 he bought the 14 islands and islets, eradicated the disease with the help of doctors, and fashioned parks from Mediterranean scrub. Thus arose a vacation retreat par excellence—not for rich Romans, as had been the case here 17 centuries earlier, but for fin de siècle Viennese and other European high-society sorts. Archduke Franz Ferdinand summered here, as did such literary lights as Thomas Mann and Arthur Schnitzler; James Joyce came here to celebrate his 23rd birthday. Two world wars ensued, however, and the islands' fate faded as they changed hands—coming under Italian rule and, later, Yugoslavian. From 1949 to 1979 the largest island, Veli Brijun, was the official summer residence of Marshal Josip Broz Tito, Yugoslavia's "president for life." Here he retreated to work, rest, and pursue his hobbies. World leaders, film and opera stars, artists, and writers were his frequent guests; and it was here that, together with Nasser of Egypt and Nehru of India, Tito forged the Brioni Declaration, uniting the so-called nonaligned nations (countries adhering to neither NATO nor the Warsaw Pact). The archipelago was designated a national park in 1983 and opened to the public.

Fodor's Choice **Nacionalni Park Brijuni.** The Brijuni islands are a group of 14 small islands
★ that were developed in the late 19th century. You'll need to pass through Fažana to get here, and though the town seems to offer little more than the usual collection of touristy restaurants along its small harbor, it is at least refreshingly quiet compared to some other tourist-traveled spots along Istria's west coast. Fažana's main cultural attractions—all just a short walk from the harbor—are the 15th-century **Church of Saints Kosmas and Damian,** whose bell may be in need of oiling, as it sounds like a fork striking a plate; and the smaller but older 14th-century **Church of Our Lady of Mount Carmel,** which you enter through an atmospheric loggia and whose ceiling features several layers of fascinating 15th-century Renaissance frescoes. But you are presumably here to visit the archipelago. Before doing so, call or email the Brijuni National Park office in Fažana at least one day in advance to make a reservation; you can also do so in person, but especially in midsummer there is a substantial risk that there won't be space. (Though various private tourist agencies in Fažana and Pula offer excursions, they do not generally measure up, in cost or quality, to making your arrangements directly with the national park. Some of the tourist agencies simply reserve you a spot on the "official" tour, adding their own commission when doing so.) Take the National Park ferry from Fažana, which is about 15 minutes. The entire tour of the park takes about four hours. Your first view is of a low-lying island with a dense canopy of evergreens over blue waters. Ashore on Veli Brijun, the largest island, a **tourist train** takes you past villas in the seaside forest and relics from the Roman and Byzantine eras. The network of roads on this 6½-km-long (4-mile-long) island was laid down by the Romans, and stretches of original Roman stonework remain. Rows of cypresses shade herds of deer, and peacocks strut along pathways. The train stops at the **Safari Park,** a piece of Africa transplanted to the Adriatic, its zebras, Indian holly cattle, llamas, and elephants all gifts from visitors from faraway lands. In the **museum,** an archaeological exhibition traces life on Brijuni through the centuries, and a photography exhibition, "Tito on Brijuni," focuses on Tito and his guests.

Those who have made the rounds of Kupelwieser's golf course—the oldest golf course in Croatia—report that it is more a historic experience than anything else, since it looks much the same as it did when built in 1923, with "natural," sandy tees and deer grazing where there is grass; it's blessed by an absence of fertilizers. Even if it isn't quite up to snuff by modern golfing standards, how often do you find a course that allows you to take a dip in the sea between holes? ⊠ *Brionska 10, Fažana* ☎ *052/525–883, 052/525–882* ⊕ *www.brijuni.hr* ⊠ *July and Aug., 210 Kn; June and Sept., 200 Kn; Apr., May, and Oct., 170 Kn; Nov.–Mar., 125 Kn* ⊗ *Apr.–June, Sept., and Oct., 1 tour daily at 11:30 am; July and Aug., 3 tours daily at 9 am, 11:30 am, and 1:30 pm; Nov.–Mar., by request.*

WHERE TO STAY

You can save money by booking a room in Fažana and taking a day trip to the islands.

Stefani Trade. This accommodations and travel agency in Fažana can help you arrange a place to stay, not to mention tours around the region. ✉ *Župni Trg 3, Fažana* ☎ *052/521–910* ⊕ *www.fazana-brijuni.com.*

$$$ 🏨 **Neptun-Istra Hotel.** The most comfortable of all the hotels and vil-
HOTEL   las on Veli Brijun has bright, spacious rooms, and the rates include unlimited passages on the National Park boats between the islands and the mainland. **Pros:** location can't be beat. **Cons:** partly renovated; outdated interior design in the Neptun wing; pricey for the level of service. Ⓢ *Rooms from: 1430 Kn* ✉ *Nacionalni Park Brijuni, Brijuni* ☎ *052/525–807* 🖷 *052/521–367* ⊕ *www.brijuni.hr* 🛏 *92 rooms, 18 suites* 🍽 *Breakfast.*

ROVINJ

35 km (22 miles) northwest of Pula.

Fodor's Choice   It is hard to imagine how Rovinj could be more beautiful than it is.
★   In a fantastic setting, with centuries-old red-roofed houses clustered around the hill of a former island, Istria's cultural mecca is crowned by the monumental baroque Crkva Sv Eufemije (Church of St. Euphemia), which has a typical Venetian bell tower topped by a gleaming bronze figure of St. Euphemia. Far below, a wide harbor crowded with pleasure boats is rimmed with bright awnings and colorful café umbrellas. Artists, writers, musicians, and actors have long gravitated to this ravishing place to carve out apartments in historic houses. Throughout the summer, the winding cobbled streets are crowded with vacationers from all reaches of Europe, who are more often than not staying in nearby resort developments. South of the harbor lies the beautiful nature park of Zlatni Rt, planted with avenues of cedars, oaks, and cypresses and offering numerous secluded coves for bathing.

GETTING HERE AND AROUND
There is a shuttle bus from Pula airport to Rovinj. There are also buses daily between Pula central bus station and Rovinj, along with Zagreb and Rovinj. The town is easily reachable by car, but the best way to get around Rovinj is on foot of bicycle, but you cannot really cycle within the old town.

EXPLORING

Practically all of Rovinj's key cultural and commercial attractions are packed into the compact, one-time island and present-day peninsula that juts like the tip of a hitchhiker's thumb westward into the sea. The main square, Trg M. Tita, is at the southern juncture of this little peninsula with the mainland; from there you can either cut straight up the center of the peninsula (i.e., west) along Grisia toward the cathedral or walk around the outer edge of the peninsula, or you can go south along the harbor to some fine restaurants and the beaches of Zlatni Rt beyond.

Exploring ▼
Akvarij **5**
Crkva
Sv Eufemije **1**
Galerija
Sv. Toma **2**
Kuća o Batani ... **3**
Trg M. Tita **4**

Restaurants ▼
Blu **6**
Giannino **5**
Kantinon **4**
Monte **1**
Orca **8**
Pizzeria
Da Sergio **2**

Hotels ▼
Hotel Lone **10**
Hotel
Monte Mulini . **11**
Hotel Villa
Valdibora **3**
Island Hotel
Katarina **9**
Stancija 1904 ... **7**

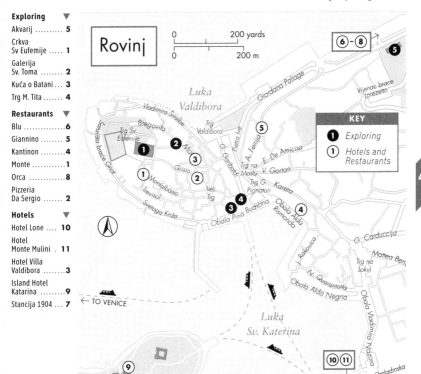

FAMILY **Akvarij** (*Aquarium*). Opened in 1891, making it one of the oldest institutions of its type in Europe, the Rovinj aquarium displays tanks of Adriatic marine fauna and flora. It's housed within the Ruđer Bošković Institute's Center for Maritime Research. ⌧ *Centra za istraživanja mora—Akvarij, Giordana Paliage 5* ☎ *052/804–712* 💰 *30 Kn* ☉ *May–Sept., daily 10–5; Oct.–Apr., by appointment only.*

NEED A BREAK?

Havana Club. The Adriatic may not be quite as warm as the Caribbean, but at the Havana Club—a spacious, tropical-themed cocktail bar-cum-café right on the harbor—you can sip a piña colada or, if you dare, a Sex on the Beach (vodka, peach, and melon juices, plus "sex mix"). There are also nonalcoholic cocktails, including, of course, Safe Sex on the Beach, as well as iced tea and coffee. Kick back and relax in a wicker chair under one of five huge, bamboo umbrellas while listening to reggae. That's not to mention the Cuban cigars you can puff for anywhere between 40 Kn and 120 Kn. Ah, the life! ⌧ *Obala Alda Negria.*

Fodor's Choice **Crkva Sv Eufemije** (*Church of St. Euphemia*). Inside the 18th-century
★ baroque church, the remains of Rovinj's patron saint are said to lie within a 6th-century sarcophagus. Born near Constantinople, Euphemia was martyred in her youth, on September 16 in AD 304, under the reign

of Emperor Diocletian. The marble sarcophagus containing her remains mysteriously vanished in AD 800 when it was at risk of destruction by iconoclasts—and, legend has it, it somehow floated out to sea and washed up in faraway Rovinj. (Note the wall engraving just to the right of the entrance of St. Euphemia holding Rovinj in her arms.) Not surprisingly, Euphemia has long been among the most popular names in Istria for girls, and on September 16 of each year many people gather to pray by her tomb. In the church a large mural in the sarcophagus room portrays Euphemia being picked at by two lions who,

> ### SWIMMING IN ROVINJ
>
> Swimming in the sea in Rovinj is a rocky business. There are no sandy beaches in the town itself; most of the swimming is done off the rocks or cement slabs (with ladders in some places) that jut into the sea. Head out to Crveni Otok (Red Island) or uvala Lone (Lone Bay) for a pebble beach and a place to lay your towel, but don't forget to bring some rubber water sandals, as entering the water there, as in the rest of Istria, is a bit rough on your feet.

legend has it, didn't eat her after all. As at other churches in Croatia, a sign at the entrance makes it clear that no short-shorts or miniskirts (or dogs, or ice-cream cones, or lit cigarettes) are allowed inside. Judging from the scanty dress of some folks streaming inside in the summer heat, such rules can be bent, but you won't be let up the campanile unless you abide. ⊠ *Trg Sv. Eufemije* ☎ *052/815–615* 🖃 *Church and sarcophagus room free, campanile 20 Kn* ☉ *May–Sept., daily 11–4.*

Galerija sv.Toma (*St. Thomas Gallery*). Today a public art gallery, this small, bright yellow church dates to the Middle Ages but was rebuilt in 1722. It's on your way back down the hill from the main cathedral, and right after you pass by it, you will pass under a lovely, arched hall some 50 feet long, its ceiling replete with wooden beams. On your left, you'll notice a small courtyard, encircled by pastel painted houses with green and blue shutters and colorful flowers in the window. ⊠ *Bregovita ulica* 🖃 *Free* ☉ *June–Sept., Tues.–Sun. 6:30 pm–10 pm.*

Kuća o Batani (*House of Batana Ecomuseum*). Devoted to Rovinj's *batana* (traditional wooden boat), this small museum in a typical multistory house has a permanent exhibition of boats and fishing tools. It also hosts various cultural events and educational programs, and during the summer the museum organizes gourmet evenings (110 Kn) in a *spacio*, a typical Rovinj tavern or wine cellar. These start with a *batana* ride from the Mali mol around Rovinj's Old Town to the tavern, where guests taste typical dishes like salted anchovies or marinated sardines and local wine. ⊠ *Obala Pinia Budicina 2* ☎ *052/812–593* ⊕ *www.batana.org* 🖃 *10 Kn* ☉ *Mar.–June and Oct.–Dec., Tues.–Sun. 10–1 and 4–6; June–Sept., daily 10–2 and 7–11.*

OFF THE BEATEN PATH

San Tommaso Winery. This small family-run winery in Golaš, a small village 17 km (10½ miles) south of Rovinj, is housed in a beautifully restored farmhouse with exposed stones and large wooden beams. It features a wine cellar, tasting room with a big open fireplace, and a small ethnographic museum displaying old family photos and equipment that once was used in the winemaking process in Istria. Don't let their Malvazija Istarska fool you! Although the wine is fresh, easy to drink, and sweet, it contains 14% alcohol. They also produce a few reds (merlot, Terrano), rosé, and the sweet dessert wine Muscat Žuti. If the owner, Janja, happens to be there, ask her to let you taste her raisin wine, which isn't for sale. ⊠ *Golaš 13, Bale* ☎ *098/309–594* ⊕ *www. santommaso-debeljuh.hr* ⊙ *Apr.–Sept., Tues.–Sun. 10–6.*

Trg M. Tita. Standing on the Old Town's main square, you can't help but notice the **Balbi Arch,** which at one time was the gate to Rovinj's fish market. Notice the Venetian lion with an open book (a symbol of acceptance of Venetian rule without a fight) and a Venetian head on one side, and the Turkish head on the other, the symbolism of which hasn't yet been explained. At the top, between the two Balbi coats of arms, is a Latin epigraph. Also quite prominent on the square is the city's pinkish-orange **watchtower,** whose base houses the tourist agency. Although it looks Venetian, the tower was erected in 1907. That said, the winged-lion relief on one side is indeed from the 16th century. ⊠ *Trg Maršala Tita.*

OFF THE BEATEN PATH

Dvigrad. When its residents abandoned Dvigrad suddenly in the mid-17th-century—fleeing the combined misfortune of plague and attacks by Uskok raiders—and established nearby Kanfanar, surely they didn't foresee that more than three centuries later tourists would delight in what they left behind. In any case, if exploring ruins is your (or your child's) thing, this is the place for you. Along an isolated road 23 km (14 miles) east of Rovinj, outside the sleepy town of Kanfanar (a short detour if you're headed north toward Poreč, Motovun, or Grožnjan), this huge maze of dirt paths surrounded by high stone walls makes for an adventuresome, imagination-stirring walk. Indeed, just enough restoration has been done to let your imagination "reconstruct" the rest: some of the walls, which rise to around 20 feet (with signs warning of loose brickwork), are vine-covered, and much of the place is overgrown with vegetation. Nor is there a single explanatory sign, in any language. All this combines to give you the sense that you are discovering this eerie ghost town of a fortress city, even if a few other tourists are also wandering about. The battlements are impressively intact, and toward the center of the fortress you will find the remains of St. Sophia's Church, replete with depressions in the ground that contained the crypts of very important persons. To get here, take the main road east out of Rovinj toward Kanfanar. Just before you cross the railroad tracks and enter Kanfanar, you'll see a sign pointing to Dvigrad, which is to your left; from the sign the ruins are about 4 km (2½ miles) down an isolated, scrub-lined road. ⊠ *Dvigrad.*

WHERE TO EAT

$$$$
MEDITERRANEAN

✕ **Blu.** Three km (2 miles) north of Rovinj's old town, perched on the sea in the Borik section of town, Blu is the epitome of Istrian seaside elegance. The cozy dining room has a wall of windows to the sea, a couple of stone terraces, tables on a patio, and a spectacular canopied table at the breakwater's edge. There's simply no bad table here. One terrace juts out into the sea, where you're so close you can look at the crustaceans on the sea floor in between courses. Expect refined seafood dishes that showcase the bounty of the Adriatic waters; for example, tagliatelle with scampi, or delicious baked octopus. It's hard to beat this class act for a quiet, romantic dinner. ⓢ *Average main: 150 Kn* ⊠ *Val de Lesso 9* ☎ *052/811–265* ⊕ *www.blu.hr* 🍴 *Reservations essential* ⊘ *Closed Nov.–Easter.*

$$$$ ✕ **Giannino.** Tucked away on a small square in a residential area of
MEDITERRANEAN   the old town, Gannino is equally popular among locals and tourists. Established in 1982 and renovated in 2014, the large restaurant is modern, except for a gallery-seating area rustically decorated with a vaulted brick ceiling; you may opt for a spot on the large patio. White tablecloths make the place look classy, but the atmosphere is convivial and relaxed and the staff very friendly. Giannino's food is simple but fresh, made with a great care, and delicious. Ask for Adriatic shrimp in vinegar or pasta with lobster. To find it, at the beginning of Car-rera ulica, Rovinj's main street, turn right—opposite of where all the crowds will be heading. ⓢ *Average main: 110 Kn* ⊠ *Agusta Ferrija 38* ☎ *052/813–402* ⊘ *Closed Nov.–Mar. Closed Tues.*

$$$$ ✕ **Kantinon.** Wine cellar or restaurant? Regardless of the answer, the
MEDITERRANEAN   food here is really good, and the ambience is inviting. Stone floors, long wooden tables, huge wine barrels, and high vaulted ceilings befitting a wine-cellar restaurant combine scrumptiously with standard but good seafood, pasta, and meat specialties. Ask the waiter to recommend a good Croatian wine to pair with your meal. Order mussels and clams in sauce and they'll come served in a small black pot. And instead of a classical dessert, order a plate of Kumparicka goat cheese with homemade caramel. ⓢ *Average main: 80 Kn* ⊠ *Obala A. Rismonda 6* ☎ *052/816–075* ⊘ *Mar.–June and Sept.–Jan., noon–10 pm daily except Mon.* ⊘ *Closed Jan. and Feb. Closed Mon. Mar.–June and Sept.–Dec.*

$$$$ ✕ **Monte.** Upscale Italian-Istrian dishes like monkfish poached in olive oil
MEDITERRANEAN   are what you'll find at this lovely restaurant not far from Grisia. Crisp
Fodor's Choice   white tablecloths on wrought-iron patio tables dot the shady terrace,
★   where you can sip glasses of local *malvazija* (white wine) and while away the evening in peace and quiet, a surprise given the restaurant's location just below St. Euphemia's. The menu changes often, but usu-ally includes *mare crudo,* an eye-popping feast of super-fresh seafood carpaccio, or try a bit of everything with a five- or seven-course tasting menu. The place is known locally as Casa Đekić after the family that owns it. ⓢ *Average main: 210 Kn* ⊠ *Montalbano 75* ☎ *052/830–203* ⊕ *www.monte.hr* 🍴 *Reservations essential* ⊘ *Closed mid-Oct.–Easter. No lunch Mon. and Wed.*

$$$$ ✕ **Orca.** Local, fresh, traditional food makes this restaurant on the out-
MEDITERRANEAN   skirts of town a favorite among locals. Its location on the main road may not draw visitors in, but the food is excellent and a great value. This large restaurant with an open fireplace and outdoor terrace is open year-round serving typical Istrian meat, fish, and pasta. Locals rave about their tagliatelle with scampi and mushrooms as well as the meat plate. ⓢ *Average main: 80 Kn* ⊠ *Gripole 70* ☎ *052/816–851* ⊕ *www. orca-rovinj.com* ⊘ *Closed Nov. Closed Tues.*

$$ 🍴 **Pizzeria Da Sergio.** With 40-plus varieties of delicious thin-crust pizzas, PIZZA there's plenty to choose from at this conveniently located venue along the narrow road leading up to the main cathedral. Pizzas are delicious, and all baked in a wood-burning oven. Inside it's pleasantly cool, even on a hot day. The interior spreads out over two floors, but try to get a table downstairs, where wooden tables and benches give it the feel of an old Italian tavern and the atmosphere is more vibrant. [$] *Average main: 50 Kn* ✉ *Grisia 11* ☎ *052/816–949* 💳 *No credit cards.*

WHERE TO STAY

4

$$$$ 🏨 **Hotel Lone.** Superbly designed by an all-star Croatian team, the Hotel HOTEL Lone blends perfectly with its lush surroundings; rooms are modern, spacious, and comfortable, with sleek bathrooms and huge balconies. **Pros:** contemporary design; cool ambience and airy interior; easy access to the beach; located within a wonderful forest park. **Cons:** pool is shared with nearby Eden Hotel; limited garage and parking spaces; service a bit lax; large hotel that caters to business travelers. [$] *Rooms from: 2900 Kn* ✉ *L. Adamovića 31* ☎ *052/800–250, 052/632–000* 🌐 *www.lonehotel.com* 🛏 *236 rooms, 12 suites* 🍽 *Breakfast.*

$$$$ 🏨 **Hotel Monte Mulini.** Considered one of the top luxury hotels in Croa- HOTEL tia, the Hotel Monte Mulini has a stunning location a 20-minute walk from Rovinj's old town, in a landscaped park next to the nature park Zlatni Rt and 50 meters from the sea. **Pros:** great location by the sea; within walking distance to town; first-class facilities; spacious rooms. **Cons:** pricey; outdoor swimming pool is heated but sometimes too cold. [$] *Rooms from: 3500 Kn* ✉ *A. Smareglia 3* ☎ *052/636–000* 🌐 *www.montemulini.com* 🛏 *98 rooms, 15 suites* ⏲ *Closed Oct.–Easter* 🍽 *Breakfast.*

$$$ 🏨 **Hotel Villa Valdibora.** A cross between a villa rental and a small luxury HOTEL hotel, the Valdibora has apartments and studios with kitchens, daily maid service, breakfast included, and a location—just a stone's throw away from the Church of St. Euphemia—that can't be beat. **Pros:** atmospheric 17th-century building; kitchens are well equipped; rental bikes on-site. **Cons:** the hotel cannot be reached by car, so guests rely on staff driving golf carts. [$] *Rooms from: 1500 Kn* ✉ *Chiurca Silvana 8* ☎ *052/845–040* 🌐 *www.valdibora.com* 🛏 *5 apartments, 3 studios, 6 rooms* 🍽 *Breakfast.*

$$ 🏨 **Island Hotel Katarina.** Located on Santa Katarina Island, a 15-minute HOTEL boat ride from the Old Town, Island Hotel Katarina is partly housed in an old family castle from the early 20th century with basic and outdated but spacious rooms, some with breathtaking views over the old town. **Pros:** wonderful island location; surrounded by beautiful parks; nice views. **Cons:** not all rooms are air-conditioned; dependent on a boat schedule; outdated decor in the rooms. [$] *Rooms from: 1200 Kn* ✉ *Otok Katarina 1* ☎ *052/800–250* 🌐 *www.maistra.com* 🛏 *110 rooms, 10 suites* ⏲ *Closed Oct.–May* 🍽 *Multiple meal plans.*

$$ 🏨 **Stancija 1904.** This lovingly restored turn-of-the-century villa is an HOTEL excellent place to stay—and a good example of what you're likely to find if you venture into the agritourism section of the Istria brochure. **Pros:** secluded property but still convenient to major tourist

sites; friendly owners; great homemade meals offered on-site. **Cons:** no swimming pool or spa facilities; car is essential [$] *Rooms from: 1260 Kn* ✉ *Smoljanci 2–3, Svetvinčenat* ☎ *052/560–022, 098/738–974* 🌐 *www.stancija.com* 🛏 *1 house, 2 apts.* 🕓 *Closed Nov.–Jan.*

NIGHTLIFE AND PERFORMING ARTS

Croatian Summer Salsa Festival. Already in its 10th year, the Croatian Summer Salsa Festival offers 10 days of dance, fun, beach and pool parties, workshops, DJs, and more than 2,000 attendees the last week of June. 🌐 *www.crosalsafestival.com.*

Piassa Grande Wine Bar. Rovinj's must-visit bar for wine aficionados, Piassa Grande features over 70 white, red, rosé, dessert, and sparkling wines by the glass. Istrian wines dominate the wine list. Run by two sisters, both passionate about wine, this is a perfect place to taste, enjoy, and learn about Istrian wines and winemakers. Located at the small square right in the old town, Piassa Grande also serves simple food like bruschetta, salad, local cheeses, and cold cuts. ✉ *Veli trg 1* ☎ *98/824–322.*

Puntulina Wine & Cocktail Bar. Take the steps down to Puntulina's terrace, where you can enjoy a glass of Istrian or other Croatian wine in a pleasant atmosphere yards from the sea, with light pop music setting the tone, plus amazing sunsets. And, yes, you can take a few more steps down if you wish, to the rocks, and take a dip before or after being served—for this is where Rovinj's free, public swimming area begins. It's not especially a "night" spot, so you may wish to confine your wine-sipping to daylight hours. There's also an excellent restaurant on the upper level. ✉ *Sv Križ 38* ☎ *052/813–186* 🕓 *Closed Nov.–Mar.*

Valentino. Will it be on the rocks? Yes? Then it'll be either the setting or a cocktail at the Valentino, situated idyllically on the rocks across from Katarina Island, with the sea illuminated by the club's theatrical lighting. When the weather turns foul, the crowds squeeze into the small, altarlike interior. ✉ *Santa Croce 28* ☎ *052/830–683* 🌐 *www.valentino-rovinj.com* 🕓 *Closed Oct.–Mar.*

Wine Bar San Tommaso. This newly opened wine bar at Rovinj's seafront promenade is small, with only four interior tables, but the outdoor terrace—right at the seafront—is a great place to enjoy your glass of wine and nibble a variety of cheeses and cold cuts. Wines offered here include San Tommaso's own wines and others from Rovinj and its surroundings. ✉ *Obala A. Rismonda BB* ☎ *052/815–915* 🕓 *Closed Nov.–Mar.*

SPORTS AND THE OUTDOORS

As elsewhere along the coast, the Rovinj area has its share of places to dive, and several diving centers to go along with them—most of which will take you by boat for supervised dives to shipwrecks and other fascinating spots, not least the famous wreck of the *Baron Gautsch*, an Austrian passenger ferry that sank in 1914 just 13 km (8 miles) from Rovinj.

DIVING

Puffer. This diving center offers shore dives, off-site island and wreck dives, and night diving (€15–€60). The *Baron Gautch* shipwreck dive is the most popular around Rovinj, but at €60 it's also the most expensive. Puffer also offers diving courses, a two-hour discovery dive, and specialized courses for advanced divers. ✉ *Hotel Istra, Otok Sveti Andrija* ☎ *052/802–540, 095/902–5543* ⊕ *www.rovinj-diving.hr.*

SHOPPING

Rovinj is worth visiting for its beauty, not its boutiques. The souvenir market is nothing to write home about, but there are at least a couple of shops with fine Istrian and/or Croatian products worth checking out.

4

Art Studio. It has a pretty unimaginative name, to be sure, but Art Studio is one gem of a little shop. Zagreb jewelry maker (and documentary filmmaker) Radovan Sredić spends his summers here selling lovely jewelry that he creates by hand from rare, natural materials, mostly from Asia. The shop is on your left on the way up the hill before the main cathedral. ✉ *Grisia 48* ☎ *052/649–529.*

House of Batana. Original souvenirs based on Rovinj's fishing heritage—including replicas of Rovinj's traditional vessel, the batana; key-chains; and T-shirts—can be bought at the House of Batana museum. Besides batana-inspired souvenirs, you can pick up a small recipe book with old, almost-forgotten recipes from Rovinj fishermen, also available in English. ✉ *Obala Pina Budicina 2* ☎ *052/812–593* ⊕ *www.batana.org.*

EN ROUTE If you go to Poreč from Rovinj, you can skirt the Limski kanal. Ten km (6 miles) north of Rovinj you'll pass right by the Matošević winery in Sv. Lovreč.

Wine Cellar Krunčići. A first-class spot to get a tour of Istrian vineyards and taste the local wine, Wine Cellar Krunčići has tastings on a stone patio attached to a farmhouse; the owner, Ivica Matošević, is usually on hand to tell you about his vintages including the Alba wine, an Istrian malvazija considered one of the region's best. Call ahead to arrange tastings. There is an apartment to rent if the tastings last into the evening. ✉ *Krunčići 2, Sv. Lovreč* ☎ *052/448–588, 098/367–339* ⊕ *www.matosevic.com* ⊙ *May–Sept., weekdays 9–7, weekends 10–6.*

POREČ

55 km (34 miles) northwest of Pula.

A chic, bustling little city founded as a Roman castrum (fort) in the 2nd century BC and swarming with tourists more than 2,000 years later, Poreč may not be quite as lovely as Rovinj—nor does it enjoy the benefits of a hilltop panorama—but it is nonetheless a pretty sea of red-tile roofs on a peninsula jutting out to sea. Within the historic center, the network of streets still follows the original urban layout. Dekumanova, the Roman *decumanus* (the main traverse street), has maintained its character as the principal thoroughfare. Today it is a worn flagstone passage lined with Romanesque and Gothic mansions and patrician palaces, some of which now house cafés and restaurants. Close by lies the magnificent UNESCO-listed Eufrazijeva Basilica (St. Euphrasius Basilica), Istria's prime ecclesiastical attraction and one of the coast's major artistic showpieces. Although the town itself is small, Poreč has an ample capacity for overnight stays, thanks to the vast hotel complexes of Plava and Zelena Laguna, situated along the pine-rimmed shoreline a short distance from the center. Although you can cover the main sights in two or three hours, Poreč surely merits a one-night stay, or more if you figure in a day trip to a nearby attraction such as the Baradine Cave or the Limski kanal.

GETTING HERE AND AROUND

Getting to Poreč is easier straight from Pula than from Rovinj, as you simply take the main inland highway north for 42 km (26 miles) and then follow the signs before turning west onto the secondary road that leads you another 13 km (8 miles) to Poreč—a 45- to 60-minute drive in all, depending on the traffic and how much pressure you apply to that pedal.

VISITOR INFORMATION

Tourist Information Center Poreč. Just yards away from the main square, the helpful Tourist Information Center Poreč has a detailed brochure-cum-map of the town. ⊠ *Zagrebačka 9* ☎ *052/451–293, 052/451–458* ⊙ *June–Sept., Thurs.–Mon. 8 am–9 pm, Tues. and Wed. 8–6; Apr., May, and Oct., daily 8–4; Nov.–Mar., weekdays 9–5, Sat. 8–1.*

EXPLORING

FAMILY   **Aquarium Poreč.** Since its opening in 2005, families with small kids have been flocking to Aquarium Poreč, which is just yards from the main square, Trg Slobode. It's not the most spectacular aquarium, but it will give you a good introduction to the marine species of the Adriatic including some 80 species from sea horses to sea urchins, from small sharks to arm's-length octopi and foot-long crabs. ⊠ *F. Glavinića 4* ☎ *052/428–720* ⊕ *www.aquarium.hr/en* ⊠ *40 Kn* ⊙ *Apr.–June and Sept., daily 10–5; July, daily 10 am–11 pm.*

Fodor's Choice   **Eufrazijeva Basilica** (*St. Euphrasius Basilica*). The magnificent Eufrazijeva
★   Basilica is among the most perfectly preserved early Christian churches in Europe, and one of the most important monuments of Byzantine art on the Adriatic. It was built by Bishop Euphrasius in the middle of the 6th century and consists of a delightful atrium, a church decorated with stunning mosaics, an octagonal baptistery, a 17th-century bell tower you can climb (for a modest fee), and a 17th-century Bishop's Palace whose foundations date to the 6th century and whose basement contains an exhibit of stone monuments and of mosaics previously on the basilica floor. The church interior is dominated by biblical mosaics above, behind, and around the main apse. In the apsidal semidome, the Virgin holding the Christ child is seated in a celestial sphere on a golden throne, flanked by angels in flowing white robes. On the right side there are three martyrs, the patrons of Poreč; the mosaic on the left shows Bishop Euphrasius holding a model of the church, slightly askew. High above the main apse, just below the beamed ceiling, Christ holds an

open book in his hands while apostles approach on both sides. Other luminous, shimmeringly intense mosaics portray further ecclesiastical themes. ⊠ *Eufrazijeva* 🖾 *40 kn* 🕙 *June–Aug., Mon.–Sat. 9:30 am–10 pm, Sun. 2–10; Jan.–May and Sept.–Dec., Mon.–Sat. 9:30–4.*

Trg Marafor. This square toward the tip of the peninsula was the site of Poreč's Roman forum, whose original stonework is visible in spots amid the present-day pavement. Beside it is a park containing the ruins of Roman temples dedicated to the gods Mars and Neptune.

NEED A BREAK? **Torre Rotonda Coffee Bar.** Do not be deterred by the cannon facing you as you enter the 15th-century tower that now houses the Torre Rotonda café and bar. Climb up a spiral staircase to a second floor replete with several intimate nooks, or go one more flight to the roof for an unbeatable view of Poreč and its harbor. ⊠ *Narodni trg 3a* ☎ *098/255-731* ⊕ *www. torrerotonda.com* 🕙 *May–Oct. daily 10 am–2 am.*

4

OUTSIDE OF TOWN

FAMILY **Jama Baredine** (*Baredine Cave*). Far from sun and sea though it may be, the Baredine Cave has long been one of the Poreč area's top natural attractions. About 8 km (5 miles) northeast of town, near Nova Vas, this wonderful world of five limestone halls includes not only the miniature olm—known as the cave salamander—and insects but, of course, stalactites, stalagmites, and dripstone formations—from "curtains" 10 yards long to "statues" resembling the Virgin Mary, the Leaning Tower of Pisa, and the body of the 13th-century shepherdess Milka, who supposedly lost her way down here while looking for her lover Gabriel (who met the same fate). One of the halls includes a hatch some 70 yards deep that leads to underground lakes. Groups leave every half hour on a 40-minute guided tour. You can also partake of either a brief round of "speleoclimbing" that allows you to try out caving techniques with equipment and under the watchful eye of a professional spelunker; or a more involved, five-hour "speleo-adventure" that gives you even more technical training (plus a certificate at the end) as you explore various other caves nearby. Less adventurous visitors can visit a nearby exhibition of antique tractors. Those without car transport may wish to contact one of the various private agencies in Poreč and other nearby towns that offer excursions to Baredine Cave. ⊠ *Nova Vas* ☎ *052/421–333, 098/224–350* ⊕ *www.baredine.com* 🖾 *60 Kn* 🕙 *July and Aug., daily 9:30–6; May, June, and Sept., daily 10–5; Apr. and Oct., daily 10–4; Nov.–Mar., by appointment.*

Limski kanal. There's even a bit of Norwegian-style fjord in Croatia. The Limski kanal is a 13-km-long (8-mile-long) karst canyon, whose emerald-green waters are flanked by forested valley walls that rise gradually to heights of more than 300 feet inland. The canyon was formed in the last Ice Age, and it is Istria's most fertile breeding area for mussels and oysters—hence, you'll find the excellent Viking seafood restaurant on-site. Tours are available from both Poreč and Rovinj with various agencies and independent operators, whose stands and boats are impossible to miss. A reservation a day or two in advance can't hurt, though, particularly in midsummer. Kompas offices in either Poreč or

Rovinj can arrange tours, as can Excursions Delfin in Rovinj; expect to pay approximately 150 Kn for the four-hour tour or 230 Kn for a daylong tour that includes a "fish picnic." You can also visit the Limski kanal on your own by car. And hiking enthusasts can take a trail to the Romualdova Cave, open daily from June to September. ✉ *D21, halfway between Rovinj and Poreč, Sveti Loreč.*

Vrsar. This pretty, medieval hilltop town just 10 km (6 miles) south of Poreč is near the fjord's northern juncture with the sea (and yet another place you can catch a tour of the fjord). Famous since Roman times for its high-quality stone, which helped build Venice, Vrsar is home to the 12th-century Romanesque church St. Marija Od Mora (St. Mary of the Sea), which has three naves. In his memoirs, the Venetian adventurer Casanova fondly recalled the local red wine, teran. Just a couple of miles south, by the way, is Croatia's oldest and largest naturist resort, FKK Park Koversada.

WHERE TO EAT

$$$$ EUROPEAN 🍴 **Konoba Daniela.** Steak tartare isn't everyone's cup of tea, but if it's yours, visit Tavern Daniela for the best in Istria. They also have a great selection of seafood like grilled sole, mussels, or calamari; homemade pasta; and succulent meat dishes. In the village of Veleniki just a few miles from Poreč, this rustic, family-run tavern has exposed stone walls, wooden beams, and an outdoor terrace in an enclosed courtyard. With its simple and honest food, friendly staff, and huge portions, Tavern Daniela offers excellent value for money. It's a locals' favorite in and around Poreč, but also very popular among tourists, especially Italians. [$] *Average main: 80 Kn* ✉ *Veleniki 15a, Veleniki* ☎ *052/460–519* 🌐 *www.konobadaniela.com.*

$$ PIZZA 🍴 **Pizzeria Nono.** Right across the street from the main tourist office, the Nono is teeming with folks saying "yes, yes!" to scrumptious budget fare from pizzas and salads to such seafood standards as grilled squid. [$] *Average main: 60 Kn* ✉ *Zagrebačka 4* ☎ *052/453–088* 🕒 *Closed Mon. Nov.–Feb.*

$$$$ CONTEMPORARY 🍴 **Restaurant Divino.** For upscale dining in Poreč, the lovely seafront terrace at Restaurant Divino is hard to beat. It's sophisticated but not stuffy atmosphere, contemporary dishes, wine pairing, and friendly service make this one of the best places in town. Order a seafood carpaccio, pasta with truffles and langoustine, or an excellent beefsteak. [$] *Average main: 130 Kn* ✉ *Obala Maršala Tita 20* ☎ *052/453–030* 🌐 *www.divino.hr* 🕒 *Closed mid-Jan.–mid-Feb.*

$$$$ CONTEMPORARY 🍴 **Sv Nikola Restaurant.** Those with a discriminating palate and a not so discriminating pocketbook should try this restaurant. Service is included in the price, which is a good thing, since the price is nothing to sneeze at in this sparkling, air-conditioned venue right across from the harbor. The menu offers such delicacies as fish fillet in scampi and scallops sauce, cream soup with truffles and mushrooms, and beefsteak Sv. Nikola. You can set forth on this culinary adventure with a plate of raw octopus and oysters from Istria's west coast or Istrian prosciutto. Or sample many dishes with one of their tasting menus. As good as the

food may be, though, the elegant, spotless interior isn't exactly brimming with character, but the seafront terrace is lovely. $ *Average main: 150 Kn* ⊠ *Obala maršala Tita 23* ☎ *052/423–018* ⊕ *www.svnikola.com* ⚎ *Reservations essential.*

WHERE TO STAY

$$$ 🏨 **Grand Hotel Palazzo.** Its outstanding location on the head of a small
HOTEL peninsula in Poreč's old town sets this hotel apart; built in 1910, it housed the very first hotel in town. **Pros:** excellent location; surrounded by the sea on three sides; historical building with character. **Cons:** smallish rooms; hotel lacks its own beach; it can be noisy at night. $ *Rooms from: 1600 Kn* ⊠ *Obala Maršala Tita 24* ☎ *052/858–800* ⊕ *www.hotel-palazzo.hr* ⚎ *70 rooms, 4 suites* ❘⊙❘ *Breakfast.*

$$$ 🏨 **Hotel Valamar Diamant.** Located a mile south of the Old Town in
HOTEL the Brulo neighborhood, this large hotel is surrounded by pines and
FAMILY close to the sea; most rooms have balconies, but thick pine woods block the view on lower floors, so ask to stay higher up. **Pros:** superlative sports facilities; excellent buffet food; modern and comfy rooms. **Cons:** 15-minute walk from Poreč; small spa for the size of the hotel; caters to business travelers, too. $ *Rooms from: 1500 Kn* ⊠ *Brulo 1* ☎ *052/465–000, 052/400–000* ⊕ *www.valamar.com* ⚎ *220 rooms, 26 suites* ❘⊙❘ *Some meals.*

$$$ 🏨 **Valamar Riviera Hotel.** On the seafront promenade, where Poreč's old-
HOTEL est hotels are found, the Valamar Riviera is widely considered the best hotel in town. **Pros:** easy access to the Old Town and the sea; private beach served by taxi-boat. **Cons:** noise from the promenade reaches the rooms; limited parking in front of hotel. $ *Rooms from: 1550 Kn* ⊠ *Obala M. Tita 15* ☎ *052/465–000, 052/400–800* ⊕ *www.valamar.com* ⚎ *97 rooms, 9 suites* ⊘ *Closed Nov.–Mar.* ❘⊙❘ *Multiple meal plans.*

NIGHTLIFE AND PERFORMING ARTS

Fodor's Choice **Jazz in Lap Festival.** Live jazz performances can be heard once a week
★ through July and August, usually on Wednesday evening, behind the 18th-century baroque palace housing the Zavičajni muzej (Regional Museum), at Decumanus 9. ⊠ *Decumanus 9.*

Street Art Festival. In the third week of August, Poreč's annual Street Art Festival enlivens the Old Town's streets and squares with musical, theatrical, art, multimedia, and acrobatic events.

Tequila Beach Bar. An open-air beach bar in the shadow of pines at Pical Beach, just half a mile north of the Old Town, this is a favorite among locals for a nightcap with live rock performed by bands from all over Croatia. Resident DJs play mostly rock, funk, and pop. ⊠ *Pical Beach, below Valamar Hotel Zagreb* ⊘ *Closed Oct.–mid-May.*

Villa Club. Located near the marina, right by the beach, the Villa Club is a popular hangout with lounge chairs, wicker canopy beds, and lounge music during the day. Night brings DJs, thematic parties, live bands playing dance music, and go-go dancers until dawn. ⊠ *By beach south of Poreč marina* ⊕ *www.villa-club.net* ⊘ *Closed Oct.–Apr.*

SPORTS AND THE OUTDOORS

BEACHES

Walk 10 minutes south of Poreč along the shore, past the marina, and you'll meet with the thoroughly swimmable, if typically rocky, pine-fringed beaches of the Brulo and Plava Laguna resort area. Keep walking until you're about 5 km (3 miles) south, and you'll be right in the center of the Zelena Laguna, which, though more concrete than rock, is one of the best-equipped tourist resorts on the Adriatic coast. Every day in the summer months (from May through September), two charming little "tourist trains," tiny open-walled buses, run hourly from 9 am to midnight between the town center and the Zelena Laguna resort, as well as the Hotel Luna to the north—costing you 20 Kn but saving you the walk and providing you a virtual rail experience in a part of Istria otherwise without. Those who prefer traversing the brief distance by sea can do so by way of a ship that runs from 8:30 am to midnight daily, likewise May through September, between Zelena Laguna and the center, making a couple of stops at other resort areas in between. Tickets can be purchased on board.

DIVING

Starfish Diving Center. Divers—aspiring or advanced—can contact this outfitter for daily diving tours to local shipwrecks, reefs, and caves or a four-day beginners' course that yields an international diving certification. ⊠ *Autocamp Porto Sole, 10 km (6 miles) south of Poreč, Vrsar* ☏ *052/442–119, 098/334–816* ⊕ *www.starfish.hr.*

NOVIGRAD

15 km (9½ miles) northwest of Poreč.

Imagine a mini Rovinj of sorts, not quite so well preserved, it's true, and without the hill. This is Novigrad—a pretty little peninsula town that was the seat of a bishopric for more than 1,300 years, from 520 to 1831, and, like Rovinj, was at one time an island (before being connected with the mainland in the 18th century). With its medieval structure still impressively intact, along with its Old Town wall, it merits a substantial visit and perhaps a one-night stay as you make your way up and down the coast or before heading inland toward the hill towns of Grožnjan and Motovun. At first glance, as you enter town on an uninspiring main road bordered by communist-era, concrete-box apartment buildings, you might wonder if it was worth coming this far. Drive on (or let the bus take you), for you then arrive at a little gem: to your right is a pint-size, protected harbor, the Old Town is in front of you, and to your left is a peaceful park. The bustling, harborside square has a few bars and restaurants. A nearby ice-cream stand is manned by enterprising, acrobatic young men who wow the crowds repeatedly by hurling scoops 50 or more feet into the air to open-mouthed colleagues who then discreetly spit them into napkins, garnering much applause (and generating long lines). If you continue walking past the harbor on the left, you'll arrive at Vitriol, one of the most popular sunset bars in all of Istria.

GETTING HERE AND AROUND

There are daily buses from Pula to Novigrad. The town is also connected by bus with Zagreb, Rijeka and Trieste. Novirad is easily reachable by car, but the best way to get around town is on foot, or by bicycle. The electric tourist train connects resort complex to the south with Novigrad harbor. The train runs seasonally, from June to September.

EXPLORING

The 13th-century **Crkva svetog Pelagija** (Church of St. Pelagius), built on a 6th-century foundation and containing some elaborate baroque artwork, stands near the tip of the peninsula with its towering late-19th-century campanile. As in Rovinj, the main church faces the sea, and the statue atop the campanile doubled as a weather vane for the benefit of sailors.

On nearby Veliki trg is Novigrad's pale-red **city hall,** topped by a watchtower and contrasting sharply with the yellow building beside it. Here and there, Gothic elements are in evidence on the medieval architecture about town (e.g., two windows on a 15th-century building at Velika ulica 33).

NEED A BREAK?

Istralandia. The first water park in Istria opened in 2014, featuring 20 waterslides, including an almost 90-foot-high free-fall waterslide; family rafting in inflatable rafts; three pools, including a children's pool with water castle, pirate ship, and several smaller slides; sand volleyball; and a badminton court—a great place to spend a day! Direct buses from major coastal towns run throughout the day in July and August. ✉ ***Nova Vas*** ☎ ***052/866-900, 052/866-901*** 🌐 ***www.istralandia.hr*** 🕐 ***June–Sept., daily 10–6:30.***

WHERE TO EAT

$$$$ SEAFOOD Fodor's Choice ★

🍴 **Damir e Ornella.** Tucked away in a quiet side street, this superb (and pricey) little family-run establishment is a secret wonder you may want to share only with your fellow *gourmands* who appreciate Japanese-style raw-fish specialties. Indeed, it may be the one restaurant in Istria where fish—the fresh catch of the day, that is—is brought to the table this way and served with such care. The service is elegant and friendly. Although the main reason to dine here is the raw fish, you can also delight in grilled seafood and gnocchi, not to mention some fine pastries. There's no menu, but the owners tell you their daily menu, and the owners' daughter, who is always on hand, speaks English. You don't go here to eat a plate of pasta, but instead to indulge in a three-course meal (500 Kn). [$] *Average main: 500 Kn* ✉ *Ul. Zidine 5* ☎ *052/758–134* ✍ *Reservations essential* 🕐 *No lunch Sept.–May.*

$$$$ CONTEMPORARY

🍴 **Restaurant Marina.** Set on the first floor of what looks like a typical family house, this seafood restaurant has a surprisingly elegant and stylish interior. Husband-and-wife duo Marina and Davor don't have a fixed menu, but rather changing offerings recited by the young owner. The food is delicious, fresh, and innovative; the meatballs made of shrimp, rice, and veggies and covered in black sesame seeds are yummy. They also offer three-, five-, and eight-course tasting menus. ⚠ **Don't confuse this place with a restaurant in the town's marina. Restaurant Marina is just across the street from the marina.** [$] *Average main: 110 Kn* ✉ *Sv. Antona 38* ☎ *099/812–1267, 052/726–691* ⏲ *Closed Jan. and Feb. Closed Tues.*

$$$$ SEAFOOD 🍴 **Tavern Čok.** Just steps from the Old Town, this family-run restaurant offers fresh and tasty seafood dishes and a great selection of home-made pasta. The restaurant serves Croatian classics like fresh oysters, lobster pasta, and grilled sea bass, and the daily menu depends on the day's catch—your server will bring the tray full of raw fish and other seafood delicacies for you to choose which you'd like prepared for you. The interior is rustic and cozy, and while the covered outdoor terrace offers al fresco dining, unfortunately it overlooks the main road. The service can be a bit rough around the edges, but the food is fresh and delicious. [$] *Average main: 130 Kn* ✉ *Sv. Antona 2* ☎ *052/757–643* ⏲ *Closed Jan. Closed Wed.*

WHERE TO STAY

Though hotels are also available in a resort area southeast of town, the in-town alternatives are more attractive and quite reasonably priced by Istrian standards.

Go Adria Travel Agency. For private rooms and apartments, check with the Go Adria tourist agency. ✉ *Mirna 2* ☎ *052/555–555* 🌐 *www.adriatravel.hr/en/* .

$$ HOTEL 🏨 **Hotel Cittar.** The facade of this hotel is part of the medieval Old Town wall; inside, a glass-covered vestibule imaginatively separates the wall from the hotel lobby. **Pros:** central location; pleasant patio and breakfast room; friendly staff. **Cons:** somewhat sterile modern interior; smallish rooms. [$] *Rooms from: 990 Kn* ✉ *Prolaz Venecija 1* ☎ *052/758–780* 🌐 *www.cittar.hr* 🛏 *14 rooms* 🍽 *Breakfast.*

$$$ HOTEL 🏨 **Hotel San Rocco.** Nine km (6 miles) up the road from Novigrad (on the road to Buje), the Hotel San Rocco is a real change of pace from the coast: among rolling hills surrounded by olive trees and vineyards, this upscale boutique hotel makes an impressive entrée to the Istrian interior. **Pros:** excellent (though pricey) restaurant on-site; magnificent views. **Cons:** not regularly accessible by public transportation; terrace is within earshot of busy road. [$] *Rooms from: 1400 Kn* ✉ *Srednja ulica 2, Brtonigla–Verteneglio* ☎ *052/725–000* 🌐 *www.san-rocco.hr* 🛏 *12 rooms* 🍽 *Breakfast.*

$$$ HOTEL 🏨 **Nautica Hotel.** Sparkling bathrooms and plasma-screen TVs in every room promise comfort of the highest order in this modern hotel a few steps from the marina in Novigrad. **Pros:** great location with lovely views over marina; hearty breakfast. **Cons:** nautical theme a bit over-the-top. [$] *Rooms from: 1300 Kn* ✉ *Sv. Anton 15* ☎ *052/600–400* 🌐 *www.nauticahotels.com* 🛏 *38 rooms, 4 apartments* 🍽 *Breakfast.*

$ B&B/INN 🏨 **Torci 18.** This family-run hotel offers modern rooms at good rates, plus one of Novigrad's best-reputed restaurants, which serves the family's own wine and olive oil. **Pros:** excellent restaurant. **Cons:** hotel only has 12 rooms, so books up fast; simple decor. $ *Rooms from: 550 Kn* ✉ *Ul Torci 34* ☎ *052/757–799* ⊕ *www.torci18.hr* ⇱ *12 rooms* ⦿ *Breakfast.*

EN ROUTE

As you head north to Umag or northeast toward the interior hill towns remember that you're driving through some of Istria's most fertile olive-oil territory. The tourist offices in Novigrad and Umag can give you a map outlining an olive-oil route with directions to several production facilities that offer tastings.

UMAG

4

14 km (8¾ miles) northwest of Novigrad.

Yet another onetime island, the peninsula town of Umag draws the fewest tourists of any of the major towns along Istria's western coast, even if it has more than its share of the usual beach resorts nearby. Perhaps it's the frustration with waiters who, while twiddling their thumbs in front of their restaurants, call out to every passing tourist, "Italiano? Deutsch? English?" and, less often, "Français?"

And yet Umag is a nice enough place to stroll for a couple of hours if you are passing this way, even if you might not be moved to stay for the night. Although the town grew up under the rule of Rome, practically none of its ancient roots are apparent in what remains of the historic core, which dates to the Middle Ages.

A spacious main square, **Trg Slobode** (Piazza Liberta—i.e., Freedom Square) is a jarring architectural mix from the medieval to the 20th-century mundane. It's where you'll find the towering **Church of the Assumption of the Virgin Mary & St. Pelegrin,** built in 1757 on the site of the original church. Among its main attractions are a wooden, 14th-century Venetian triptych and a 16th-century painting depicting the resurrected Christ.

Just off Trg Slobode is the town's best-preserved historic street, **Riječka ulica,** where the souvenir vendors tend to congregate. The palm-lined main road leading through town from the coastal road to the square is a pleasant, comparatively modern, somewhat bustling thoroughfare. Along it you'll pass a large open square to your left that is home to both the tourist office and Istria's newest aquarium. A bit farther down, the **Church of St. Roche,** a lovely little stone structure, was erected in 1514 to mark the end of a plague outbreak some years earlier.

GETTING HERE AND AROUND

The best way to get to Umag is by car. The town isn't located along the main Istrian bus routes. This quaint historic town is best explored on foot.

EXPLORING

FAMILY **Aquarium Umag.** Modeled after its counterparts in Pula and Poreč, this aquarium opened in 2005 to bring the nearby world of Adriatic sea life closer to home—in the form of dozens of species from sea horses to sea stars, morays to rays, and corals to crabs. ✉ *Ulica Prvog Svibnja BB*

☎ 052/721–041 ⊕ www.aquarium-travel.com ✉ 40 Kn ⊗ Apr., May, and Oct., daily 10–3; June, July, and Sept., daily 10–9; Aug., daily 10–10.

Cuj Winery. The Cuj olive oils (and wines) are a true labor of love and passion. Owner Danijel Kraljevic—Cuj—will infuse you with both when you visit his wine and olive oil estate in the village of Farnažine near Umag. A beautifully restored old stone building houses an olive mill, wine cellar, and tasting room with an open fireplace. He produces three single-sort extra virgin olive oils—Buža, Črna, and Bjelica—and one multisort extra virgin olive oil—Selekcija. Call in advance to arrange a visit. ✉ Farnažine BB, Farnažine ☎ 098/219–277 ⊕ www. cuj.hr ⊗ Daily 8–4.

Kabola Winery. Near the small medieval hill town of Momjan, the Kabola Winery is a must-visit for wine and olive oil aficionados. A wine cellar, small wine museum, and tasting room are set in a traditional Istrian farmhouse; views over the surrounding landscapes are breathtaking. Kabola only produces one extra virgin olive oil, a blend of three kinds of olives: indigenous Istarska Bjelica mixed with Leccino and Pendolino. Fresh, well rounded, and balanced, it marries perfectly with seafood, cheese, and salads. Call in advance to arrange a visit. ✉ Kanedolo 90, Momjan ☎ 099/720–7106, 052/779–208 ⊕ www.kabola.hr ⊗ Mon.–Sat. 10–6.

Kozlović Winery. At the Kozlović family's stylish, modern winery, which opened in 2012 and blends perfectly with the scenic countryside, you can taste their single extra virgin olive oil along with their wines. Next door is the Stari Podrum, one of the best taverns in Istria. ✉ Vale 78, Momjan ☎ 052/779–177 ⊕ www.kozlovic.hr ⊗ Mon.–Sat. 10–5.

WHERE TO EAT

$$$$
MEDITERRANEAN

✕ **Restaurant Sole.** Its large parking area and bland exterior don't do justice to this family-run restaurant with excellent food and a friendly atmosphere. Based more on seafood than meat, everything on the menu is prepared using fresh, locally sourced, and homegrown produce. Their homemade eggless bigoli pasta with wild asparagus, crabmeat, and scampi is delicious, as are the seared baby calamari. $ Average main: 100 Kn ✉ Donji Picudo, Sošići 58, Sošići ☎ 052/730–123 ⊕ www. konoba-sole.hr ⊗ Closed Tues.

$$$
VENETIAN
FAMILY

✕ **Tavern Nono.** Extremely popular and always busy, Tavern Nono is in Petrovija, a mile east of Umag. This family-run tavern offers hearty Istrian seafood, meat, and pasta dishes in a cozy and friendly atmosphere. The interior is rustic but classy, while the enclosed terrace features ceiling decorations like a hanging bicycle and a collection of hats. The staff is friendly. ■ TIP➔ Children like to visit the small farm behind the restaurant with animals like rabbits, ducks, chicken, goats, and donkeys. $ Average main: 80 Kn ✉ Umaška 35, Petrovija ☎ 052/740–160 ⊕ www.konoba-nono.com ⊗ Closed Tues.

■ EN
ROUTE

Istria's interior hilltop villages have been much celebrated in recent years, both for their beauty and their gastronomical traditions. We recommend renting a car, even for a day, for a drive into the interior in the late afternoon, when fewer tour buses are likely to be on the road. Aside from Motovun and Grožnjan, Buje and Momjan to the northwest, Buzet and Hum to the east, and Gračišće to the south are all picturesque villages with their own medieval churches, old clock towers, and small-town restaurants.

MOTOVUN

30 km (19 miles) east of Poreč.

Fodor's Choice ★ It is an understatement to say that a day exploring the undulating green countryside and medieval hill towns of inland Istria makes a pleasant contrast to life on the coast. Motovun, for one, is a ravishing place. The king of Istria's medieval hill towns, with a double ring of defensive walls as well as towers and gates, may even evoke a scene straight from *Lord of the Rings*. Motovun is *the* place to visit if you opt to travel inland for a day or two from the sea. Be warned though, the town sees lots of tour buses. That said, a walk around the ramparts offers views across the oak forests and vineyards of the Mirna Valley. At the town's main square stands a church built according to plans by Palladio. In late July Motovun transforms for about five days into one of Croatia's liveliest (and most crowded) destinations—for the famed **Motovun Film Festival.**

GETTING HERE AND AROUND

The best way to get to Motovun is by car. The town isn't located along the main Istrian bus routes, and travelling to Motovun by bus isn't a viable option. This small hilltop town is best explored on foot.

WHERE TO EAT

$$$$ VENETIAN 🍴 **Mondo.** Located on a narrow cobblestone street leading up to the Old Town, just few yards before the town's gate, this tavern is perhaps the best place to eat in town. Sure, being featured in the *New York Times* raised its profile among visitors to Motovun, but locals loved it even before. The interior is rustic with roughly plastered stone walls, while the side-street terrace is breezy and perfect for dining alfresco. The menu screams truffles—almost every dish features them: homemade pasta, steaks, and even panna cotta come with shaved black truffles atop. Locals also rave about their olive and truffle tapanade amuse-bouche. [$] *Average main: 100 Kn* ✉ *Barbacan 1* ☎ *052/681–791* ⏲ *Closed Sept.–May. Closed Tues.*

$$$ MEDITERRANEAN 🍴 **Pod Voltom.** Centrally located, Pod Voltom offers authentic local dishes, many flavored with either black or white truffles, plus open-air dining on a romantic terrace by the town walls with terrific sunset views. Look out for excellent homemade *fuži* (Istrian pasta), succulent steaks, and a delicious panna cotta. The owner's red wine, served by the carafe, is also worth a mention. [$] *Average main: 120 Kn* ✉ *Trg Josefa Ressela 6* ☎ *052/681–923* ⏲ *Closed Jan.–Mar.*

$$$ VENETIAN **Fodor's Choice ★** 🍴 **Tavern Tončić.** This rustic tavern with exposed stone walls, wooden beams, and large open fireplace offers traditional hearty Istrian meat dishes. Located off the beaten path well past Oprtalj, the outdoor terrace has scenic views over the rolling hills, valley, and mountain in

CLOSE UP

A Scent to Swoon Over

A ball-shape candy often coated with cocoa? (That's what *Webster's* says about the truffle.) Think again. Such truffles are a dime a dozen compared to the real thing—namely, the sort of record-breaking, 1,310-kilogram (2,882-pound) truffle Giancarlo Zigante unearthed on November 2, 1999, with the help of his sharp-nosed dog in the village of Livade, near Motovun. What he found was—as attested to by the 100 guests he served in an effort to promote the cause of the Istrian truffle—the most delicious fungus you are likely to find.

For one thing, truffles grow underground, in a symbiotic relationship with the roots of oaks and certain other trees. As such, they cannot readily be seen. It is their scent that gives them away—a swoon-inducing scent. Sows were once the truffle hunter's favored companion, as truffles smell a lot like male hogs. (To be fair, the earthy aroma and pungent taste of truffles, which has also been likened to garlic, is prized by gourmands the world over.) These days, dogs are the truffle hunter's best friend.

For another thing, truffles are extremely rare. Most efforts to grow them domestically have failed, not least because you first need to grow a forest full of trees whose roots are just right for truffles. The white truffle, prized for its superior scent—the "white diamond," it's often called—sells for up to $3,500 a pound. This was the sort unearthed by Zigante, whose family owns a chain of truffle-oriented shops in Istria. In addition to the white truffle, Istria is also home to three sorts of black truffle, which sell for a mere $1,200 a pound.

In Istria truffles have been extracted since ancient times. Even Roman emperors and Austro-Hungarian aristocrats had a taste for truffles, not least because of the aphrodisiac qualities attributed to them. Truffles were once consumed and gathered like potatoes—that's how plentiful they were. That was in the 1800s. No longer, of course. Still, their fine shavings impart an unforgettable, earthy aroma and an irresistibly pungent, vaguely garlicky taste to pastas, salads, omelets, beef specialties, sauces, and more.

Economics and truffle scarcity being what they are, the Istrian truffle has become a hot commodity indeed. These days, for example, much of what is sold by Italy as Italian white truffles actually comes from Croatia—not least from the moist woods around Motovun, near the river Mirna.

Istriana Travel. If you'd like to join a truffle hunt, reserve a spot on a truffle-hunting excursion that departs from the village of Vrh from April to November. Accompanied by an English-speaking guide, you'll meet a truffle hunter and his trained truffle-sniffing dogs at the hunter's house, spend 45 minutes hunting in the woods, and enjoy a light lunch or dinner. ✉ *Vrh 28, Vrh, Buzet* ☎ *052/667–022* ⊕ *www.trufflehuntingcroatia.com.*

the background. Lots of regular guests and the friendly owners make you feel welcome in this family-run tavern, where you can try their homemade ravioli with black truffles or gnocchi with rooster stew. It's open weekends only. [$] *Average main: 70 Kn* ✉ *Čabarnica 42, Zrenj, Oprtalj* ☎ *052/644–146* ✍ *Reservations essential* ⏲ *Closed weekdays. Closed July.*

WHERE TO STAY

$ HOTEL 🏨 **Hotel Kaštel.** Just outside the Motovun town walls—but nonetheless nestled in a cloistered niche atop the hill—this peaceful, old-fashioned hotel makes an ideal retreat if you prefer green hills to sea and islands. **Pros:** quiet location; indoor pool and spa facilities; nice views over the valley from some rooms. **Cons:** uphill walk to the hotel; no car access; not all rooms are air-conditioned. [$] *Rooms from: 750 Kn* ✉ *Trg Andrea Antico 7* ☎ *052/681–607, 052/681–735* 🌐 *www.hotel-kastel-motovun.hr* 🛏 *31 rooms, 2 suites* 🍴 *Breakfast.*

EN ROUTE

As you near Grožnjan, you can take a small detour for a stop in the hilltop village of Buje. Drive up the hill through this quiet, lovely town, and take a stroll around its hushed little square shaded by plane trees, under which is a statue of a goat that seems to be reaching in vain for the leaves inches above its head. The pale yellow Church of the Madonna of Mercy is around the corner.

GROŽNJAN

10 km (6 miles) east of Motovun.

Close to Motovun and a reasonable drive from Poreč, Novigrad, or Umag, Grožnjan is also among Istria's preeminent hill towns, with a Renaissance loggia adjoining the town gate. Much visited by busloads of summer tourists, it is quite empty the rest of the year. In 1358, after at least 250 years in existence as a walled city, Grožnjan came under Venetian rule and remained so for more than 400 years. Though most of its population left after World War II, when decades of Italian rule came to an end and it officially became part of Yugoslavia, from the mid-1960s the government encouraged artists and musicians to settle here. This explains the number of painting and sculpture galleries you will encounter in this otherwise unassuming village. During the summer, an international federation of young musicians meets for training and workshops, presenting concerts beneath the stars through July and August.

GETTING HERE AND AROUND

The best way to get to Grožnjan is by car. Grožnjan is located off the main bus routes, and there aren't any buses connecting Pula or other coastal towns with Grožnjan. This small hilltop town is best explored on foot.

EXPLORING

Crkva svetog Vida i Modesta (*Church of St. Vitus and St. Modestus*).
Walk straight ahead from the small parking area just outside Grožnjan
and you will come to the Crkva svetog Vida i Modesta. Reconstructed
in baroque style from an earlier, 14th-century church, it stands on a
relatively unassuming, parklike space a bit removed from the gallery
scene, with panoramic views of the surrounding countryside and pla-
teaus of Istria all the way to the sea. ⊠ *Obzidna 2, at main entrance
to Grožnjan on left.*

**NEED A
BREAK?**

Bastia Konoba. If you are looking for a more substantial meal in Grožnjan,
visit the chic if a bit smoky Bastia Konoba, which is right on the main
square. Look out for local specialties such as *fuži* (Istrian pasta) and steak
with truffles. ⓢ *Average main: 80 Kn* ⊠ *1. Svibnja 1* ☏ *052/776–370.*

Vina Desković. For a bit of wine tasting with Istrian prosciutto and similar hearty fare to accompany the elixir, stop by this house-cum–wine
cellar on a lonely country road about 10 minutes outside Grožnjan by
car. You can get not only a tasty selection of five Istrian wines—for
example, malvazija among the whites and teran among the reds—but
also a selection of hearty snacks from its simple menu and even a breathtaking view of the tiny village of Kostanjica several hundred yards away.
Though the friendly family members here speak little English, communication need not be a barrier to a pleasant experience; you need to
be able to say little more than "vino" and "prosciutto." Figure on at
least 120 Kn per person for a full meal and a glass of wine. Since finding your way there through the hills outside Grožnjan is much easier
said than done, do check with the town's tourist-information office
for directions here and/or to similar wine-tasting opportunities nearby.
Call in advance to arrange a visit. ⊠ *Kostanjica 58* ☏ *052/776–315,
052/776–316, 098/197–7985* ⊕ *www.vina-deskovic.hr.*

Zigante Tartufi. Grožnjan may be small and out of the way, but enough
tourists visit to merit yet another outlet in the Zigante family's Zigante
Tartufi chain. The shop sells truffles and everything truffle-related you
can imagine, as well as local products from aromatic herb brandies to
honey to dried *Boletus* mushrooms. It is attached to the town's loggia.
⊠ *Ul Gorjan 5* ☏ *052/776–099 store* ⊕ *www.zigantetartufi.hr.*

EASTERN ISTRIA: LABIN AND RABAC

Labin is 44 km (28 miles) northeast of Pula.

Few travelers take time to explore Istria's often-overlooked eastern
coast. Although the region's mostly mountainous terrain offers a relative dearth of large towns abounding in historical sights and easy-to-
access, swimmable stretches of sea, the region does contain one notable
exception: Labin.

GETTING HERE AND AROUND

There are nine buses daily from Pula to Labin, and couple of more during the weekdays. From Labin you can easily reach Rabac using local buses. The best way to get around Rabac and Labin is on foot. An electric tourist train is also available in Rabac from mid-June to mid-September, and it runs between two resorts: Maslenica and Girandella.

Labin. Perched in all its compact medieval redolence atop a hill a short drive or walk from the sea, Labin is Croatia's former coal-mining capital and the birthplace of Matthias Flacius Illyricus, a Reformation-era collaborator of Martin Luther. Its narrow, historic streets are well deserving of a good walk, followed, if time allows, by a dip in the sea at Rabac, the relatively crowded and less inspiring complex of hotels and beaches 3 km (2 miles) away. From Labin's endearing little main square, **Titov trg**, with its 16th-century loggia and bastion, it's an easy stroll to Šetališste San Marco, a semicircular promenade with a spectacular view of the sea. Walk to the end, past a half dozen or so busts of historical luminaries, and take a sharp left up the cobblestone road. By following the spray-painted "Panorama" signs on the stone walls, you will soon reach the top of the hill, where (for 5 Kn) you can climb another 98½ feet up for an even better view from the town's onetime fortress, the **Fortica**. From here Labin's relatively bustling commercial center, which seemed nonexistent a few minutes ago, comes fully into view below, as do the dry, craggy hills of inland Istria. Making your way down the other side of the hill back toward the main square, you will pass by Labin's other major attractions, not least the **Crkva Rođenja Blažene Djevice Marije** (Church of the Birth of the Virgin Mary). With a facade featuring a 14th-century rose window and a 17th-century Venetian lion of the sort you will encounter elsewhere in Istria, the church was thoroughly renovated in 1993 to repair serious damage from mining under the Old Town in the 1960s. That said, its mix of architectural styles essentially dates from a late-16th-century renovation, though its foundations may date to the 11th century—and, farther back, to an earlier church built here by the Avars in AD 611. ✉ *Labin* ⊕ *www.rabac-labin.com.*

Rabac. Your first thought on arriving (buses run hourly from Labin for 10 Kn) at Rabac may be: Why come all the way to Europe for a place that looks much like a generic beach resort anywhere? Its series of huge, honeycomb-shaped, Italian-owned hotel monstrosities with names like Narcis, Casino, and Mimosa are truly the last place the writer of these lines, for one, would want to stay. But wait. Make a *right* on entering town rather than a left, then walk down the hill by road or the steps to the harbor. Once you reach the harbor, go *left* and then along the harborside promenade, rather than right. Doing so will reveal a side of Rabac that, although still somewhat touristy, also retains something of the idyllic—with its quiet harbor replete with small yachts, motorboats, and other pleasure craft, not to mention dozens of tiny, harborside coves you can walk down into for a quick dip via short flights of concrete steps. Although you can rent a plastic beach chair, making yourself comfortable on the smooth, roundish stones isn't nearly as difficult as it sounds; and even in midsummer, you can usually find yourself a rock to sprawl out on. ⊠ *Rabac* ⊕ *www.rabac-labin.com.*

WHERE TO EAT

$$$$

MEDITERRANEAN

Fodor's Choice

★

✕ **Due Fratelli.** Owned by a family that also has a fishing boat down on the bay, this restaurant has plenty of fresh, delicious seafood specialties on offer in addition to a good selection of meat and poultry dishes. Getting to this well-reputed restaurant, whose decor is pleasantly folksy and which has a cool, shaded terrace with a lush wall of pink flowers and grapevines out front, is easy if you're driving; keep your eyes peeled along the winding road downhill from Labin to Rabac for the restaurant's little sign to the left as the road curves right. If you're on foot, the walk is a bit of a haul. $ *Average main: 110 Kn* ⊠ *Montozi 6, Labin* ☎ *052/853–577* ⊕ *www.due-fratelli.com* ⚑ *Reservations essential.*

$$$$

SEAFOOD

Fodor's Choice

★

✕ **Martin Pescador.** A drive to seafood restaurant Martin Pescador will take you along the Rasa River, past the abandoned-looking bulk port Bršica, to the small fishing village of Trget, where you'll find the restaurant where the road dead ends. The cozy interior has exposed stone walls, an open fireplace, and an old wooden boat made into a bar. But the real deal here is the outdoor terrace, located directly at the sea: the turquoise water, the bay dotted with pleasure boats small and large, wooden piers—the view doesn't get any better than this. Praised for its laid-back atmosphere, fresh seafood, and simple tasty dishes like scampi tagliatelle, mussels *buzara* (in white wine with garlic, parsley, and breadcrumbs), and crab salad, Martin Pescador is perhaps the best restaurant in the vicinity of Rabac and Labin. $ *Average main: 100 Kn* ⊠ *Trget 20, Trget, Labin* ☎ *052/544–976* ⚑ *Reservations essential* ☾ *Closed Mon. Oct.–May.*

WHERE TO STAY

$$$

HOTEL

▦ **Hotel Adoral.** This family-run hotel has an excellent location right across the seafront promenade just a few yards from the water, and its spacious, modern, and well-equipped rooms have balconies overlooking the sea. **Pros:** location right at the seafront; modern and spacious rooms; attentive staff. **Cons:** checkout time could be a bit later. $ *Rooms from: 1400 Kn* ⊠ *Obala M. Tita 2a, Rabac* ☎ *052/535–840* ⊕ *www.adoral-hotel.com* ⇦ *5 rooms, 7 suites* ▯❑│ *Breakfast.*

$$$

HOTEL

▦ **Villa Annette.** Although you'll pass by quite a few ugly hotels on the way, once you arrive at Villa Annette, perched on top of a cliff overlooking Rabac harbor, you'll be happy you persevered. **Pros:** spacious rooms with undisturbed views. **Cons:** not easily accessible without a car. $ *Rooms from: 1450 Kn* ⊠ *Raška 24, Rabac* ☎ *052/884–222* ⊕ *www.villa-annette.com* ⇦ *12 suites* ▯❑│ *Multiple meal plans.*

KVARNER

Updated
by Vera
and Frank
Galparsoro

Majestic scenery and natural diversity characterize the Kvarner region: the mainland is dominated by a tiny stretch of coast backed by high-rising mountains, while some of the largest Croatian islands fill the heart of Kvarner Bay. Hike the wild Gorski Kotar Mountains, explore Krk Island on two wheels, beach-hop on the island of Cres, enjoy the mild climate and abundant vegetation of Lošinj, and experience the best of Croatian cuisine along the Opatija Riviera.

The Kvarner Gulf is a large, deep bay with the Istrian peninsula to the north and Dalmatia to the south. Four major islands, Cres, Krk, Lošinj, and Rab, along with numerous smaller specks of land, fill the heart of the bay and can be viewed from the gentle resort towns strung around the coastal arc. The lush, rolling hills of this coastal strip wind their way around the gulf from Opatija. East of Rijeka, the scenic Magistrala costal highway cuts into the solid rock of the foothills on its way to the southern tip of Croatia.

The wild Gorski Kotar mountain district is on the mainland northeast of Rijeka. Across the narrow range sits the inland part of Primorsko–goranska županija (Primorje–Gorski Kotar county), a region of small towns, thick forests, and agricultural land, through which you pass if you are traveling overland to Zagreb. Although the entire northern stretch of the Croatian coast exhibits a strong Italian influence, thanks to centuries of control from across the Adriatic, most of the mainland resorts developed during Habsburg rule. Robust and sophisticated Austro-Hungarian architecture and infrastructure predominate in these towns.

In contrast, the islands tend toward the cozier, less aspirational features of Italy. Dwellings are simpler, often of stone, and set in less geometric layouts. The elder population may struggle with any language other than Italian, and that includes Croatian.

Krk, entered via a short bridge from the eastern shore of the gulf region, reflects the mainland's arid nature more than its brethren. On Cres the northern stretches are a twisted knot of forest peaks and rocky crags, while gentler, cultivated slopes appear toward the center. Pine forests marching down to the shores provide welcome shade in the middle of the day. On the island's southern end, hollows have filled up to make freshwater lakes that provide the island's drinking water, counterbalancing the salty sea that licks at the land just a hill crest away. At the foot of Cres, a hop across a narrow stretch of the Adriatic brings you to Lošinj. This lush, Mediterranean oasis owes much of its charm to the gardens and villas that were built here during the seafaring heydays of the 19th century. As you approach from the north, the silhouette of Rab resembles the humped back of a diving sea monster. The high north of the island is dry and barren, almost a desert of rock and scrub, whereas the lower southern hemisphere is lush and fertile.

ORIENTATION AND PLANNING

GETTING ORIENTED
The Kvarner region is a stretch of Adriatic coast dotted with some of the largest Croatian islands. Rijeka, the region's administrative center and largest town, is within a five-hour drive of European hubs like Munich, Milan, Vienna, Budapest, Zagreb, and Ljubljana. The Kvarner's principal city, Rijeka, is a somewhat dilapidated port (although the 21st century has seen it making a reasonably committed effort at a comeback), with good road and rail connections to Zagreb. Genteel Opatija was founded by the Habsburgs in the mid-19th century as Croatia's first seaside resort. The regional airport is found on the island of Krk.

WHEN TO GO
The Kvarner region gets very busy in high summer, so don't even dream of heading, for instance, to Opatija or Krk in August without accommodations lined up. Late May through early June and September are ideal times to visit, since you can expect good weather, warm seas, and open facilities. Early May and October are good if you're looking for peace and quiet, but remember that few tourist-related activities are on offer and you still need to book accommodations in advance.

GETTING HERE AND AROUND
AIR TRAVEL
Rijeka's airport is on Omišalj on Krk Island, with regular bus service provided by Autotrans to downtown Rijeka and the beach towns on Krk island as well as to Mali Lošinj and Cres (though not to Rab). The airport is served by Ryanair from London, Norwegian Air Shuttle from Oslo, Croatia Airlines from Zagreb, Germanwings from Cologne, as well as charter-flight companies from several other cities in Germany. These charter companies usually sell air tickets only in combination with holiday packages, and flights cannot be booked separately.

Airline Contacts **Autotrans** ☎ *051/660–660* ⊕ *www.autotrans.hr*. **Croatia Airlines** ✉ *Jelačićev trg 5, Rijeka* ☎ *051/330–207* ⊕ *www.croatiaairlines. com*.**Germanwings** ☎ *0330/365–1918* ⊕ *www.germanwings.com*. **Norwegian Air Shuttle** ☎ *800/357–4159 from U.S.* ⊕ *www.norwegian.com*. **Ryanair** ☎ *44871/246–0002 in U.K.* ⊕ *www.ryanair.com*.

Airport Contacts **Rijeka Airport** ✉ *Hamec 1, Omišalj* ☎ *051/842–040* ⊕ *www. rijeka-airport.hr*.

BOAT AND FERRY TRAVEL
From June through September only, Jadrolinija ferries travel between Dubrovnik and Rijeka (journey time approximately 24 hours), stopping at Split, Stari Grad (island of Hvar), Korčula, and Sobra (island of Mljet) en route. The fare between Dubrovnik and Rijeka is €103 for a reclining seat in your own two-berth cabin with bathroom and TV. The cheapest way to go with no booked seat at all is €47. In good weather you'll find the rear decks of the ship smothered with passengers camping

GREAT ITINERARIES

IF YOU HAVE 3 DAYS

With only three days, start off on **Krk** to enjoy a little island life, heading straight to the action on Baška beach. From here, either choose another town like Malinska or Krk Town, or make your way to **Rijeka,** visiting the fruit and vegetable market and possibly taking in a cultural exhibit or two. On the final day, scoot farther west for some classic seaside resorting in **Opatija,** and don't miss an afternoon stroll along the Lungomare.

IF YOU HAVE 5 DAYS

Begin your trip either in Opatija or Krk, reversing the three-day itinerary to suit your fancy, and add a visit to the relatively wild island of **Cres.** Ferries connect northern Cres (Porozina) to Brestova west of Opatija and central Cres (Merag) with Krk at Valbiska. A day divided between swimming at the beaches

and relaxing in a café or ice-cream parlor in Cres Town can be enhanced by a second day exploring the more remote areas of the island, taking in some of the smaller villages or the rugged north.

IF YOU HAVE 7 DAYS

With a full week, explore the upscale marina at **Mali Lošinj** for one day (reachable by bus from Cres Town). You'll have to work your way back to Rijeka or Krk at this point to get to Rab, as ferries don't connect Cres and Lošinj to Rab. On your way, spend an extra day on the Opatija Riviera, taking in the pretty towns of **Lovran** and **Ičići.** From Rijeka jump on a bus or, in summer, a catamaran and head south to sample some of the region's only sandy beaches on the beautifully lush island of **Rab.** Spend at least a day admiring the medieval churches and campaniles of **Rab Town.**

out beneath the stars, which lends the journey a special atmosphere. Prices vary according to the season, with rates falling as much as 30% in low season. Cars cost €82. Round-trip tickets save 20%. Hourly on the half-hour, ferries leave Brestova for Cres; these ferries arrive at Porozina. Ferries also leave Valbiska on Krk to dock at Merag on Cres. Each brief hop across the channel sets you back €2.40 per person, €15.50 if you have a car.

Every day in high season, U.T.O Kapetan Luka ferries leave Rijeka at 5 pm to call at Ilovik, Sušak, Unije, Cres, and Mali Lošinj; the entire trip from Rijeka to Mali Lošinj takes around four hours. Meanwhile, a catamaran service heads out to Rab at 5 pm and drops into the northern Dalmatian island of Pag about 2½ hours later. Four times per day from 6 am to 6 pm, LNP ferries head out from Baška on Krk toward Lopar on Rab. The trip costs €5, €30 for a car. Tourist boats and water taxis offering transport on shorter stretches are also abundant at many resorts.

Contacts Jadrolinija ☎ *051/211–444, 060/321–321 recorded ferry timetable* ⊕ *www.jadrolinija.hr.* **LNP** ☎ *021/352–527* ⊕ *www.lnp.hr.* **U.T.O. Kapetan Luka** ☎ *021/645–476* ⊕ *www.krilo.hr.*

TOP REASONS TO GO TO KVARNER

■ **The Ultimate Waterfront Path:** Opatija's Lungomare—more than 11 km (7 miles) long—is ideal for a leisurely stroll anywhere between Lovran and Volosko.

■ **Fun in the Sand:** For a day of seaside family fun—windsurfing, sandy expanses, and ice-cream stands galore—take a trip to Krk's Baška beach, on the southern end of the island.

■ **Beautiful Remote Beaches:** Take a taxi boat or join one of the many daily excursions to the remote beaches below the hilltop village

of Lubenice on Cres Island. The famed Sv. Ivan beach is one of the prettiest in Croatia. Not far from it, at the beach Zanja, you can visit a sea cave.

■ **Towering Views:** The view from the top of the Great Bell Tower, Rab Town's tallest and most beautiful (there are four), is of a perfectly preserved medieval square.

■ **Yacht Gazing:** Watch yachts come in to the picturesque harbor of Lošinj and dock in front of stately 19th-century villas on both sides of the marina.

BUS TRAVEL

There's daily international bus service to Rijeka from Italy (Trieste), Slovenia (Ljubljana and Nova Gorica), and Germany (Dortmund, Frankfurt, Munich, and Stuttgart). You can also reach destinations all over mainland Croatia from Rijeka. Timetable information is available from the Rijeka Bus Terminal.

Buses travel from Rijeka to all the major towns on the mainland and the islands at least once a day. If you're traveling independently, you'll find that buses to the various islands are roughly scheduled to tie in with ferry services.

Information Autotrans ✉ *Rijeka Bus Terminal, Žabica 1, Rijeka* ☎ *051/660–660* ⊕ *www.autotrans.hr.* **Rijeka Bus Terminal** ✉ *Žabica 1, Rijeka* ☎ *060/302–010.*

CAR TRAVEL

Although local buses and ferries are an excellent, stress-free method of touring the region (buses are scheduled in tandem with the docking of ferries, so don't fear that you'll be left stranded at an empty dock), touring the Kvarner by car does offer the opportunity to nose your way around some of the smaller and more remote villages on the islands and up in the mountains. In addition, despite a poor safety record and heavy traffic in high season, there are few roads more scenic than the Magistrala. A car is also useful if you plan to leave Kvarner and head for Istria (passing through the Učka Tunnel). However, good train and bus services to Zagreb and a comfortable overnight ferry to Dalmatia mean that a vehicle is not really essential for moving on to other areas.

Car Rental Contacts Europcar ✉ *Rijeka Airport, Hamec 1, Omišalj* ☎ *098/231–078* ⊕ *www.europcar.com.* **Oryx Rent A Car** ✉ *Riječki lukobran 4, Rijeka* ☎ *051/338–800* ⊕ *www.oryx-rent.hr.*

TRAIN TRAVEL

There are three trains daily from Rijeka to Zagreb (journey time is approximately 4 hours) and two trains daily to Ljubljana (2½ hours).

Contacts Hrvatske Željeznice (Croatian Railways) ☎ *060/333–444* ⊕ *www. hzpp.hr.* **Rijeka Train Station** ✉ *Krešimirova 5, Rijeka* ☎ *051/213–333.*

RESTAURANTS

Without wanting to force square pegs into round holes, there are essentially four types of restaurants in Kvarner, if not the whole of the country. Unsurprisingly, many of them fall heavily under the influence of the Italian *tricolore*. In place of faith, hope, and charity, expect white pasta, green salads, and red pizza. The many pizza and pasta spots tend to be the cheaper and more casual alternatives.

Possibly the most delightful Croatian establishment is the *konoba*. Originally, the konoba was a humble cottage or shed, where fishermen would gather after returning to shore and might toast to surviving another day's trip out to sea by raising a few glasses, followed by a sample of their catch cooked to soak up the booze. These rustically styled fish restaurants have cropped up everywhere in the last few years. Especially on the islands, you'll see quite a few originals around.

Few dishes come specifically from Kvarner, but several parts of the region carry a healthy reputation for certain produce. In Rijeka try *jota,* a thick soup with sauerkraut or pickled beets with meat. *Maneštra* is a bean soup with corn, sauerkraut, and sometimes cured meats. The Gorski kotar region serves a mean polenta made with potatoes, local cheese, blood sausage, and game. On Krk try *Krk–Šurlice*, the local version of pasta; handmade on a spindle, it's often served with wild-game goulash. Cres has a fierce rivalry with the northern Dalmatian island of Pag regarding who serves the best lamb in Croatia. Calamari cooked in herbs and wine is a good bet on Lošinj. In Kvarner, *mrkač* is the local word for octopus; it's *hobotnica* in the rest of the country. If you order white fish, either grilled (*na žaru*) or baked in salt (*u soli*), you'll be charged by the kilogram, whereas squid (either grilled or fried) and shrimp (often cooked in white wine, *na buzaru*) come in regular portions. The classic accompaniment to fish is chard (*blitva*) and potatoes (*krumpir*). Many choices will come smothered in olive oil and garlic; you'll likely be told that this is what keeps the population so healthy. Krk and Sušak are home to the most highly regarded wines from the region, with the dry white *Vrbnićka žlahtina* a strong candidate for "best." *Rakija* (fruit and herb brandies) are, of course, the common end to a meal and the start of a long night.

HOTELS

Opatija, Krk, and Lošinj have a healthy selection of quality hotels, but outside these (relatively) major resorts, hotels become a rarer commodity. Much more common is renting a house or apartment. There are multitudes of these holiday homes available across the region, and many local agencies can assist in booking. Expect anything from a room in a block that shares a common kitchen, to a full-blown private house. Terraces are a standard and range from a simple tiled slab with metal rails to prevent you toppling off to a beautifully appointed perch shaded by a vine-smothered trellis and with an open grill for alfresco cooking. If you want to save money, consider renting a room in a private home. This arrangement rarely involves food, so you'll have to get up and out in the morning for your breakfast. At major transport hubs you'll often be accosted by elderly ladies attempting to entice you to their spare room. (They shout out, "Soba!" meaning "room.") Having a map in hand to understand exactly the location of the room being offered is wise, because out-of-town rooms often mean navigating the public transport system late in the evening or shelling out for a taxi ride. Croats are a house-proud race, so in general rented rooms are likely to be very clean and comfortable, with private bathrooms. Your welcome will probably be very warm, with drinks—especially strong coffee—thrust under your nose the moment you step across the threshold. There's no better way to get a real feel for how Croats live. *Hotel reviews have been shortened. For full information, visit Fodors.com.*

■ TIP → It can be close to impossible to get accommodations for fewer than two consecutive nights in high season, so plan to stay at least that long in each place you overnight.

WHAT IT COSTS IN EUROS (€) AND CROATIAN KUNA (KN)			
	$	**$$**	**$$$**	**$$$$**
Restaurants	under 35 Kn	35 Kn–60 Kn	61 Kn–80 Kn	over 80 Kn
	under €5	€5–€8	€9–€10	over €10
Hotels	under 925 Kn	925 Kn–1,300 Kn	1,301 Kn–1,650 Kn	over 1,650 Kn
	under €121	€121–€170	€171–€216	over €216

Restaurant prices are the average cost of a main course at dinner or, if dinner is not served, at lunch. Hotel prices are the lowest cost of a standard double room in high season.

VISITOR INFORMATION

Tourist information offices can help you with information about accommodations and activities and excursions like diving, windsurfing, and sightseeing. Most offices give out maps and ferry schedules for free.

Contacts Cres Tourist Information ⊠ Cons 10, Cres Town ☎ 051/571–535 ⊕ www.tzg-cres.hr. **Krk Tourist Information** ⊠ Vela placa 1/1, Krk Town ☎ 051/221–414 ⊕ www.tz-krk.hr. **Lošinj Tourist Information** ⊠ Riva lošinjskih kapetana 29, Mali Lošinj ☎ 051/231–884 ⊕ www.tz-malilosinj.hr. **Opatija Tourist Information** ⊠ Vladimira Nazora 3, Opatija ☎ 051/271–710 ⊕ www. opatija-tourism.hr. **Rab Tourist Information** ⊠ Trg Municipum Arba 8, Rab Town ☎ 051/724–064, 051/771–111 ⊕ www.tzg-rab.hr. **Rijeka Tourist Information** ⊠ Korzo 14, Rijeka ☎ 051/335–882 ⊕ www.tz-rijeka.hr.

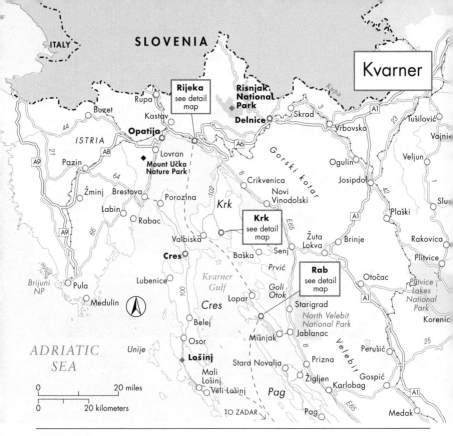

RIJEKA

165 km (103 miles) southwest of Zagreb.

Water is the essence of Kvarner, and the region's largest city expresses this simply. Whether in Croatian or Italian (Fiume) the translation of the name to English is the same: *river*. Although the history of Croatia's third city goes back to the days of Imperial Rome, modern Rijeka evolved under the rule of Austria-Hungary. The historic core retains vestiges of the old Habsburg monarchy from the time when Rijeka served as the empire's outlet to the Adriatic. During the 1960s, under Yugoslavia, the suburbs expanded rapidly. Rijeka is the country's largest port, with a huge shipyard, massive dry-dock facilities, refineries, and other heavy industries offering large-scale employment. Since the breakup of Yugoslavia, however, Rijeka's role as a shipping town has declined significantly. Much business shifted north to the smaller Slovene ports during the crippling wars of the 1990s, and although some has returned, the volume remains less than half that seen in 1980.

At the city's core sits Korzo, a pedestrian street of shops and cafés running parallel with the harbor and just to the south of where the land begins to rise toward the peaks of the mountains that back the bay. The high ground ensures that the suburbs stretch out to the east and the west, with little space to expand to the north. The general rule is that Rijeka is more of a transit town than a holiday destination, and it's not known for its points of interest, apart from the hilltop fortress of Trsat. However, the city is well worth investigating more thoroughly than most would have you believe.

Many visitors stay in the nearby seaside resort of Opatija, and locals will often head that way in their free time as well. That said, Rijeka is a perfectly pleasant small city (approximately 130,000 people call it home); if it did not command the wonderful bay that it does, it would also be unremarkable. This makes it one of the more authentically Croatian spots in the region in summer. Those looking to avoid the hordes could do much worse than to stay in Rijeka—albeit with very few options for accommodation—and use the excellent network of ferries to explore the rest of Kvarner.

Rijeka is the home port of Jadrolinija, the coast's major ferry company. Local ferries connect with all the Kvarner islands and will take you farther afield as well. If you're planning on heading south and would rather dodge the slow and dangerous roads that head that way, then let the boat take the strain. Ferries leaving Rijeka weave through islands all the way down to Dubrovnik, stopping at most major points on the way. Sunsets, sunrises, plus a mingling of stars and shore-anchored town lights in between, help transport one further than just the few hundred kilometers to the other end of the country.

GETTING HERE AND AROUND

Rijeka is linked with Zagreb by the new A6 motorway, which is clean and fast, though tolls add up on the journey. To reach the Dalmatian coast from Rijeka, you'll have to backtrack 75 km (47 miles) away from the coast and get on the motorway heading south toward Split and Dubrovnik. Rijeka is also the start of the Jadranska Magistrala (the coastal highway), which follows the coast south, all the way to the Montenegro border.

EXPLORING

TOP ATTRACTIONS

City Market. A set of three turn-of-the-20th-century halls host the city's main market, one of the liveliest spots in Rijeka on a weekday or Saturday morning. Get here before midday to enjoy the trading in full cry. The original constructions from the 1880s have suffered a little from later additions, but the fish market, the last to be built, is a wonderful example of art nouveau design. The castings by well-known Venetian artist Urbano Bottasso ape the fish and crustaceans being sold below. ■ TIP➔ **The streets surrounding the market are filled with no-frills eateries that are good for a quick lunch, and it's a good bet that their offerings will be fresh.** ✉ *Demetrova 3* ⊙ *Mon.–Sat. 6:30 am–2 pm, Sun. 6:30 am–noon.*

Guvernerova palača (*The Governor's Palace*). High on a hill, the palace affords a grand view over the harbor from all the front windows, from its gardens, and from the approach. Built in 1893 by Alajos Hauszmann, who also worked on Budapest's castle and Palace of Justice for

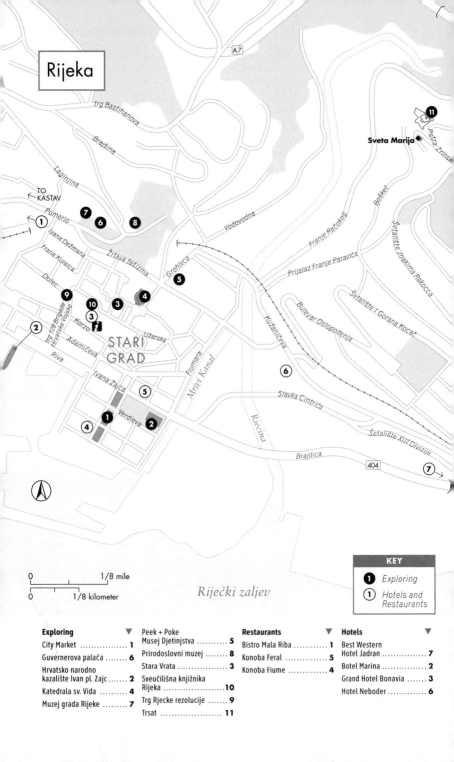

Rijeka

A7

trg Bastihanova

Brajšina

Lagnjina

TO
← KASTAV

Pomerio

Ivana Dežmana

Frana Kurelca

Dolac

Žrtava fašizma

Grohvca

Vodovodna

Franje Račkog

Prijalaz Franje Paravića

Bešket

Šetalište Joakima Rakocca

Šetalište I Gorana Kočara

Bulevar Ostopodenja

Kuzaničeva

Mrtvi Kanal

Frumara

Užarska

STARI
GRAD

trg 128 Brigade
Hrvatske Vojske

Korzo

Adamičeva

Riva

Ivana Zajca

Verdieva

Slavka Cintrića

Riccina

Brajdica

404

Šetalište XIII Divizije

Sveta Marija

Petra Zrinsk

Riječki zaljev

Exploring ▼
City Market **1**
Guvernerova palača **6**
Hrvatsko narodno
kazalište Ivan pl. Zajc ... **2**
Katedrala sv. Vida **4**
Muzej grada Rijeke **7**

Peek + Poke
Musej Djetinjstva **5**
Prirodoslovni muzej **8**
Stara Vrata **3**
Sveučilišna knjižnika
Rijeka **10**
Trg Rjecke rezolucije **9**
Trsat **11**

Restaurants ▼
Bistro Mala Riba **1**
Konoba Feral **5**
Konoba Fiume **4**

Hotels ▼
Best Western
Hotel Jadran **7**
Botel Marina **2**
Grand Hotel Bonavia **3**
Hotel Neboder **6**

KEY

❶ Exploring

① Hotels and
Restaurants

0   1/8 mile
0   1/8 kilometer

the then-governor of Hungary, the building itself is no eyesore either. The large columned facade communicates the self-confidence of the robust Habsburg empire, as do the numerous statues placed throughout its grounds. The **Maritime & Historical Museum of the Croatian Littoral,** which investigates the Kvarner's seafaring traditions and the region's cultural heritage from both the Mediterranean and Central Europe, is housed here. You can also admire the rest of the interior while viewing a temporary exhibition in the atrium or attending a meeting or concert in the impressive Marble Hall. ✉ *Muzejski trg 1* ☎ *051/213–578* ⊕ *www.ppmhp.hr* ✎ *15 Kn* ⊗ *Mon.–Sat. 9–8, Sun. 4–8.*

Katedrala sv. Vida (*St. Vitus's Cathedral*). Unusual in this part of the world, the church centers on a rotunda, although numerous additions and mixtures of style blunt its effect on the onlooker. Fine baroque statues are sheltered by baroque and Gothic construction. Founded by the Jesuits in 1638, the cathedral was named for Rijeka's patron saint. An 18th-century gallery was reportedly built to protect young novice monks from the tempting sights presented when the local lovelies attended services. At the main entrance you can find a cannonball in the wall, apparently sent from a British ship during the Napoleonic wars. ✉ *Grivića 11* ☎ *051/330–897* ⊗ *Daily 6:30–noon and 4:30–7.*

Trg Rijecke rezolucije (*Rijeka Resolution Square*). The buildings housing the **municipal palace** were originally part of an Augustinian monastery, and they connect to St. Jerome's Church. Named for the resolution that was drawn up here in 1905—and which contributed to the formation of Yugoslavia—the square's lemon-meringue buildings cluster around the foot of the city **flagpole,** erected on a high base in the 16th century and featuring a likeness of the city's patron saint, St. Vitus, holding a scale model of Rijeka protectively in his hand. ✉ *Rijeka.*

Fodor'sChoice
★ **Trsat** (*Trsat Castle*). The medieval castle was built on the foundations of a prehistoric fort. In the early 1800s it was bought by an Austrian general of Irish descent, who converted it into a kind of pre-Disneyland confection that even includes a Greek temple with Doric columns. Today it hosts a popular café, offering stunning views of the Kvarner Bay; throughout the summer, open-air theater performances and concerts take place here. Across the street, the pilgrimage church of **Sveta Marija** (St. Mary) was constructed in 1453 to commemorate the Miracle of Trsat, when angels carrying the humble house of the Virgin Mary are said to have landed here. Although the angels later moved the house to Loreto in Italy, Trsat has remained a place of pilgrimage. The path up to Trsat from the city center takes you close to Titov trg, at a bridge across the Rječina. It passes through a stone gateway, then makes a long, steep climb up 538 steps. Local Bus 2 will get you here, too. ✉ *Petra Zrinskog BB* ✎ *15 Kn* ⊗ *June–Sept., daily 9–8; Oct.–May, daily 9–5.*

WORTH NOTING

Hrvatsko narodno kazalište Ivan pl. Zajc (*Croatian National Theatre Ivan Zajc*). Designed by specialist Viennese architects Fellner and Helmer, Rijeka's National Theatre opened in 1885. In high summer the theater plays host to a Festival of Summer Nights, held beneath wonderful ceiling paintings by Gustav Klimt and emerging from behind a stage curtain decorated by Croatian artist Oton Gliha. However, you'll have to buy a ticket to a performance to see the inside of the theater. ⊠ *Verdijeva 5a* ☎ *051/355–917* ⊕ *www.hnk-zajc.hr.*

Muzej grada Rijeke (*The Museum of the City of Rijeka*). In a cube-shape building on the grounds of the Governor's Palace, the museum has 11 collections but no permanent exhibit. There's always a mix of military artifacts along with cultural and scientific displays, and the temporary exhibits can be interesting. ⊠ *Muzejski trg 1/1* ☎ *051/336–711* ⊕ *www. muzej-rijeka.hr* 🎫 *15 Kn* ☉ *Mon.–Sat. 9–8, Sun. 10–3.*

Peek + Poke Muzej Djetinjstva (*Peek + Poke Museum of Childhood*). Return to your childhood through the museum's exhibit of toys and games. Among the 600 items on display, mostly donated by people from Croatia and around the world, the oldest is a scrapbook dating to 1900. The collections are displayed thematically: construction games, a "fossil" zone displaying the oldest items, board games, literature, a school corner, doll collection, and outdoor games and toys. Among the most interesting items are Richter's Stone Building Set from 1902 and a large replica of the Croatian National Theater made of Lego blocks. ⊠ *Ivana Grohovca 2* ☎ *051/562–100* 🎫 *20 Kn* ☉ *Weekdays 11–8, Sat. 11–4, Sun. 2–6.*

Prirodoslovni muzej (*Natural History Museum*). Exploring the geology and biology of the region invariably involves holding a sizable chunk of marine life up to the eyes. The shark and ray display here is predictably popular, starring a brigade of stuffed sharks swimming in strict formation while suspended from the ceiling. A multimedia center based on an aquarium adds to the extensive collection of nonmammalian species, which boasts 90,000 specimens in total, but includes rocks, plants, and other less animated elements of the locality. The botanical garden contributes more exotic plants to the array from the museum's grounds. Considering the fearsome appearance of some of the more fascinating inhabitants of the museum, it may be worth considering putting off a visit here until the end of your stay on the coast, lest your imagination get the better of you while bathing off the beaches. ⊠ *Lorenzov prolaz 1* ☎ *051/553–674* ⊕ *www.prirodoslovni.com* 🎫 *10 Kn* ☉ *Mon.–Sat. 9–7, Sun. 9–3.*

Stara Vrata (*The Roman Gate*). This enormous stone arch—the oldest structure in the city—is an ancient town gate. Today it's partly engulfed by additions from more recent times, but it was from this site many centuries ago that the chain of mountain fortresses in the region was commanded by the Romans. These days, the Roman elite's enthusiasm for comfort is catered to with a handful of park benches amid what is left of the ancient walls and columns. ⊠ *Trg Ivana Koblera.*

Sveučilišna knjižnica Rijeka (*University Library*). Formerly a school, the University Library now houses a permanent exhibition about the Glagolitic script. Stone tablets written in the ancient Slavic script, including the important Baška tablet from Krk, are the stars. Books, paintings, masonry, and frescoes are also displayed. Call in advance to view the exhibition. ⊠ *Dolac 1* ☎ *051/336–129* 🎫 *10 Kn* ☉ *Mon. and Thurs. 2–7, Tues., Wed., and Fri. 9–2.*

OFF THE BEATEN PATH

Kastav. One of the finest spots from which to admire the splendors of the Kvarner bay is Kastav, 11 km (7 miles) northwest of Rijeka. Originally a medieval fortress comprising nine defensive towers, the old hilltop village sits at 1,200 feet in elevation and is home to 900-some people. Without the crowds of Rijeka, you, along with city residents that spend their leisure time here, can concentrate more properly on the quality of your relaxation. The local vintage, Kastavska Belica, is a decent white wine that is gulped merrily at Kastav Cultural Summer and on the feast day of patron St. Helena (as featured on the coat of arms), May 22. Having been home to wealthy and powerful clans in times past, the tiny town has many splendid—if not officially noted—buildings from throughout the ages. ✉ *Kastav* 🌐 *www.kastav-touristinfo.hr.*

WHERE TO EAT

$$$ SEAFOOD

🍴 **Bistro Mala Riba.** Fish marinated in lemon juice, sea-snail salad, fried olives, barley and squid stew—these are just some of the Kvarner-style tapas offered at this cozy seafood tavern. Located on the main road Matulji–Kastav, Mala Riba doesn't have a prime location, but the interior is homey and the outdoor terrace is pleasant. [$] *Average main: 65 Kn* ✉ *Tometići 33a, Tometići, Kastav* ☎ *051/277–945* 🌐 *www.mala-riba.com.*

$$$$ SEAFOOD

🍴 **Konoba Feral.** This excellent informal seafood restaurant lies on a side road close to the City Market. House specialties are *crni rižot* (cuttlefish-ink risotto), seafood tagliatelle, and *fuži* (homemade pasta) with asparagus and scampi. Fish is charged by weight. Adriatic blue fish, like sardines, is delicious and very affordable here. [$] *Average main: 80 Kn* ✉ *Matije Gupca 5b* ☎ *051/212–274* 🌐 *www.konoba-feral.com* ⏲ *No dinner Sun.*

$$$$ MEDITERRANEAN

🍴 **Konoba Fiume.** Tucked away in an alley right next to Rijeka's fish market, quaint Fiume fills with locals at lunchtime. Unpretentious and friendly with a small street-side terrace, the tavern serves mostly seafood, but also meat and pasta dishes. Prices are pleasantly affordable. [$] *Average main: 80 Kn* ✉ *Vatroslava Lisinskog 12* ☎ *051/312–108* ⏲ *Closed Sun. No dinner.*

WHERE TO STAY

The selection of hotels in Rijeka reflects the city's status as a simple transit town.

Homeaway Holiday Rentals. This U.K.-based travel agency lists a good selection of private rooms and apartments in Rijeka. ☎ *+44 208/827–1971* 🌐 *www.homeaway.co.uk.*

$ HOTEL

🏨 **Best Western Hotel Jadran.** It's a good 15-minute walk (or 10-minute bus ride) from central Rijeka to this pleasant hotel right on the water, but views of the Gulf of Kvarner don't come much better than this. **Pros:** substantial breakfast; unfettered sea views. **Cons:** a bit out of town to take in any nightlife; walk into town is along a busy street. [$] *Rooms from: 760 Kn* ✉ *Šetalište XIII divizije 46* ☎ *051/216–600* 🌐 *www.jadran-hoteli.hr* 🛏 *66 rooms, 3 suites* 🍽 *Breakfast.*

$ HOTEL **Botel Marina.** Docked at the pier in Rijeka, the first Croatian boat hotel features 35 modern rooms, from doubles to dorms, furnished with comfy beds and en suite bathrooms—a cool place to stay. **Pros:** centrally located; nice ambience; friendly staff. **Cons:** no elevators, so carrying laguage to the rooms on lower decks can be inconvenient; no TV in rooms. [$] *Rooms from: 380 Kn* ✉ *Adamićev gat* ☎ *051/410–162* 🌐 *www.botel-marina.com* 🛏 *35 rooms* 🍴 *Breakfast.*

$$ HOTEL **Grand Hotel Bonavia.** In the city center, one block back from the Korzo, this modern, luxury high-rise has comfortable rooms with specially designed furnishings and original oil paintings. **Pros:** spacious rooms; good service; excellent location. **Cons:** getting a bit outdated; also caters to business guests. [$] *Rooms from: 950 Kn* ✉ *Dolac 4* ☎ *051/357–100* 🌐 *www.bonavia.hr* 🛏 *114 rooms, 7 suites* 🍴 *Breakfast.*

$ HOTEL **Hotel Neboder.** Although by no means luxurious, the hotel is in the very center of Rijeka near all of the city's attractions, and a room in the upper floors of this white skyscraper offers decent views of the city. **Pros:** central location; friendly staff. **Cons:** rooms are dated with a budget feel; rear-facing room get some railway noise. [$] *Rooms from: 550 Kn* ✉ *Strossmayerova 1* ☎ *051/373–538* 🌐 *www.jadran-hoteli.hr* 🛏 *54 rooms* 🍴 *Breakfast.*

NIGHTLIFE AND PERFORMING ARTS

BARS

Celtic Cafe Bard. A hangout spot for beer lovers, this bar on a small town square next to St. Vitus Cathedral is decorated with wood and brass. This cozy spot offers an excellent choice of Croatian and international beer in a friendly atmosphere to the rhythm of Celtic music and some jazz. ✉ *Trg Grivica 6b* ☎ *051/215–235.*

Cukarikafe. Perhaps the most popular daytime café-bar in Rijeka, this shabby chic spot is packed with unique decor, much of it culled from the dump and flea market. People from all walks of life come here for the excellent selection of wine by glass, beer, local spirits, teas, and freshly squeezed juices. Cukarikafe also serves as an exhibition venue for local artists and designers. ✉ *Trg Jurja Klovića 4* ☎ *099/583–8276.*

Karolina. In an upmarket pavilion right on the quayside, Karolina serves cocktails and wine to the smart set as they watch the tide flow in and out of the bay. ✉ *Gat Karoline Riječke* ☎ *091/490–4042.*

Phanas Pub. The best party place in town, this nautically themed pub is like an old sailboat with its dark wood, long bar, and maritime decorations. Music ranges from acoustic and R&B to dance, and you can enjoy it until 6 am from Thursday through Sunday. ✉ *Ivana Zajca 9* ☎ *051/312–377* 🌐 *www.phanas.hr.*

River Pub. For those who might remember summer nights sitting on a terrace, drinking, dancing, chatting, and actually being able to hear what others are saying, the River Pub is the place to make it all come back. ✉ *Frana Supila 12* ☎ *091/151–6754* 🕒 *Closed Sun.*

Tunel. In a real tunnel under the railway in the Skoljić area of town, one of Rijeka's favorite bars has a great atmosphere, friendly staff, and cool crowd. Some nights jazz, rock, and funk bands take the small stage; other nights DJs play electronic music. They have a good choice of local brandies, Croatian wines, and international beers. ⊠ *Školjić 12* ☎ *051/327–116* ⊘ *Closed Sun.*

FESTIVALS

Rijeka Carnival. From the end of January until mid-February the streets of the city are taken over by crazy antics and costumes during the Rijeka Carnival. The carnival kicks off with the Carnival Queen Pageant, continues with weeks of fun activities and masked parties all over town, and ends with the Children's Carnival Parade and the International Carnival Parade. ⊠ *Rijeka* ⊕ *www.rijecki-karneval.hr.*

Rijeka's Summer Nights. Beginning in late June, the four-week annual Rijeka's Summer Nights festival ensures that venues, streets, and squares are filled with cultural performances. You can experience classical music and theater as well as contemporary music and performance art. ⊠ *Rijeka* ⊕ *www.rijeckeljetnenoci.com.*

Summer on Gradina. From mid-July through mid-September, this cultural festival brings theater plays, live concerts, and conceptual and themed events to Trsat Fortress. ⊠ *Trsat Fortress, Petar Zrinskog BB* ⊕ *www. trsatskagradina.com.*

SHOPPING

Appearance is of great importance to Croatians, and the local ladies will invariably be exhibiting style and glamour even as they sip coffee or shop for vegetables on any given weekday morning. To serve this fashion-conscious crowd, many hip little boutiques offer the latest styles in imported clothing and shoes (mostly from Italy). Prices are generally higher than what you'd pay in Italy, so unless you're caught short needing some posh clothes, it's better for your wallet to do your high-fashion shopping elsewhere. The Korzo, a pedestrian strip that strides through the center of Rijeka, is the best place to go should you be unable to contain your shopping urges.

Fresh local produce, fish, cheeses, olive oils, wines, and *rakijas* (fruit brandy) are the items that should be on your Kvarner shopping list. The best place to buy these is the City Market on Verdijeva. Although there are "professional" traders present, many of the stallholders are still locals who bring their home-produced wares to sell. Noisy and colorful, Rijeka's central market is the place to haggle over fresh produce, swap gossip, and, of course, drink coffee. Pick up a picnic lunch of cheeses, salads, fruit, and nuts here, then pop into one of the multitude of bakeries for freshly baked *burek* (cheese and meat pies) to complete the feast. Although a little tricky to transport, homemade olive oil, apple-cider vinegar, and *rakija*—usually sold in recycled bottles—are good buys as well. Smaller containers of dried herbal tea leaves and spices like rosemary and oregano are a good alternative if your luggage is already tightly packed.

Mala galerija. All things that glitter or smash easily are available at the Mala galerija. Although not entirely exclusive to Rijeka (you'll find similar, if more ostentatious, artifacts in Venice), the *Morčić* is the figurehead of a Moor wearing a white turban and is associated with the luck that all seafarers rely on. This small shop has many items bearing the "little Moor." ⊠ *Užarska 25* ☎ *051/335–403* ⊕ *www.mala-galerija. hr* ⊙ *Weekdays 8–8, Sat. 9–2.*

ZTC. This mall right at the seafront is the favorite shopping destination of Rijeka residents. Shops include fashion brands like Benetton, H&M, and S'Oliver; Lush and L'Occitane cosmetics; and sport store Hervis. ⊠ *Zvonimirova 3* ☎ *051/561–014* ⊕ *www.ztc-shopping.hr.*

SPORTS AND THE OUTDOORS

BEACHES

Since it serves as the country's largest port, there aren't too many beautiful beaches in the middle of Rijeka. However, you don't imagine locals stay here the whole summer without having a few spots they try to keep secret from the tourists, do you? Favorite beaches easily accessible from the city include the **Bivio Cove,** near Kantrida to the west. In the opposite direction around the coast, **Uvala Žurkovo,** at Kostrena, is wonderful. Within the city itself, the popular place is Pecine to the east, where you can swim off rocky beaches and admire the local villas.

FISHING

The Croatian coast is well known for its population of blue fin tuna.

Ministry of Agriculture, Forestry & Water Management. You need a fishing license to hunt for any marine life using a line or gun. Prices start from 60 Kn per day. In Rijeka licenses are available from the local office of the Ministry of Agriculture, Forestry & Water Management, or online through the ministry's website. ⊠ *Demetrova 3* ☎ *051/213–626* ⊕ *www.mps.hr.*

HIKING AND CLIMBING

The mountains around Rijeka—and indeed throughout the Kvarner—are riddled with tracks with international signs. Many lovely starting spots can be reached by car.

Kamenjak Mountaineering Club. The friendly folks here will give you information about routes and mountain huts for overnight tramps. But be prompt; they're only open on Tuesday and Friday evenings between 6 and 8 pm. ⊠ *Korzo 40/I* ☎ *051/331–212.*

OUTFITTERS

Raspadalica. This outfitter can help out if you want to do some exploring on two wheels, on foot, underground, or in the air: paragliding and free flying above the clouds in Mount Učka Nature Park. They also offer Robinson Crusoe–style camping (no hot water, electricity, or other amenities). ⊠ *Ćićarija, Buzet* ☎ *098/924–7300, 098/167–8737* ⊕ *www.raspadalica.com.*

RISNJAK NATIONAL PARK

40 km (25 miles) northeast of Rijeka.

The northern outpost of the forested and karst-peaked Gorski kotar region, Veliki Risnjak is the major peak in this national park, peering over Rijeka from 5,013 feet. The thick pine-forest meadows are stuffed with wildflowers in the spring, and limestone peaks, crevices, and caves cover around 60 square km (25 square miles).

Risnjak National Park. Risnjak is a popular destination year-round. In winter you'll find a healthy contingent of snow aficionados desperately trying to avoid a trip up to Austria to sample the real thing. In summer, however, as the sun and the tourists beat down upon the coast, this is perhaps the best place to be. The cooling mountain air—the average temperature in these heights in July is around 12°C (53°F)—is a bonus to Risnjak's virtually deserted landscape.

You'll be free to commune with the locals, which include deer, bear, wildcat, and lynx (*ris*), from which the park takes its name. Geologic and botanical features are occasionally explained by English-language information points over which you may stumble on one of the more popular walking routes. Marked trails can occupy you for an hour's evening stroll to a full seven-day trek on the monstrous Rijeka Mountain Transversal from one side of Gorski kotar to the other. Hiking huts are strung across the peaks to accommodate such ambitious expeditions. More information regarding these multiday hiking trips is available from the Croatian Mountaineering Association.

The park information office is in the village of Crni lug, at the eastern entrance to the park; in the off-season, from October through April, you can pick up information at the reception desk of the Motel Risnjak. You can easily explore the gentler trails on day trips from either Rijeka or Delnice. Paths from the villages of Razloge and Kupari lead up to the source of the wild Kupa River, which can then be followed down the slopes through the "Valley of the Butterflies." ⊠ *Bijela vodica 48, Crni lug* ☎ *051/836–133* ⊕ *www.risnjak.hr* ✉ *45 Kn* ☉ *Park information office May–Sept., daily 9–5.*

OPATIJA

15 km (9 miles) west of Rijeka.

In the late 19th century, Opatija (Abbazia in Italian) was among the most elegant and fashionable resorts in Europe. Its history as a resort town dates from the 1840s, when villas were built for members of minor royalty. In 1882 the start of rail service from Vienna and Budapest, along with an aggressive publicity campaign, put Abbazia on the tourist map as a spa of the first magnitude. With the high mineral content of the sea water, iodine in the air, and an annual average of 2,230 hours of sunshine, it qualified as a top-rated climatic health resort, and emerged as a favorite wintering spot for Central European nobility and high society.

A hint of the formality that shrouded Opatija in its heyday still survives; the narrow pines and grand buildings remind one of the Italian lakes. This means that many visitors from all over Europe continue to head to the Opatija Riviera in the summer. At the same time, this stretch of coast has not gone unnoticed by the locals. Until recent years the town was a weekend haunt for some younger, motorized Rijeka citizens. Thanks to these driving forces, the upmarket hotel guests still share the resort with some of the region's more upwardly mobile restaurants. However, their number is dwindling, while the town's once admirable nightlife has packed up and headed back to the cooler parts of Rijeka, leaving Opatija to wealthy and more elderly visitors from the surrounding countries. These guests seem more eager to sip the waters than wine and spirits.

The main street, ulica Maršala Tita, runs parallel to the coast for the length of town, and you can go from one end of town to the other on foot in about half an hour, passing numerous terrace cafés along the way. The best seafood restaurants are in the neighboring fishing village of Volosko, a 15-minute walk along the seafront. The mild climate year-round and resulting subtropical vegetation, frequently sunny skies, and shelter from cold north winds provided by Mt. Učka give Opatija pleasant weather for much of the year. In summer, fresh sea breezes tend to dispel any oppressive heat, making the city an ideal seaside resort.

EXPLORING

TOP ATTRACTIONS

Lungomare. If you enjoy walking by the sea, set off along the magnificent paved, waterfront Lungomare. Built in 1889, this 12-km (7½-mile) path leads from the fishing village of Volosko, through Opatija—passing in front of old hotels, parks, and gardens and around yacht basins—and all the way past the villages of Ičići and Iká to Lovran. In the middle you'll find the popular town beach that fronts the center of Opatija. Close to many cafés, ice-cream shops, and other essentials, the beach also has a couple of protected sections of water for safe swimming. These would be handy for kids if it weren't for the fact that the concrete sides and underwater steps feature extremely sharp stones that can slice skin quite nastily if met with sufficient force. ⊠ *Obalno Šetalište Franza Josefa.*

Mount Učka Nature Park. From gentle hiking to mountain biking, climbing and paragliding, all are available in the 160 square km (62 square miles) of Mount Učka Nature Park, a series of peaks that help shelter the Liburnia Riviera (which is actually the official name for the stretch of coast centered on Opatija) and the islands from weather systems to the north. Paths toward the summit of the range start from all the resorts along the coast. A climb up to the highest peak, Vojak (4,596 feet), with a fine stone lookout tower at its summit, can be well worth it, particularly on a clear day. The view offers a cheap (but somewhat distant) tour of the islands of Kvarner Bay, the Italian Alps, and perhaps even an indistinct version of Venice. Most routes up to the heights lead through forest, so you can make the trek in summer without overheating. Along the way you'll find natural springs from which to quench your thirst, along with ponds, tumbling waterfalls (in the wetter months), impressive natural stone columns and several hundred caves. The local inhabitants include deer, wild boar, and, in the northernmost sections of the park, bears. Humans have been living in these hills for centuries also, rearing cattle, farming, and working the forest; you'll come across numerous tiny villages and historic sites if you roam far enough. If you're running short of time, there are many mountain-biking tracks throughout the park offering the chance to expand your lungs on the way up and test your nerve rattling back down to the coast. ⊠ *Liganj 42, Lovran* ☎ *051/293–753* ⊕ *www.pp-ucka.hr* ✉ *Free.*

WORTH NOTING

Croatian Museum of Tourism (*Villa Angiolina*). Visit this museum to get a good understanding of Croatian, and particularly Opatija's, tourism in the 19th century. Slated to fill the gorgeous pink Villa Angiolina in the botanical gardens, the museum's permanent collection includes postcards and photographs, souvenirs, and hotel inventory and equipment such as 19th-century hotel silverware and furniture. The villa's neoclassical design includes superb mosaic floors and frescoes. Local artists often exhibit at this appealing building and grounds. ⊠ *Park Angiolina 1* ☎ *051/603–636* ⊕ *www.hrmt.hr* ✉ *10 Kn* ☉ *Daily 10–6.*

Park Angiolina. The grounds of Park Angiolina are a wonderful spread of palm-punctuated lawns with a botanical garden. The vegetation is strikingly lush, including cacti, bamboo, and magnolias, plus neatly kept beds of colorful flowers and sweet-scented shrubs. Indeed, Opatija as a whole is a town saturated with botanical splendor. Iginio Scarpa, an aristocrat from Rijeka and the first settler in Opatija, began importing exotic plants, and the tradition has survived into the present. The camellia is the symbol of the city. ⊠ *Between Maršala Tita and seafront* ⊕ *www.opatija-tourism.hr* ✉ *Free* ☉ *Tues.–Sun. sunrise–sunset.*

OFF THE BEATEN PATH

Lovran. Just 5 km (3 miles) southwest of Opatija, the lovely town of Lovran is home to good swimming coves, Habsburg villas, and paths up to Mount Učka Nature Park. Massive chestnut trees dot the medieval town, giving shady relief from the sun on long summer days. If the crowds of Opatija leave you no place for peace and quiet, walk along the Lungomare through Ičići and Ika (or take bus No. 32) to Lovran, where you can take in the sea air that lured Austrian royalty to winter here. If you find yourself on the Opatija Riviera in October, don't miss Lovran's **Marunada,** or chestnut festival. Contact the Lovran Tourist Office (*Trg Slobode 1, Opatija, 051/291–740, www.tz-lovran.hr*) for information. ⊠ *Lovran*

WHERE TO EAT

$$$$ ✕ **Istranka.** With a delightful covered terrace flanked by a twisting tree,
VENETIAN this small restaurant is Opatija's best option for those who are not the greatest fans of seafood (although if that's you, what you're doing in Kvarner is a mystery). Taking its influence from the neighboring region of Istria, the menu concentrates more on landlubber food: hams,

cheeses, and of course, the famous Istrian truffle! $ *Average main: 80 Kn* ⊠ *Bože Milanoviča 2* ☎ *051/271–835.*

$$$$ ✕ **Plavi Podrum.** Although this is one of the more traditional fish res-
SEAFOOD taurants in Volosko, don't be fooled into thinking it's not classy. The owner has been "Sommelier of the Year" twice in this young century. All the usuals are cooked to perfection here, but *jaja od hobotnice* ("octopus egg") is a house special featuring squid, octopus, caviar, mustard, and fresh spinach. The terrace is a little more relaxed than inside. $ *Average main: 130 Kn* ⊠ *Obala Frana Supila 12, Volosko* ☎ *051/701–223.*

$$$$ ✕ **Tramerka.** Located in Volosko, just above more famed Plavi Podrum,
SEAFOOD this small seafood tavern offers fresh, creative seafood dishes in a cozy
Fodor'sChoice interior with exposed stone walls; a tiny streetside terrace has only a
★ few tables. Locals rave about their bonito tartare, monkfish stew, and "dirty" calamari (baby calamari too small to be thoroughly cleaned before cooking, thus "dirty"). For the ultimate seafood feast, order a little bit of everything—just ask for smaller portions. $ *Average main: 90 Kn* ⊠ *Dr. Andrije Mohorovicica 15, Volosko* ☎ *051/701–707* ✍ *konobatramerka@gmail.com* ☾ *Closed Mon.*

WHERE TO STAY

$$ ⊞ **Astoria Design Hotel.** Sleek flat-screen TVs and Wi-Fi in every room
HOTEL aren't what you'd expect in a hotel in this price category in a city popular with Austrian pensioners. **Pros:** boutique touches like flat-screen TVs and deluxe toiletries. **Cons:** superior rooms are on the small side; not directly on the seafront. $ *Rooms from: 1100 Kn* ⊠ *Maršala Tita 174* ☎ *051/706–350* ⊕ *www.vi-hotels.com* ⇆ *46 rooms, 4 suites* ⦿ *Breakfast.*

$$$ ⊞ **Milenij Hotel Opatija.** On the coastal promenade, this bright pink villa
HOTEL is part old and part new; rooms are furnished accordingly, with either Louis XV–style antiques heavily striped in silk or modern designer pieces. **Pros:** centrally located and at seafront; homemade pralines and a good choice of other cakes and pastries in hotel's café. **Cons:** small pool with few lounge chairs; lack of parking spaces. $ *Rooms from: 1450 Kn* ⊠ *Maršala Tita 109* ☎ *051/202–000, 051/278–007* ⊕ *www. milenijhoteli.hr* ⇆ *99 rooms* ⦿ *Breakfast.*

$$$ ⊞ **Remisens Premium Hotel Ambasador.** This 10-floor skyscraper may
HOTEL not look appealing from the outside, but this five-star hotel is surprisingly elegant on the inside, with an airy lobby area and floor-to-ceiling windows overlooking the sea. **Pros:** view from sea-facing rooms is gorgeous; nice pool area; friendly staff. **Cons:** parking fees; hotel also caters to business travelers. $ *Rooms from: 1550 Kn* ⊠ *Feliksa Peršića 5* ☎ *051/710–444* ⊕ *www.remisens.com* ⇆ *180 rooms, 20 suites* ⦿ *Breakfast.*

$$ ⊞ **Remisens Premium Hotel Kvarner.** The former summer residence of Euro-
HOTEL pean royalty, Kvarner's oldest hotel first opened its doors to guests in 1884. **Pros:** Habsburg-era grandeur; spacious patio overlooking the sea. **Cons:** noise from wedding parties sometimes hosted in the Crystal Ballroom. $ *Rooms from: 1220 Kn* ⊠ *Park Tomašica 1–4* ☎ *051/271–233, 051/710–444* ⊕ *www.remisens.com* ⇆ *54 rooms, 4 suites* ⦿ *Breakfast.*

NIGHTLIFE AND PERFORMING ARTS

There was a time when folk from Rijeka used Opatija as their playground; then, the town offered superb nightlife options. These days, however, the big city along the coast is reclaiming its post as the cultural hot spot of the region, and Opatija has been busy transforming itself back into Central and Eastern Europe's health resort. The wealthy, older Italians and Austrians who dominate here have done little to inspire energetic evenings.

Hemingway. A Croatian chain of cocktail bars for the upwardly mobile, Hemingway is spreading across the country and tends to thrust its nose in the air wherever it goes. Pack your wallet with at least one gold card if you're planning on gaining entry to *the* elite bar in this most elite of resorts. Wood is big here, and it gives a warmer feel than might be expected among the dressed-up clientele. The two floors offer a rainbow of cocktail choices on three terraces, including one up on the roof that spies down on the small harbor. ✉ *Zert 2* ☎ *098/324–456* ⊕ *www.hemingway.hr.*

Monokini. Right on the main road that winds through town along the seafront, Monokini has a shaded, street-side terrace with plenty of comfortable seating, whereas inside all is funky and modern. You'll find good music, a friendly staff, good drinks, cocktails and a selection of teas, and an atmosphere that invites locals to meet up here for a chat. ✉ *Maršala Tita 96* ☎ *051/718–441.*

SPORTS AND THE OUTDOORS

Mount Učka Nature Park, accessible from virtually any point along the coast, offers the easiest opportunity for active exploring, including mountain-bike and hiking trails up through the forested slopes. **Raspadalica,** in nearby Buzet, can help you explore.

CRES

Brestova is 30 km (18 miles) south of Opatija, then a 20-minute ferry ride.

Twisting down the entire length of the Kvarner Bay on its eastern side is Cres, whose latest claim to fame is that it is the largest of all Croatian islands. For many years, squat neighbor Krk was awarded this distinction, but recent recalculations have rectified a long-standing error. Ferries to Cres has been known as one of the most unspoiled islands in the Adriatic for a long time. More difficult to get to than Krk or Rab, and with a wilder and more rugged topography, Cres is quite frankly a delight. Its natural stretches are punctuated with olive groves and tiny towns and villages that remain authentic for the most part. Even in the capital, Cres Town, you'll find older inhabitants who struggle to speak Croatian, having been brought up under the much stronger Italian influence.

GETTING HERE AND AROUND

Cres take about 20 minutes, embarking from Brestova, which is on the mainland southwest of Opatija, to Porozina; another ferry goes from Valbiska on Krk to Merag, on the east side of Cres.

EXPLORING

Cres Town. Tucked into a well-protected bay, midway down the island, Cres Town is set around a lovely little fishing harbor, small but perfectly formed, with numerous Gothic and Renaissance churches, monasteries, and palaces. For the most part these are in the Old Town, which sits protected by winged Venetian lions atop three 16th-century gates, the only remains of a defensive wall. A small harbor (*Mandrać*), as well as municipal loggia built in the 15th-century, remain the soul of the town.

The **town beach**, at Kovačine campsite, holds a Blue Flag award for cleanliness. To get there, follow the path around the harbor from the main road and keep going for at least 15 minutes along the promenade, where you'll find spots to jump into the water and the odd café or restaurant to keep you fueled. Although the seaside here is man-made, for the most part it somehow doesn't detract too much from the experience. ✉ *Cres Town* ⊕ *www.tzg-cres.hr.*

Fodor's Choice ★   **Lubenice.** One of the most tempting beaches on the island is on the western coast of Cres at the foot of a steep cliff, at the top of which is the tiny village of Lubenice, which offers great views out to sea and up the western coast. This picturesque collection of houses that surround the 15th-century Church of St. Anthony the Hermit has been clinging to its outcrop for around 4,000 years. The hamlet is popular among arty types and hosts exhibitions and music performances in the summer. From the beach below, a short walk through vineyards will bring you to Žanja Cove, which has a blue grotto, a cave at water level that enjoys brilliant blue light as strong sunlight filters through the azure water. ✉ *Lubenice* ⊕ *www.tzg-cres.hr.*

Osor. At the southwestern tip of Cres is the town of Osor, whose strategic position on the channel between the island Cres and Lošinj ensured that wealth flowed into the town from trade ships. A tour of the town makes for a pleasant afternoon. Reflecting its former status, there's even a cathedral, and many important archaeological sites have been discovered in the vicinity. ✉ *Osor* ⊕ *www.tz-malilosinj.hr.*

Osor Archaeological Collection. Housed at city hall, this collection contains booty from throughout the ages, including artifacts from across the Roman empire. ✉ *Gradska vijecnica, Osor* ☎ *051/233–892* ⊕ *www.muzej.losinj.hr* 🎟 *8 Kn* ⊙ *Tues.–Sun. 10–1 and 7–10.*

Valun. Across the bay from Cres, the village of Valun has a nice beach. The town's claim to fame is the "Valun Tablet," a gravestone that is one of the oldest known examples of Glagolitic script. The tablet is now kept in the parish church, right on the waterfront. Get to Valun by car or by taking the wooden boat that sits just outside the Cres Harbor wall; it's easily spotted from the main square. ✉ *Valun.*

WHERE TO EAT

$$$$ ✗**Hibernica.** A nice little terrace right by the bell tower in the heart
MEDITERRANEAN of the stone hilltop village of Lubenice is the perfect location for a
light lunch of *pršut* (prosciutto), cheese, olives, and a glass of local
wine. Lamb is a specialty on Cres, so if you feel like a hearty meal,
order lamb stew gnocchi or lamb liver with polenta. $ *Average main:
80 Kn* ✉ *Lubenice 17, Lubenice* ☎ *051/525–040* ▬ *No credit cards*
🕑 *Closed Oct.–Apr.*

$$$$ ✗**Konoba Bonifačić.** The subtitle on the road signs reads *nonina kuhinja*
MEDITERRANEAN (granny's cooking), and you were a spoiled child indeed if your
grandma turned out dishes of this standard for you. The shady garden in the heart of ancient Osor is a perfect setting in which to enjoy
the typical plates of the Konoba: meat, seafood, pasta, and salads.
$ *Average main: 80 Kn* ✉ *Osor 64, Osor* ☎ *051/237–413* ⊕ *www.
jazon.hr* 🕑 *Closed Nov.–Mar.*

$$$$ ✗**Konoba Bukaleta.** Cres is famous for its lamb, and although the major-
MEDITERRANEAN ity of restaurants have it on the menu, Bukaleta is *the* place for the
Fodor's Choice best on the island. Located in the small village of Loznati, just 10
★ km (6 miles) south of Cres Town, Bukaleta has been run by the same
family for over 30 years. The cozy interior is rustic with a large open
fireplace, a collection of old tools and pots, and its namesake *bukaleta*,
a traditional jug made of clay. The large outdoor terrace can accommodate 100 people. $ *Average main: 100 Kn* ✉ *Loznati 9a, Loznati*
☎ *051/571–606* 🕑 *Closed Oct.–Mar.*

$$$$ ✗**Riva.** The colorful square on the edge of Cres Town harbor is lined
SEAFOOD with many restaurants serving seafood, pasta, and risotto, and Riva is
an excellent choice. Tables edge out onto the flagstones of the square,
meaning the steady stream of strollers through the town will eye your
plate with appreciative glances. A good selection of shellfish is up for
grabs, including the seafood spaghetti, which is wonderful. It's a good
idea to reserve a table in the evening. $ *Average main: 90 Kn* ✉ *Riva
creskih kapetana 13, Cres Town* ☎ *051/571–107* ▬ *No credit cards*
🕑 *Closed Nov.–Mar.*

WHERE TO STAY

Reflecting its splendid, undeveloped nature, Cres offers very few hotels,
though there are plenty of apartments and guest rooms available for
rent on the island.

HomeAway. A good place to start a search for private accommodation is
U.K.-based HomeAway's website, which offers a good choice of holiday
rentals throughout the island. ☎ *+44 208/827–1971 in U.K.* ⊕ *www.
homeaway.co.uk.*

$ 🏨**Hotel Kimen.** Tucked away in a shady pine forest just a stone's throw
HOTEL from the town beach and a 10-minute walk from the center, Kimen's
four stories provide the only hotel accommodation in Cres Town. **Pros:**
enviable position on an attractive cove. **Cons:** smallish rooms. $ *Rooms
from: 920 Kn* ✉ *Melin 1, Cres Town* ☎ *051/573–305* ⊕ *www.hotel-
kimen.com* 🕑 *Closed Nov.–Mar.* ⇆ *126 rooms, 2 suites* ⦿⃓ *Breakfast.*

5

$ ⛶ **Zlatni lav.** A delightful 20-minute drive south from Cres Town, in the
HOTEL   small, west coast resort of Martinšćica, Zlatni lav is a large, new building looking across 100 meters of land to the Adriatic. **Pros:** spectacular views; high-quality fittings in public spaces and bathrooms. **Cons:**
far from any nightlife. $ *Rooms from: 875 Kn* ✉ *Martinšćica 18d,
Martinšćica* ☎ *051/574–020* ⊕ *www.hotel-zlatni-lav.com* ✆ *Closed
Nov.–Mar.* ⇌ *24 rooms, 5 suites* ❍ *Breakfast.*

NIGHTLIFE AND PERFORMING ARTS

The half-dozen or so bars around the main harbor are great for casual
drinking and chatting while you sit outside on balmy evenings listening
to the chinking chains of boats. Head inside for quicker quaffing and
shouting above Croatian high-energy pop music, where you'll share the
space with German yachtsmen. If you're looking for livelier options,
unfortunately you're on entirely the wrong piece of land for that sort
of nonsense.

SPORTS AND THE OUTDOORS

BOATING

Alan Excursion Boat. This wooden sailing ship offers differing routes
around the island's coast. A full-day trip to Valun including a lunch
costs 270 Kn. The ship offers regularly scheduled sailings. ✉ *Cres Harbor* ☎ *051/571–070, 091/257–1070.*

CYCLING

Camp Kovačine. The staff at Camp Kovačine, which is nicely set under
shady pines and right on the main town beach, can rent you bikes and
boats, organize diving trips, beach volleyball, and even paragliding.
✉ *Melin 1, Cres Town* ☎ *051/573–150 sales office, 051/571–423 front
desk* ⊕ *www.camp-kovacine.com* ✆ *Closed mid-Oct.–Mar.*

DIVING

Diving Cres. If you prefer to explore beneath the waves, Diving Cres
can be found in the Camp Kovačine, about a 10-minute walk from the
harbor. A single orientation dive can be tried for €10. ✉ *Melin I, Cres
Town* ☎ *051/571–706* ⊕ *www.diving.de.*

LOŠINJ

Mali Lošinj is 26 km (16 miles) from Cres Town.

As you approach the southern tip of Cres, you'll see the steep slopes
of Osorčica Mountain on nearby Lošinj. Sheltered from poor weather
by the Alps and closer ranges such as the Velebit, the excellent climate
prompted the creation of a health resort here in 1892.

Blink and you might miss the bridge that connects Cres to Lošinj,
unless you happen to arrive when the span is raised to allow a ship
through the narrow channel that splits the two islands. In fact, until
Roman times the two islands were one, connected near Osor. Mother
Nature's inconsiderate arrangement did much to frustrate trade ships;

entire vessels would be hauled across the few feet of land that blocked the route here rather than sail around the southern tip of the archipelago. Eventually, some bright spark decided to cut the present-day channel, opening the shipping lanes. Lošinj is an elongated, low-lying island covered with a pine forest. Viewed from the hills of Cres, the slim green outline of the main island and its surrounding islets, with a backbone of hills in the middle, resembles a long frog splayed out in the water, basking in the sun and contrasting beautifully with the water. Lošinj's past and present are very much connected to the shipping industry. The sea captains who populated the towns of Veli and Mali Lošinj when the island reached its golden age in the 19th century are very much responsible for bringing exotic plant life here from around the world and for building the fine villas that have made this a colorful destination for vacationers, who contribute much more to the island's economy today. The smaller islands that make up the archipelago include Unije, Sušak, and Ilovik—all of which are large enough to provide some type of accommodation—and even smaller islands such as Vele and Male Srakane, Orjule, and Sveti Petar, which can be reached by tourist boats from the resorts on Lošinj.

EXPLORING

Čikat Bay. The road that runs along the Mali Lošinj harbor leads to Čikat Bay, a pine-covered area dotted with impressive Habsburg-era villas and pebbled beach coves. Nearby hotels and campsites, plus good parking, lots of cafés, and ice-cream stands make these beaches popular. There's a gracious promenade along the bay that's perfect for strolling, a windsurfing school for the adventurous, and paddleboat rentals. ⊠ *Čikat Bay.*

Mali Lošinj. With 8,000 inhabitants sheltered around an inlet, Mali Lošinj is the largest island settlement in the Adriatic. In the 19th century Mali and Veli Lošinj experienced a golden age, when many wealthy sea captains lived on the island. Brightening the waterfront, the mansions and villas they constructed contribute greatly to the towns' appeal. A long tradition of tourism means that you'll find a healthy selection to choose from. A number of attractive churches will catch your gaze as you wander around town. Somewhat scruffy and announcing its presence with a tall, square tower that tapers to a spike at the summit, the 15th-century **St. Martin's Church** was the original centerpiece around which the town was built. The cemetery it lords over amalgamates much of the history of the town. If you wish to dig a bit deeper, the **Church of Our Little Lady** hosts many fine examples of religious art. ⊠ *Mali Lošinj, Mali Lošinj* ⊕ *www.tz-malilosinj.hr.*

Miomirisni otočki vrt (*Garden of Fine Scents*). After a few days of dipping your toes in the water and basking in the sun, you might be itching for a diversionary outing. The Miomirisni otočki vrt is a pleasant place to spend the afternoon—rain or shine—sitting on the terrace admiring the sea of lavender on the hilltop. Donkeys, rabbits, and ponies prance around delighting visitors, especially children. A small shop in a wooden building sells organic products like soaps, candles, and of course, lavender oil. ✉ *Bukovica 6, Mali Lošinj* ☎ *098/326–519* ⊕ *www.miomirisni-vrt.hr* 🎟 *Free* ⊙ *July and Aug., 8:30–12:30 and 5:30–8:30; Feb.–June and Sept.–Dec., 8–3.*

Veli Lošinj. The sea captains of Veli Lošinj evidently preferred to escape their working environment during their time off, and thus built their villas away from the waterfront, surrounding themselves with exotic plants brought back from their travels. Archduke Karl Stephen built a winter residence in Veli Lošinj; it's now a sanatorium surrounded by wonderful gardens, again with a range of exotic plants, and an arboretum. It's possible to stay in the sanatorium, even for the healthy. A short walk beyond the main harbor is the little fishing cove of Rovenska. Beyond, there's a pebble beach and some nice restaurants. The breakwater was established by Habsburg archduke Maximilian. ■**TIP→ Walking in the other direction brings you to a great rocky Blue Flag beach, where water-sports equipment can be rented in the Vitality Hotel Punta complex.** ✉ *Veli Lošinj, Veli Lošinj.*

Church of St. Anthony the Hermit. The intimate harbor is the centerpiece of Veli Lošinj, at the entrance to which is the delightful Church of St. Anthony the Hermit, with a separate bell tower in pink and cream stone. Built on the site of a former church in 1774, the church has always had a congregation of seafarers, who have filled it with religious art and altars from spots such as Venice. ✉ *On Veli Lošinj waterfront, Lošinj* ⊙ *July and Aug., daily 9–12:30 and 7–9; other months on request or during mass.*

Kula (*The Tower*). Opposite the harbor, but now hidden by a row of houses, are the battlements of a defensive tower that dates from 1455. The squat construction, known as the Tower, now houses an art gallery staging temporary exhibitions by notable Croatian artists. The permanent exhibition tracing the town's history includes a copy of a Greek statue of Apoksiomen, which was discovered on the seabed in 1999. ✉ *Kaštel BB, Veli Lošinj* ☎ *051/236–594* ⊕ *www.muzej.losinj.hr* 🎟 *10 Kn* ⊙ *Tues.–Sun. 10–1 and 7–10.*

Lošinj Marine Education Centre. A community of around 150 bottlenose dolphins makes its home just off the coast of Lošinj, and the nonprofit Lošinj Marine Education Centre will tell you all about them. Excellent displays and videos take you right into their underwater world, fascinating stuff for kids and adults alike. You may even end up adopting your own dolphin, although you can't take it home with you. For a mere €30 you'll receive a bundle of stuff such as certificates and T-shirts and, of course, that warm fuzzy feeling of doing something good for the world. The best bit is that you'll be able to visit your newfound family member in his or her natural environment every time you swing through town. ✉ *Kaštel 24, Veli Lošinj* ☎ *051/604–666* ⊕ *www. blue-world.org* 🎟 *15 Kn* ⊙ *July and Aug., daily 10–9; May, June, and Sept., weekdays 10–4, Sat. 10–2; Oct.–Apr., weekdays 10–2.*

When It All Gets Too Much

If the pace of life on the major islands is too hectic, knock your engine down to quarter-speed and head out to one of the tiny islands that pepper the seas around the coast of Lošinj. The island of **Unije** is by far the largest, managing to fit in a population of 90, although many of them are summer-only residents. The tiny town of the same name has a handful of restaurants settled around a large pebble bay, although exploring the northern coasts, by foot or by boat, should reveal many private swimming spots. **Ilovik** is the southernmost island of the group. Its nickname, "Island of Flowers," is accurate; oleanders and roses surround almost every home. Watch yachts at close quarters cutting through the channel between Ilovik and the islet of Sveti Petar, on which there was once a convent. The graveyard remains, and burial processions

by fishing boat still take place. Parzine, on the southeastern coast, has a large sandy beach.

If you're from New Jersey, you may have a good chance of being related to one of the 188 people living on **Sušak** since many folk from here have settled in the Garden State. Sušak, flung farther out into the sea than any of the other islands, is a very different beast. First, while the rest of the Kvarner is composed of limestone karst, Sušak consists entirely of sand, so its coast is far gentler both in elevation and indentation. Not wanting to be outdone, the population retains a distinctive character and culture. Their dialect is difficult for other Croats to follow, and it's not uncommon to spot women in full folk costume. The only wheeled transport on the island are wheelbarrows.

WHERE TO EAT

$$$$
MEDITERRANEAN
Fodor's Choice
★
✕**Artatore.** Ten kilometers (6 miles) north of Mali Lošinj, in the small village of Artatore, you'll find the restaurant of the same name. Locals claim the restaurant, which they call *Kod Janje* (Chez Janje), is the best on the entire island. Seafood here is *à l'ordre du jour*; order the scampi in white wine with polenta, grilled fish, or lobster tagilatelle. For meat eaters, the house specialty is lamb from the wood-burning oven with fried crepes filled with fresh cheese and asparagus. End the meal with a delicious chocolate cake with fresh figs. $ *Average main: 100 Kn* ⊠ *Artatore 132, Artatore* ☎ *051/232–932* ⊘ *Closed Nov.–Mar.*

$$$$
SEAFOOD
✕**Baracuda.** Many of the yachts that line the harbor unload their human cargo at this small restaurant, which enjoys a big reputation for fresh-fish dinners. Tuna carpaccio, shark on the grill, and lobster *na buzaru* (cooked with wine) are all great. Carnivores will be pleased with a couple of land-based courses, such as pork medallions with asparagus. The restaurant's terrace is lively and leafy. ■TIP➜ **Baracuda's size, matched with its good name, make an early arrival or a reservation advisable.** $ *Average main: 130 Kn* ⊠ *Priko 31, Mali Lošinj* ☎ *051/233–309* ⊟ *No credit cards* ⊘ *Closed Oct.–Apr.*

$$$$
MEDITERRANEAN
✕**Bora Bar.** Creative Italian dishes like tuna carpaccio with celery root and truffles are what you'll find at this friendly restaurant in the Rovenska bay. The place bills itself as a "tartuferia," and in case your trip

5

to Croatia didn't include a visit to Istria to taste the truffles, this is a good place to try the local delicacy. The dynamic owners—part Croatian, part expat—bring a very local joie de vivre to the place and check up on you to see you're enjoying your meal. [$] *Average main: 130 Kn* ✉ *Rovenska 3, Veli Lošinj* ☎ *051/867–544* 🌐 *www.borabar.net* ⏲ *Closed Oct.–Easter.*

$$$$ SEAFOOD 🍴 **Konoba Lanterna.** From this former lighthouse, which is in a working-class district by the seashore, you'll see (and hear) boats being mended. The tiny stone building has the feel of an old pub inside, and the simple terrace seems far away from the packed quayside tourist restaurants in the main Lošinj square. Tangled nets, small fishing boats, and buoys provide the scenery, with the occasional diving seagull for excitement. At lunchtime you are likely to be joining a crowd of mostly elderly gents from the neighborhood. But who cares that the clientele isn't so glamorous when you can enjoy tasty traditional food such as baked fish, or sausages cooked in wine? [$] *Average main: 100 Kn* ✉ *Sveti Marije 12, Mali Lošinj* ☎ *051/233–625* ⏲ *Closed Nov.–Mar.*

WHERE TO STAY

$$ HOTEL 🏨 **Hotel Apoksiomen.** Named after a Greek statue that was recovered from the seabed near Mali Lošinj in 1999, this renovated villa imposes itself on the seafront close to the main square and offers a good example of how to run a small establishment. **Pros:** seafront location in the heart of town; delicious pastries at the café. **Cons:** rooms don't match the gorgeous hotel exterior. [$] *Rooms from: 1150 Kn* ✉ *Riva Lošinjskih kapetana 1, Mali Lošinj* ☎ *051/520–820* 🌐 *www.vi-hotels.com* 🛏 *24 rooms, 1 suite* ⏲ *Closed Oct.–Apr.* 🍽 *Breakfast.*

$$ HOTEL 🏨 **Hotel Villa Deis.** Set in a wonderful 19th-century villa and surrounded by bougainvilleas, palms, and pines, this hotel has spacious and bright rooms, some of them with a balcony and a sea view. **Pros:** beautiful garden; spacious rooms; friendly staff. **Cons:** 500 yards away from the beach. [$] *Rooms from: 1250 Kn* ✉ *Ambroza Haracica 13, Mali Lošinj* ☎ *051/520–950* 🌐 *www.villadeis.com* 🛏 *11 rooms* ⏲ *Closed Oct. and Nov.* 🍽 *Breakfast.*

$$ HOTEL 🏨 **Vitality Hotel Punta.** The attractive, colored blocks of this newly renovated four-star property in Veli Lošinj line the seashore in a style that complements the island's traditional architecture surprisingly well. **Pros:** terrace restaurant; near both the sea and the town of Veli Lošinj. **Cons:** small pool complex; large hotel complex can feel a bit impersonal. [$] *Rooms from: 1265 Kn* ✉ *Šestavine 17, Veli Lošinj* ☎ *051/662–000* 🌐 *www.losinj-hotels.com* 🛏 *216 rooms, 19 apartments* ⏲ *Closed Oct.–Apr.* 🍽 *Breakfast.*

NIGHTLIFE AND PERFORMING ARTS

Both Mali and Vela Lošinj offer a healthy selection of bars, where you can sit outside on warm evenings, sip drinks, and chat. Those looking for brighter lights had better move on to Krk or the mainland.

SPORTS AND THE OUTDOORS

BIKING

Sanmar Tourist Agency. You can rent bikes for 100 Kn per day in July and August, 70 Kn per day the rest of the year. ✉ *Priko 24, Mali Lošinj* ☎ *051/238–293.*

DIVING AND SAILING

Diver Sport Center. The center offers a full-day guided diving boat cruise with lunch and drinks for about 600 Kn per person. An orientation dive costs a whopping 420 Kn, and you can take a five-day course with certification for about 2,600 Kn. ✉ *Uvala Čikat 13, Mali Lošinj* ☎ *051/233–900* ⊕ *www.diver.hr.*

FLIGHTSEEING

Airport Lošinj. To put it all in perspective, from Airport Lošinj, you can take a panoramic 15-minute flight over the archipelago for about 650 Kn. The airport is open year-round. ✉ *Privlaka 19, Mali Lošinj* ☎ *051/231–666* ⊕ *www.airportmalilosinj.hr.*

KRK

Krk Town is 50 km (31 miles) southeast of Rijeka.

It's no surprise—since Krk is one of the largest Croatian islands, hosts the regional airport, and is connected to the mainland by a bridge—that the robust island is one of the most developed in the country. The dusty edges and agricultural interior get very busy during the high season, and if you visit then you will likely find yourself in traffic jams along the snaking routes between the resort towns. Add the sight of the oil refinery on the mainland near the bridge and the terminal for tankers near Omišalj on the northern coast of the island, and you may think twice about heading here. The sights aren't exactly what you'd call picturesque, but don't be put off so easily. Krk still offers many of the same delights found in the rest of the region: great beaches, interesting history, and pretty old towns. Although other islands may offer a slower pace, Krk compensates by offering more facilities and convenience. With numerous accommodation options and more entertainments, it may very well be the best choice for families that have easily bored children in tow.

EXPLORING

Baška. On the southern end of the island, this town has a great beach as well as the conveniences of civilization. However, this naturally means that you must sometimes fight to find a spot in season. The 2-km (1-mile) beach is fronted by houses (and hotels at the southern end), which are often painted in bright colors and adorned with interesting nooks and stairways, all lending a fun and slightly eccentric air to the town. Cute backstreets behind the houses offer a selection of thirsty cafés and ice-cream shops. ✉ *Baška* ⊕ *www.tz-baska.hr.*

Crkva Sv. Lucije (*Church of St. Lucy*). Driving into Baška, you'll pass through Jurandvor and then find yourself in Baščanska draga. While

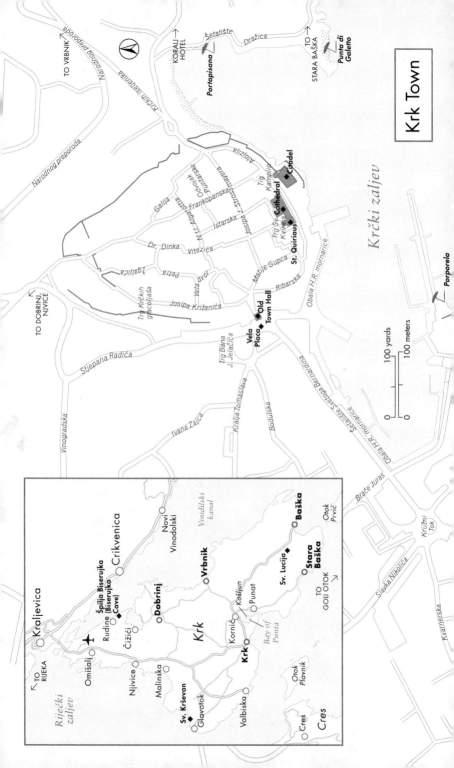

Krk Town

Krčki zaljev

Porporela

TO VRBNIK
Narodnog preporoda
Nacionalnog preporoda
Krčkih iseljenika
KORAU HOTEL
Šetalište
Dražica
Portapisana
TO STARA BAŠKA
Punta di Galetto

eliziou
Trg Kamplin
Citadel
Galija
Puntarska
Odvojak Puntarska
N-I-I-I-L-I
Josipa Jurasa
Frankopanska
Istarska
Trg Sv. Kvirina
Cathedral
St. Quiriaus
Dr. Dinka
Vitezića
Matije Gupca
Petra
Vela dvor
Žgaljica
Trg Krčkih glagoljaša
Josipa Križanića
Ribarska
Obala H.R. mornarice
TO DOBRINJ, NJIVICE
Stjepana Radića
Ivana Zajca
Trg Bana J. Jelačića
Vela Placa
Old Town Hall
Kralja Tomislava
Bodulska
Šetalište Svetoga Bernardina
Obala H.R. mornarice
Braće Juras
Slavka Nikolića
Kvarnerska
Kružni Tok

Vinogradska

100 yards
100 meters
0

Rijecki zaljev
TO RUEKA
Kraljevica
Omišalj
Njivice
Malinska
Sv. Kršévan
Glavotok
Valbiska
Cres
Cres
Otok Plavnik
Krk
Kornić
Bay of Punta
Punat
Košljun
Sv. Lucija
Stara Baška
TO GOLI OTOK
Baška
Otok Prvić
Vrbnik
Dobrinj
Čižići
Rudine
Špilja Biserujka (Biserujka Cave)
Crikvenica
Novi Vinodolski
Vinodilski kanal
Kvarnerska

on this road, take the chance to visit the Church of St. Lucy, which has achieved cultlike status since the discovery of the glagolithic Baška Tablet on its grounds in 1851. ⊠ *Jurandvor* ☎ *051/860–184* ⊕ *www. azjurandvor.com* ✉ *25 Kn* ⊙ *May–Sept., daily 9–9.*

Krk Town. In terms of its importance and the pride of the 4,000 locals, the island's capital could perhaps even be called a city. The old city walls were built around the 1st century BC, and there's an inscription speaking of the dimensions of the fortifications at that time (111 feet long and 20 feet high). The present-day walls, however, date mainly to the Middle Ages. The city walls have four gates.

The seafront has a pleasant green area that takes you past cafés and a fish market. The main square, **Vela Placa,** is just behind the first row of houses. There's a beach underneath the town walls with a lovely view of the town.

The **old town hall** on Vela Placa was built in the 15th century. Its clock shows all 24 hours: daytime on the upper part, nighttime on the lower.

Krk Town has two well-known visual anchors. The first is the imposing **citadel** that sits on Trg Kamplin. Summer concerts, theater performances, and a jazz festival are held on the square and within the citadel walls. The bell tower of **St. Quirinius** is the other, with its angular onion dome typical of Krk.

Here's a useful tip: Streets that are thoroughfares have a straight line of stones running down the middle; those without are most likely dead ends. ⊠ *Krk Town.*

NEED A BREAK?

Stanic. This wonderful gallery is chockablock with works by local artists, as well as lamps, mirrors, and souvenirs. If you're not into shopping, you can simply remain downstairs at the café–bar, or the many other watering holes around Vela Placa. ⊠ *Vela Placa 8, Krk Town* ☎ *051/220–052* ⊕ *www. helena.hr.*

FAMILY **Stara Baška.** If you're looking for a more secluded spot, head to this town that sits just above the beaches that trim a wide cove and peninsula. The road here is a single track through the tiny village, so you may find yourself performing intricate maneuvers in your car should you be unlucky enough to meet the local water truck that keeps the houses supplied. ⊠ *Croatia.*

OFF THE BEATEN PATH

Goli Otok. Like Communist history? Consider a day trip to this uninhabited former Yugoslavian prison island just off the coast of Rab. Goli Otok means "naked island" and was so named for the lack of vegetation and habitable conditions on the island. After Tito broke ranks with Stalin in 1948, the island became infamous as a place where Yugoslav political prisoners sympathetic to the Soviet Communist agenda were imprisoned. Men were incarcerated here while women were taken to nearby Grgur island. The treatment of these prisoners is wholly unknown, as very few prisoners lived to tell of their experiences, but a stone quarry indicates that prisoners were forced to do hard labor quarrying stone. Conditions on Goli Otok were harsh, with blistering temperatures in the summer, and brutal *Bura* winds ripping across the

5

barren island in the winter. Any mention of Goli Otok was strictly forbidden in Yugoslavia until after Tito's death. The prison was completely abandoned in 1989, but prison barracks remain there. You can make a short trip to this legendary gulag by taxi boat with one of the many charter companies in Baška or Punat on Krk Island. Or book a full-day excursion aboard tour boats, which depart from all major coastal towns; expect to pay around 260 Kn for a full-day excursion to Goli Otok with lunch. ✉ *Croatia.*

Špilja Biserujka (*Biserujka Cave*). North of Vrbnik, near Rudine, this cave is only one of many caverns on Krk; however, it's the only one open to the public. The stalactites, stalagmites, and calcine pillars inside are lighted for your pleasure. ✉ *One-half km (mile) from Rudine* ☎ *098/211–630, 051/852–203* 🌐 *www.spilja-biserujka.com.hr* 🎟 *20 Kn* ⏲ *Apr. and Oct., daily 10–3; Sept., daily 10–5; May and June, daily 9–5; July and Aug., daily 9–6.*

Vrbnik. Lovers of majestic views or high-diving should head to this cliff-top town on the northeast coast. Clustered on a hilltop 48 meters above a small harbor, it's a mass of confusing, winding streets. Happily, as in Krk Town, you can simply follow the lines set in the streets. The bumpy terrain means that staircases crop up around most corners. One of the oldest settlements on Krk, Vrbnik may be a little ramshackle, but it's utterly charming. That's certainly what the busloads of tourists seem to think anyway. Vrbnik's fragrance is of the vine; you'll see old barrels lying around everywhere. These might once have been filled with Žlahtina, a great white wine that some claim is the best to come from the Kvarner region. The vineyards are but a short hop from town. ✉ *Croatia.*

WHERE TO EAT

In the summer you'll be sharing tables with busloads of tourists at many of Krk's best restaurants, all of which tend to be outside the capital. However, Krk Town has many restaurants that will serve you perfectly reasonable renditions of less ambitious fare, such as fish, pasta, and pizza.

$$$$ MEDITERRANEAN 🍴 **Nada.** Considered top-notch by many islanders and Croatians who know their stuff, this tiny downstairs konoba provides an authentic Croatian atmosphere. The large restaurant upstairs has much more space, although it's still quite cozy and traditional, and has a terrace with spectacular sea views. This is a great place to try Kvarner specialties. Of course, it's extremely popular, so definitely make a reservation if you choose to wade through the tour-bus crowds. [$] *Average main: 100 Kn* ✉ *Glavača 22, Vrbnik* ☎ *051/857–065* ⏲ *Closed Nov.–Mar.*

$$$$ MEDITERRANEAN 🍴 **Pod Prevolt.** This small, family-run tavern, located in the village of Milohnići, is a bit off the beaten path and only open weekends, but it's well worth a detour. Its name, which means "under the vaulted porch," is inspired by the entrance to the traditional house that houses it. The tiny interior has just six tables and exposed stone walls. For dining alfresco, you can enjoy two outdoor terraces, but if possible, get a place at the tree-shaded terrace across the small street. The homemade, traditional

Krk dishes include octopus with veggies baked in a wood-burning oven, dried octopus macaroni, homemade prosciutto and cheese, grilled and marinated fish, and the like. Desserts are simple but absolutely delicious, like sponge cake with whipped cream, yogurt, and cherries. $ *Average main: 80 Kn* ✉ *Milohnići 21B, Milohnići, Malinska* ☎ *051/862–149* 🍽 *Reservations essential* ⊘ *Closed Mon.–Thurs. No lunch.*

$$$$
SEAFOOD
Fodor's Choice
★

✕ **Rivica.** One of the best-known restaurants in the region, Rivica has a long tradition but lacks any pretense. Try a poached fish fillet with fennel and olives while you sit on the terrace shaded from the sun. If you want your dinner to be extra special, ask the staff to recommend the catch of the day. $ *Average main: 100 Kn* ✉ *Ribarska obala 13, Njivice* ☎ *051/846–101* ⊕ *www.rivica.hr* ⊘ *Closed Nov.–Mar.*

WHERE TO STAY

$$$
HOTEL

🏨 **Atrium Residence Baska.** Located a few steps away from the famed Baška beach, Atrium Residence has spacious, well-appointed rooms and suites, and apartments feature fully equipped kitchens. **Pros:** seafront location; great beach views; spacious rooms. **Cons:** standard rooms have French balconies; parking not right at the hotel, and fees apply; lack of in-hotel facilities (guests can use facilities of the nearby hotels). $ *Rooms from: 1390 Kn* ✉ *Emila Geistlicha 39, Baška* ☎ *051/656–890 reception, 051/656–223 reservations* ⊕ *www.hotelibaska.hr* 🛏 *18 rooms, 46 apartments* ⊘ *Closed Oct.–Mar.* ⦿ *Breakfast.*

$$
HOTEL

🏨 **Hotel Kanajt.** Set in a 16th-century building that served as a bishop's residence and surrounded by palms, pine, and olive trees, this hotel in Punat has rooms that are modern, clean, and comfortable. **Pros:** comfortable rooms, some with a really large terrace; relaxing garden; historical building; easy parking. **Cons:** good beaches are a bit away from the hotel. $ *Rooms from: 980 Kn* ✉ *Kanajt 5, Punat* ☎ *051/654–340* ⊕ *www.kanajt.hr* 🛏 *21 rooms, 1 suite* ⦿ *Breakfast.*

$$$
HOTEL

🏨 **Hotel Pinia Malinska.** Located in the small seaside village of Porat, just next to Malinska, this hotel has a wonderful setting by the sea, surrounded by greenery; the hotel's beach—a nice pebbly beach, though a bit on a small side—is just a few meters down. **Pros:** great location; good on-site restaurant; spacious rooms. **Cons:** hotel beach can get very busy in July and August. $ *Rooms from: 1450 Kn* ✉ *Porat BB, Malinska* ☎ *051/866–333* ⊕ *www.hotel-pinia.hr* 🛏 *42 rooms, 3 suites* ⊘ *Closed Nov.–Mar.* ⦿ *Some meals.*

$$$
HOTEL
FAMILY

🏨 **Valamar Koralj Hotel.** For long days on the beach and all conveniences on tap, this hotel on the edge of Krk Town is a decent choice, though those who plan busy evenings may want to find somewhere closer to the center. **Pros:** great for families with kids in summer; good for couples off-season; peaceful location amid pine trees. **Cons:** small rooms; some rooms without balcony; better rooms quite pricey for the quality. $ *Rooms from: 1370 Kn* ✉ *Ul. Vlade Tomašiča, Krk Town* ☎ *051/655–400 hotel, 052/465–000 reservations* ⊕ *www.valamar.com* 🛏 *170 rooms, 20 apartments* ⊘ *Closed Oct.–Mar.* ⦿ *Some meals.*

5

NIGHTLIFE

Krk Town and Baška are the places to head for relatively low-key drinks in the evening. The center of the capital and the stretch of town above the beach at Baška offer numerous bars with music and tables out under the stars. A firm family favorite, Krk is definitely not the place for cutting-edge nightlife. However, if you really can't live without getting your club fix, there are a couple of large venues offering house DJs. Note that clubs are open only in the summer months.

Cocktail Bar Volsonis. One of the livelier nightspots in Krk Town, this bar has the appropriate, though somewhat mysterious, ruins of a wonderful sacrificial altar to love goddess Venus down in the basement. In fact, all of Volsonis is incorporated into a 2,000-year-old archaeological site that the owners, Maria Elena and Goran, found under the house. Electronic music plays on weekends in the underground Catacombs, or you can chill out with a glass of wine, beer, or coffee in their secret garden. ⊠ *Vela Placa 8, Krk Town* ☎ *051/880–249* ⊕ *www.volsonis.hr.*

Jungle Club. Located in the heart of the old town Krk, this jungle-themed club has two floors and an adjacent jungle cocktail bar—the best party place in Krk. ⊠ *Stjepana Radića BB, Krk Town* ☎ *051/221–503* ⊕ *www.junglekrk.com* ☯ *Closed Oct.–May.*

SPORTS AND THE OUTDOORS

BICYCLING

You can bike around the island for transportation or exercise.

Hotel Punat. The best place to rent a bicycle is at the Hotel Punat. ⊠ *Obala 94, Punat* ☎ *051/854–024.*

DIVING

Divesport. The most interesting sights in Kvarner Bay are wrecks. At Divesport on the Bay of Punta, a full-day diving trip (two dives) sets you back about 420 Kn, plus 150 Kn for equipment rental, if you need it. ⊠ *Dunat, Kornic* ☎ *051/867–303* ⊕ *www.dive-center-krk.com.*

HIKING

There are many marked paths in the area around Baška. For a longer hike, consider visiting the splendid remote villages at Vela and Mala Luka; take this path as part of a group, and be aware that the section of the trail through the canyon may flood if there's rain. For some nice hikes around Baška, consider the path from Baška to Mjesec Hill (5½ km [3 miles]/2 hours). Offering spectacular views over the bay, this easy route passes by St. John's Church, where you can take a breather while you contemplate higher things. The route from Baška to Jurandvor (5 km [3 miles]/2 hours) takes you through the Baška Valley and leaves you with a visit to the Church of St. Lucy, home of the Baška Tablet. The short hike between Baška and Stara Baška will give you a little exercise; a delightful stretch of small, quiet beaches is the reward for a short hike.

Krk Tourist Office. For more hiking information, contact the Krk Tourist Office. ⊠ *Trg Sv. Kvirina 1, Krk Town* ☎ *051/221–359* ⊕ *www.krk.hr.*

WATERSKIING

Cable Krk. Always fancied spraying majestic jets of water across the aquamarine seas, but sorting out a boat and someone to drive just seems too much trouble? Well, the answer lies with Cable Krk, on a calm bay just outside the resort of Punat, between Krk Town and Stara Baška. A large wooden pier with a bar and restaurant to entertain your companions is the gateway to a cableway, which is not much different than a drag-lift at a ski resort. The cable pulls you around a short course, with tuition on hand to help you get your sea legs. One hour costs about 100 Kn. ✉ *Dunat, Kornic* ☎ *091/262–7303* ⊕ *www.wakeboarder.hr* ⊘ *Closed Oct.–mid-Apr.*

DELNICE

5

45 km (28 miles) east of Rijeka.

Delnice, which sits on the road between Rijeka and Zagreb, is itself not much to write home about. However, it makes a good base for exploring the mountains of the Gorski kotar region that sits above Kvarner Bay. This is the place to head for hiking trails that swing away from civilization. It's also a convenient stopover if you're taking the slow route back to Zagreb and your transport home. Take a day or two to swap the brilliant blue domination and ramshackle culture of the coast for the bright green mountains and hearty way of life in Gorski kotar.

WHERE TO EAT

$$$$
EASTERN
EUROPEAN

✕ **Volta.** The small town of Fužine is very close to Delnice and is well known for its pine-bordered lake. *Volta,* which means vaults, tells you exactly what to expect from this vaulted, cellar-style dining room, fronted by a conservatory. The simple, publike interior is a cut above most of the restaurants in the Gorski kotar, which tend to be a little old-fashioned. Try the pasta with wild mushrooms or hunter's stew; the bold may want to try the house specialty: horse meat, made into *čevapčići* (spiced meat rolled into sausage shapes and grilled). A long list of Croatian wines rounds things off. Ⓢ *Average main: 80 Kn* ✉ *Franja Račkog 8, Fužine* ☎ *051/830–030.*

WHERE TO STAY

$
HOTEL

⛰ **Mountain Center Petehovac.** There is no better place to stay in Gorski Kotar than up in the hills, surrounded by thick pine forest, and that's exactly where you'll find Mountain Center Petehovac. **Pros:** location in nature; good and very affordable food; views over the surrounding area. **Cons:** very weak Wi-Fi signal (if any); basic facilities. Ⓢ *Rooms from: 450 Kn* ✉ *Polane 1a, Delnice* ☎ *051/814–901* ⊕ *petehovac.com. hr* ⇥ *20 rooms* ❖*Breakfast.*

SPORTS AND THE OUTDOORS

HIKING

Delnice is a good base for hiking around Risnjak and the Gorski kotar range, which have many marked walking and hiking paths.

RAFTING AND CANOEING

Outdoor Centar Foris. The Kupa River either meanders or rushes down through the mountains toward the coast. You can join expeditions organized by Outdoor Centar Foris, which start out at 9:30 am or 2 pm from a point near Delnice and tackle the rough or the smooth sections of the river. The company also runs canyoning trips, in case you want to omit the boat portion of the exercise. ⊠ *Zrinska 13, Brod na Kupi, Delnice* ☎ *051/837–139, 097/723–8464* ⊕ *www.foris.hr* ⊘ *Closed Nov.–Mar.*

RAB

Fodor'sChoice   *93 km (58 miles) south of Rijeka.*
★
Rab presents an utterly schizophrenic landscape. When you drive southward, down the Magistrala, you see that the island resembles the humped back of a diving sea monster. Once you've mounted this beast, via a short ferry ride from Jablanac to Mišnjak, you travel along the center of its back, which is almost entirely bald to the north, letting all its hair hang out to the south. The high northern coast, which bears the brunt of the northern Bora winds, is dry, rocky, and barren. Crouching below this crusty ledge, the southern half of the island could hardly differ more, and has possibly the lushest terrain found on any Croatian island. Low, green hills dip into the seas, while the ancient Dundo forest grows so voraciously that it's almost impossible to walk in.

EXPLORING

Sitting on a narrow peninsula halfway up the island's southern coast, the compact, well-preserved medieval village is best known for its distinctive skyline of four elegant bell towers, and its many churches. Author Rebecca West, who traveled through Yugoslavia in the 1930s, called Rab Town "one of the most beautiful cities of the world" in her masterpiece, *Black Lamb and Grey Falcon*. Closed to traffic, the narrow cobbled streets of the Old Town, which are lined with Romanesque churches and patrician palaces, can be explored in an hour's leisurely stroll. The urban layout is simple: three longitudinal streets run parallel to the waterfront promenade and are linked together by steep passages traversing the hillside. The lower street is Donja ulica, the middle street Srednja ulica, and the upper street Gornja ulica.

The oldest part of Rab Town is **Kaldanac,** the very tip of the narrow peninsula that juts into the sea. From here the ancient city grew in the 15th century to include Varoš, farther north, and later was widened and fortified by walls during a brief Venetian rule.

Komrčar Park. On the edge of town, the green expanse of Komrčar Park, laid out in the 19th century, offers avenues lined with pine trees for

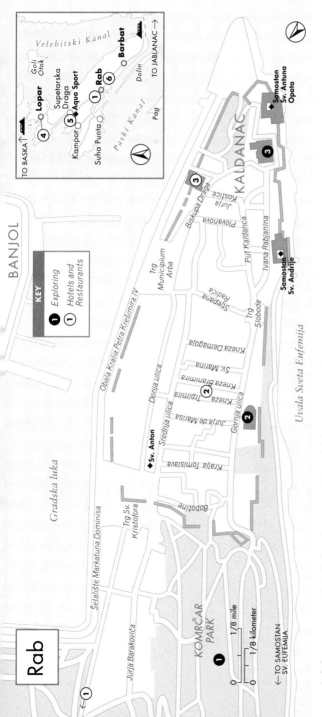

Rab

BANJOL

Gradska luka

Velebitski Kanal

Goli Otok

Lopar

Supetarska Draga

Aqua Sport

Rab

Barbat

Kampor

Suha Punta

Dolin

KALDANAC

TO JABLANAC →

Pag

Paški Kanal

TO BAŠKA ↑

KEY

● Exploring

① Hotels and Restaurants

Šetalište Markantuna Dominisa

Trg Sv. Kristofora

Junja Barakovića

KOMRČAR PARK

← TO SAMOSTAN SV. EUFEMIJA

0   1/8 mile
0   1/8 kilometer

Obala Kralja Petra Krešimira IV

Donja ulica

Srednja ulica

◆ Sv. Anton

Kralja Tomislava

Bobotine

Jurja de Marisa

Kneza Tipimira

Kneza Branimira

Sv. Marina

Gornja ulica

Kneza Demagoja

Stjepana Radića

Trg Slobode

Trg Municipium Arba

Biskupa Draga

Jurja Košlice

Plovanova

Put Kaldanca

Ivana Rabljanina

Samostan Sv. Antuna Opata ◆

③

③

Samostan Sv. Andrije ◆

Uvala Sveta Eufemija

Exploring ▶

Komrčar Park **1**
Sveta Marija Velika **3**
Veli Zvonik **2**

Restaurants ▶

Konoba Rab **2**
Marco Polo **6**
Restaurant More **5**

Hotels ▶

Arbiana Hotel **3**
Hotel Imperial **1**
Tourist Resort San Marino .. **4**

gentle strolling and access down to the sea. Although the Old Town and its immediate surroundings are Rab's chief treasures, the city is also a gateway to the great stretches of beach that rim the towns of Kampor, Suha Punta, Lopar, and neighboring islands. ✉ *Northwest of Old Town, just behind seafront promenade, Obala Kralja Petra Krešimira IV, Rab.*

Sveta Marija Velika (*Cathedral of St. Mary*). The Romanesque Sveta Marija Velika, built in the 12th century and consecrated by the pope in 1177, is the biggest church in Rab Town, and was built on the site of Roman ruins. ✉ *Ivana Rabljanina, Rab* 🌐 *www.tzg-rab.hr* 🕒 *June–Sept., daily 9–1 and 7–9; Oct.–May, on request.*

Veli Zvonik (*Great Bell Tower*). The tallest and most beautiful of Rab's campaniles, the freestanding Veli Zvonik forms part of the former cathedral complex and dominates the southwest side of the peninsula. Built in the 12th century, it stands 85 feet high. **■ TIP→ A climb to the top offers breathtaking views over the town and sea.** ✉ *Gornja ulica, Rab Town* 🎟 *10 Kn* 🕒 *June–Sept., daily 9–1 and 7–9; Oct.–May, by request through Town Hall.*

NEED A BREAK?

Paradiso Gallery. Tucked behind the town lodge, this café has a wonderful atrium brimming with stone columns and palms; it's ideal for a quick lunch or just a seat and coffee. Alternatively, peruse the gallery, or stock up on local wine. ✉ ***Stjepana Radića 2, Rab Town*** ☎ ***051/771–109*** 🌐 ***apartments-paradiso-rab.hr*** 🕒 ***Closed Nov.–Apr.***

WHERE TO EAT

$$$$ MEDITERRANEAN

🍴 **Konoba Rab.** Tucked away in a narrow side street between Srednja ulica and Gornja ulica in Rab Town, this konoba is warm and inviting, with exposed-stone walls and rustic furniture. Grilled fish and meat are the house specialties, along with a good choice of pastas and risottos. [$] *Average main: 130 Kn* ✉ *Kneza Branimira 3, Rab Town* ☎ *051/725–666* 🕒 *Closed Oct.–Apr. No lunch Sun.*

$$$$ MEDITERRANEAN

🍴 **Marco Polo.** With its superb food and convenient location right next to the large campsite Padova III, this restaurant draws crowds in to its large outdoor terrace and small but elegant interior. Veggies are home-grown, seafood is local and always fresh, and meat dishes like Viennese schnitzel or beef tenderloin never disappoint. Service is friendly and attentive. [$] *Average main: 100 Kn* ✉ *Banjol 468, Banjol, Rab Town* ☎ *051/725–846* 🌐 *www.marcopolo-rab.com* 🕒 *Closed Nov.–Mar.*

$$$$ MEDITERRANEAN

🍴 **Restaurant More.** This family-owned restaurant has an amazing location with seating right on the quay. The fish served here is caught by the owner, so the phrase "catch of the day" really means something. The upstairs terrace is more formal, and the slightly old-fashioned setting showcases the fantastic sea views and seafood specialties like lobster with pasta and truffles or fresh tuna carpaccio. Chill out during the day at the downstairs terrace with a drink and simple dishes like grilled meat, pasta, and pizza. [$] *Average main: 80 Kn* ✉ *Supetarska Draga 321, Supertarska Draga* ☎ *051/776–202* 🌐 *more-rab.com* 🕒 *Closed Oct.–Apr.*

WHERE TO STAY

You'll see plenty of private rooms advertised on the Internet, as well as signs on the side of the road. If you want to seek out private accommodations, perhaps the best place to start is the website of the tourist office in the closest main town. Costs vary wildly, but private rooms are almost always a cheaper alternative to hotels.

$$ HOTEL **Arbiana Hotel.** It's hard to imagine a more romantic setting than this harborside inn in a perfectly restored medieval villa with balconies overlooking Rab marina and the hills of Barbat in the distance. **Pros:** boutique-hotel feel; personal service. **Cons:** no pool or beach access; not all rooms have balconies. [$] *Rooms from: 1260 Kn* ✉ *Obala Kralja Petra Kresimira IV br.12, Rab* ☎ *051/725–563* 🌐 *www.arbianahotel.com* 🛏 *25 rooms, 3 suites* 🕒 *Closed Nov.–Mar.* 🍴 *Breakfast.*

$$ HOTEL **Hotel Imperial.** On the edge of the Old Town amid the greenery of Komrčar Park, this peaceful 1930s-era resort hotel has excellent sports facilities and a beach. **Pros:** good location in a wooded park near Rab Town. **Cons:** a little run-down; dated furnishings. [$] *Rooms from: 1110 Kn* ✉ *Palit, Rab Town* ☎ *051/724–522* 🌐 *www.imperialrab.com* 🛏 *136 rooms, 4 suites* 🕒 *Closed Nov.–Mar.* 🍴 *Multiple meal plans.*

$ HOTEL FAMILY **Tourist Resort San Marino.** A complex of five hotels stretches across the peninsula at this family-friendly resort wrapping around the gentle Paradise Beach. **Pros:** access to Paradise Beach couldn't be better; good value. **Cons:** sprawling complex lacks personality; rooms are on the small side and lack luxuries. [$] *Rooms from: 550 Kn* ✉ *Lopar 408, Lopar* ☎ *051/775–144* 🌐 *www.imperialrab.com* 🛏 *430 rooms, 60 suites* 🕒 *Closed Nov.–Apr.* 🍴 *Breakfast.*

NIGHTLIFE

For such a small town, Rab has a surprisingly lively nightlife, although it's certainly not extreme by any stretch of the imagination. Trg Municipium Arbe on the waterfront is lined with bars and can get noisy as the night progresses; they're mostly anchored by troops of waiters with some attitude as well as a habit of setting drinks on fire when they're not throwing them around. All-night house parties are found at Santos Beach Club on Puderica Beach, 2 km (1 mile) from Barbat toward the ferry terminal. Buses to Puderica leave Rab Town every hour from 10 am onward.

Café Bar Amadeus. This hilariously tiny bar is short on luxury but with no lack of entertainment, stuffed as it is with local fishermen pogoing to 1980s Croatian hard rock. ✉ *Biskupa Draga 25, Rab Town* ☎ *051/724–485.*

San Antonio. Those after a little glitz to show off their suntan can head to the center of Rab Town nightlife at San Antonio, open until 4 am. ✉ *Trg Municipium Arba 4, Rab Town* ☎ *051/724–145* 🌐 *www.sanantonio-club.com.*

5

SPORTS AND THE OUTDOORS

BOATING

Travel Agency Kristofor. This agency can satisfy most of your wishes, including motorboat rentals so you can explore the coast and use it as your own private diving board. Prices start at about 300 Kn per day, depending on the power. ✉ *Poslovni centar, Mali Palit, Rab Town* ☎ *051/725–543* ⊕ *www.kristofor-travel.com.*

DIVING

Aqua Sport. A single dive costs about 300 Kn, a full diving course 2,440 Kn. In addition, you can dive at various sites from their boat, and your nondiving companions are welcome to go along for the ride. ✉ *Supetarska Draga 331, Supetarska Draga* ☎ *051/776–145* ⊕ *www. aquasport.hr.*

ZADAR AND NORTHERN DALMATIA

By Sierra and Ivan Verunica

Safely protected from the northern Adriatic shore and continental Croatia by the imposing Velebit Mountain, northern Dalmatia offers a whole new set of aesthetic and cultural values. The islands get smaller and more abundant and the architecture, which varies between Roman, Venetian, socialist and modern influences, still carries the elegance of locally quarried limestone. Make Zadar, a fast-growing historical city, the focal point of your sojourn, but do not overlook Nin and the islands, especially Kornati and Telašćica. Admirers of intact, rough nature will revel in the Paklenica National Park.

Where exactly does Northern Dalmatia begin? Zadar may be the region's cultural and urban capital—it is, after all, the first sizeable city you encounter in Dalmatia on your way south from Zagreb or Rijeka—but it is not where the region begins, either culturally or geographically. Look instead to the southern reaches of Velebit Mountain, where that coastal range gives way to the flat, sandy coastline of Nin and environs. Practically speaking, though, you enter Dalmatia proper when you cross the long, bright-red span of the Maslenica Bridge going south on the route from Zagreb to Zadar.

Though it's easy enough to drive on straight to Zadar, you won't regret stopping for a visit in Nin. While today it's an unassuming little town with well-preserved 17th-century architecture, more than 1,000 years ago—and for centuries afterward—it was one of the most important Croatian towns of all.

Much of the region is not on the mainland at all but rather comprises the Zadar archipelago, including Pag Island, and, farther south, the Adriatic's largest archipelago, Kornati National Park. Farther inland, only miles from the coast, is a sweeping expanse of countryside still visibly recovering from the Yugoslav war of the 1990s, where tourists rarely tread. Benkovac, the region's center, is home to an imposing 16th-century fort; nearby are the massive ruins of the ancient city of Asseria. Zadar itself, with its mix of Roman, Venetian, communist-era, and modern architecture, has a bustling and beautiful historic center and is also the main point of access by ferry to the islands, which include the beautiful Telašćica Nature Park.

ORIENTATION AND PLANNING

GETTING ORIENTED

Getting to Zadar is easiest by car. Be it on the A1 highway from Zagreb, down a winding coastal road from Rijeka or from nearby Split, the roads are good and there are signs aplenty. If you are skipping the Kvarner region, Croatian Airlines operates flights from Pula as well as from Zagreb, and the Zadar Int'l is also serviced from England and Germany during the summer months.

WHEN TO GO

If you don't mind crowds, midsummer is a good time to visit Northern Dalmatia—when the Adriatic is at its optimal temperature for beach-going, and you can also delight in the varied music, dance, and drama of the Zadar Summer Theatre (late June to early August), the Full Moon Festival (late July) in and around Zadar, the Pag Carnival (late July or early August), and Sali's annual Saljske užance, which features raucous, horn-blown "donkey music" and donkey races (early August). However, if you don't mind missing out on midsummer culture and crowds, late spring to early autumn is preferable—when you can relax on relatively quiet beaches and enjoy discounts of up to 20% on accommodations relative to high season prices.

GETTING HERE AND AROUND

If you're driving or bussing it from the north, you can stop for an excursion to Pag Island and at Paklenica National Park before arriving in Zadar. The pretty little town of Nin, meanwhile, is just a half-hour north of Zadar and most easily done as a day trip (or even a half-day trip). Though many daily ferries can take you to the Zadar archipelago, Sali (two hours from Zadar by ferry) is a good place to base yourself for a night or two if you want to explore the outer reaches and have the best access to Telaščica Nature Park. A drive or bus trip to Murter will get you within a short boat ride of the spectacular Kornati National Park.

AIR TRAVEL

Zadar's airport is in Zemunik Donji, 9 km (5½ miles) southeast of the city. Croatia Airlines, which offers service between Zadar and Zagreb as well as Paris and other European cities, runs buses (20 Kn one-way) between the airport, the city bus station, and the harborside near the ferry port on the Old Town's peninsula.

Contact Croatian Airlines ✉ *Zadar Airport, Zadar* ☎ *023/250–101* ⊕ *www. croatiaairlines.com.*

BOAT AND FERRY TRAVEL

Jadrolinija's local ferries (*trajektne linije*) and passenger boats (*brodske linije*) run daily routes that connect Zadar not only with the surrounding islands but also with Rijeka. Do check also with Miatours, which offers alternative service to the islands and also between Zadar and Ancona, Italy. Twice a day most days of the week there is ferry service between Pula and Zadar; at eight hours and at a cost of only 123 Kn it's a decent alternative to the bus, though a downside is that the ferry from Pula arrives in Zadar at midnight. The offices are by the Harbor Gate in the city walls, across from the ferry port.

GREAT ITINERARIES

Unless you stop at Paklenica National Park, head straight for Zadar and work outward from there, depending on how much time you have. It's easier to take day trips to visit the closer parts of the Zadar archipelago, as well as Nin. To see the farther reaches of the archipelago, stay over in Sali. Keep Benkovac and environs in mind if you have some time to spare and might appreciate a look at the relatively tourist-free interior, including the ruins of the ancient city of Asseria.

IF YOU HAVE 3 DAYS

Plan on two nights in **Zadar** with excursions to the city of **Nin** and also to Ugljan Island, which is in the **Zadar archipelago**. For your final day and night, go either to **Sali** to see **Telaščica Nature Park** or,

if you're hankering for mountains, spend one night in Starigrad and see **Paklevica National Park** (unless you've already stopped there on the way south or might do so on your return north).

IF YOU HAVE 5 DAYS

Spend your first three days as outlined in the three-day itinerary, but spend the third night in Zadar. Then spend one night in Starigrad or environs to devote some quality time to Paklevica National Park, and do a loop that includes a night on Pag Island, too.

IF YOU HAVE 7 DAYS

Follow the itinerary above, adding a trip to **Murter** and perhaps inland, to Benkovac or, if you have a car, to the nearby ruins of the ancient city of Asseria.

Both Jadrolinija and Miatours run ferry routes from the port of Zadar, just outside the city walls on the western side of the Old Town, to Sali. The trip, which takes about two hours and costs from 30 Kn (Miatours) to 38 Kn (Jadrolinija), takes you initially south in the Zadarski kanal, then through a narrow strait between Ugljan and Pašman islands before proceeding to the island of Dugi Otok, where you stop briefly in Zaglav before heading on to Sali. If you don't want to base yourself in Murter, you can take a cruise straight from the Borik marina just outside Zadar all the way to Kornati National Park, that almost mythical archipelago even farther south. The *Blue Lagoon,* which holds 90 passengers, will take you on a full-day journey (8 am to 6 pm) to the national park, including stops on the islands of Mana and Kornat.

Contacts Kornat Exursions. This Zadar-based company runs day trips by boat from Zadar to the islands of Kornati National Park. Their boat, *Plava Laguna* (which means Blue Lagoon) departs from Borik marina daily through summer at 8 am, returning at 6 pm for 300 Kn, with breakfast and lunch included. ■TIP→ **The company is known by several names: Kornat Excursions, Plava Laguna, and Blue Lagune.** ⊠ *Borik marina, Obala kneza Domagoja 1, Borik, Zadar* ☎ *023/334–468* ⊕ *www.kornat-excursions.hr.* **Jadrolinija** ⊠ *Liburnska obala 7, Zadar* ☎ *023/254–800* ⊕ *www.jadrolinija.hr.*

Northern Dalmatia

BUS TRAVEL

Though sometimes crowded in midsummer, Zadar's bus station will almost certainly figure prominently in your travel plans unless you're driving or flying directly here. The trip to or from Zagreb takes around 4½ hours, for around 105 Kn. Timetables are available at the station. The luggage room (*garderobe*) is open from 6 am to 10 pm, and costs 1.20 Kn per hour.

Getting to Nin from Zadar is easy by bus. The half-hour trip follows the coastal road north; the fare is 11 Kn one-way, with buses running daily out of Zadar's station every 45 minutes or so. By bus, getting to Murter—to its tiny main square, Trg Rudina, which is where you're dropped off and get back on—from Zadar is certainly doable, if a bit complicated. You can transfer either at Šibenik or at Vodice; although the former option looks longer on the map, given the crowded confusion at Vodice's small station, Šibenik—around 12 buses daily from Zadar—may be a less trying experience (and a surer way of getting a seat) even if it might take a bit longer; about 9 buses go on from Sibenik to Murter (via Vodice). Travel time via Šibenik is 2½ hours or more (i.e., 90 minutes from Zadar to Šibenik, up to an hour of waiting time, then another 45 minutes to Murter via Vodice). The total cost: around 70 Kn via Šibenik and around 50 Kn if you go straight to Vodice (travel time is less than two hours, and an even harder-to-predict wait time, because the bus from Šibenik might be contending with heavy traffic). Numerous buses ply the one-hour route daily between Zadar and Starigrad for access to Paklenica National Park. The one-way cost to or from Starigrad—via the Zadar–Rijeka bus—is between 25 Kn and 34 Kn, depending on the company. There are two stops in Starigrad; the national park information office is between the two, and the access road to the park is near the first stop (if you're coming from Zadar).

Around half a dozen buses daily ply the one-hour route from Zadar to Pag Town, on Pag Island (35 Kn).

Last but not least, the easiest way to get either from the bus station to Zadar's town center, or from the center to the Borik complex (with its beaches, hotels, and restaurants) on the northern outskirts, is by any of several, user-friendly local buses. You can buy tickets at news kiosks for 6.50 Kn (single ride) or for 8 Kn from the driver; be sure to validate your ticket on boarding by inserting it into the stamping device.

Contact **Zadar Bus Station** ✉ *Ante Starčevića 1, Zadar* ☎ *023/319-057.*

CAR TRAVEL

With the completion of the Mala Kapela tunnel in 2005, the A1 motorway between Zagreb and Dalmatia has become a complete, uninterrupted whole. Zadar is the first major stop on the highway, which proceeds south toward Split. Barring traffic congestion, especially on weekends, the trip between Zagreb and Zadar is doable in 2½ hours. That said, you can also easily get to Zadar by bus, whether from Zagreb, Rijeka, or Split, and rent a car there if necessary. As the Zadar bus station can be a chaotic place at times, especially in midsummer, you might want to rent a car for some excursions—to Murter, for example, which otherwise involves a somewhat complicated, time-consuming trip to or toward Šibenik with a transfer. But you'll be just fine without a car in and immediately around Zadar, as bus service is both good and affordable. How to get to Pag Island? By the Pag Bridge route, Pag Town (at the island's center) is within a one-hour drive from Zadar. One good option is to take two nights and take in Paklenica National Park, then drive another 25 minutes or so north along the coastal road toward Rab Island and Rijeka, and take the ferry from the village of Prizna—roughly midway between Rijeka and Zadar, just south of Rab Island—to Žigljen, in the north of the island (14 Kn per person, 89 Kn for a car); or do the same in reverse.

Contacts **Avis** ✉ *Zadar Airport, Zemunik, Zadar* ☎ *023/205–862* ⊕ *www.avis. com.* **Hertz** ✉ *Zadar Airport, Zemunik, Zadar* ☎ *023/348–400* ⊕ *www.hertz.hr.*

TRAIN TRAVEL

It's possible to travel between Zadar and Zagreb by train. Five trains run daily from Zadar to Knin (in just over two hours with almost 20 stops in between), and from Knin you can transfer within an hour to a train that gets you to Zagreb in roughly four hours—that's around seven hours in all from Zadar to Zagreb, for about 130 Kn one way. Unless you want to see some relatively war-wearied parts of the interior, though, you'll do well to simply hop aboard one of the many daily Zagreb-bound buses at Zadar's bus station, which get you to the capital in less time and for less money (around 100 Kn). Trains also run between Knin and Split, and service and travel times are improving yearly on all these routes.

RESTAURANTS

Fresh seafood is the cuisine of choice in Northern Dalmatia, as it is elsewhere on Croatia's coast. Beyond standard coastal fare, look for Dalmatian specialties including Pag Island lamb and Paški sir (Pag cheese); prosciutto and *šokol* (smoked pork neck) from Posedarjedried; and sheep's cheese and peppery meat dishes from inner Dalmatia. And of course, there's Zadar's famous Maraschino liqueur—compliments of the area's uniquely zesty cherry and the Maraška company—whose facility is just across the town's pedestrian bridge and whose brand name graces the bottles of the best maraschino.

HOTELS

As elsewhere along practically every populated area of the Croatian coast, package-hotel resorts are easy to find, in particular in the Borik complex on the northern outskirts of Zadar. Top-notch pensions and intimate, elegant small hotels are in somewhat short supply, though a whole host of private rooms and apartments can be found, often for half the price of larger, more established accommodations, either through the local tourist-information office or through private travel agencies. And, as is the practice in other parts of Croatia, short stays (i.e., fewer than three days) often mean a surcharge of around 20%. *Hotel reviews have been shortened. For full information, visit Fodors.com.*

WHAT IT COSTS IN EUROS (€) AND CROATIAN KUNA (KN)				
	$	$$	$$$	$$$$
Restaurants	under 35 Kn	35 Kn–60 Kn	61 Kn–80 Kn	over 80 Kn
	under €5	€5–€8	€9–€10	over €10
Hotels	under 925 Kn	925 Kn–1,300 Kn	1,301 Kn–1,650 Kn	over 1,650 Kn
	under €121	€121–€170	€171–€216	over €216

Restaurant prices are the average cost of a main course at dinner or, if dinner is not served, at lunch. Hotel prices are the lowest cost of a standard double room in high season.

VISITOR INFORMATION

If there's no English speaker at the office you happen to contact, try the Zadar County Tourist Information office or the city of Zadar's corresponding office.

Contacts Zadar Tourist Information ✉ *Mihe Klaića, 2 yards from Narodni trg, Zadar* ☎ *023/316–166* ⊕ *www.visitzadar.net.*

TOP REASONS TO GO

■ From the Crkva sv. Donata, Croatia's most monumental surviving early Byzantine church, to Katedrala sv. Stošije, Dalmatia's largest basilica, ecclesiastical marvels abound.

■ The barren but beautiful Kornati Islands, Telaščica Nature Park, and the Zadar archipelago are ripe for exploration, as is Pag Island to the north.

■ Comprising 35 pipes under the quay, Zadar's incredible Sea Organ

yields a never-ending concert that delights listeners with the music of the sea itself.

■ With its extraordinary karst features towering over the sea at the southern end of the Velebit range, Paklenica National Park is easily accessible from Zadar.

■ North of Zadar—around Nin and, farther afield, on Pag Island—are some of Croatia's sandiest, and shallowest, beaches.

ZADAR

347 km (217 miles) southwest of Zagreb.

Dalmatia's capital for more than 1,000 years, Zadar is all too often passed over by travelers on their way to Split or Dubrovnik. What they miss out on is a city of more than 73,000 that is remarkably lovely and lively despite—and, in some measure, because of—its tumultuous history. The Old Town, separated from the rest of the city on a peninsula some 4 km (2½ miles) long and just 1,640 feet wide, is bustling and beautiful: the marble pedestrian streets are replete with Roman ruins, medieval churches, palaces, museums, archives, and libraries. Parts of the new town are comparatively dreary, a testament to what a world war followed by decades of communism, not to mention a civil war, can do to the architecture of a city that is 3,000 years old.

A settlement had already existed on the site of the present-day city for some 2,000 years when Rome finally conquered Zadar in the 1st century BC; the foundations of the forum can be seen today. Before the Romans came the Liburnians had made it a key center for trade with the Greeks and Romans for 800 years. In the 3rd century BC the Romans began to seriously pester the Liburnians, but required two centuries to bring the area under their control. During the Byzantine era, Zadar became the capital of Dalmatia, and this period saw the construction of its most famous church, the 9th-century St. Donat's Basilica. It remained the region's foremost city through the ensuing centuries. The city then experienced successive onslaughts and occupations—both long and short—by the Osogoths, the Croatian-Hungarian kings, the Venetians, the Turks, the Habsburgs, the French, the Habsburgs again, and finally the Italians before becoming part of Yugoslavia and, in 1991, the independent republic of Croatia.

Zadar was for centuries an Italian-speaking city, and Italian is still spoken widely, especially by older people. Indeed, it was ceded to Italy in 1921 under the Treaty of Rapallo (and reverted to its Italian name of Zara). However its occupation by the Germans from 1943 led to intense bombing by the Allies during World War II, which left most of the city in ruins. Zadar became part of Tito's Yugoslavia in 1947, prompting many Italian residents to leave. Zadar's most recent ravages occurred during a three-month siege by Serb forces and months more of bombardment during the Croatian-Serbian war between 1991 and 1995. But you'd be hard-pressed to find outward signs of this today in what is a city to behold.

GETTING HERE AND AROUND

Zadar is the only sizable city in Northern Dalmatia and quite likely your first destination in the area. It has an international airport that connects it to Europe during the summer season, mostly via budget airlines, and Zagreb and Pula throughout. You can also drive in via the A1 highway or the Adriatic "magistrala" road, but a car will be of little use in the city itself where narrow alleys are best explored on foot. There are ample regular bus lines from Zagreb, Rijeka and Split, but be advised that the bus station is not walking distance from the old city. Zadar's port is very busy with lines serving local islands and a daily international line to Ancona, Italy.

TOURS

Secret Dalmatia. Not the biggest, but certainly one of the best organized companies, Secret Dalmatia specializes in showing you parts of Dalmatia that might not be on the tourist map, but still tickle your fancy for whichever individual reason. The owner Alan is very outgoing and reliable and his team have Dalmatia well covered—from hidden little wineries to sailboats via culture. Young and professional, excellent English. ✉ *Turanj 426* ☎ *091/567–1604* ⊕ *www.secretdalmatia.com/.*

EXPLORING

There are helpful interpretive signs in English all around the Old Town, so you certainly won't feel lost when trying to make sense of the wide variety of architectural sites you might otherwise pass by with only a cursory look.

TOP ATTRACTIONS

Fodor's Choice **Crkva sv. Donata** (*St. Donatus Church*). Zadar's star attraction, this huge, ★ cylindrical structure is the most monumental early Byzantine church in Croatia. Originally called Church of the Holy Trinity, and probably inspired by plans set forth in a book by the Byzantine emperor Constantine Porphyrogenet, *On Ruling the Empire,* centuries later it was rededicated to St. Donatus, who was bishop here from 801 to 814. Legend has it that Donatus, an Irishman, was the one who had it built, using stone from the adjacent Forum. The stark, round interior features a circular center surrounded by an annular passageway; a sanctuary consisting of three apses attached to the lofty mantle of the church walls, set off from the center by two columns; and a gallery reached by a circular stairway. Although the church no longer hosts services, its fine acoustics make it a regular concert venue. During the off-season (November to March), when the church is closed, someone at the Archaeological Museum next door may have a key to let you in.

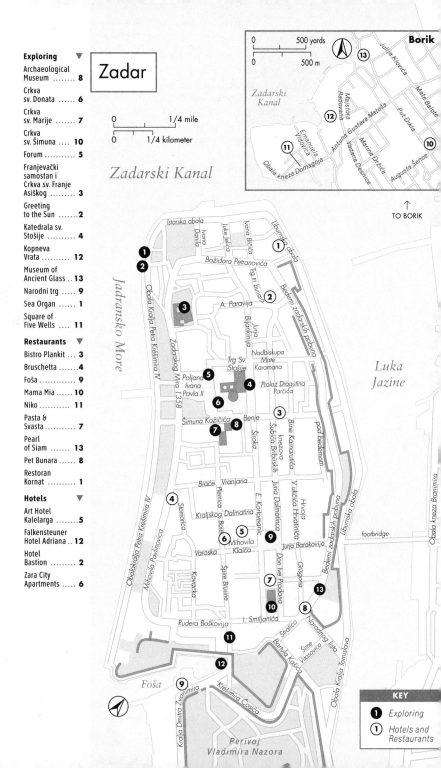

Zadar

Exploring ▼

Archaeological Museum 8

Crkva sv. Donata 6

Crkva sv. Marije 7

Crkva sv. Šimuna 10

Forum 5

Franjevački samostan i Crkva sv. Franje Asiškog 3

Greeting to the Sun 2

Katedrala sv. Stošije 4

Kopneva Vrata 12

Museum of Ancient Glass .. 13

Narodni trg 9

Sea Organ 1

Square of Five Wells 11

Restaurants ▼

Bistro Plankit ... 3

Bruschetta 4

Foša 9

Mama Mia 10

Niko 11

Pasta & Svasta 7

Pearl of Siam 13

Pet Bunara 8

Restoran Kornat 1

Hotels ▼

Art Hotel Kalelarga 5

Falkensteuner Hotel Adriana .. 12

Hotel Bastion 2

Zara City Apartments 6

Borik

Zadarski Kanal

↑ TO BORIK

Zadarski Kanal

Jadransko More

Luka Jazine

footbridge

Foša

Perivoj Vladimira Nazora

KEY

1 Exploring

1 Hotels and Restaurants

✉ *Šimuna Kožičića Benje* ☎ *023/316–166* ⊕ *www.amzd.hr* ⌨ *10 Kn* ⊙ *Apr.–Sept., 9–2 and 5–9; Oct., 9–2.*

Franjevački samostan i Crkva sv. Franje Asiškog (*St. Francis Church & Franciscan Monastery*). Dalmatia's oldest Gothic church, consecrated in 1280, is a stellar example of a so-called Gothic monastic church, characterized by a single nave with a raised shrine. Although the church underwent extensive reconstruction in the 18th century, behind the main altar is a shrine dating to 1672; inside the shrine you can see choir stalls in the floral Gothic style that date to 1394. In 1358 a peace treaty was signed in this very sacristy under which the Venetian Republic ended centuries of attack and handed Zadar over to the protection of the Croat-Hungarian kingdom. ■ **TIP→ You can walk around the atmospheric inner courtyard for free, by the way, but you must pay a fee to enter the church itself.** From mid-October through March or April, the church may keep irregular hours. ✉ *Samostan sv. Franje, Trg sv. Frane 1* ☎ *023/250–468* ⊕ *www.svetifrane.org* ⌨ *15 Kn* ⊙ *Daily 9–6.*

Katedrala sv. Stošije (*St. Anastasia's Cathedral*). Dalmatia's largest basilica was shaped into its magnificent Romanesque form in the 12th and 13th centuries from an earlier church; though it was damaged severely during World War II, it was later reconstructed. The front portal is adorned with striking Gothic reliefs and a dedication to the archbishop Ivan from the year 1324. The interior includes not only a high, spacious nave but also a Gothic, stone ciborium from 1332 covering the 9th-century altar; intricately carved 15th-century choir stalls by the Venetian artist Matej Morozon; and, in the sacristy, an early Christian mosaic. St. Anastasia is buried in the altar's left apse; according to legend, she was the wife of a patrician in Rome but was eventually burned at the stake. Bishop Donatus of Zadar obtained the remains in 804 from Byzantine Emperor Niceforos. ■ **TIP→ The late-19th-century belfry, which is separate from the main church building, offers a sweeping view to those who climb to the top for a fee, but even the 20 steps up to the ticket desk rewards you with a decent view of the square below.** ✉ *Trg sv. Stošije 2* ☎ *023/208–637* ⌨ *Church free; belfry 10 Kn* ⊙ *Belfry July and Aug., daily 9 am–midnight; June and Sept., 9 am–10 pm; Apr., May, and Oct., 10 am–5 pm.*

FAMILY

Fodor'sChoice
★

Sea Organ. Comprising 35 pipes under the quay stretching along a 230-foot stretch of Zadar's atmospheric Riva promenade, the Sea Organ yields a never-ending (and ever free) concert that delights one and all. Designed by architect Nikola Bašić with the help of other experts, the organ's sound resembles a whale song, but it is in fact the sea itself. It's hard not to be in awe as the sound of the sea undulates in rhythm and volume with the waves. ✉ *Obala kralja Petra Krešimira IV, toward end of western tip of peninsula.*

WORTH NOTING

Archaeological Museum. Founded in 1832, Zadar's archaeological museum is one of the oldest museums in this part of Europe. It occupies a plain but pleasant modern building beside the convent complex of Crkva sv. Marije (St. Mary's Church). It is home to numerous artifacts from Zadar's past, from prehistoric times to the first Croatian settlements. Head upstairs to move back in time. The third floor focuses on ceramics, weaponry, and other items the seafaring Liburnians brought home from Greece and Italy, whereas the second floor covers the classical period, including a model of the Forum square as it would have looked back then; a smaller exhibit addresses the development of Christianity in Northern Dalmatia and contains rare artifacts from the invasion of the Goths. On the first floor you'll find an exhibit from the early Middle Ages, taking you to the 12th century. ⊠ *Trg Opatice Čike 1* ☎ *023/250–516* ⊕ *www.amzd.hr* 🖾 *15 Kn* ⊗ *July–Sept., daily 9–9; Oct.–May, daily 9–3.*

Crkva sv. Marije (*St. Mary's Church*). Legend has it that a local noblewoman founded a Benedictine convent on this site in 1066, and the adjoining St. Mary's Church in 1091. Rebuilt in the 16th century, the church was supposed to incorporate a new, Renaissance look into the remnants of its earlier style: its rounded gables remained, continuing to express a certain Dalmatian touch; early Romanesque frescoes are still evident amid the largely baroque interior; and your eyes will discover 18th-century rococo above the original columns without being any worse for the effect. Most noteworthy for modern-day visitors, however, is the adjoining convent complex, two wings of which house one of Zadar's most treasured museums. The **Permanent Exhibition of Religious Art,** whose highlight is commonly called "The Gold and Silver of Zadar," is a remarkable collection of work from centuries past by local gold- and silversmiths (including Italians and Venetians who lived here), from reliquaries for saints and crucifixes, to vestments interwoven with gold and silver thread. ⊠ *Poljana Opatice Čike* ☎ *023/254–820* 🖾 *Museum 15 Kn* ⊗ *Museum Mon.–Sat. 10–1 and 6–8, Sun. 10–noon.*

Crkva sv. Šimuna (*St. Simeon's Church*). Built in the 5th century as a three-nave basilica, it was later reconstructed in Gothic style, and again in baroque style, though the terra-cotta and white exterior pales in comparison to some of the city's other churches. St. Simeon's Church is best known for housing the gilded silver sarcophagus of Zadar's most popular patron saint. The chest, which depicts intricately detailed scenes from St. Simeon's life and the city's history, was commissioned in 1381 by Elizabeth, wife of Croat-Hungarian King Ludwig I of Anjou, and made by Francesco De Sesto of Milan, one of Zadar's best silversmiths. As for St. Simeon, legend has it that his body wound up here while being transported from the Holy Land to Venice by a merchant who got caught in a storm, took refuge here, fell ill, and died—but not before drawing attention to the saintliness of the body he'd brought with him. Palm trees outside the church lend the site a pleasant, Mediterranean touch. ⊠ *Crkva sv. Šime, Trg Petra Zoranića 7* ☎ *023/211–705* 🖾 *Free* ⊗ *Weekdays 9–noon and 3–5, Sat. 9–noon. Masses 8 am weekdays, 8:30 am and 10 am weekends.*

Forum. Established in the 1st century BC by the first emperor Augustus, the Roman Forum is, more than 2,000 years later, pretty much a wide empty space with some scattered ruins. However, since it was rediscovered in the 1930s and restored to its present condition in the 1960s, the Forum has been one of Zadar's most important public spaces. A raised area on the western flank indicates the site of a onetime temple dedicated to Jupiter, Juno, and Minerva, and if you look closely you will notice what remains of its altars that served as venues for blood sacrifices. The only surviving column was used in the Middle Ages as a "Pillar of Shame," to which wayward individuals were chained. Fragments of a second column were removed from the Forum in 1729 and put back together again near the Square of Five Wells, where the column still stands today. ⊠ *Zeleni trg.*

Greeting to the Sun (*Pozdrav Suncu*). Close to the Sea Organ, the Greeting to the Sun is a 22-meter circle of multilayered glass plates set into the stone-paved waterfront. Under the glass, light-sensitive solar modules soak up the sun's energy during daylight hours, turning it into electrical energy. Just after sunset, it puts on an impressive light show, illuminating the waterfront in shades of blue, green, red and yellow. It was installed in 2008 and was created by local architect Nikola Bašić, who also made the Sea Organ. ⊠ *Obala Kralja Petra Krešimira IV, toward western tip of peninsula.*

Kopnena Vrata (*The Land Gate*). A walk around the walls of Zadar's Old Town is a walk around what was once the largest city-fortress in the Venetian Republic. One of the finest Venetian-era monuments in Dalmatia, the Land Gate was built in 1543 by the small Foša harbor as the main entrance to the city. It takes the form of a triumphal arch, with a large, central passage for vehicles and two side entrances for pedestrians, and is decorated with reliefs of St. Chrysogonus (Zadar's main patron saint) on his horse, and the shield of St. Mark (the coat of arms of the Venetian Republic). ⊠ *Ulica Ante Kumanića.*

Museum of Ancient Glass. Occupying the 19th-century Cosmacendi Palace, on the edge of the Old Town, this museum opened in 2011. It displays one of the world's finest collections of Roman glassware outside Italy, with a vast array of ancient pieces unearthed from archaeological sites across Dalmatia. Highlights include the delicate vessels used by Roman ladies to keep their perfumes, skin creams, and essential oils, as well as sacred goblets used to celebrate mass. ■ **TIP→ The museum shop offers a fine choice of replicas of Roman glassware, making great gifts to bring home.** ⊠ *Poljana Zemaljskog odbora 1* ☎ *023/363-831* ⊕ *www.mas-zadar.hr* ⊠ *30 Kn* ☯ *Mid-June–mid-Oct., daily 9–9; mid-Oct.–mid-June, Mon.–Sat. 9–4.*

Narodni trg (*People's Square*). One of the Old Town's two main public spaces, the ever bustling Narodni trg is home of the Gradska Straža (City Sentinel), which was designed by a Venetian architect in late-Renaissance style with a large, central clock tower. The sentinel's stone barrier and railing, complete with holes for cannons, were added later. This impressive tower once housed the ethnographic section of the National Museum and is today a venue for various regular cultural exhibits. ⊠ *Narodni trg.*

Square of Five Wells. The square is the site of a large cistern built by the Venetians in the 1570s to help Zadar endure sieges by the Turks. The cistern itself has five wells that still look quite serviceable, even though they have long been sealed shut. Much later, in 1829, Baron Franz Ludwig von Welden, a passionate botanist, established a park above an adjacent pentagonal bastion that was also built to keep the Turks at bay. ✉ *Pet Bunara.*

WHERE TO EAT

$ CAFÉ FAMILY 🍴 **Bistro Plankit.** Casual and affordable with respectable fare, Bistro Plankit offers relaxed diners a varied menu. The pizza is a sure bet, as are the salads. The waiters are friendly and the setting laid back, a good choice for families and travelers looking for a quick bite. [$] *Average main: €8* ✉ *Šimuna Kožičića Benje 3* ☎ *098/756–998* 🌐 *www.restorani-zadar.hr.*

$$ MEDITERRANEAN 🍴 **Bruschetta.** With outdoor tables on a lovely terrace, overlooking the sea in the Old Town, Bruschetta serves reasonably priced and well-presented Mediterranean cuisine. Popular with locals and visitors alike, it's especially known for its pizzas and pasta dishes, but it also does excellent steaks and fresh fish, as well as an irresistible tiramisu. [$] *Average main: 100 Kn* ✉ *Mihovila Pavlinovica 12* ☎ *023/312–915* 🌐 *www.bruschetta.hr .*

HOW SWEET—AND DRY—IT IS

Zadar's famous maraschino cherry liqueur, one of the world's few liqueurs produced by distillation, manages to be subtly sweet and robustly dry at the same time. Look for bottles labeled Maraška, the Zadar company that produces this transparent spirit from the area's zesty sour cherries. It is typically enjoyed as either an aperitif or digestif.

$$$ SEAFOOD 🍴 **Foša.** One key reason to eat at the Foša, whose name includes the tag "Riblji [Fish] restaurant," is the choice setting just outside the city walls a stone's throw from the Kopnena Vrata. And then there's the excellent seafood, of course. Whether you opt to sit at a white-tablecloth-and-candle adorned table inside or on the hugely appealing outdoor terrace overlooking quiet little Foša harbor, your palate is likely to be pleased—whether on account of a staple like grilled squid or, say, Dalmatian-style tuna with Swiss chard. [$] *Average main: 500 Kn* ✉ *Kralja Dimitra Zvonimira 2* ☎ *023/314–421* 🌐 *www.fosa.hr.*

$$ PIZZA 🍴 **Mama Mia.** Mama Mia is a popular place for locals and tourists, and with good reason: generous portions at fair prices that are tasty to boot! The pizzas are the stars here, with an impressive spread of toppings to choose from, and the cuttlefish risotto and daily specials never disappoint. It tends to get crowded, especially when the games are on, but the staff is attentive and the atmosphere is friendly. The pizzas are plenty big enough to share—but you definitely won't want to. [$] *Average main: 80 Kn* ✉ *Put Dikla 54* ☎ *023/337–713.*

$$$ MEDITERRANEAN Fodor's Choice ★ 🍴 **Niko.** Just across from a public beach and near the Borik resort complex, this distinguished restaurant has been serving up a delicious array of seafood, beef, veal, pork, and pasta dishes since 1963. You can choose between such lower-end fare as spaghetti with scampi or more expensive delights like scampi on the skewer. That's not to mention the mouthwatering banana splits. Upstairs are 12 spacious, elegant, peach-toned, pricey rooms, at €150 for a double with breakfast. [$] *Average*

main: €120 ✉ *Obala Kneza Domagoja 9* ☎ *023/337–880* 🌐 *www.hotel-niko.hr.*

$$ ITALIAN 🍴 **Pasta & Svasta.** Charming and cozy (with limited but coveted seating) visit this tucked-away spot for a comprehensively pleasant experience. Pick a clear night and sit in the courtyard, enjoying a palatable house wine that complements both the lighter fare and pasta plates. Knowledgeable waiters will help you pair the fresh pastas and sauces. The gnocchi are heavenly potato pillows. Complimentary aperitifs are common, as are kind words from the managers as they ensure their customers are happy. Not a complaint to be had about this establishment, although your waistband may beg to differ. [$] *Average main: 80 Kn* ✉ *Poljana Šime Budinića 1* ☎ *099/731–0232.*

$ THAI 🍴 **Pearl of Siam.** If it is true that we first eat with our eyes, Pearl of Siam is delivering a bountiful feast. The decor is noteworthy and gorgeous. Welcoming servers are happy to help decipher the menu, and while some selections could stand a touch more ginger and galangal, the coconut cream and pineapple dessert is perfect every time. This restaurant creates excitement for Thai food in a region that is otherwise deficient in Asian cuisine. [$] *Average main: €5* ✉ *Put Dikla 9* ☎ *023/337–713.*

$$$ MEDITERRANEAN Fodor's Choice ★ 🍴 **Pet Bunara.** If you are in need of a break from the tourist bustle, head for the Pet Bunara, a slow-food restaurant situated in a quiet little nook just off the Pet Bunara square. The fare is very creative and changes weekly, if not daily, according to the local produce available. Every dish is centered on local food, from seafood to signature lamb, and the addition of home-made fig jam and roasted almonds really sparks up the palate. The staff are very wine-savvy and unobtrusive and they help turn your dinner into an authentic culinary experience. The prices are surprisingly fair for an establishment of this caliber, so take some time out of the schedule and let them spoil you with the best comestibles of the Zadar region. [$] *Average main: €25* ✉ *Stratico St., near Trg pet bunara* ☎ *023/224–010* 🌐 *www.petbunara.hr.*

$$$ SEAFOOD 🍴 **Restoran Kornat.** Just outside the city walls on the tip of the peninsula, the Kornat offers fine dining. You may find the space a tad dull despite (or because of) all the sparkling elegance, marked by warm yellow hues that extend to the cloth napkins. On the ground floor of a four-story concrete-box building, the restaurant serves original, first-rate cuisine, with an emphasis on seafood—try the monkfish fillet with truffle sauce—plus a limited choice of hearty meat dishes, including leg of lamb with roasted potatoes. Desserts include melon with champagne. There's also an extensive wine list, from the best of Croatian elixirs to the smoothest syrah. [$] *Average main: €120* ✉ *Liburnska obala 6* ☎ *023/254–501* 🌐 *www.restaurant-kornat.com.*

6

WHERE TO STAY

There are very few hotels in or near Zadar's Old Town—the pension-style Venera used to be the only option until the opening of the Bastion Hotel in 2008. As you leave the center, you'll find either fairly expensive, top-end hotels or relatively simple, budget places, but not much in the middle price ranges. In midsummer, you can step off the ferry from Pula at midnight and be reasonably assured that some relatively trustworthy person—more likely than not a pensioner who speaks more Italian than English—will offer you a room in a centrally located apartment for around 300 Kn for two people. But your best bet is to book a room— for a slightly higher cost—through one of the following travel agencies, which also offer excursions to nearby islands and national parks.

$$$$
HOTEL
Fodor's Choice
★

Art Hotel Kalelarga. Carefully curated modern furnishings create a cool relief after a day of hustling through Zadar's narrow streets. **Pros:** fantastic restaurant; one of the few hotels in the old town; good off-season packages. **Cons:** atmosphere can be stuffy; pricey. $ *Rooms from: €260* ⊠ *Majke Margarite 3* ☎ *023/233–000* ⊕ *www.arthotel-kalelarga.com* ⤴ *10 rooms* ❍❙ *Breakfast.*

$$$
RESORT

Falkensteuner Hotel Adriana. Flanked beachside by a grove of tall pines, and encircled by a security fence (more to keep nonguests from enjoying the hotel's outdoor pool than for the sake of safety), this is an appealing place to stay even if the long, narrow lobby does resemble an airport terminal. **Pros:** bright, spacious rooms; lovely private beach; substantial discounts for stays of three nights or more. **Cons:** pricey; in a huge, somewhat characterless complex; far from the town center. $ *Rooms from: €282* ⊠ *Majstora Radovana 7, Borik* ☎ *023/206–300* ⊕ *www. falkensteiner.com* ⤴ *48 rooms* ❍❙ *Some meals.*

$$$
HOTEL
Fodor's Choice
★

Hotel Bastion. Elegant, with artistic decoration and a refined ambience, Hotel Bastion offers a chic respite for travelers with a taste for sophistication. **Pros:** perhaps the best slow-food restaurant in the country; location in the old town; stylish interior. **Cons:** small, so often fully booked in high season; old town is pedestrian-only and parking nearby can be problematic; guests pay to use the spa. $ *Rooms from: €219* ⊠ *Bedem zadarskih pobuna 13* ☎ *023/494–950* ⊕ *www.hotel-bastion. hr* ⤴ *23 rooms, 5 suites* ❍❙ *Breakfast.*

$$
RENTAL

Zara City Apartments. Renting an apartment will be a good fit for travelers looking for the ability to prepare meals for themselves. **Pros:** all within walking distance to main attractions; air-conditioning; affordable. **Cons:** some apartments are smaller than you'd hope; some apartments are on noisy streets. $ *Rooms from: €90* ⊠ *Borelli ulica 6* ☎ *095/891–9203* ⊕ *www.zaracityapartments.com* ⤴ *6 apts.*

NIGHTLIFE AND PERFORMING ARTS

BARS AND CLUBS

Beach & Cocktail Bar Bamboo. The big wooden deck clad with wooden benches, deck chairs, and grass umbrellas right on the beach certainly has its appeal. Beach & Cocktail Bar Bamboo overlooks the old city and outward to the islands. They know how to keep it simple and their version of simple is pretty good. ⊠ *Obala Kneza Domagoja BB* ☎ *098/756–998* ⊕ *www.restorani-zadar.hr/beach-bar-bamboo.*

The Garden. Cloistered in a walled garden right atop the city walls, The Garden is a minimalist and exceedingly popular place to drink, soak in the sun and the views, play a game of chess, and even dance to the jazz, Latin, and down-tempo electronica. It's open daily from 10 am to 1:30 am. ⊠ *Bedemi Zadarskih Pobuna* ☎ *023/364–320* ⊕ *www. watchthegardengrow.eu/the-garden-zadar/.*

SUMMER FESTIVALS

Musical Evenings in Saint Donat. Despite its name, not all the month-long series of classical music concerts and recitals, staged between early-July and early-August, are held in the splendid St. Donat's Church. ✉ *Trg Petra Zoranića 1* ⊕ *www.donat-festival.com.*

Zadar snova (*Zadar of Dreams*). Talk about eclectic. The Zadar Snova festival, in the second week of August, welcomes everything from contemporary dance and films to comic-strip exhibits and workshops, to theatrical events, to a rich array of music, and more. ✉ *I. Meštrovića 9* ⊕ *www.zadarsnova.hr; www.facebook.com/zadarsnova/.*

Zadar Summer Theatre. From late June to early August the annual Zadar Summer Theatre festival sees a whole range of music, dance, and drama performed in various squares, churches, and other buildings about town.

SPORTS AND THE OUTDOORS

BEACHES

As in many another coastal city, you can feel free to take a short dip off the quay in the Old Town—the most atmospheric place to do so being the **Riva** promenade and especially the tip of the peninsula directly over the Sea Organ, as nature's music accompanies your strokes. But for a more tranquil swim, head to the **Kolovare** district, just southeast of the Old Town, with its long stretch of park-flanked beach punctuated here and there by restaurants and cafés. This is not to mention the resort complex in **Borik**, where relatively shallow waters and a sandy bottom may be more amenable to kids. Last but not least, by driving or bussing it 30 minutes north along the coast you can reach the famously sandy beaches of **Zaton** and **Nin.** For true peace and quiet, though, your best bet is an excursion by ferry and then on foot, by bicycle, or in a rental car out to some more isolated stretch of beach on an island of the Zadar archipelago.

BICYCLING

TČT. Being relatively flat with lots of relatively quiet thoroughfares both in the Old Town and on the outskirts of the city, Zadar is indeed a bicycle-friendly place. You can rent a bike at TČT. ✉ *Dr. Franje Tuđmana 14* ☎ *023/241–243.*

DIVING

Zadar Sub. Since diving on your own is possible only with two pricey permits, it is advisable to take that deep dip through a diving center (i.e., with the supervision of a licensed instructor). Just one of the many such centers in Zadar and on the surrounding coast and islands is Zadar Sub. ✉ *Dubrovačka 20a* ☎ *023/214–848* ⊕ *www.zadarsub.hr.*

SHOPPING

As hip as it otherwise is, Zadar is low on high fashion and has few outlets for quality souvenirs (as opposed to the usual kitsch, which there is plenty of). That said, those interested will be happy to know that jewelry stores are in no short supply. Also, one of the first shopping opportunities you will pass if you enter the Old Town via the main pedestrian bridge is a large enclosed hall with an antiques market inside; keep your eyes open for the open doorway to your right on Jurja Barakovića, just before you reach H. Vukšića Hrvatinića (9–2 and 5–10 daily).

Fodor's Choice
★ **Arsenal.** Arsenal, where the Venetians used to repair their galleys in the 18th-century, is a multipurpose cultural space that hosts art exhibitions and concerts, as well as a lounge bar, a restaurant, and a wine shop. ⊠ *Trg Tri Bunara 1* ☎ *023/253–821* ⊕ *www.arsenalzadar.com.*

Fodor's Choice
★ **Boutique MAR&VAL.** A multibrand store full of unique pieces from prominent Croatian fashion designers. ⊠ *Don Ivo Prodan 3* ☎ *023/213–239.*

Croatian Design Superstore. If you find yourself in Zadar over the summer months, make sure to check out the Croatian Design Superstore, an unusual gifts and souvenirs shop only opened in July, August, and September. It hosts everything from high fashion and furniture to design crafts and gastro treats, and rest assured that everything is locally made. ⊠ *Rector's Palace, Poljana Šime Budinića* ⊕ *www.croatiandesignsuperstore.com.*

Galerija Morsky. Galerija Morsky sells fine paintings by local artists. ⊠ *Ulica Borelli 3* ☎ *091/780–6101.*

NIN

14 km (9 miles) north of Zadar.

On a tiny, 1,640-foot-wide island in a shallow, sandy lagoon that affords a spectacular view of the Velebit range to the northeast, Nin is connected to the mainland by two small bridges. The peaceful town of 1,700, a compact gem whose present-day size and unassuming attitude belie a stormy history, is well worth a visit, whether on the way to Zadar or as a day trip from there, assuming that the beautiful sand beaches stretching for miles around Nin don't inspire you to stay a bit longer.

Nin was a major settlement of the Liburnians, an Illyrian people who also settled Zadar, hundreds of years before the Romans came, conquered, and named it Aenona. A vital harbor for centuries, it was the first seat of Croatia's royalty, and was long the region's episcopal see, whose bishop was responsible for the conversion to Christianity of all Croatian territory. In 1382 the Venetians seized it and prospered from the trade in salt, livestock, and agriculture. However, the Venetian-Turkish wars eventually brought devastating onslaughts, including Nin's destruction in 1571; later, the Candian Wars of 1645–69 led to the decimation of Nin and the surrounding area yet again.

Aside from its historic buildings and monuments that testify to a rich past, Nin's draw also includes the only sandy beaches on this stretch of the Adriatic, not to mention the area's medicinal seaside mud. Since the sea here is shallow, water temperatures are warmer than in the rest of the Adriatic; moreover, the water is more saline, accounting for Nin's major export product—salt. But what would a Croatian coastal town be without the usual resort complex on its fringes? Holiday Village Zaton is a 15-minute walk from the Old Town.

If you're coming from Zadar, soon before you reach Nin proper, look to your left (your right if headed back toward Zadar) to see the squat, stony, 12th-century form of **St. Nicholas's Church** on a hillock out in the middle of a field, looking rather like a cake ornament, with a lone Scotch pine at the foot of the little hill keeping it company, as it were. You can enter Nin via one of two small bridges—the most likely of the two being the charming, pedestrian **Donja most** (Lower Bridge), only yards from the tourist-information office, which provides a helpful map that folds small enough to fit in your palm. If you're coming by car, you can park in a lot on the right just beyond the office and then cross the bridge, or else find a semi-legal spot along the road roughly opposite the lot, which plenty of enterprising visitors prefer.

GETTING HERE AND AROUND
The best way to Nin is a 15-km (9-mile) drive from Zadar, be it by car or one of the hourly regular buses. Once there, you can only get around on foot.

EXPLORING

Arheološki muzej (*Archaeological Museum*). Nin's shallow coast and centuries of sand deposits preserved numerous remains from prehistory to the Middle Ages under the sea. The Arheološki muzej has a rich collection for a town of this size, including replicas of two small, late-11th-century fishing boats discovered only in 1966 and carefully removed from the sea in 1974. One of these boats has been completely reconstructed, the other only to the extent to which it had been preserved underwater. The main themes in each room are elucidated in clear English translations. ⊠ *Trg Krajlevac 8* ☎ *023/264–160* ⌨ *15 Kn* ⊗ *May and Sept.: 9 am—noon and 5pm-9pm; June–Aug.: 9 am–10 pm; Oct.–Apr.: 8–2.*

Crkva sv. Anselma (*St. Anselmo's Church*). The 18th-century Crkva sv. Anselma, dedicated to a 1st-century martyr believed to have been Nin's first bishop, was built on the site of Nin's former, 9th-century cathedral, the first cathedral of the medieval Croatian principality. To the right of the altar is a 15th-century statue of the Madonna of Zečevo, inspired by the appearance of the Virgin Mary to a woman on a nearby island. Though the church is plain—the ceiling is adorned with only a nice chandelier and a smoke detector—the foundations of the onetime cathedral are still much in evidence. Beside the church is the belfry, and next door is the treasury, which houses a stunning little collection of reliquaries containing various body parts of St. Anselmo. ⊠ *Branimirova, near Višeslavov trg* ⌨ *10 Kn* ⊗ *Treasury: May–Sept., Mon.–Sat. 10–noon and 5:30–9:30.*

Crkva sv. Križa (*Church of the Holy Cross*). Croatia's oldest church, the 8th-century Crkva sv. Križa is also known locally as the "world's smallest cathedral." Indeed, the unadorned, three-naved whitewashed structure—which has a solid, cylindrical top and a few tall, Romanesque windows (too high to peek inside)—has an unmistakable monumental quality to it even though it's no larger than a small house. There's little to see inside, though it is sometimes open, erratically, in summer; check with the tourist office or the Archaeological Museum. ✉ *Petra Zoranića.*

Nin Saltworks. Historically, Nin's riches came from an unlikely source: salt. Making the best of a rare geographical location with lots of sun, lots of wind and shallow sea basins, Nin Saltworks produces salt in a traditional, ecological way to this date. To commemorate salt's vast influence on the development of the city, Nin opened up a small but charming salt museum, which opens our eyes to how this common table adornment was produced back in the day. While there, make sure to pick up a bag of *fleur du sel,* the flower of salt ultrarich in minerals. For a fee, you can take a tour led by a professional guide (offered on the hour). ✉ *Ilirska cesta 7* ☎ *023/264–764* 🌐 *www.solananin.hr* 🎫 *Free; tours 35 Kn* ⏲ *Daily 8–8; tours 8–1 and 5–7 (hourly).*

Temple of Diana. Around the corner from the Archaeological Museum are the ruins of the large Temple of Diana, one of the few remaining testaments in Nin to the Roman era. ✉ *Sv. Mihovila.*

WHERE TO EAT

$$ MEDITERRANEAN FAMILY

🍴 **Bepo.** Even if you are not staying at Holiday Village Zaton, you might find yourself at Zaton's Konoba Bepo in search of a good meal because Nin does not have many worthy alternatives. Bepo's charming atmosphere is lively and their menu is a good representation of local Mediterranean fare that's suitable for all taste buds. As a nice touch, they use olive oil produced by the reputable local producer, Ivica Vlatković. And their domestic desserts will leave you satisfied. [$] *Average main: €14* ✉ *Zaton Holiday Resort, Dražnikova 76t* ☎ *023/280–336* 🌐 *www.konoba-bepo.hr.*

$$ EASTERN EUROPEAN

🍴 **Konoba Branimir.** Strategically located yards away from the Church of the Holy Cross—indeed you might enter the restaurant by mistake, thinking you are proceeding to the churchyard from a back entrance—this is the most pleasant place to dine in Nin. The well-prepared fare ranges from fresh seafood to meats, and desserts such as pancakes with fig marmalade. Note that the spaghetti, though listed as a children's meal, makes for a hearty "light" (and budget) meal even for an adult. [$] *Average main: €15* ✉ *Višeslavov trg 2* ☎ *023/264–866.*

SPORTS AND THE OUTDOORS

With its long sandy **beaches,** the coastline in and around Nin, and Pag Island just to north, is widely regarded as the most beautiful—and most swimmable—in Dalmatia.

DIVING

Scuba Adriatic. The Holiday Village Zaton resort complex, a 15-minute walk from Nin, is home to Scuba Adriatic, which offers diving excursions for advanced and beginning divers, formal diving instruction, as well as a two-hour "Discovery Diving" course. ✉ *Holiday Village Zaton* ☎ *023/280–350.*

SALI AND TELAŠČICA NATURE PARK

Sali is approximately 30 km (19 miles) south of Zadar; Telaščica Nature Park is 10 km (6 miles) south of Sali.

Situated toward the southeastern tip of the 52-km-long (32-mile-long) island, which is no more than 4 km (2½ miles) wide, Sali is Dugi Otok's largest settlement—with around half of the island's 1,800 inhabitants, the rest of whom reside mostly in its 10 other villages—but it's an awfully peaceful little place you arrive in after the two-hour ferry ride from Zadar.

GETTING HERE AND AROUND

Sali is on Dugi Otok Island and functions as a gateway to Telašćica Nature Park. You can get to Sali via the regular ferry line from Zadar to Dugi Otok or hop on one of many organized tours leaving from the area. Telašćica is a special treat, of course, for those chartering their own boat.

EXPLORING

6

The largest and most westerly island of the Zadar archipelago, facing the open sea, Dugi Otok culminates at its southern end with a spectacular nature preserve in and around Telašćica Bay, the town of Sali being the ideal access point.

Sali. Once an out-of-the-way fishing village, Sali draws tourists these days due to its location in and near such natural splendors. It is home to several old churches, including the 12th-century **St. Mary's church,** whose baroque altar was carved in Venice. Adding to the village's appeal is its annual **Saljske užance** (Donkey Festival) during the first full weekend in August, which includes an evening ritual during which lantern-lit boats enter Sali harbor and there are donkey races and *tovareća muzika* (donkey music) produced by locals blowing or braying raucously into horns. Spending at least a night or two here can provide a relatively peaceful, nature-filled respite from the rigors of tourism on the mainland or, for that matter, on more tourist-trodden reaches of the Zadar archipelago. ⊠ *Sali.*

Telašćica Nature Park. Telašćica Nature Park encompasses Telašćica Bay, which cuts 7 km (4½ miles) into the southern tip of Dugi Otok with an inner coastline so indented that it is really a series of smaller bays and a handful of islands. Flanked by high vertical cliffs facing the open sea to the west, with low, peaceful bays on the other side, it has a variety of vegetation. Relatively lush alpine forests and flower-filled fields as well as vineyards, olive groves, and onetime cultivated fields give way, as you move south, to bare rocky ground of the sort that predominates on the Kornati Islands, whose northern boundary begins where Telašćica Nature Park ends. Aside from Telašćica's other attractions, most of which are accessible only by boat, one of the park's key highlights—accessible by land on a 20-minute drive from Sali—is the salt lake **Jezero mir,** which was formed when a karst depression was filled by the sea. Small boats (generally with eight to 12 passengers) bound for both Telašćica Nature Park and the northern fringes of Kornati

National Park leave the east side of Sali's harbor (i.e., where the Zadar ferry arrives) at 9 or 9:30 each morning and return by 6 or 6:30 in the evening. Expect to pay 200 Kn per person, sometimes less. The best way to arrange this is in person—by going to the harborside square near the post office around 8 pm on the day before you wish to leave (which means at least a one-night stay in Sali), when boat captains gather there looking for passengers for the next day's excursion. However, the tourist-information office in Sali can put you in touch with operators by phone as well. ⊠ *Put Danijela Grbina, Sali* ☎ *023/377–096* ⊕ *www.telascica.hr.*

Zadar archipelago. The Zadar archipelago is so close and yet so far away. Ugljan and Pašman are just two of the myriad islands comprising the lacelike islands, and yet they are among the largest and the easiest to reach from Zadar. More than 15 ferries a day run the 5-km (3-mile) distance between Zadar and Ugljan, a 19-km-long (12-mile-long) island whose narrow width of just a couple of kilometers runs parallel to the mainland, with its midway point across from Zadar. From the ferry landing on Ugljan, your best bet may be to head north along the seafront 10 minutes on foot to the heart of **Preko,** a fine access point to several worthwhile destinations (very) near and (not too) far. Going south will get you in roughly the same time to the unassuming fishing village of Kali. From Preko's harbor you can walk about 1 km (½ mile) farther north to a shallow bay locals like to swim in; or better yet, take a taxi-boat to **Galevac,** a charming wooded islet less than 100 yards from Preko that not only has splendid swimming but also a 15th-century Franciscan monastery set in a lush green park. And then there's the **Tvrđava sv. Mihovila** (Fortress of St. Michael), a 13th-century landmark atop a hill roughly an hour's walk west of town. Though largely in ruins, the fortress offers spectacular views not only of nearby Zadar, to the west, but on a cloudless day the Italian coast as well. Meanwhile, 10 km (6 miles) farther north is the quiet village of **Ugljan,** accessible from the ferry port by a handful of buses daily. For a somewhat sleepier island experience, hop aboard one of eight buses daily from Preko to the village of **Pašman.** Continuing on, you can eventually get to Tkon, Pašman island's largest village, from which some 10 ferries daily can get you back to the mainland south of Zadar. ⊠ *Zadar.*

WHERE TO·EAT

$$ ✕ **Konobe Kod Sipe.** There are plenty of tourist places harborside in Sali,
EASTERN   but if you want to have a hearty meal well above the fray, you'll have
EUROPEAN   to do some climbing. Start at the steps between the Suvenirica Porat store and the Gelateri Contes café, near the tip of the harbor, and walk up more than 100 of them, passing two pretty little churches on your left along the way. After the second church, follow the "Konoba" signs to this popular restaurant that serves everything from grilled calamari and pork chops to cuttlefish spaghetti and "octopus under a baking lid." The rustic decor is pleasingly punctuated by a barrel theme, with both the chairs and the tables on barrels, and the usual fishnets hanging from the ceiling's wooden beams. The outdoor terrace is shaded by

grapevines (and, yes, some fishnet) and has an enticing open hearth. All this, in a villagelike atmosphere where tourists rarely tread. $ *Average main: €15* ⊠ *Ulica sv. Marije, Sali* ☎ *023/377–137* ▭ *No credit cards.*

WHERE TO STAY

The tourist-information office can put you in touch with locals who rent private rooms, at around 220 Kn per night in high season. Large hotels will generally accept payment in either euros or kunas.

$$
HOTEL **Sali Hotel.** A 10-minute walk from the harbor on the quiet waters of Sašćica, the next bay north, this low-key hotel occupies a pair of two-story, concrete-boxish buildings perched on a lovely, pine-covered hill leading down to a beach on a pristine bay worlds away from the hubbub of busier coastal resorts. **Pros:** lovely setting on private beach; diving center yards away. **Cons:** rooms have smoky smell; hotel bland and boxlike on the outside; few frills. $ *Rooms from: €85* ⊠ *Adresa, Sali* ☎ *023/377–049* ⊕ *www.hotel-sali.hr* ⤴ *52 rooms* ⭗ *Breakfast.*

SPORTS AND THE OUTDOORS

DIVING

Diving Center. "Diving is not about sitting around on land, sipping wine, and watching the sea," says the chief instructor of Sali's Diving Center, as several clients huddle nearby sipping coffee and watching the sea— true, it's cold and rainy just now. This German-owned firm, which operates out of a compact cabin on the pine-covered hillside below the Sali Hotel, offers everything from a 30-minute resort course to a five-day certification course, in English if you prefer. Diving can be done both from shore or farther afield from a boat, whether on Sašćica Bay itself or farther out, in Teščica Nature Park or on the fringes of Kornati National Park. Cash only. ⊠ *Adresa, Sali* ☎ *023/646–678* ⊕ *www.dive-kroatien.de.*

MURTER AND THE KORNATI ISLANDS

70 km (44 miles) south of Zadar.

Built near the ruins of the 1st-century Roman settlement of Colentum, Murter has that unmistakable tourism-driven hustle and bustle in midsummer that Sali doesn't—both because it is the key gateway to one of Croatia's chief offshore natural splendors, Kornati National Park, and because it is easily accessible by road from Zadar.

GETTING HERE AND AROUND

Murter Island is serviced by a regular ferry line from the town of Tisno, halfway between Zadar and Šibenik. If only visiting Kornati Islands National Park for a day, there are many daily boats leaving from Zadar (north of the NP) and Vodice (south of the NP).

TOURS TO KORNATI NATIONAL PARK

Plava Laguna. If you prefer to save yourself the long and meandering drive to Murter, or don't have wheels to begin with, you can catch a tour on one of several boats that ply the waters straight from Zadar,

6

for a daylong excursion price of around 300 Kn per person. One good option is the boat Plava Laguna, which departs from the Borik marina at 8 am daily and returns by around 6 pm. ⊠ *Borik Marina, Obala kneza Domagoja 1, Zadar* ☎ *098/875–746, 023/334–68* ⊕ *www. kornat-excursions.hr.*

EXPLORING

Fodor'sChoice
★

Kornati National Park. The largest archipelago in the Adriatic, Kornati National Park comprises more than 100 islands that are privately owned, mostly by residents of Murter, who purchased them more than a century ago from Zadar aristocrats. The new owners burned the forests to make room for sheep, which in turn ate much of the remaining vegetation. Although anything but lush today, the islands' almost mythical beauty is ironically synonymous with their barrenness: their bone-white-to-ochre colors represent a striking contrast to the azure sea. However, owners tend vineyards and orchards on some, and there are quite a few small buildings scattered about, mostly stone cottages—many of them on **Kornat,** which is by far the largest island, at 35 km long (22 miles long) and less than a tenth as wide. Indeed, some of these cottages are available for so-called *Robinson turizm* (ask at the Murter tourist office, or ask around town). In 1980 the archipelago became a national park. It was reportedly during a visit to Kornati in 1936 that King Edward of England decided between love for his throne and love for Wallis Simpson, the married woman who was to become his wife a year later. ⊠ *An archipelago lying off coast of North Dalmatia, between mainland coastal cities of Zadar and Šibenik, Zadar* ☎ *022/435–740* ⊕ *www.kornati.hr* ✉ *The entrance ticket is included in price of excursion, departing from Zadar.*

Murter. However you go to Murter, you'll pass through Biograd-Na-Moru, a relatively big, bustling—but thoroughly tourist-trampled—town, where the resorts have long come to predominate in what was once a charming place; Biogrand-Na-Moru also serves as another access point for ferries to the Kornati Islands.

Murter, a town of 2,000 on the island of the same name that lies just off the mainland, is accessible by road from the main coastal route that runs south from Zadar toward Split. As important as tourism is to its present-day economy, boatbuilding has, not surprisingly, long been vital to Murter as well. This is not to mention its olive oil, which was once so famous that it made its way to the imperial table in Vienna.

WHERE TO EAT

$$
MEDITERRANEAN
FAMILY

✕ **Boba.** Beyond its outstanding selection of seafood, Boba offers a variety of regional delicacies sure to please even finicky diners. The outdoor terrace and shaded gardens provide a quiet respite, and while the restaurant is very popular it doesn't feel crowded. Locals and visitors alike enjoy friendly service and crisp Croatian white wines, offered at moderately expensive prices. The good word is out on Boba—a short wait to be seated may be expected, or reserve a table in advance. $ *Average main: €15* ✉ *Butina 22* ☎ *098/948–5272.*

$$$ ✕ **Tic-Tac.** The chef likes putting seafood in wine sauce here, to grati-
SEAFOOD fyingly delicious effect. In this elegant little restaurant near the main square, with tables lining the length of the narrow, historic alleyway where you'll also find the main entrance, you can begin with an appetizer such as mussels in wine sauce and move on to monkfish tail or grilled scampi—both also in wine sauce. Whatever you get, accompany it with a glass of Graševina, the house white. $ *Average main: €40* ✉ *Hrokešina 5* ☎ *022/435–230* ⊕ *www.tictac-murter.com.*

WHERE TO STAY

Check with local agencies, which can find you a private room for around €30 for two.

$$$ ☷ **Hotel Tisno.** Like many regional lodging options, Hotel Tisno marries
HOTEL historical elegance with modern amenities. **Pros:** beautiful surrounding scenery; complimentary bikes; welcoming staff. **Cons:** limited number of rooms, so book in advance; decor is pleasant but lacks personality. $ *Rooms from: €190* ✉ *Zapadna Gomilica 8, Tisno* ☎ *022/438–182* ⊕ *www.hoteltisno.hr* ⇄ *9 rooms* ⦿| *Breakfast.*

SPORTS AND THE OUTDOORS

DIVING

Whether for exploring shipwrecks or reefs or underwater cliffs, Kornati National Park is among Croatia's most popular diving destinations. That said, you can't dive alone here, only through a qualified diving center. The permit for diving in the park is 150 Kn, which includes the park entrance fee.

Aquanaut Diving Center. Aquanaut Diving Center offers a small menu of choice courses and excursions (to more than 100 sites), including a daylong boat trip that includes two dives and a stopover in the Kornati Islands. Nondiving companions are also welcome to join at a reduced fee. ✉ *Luke, near intersection of Kornatski, across from supermarket, J. Dalmatinca 1* ☎ *098/202–249* ⊕ *www.divingmurter.com.*

NIGHTLIFE AND PERFORMING ARTS

FESTIVALS

Tisno Music Festivals. An array of hip music festivals come to the strait of Tisno every summer. Slightly varying by date, check festival specific websites for up-to-date information. Some Tisno festivals include: Garden Festival, Electric Elephant, Soundwave Croatia, SuncéBeat, and Stop Making Sense. ✉ *Tisno* ⊕ *www.tz-tisno.hr/en/festivals-tisno.*

PAKLENICA NATIONAL PARK

50 km (31 miles) northeast of Zadar.

For mountain scenery at its most spectacular and mountain tourism at its most advanced, you need go no further from Zadar than Paklenica National Park.

Paklenica National Park. The Velebit mountain range stretches along the Croatian coast for more than 100 km (62 miles), but nowhere does it pack in as much to see and do as in this relatively small, 96-square-km (37-square-mile) park at the southern terminus of the range. Here, less than an hour from Zadar, is a wealth of extraordinary karst features from fissures, crooks, and cliffs to pits and caves. The park comprises two limestone gorges, Velika Paklenica (which ends, near the sea, at the park entrance in Starigrad) and Mala Paklenica, a few kilometers to the south; trails through the former gorge are better marked (and more tourist-trodden).

All that dry rockiness visible from the seaward side of the range turns resplendently green as you cross over the mountains to the landward side. Named after the sap of the black pine, *paklina,* which was used long ago to prime boats, the park is in fact two-thirds forest, with beech and the indigenous black pine a key part of this picture; the remaining vegetation includes cliff-bound habitats featuring several types of bluebells, and rocky areas abounding in sage and heather. The park is also home to 4,000 different species of fauna, including butterflies that have long vanished elsewhere in Europe. It is also the only mainland nesting ground in Croatia for the stately griffin vulture.

The park has more than 150 km (94 miles) of trails, from relatively easy ones leading from the **Velika Paklenica Canyon** (from the entrance in Starigrad) to the 1,640-foot-long complex of caverns called Manita Peć cave, to mountain huts situated strategically along the way to the Velebit's highest peaks, Vaganski Vrh (5,768 feet) and Sveto brdo (5,751 feet). The most prominent of the park's large and spectacular caves, **Manita Peć** is accessible on foot from the park entrance in Starigrad; you can enter for a modest additional fee, but buy your ticket at the park entrance. Rock climbing is also a popular activity in the park. Meanwhile, mills and mountain villages scattered throughout Paklenica evoke the life of mountain folk from the not-too-distant past.

About a half-mile down the park access road in Starigrad, you pass through the mostly abandoned hamlet of **Marasovići,** from which it's a few hundred yards more downhill to the small building where you buy your tickets and enter the park (from this point on, only on foot). From here it's 45 minutes uphill to a side path to Anića kuk, a craggy peak, and from there it's not far to Manita Peć. However, if you don't have time or inclination for a substantial hike into the mountains, you will be happy to know that even the 45-minute walk to the entrance gate and back from the main road affords spectacular, close-up views of the Velebit range's craggy ridgeline and the gorge entrance. Also, be forewarned that if you are looking to escape the crowds, you will be hard-pressed to do so here in midsummer unless you head well into the mountains or, perhaps, opt for the park's less-frequented entrance at Mala Paklenica; more likely than not, you will be sharing the sublimities of nature with thousands of other seaside revelers taking a brief respite from the coast.

A further point of interest at the park are the Bunkers, an intricate system of underground shelters built by Marshall Tito in the early 1950s. With relations between Yugoslavia and the USSR then being at their worst, Tito used the geographical benefits of the gorges to build an A-bomb shelter. All the work was done in complete secrecy and very few people knew of the Bunkers. After Stalin's death, they were closed down and only reopened in 1991.

Although the park headquarters is on the main coastal road in the middle of Starigrad, fees are payable where you actually enter the park on the access road. Beyond the basic park admission and the supplemental fee to enter Manita Peć cave, the park offers every imaginable service and presentation that might encourage you to part with your kunas, from half-day group tours (400 Kn) to presentations every half hour from 11 to noon and 4 to 7 on the park's birds of prey and on falconry. ✉ *Dr. Franje Tuđmana 14a* ☎ *023/369–202* 🌐 *www.paklenica.hr* 🎫 *50 Kn, guided 400 Kn* 🕒 *Park: July and Aug., daily 7 am–9 pm; Apr.–June, Sept., and Oct., daily 8 am–noon and 4–8 pm. Cave: daily 10–1.*

6

WHERE TO EAT

$$ EASTERN EUROPEAN 🍴 **Taverna-Konoba Marasović.** An excellent choice for travelers looking to experience traditional Croatian-style architecture, this konoba is a transformed village house replete with period furniture and a customary front terrace. The kitchen prepares local, seasonal ingredients with care, producing meals that will satisfy the desire for an authentic Dalmatian experience. Come here for a rustic atmosphere, cold beer, fresh fish, and an enjoyable evening alfresco. The konoba and the adjoining ethno-house are managed by the National Park itself and its reconstruction was partly allowed by EU funding. [$] *Average main: €13* ✉ *Trg Marasovica* ☎ *023/369–155* ✉ *np-paklenica@paklenica.hr.*

WHERE TO STAY

$$$ HOTEL 🏨 **Hotel Alan.** Once inside this high-rise hotel, you might easily forget that you are, in fact, in a concrete box that still looks rather like a college dormitory. **Pros:** great views; beach and pool; bright and modern interiors. **Cons:** bland high-rise look on the outside; pricey; smallish rooms. [$] *Rooms from: €150* ✉ *Dr. Franje Tuđmana 14* ☎ *023/209–050* 🌐 *www.hotel-alan.hr* 🛏 *138 rooms* 🍽 *Breakfast.*

$ HOTEL 🏨 **Hotel Rajna.** On an isolated stretch of the main road just before you enter Starigrad from the south—and close to the national park access road—this friendly little hotel is a bit concrete-boxish in appearance. **Pros:** pleasantly isolated spot near park-access road; fine mountain views; good on-site dining; friendly service. **Cons:** 15-minute walk from the village center; bland on the outside; rooms a tad worn. [$] *Rooms* *from: €60* ⊠ *Dr. Franje Tuđmana* ☎ *023/359–121* ⊕ *www.hotel-rajna. com* ⤴ *10 rooms* ⧈ *Breakfast.*

SPORTS AND THE OUTDOORS

TOURS

Koma-Maras. Koma-Maras rents bicycles and sells tickets for various excursions in the national park as well as tickets for daylong boat trips up the lovely Zrmanja River gorge and its waterfalls, which are near Obrovac, toward the southern end of the Velebit range; the boat tours cost about 300 Kn per person. There's an ATM by the agency entrance. ⊠ *Dr. Franje Tuđmana 14* ☎ *023/359–206* ⊕ *www.koma-maras.hr.*

PAG ISLAND

48 km (30 miles) north of Zadar.

Telling an urbane resident of architecturally well-endowed Zadar that you are headed to Pag Island for a night or two will make them think you want to wallow on a sandy beach all day and party all night. Indeed, Pag Island has developed a reputation in recent years as a place to sunbathe and live it up rather than visit historic sites. The town of Novalja, in the north, has quite a summertime population of easy-livin' revelers. But to be fair, this narrow island, one of Croatia's longest, stretching 63 km (40 miles) north to south, has long been famous for other reasons, among them its cheese, salt, and, not least, its lace. Moreover, Pag Town in particular has an attractive historic center, a surprising contrast to the modern, resortish feel of its outskirts, and a contrast to the breathtaking natural barrenness of so much of the island.

Inaccessible for centuries except by sea, Pag Island saw a dramatic boost in tourism starting in 1968 with the completion of the Paškog mosta (Pag Bridge), which linked it with the mainland and the Zagreb-Split motorway. The first thing you notice on crossing over the bridge onto the island is that practically all vegetation disappears. You are on a moonlike landscape of whitewashed rocks scattered with clumps of green hanging on for dear life. But, sure enough, soon you also notice the sheep so instrumental in producing both Pag cheese—that strong, hard, Parmesan-like product that results from the sheep munching all day long on the island's salty herbs—and, yes, Pag lamb. Then, five minutes or so apart, you pass through a couple of small villages and, finally, the huge salt flats stretching out along the road right before you pull into Pag Town.

GETTING HERE AND AROUND

Pag is easiest to reach by car or bus from Zadar via the toll-free Pag bridge. There are 10 to 15 inexpensive bus connections a day. If driving along the "magistrala" from Rijeka, you will do well to take the ferry from Prizna, while nondrivers have the option of a daily fast boat connection from Rijeka to Novalja at the southern tip of the island.

EXPLORING

Lest you think the modern vacation homes lining the bay are all there is to Pag Town, park your car (or get off the bus) for a walk into the historic center, the narrow streets of which provide not only a rich sense of centuries past but also a refuge of shade on a hot summer day. Pag Town was founded in 1443, when Juraj Dalmatinac of Šibenik, best known for designing Šibenik's magnificent cathedral, was commissioned by the Venetians to build a fortified island capital to replace its predecessor, which was ravaged by invaders in 1395. Today a few odd stretches remain of the 7-meter-high wall Dalmatinac built around the town, and a walk around the center reveals several Renaissance buildings and palaces from his era as well as baroque balconies and stone coats of arms from the 15th to 18th centuries. Pag Town's compact main square, **Trg Kralja Petra Krešimira IV,** is home to three of the town's key landmarks, two of them original buildings designed in the mid-14th century by Juraj Dalmatinac. The bay stretches far, with sandy, shallow beaches aplenty—making Pag Island a great place to sunbathe and swim for a day or two, especially with children. The best and biggest beaches, amid pretty groves of pine and Dalmatian oak, are in Novalja.

> ## PAG CHEESE
>
> Thanks to its many sheep, Pag Island is known as the home of one of Croatia's most esteemed cheeses—*Paški sir* (Pag cheese). You can buy some for 150 Kn per kilogram, or 15 Kn for a decagram, which is a small piece indeed. If that sounds expensive, just try ordering a bit as an appetizer in a restaurant, where it's more than twice as much. You can easily find it on sale in private homes on some of the narrow streets off the main square. Celebrated local complements to the cheese include the lamb, an herb brandy called travarica, and Pag prosciutto.

Crkva Sveta Marija (*St. Mary's Church*). Most notably, there is the Crkva Sveta Marija (St. Mary's Church), a three-nave basilica whose simple front is decorated with a Gothic portal, an appropriately lace-like Renaissance rosette, and unfinished figures of saints. A relief over the entrance depicts the Virgin Mary protecting the townsfolk of Pag. Begun in 1466 under Dalmatinac's direction, it was completed only decades later, after his death. Inside, note the elaborate, 18th-century baroque altars, and the wood beams visible on the original stone walls. The church is open daily 9–noon and 5–7. ⊠ *Glavni Trg, 6 Ulica Jurja Dalmatinca* ⊕ *www.pag.hr.*

Knežev dvor (*Duke's Palace*). Across the square is the imposing Knežev dvor with its magnificent, richly detailed portal, a sumptuous 15th-century edifice built to house the duke. Until the early 1990s, it housed a grocery store and a café; now it is a cultural and exhibition venue, hosting concerts, plays, and manifestations during the summer months. The upper floors have been converted into the City Hall. ⊠ *Glavni Trg.*

Stari grad. A mere 20-minute walk south of the present town center lays the ruins of the previous, 9th-century town, Stari grad (Old Town). You

CLOSE UP

White Gold

There was a time when paške čipke was passed off abroad as Greek, Austrian, or Italian. Those days are long over. Today an officially recognized "authentic Croatian product" that is sometimes called "white gold," Pag lace is the iconic souvenir to take home with you from a visit to Pag Island—unless you are confident that a hulking block of Pag cheese won't spoil. An integral component of the colorful folk costumes locals wear during festivals, this celebrated white lace is featured most saliently as the huge peaked head ornament ladies don on such occasions, which resembles a fastidiously folded, ultra-starched white cloth napkin.

Originating in the ancient Greek city of Mycenae, the Pag lace-making tradition endured for centuries before being popularized far and wide as a Pag product beginning in the late-19th century. A lace-making school was founded in Pag Town in 1906, drawing orders from royalty from distant lands. In 1938 Pag lace makers participated in the world exhibition in New York.

Pag lace differs from other types of lace in two key respects: a thin thread and exceptional durability. Using an ordinary mending needle against a solid background, and usually proceeding without a plan, the maker begins by creating a circle within which she (or he) makes tiny holes close together; the thread is then pulled through them. The completed lace has a starched quality and can even be washed without losing its firmness. It is best presented on a dark background and framed.

The process is painstaking, so Pag lace is not cheap: a typical small piece of around 20 centimeters in diameter costs at least 200 Kn from a maker or perhaps double that from a shop.

can wander around for free, taking in the Romanesque-style Crkva svete Marije (St. Mary's Church), first mentioned in historical records in 1192; the ruins of a Franciscan monastery; and a legendary, centuries-old well whose filling up with water after a drought was credited to the intervention of the Holy Virgin. On August 15, one of only two days St. Mary's Church is open to the public (the other is September 8), a procession of locals carries a statue of the Virgin Mary from here to the church of the same name on present-day Pag's main square. On September 8 they return. To get to Stari grad, walk across the bridge and keep left on Put Starog Grada, the road that runs south along the bay.

WHERE TO EAT

$$ EASTERN EUROPEAN 🍴 **Bistro Na Tale.** An easy choice if you are looking to sample Pag's signature local lamb or specialty Paški Sir (cheese produced by sheep consuming grass laced with salty sea water). While more unique eateries are to be had, Bistro Na Tale is nevertheless a popular spot that serves quality dishes in a pleasant atmosphere. Enjoy a seat on the terrace facing the salt flats and dine casually while planning your next excursion. [$] *Average main: €18* ✉ *Radiceva 2* ☎ *023/611–194* 🕓 *Closed Dec. 23–Feb. 1.*

$$$ EASTERN EUROPEAN 🍴 **Konoba Bodulo.** The menu may be small at this family-owned spot, but it manages to squeeze in everything from staple pastas and risottos to grilled meats and steak—and the service is friendly. You can enjoy this combination under the courtyard's grapevine or next to the interior's stone walls, with Croatian pop for background music. [$] *Average main: €42* ✉ *Vangrada 19* ☎ *023/611–689.*

$$ EASTERN EUROPEAN 🍴 **Konoba Giardin.** The Konoba Giardin has mastered the art of cooking with flame, producing delectably grilled entrées from a real wood fire nestled within a brick oven. Select a whole fish from the day's fresh catch, sold by the kilogram, or share a grill platter of mixed cuts of beef piled high atop potatoes and salads. Lamb and octopus are equally top choices. Proprietors Nikola and Josip are apt to produce a guitar as the evening stretches to night, serving merriment and local wine into the wee hours. [$] *Average main: €18* ✉ *Vanđelje 1, Kolan* ☎ *023/698–007* 🌐 *www.konoba-giardin.com.*

WHERE TO STAY

$$$ B&B/INN Fodor's Choice ★ 🏨 **Boškinac.** Nestled amid the vines of vineyards and olive groves, refined serenity awaits guests to Boškinac. **Pros:** phenomenal restaurant; great vineyard tour; luxurious everything. **Cons:** remote; vehicle needed. [$] *Rooms from: €170* ✉ *Novaljsko Polje BB, Novalja* ☎ *053/663–500* 🌐 *www.boskinac.com* 🛏 *11 rooms* 🍽 *Breakfast.*

$$$ RESORT 🏨 **Luna Island Hotel.** If you're looking for a place to relax and have your meals, spa treatments, and lounge chair easily available within just a few steps, at Luna Island Hotel you have arrived. **Pros:** air-conditioning; service; beachside; good distance from the party beach of Zrće (the Ibiza of Croatia). **Cons:** vehicle is helpful; pleasant yet bland furnishings; pricey. [$] *Rooms from: €200* ✉ *Jakisnica BB* ☎ *+385 05/365–4700* 🌐 *lunaislandhotel.com* 🛏 *96 rooms* 🍽 *Breakfast.*

NIGHTLIFE AND PERFORMING ARTS

FESTIVALS

Pag Carnival. Pag Carnival, featuring a range of music on and around the main square, dance and folk-song performances—and, not least, the annual reenactment of a 16th-century folk drama, Paška robinja "Slave Girl of Pag," which tells the story of buying back an enslaved girl, the granddaughter of the ruler Ban Derenčin, who was defeated by the Turks. The Pag Carinval takes place immediately before Lent, which is usually in February, but varies from year to year.

Pag Music Festivals. An array of hip music festivals come to the island of Pag every summer. Slightly varying by date, check festival specific websites for up to date information. Some island festivals include: Hideout Festival, Sonus Festival, and Fresh Island Festival.

SHOPPING

Galerija Paške Čipke (*Pag Lace Gallery*). You needn't venture farther than the main square and surrounding narrow streets of Pag Town to find a white gold jewelry seller—whether an old lady or an equally enthusiastic child. Of course, you can also try Pag Town's very own Galerija

6

Paške Čipke, open mid-June through mid-September, daily 9–1, or else any of several local shops that you are certain to encounter near the main square in Pag Town. ⊠ *Trg Krajla Petra Krešimira IV, Pag Town.*

SPORTS AND THE OUTDOORS

BEACHES

Deciding where to swim once you reach Pag Town is a no-brainer; you can pick practically anywhere in the huge, sheltered bay that stretches out from the short bridge in the town center. If you have kids, all that sand and shallow water is an added plus, compared to Zadar and so many other stretches of Croatia's often deep, rocky coast. Most of the 27 km (17 miles) of public beaches in the bay are accessible by car. For even better swimming, if that is possible, try heading north to Novalja and environs. The tourist-information office has a free map showing the locations of the best beaches.

SPLIT AND CENTRAL DALMATIA

By Elizabeth Hughes-Komljen

Central Dalmatia's wild beauty is often characterized as harsh, hot, and edgy because of its scorching summers, rocky coastal beaches, steep mountains, and rugged inland. Those same words could also be used to describe the collective personality of the people that come from this region. It is precisely that combination of wild raw beauty that makes central Dalmatia stand out from its northern and inland neighbors and what attracts outsiders. The capital city of Dalmatia, Split, is an historic city that was once an industrial and trade center that has transformed dramatically since the war for independence.

Split has blossomed in the past 10 years into a bustling coastal destination. The layers of history contained within the walls of the Diocletian palace beg to be uncovered with more than just a few snapshots and a stroll through the labyrinth-like side streets, which contrast sharply with the modern life of the citizens that currently live in and around the old walls and make Split the most eclectic of all Croatian cities.

From Split you can take an overnight ferry to Ancona, Italy or hop on one of the regular ferries or catamarans to one of the outlying islands. Split is also Central Dalmatia's main base for yacht-charter companies. A 90-minute drive up the coast, northwest of Split, lies Šibenik, home to a Gothic-Renaissance cathedral. Once an important industrial center, Šibenik has fallen into economic decline, but it still makes a good base for visiting the cascading waterfalls of Krka National Park, and the peaceful riverside town of Skradin. Moving back from Šibenik toward Split is Trogir. The historic city of Trogir is a remarkable conglomeration of Roman, Greek, and Venetian ancient stone architecture contained on a tiny island that residents call their living museum. A 30-minute drive down the coast from Split brings one to Omiš and the mouth of the River Cetina. This river forms a steep-sided valley renowned for adventure sports like rafting and rock climbing (called free climbing in Croatia). However, for many people, what makes Central Dalmatia so special are the islands. The nearest, Brač, most often recognized for its famous Zlatni Rat (Golden Cape) beach is an island of exceptional beauty that will leave you with a lasting impression because of the traditions, culture, and history that remain undiscovered yet pervade every aspect of the food, work, and life on this island. West of Brač lays the island of Šolta. Although there is little of cultural interest here, those lucky enough to be sailing along the south side of the island will find several idyllic bays that are accessible only by sea. South of Brač rises the island of Hvar, home to Central Dalmatia's most exclusive party destination, Hvar Town. Sixteenth-century Venetian buildings ring three sides of the Hvar Town harbor with its magnificent main square that is overlooked by a baroque cathedral, and a proud hilltop castle that beckons visitors to take in the view from higher ground. Farther out to sea still lies wild, windswept Vis, Croatia's most distant inhabited island. There are only two real settlements here: Vis Town and Komiža, the latter making the best starting point for a day trip to Modra Spilja (Blue Cave) on the island of Biševo. Back on the mainland, a two-hour drive down the coast south of Split brings you to Makarska, a popular seaside area built around a bay filled with fishing boats and backed by the rugged silhouette of the Biokovo Mountains. Biokovo's peak, Sveti Jure (5,780 feet) is the third highest of Croatia's mountains and offers stunning views over the entire region.

Lastovo, Croatia's second–most distant inhabited island (after Vis), remains firmly off the beaten track. Although it is part of Southern Dalmatia, it is not connected to the region by boat. The islanders there opted instead to remain connected to Split via ferry and catamaran services.

ORIENTATION AND PLANNING

GETTING ORIENTED

Split is the main jumping-off point for exploring all of Dalmatia, not just Central Dalmatia. From there it is easy to catch a bus, boat, train, or rental car in any direction to see everything Dalmatia offers, on and off the beaten path. In each direction of Split, there are many nearby places worth exploring. Directly south of Split are the islands of Brač and Šolta, both easily accessed by ferry in less than one hour. Northeast of Split is Omiš and the Cetina river valley, and directly west across the bay from the Split port is the ancient walled city of Trogir, which can be reached in 20 minutes by taxi boat. To the north of Split and a 30-minute drive are the Klis fortress and the Vranjaca cave, which offers spectacular views over Split and are often overlooked by tourists. Southwest toward Dubrovnik is the Makarska Riviera with its plethora of hidden coved beaches that can be reached in about 45 minutes by car from Split. In the opposite direction of Makarska, along the main coastal highway, there is Krka National park, about a two-hour drive from Split but also accessible by boat via the Skradin bay. Međugorje, which is across the border in Bosnia and Herzegovina, is less than a two-hour drive from Split and is also a short distance from Mostar.

WHEN TO GO

High season runs from July through August, when the region is inundated with foreign tourists. During the summer of 2014 more than 45 different airlines had scheduled flights into Split, making it the most accessible of all Croatian destinations. Prices at this time rise significantly, and it can be difficult to find a place to sleep if you haven't reserved in advance, restaurant staff are overworked, and beaches are crowded. On top of everything, it can be very hot. On the positive side, some museums and churches have extended opening hours, the season's open-air bars and clubs bring nightlife to the fore, and there

are numerous cultural festivals with performances starring international musicians, dancers, and actors. Low season runs from November through April, when many hotels and restaurants close completely, the exception being over the New Year's period, when some of the more sophisticated establishments (for example in Hvar Town) open their doors for the holidays. At this time of year the weather is unreliable, but if you're lucky you could find yourself drinking morning coffee in the sunshine below a deep blue sky, against a backdrop of snowcapped mountains.

However, for most people the best time to visit is midseason, May through June and September through October. During these periods you'll miss the crowds, the weather should be sunny and dry, and the sea will be warm enough to swim in; the region's hotels and restaurants will be open, but their pace slow enough to lend an air of true relaxation.

GETTING HERE AND AROUND

AIR TRAVEL

Split is served by Split Airport (SPU) at Kaštela, 25 km (16 miles) northwest of the city center. The island of Brač is served by Brač Airport at Veško Polje, 14 km (9 miles) northeast of Bol.

The national carrier, Croatia Airlines, operates domestic flights from Split to Zagreb, Dubrovnik, Pula, and Osijek. During the summer high

TOP REASONS TO GO

■ Explore Diocletian's Palace, a massive 3rd-century Roman edifice that contains Croatia's most defiant and alternative population within its walls. Arrange to take a tour in the early morning hours before the buzz of daily life drowns out the voices of the past in this amazing historical location.

■ Come to Hvar and hire a taxi boat or a one-day sailing charter to bring you to your own private island and experience the purity of island life and what it inspires.

■ Plunge into the clear waters of Sutivan on Brač after climbing to Vidova Gora, the highest point on all the Croatian islands, or walking the Dolce Vita trail through the island's olive groves where the country's premiere olive oil is produced.

■ Sail into Komiža harbor on Vis island aboard a yacht after a long day on the water, perhaps having visited Modra Spilja (the Blue Cave) on the nearby island of Biševo.

■ Climb Biokovo Mountain at sunrise, take a moonlight swim in Tucepi, and be awed by the Makarska riviera's majestic mountain from above and below.

season you can fly directly to Split from Amsterdam, Bari, Brussels, Catania, Copenhagen, Frankfurt, Gothenburg, Hamburg, Helsinki, Istanbul, Lisbon, London, Lyon, Manchester, Milan, Munich, Oslo, Palermo, Paris, Prague, Rome, Sarajevo, Skopje, Stockholm, Tel Aviv, Turin, Vienna, Warsaw, and Zurich. Also through summer, Croatia Airlines flies nonstop from the island of Brač to Zagreb, Munich, and Frankfurt. Adria, British Airways, ČSA and Malev also fly to Split. In addition, through the summer the low-cost airlines EasyJet and Wizzair operate between London and Split.

You can take an airport bus to obala Lazereta, near the Split Bus Station. For your return, the airport bus leaves Split 90 minutes before each flight. A one-way ticket costs 30 Kn, and the travel time is 40 minutes. Brač airport is not served by bus but taxis are available.

Airline Contacts Adria Airways ✉ *Praška 9, Zagreb* ☎ *021/20–33–31* ⊕ *www.adria.si.* **Air Mediterranee** ✉ *Split* ☎ *581/312–999* ⊕ *www.air-mediterranee.fr.* **Austria Airlines** ✉ *Zagreb* ☎ *1/62–65–900* ⊕ *www.austrian.com.* **British Airways** ✉ *Split Airport, Kaštela* ☎ *021/797–303.* **Croatia Airlines** ✉ *Obala Hrvatskog Narodnog Preporoda 9, Grad, Split* ☎ *021/203–305* ⊕ *www.croatiaairlines.com.* **EasyJet** ✉ *Split* ⊕ *www.easyjet.com.* **Jet2.com** ✉ *Split* ⊕ *www.jet2.com.* **Lufthansa** ✉ *Kaštela* ☎ *1/390–7284* ⊕ *www.lufthansa.com.* **Wizzair** ✉ *Split* ⊕ *www.wizzair.com.*

Airport Contacts Split Airport ✉ *Kaštela* ☎ *021/203–555 general information, 021/203–218 lost and found* ⊕ *www.split-airport.hr.* **Brač Airport.** Brac airport is open for charter flights in summer only. ✉ *Supetar, Veško Polje* ☎ *021/559–711 general information* ⊕ *www.airport-brac.hr.*

Airport Transfer Contacts Split airport bus. The Croatia Airlines shuttle service travels daily to and from the airport to the port of Split. The shuttle departs from the main Split bus station platform 5. One-way ticket is 30 Kn,

GREAT ITINERARIES

Central Dalmatia warrants weeks of discovery; even many locals admit that they haven't even seen it all. However, if your time is limited, the itineraries listed below aim to give you a taste of the major attractions.

IF YOU HAVE 3 DAYS

Devote Day 1 to **Split,** exploring the historic monuments within the walls of Diocletian's Palace and attending an open-air opera performance if the Split Summer Festival is in progress. On the next day, take an early morning ferry to Supetar on the island of Brač, then a local bus to **Bol,** for an afternoon bathing on Croatia's finest beach, Zlatni Rat. Catch the late-afternoon catamaran to Jelsa on the island of Hvar, then a local bus to **Hvar Town,** the region's hippest island resort, where you should sleep. Next morning, either check out Hvar's Venetian-style architecture or take a taxi boat to Pakleni Otoci for a swim. Catch the late-afternoon ferry back to Split for your final night.

IF YOU HAVE 5 DAYS

Spend your first day in Split. On the next morning, drive or take a local bus to **Trogir,** a compact settlement of stone houses built on an island linked to the mainland by a bridge, then proceed up the coast for an afternoon in **Šibenik,** where the most-visited monument is the Gothic–Renaissance cathedral. Spend the night in either Šibenik or **Skradin.** Give Day 3 to the waterfalls and dense woodland of **Krka National Park,** returning to Split for the night. Days 4 and 5 should be dedicated to the islands of **Brač** and **Hvar** (see above), returning to Split for the final night.

IF YOU HAVE 7 DAYS

Spend your first day in Split, the second and third days in Trogir, Šibenik, Skradin, and Krka National Park, as outlined above, returning to Split on the third night. Days 4 and 5 can then be given over to the islands of Brač and Hvar (as described above), returning to Split for the fifth night. On the next morning, either drive or take a local bus down the coast to **Omiš,** from which you can set off up the **Cetina Valley** and participate in adventure sports (by prior arrangement). In the evening continue down the coast to **Makarska,** where you should sleep. The final day you can explore Makarska and its beaches, or venture up Biokovo Mountain for spectacular views over the entire region. Return to Split for your last night.

return on same day is 40 Kn. There is another shuttle service offered from April to October, adjacent to the ferry terminal and next to the bus station. Price is 30 Kn. ✉ Split ☎ 021/203–119 ⊕ www.plesoprijevoz.hr.

BOAT AND FERRY TRAVEL

From June through September, Jadrolinija and Blue Line both run regular services to Ancona (Italy), departing at 9 pm from Split and arriving in Ancona at 7 am the following day. The same vessels depart at 9 pm from Ancona to arrive in Split at 7 am. Journey time is approximately 10 hours in either direction. In peak season only, Blue Line also runs day crossings departing from Ancona at 11 am on Saturday, Sunday, and Monday. Through winter these services are reduced slightly.

From June to September the Italian company SNAV runs Croazia Jet, a daily catamaran service between Ancona (Italy) and Split, departing at 5 pm from Split and arriving in Ancona at 9:30 pm. The same vessel departs at 11 am from Ancona to arrive in Split at 3:30 pm. The journey time is 4½ hours in either direction. The same company runs Pescara Jet, a daily catamaran service between Pescara (Italy) and Split, stopping at Stari Grad (island of Hvar) en route. The vessel departs at 5 pm from Split and arrives in Pescara at 11 pm, then leaves Pescara the following morning at 10:30, arriving in Split at 4:15 pm. On Saturday only, a corresponding catamaran connects from Stari Grad (Hvar) to Bol (Brač). Jadrolinija operates coastal ferries that run from Rijeka to Dubrovnik. Ferries depart from Rijeka twice a week in the evening, and arrive in Split in the early morning on the following day (journey time is approximately 10 hours) and then continue down the coast to Dubrovnik (journey time is approximately 9 hours), stopping at Stari Grad (island of Hvar) and Korčula en route. From Dubrovnik, they then cover an overnight stretch to Bari in Italy. Jadrolinija runs daily ferries to Supetar (island of Brač), Stari Grad (island of Hvar), and Vis from Split. Jadrolinija runs a daily catamaran from Split to Hvar Town (island of Hvar), which then continues to Vela Luka (island of Korčula) and Ubli (island of Lastovo). A separate service runs to Bol (island of Brač) and then continues to Jelsa (island of Hvar). It is now possible to book most boat and ferry travel online, sometimes at a reduced price. It is highly recommended to purchase online in advance whenever possible, especially during high season when waiting until the last minute could often mean waiting an extra day.

Contacts Blue Line ✉ Split ☎ 021/352–533 ⊕ www.blueline-ferries.com. **Jadrolinija** ✉ Split ferry port, Gat Sv.Duje BB, Split ☎ 021/338–333 ⊕ www. jadrolinija.hr. **Krilo** ✉ Poljička cesta, Krilo Jesenice ☎ 021/645–476 ⊕ krilo.hr. **SNAV** ✉ Split ☎ 021/322–252 ⊕ www.snav.it.

BUS TRAVEL

International buses arrive daily from Trieste, Ljubljana, Belgrade, Sarajevo, Munich, and Stuttgart. There are buses once a week from Vienna, and London via Paris.

There are good bus connections to destinations all over Croatia. There are approximately 30 buses per day to Zagreb, 12 to Dubrovnik (in Southern Dalmatia), 14 to Zadar (in Northern Dalmatia), and 12 to Rijeka (in Kvarner). Buses traveling south to Dubrovnik stop at Makarska en route, while those going north to Zadar stop at Šibenik. In addition, regular local buses run every 30 minutes up the coast to Trogir and down the coast to Omiš. Timetable information is available from the Split Bus Station, or from their website (*see below*).

Contacts Split Bus Station ✉ Obala Kneza Domogoja 12, Split ☎ 060/327–777 ⊕ www.ak-split.hr.

CAR TRAVEL

While visiting Split and the nearby islands of Brač, Hvar, and Vis, you are certainly better off without a car. However, you may wish to rent a vehicle to drive up the coast to Šibenik and Krka National Park, or down the coast to Omiš and Makarska, although these destinations are also well served by buses. Renting a car once you arrive on the islands is also an affordable option to be able to see the entire island at your own pace.

Contacts Dollar Thrifty ⌧ *Trumbićeva Obala 17, Split* ☎ *021/895–320* ⊕ *www. subrosa.hr* ⌧ *Split Airport, Kaštela* ☎ *021/399–000* ⊕ *www.subrosa.hr.* **Hertz** ⌧ *Trubićeva Obala 2, Split* ☎ *021/360–455* ⊕ *www.hertz.hr* ⌧ *Split Airport, Kaštela* ☎ *021/203292* ⊕ *www.hertz.hr.* **Rapidus rent-a-car.** Rent a bright-color convertible Bug for the day and you can explore the island in style and at your own pace. They have a fleet of quirky cars that can be picked up and dropped off in Hvar Town, Stari Grad, Jelsa and even on Brac or Vis. ⌧ *Hvar* ⊕ *www. rapidus.hr/en-hvar.php.*

TAXI TRAVEL

In Split the main taxi ranks lie at each end of the *Riva* (Obala Hrvatskog Preporoda), in front of the *pazar* (open-air market), and in front of Hotel Bellevue. You will also find taxis waiting outside the train station (Obala Kneza Domagoja). Or you can call for a taxi in Split.

TRAIN TRAVEL

There are three day trains and two night trains (with sleeping cars) daily between Split and Zagreb (journey time 5½ hours daytime; 8½ hours nighttime). In addition, there are three day trains daily between Split and Šibenik (journey time approximately 3½ hours, with a change at Perković).

Contact Split Train Station ⌧ *Obala Kneza Domagoja 9, Split* ☎ *060/333–444* ⊕ *www.hzpp.hr.*

RESTAURANTS

Eateries fall into two main categories: you can eat in a *restoran* (restaurant) or *konoba* (tavern). Restaurants are more formal affairs, catering mainly to tourists and offering Croatian cuisine plus a choice of popular international dishes. In contrast, a konoba serves typical regional dishes; many offer a *marenda* (cut-price lunch), and at those you are likely to see locals as well as tourists. Central Dalmatian specialties are mainly seafood-based. *Rižot* (risotto) reflects the region's historic ties with Venice, as does *brodet* (fish stewed in a rich tomato, onion, and wine sauce). Fish are divided into two categories: "white" fish, including *brancin* (branzino, or sea bass) and *san pjero* (John Dory), being the more expensive, while "blue" fish, including *srdele* (sardines) and *skuša* (mackerel) are cheaper but less frequently on offer. In restaurants, be aware that fresh fish is priced by the kilogram, so prices vary dramatically depending on how big your fish is. A popular new trend in dining are the wine bars that have popped up all over Dalmatia featuring the regions best local wines, cheeses, and prosciutto. Some offer a wide selection of original tapas, and almost all are eager to educate their clientele about local wines and provide suggestions.

HOTELS

Central Dalmatia's best and most expensive hotels are in Hvar Town on the island of Hvar. The region's socialist-era resort hotels are gradually being privatized and refurbished, and a number of small family-run and boutique luxury hotels have opened as well. However, many visitors still prefer to rent a private room or apartment, a solution that offers value for money, direct contact with the locals, and (if you are lucky) an authentic stone cottage opening onto a terrace lined with potted geraniums and a blissful sea view. The season runs from Easter to late October, and peaks during July and August, when prices rise significantly and when it may be difficult to find a place to sleep if you have not booked in advance. *Hotel reviews have been shortened. For full information, visit Fodors.com.*

WHAT IT COSTS IN EUROS (€) AND CROATIAN KUNA (KN)			
$	**$$**	**$$$**	**$$$$**
Restaurants under 35 Kn	35 Kn–60 Kn	61 Kn–80 Kn	over 80 Kn
under €5	€5–€8	€9–€10	over €10
Hotels under 925 Kn	925 Kn–1,300 Kn	1,301 Kn–1,650 Kn	over 1,650 Kn
under €121	€121–€170	€171–€216	over €216

Restaurant prices are the average cost of a main course at dinner or, if dinner is not served, at lunch. Hotel prices are the lowest cost of a standard double room in high season.

TOURS

There are many tour options to choose from in Split. New agencies pop up every year offering different options of the same basic tours. There are some agencies more committed to preserving the natural beauty, culture, and traditions of Dalmatia. These agencies are very proud of Croatia and seek to provide tourists with authentic and individual experiences that are not focused on mass tourism.

Opcija Tours. Opcija Tours is well known not only for their walking tours of Diocletian's palace but also for their private one-day charters to nearby islands and restaurants. ⊠ *Papalićeva ulica 2, Split* ☎ *021/345244* ⊕ *www.opcijatours.hr.*

Secret Dalmatia. Secret Dalmatia custom-designs their signature tours and is a good choice if you want to experience Dalmatia up close and personal. ⊠ *Turanj 426, Sv Filip Jakov* ☎ *091/567-1604* ⊕ *www.secretdalmatia.com.*

Split Excursions. Split Excursions offers tours both of the city and the surrounding area, including Plitvice National Park. ⊠ *Split* ☎ *021/360-061* ⊕ *www.split-excursions.com.*

VISITOR INFORMATION

Contacts Bol Tourist Information Center ⊠ *Porat Bolskih Pomoraca BB, Bol* ☎ *021/635-638* ⊕ *www.bol.hr.* **Hvar Town Tourist Information Center** ⊠ *Trg Sv. Stjepana BB, Hvar* ☎ *021/741-059* ⊕ *www.tzhvar.hr.* **Lastovo Tourist Office** ⊠ *Pjevor BB, Lastovo* ☎ *020/801-018* ⊕ *www.lastovo-tz.net.* **Makarska Tourist Information Centre** ⊠ *Obala Kralja Tomislava 16, Makarska* ☎ *021/612-002* ⊕ *www.makarska-info.hr.* **Split & Dalmatia County Tourist Board** ⊠ *Prilaz brace Kaliterna 10/I, Split* ☎ *021/490-032* ⊕ *www.dalmatia.hr.* **Split Tourist Information Center** ⊠ *Hrvatskog narodnog preporoda 7, Split* ☎ *021/348-600* ⊕ *www.visitsplit.com.* **Šibenik Tourist Information Center** ⊠ *Obala dr. Franje Tuđmana 5, Šibenik* ☎ *022/214-448* ⊕ *www.sibenik-tourism.hr.* **Trogir Tourist**

Information Center ⊠ *Trg Ivana Pavla II 1, Trogir* ☎ *021/885–628* ⊕ *www. tztrogir.hr.* **Vis Tourist Information Center** ⊠ *Šetalište Stare Isse 5, Vis Town* ☎ *021/717–017* ⊕ *www.tz-vis.hr.*

SPLIT

Split is 365 km (228 miles) south of Zagreb.

Split's ancient core is so spectacular and unusual that a visit is more than worth your time. The heart of the city lies within the walls of Roman emperor Diocletian's retirement palace, which was built in the 3rd century AD. Diocletian, born in the nearby Roman settlement of Salona in AD 245, achieved a brilliant career as a soldier and became emperor at the age of 40. In 295 he ordered this vast palace to be built in his native Dalmatia, and when it was completed he stepped down from the throne and retired to his beloved homeland. Upon his death, he was laid to rest in an octagonal mausoleum, around which Split's magnificent cathedral was built.

In 615, when Salona was sacked by barbarian tribes, those fortunate enough to escape found refuge within the stout palace walls and divided up the vast imperial apartments into more modest living quarters. Thus, the palace developed into an urban center, and by the 11th century the settlement had expanded beyond the ancient walls.

Under the rule of Venice (1420–1797), Split—as a gateway to the Balkan interior—became one of the Adriatic's main trading ports, and the city's splendid Renaissance palaces bear witness to the affluence of those times. When the Habsburgs took control during the 19th century, an overland connection to Central Europe was established by the construction of the Split–Zagreb–Vienna railway line.

After World War II, the Tito years saw a period of rapid urban expansion: industrialization accelerated and the suburbs extended to accommodate high-rise apartment blocks. Today the historic center of Split is included on UNESCO's list of World Heritage Sites.

GETTING HERE AND AROUND
Central Dalmatia's capital, this coastal city is easy to get around and offers ferries to popular tourist spots like the islands of Brač and Hvar. There are also local buses available to visit surrounding towns like Bol and Trogir.

EXPLORING

The Old Town (often referred to as the Grad), where most of the architectural monuments are found, lies within the walls of Diocletian's Palace, which fronts on the seafront promenade, known to locals as the Riva. West of the center, Varoš is a conglomeration of stone fishermen's cottages built into a hillside, behind which rises Marjan, a 3½-km-long (2-mile-long) peninsula covered with pinewoods. Southeast of the center, the ferry port, bus station, and train station are grouped close together on Obala Kneza Domagoja. The newly constructed waterfront area, known as westcoast to locals, is a three-minute walk from the Riva and is modernly designed and offers a fresh new spacious view of Split.

TOP ATTRACTIONS

Fodor'sChoice **Dioklecijanova Palača** (*Diocletian's Palace*). The original palace, which
★ took about 10 years to complete, was built in AD 298. The palace was both a luxurious villa and a Roman garrison. Its rectangular shape has two main streets that divide the palace into four quarters: Dioklecijanova Ul, which runs north to south, and Poljana Krajlice Jelene, which runs east to west. Each of the four walls have a main gate, the largest and most important being the northern *Zlatna Vrata* (Golden Gate), which once opened onto the road to the Roman settlement of Salona. The entrance from the western wall was the *Željezna Vrata* (Iron Gate), and the entrance through the east wall was the *Srebrena Vrata* (Silver Gate). The *Mjedna Vrata* (Bronze Gate) on the south wall faces directly onto the sea, and during Roman times boats would have docked here. The city celebrated the palace's 1,700th birthday in 2005 and continues to share the heritage of its Roman emperor by annually marking the last Friday in July as Diocletian's Night. ■TIP➔ Hire an experienced private guide that can give you a walking tour in the early morning hours in order to experience the true history of the palace walls. Currently more than 1,000 people live within what once was a Roman emperor's palace, which can make it more difficult to uncover this treasure as it once was. ✉ *Obala Hrvatskog Narodnog Preporoda, Grad, Split.*

Galerija Meštrović (*Meštrović Gallery*). A short walk from the Riva, this must-see gallery is located in a tranquil location that overlooks the sea and is surrounded by extensive gardens. Ivan Mestrovic, considered to be the Rodin of Croatia, designed this building as his summer residence during the 1920s and '30s. Some 200 of his sculptural works in wood, marble, stone, and bronze are on display, both indoors and out. The gallery is a green oasis in the center of the city with an open-air café that is frequented by children and families durnig the day and young locals in the evening. ✉ *Šetalište Ivana Meštrovicá 46, Meje, Split* ☎ *021/340–800* ⊕ *www.mdc.hr* ✉ *30 Kn* ☽ *May–Sept., Tues.–Sun. 9–7; Oct.–Apr., Tues.–Sat. 9–4, Sun. 10–3.*

Kaštelet. Entrance to the Galerija Meštrović is also valid for the nearby Kaštelet, housing a chapel containing a cycle of New Testament bas-relief wood carvings that many consider Meštrović's finest work. ✉ *Šetalište Ivana Meštrovicá 39, Meje, Split* ⊕ *www.mestrovic.hr.*

Vestibul. The cupola of this domed space would once have been decorated with marble and mosaics. Today there's only a round hole in the top of the dome, but it produces a stunning effect: the dark interior, the blue sky above, and the tip of the cathedral's bell tower framed in the opening. ✉ *Peristil, Grad, Split.*

Zlatna Vrata (*Golden Gate*). Formerly the main entrance into the palace, Zlatna Vrata, on the north side of the palace, is the most monumental of the four gates—two guards in Roman costume stand here through summer. Just outside the Zlatna Vrata stands Meštrović's gigantic bronze **statue of Grgur Ninski** (Bishop Gregory of Nin). During the 9th century, the bishop campaigned for the use of the Slav language in the Croatian

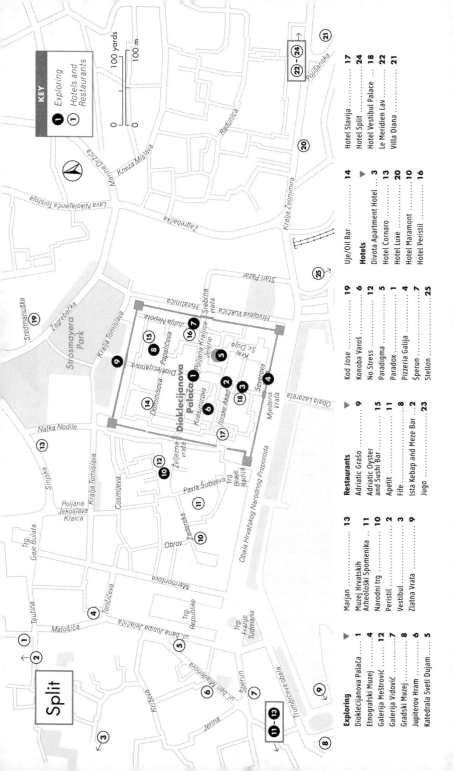

Split

KEY
- ● **1** Exploring
- ① Hotels and Restaurants

Exploring ▶
Dioklecijanova Palača	1
Etnografski Muzej	4
Galerija Meštrović	12
Galerija Vidović	7
Gradski Muzej	8
Jupiterov Hram	6
Katedrala Sveti Dujam	5
Marjan	13
Muzej Hrvatskih Arheološki Spomenika	11
Narodni trg	10
Peristil	2
Vestibul	3
Zlatna Vrata	9

Restaurants ▶
Adriatic Grašo	9
Adriatic Oyster and Sushi Bar	15
Apetit	11
Fife	8
Ista Kebap and Meze Bar	2
Jugo	23
Kod Jose	19
Konoba Varoš	6
No Stress	12
Paradigma	5
Paradox	1
Pizzeria Galija	4
Šperun	7
Stellon	25
Uje/Oil Bar	14

Hotels ▶
Divota Apartment Hotel	3
Hotel Cornaro	13
Hotel Luxe	20
Hotel Maramont	10
Hotel Peristil	16
Hotel Slavija	17
Hotel Split	24
Hotel Vestibul Palace	18
Le Meridien Lav	22
Villa Diana	21

Church, as opposed to Latin, thus infuriating Rome. This statue was created in 1929 and placed on Peristil to mark the 1,000th anniversary of the Split Synod, then moved here in 1957. Note the big toe on the left foot, which is considered by locals to be a good luck charm and has been worn gold through constant touching. ⊠ *Dioklecijanova, Grad, Split.*

WORTH NOTING

Etnografski Muzej (*Ethnographic Museum*). Occupying a splendid location within the walls of Diocletian's Palace, the museum displays traditional Dalmatian folk costumes and local antique furniture. ■**TIP→** If you are staying in Split for more than 3 days be sure to pick up your free Split Card, which gives you free entry to certain museums and galleries and reduced rates at others including some restaurants and cafés. Just ask the staff at your hotel or go to the nearest Tourist Information Bureau to pick one up. ⊠ *Iza Vestibula 4, Grad, Split* ☎ *021/344–161* ⊕ *www. etnografski-muzej-split.hr* ☒ *15 Kn, free if you have SplitCard* ☉ *June– Sept., weekdays 9–7, Sat. 9–1; Oct.–May, weekdays 9–4, Sat. 9–1.*

Galerija Vidović (*Vidović Gallery*). Emanuel Vidović (1870–1953) is acknowledged as Split's greatest painter. Here you can see 74 of his works, donated to the city by his family. Large, bold canvasses depict local landmarks cast in hazy light, while the sketches done outdoors before returning to his studio to paint are more playful and colorful. ⊠ *Poljana Kraljice Jelene BB, Grad, Split* ☎ *021/360–155* ⊕ *www. galerija-vidovic.com* ☒ *10 Kn* ☉ *June–Sept., Tues.–Fri. 9–9, weekends 9–4; Oct.–May, Tues.–Fri. 10–5, Sat. 9–1, Sun. 10–1.*

Gradski Muzej (*City Museum*). Split's city museum is worth a quick look both to marvel at the collection of medieval weaponry and to see the interior of this splendid 15th-century town house. The dining room, on the first floor, is furnished just as it would have been when the Papalić family owned the house, giving some idea of how the aristocracy of that time lived. ⊠ *Papaličeva 1, Grad, Split* ☎ *021/360–171* ⊕ *www.mgst. net* ☒ *20 Kn* ☉ *May–Oct., Tues.–Fri. 9–9, Sat.–Mon. 9–4; Nov.–Apr., Tues.–Fri. 10–4, Sat. 9–1, Sun. 10–1.*

Jupiterov Hram (*Jupiter's Temple*). Roman Emperor Diocletian constructed this temple to worship the god Jupiter. It was converted during the Middle Ages into a baptistery by Christians, who were greatly persecuted during the emperor's reign. The entrance is guarded by a black-granite sphinx that stands in front of the cathedral. The sphinx, brought to the palace from ancient Egypt by Diocletian, was partially destroyed by Christians as revenge for the persecution they suffered during his rule. Inside, beneath the coffered barrel vault and ornamented cornice, the 11th-century baptismal font is adorned with a stone relief showing a medieval Croatian king on his throne. Directly behind it, the bronze statue of St. John the Baptist is the work of Meštrović. ⊠ *Kraj Sv Ivana, Grad, Split* ☒ *15 Kn* ☉ *May–Oct., daily 8–7.*

Katedrala Sveti Dujam (*Cathedral of St. Dominius*). The main body of the cathedral is the 3rd-century octagonal mausoleum designed as a shrine to Emperor Diocletian. During the 7th century, refugees from Salona converted it into an early Christian church, ironically dedicating it to Sv Duje (St. Domnius), after Bishop Domnius of Salona, one of the many Christians martyred during the late emperor's persecution campaign. The cathedral's monumental main door is ornamented with magnificent carved wooden reliefs, the work of Andrija Buvina of Split, portraying 28 scenes from the life of Christ and dated 1214. Inside, the hexagonal Romanesque stone pulpit, with richly carved decoration, is from the 13th century. The high altar, surmounted by a late-Gothic canopy, was executed by Bonino of Milan in 1427. Nearby is the 15th-century canopied Gothic altar of Anastasius by Juraj Dalmatinac. The elegant 200-foot Romanesque-Gothic bell tower was constructed in stages between the 12th and 16th centuries; the tower is sometimes closed in winter during bad weather. ⊠ *3 Ul. Kraj Sv. Duje, Grad, Split* ▭ *Cathedral 25 Kn (including crypt); bell tower 15 Kn* ⊙ *Nov.–Apr, daily 8–6; May–Oct., daily 8–7.*

Marjan (*Marjan Hill*). Situated on a hilly 3½-km-long (2-mile-long) peninsula that is covered with pine trees and Mediterranean shrubs, Marjan Hill has been a protected nature reserve since 1964. It is known to locals as the "lungs of the city" because of its vast green area and is frequented by locals on weekends as a nearby recreational area. There are stunning views from the top, and rocky beach areas circling the penninsula. A network of paths crisscross the grounds that are suitable for biking and jogging. There are seven small churches throughout the park; one in particular is St. Jerome (Sv. Jere), built in 1500 into a rock face and which includes Renaissance-style stone reliefs on the the walls. ⊠ *Cattanijin put 2, Marjan, Split* ⊕ *www.marjan-parksuma.hr.*

NEED A BREAK? **Vidilica.** Having reached this point, you're undoubtedly in need of refreshment. Sit on a sofa at Vidilica, a lounge-style café terrace, and order a long, cold drink. Then sit back and enjoy the breathtaking view. ⊠ *Nazorov Prilaz, Marjan, Split.*

Muzej Hrvatskih Arheološki Spomenika (*Museum of Croatian Archaeological Monuments*). One of the oldest Croatian museums, it houses more than 20,000 Croatian archaeological artifacts, only a quarter of which are on display. The most interesting exhibits are fine stone carvings decorated with plaitwork designs, surprisingly similar to the geometric patterns typical of Celtic art. In the garden are several stećci, monolithic stone tombs dating back to the Bogomils. The museum also conducts archaeological excavations in the southern Croatian regions between the Cetina and Zrmanja rivers and has a large collection of cultural/historical guidebooks on early medieval monuments in Croatia. ⊠ *Stjepana Gunjace BB, Meje, Split* ▦ *021/323–901* ⊕ *www.mhas-split.hr* ▭ *Free* ⊙ *Weekdays 9–1 and 5–8, Sat. 9–2.*

Narodni trg (*People's Square*). Narodni Trg, or People's Square, is the main city square and can be accessed from Diocletian's Palace through the western gate. Locals refer to this square as *pjaca*, which means square, as this was, and still is, the primary gathering place for *Splicani* (people from Split). In the 15th century the Venetians constructed several important public buildings here: the Town Hall (that today houses a contemporary art gallery, with erratic opening hours), plus the Rector's Palace and a theater, the latter two sadly demolished by the

CLOSE UP

Imperial Quirks

Many powerful state leaders tend toward eccentricity, and Roman emperor Diocletian was no exception. Born to a humble family in Dalmatia, he went on to govern the empire for 20 years, proving to be an astute and innovative leader. However, he was also something of a megalomaniac. Believing himself to be Jupiter's representative on Earth, he set about persecuting Christians, ordering religious scriptures to be burnt, churches destroyed, and thousands of believers executed. He dressed in robes of satin and gold, along with a crown embedded with pearls and shoes studded with precious stones. His imperial apartments were guarded by eunuchs, and anyone who came into his presence was obliged to fall prostrate on the ground out of respect. The best-known of his many massive building schemes is the Baths of Diocletian in Rome, a vast complex of marble and mosaics, constructed by 10,000 Christian prisoners for the pleasure of some 3,000 bathers.

Habsburgs in the 19th century. The Austrians, for their part, added a Secessionist building at the west end of the square. Once the heart of the city for civic life, it is now a prime location for people-watching from one of the many restaurants or cafés that line the whie marble square. ⊠ *Narodni Trg, Grad, Split*.

Peristil (*Peristyle*). From Roman times up to the present day, the main public meeting place within the palace walls, this spacious central courtyard is flanked by marble columns topped with Corinthian capitals and richly ornamented cornices linked by arches. There are six columns on both the east and west sides, and four more at the south end, which mark the monumental entrance to the Vestibul. During summer, occassional live concerts are held here. ⊠ *Grad, Split*.

NEED A
BREAK?

Luxor Café. This is a perfect place to sit over coffee or a glass of local wine and absorb the 2,000 years of magnificent architecture that surround you. There are no longer outdoor tables, but they put cushions on the stone steps and bring your drinks on a tray. There are also English language newspapers and magazines available for browsing. Luxor also stages occassional live music and open-air dancing in summer. ⊠ *Kraj Sv. Ivana 11, Grad, Split* ☎ *021/341–082* ⊕ *lvxor@lvxor.hr*.

WHERE TO EAT

In the past two years the gastro scene in Split has exploded. There are a great number of new and exciting places to eat that showcase the region's growing culinary sophistication. This comes as a great relief for foreign travelers looking for more than a good pizza and fresh grilled fish, the only options once found in most restaurants. A new generation of young well-traveled entrepreneurs have come back to Croatia and are giving the food scene a much needed face-lift. The fact that in Split there are three sushi bars, an authentic Turkish mezza, a specialty olive oil and farm food restaurant, numerous healthy lunch options besides sandwiches, several serious fine dining options, and, of course, the original wine and cheese bar that not only spurred a Croatian trend but a business that sees its customers as partners with whom they would like to share their love of food and wine speaks volumes about the dining changes that have hit Split in recent years.

$$$$ ✕ **Adriatic Grašo.** Above the ACI marina, at the foot of Marjan hill and
SEAFOOD close to the gardens of Sveti Stipan, this seafood restaurant has a light and airy minimalist interior, and a summer terrace where you can watch the yachts sail in and out of port. In the vein of "slow food," the kitchen gives great care to seasonal ingredients and presentation. The owner, Zoran Grašo, is a retired basketball player, so you may spot some well-known sporting stars from time to time among the diners. There is also a pizzeria in the same location that is a separate restaurant. $ *Average main: 120 Kn* ✉ *Uvala Baluni BB, Zvončac, Split* ☎ *021/398–560* ⊕ *www.adriaticgraso.com.*

$$ ✕ **Adriatic Oyster and Sushi Bar.** Croatians are not known for being big
SUSHI sushi lovers, but this sushi bar with its fresh catch and simple, yet direct approach is changing that. Eighty percent of the menu comes directly from the Adriatic ocean and everything in the restaurant is sourced within a 50-km (30-mile) radius of the premises, from the yellowfin tuna to the award-winning Paski sir, to the scampi and oysters and Dalmatian prosciutto. Located in the *get* (taken from the word ghetto, a term locals use to refer to the location inside the palace walls), you may have to turn a few corners to find it, but it is worth the hunt. The atmosphere is relaxed and the wine menu has been well-researched for sushi pairings. $ *Average main: €20* ✉ *Carrarina Poljana, 4, Grad, Split* ☎ *021/610–644.*

$$ ✕ **Apetit.** A small low-key restaurant, tucked away on the second floor
MEDITERRANEAN of a 15th-century palazzo just off the main square, Apetit serves traditional local dishes with a twist. Look out for favorites such as *tuna ala pašticada* (fresh tuna cooked in wine and served with gnocchi), or the house speciality, *rezanci Apetit* (homemade tagliatelle with shrimp, salmon, and zucchini). The restaurant recently added several dishes to its menu that offer Istrian "Boksarin" cattle. The Boksarin cattle are an indigenous ancient cattle that has recently been brought back into production in a sustainable way and is offered in select gourmet restaurants. $ *Average main: 90 Kn* ✉ *Šubićeva 5, Grad, Split* ☎ *021/332–549* ⊕ *www.apetit-split.hr.*

$ ✕ **Fife.** This casual local hangout offers traditonal dishes commonly
EASTERN found on Dalmatian dinner tables. Fife is a popular local eatery where
EUROPEAN the seating both inside and out is often crowded, especially in summer. But that is not without reason, for the food is hearty, filling, and affordable. There is a daily selection of local specialties like *kokos na tingul,* a chicken tomato stew spiced with bay and clove, lamb and peas, or tripe. You will not find high-end fish on offer, like sea bass, but there will be plenty of fish dishes that include sardines, mackerel, and mullet, depending on the catch of the day. $ *Average main: 55 Kn* ✉ *Trubičeva Obala 11, Matejuška, Split* ☎ *021/345–223* ⊟ *No credit cards.*

$ ✕ **Ista Kebap and Meze Bar.** Pop into this authentic Turkish delight for a
TURKISH true halal kebab accompanied by a wide range of Turkish spiced sides.
The bean and tomato dip with coriander and cucumber yogurt salad
will refresh your palate and leave you wondering whether you are in
Istanbul and not in Split. Try the Istah mini-meze to sample a range
of Turkish flavors. Although Ista Kebap is a snack place, the dishes
can easily be full meals, with lots to offer vegetarians and meat lovers alike. A tiny little place with excellent value and superior baklava.
■ TIP➜ Try one of thier original drinks like salep, a warm milk spiced with
orchid flowers. $ *Average main: €15* ✉ *Put Supavla 1 Poljud, Grad,
Split* ☎ *021/380–640.*

$$$ ✕ **Jugo.** In a modern white building with floor-to-ceiling glass windows
MEDITERRANEAN and a large roof terrace above the ACI marina, Jugo offers great views
back to town across the bay, with rows of sailing boats in the fore-
ground. The menu includes Dalmatian seafood specialties and barbe-
cued meats, with pizza as a cheap option. $ *Average main: 85 Kn*
✉ *Uvala Baluni BB, Zvončac, Split* ☎ *021/398–900.*

$$$ ✕ **Kod Joze.** This typical Dalmatian *konoba* is relaxed and romantic,
EASTERN with exposed stone walls and heavy wooden furniture set off by candle-
EUROPEAN light. The waiters are wonderfully discreet, and the *rižot frutta di mare*
(seafood risotto) delicious. You'll find it just outside the palace walls, a
five-minute walk from Zlatna Vrata (Golden Gate)—it's slightly hidden
away, so many tourists miss it. There are also tables outside on a small
open-air terrace if you come here in summer. $ *Average main: 120 Kn*
✉ *Sredmanuška 4, Manuš, Split* ☎ *021/347–397.*

$$$ ✕ **Konoba Varoš.** The dining-room walls are hung with seascapes and
EASTERN fishing nets, and the waiters wear traditional Dalmatian waistcoats. The
EUROPEAN place can seem a little dour at lunchtime, but mellows when the candles
are lighted during the evening. The fresh fish and *pržene lignje* (fried
squid) are excellent, and there's also a reasonable choice of Croatian
meat dishes. It's a five-minute walk west of the center, at the bottom
of Varoš, and has a couple of tables outside by the entrance. $ *Aver-
age main: 120 Kn* ✉ *Ban Mladenova 7, Varoš, Split* ☎ *021/396–138.*

$$ ✕ **No Stress.** No Stress is on the *pjaca,* smack-dab in the middle of every-
EUROPEAN thing, yet this bistro does not define itself by its great location, but by
its premium ingredients, eclectic menu, and friendly service. The trio
of seafood tartar with sea bream on lima beans, wasabi tuna on diced
tomatoes, and shrimp on truffle cheese gets sparkling reviews, as do the
more traditional lunch fare of burgers and club sandwiches, which are
world-class. They bake their own whole wheat bread and have branded
some traditional Hvar wines, Bogdanusa and Pharos, with their own
label. Try the eggs Benedict for breakfast or sit back over dessert and
enjoy the people-watching. During high season they discourage guests
from sitting without dining. ■ TIP➜ For an adventurous change of pace
surprise yourself by trying the donkey medallions in donkey milk! $ *Aver-
age main: €20* ✉ *Iza Loza 1, Grad, Split* ☎ *099/498–1888.*

$$$$ ✕ **Paradigma.** Paradigma's entry into the Split gastro scene has undecid-
MODERN edly lifted the bar on all levels for a quality dining experience, and not
EUROPEAN just for Split. The menu offers a fresh take on classic Mediterranean
cuisine (that is, French, Spanish, Italian, *and* Croatian) that features

spectacular ingredients and creative cooking. The wine list is also exclusively Mediterranean but also includes some rare finds. Starters like pan-seared scallops with foie gras on a cauliflower pate with proscioutto powder beg to be tasted slowly and carefully. You will hardly be able to stop yourself from drinking every drop of the seafood bouillabaisse that has hints of anise liquor in its red sauce. Paradigma's rooftop dining provides an unparalleled view of the port, and the friendly sommelier is happy to provide expert recommendations. ■**TIP→ Ask for a seat along the glass wall for the best view.** [$] *Average main: €25* ✉ *Ulica Bana J. Jelačića 3, Grad, Split* ☎ *021/645–103* 🌐 *www.paradox.hr.*

$$ WINE BAR Fodor's Choice ★ 🍴 **Paradox.** Paradox is a standout restaurant/bar not just because of its extensive wine and cheese selection but for its superb service, which expertly guides and educates you through your selection of wine and tapas. The staff are well versed in their craft and eager to share their knowledge of more than 100 different labels and the right tastes with which to pair them. This is a happening place that quickly achieved cult status among Split's overthirty crowd and has reportedly changed the night scene for *Splicani.* According to local wine aficionados it is *the* wine place to gather for drinks and a few bites. The outdoor seating is casual and conducive for mingling and they occasionally have live music and showcase local artists' work. [$] *Average main: €20* ✉ *Poljane Tina Ujevica 2, Grad, Split* ☎ *021/395–854* ⊗ *Closed Mon.*

$$ PIZZA 🍴 **Pizzeria Galija.** Considered an institution by locals for pizza, Galija also offers pasta dishes and a range of colorful salads, good draft beer and wine sold by the glass. The dining room is bustling and informal, with heavy wooden tables and benches. There's also a terrace for open-air dining out front. Service can be rather slow when it is busy. The owner, Željko Jerkov, is a retired Olympic gold medal–winning basketball player. [$] *Average main: 65 Kn* ✉ *Tončićeva 12, Grad, Split* ☎ *021/347–932* 💳 *No credit cards.*

$$ SEAFOOD 🍴 **Šperun.** This cozy restaurant has become popular because of its reasonably priced menu and quaint atmosphere. There are just eight tables plus four on the sidewalk, although it is recommended to sit inside. It is decorated with antiques and brightly colored modern oil paintings. The Italo-Dalmatian menu features pasta dishes, seafood risottos, and old-fashioned local fish specialties such as *bakalar* (salt cod cooked in a rich tomato and onion sauce) and *brudet* (fish stew). Šperun II, across the road, is also open for breakfast. [$] *Average main: 80 Kn* ✉ *Šperun 3, Varoš, Split* ☎ *021/346–999.*

$$ MEDITERRANEAN 🍴 **Stellon.** Situated on a terrace that overlooks the popular Bacvice bay and nearby islands, Stellon offers an undisputable view and a classy upscale atmosphere that is contemporary and inviting. The food includes classic Mediterranean fare with some surprising international touches. Rigatoni with curry sauce and tuna steak with wasabi are decidedly unconventional flavors for Croatian food but a welcome diversion. The restaurant also has a hip lounge area and occasional live music during summer. [$] *Average main: 90 Kn* ✉ *Kupalište Bačvice BB, Bačvica, Split* ☎ *021/489–200* 🌐 *www.restaurant-stellon.com.*

$$ MEDITERRANEAN 🍴 **Uje/Oil Bar.** Stop in at Uje Oil bar and sample some of the region's best olive oil along side a choice selection of Croatia's best cheese,

prosciutto, and wine. This quaint back-alley tapas bar or *pikulece,* a term the owner cleverly coined to mean tapas in Dalmatian dialect, has quickly gained attention among local food lovers for doing something different. They showcase popular local chefs during off-season and change the menu regularly. It's one of the few local eateries that makes a great effort to source all produce from a local organic family farm. They have a wide selection of olive oils for sale on the premises and a wine bar across the alley. The menu can feel overwhelming, so sticking to the daily specials is recommended. **TIP→ Go in the early afternoon or late evening to get the attention and service that makes eating here worth it.** [$] *Average main: €20* ✉ *Dominisova 3, Grad, Split* ☎ *095/200–8008* 🌐 *www.uje.hr.*

WHERE TO STAY

Split is no longer just a transit destination, and travelers today have excellent options for making it their primary vacation spot. The demand for more upscale and affordable sleeping options has been met with a solid selection from which travelers can choose. From luxury boutique hotels and apartments, to clean and modern hostels, to green hotels and spa and wellness centers, there are new places popping up constantly around the city. Even the most affordable places will feel overpriced in high season, so do your research to find the best deals.

7

$$$ B&B/INN 🏨 **Divota Apartment Hotel.** Spend the night in one of Divota's 15 renovated stone apartments and rooms and experience Split as it once was for the villagers that occupied these closely situated ancient structures hundreds of years ago. **Pros:** quiet location yet walking distance to city attractions; unique residential living experience; some units with laundry machines. **Cons:** apartments may be too close for comfort for guests looking for more anonymity; not a standard hotel setup, which means reception is in a separate nearby office. [$] *Rooms from: €158* ✉ *Plinarska 75, Varoš, Split* ☎ *021/782–700* 🌐 *divota.hr* 🛏 *6 rooms, 9 apartments* 🍴 *Breakfast.*

$$$ HOTEL 🏨 **Hotel Cornaro.** A newcomer to the hotel scene in 2014, Hotel Coronaro seeks to set a new standard by providing its guests with the technology and comfort to make a stay here seamless. **Pros:** extensive breakfast offer; quiet enclosed terrace with excellent wine selection. **Cons:** parking is 15 euro per day; new and has yet to establish itself with targeted clientele. [$] *Rooms from: €229* ✉ *Sinjska 6, Split* ☎ *021/644–200* 🌐 *www.cornarohotel.com* 🛏 *34, plus 2 luxury suites* 🍴 *Breakfast.*

$$$ HOTEL 🏨 **Hotel Luxe.** The contemporary style of Hotel Luxe represents the mood of Split as an alternative fresh-minded city that is confidently moving beyond its conservative past. **Pros:** nearby free parking; a well-organized and functional fitness and wellness area; children under 16 are free. **Cons:** additional meals must be catered by a nearby restaurant; some rooms on first floor have no sea view. [$] *Rooms from: €200* ✉ *K. Zvonimira 6, Grad, Split* ☎ *021/314–444* 🌐 *www.hotelluxesplit.com* 🛏 *27 rooms, 3 suites* 🍴 *Breakfast.*

$$$$ HOTEL 🏨 **Hotel Marmont.** Tucked away in the heart of the city, this 15th-century stone building offers guests a quiet retreat from the hustle and bustle of Split's Old Town. **Pros:** 10% discount for hotel guests in restaurant;

smart and pleasant staff. **Cons:** no parking nearby; some rooms have unattractive views of adjacent walls or windows. $ *Rooms from: €350* ✉ *Zadarska 1, Grad, Split* ☎ *021/308–060* ⊕ *www.marmonthotel.com* ⤴ *21 rooms, 1 suite* �‖ *Breakfast.*

$$
HOTEL
⌂ **Hotel Peristil.** One of only a handful of hotels within the palace walls, Hotel Peristil lies behind the cathedral, just inside Srebrena Vrata, the city gate leading to the open-air market. **Pros:** good value for money based on location; small (so guests receive individual attention); lovely open-air restaurant terrace. **Cons:** often fully booked; nearby parking difficult; limited facilities. $ *Rooms from: €162* ✉ *Poljana Kraljice Jelena 5, Grad, Split* ☎ *021/329–070* ⊕ *www.hotelperistil.com* ⤴ *12 rooms* �‖ *Breakfast.*

$$
HOTEL
⌂ **Hotel Slavija.** Split's first hotel when it opened in 1900, Slavija occupies an 18th-century building within the palace walls. **Pros:** offers discounts for longer stays and other similar incentives; nightlife nearby; several four-bed family rooms. **Cons:** no restaurant; undergoing reconstruction to include new elevator. $ *Rooms from: €175* ✉ *Buvinina 2, Grad, Split* ☎ *021/323–840* ⊕ *www.hotelslavija.com* ⤴ *25 rooms* �‖ *Breakfast.*

$$$
ALL-INCLUSIVE
⌂ **Hotel Split.** Located on the outskirts of the city, Hotel Split offers every guest an eco-friendly room with a sea view, comfortable bright rooms with quality furnishings, and an à la carte room accommodation that can be customized to include everything from in-room fitness equipment with private trainer, to gourmet in-room meals with cooking classes, to a welcoming massage in your aromatherapy-designed room. **Pros:** spa and fitness facilities; panoramic elevator; easy acess into city. **Cons:** on-site parking 8 euros per day; crowded breakfast area during peak season. $ *Rooms from: €214* ✉ *Strožanačka 20, Podstrana, Split* ☎ *021/420–420* ⊕ *www.hotel-split.hr* ⤴ *40 rooms* �‖ *All-inclusive.*

$$$$
B&B/INN
Fodor$Choice
★
⌂ **Hotel Vestibul Palace.** Three palaces from different eras have been combined to form this intimate Old Town standout with interiors that have been carefully renovated to expose Roman stone- and brick-work, along with more modern, minimalist designer details. **Pros:** history and standout architecture; inside the palace walls; beautiful interior; small and intimate; individual attention. **Cons:** expensive for most of the season; often fully booked; no sports facilities. $ *Rooms from: €328* ✉ *Iza Vestibula 4, Grad, Split* ☎ *021/329–329* ⊕ *www.vestibulpalace.com* ⤴ *7 rooms, 4 suites* �‖ *Breakfast.*

$$$
RESORT
⌂ **Le Meridien Lav.** A world unto its own, this vast, self-contained complex lies 5 miles (8 km) south of Split. **Pros:** beautifully designed modern interior; excellent sports facilities; luxurious spa. **Cons:** far from the center of Split (5 miles); expensive; large (so the hotel can seem somewhat impersonal). $ *Rooms from: €230* ✉ *Grljevačka 2A, Podstrana, Split* ☎ *021/500–500* ⊕ *www.lemeridienlavsplit.com* ⤴ *364 rooms, 17 suites* �‖ *Breakfast.*

$$
B&B/INN
⌂ **Villa Diana.** On a peaceful side street just a five-minute walk east of the Old Town, Villa Diana is a traditional Dalmatian stone building with green wooden shutters. **Pros:** close to Old Town; more affordable alternative to nearby larger more expensive hotels; intimate setting that provides individual attention. **Cons:** often fully booked; located on a

busy road leading into Split. [$] *Rooms from: €149* ✉ *Kuzmanića 3, Radunica, Split* ☎ *021/482–460* 🌐 *www.villadiana.hr* 🛏 *5 rooms, 1 suite* 🍴 *Breakfast.*

NIGHTLIFE AND PERFORMING ARTS

Split is much more lively at night during the summer season, when bars stay open late, discos hold open-air parties by the sea, and the Split Summer Festival offers a respectable program of opera and classical-music concerts.

NIGHTLIFE

Through summer, many bars have extended licenses and stay open until 2 am. The clubbing scene is rather tame, but the local twentysomethings frequent the discos. In August, rock musicians from Croatia and the other countries of the former Yugoslavia perform open-air concerts. There's no particular source of information about what's on, but you'll see posters around town if anything special is planned.

BARS

Dva Tona. The closest thing to a microbrewery is a bar with a great selection of mircobrews, aka Dva Tona. Each week they introduce their patrons to new microbrews from around the world. There are more than 30 different types of bottled beer, Guiness on tap, and great whiskey and cognac, too. Topped off with lively music and energetic bartenders, it's a no-brainer for a night out. ✉ *Carrarina poljana 1, Grad, Split* ☎ *091/444–1050.*

Galerija Plavca. Hidden away on a narrow side street off Trg Braće Radića (better known to locals as Voćni trg), Galerija Plavca this is a laid-back café-bar with outdoor seating in a pleasant courtyard, plus occasional art and photography exhibitions. ✉ *Ulica Marka Marulića 3, Grad, Split.*

Ghetto Klub. With a colorful, bohemian interior and a courtyard garden lit with flaming torches, Ghetto Klub pulls in the cool, young, artsy crowd and hosts occasional exhibitions and concerts. ✉ *Dosud 10, Grad, Split* ☎ *021/346879.*

Teak. Close to Zlatna Vrata, Teak is a small café with an exposed-stonework-and-wood interior plus tables outside through summer. It's popular with highbrow locals, who come here to leaf through the piles of international newspapers and magazines. ✉ *Majstora Jurja 11, Grad, Split.*

To Je To. Check out this new café-bar, owned and run by an American, that is already making its mark with great coffee, cocktails, and karaoke. The bar's name translates as "That's It," and that is exactly how you feel once you get here, "That's It"—let's stay. The fun vibe of To Je To is sure to leave you with a smile. ■ **TIP→ Great iced coffees and Bloody Marys.** ✉ *Nigerova ulica 2, Grad, Split* ☎ *95/0000–0000.*

Tri Volta. An unpretentious place in a slightly pretentious location, this bar is a working man's hangout. Tri Volta, or *trica* as locals refer to it, is just a bar to sit and have a beer without all the fuss. There are a thousand bars like this throughout Croatia, where regular people come to drink and meet. Apropos of the decor, it is reportedly the most afford-able beer in town. ⊠ *Dosud 9, Grad, Split* ☎ *021/346–683.*

Tropic Club Equador. One of several amusing but vaguely pretentious bars overlooking Bačvice Bay, Tropic Club Equador serves pricey cocktails to a background of live DJ music (with a Caribbean vibe) and fake palms. ⊠ *Kupalište Bačvice, Bačvice, Split* ☎ *021/323574.*

CLUBS AND DISCOS

Club Bacvice. After hanging out on a local *zidic* (wall for hanging out), and "preparing" (i.e., drinking) for the nightclub scene, most young people then make their way to the Bacvice beach complex. Club Bacvice is at the center of this but there is a whole slew of venues along the way with pulsating music 'til the wee hours. ⊠ *Preradovićevo šetalište 2, Bačvica, Split.*

Gaga. Just behind the main square or *pjaca*, Gaga is the primary eve-ning hangout within the palace walls. The cocktails are less expensive and the music is good. In summer it is frequented mostly by young tourists sharing their Croatian experiences. ⊠ *Iza Luže 5, Grad, Split* ☎ *021/348–257.*

Kocka. Run by a coalition of local youth organizations, Kocka is the primary underground alternative club. Over the past 20 years they have hosted thousands of bands and artists from the region and from around the world with shows, exhibits, and other events. Located in the basement of the *Dom omladina*, the stage area can hold up to 700, listening to everything from dub and trip-hop to ska and metal. Closed during summer. ⊠ *Ulica Slobode 28, Split* ☎ *021/540–537* ⊕ *www. kum-split.hr.*

O'Hara. O'Hara, formerly Shakespeare, includes an open-air disco with the capacity to host 3,000 persons, a popular venue for rock concerts and DJ sessions. They host a wide variety of musical events from reg-gae to the Dalmatian summer Klapa Festival, and on Monday nights they host Croatian trash dance music. ⊠ *Uvala Zenta 3, Zenta, Split* ☎ *095/504–9909.*

Vanilla. In summer Vanilla hosts pool parties for "The Yacht Week" partygoers and foreign DJs every Friday night. Located about a 20-min-ute walk from the center of town near the public pools, they have a great terrace and a rotating bar. During the year, it is a trendy place for fans of Croatian pop and folk music. ⊠ *Poljudsko šetalište BB, Split* ☎ *098/292–522* ⊕ *www.vanilla.hr.*

PERFORMING ARTS

FESTIVALS

Split Summer Festival. Running from mid-July to mid-August, the Split Summer Festival includes a variety of open-air opera, classical-music concerts, dance and theatrical performances, the highlight being opera on Prokurative (Republic Square). ■ **TIP→ Tickets can be purchased on-line or from the theater box office.** ⊠ *Croatian National Theater, Trg Gaje Bulata 1, Grad, Split* ☎ *021/347–377* ⊕ *www.split-summer-festival.hr* 🖾 *10–40 euro.*

FILM

Kino Bačvice. Kino Bačvice is an open-air summer cinema in the pine woods above Bačvice Bay. The Bačvice location is one of three movie locations which operates as one complex. Predominantly English-language, top Hollywood films are shown in original version with subtitles. Special movie event nights that feature different foreign and local films are mostly shown at the Bačvice location. Discount seats on Monday. ⊠ *Trg Republike 1, Bačvice, Split* ⊕ *www.ekran.hr* ☏ *25 Kn.*

SPORTS AND THE OUTDOORS

BEACHES

FAMILY

Fodor's Choice

★

Uvala Bačvica (*Bačvice Bay*). The largest beach area in Split is a 10-minute walk east of the Old Town. If you don't mind the crowds, you can rent beach chairs and umbrellas, and there's a string of cafés and bars along this stretch of coast. It's one of the few sandy beaches on the Dalmatian coast, with a shallow swimming area. **Amenities:** food and drink; showers. **Best for:** partiers; swimming; *picigin,* a local water volleyball–type game. ⊠ *Šetalište Petra Preradovića, Bačvica, Split.*

SAILING

Well connected to the rest of Europe by plane and ferry—and within just a few hours' sailing of several of the Adriatic's most beautiful islands—Split is the center of the yacht-charter business in Dalmatia.

ACI marina. The 355-berth ACI marina is southwest of the city center. It stays open all year, and is a base for dozens of charter companies organizing sailing on the Adriatic. Prices for berth rental and ammenities can be found on their website. ⊠ *Uvala Baluni 8, Zvončac, Split* ☏ *021/398–599* ⊕ *www.aci-club.hr.*

SHOPPING

Dalmatian women—and those from Split in particular—are renowned for their sense of style. Despite a poor local economy, you'll find a good number of exclusive boutiques selling original women's clothes, jewelry, and housewares, not to mention the numerous shoe and dress shops with goods imported from Italy. Art galleries throughout the region will often feature some unique handmade products that are not able to be found elsewhere because of the difficulty local artists and crafters have in distributing their work. The city's most memorable shopping venue remains the *pijaca,* the colorful open-air market held each morning just outside the palace walls, where you can find everything from lavender and Brac stone souvenirs to purses, dresses, and fresh vegetables and Dalmatian delicacies. Dalmatia is known for producing some of the country's best wine, olive oil, and *pršut* (prosciutto), all of which can be found in the market in Split.

Croata. Overlooking Trg Brace Radića, close to the seafront, Croata specializes in "original Croatian ties" in presentation boxes. ⊠ *Mihovilova Širina 7, Grad, Split* ☏ *021/346–336* ⊕ *www.croata.hr.*

Get Get Get. "Unique, unusual, and offbeat" is how this concept store describes their original Croatian-made products. With a focus on products designed by natives from Split, they also showcase the work of other Croatian designers/artists not all professional but all of whom have "produced something good." From clothing to jewelry to toys and furniture, there is an interesting mix of things to choose if you want to bring something truly original from Croatia back home. ■**TIP→ Check out the bow ties and ties from Fjok i Grop or the artsy porcelain bowls from Marina Marinski.** ⊠ *Dominisova 16, Grad, Split* ☎ *021/341–015* ⊕ *www. getgetget.com.hr* ☉ *Closed Sun.*

Vinoteka Terra. Vinoteka Terra is a stone cellar close to Bačvice bay, where you can taste Croatian regional wines, accompanied by savory appetizers, before purchasing bottles. They also offer truffle products and olive oils and range of artistically designed wooden boxes for packing. ⊠ *Prilaz Braće Kaliterna 6, Bačvice, Split* ☎ *021/314–800* ⊕ *vinoteka.hr.*

ŠIBENIK

75 km (47 miles) northwest of Split.

Šibenik's main monument, its Gothic-Renaissance cathedral, built of pale-gray Dalmatian stone and designated a UNESCO World Heritage Site, stands on a raised piazza close to the seafront promenade. From here a network of narrow, cobbled streets leads through the medieval quarter of tightly packed, terra-cotta–roof houses, and up to the ruins of a 16th-century hilltop fortress. The city has never been a real tourist destination. Before the Croatian war for independence, it was a relatively prosperous industrial center, but when the factories closed, Šibenik sank into an economic depression. However, the cathedral more than warrants a look.

GETTING HERE AND AROUND

The narrow cobble-stone streets of this small city are most easily accessed on foot. Šibenik also makes for a decent base for visiting the nearby waterfalls of Krka National Park.

EXPLORING

Katedrala Sv Jakova (*Cathedral of St. Jacob*). Šibenik's finest piece of architecture, the Katedrala Sv Jakova, was built in several distinct stages and styles between 1431 and 1536, and today it is a UNESCO World Heritage Site. The lower level is the work of Venetian architects who contributed the finely carved Venetian-Gothic portals, whereas the rest of the building follows plans drawn up by local architect Juraj Dalmatinac, who proposed the Renaissance cupola. Note the frieze running around the outer wall, with 74 faces carved in stone, depicting the locals from that time. The cathedral's best-loved feature, the tiny baptistery with minutely chiseled stone decorations, was designed by Dalmatinac but executed by Andrija Aleši. ■**TIP→ As you leave, take a look at the bronze statue just outside the main door: that's Dalmatinac himself, by Croatia's greatest 20th-century sculptor, Ivan Meštrović.** ⊠ *Trg Republike Hrvatske, Šibenik* 🖭 *Free* ☉ *Daily 9–7.*

WHERE TO EAT

$$$ MEDITERRANEAN Fodor's Choice ★ 🍴 **Pelegrini.** In a carefully restored 14th-century palazzo opposite the historic St. James Cathedral in Šibenik, Konoba Pelegrini was once again rated the top restaurant in Dalmatia and the third-best restaurant in Croatia in 2014. The menu features traditional Dalmatian cuisine that is innovatively prepared, with exquisite flavor being the restaurant's guiding principle. Look out for mussels with leeks, smoked bacon, and cider; pappardelle with truffles, prosciutto, and sheep's cheese; tuna sausage with arugula salad; and lavender ice cream. The service is impeccable, the atmosphere unique, and the wine list is a thorough presentation of local and international labels. They also host occasional wine tasting in their wine cellar. ■ **TIP→ Ask to be seated along the pathway overlooking the cathedral.** [$] *Average main: 110 Kn* ✉ *Jurja Dalmatinca 1, Šibenik* ☎ *022/213–701* 🌐 *www.pelegrini.hr.*

$ MEDITERRANEAN 🍴 **Vino&Ino.** It's hard to pass Vini&Ino in the center of Sibenik and not stop in either for a coffee or a glass of wine and tapas. One glass of wine inevitably turns into two here because there is a relaxed feeling about the place that makes you want to stay. This is a place where you will always find a balanced mix of locals and tourists. Try some stuffed peppers with a glass of Bibich. Their coffee is extraordinarily good, and in summer they have a nice selection of live music. [$] *Average main: €20* ✉ *Fausta Vrančića BB, Šibenik* ☎ *091/250–6022* 🌐 *www.vinoiino.hr.*

WHERE TO STAY

$ B&B/INN FAMILY 🏨 **Agroturizam Kalpic.** Experience the peacefulness of the Croatian countryside at the Kalpic family estate while exploring both Sibenik and Krka National park. **Pros:** shady garden for kids to play; excellent local *pršut* and cheese. **Cons:** must have a car to reach; too rural for city folk. [$] *Rooms from: €70* ✉ *Kalpići 4, Lozovac* ☎ *091/584–5520* 🌐 *www.kalpic.com* 🛏 *8 rooms* 🍽 *All meals.*

$$ B&B/INN 🏨 **The Konoba.** In the medieval, pedestrian-only Old Town, this B&B occupies two traditional stone buildings. **Pros:** in the Old Town; small (so guests receive individual attention from the owner); excellent breakfast for additional 7 euro. **Cons:** access is difficult; no credit cards. [$] *Rooms from: €95* ✉ *Andrije Kačića 8, Šibenik* ☎ *091/601–9789* 🌐 *www.bbdalmatia.com* 🛏 *5 rooms* 💳 *No credit cards* 🍽 *Breakfast.*

PRVIĆ

Prvić lies 4.5 nautical miles west of Šibenik by ferry.

Beyond Šibenk Bay lie the scattered islands of the Šibenik archipelago, four of which—Zlarin, Prvić, Kaprije, and Žirje—are accessible by ferry from Šibenik. For a quick taste of island life, the nearest, Zlarin and Prvić, can be visited as day trips, but if you intend to stay overnight, Prvić is the better equipped, with a lovely, small hotel, rooms to rent, and half a dozen rustic eateries. Tiny, car-free Prvić is just 3 km long (2 miles long) and has a year-round population of 540. Its two villages, Prvić Luka and Šepurine, are made up of centuries-old traditional stone cottages and connected by a lovely footpath leading through a stand of pine trees that takes about 15 minutes to walk. Though some of the locals work in Šibenik, others still live by cultivating figs, olives, and vines and by fishing. There are no large beaches, but plenty of small, secluded pebble coves with crystal-clean water, perfect for swimming.

GETTING HERE AND AROUND

Through high season, there are four ferries per day from Šibenik, calling at Zlarin (30 minutes), Prvić Luka (45 minutes), Šepurine (1 hour), and Vodice (1 hour 10 minutes). All four then return to Šibenik, doing the same journey in reverse. Alternatively, you can take a water taxi from the Šibenik seafront to Prvic'c Luka (expect to pay a hefty 1,200 Kn, as opposed to the ferry, which charges 10 Kn).

WHERE TO EAT

$ PIZZA 🍴 **Konoba Nanini.** This down-to-earth, family-run eatery occupying an old stone building furnished with heavy wooden tables offers a decent selection of Dalmatian dishes, with an emphasis on fresh seafood. It stays open all year and is a popular spot for local wedding receptions. [$] *Average main: €10* ✉ *Prvić Luka BB, Prvić* ☎ *091/212–0684.*

WHERE TO STAY

$$ HOTEL 🏨 **Hotel Maestral.** On the seafront in Prvić Luka, this 19th-century stone building was once the village school. **Pros:** delightful island location; small (so guests receive individual attention); good restaurant. **Cons:** if you miss the ferry, you could end up stranded; often fully booked; limited nightlife possibilities. [$] *Rooms from: €104* ✉ *Prvić Luka BB, Prvić* ☎ *022/448–300* 🌐 *www.hotelmaestral.com* 🛏 *11 rooms, 1 suite* 🍽 *Breakfast.*

SPORTS AND THE OUTDOORS

SWIMMING

Swim Trek. Swim Trek is a Britain-based agency whose motto is "Ferries are for wimps—let's swim." The company offers a challenging and unusual one-week holiday, including swimming around the islands of the Šibenik archipelago. Participants cover an average of 4 km (2½ miles) per day, including the stretch between the islands of Zlarin and Prvić. Overnight accommodation is in the Hotel Maestral in Prvić Luka. ☎ *+44 1273/739–713 in U.K.* 🌐 *www.swimtrek.com.*

KRKA NATIONAL PARK

Skradin is 16 km (10 miles) north of Šibenik.

The Krka River cuts its way through a gorge shaded by limestone cliffs and dense woodland, tumbling down toward the Adriatic in a series of spectacular pools and waterfalls. The most beautiful stretch has been designated as the Krka National Park.

GETTING HERE AND AROUND

Drive from Šibenik to the town of Skradin, then take a 25-minute boat ride up the Krka River on a national-park ferry.

Nacionalni Park Krka (*Krka National Park*). There are several entrances into the park, but the easiest and most impressive route of arrival is to drive from Šibenik to the town of Skradin, then take a 25-minute boat ride up the Krka River on a national-park ferry (price is included in the entrance fee). The ferry will bring you to the park entrance close to Skradinski Buk and from there you can get off and go for a swim in the crystal-green waters or take a walk along the wooden bridges and explore the park further. There are a couple of snack bars, plus wooden tables and benches for picnics. However, for a full-blown meal, your best bet is to return to Skradin, a town that dates back to Roman times, which is itself well worth a look.

A series of seven waterfalls is the main attraction, the most spectacular being Skradinski Buk, where 17 cascades of water fall 40 meters into an emerald-green pool. Moving upriver, a trail of wooden walkways and bridges crisscrosses its way through the woods and along the river to Roški Slap, passing by the tiny island of Visovac, which is home to a Franciscan monastery that can be visited by boat. There is also an old mill with an ethno museum that demonstrates the fascinating different ways the mill was used centuries ago. From here one can better understand how the power of these waters inspired Nikola Tesla, whose boyhood home is not far from the national park. In 1895 the first hydroelectric plant became operational here, only two days after Tesla's hydroelectric plant on Niagra Falls. This made the residents of Skradin the first European citizens to have electricity.

More than 860 species of plant life have been identified throughout the park and more than 200 bird species live there, making it one of the most valuable ornithological areas in Europe. Something many visitors miss is a hawk training center where you can observe birds of prey being trained by ornithological experts. For bird enthusiasts there is also Gudućá Nature reserve where various species are closely studied and can be observed from boats. The Krka National Park office is located in Šibenik. ■**TIP→** For the more active, there is a 8½-km-long (5-mile-long) hiking trail, Sitnice-Roški Slap-Ozidana Cave, that takes about 2½ hours and has educational panels along the way that explain plant/animal life, geological phenomena, and historic sites. ✉ *Krka National Park* ☎ *022/201–777* ⊕ *www.npkrka.hr* ✉ *110 Kn June–Sept., 80 Kn Oct. and Mar.–May, 30 Kn Nov.–Feb.* ☉ *May–Oct., daily 8–7; Nov.–Apr., daily 9–5.*

WHERE TO EAT

$$ ✕ **Cantinetta.** Hidden away in the Skradin Bay, in a quiet location where
MEDITERRANEAN the fresh waters from Krka National Park flow into the sea, Cantinetta is well-recognized among local residents as the best place to eat in Skradin. From a humble family konoba to a serious culinary destination, this restaurant takes great pride in the well-preserved old recipes that have been passed on from generation to generation. Dishes like

the veal risotto which must be slowly cooked for at least six hours and whose actually recipe is a family secret, must be ordered well in advance. For a light dish try *ćokalica*, a tiny fish, which has a particular taste because of the combination of salt and fresh waters in which it lives. Fresh seafood and great meat dishes at reasonable prices make this an easy choice after a long day sightseeing. $ *Average main: €12* ✉ *Svilara 7, Skradin* ☎ *022/771–183.*

$$$ ✕ **Zlatne Školjke.** A favorite among the yachting crowd, due in part to
SEAFOOD its location near the ACI marina, Zlatne Školjke occupies a natural stone building with a terrace overlooking the water. The restaurant is aptly named Zlatne Školjke, which means golden shell, because of the plethora of shellfish farms nearby. Fresh oysters, mussels, scallops, lobster, scampi, and shrimp—they have it all, and prepare everything to perfection. Be sure also to try some of the Skradin local dishes like Skradin veal risotto, and Skradin cake, a light dessert with almonds, walnut, and honey. A sommelier can help you choose a wine, but a glass of Debit white wine from the Skradin Bedrica winery is a wise choice to complement a visit to Skradin. $ *Average main: 100 Kn* ✉ *Grgura Ninskog 9, Skradin* ☎ *022/771–022* ⊕ *www.zlatne-skoljke.com.*

WHERE TO STAY

$$ ▦ **Hotel Skradinski Buk.** A friendly, family-run hotel in a refurbished stone
HOTEL town house in the center of Skradin is also the only hotel in town. **Pros:** great location in pretty village close to the entrance of Krka National Park; friendly staff; good breakfast. **Cons:** only hotel in town and often fully booked; limited nightlife in Skradin. $ *Rooms from: €89* ✉ *Burinovac, Skradin* ☎ *022/771–771* ⊕ *www.skradinskibuk.hr* ⤴ *25 rooms, 4 suites* ⦿❙ *Breakfast.*

SPORTS AND THE OUTDOORS

Skradin, approached by boat through the Šibenik Channel, is a favorite retreat for those **sailing** on the Adriatic. It's also a popular place to leave boats (especially wooden ones) for the winter, as the water is less saline here, thanks to the fresh water running down from the Krka River.

ACI Marina. The 180 berth ACI Marina stays open year-round, and can receive up to 70m long mega yachts. ✉ *Obala Pavla Šubića 18, Skradin* ☎ *022/771–365* ⊕ *www.aci-club.hr.*

SHOPPING

Vinarija Bedrica. While in Skradin, pay a visit to Vinarija Bedrica, an old-fashioned family-run wine cellar where you can taste and buy bottles of locally produced wine and rakija. ■ **TIP→ Try the famous Skradin rakija of rose petals.** ✉ *Fra Luje Maruna 14, Skradin* ☎ *022/771–095* ⦿ *June–Sept. 6 pm–10 pm and by appointment.*

TROGIR

27 km (17 miles) west of Split.

On a small island no more than a few city blocks in length, the beautifully preserved medieval town of Trogir is connected to the mainland by one bridge and tied to the outlying island of Čiovo by a second. The settlement dates back to the 3rd century BC, when it was colonized by the Greeks, who named it Tragurion. It later flourished as a Roman port. With the fall of the Western Roman Empire, it became part of Byzantium and then followed the shifting allegiances of the Adriatic. In 1420 the Venetians moved in and stayed until 1797. Today it is a UNESCO World Heritage Site, and survives principally from tourism. You can explore the city in about an hour. A labyrinth of narrow, cobbled streets centers on Narodni trg, the main square, where the most notable buildings are located: the 15th-century loggia and clock tower, the Venetian-Gothic Čipko Palace, and the splendid cathedral, with its elegant bell tower. The south-facing seafront promenade is lined with cafés, ice-cream parlors, and restaurants, and there are also several small, old-fashioned hotels that offer a reasonable alternative to accommodations in Split.

GETTING HERE AND AROUND

It is more convenient and affordable to take a short boat ride from Split to Trogir if visiting for a day as parking is limited and expensive during high season.

EXPLORING

Fodor's Choice ★ **Katedrala Sveti Lovrijenac** (*Cathedral of St. Lawrence*). The remarkable Katedrala Sveti Lovrijenac, completed in 1250, is a perfect example of the massiveness and power of Romanesque architecture. The most striking detail is the main (west) portal, adorned with superb Romanesque sculpture by the Croatian master Radovan. The great door, flanked by a pair of imperious lions that form pedestals for figures of Adam and Eve, is framed by a fascinating series illustrating the daily life of peasants in a kind of Middle Ages comic strip. In the dimly lit Romanesque interior, the 15th-century chapel of Sveti Ivan Orsini (St. John Orsini) of Trogir features statues of saints and apostles in niches facing the sarcophagus, on which lies the figure of St. John. The bell tower, built in successive stages—the first two stories Gothic, the third Renaissance—offers stunning views across the ancient rooftops. ☒ *Trg Ivana Pavla II, Trogir* ☎ *021/881–550* ⊠ *25 Kn* ☉ *June–Sept., daily 8–6; May and Oct., daily 8–noon and 4–6; Nov.–Apr., phone in advance.*

WHERE TO EAT

$$$
MEDITERRANEAN

✕ **Calebotta.** Retreat to a quiet closed-in courtyard, where the Trogir cinema once sat, and allow the Calebotta family to take you away with their first-class service and menu of fresh ingredients expertly prepared like no other restaurant in Trogir. The sea-bream citrus carpaccio is a perfect way to start a meal on a hot summer afternoon. Leave room for dessert because each one is exceptional, the chocolate mousse, for example, is indescribably good. The menu can seem long, so ask the waiter for recommendations. The bar is also a good place to come for an evening drink. [$] *Average main: €25* ✉ *Gradska 23, Trogir* ☎ *021/796–413.*

$$$ MEDITERRANEAN 🍴 **Konoba Trs.** With a tremendous sense of style, Trs combines traditional food with some modern ingredients that are freshly sourced from their family farm in a nearby Trogir village. Chickpeas are tossed in with a traditional octopus salad, and grilled scampi is served up on grapefruit and sprinkled with pistachios. These unusual combinations are a welcome change and still subtle enough to allow the strength of the traditional Dalmatian food to dominate. **■ TIP→ Try the rabbit lentil and gnocchi stew with the house red winefor a nice change.** [$] *Average main: €30* ✉ *Ulica Matije Gupca 14, Trogir* ☎ *021/796–956* 🌐 *www.konoba-trs.com.*

$ SEAFOOD 🍴 **Škrapa.** More down-to-earth than the expensive seafood restaurants that line the seafront, this eatery is much loved by locals and visitors alike, who come here to feast on platters of fried seafood, with no more elaborate accompaniment than a sprinkle of salt and a dash of lemon. [$] *Average main: €15* ✉ *Hrvatskih Mučanika 9, Trogir* ☎ *021/885–313* 💳 *No credit cards* 🕒 *Closed Sun. Oct.–Apr.*

$$ MEDITERRANEAN FAMILY 🍴 **Vanjaka.** In an elegant 17th-century stone building in the old town, close to the cathedral, this welcoming family-run restaurant serves Dalmatian specialties such as black risotto, gnocchi, and fresh fish, as well as a good choice of local wines. Sit outside on the open-air terrace, or take a table in the intimate air-conditioned dining room. **■ TIP→ Vanjaka doubles as a highly regarded B&B with just three rooms upstairs.** [$] *Average main: €25* ✉ *Radovanov trg 9, Trogir* ☎ *021/884–061* 🌐 *www.vanjaka.hr.*

WHERE TO STAY

$ HOTEL 🏨 **Hotel Fontana.** In the Old Town overlooking the Trogir Channel, this old building has been tastefully refurbished to form a small hotel above a popular restaurant. **Pros:** location on seafront promenade in the Old Town; breakfast served on the seafront terrace. **Cons:** some rooms rather small; basic furnishings; Wi-Fi does not work. [$] *Rooms from: €50* ✉ *Obrov 1, Trogir* ☎ *021/885–744* 🌐 *www.fontana-trogir.com* 🛏 *13 rooms, 1 suite* 🍽 *Breakfast.*

$$$ B&B/INN 🏨 **Hotel Pašike.** In the Old Town, in a typical Dalmatian stone building, this small hotel has seven rooms with heavy wooden antique furniture and modern en suite bathrooms, plus one apartment with a hydromassage tub. **Pros:** location in the Old Town; cozy and atmospheric rooms but modern facilities; friendly and helpful staff. **Cons:** some rooms are dark; lack of elevator could pose a problem for some visitors; reception is sometimes left unattended. [$] *Rooms from: €135* ✉ *Sinjska BB, Trogir* ☎ *021/885–185* 🌐 *www.hotelpasike.com* 🛏 *13 rooms, 1 suite* 🍽 *Breakfast.*

$$ B&B/INN 🏨 **Palace Domus Maritima.** This small family-run bed-and-breakfast is perfectly located a few minutes' walk from bustling Trogir and just across the street from the ACI Marina. **Pros:** great garden for relaxing at the end of the day; free parking close by. **Cons:** you must order meals

in advance if you want to eat; can be noisy at night. $ *Rooms from:*
€85 ✉ *Put Cumbrijana 10, 21220, Trogir* ☎ *091/513–7802* ⊕ *www.*
domus-maritima.com ✍ *8 rooms* ❘○❘ *Breakfast.*

$$$ ⊞ **Tragos.** Occupying an 18th-century baroque palace in the heart of
HOTEL   the Old Town, two blocks from the cathedral, Tragos has 12 simply
furnished, modern rooms, decorated in warm hues of cream, yellow,
and orange, each with a modern, spacious tiled bathroom. **Pros:** located
in Old Town; friendly and helpful staff; good restaurant. **Cons:** rooms
can be noisy from downstairs restaurant; no elevator could be a prob-
lem for some visitors. $ *Rooms from: €110* ✉ *Budislavićeva 3, Trogir*
☎ *021/884–729* ⊕ *www.tragos.hr* ✍ *12 rooms* ❘○❘ *Breakfast.*

$$$ ⊞ **Villa Sikaa Hotel.** This 18th-century villa has been converted into a
B&B/INN   small, family-run hotel overlooking the Trogir Channel. **Pros:** seafront
location offers great views of Trogir's Old Town; friendly and helpful
staff; beautiful old building with modern facilities. **Cons:** front rooms
can be noisy (loud music and motorbikes); two hotels are in the same
building (which can be confusing); parking can be difficult. $ *Rooms*
from: 744 Kn ✉ *Obala kralja Zvonimira 13, Trogir* ☎ *021/881–223*
⊕ *www.vila-sikaa-r.com* ✍ *8 rooms, 2 suites* ❘○❘ *Breakfast.*

SPORTS AND THE OUTDOORS

Several charter companies have their boats based in Trogir, making the
town a key destination for those sailing on the Adriatic.

ACI Marina. The 162-berth ACI Marina is open year-round. ✉ *Put Cum-*
brjana 22, Trogir ☎ *021/881–544* ⊕ *www.aci-club.hr.*

OMIŠ AND THE CETINA VALLEY

28 km (17½ miles) southeast of Split.

An easy day trip from Split, Omiš is a pleasant seaside town with a
colorful open-air market and a conglomeration of old stone houses
backed by a small hilltop fortress. What makes it special is its location
at the mouth of a dramatic gorge, where the Cetina River meets the
sea. It is also the venue of the Dalmatian Klapa Festival, which attracts
singers from all over Croatia. The Cetina River carves a spectacular
gorge with the fertile, green **Cetina Valley** at the bottom, surrounded by
sheer limestone cliffs. As the river tumbles its way down toward the sea
over a series of rapids, it has become a popular and challenging site for
rafting and rock climbing. An asphalt road follows the course of the
river upstream from Omiš, leading to a couple of pleasant waterside
restaurants.

GETTING HERE AND AROUND

Omiš is an easy day trip from Split by rental car.

WHERE TO EAT

$$ EASTERN EUROPEAN FAMILY 🍴 **Radmanove Mlinice.** This renovated water mill is well known for miles around for its fresh *pastrva* (trout) and *janjetina* (roast lamb) served at tables under the trees in a picturesque riverside garden. Throughout July and August, on Wednesday evenings, it also stages live folk music and dancing from 8 pm onward. It lies 6 km (4 miles) from Omiš, up the Cetina Valley. [$] *Average main: 90 Kn* ✉ *Cetina Valley regional road, in direction of Zadvarje, Omiš* ☎ *021/862–073* 🌐 *www.radmanove-mlinice.hr* ⏲ *Closed Nov.–Mar.*

> **KLAPA**
>
> When visiting towns and villages along the Dalmatian coast, you may be lucky enough to come across a group of locals giving an impromptu *klapa* (Dalmatian plainsong) performance. Traditionally, klapa groups are formed by men, who sing occasionally and for pleasure, the classic themes being love, family life, and local gossip. Each July the town of Omiš hosts a three-week Klapa Festival.

WHERE TO STAY

$ HOTEL 🏨 **Hotel Settlement Brzet.** The Brzet overlooks a pebble beach and is backed by a pine forest. **Pros:** seafront location with a small beach; all rooms have balconies and sea views. **Cons:** rooms rather basic; Omiš offers limited nightlife. [$] *Rooms from: €51* ✉ *Brzet 13, Omiš* ☎ *021/756–880* 🌐 *www.brzet.hr* 🛏 *88 rooms* 🍽 *Breakfast.*

$$$ HOTEL 🏨 **Hotel Villa Dvor.** Built into a sheer cliff face overlooking the River Cetina, the hotel is reached through a tunnel and then a glass elevator brings you to the reception. **Pros:** hillside location offers stunning view across river to Old Town and sea; elevator that must be first entered through a cave; rooftop Jacuzzi. **Cons:** the location/view outshines the hotel itself; Omiš offers limited nightlife. [$] *Rooms from: €122* ✉ *Mosorska Cesta 13, Omiš* ☎ *021/863–444* 🌐 *www.hotel-villadvor.hr* 🛏 *23 rooms* 🍽 *Breakfast.*

PERFORMING ARTS

FESTIVALS

Dalmatian Klapa Festival. Klapa singing, which is an integral part of the Dalmatian culture, is widely celebrated all summer long with festivals devoted specifically to this cherished tradition. The Dalmatian Klapa Festival celebrated in Omis brings together the best Klapa from the region; it starts in late June and usually last three weeks. Performances are staged in the parish church and on the main square. ✉ *Ivana Katušića 5, Omiš* ☎ *021/861–015* 🌐 *fdk.hr/festival-in-omis.*

SPORTS AND THE OUTDOORS

The Cetina Valley has become a destination for both white-water rafters and rock climbers, who appreciate the sheer limestone cliffs of the canyon. Several small adventure-tour companies can arrange Cetina

Valley trips. There's also a company in Split that organizes one-day rafting trips on the Cetina.

Active Holidays. Active Holidays offers rafting, canyoning and rock climbing in the Cetina Valley, as well as windsurfing and sea kayaking off the coast at Omiš. ⊠ *Knezova Kačić, Omiš* ☎ *021/861–829* ⊕ *www. activeholidays-croatia.com.*

Falco Tours. In addition to their Cetina river canoe safari, Falco Tours also offer bird-watching and sea kayaking. Their philosophy is to take it slow so that you can really enjoy the nature that surrounds you. ⊠ *Omiš* ☎ *021/548–646* ⊕ *falco-tours.com.*

BRAČ

9 nautical miles south of Split by ferry.

Well-connected to Split by ferry and catamaran services, the island of Brač makes for the perfect island escape. It can be easily visited as a day trip from Split, but it is recommended to stay a few nights in order to uncover the true gifts the island has to offer. With much of the attention in recent years focusing on Hvar, Brač has been left to quietly develop as a solid, more sustainable tourist destination. Despite its proximity to the mainland, the slow pace of island life pervades the island's main attractions from the Blaca Monastery to the Dragon's cave to the Pučišća stone masonry school. Organizing a walking tour through the Dolce Vita trail to see, touch and taste where the country's best olive oil comes from is a good place to start your explorations. Hooking up with one of the many outdoor adventure sports companies for kayaking, climbing, windsurfing, or sailing are well worth it. Although a visit to the famous Zlatni Rat beach, which is also a prime windsurfing spot, can seem a bit overrated, exploring the waters on the more hidden sides of the island like Bobovisće or Sutivan will reveal the most crystal clear water in the entire Adriatic. The top resort area is Bol.

GETTING HERE AND AROUND

Brač is accessible by ferry or boat. To get there, either catch an early morning Jadrolinija ferry from Split to Supetar (9 nautical miles) and then take a bus across the island to the south coast, or catch the mid-afternoon Jadrolinija catamaran from Split to Bol (24 nautical miles), which then continues to Jelsa on the island of Hvar.

EXPLORING

Dominikanski Samostan (*Dominican Monastery*). With its beautiful gardens overlooking the sea, the *Dominikanski Samostan* or Dominican Monastery on the western edge of Bol, was founded in 1457. The monastery church is home to a valuable 16th-century painting by the Venetian Tintoretto, and the small museum displays ancient Greek coins and amphorae found on the nearby islands of Hvar and Vis. In addition to the museum and church, the Dominican monastery is an active community of priests studying and carrying out the Dominican mission in Croatia and Europe. ✉ *Andjelka Rabadana 4, Bol* ☎ *021/778–000* 💷 *10 Kn* ⏱ *May–Sept., daily 9–noon and 5–7.*

Galerija Branislav Dešković (*Branislav Dešković Gallery*). In a fine baroque building on Bol's seafront, the Galerija Branislav Dešković displays over 300 paintings and sculptures by 20th-century Croatian artists who have been inspired by the sea and landscapes of Dalmatia. ✉ *Porat bolskih pomoraca BB, Bol* ☎ *021/635–270* 💷 *10 Kn* ⏱ *June–Oct., Tues.–Sun 10–noon and 6–10; Nov.–May, weekdays 9–3, Sat. 9–noon.*

Pustinja Blaca (*Blaca Hermitage*). Local travel agencies arrange boat trips to the 16th-century Pustinja Blaca, built into a cliff face overlooking the sea, 13 km (8 miles) west of Bol. You can also arrive by car from Nerežišća over Vidova Gora to Dragovoda and then walk about 30 minutes up to the monastery. The hike up is worth it to understand the sacrifice the monks made in constructing the site without modern amenities. The monks who built the hermitage in the 16th century were fleeing from the Turks. The monks also turned vast forests into rich vineyards and olive groves. From the bay below the complex, it's a 2-km (1-mile) hike uphill. Inside, visitors can see a fine collection of period furniture and old clocks. In its heyday, the hermitage had a printing press, a school, and an observatory. There are no longer any monks living there. It is now on the UNESCO World Heritage Site "tentative" list. ✉ *Blaca Bay, Brač* 💷 *40 Kn.*

FAMILY **Sutivan Sports Rehabilitation Center.** If you grow tired of swimming and lying on the beach, this Nature Park is a great place to make an afternoon picnic with kids. There is a small animal park that shelters a wide variety of domestic animals including ducks, pigs, goats, turtles, peacocks, and cows. There are even donkeys and horses available for riding with a professional guide. The park is located about 3 km (2 miles) from Sutivan toward Mlin and has a large playground, a barbecue area, a botanical garden with a fountain, and also an amphitheater for performances and events. ✉ *Sutivan* ☎ *098/133–7345* ⊕ *www.park-prirode-sutivan.com.*

Vidova Gora. The village of Bol is backed by the highest peak on all the Croatian islands, Vidova Gora. From here, at a height of 2,552 feet above sea level, the Adriatic sea and the islands of Hvar and Vis spread out before you like a map. It's possible to reach the top following a clearly marked footpath from Bol, but be sure to wear good hiking boots, take plenty of water, and expect to walk at least two and a half hours to reach the summit. Alternatively, rent a mountain bike from Big Blue and cycle up—note that you need to be pretty fit to face the challenge. ■TIP➜ **If you have a head-lamp and are relatively fit, wake early and hike up before sun rises, or go in the late afternoon and watch the sun set from Croatia's highest island peak.** ✉ *Bol* ⊹ *4 km (2½ miles) north of town center.*

BRAČ WHERE TO EAT

$
DELI

✕ Arguola. If you're looking for a quick bite to eat at lunch or late at night, this sandwich bar will do the trick. They make their salads and bread fresh and the portions are perfect. Arguola is located in the center of Bol across from the Ina gas station on the way to the Zlatni Rat beach. They also pack lunches to go and do a good business late at night when you get those cravings for fast food. The staff and owner are young and eager to please. $ *Average main: €3* ✉ *Vladimir Nazora 6, Bol* ☎ *091/518–8295* 🚫 *No credit cards* 🕙 *Closed Nov.–Apr.*

$$
MEDITERRANEAN

✕ Kaštil Gospodnetic/Konoba Margera. This 16th-century konoba tucked high up in the village of Dol (which means valley) not only offers an amazing view of the valley all the way to the sea, but also offers guests a chance to step back in time with a tour though the historic building before sitting down to a home-cooked meal. The meal price includes an appetizer, main meal, and dessert, and is recommended to be ordered in advance. The restaurant is run by young family members who are warm and inviting and eager to share their heritage with guests. Order the grilled fish if you pop in unannounced and do not have the inclination to wait for the *peka*-cooked meals, or just take in the view over the local sweet cake *hrapacusa*. $ *Average main: €20* ✉ *Dol BB, Dol* ☎ *091/799–7182* 🌐 *www.konobadol.com.*

> ### BRAČ MARBLE
>
> The island of Brač is well known for its fine white marble, quarried in the village of Pučišća, on the north coast. Through the centuries, it has been used for world-famous buildings, including Diocletian's Place in Split, the U.S. White House, and the Parliament building in Budapest. Today it is used by sculptors and for the reconstruction of historic monuments. The specific conditions of Brač produce a very particularly strong herbal tasting olive oil. In days past, it was said that a man from Brač could not be married before he planted 100 olive trees.

$$
MEDITERRANEAN

✕ Konoba Kopacina. It is hard to spend more than a day on the island of Brac and avoid the suggestion to try some roasted lamb; many people choose Konoba Kopacina as the place to enjoy this island delicacy. The sheep on Brac feed only on their mother's milk and wild herbs like rosemary and sage which thrive on the island's rocky terrain. While waiting for your lamb, Konoba Kopacina prepares a good *vitalac,* an island delicacy which includes the sheep's innards wrapped in gauze or membrane and roasted on a spit and served as an appetizer. There is also a good selection of local wines for which you can trust your waiter to provide good recommendations. $ *Average main: €15* ✉ *Vjaksić, 21423, Nerežišća* ☎ *021/647–707* 🌐 *www.konoba-kopacina.com.*

$$
MEDITERRANEAN
FAMILY
Fodor's Choice
★

✕ Konoba Ranjak. Konoba Ranjak stands out not just because of the high-quality homegrown and well-prepared food, but also because of the experienced olive-growing owners who have invested their heart and soul into the entire offer surrounding their 500-year-old organic olive grove. Nearly all of the food (and drink!) on the menu is produced by them or by a nearby family-run farm. Depending on the season when you visit, the menu is chock-full of solid farm food from stuffed zucchini flowers with mozzarella, to the olive and bean spreads on homemade bread, to the delectably roasted lamb. It is easy to lose track of time here while sitting at one of the large wooden tables that are comfortably set in an olive grove and which transforms into a magical garden at night with the lights decorating the olive trees. The kids will feel right at home with lots of space and a small playground to entertain themselves. ■ TIP➔ Purchase a bottle of their award-winning organic olive oil, known for its herbal and healing qualities. $ *Average main: €10* ⊠ *Gornji Ranjak, Supetar* ☎ *091/631–6699* ⊕ *www.agroturizam-ranjak.hr* ⊘ *Closed Nov.–Apr. except by special arrangement.*

$$$ ✕ **Ribarska Kučica.** On the waterside footpath near the Dominican mon-
SEAFOOD   astery, with romantic nighttime views over the open sea, this friendly eatery serves seafood dishes, with pizza or pasta as a cheaper option. Look for the delicious gnocchi with Gorgonzola and prosciutto. The service can be a little slow when it's busy. There's also an adjoining cocktail bar on the small beach to the east. $ *Average main: €20* ⊠ *Ante Starčević BB, Bol* ☎ *021/635–033* ⊕ *www.ribarska-kucica. com* ⊘ *Closed Oct.–May.*

WHERE TO STAY

$$ ⛺ **Bluesun Hotel Borak.** Set amid pine trees on the path to Zlatni Rat
HOTEL   beach—and just a 10-minute walk from Bol's Old Town—Hotel Blue-
FAMILY   sun Borak occupies a modern, three-story white building with a res-
taurant terrace and a pool out front. **Pros:** proximity to Zlatni Rat beach; good sports facilities; family rooms available for those with kids. **Cons:** large and slightly impersonal; popular with large tour groups. $ *Rooms from: €110* ⊠ *Bračka Cesta 13, Brač* ☎ *021/306–202* ⊕ *www.bluesunhotels.com* ⤲ *136 rooms, 48 suites* ⊘ *Closed Nov.–Apr.* ⛾ *Breakfast.*

$$$$ ⛺ **Hotel Bracka Perla.** This luxurious boutique-style hotel with only 11
RESORT   rooms is perfect for those seeking a quiet romantic getaway surounded by a pine forrest and within walking distance to the beach. **Pros:** the grand piano in the breakfast area is a great place to take a break; knowledgeable, attentive, and unassuming staff; Jacuzzi, sauna, and fitness room on first floor. **Cons:** breakfast is small and not included; a little too quiet for some. ■ TIP➔ Booking direct is expensive, if you do a good Internet search you can find deals to stay at more reasonable prices. $ *Rooms from: €185* ⊠ *Put Vele Luke 53, Brač* ☎ *021/755–530* ⤲ *8 suites, 3 rooms* ⛾ *Breakfast.*

$$$ ⛺ **Hotel Osam.** This sleek adults-only new hotel with rooftop bar and
HOTEL   swimming pool offers something not found elsewhere on Brač: an urban-style island retreat. **Pros:** excellent buffet breakfast; extremely convenient location; great restaurant. **Cons:** rooms are not sound-proofed; swimming pool is small. $ *Rooms from: €125* ⊠ *Put Vele luke 4, Supetar* ☎ *021/587–478* ⊕ *www.hotel-osam.com* ⤲ *26 rooms* ⛾ *All meals.*

$ ⛺ **Villa Giardino.** Set in a quiet garden with Mediterranean plantings and
B&B/INN   an English lawn, this hotel is a five-minute walk from the harbor. **Pros:** atentive staff make all the difference; small so guests receive individual attention; peaceful yet centrally located; breakfast served in lovely

garden. **Cons:** often fully booked, limited facilities. $ *Rooms from: €120 ⊠ Novi Put 2, Brač ☎ 021/635–900 ✎ villa.giardino@st.t-com. hr ⟿ 5 rooms ⊘ Closed Nov.–Apr. ⦿ Breakfast.*

SPORTS AND THE OUTDOORS

ADVENTURE TOURS

Aldora Sports. If you want to explore the island of Brac with local outdoor enthusiasts committed to preserving the traditions and beauty of the island, the experts at Aldora Sports have you covered. From beginner to experienced enthusiasts they offer unparalleled excursions and tours in walking, sailing, biking, kayaking, and hiking. ⊠ *Porat BB, Sutivan ☎ 021/638–512 ⊕ www.aldura-sport.hr.*

BEACHES

Fodor's Choice ★ **Zlatni Rat.** The obvious spot for swimming and sunning is the glorious Zlatni Rat beach, complete with a café and snack bar, plus sun beds and parasols, and paddleboats and Jet Skis for rent through peak season. To the west of Zlatni Rat lies a small beach reserved for nudists. Regular taxi-boats run from the Old Town harbor to Zlatni Rat beach, if the 20-minute walk is too much. **Amenities:** food and drink; showers; toilets; water sports. **Best for:** windsurfing. ⊠ *Brač.*

EVENTS

Extreme Sports Festival. This Extreme Sports and Film Festival held on Brac every summer since 1999, brings together climbers, windsurfers, mountain bikers, kayakers, and free divers from all over Europe for a week of adrenaline-soaked events that is referred to by locals as the *Vanke Regule*, meaning "out of bounds" in Dalmatian dialect. Each year they add a new sport, the most recent of which was a slacklining race featuring a 30-meter-long walk on a rope only 3 centimeters in diameter. ⊠ *Sutivan ⊕ vankaregule.com.*

WATER SPORTS

Big Blue. For windsurfing and scuba-diving training and equipment rentals, this well established local company also rents sea kayaks and mountain bikes. ⊠ *Podan Glavice 2, Bol ☎ 021/635–614 ⊕ www.big-blue-sport.hr.*

> **A WORD ABOUT WINE**
>
> The island of Hvar makes some of Croatia's top wines. On the south coast, the steep, rugged, seaward-facing slopes between the villages of Sveti Nedelja and Ivan Dolac produce full-bodied reds, made predominantly from the *plavac mali* grape. In contrast, the vineyards in the flat valley between Stari Grad and Jelsa on the north side produce whites, such as the greenish-yellow Bogdanuša.

HVAR

Hvar Town is 23 nautical miles south of Split by ferry.

The island of Hvar bills itself as the "sunniest island in the Adriatic." Not only does it have the figures to back up this claim—an annual

average of 2,724 hours of sunshine with a maximum of two foggy
days a year—but it also makes visitors a sporting proposition, offering
them a money-back guarantee if there is ever a foggy day (which has
been known to happen).

GETTING HERE AND AROUND

The easiest way to reach Hvar Town is to catch a mid-afternoon Jadrolinija catamaran from Split, which stops at Hvar Town (23 nautical
miles) before continuing to the South Dalmatian islands of Korčula
and Lastovo. Alternatively, take an early morning Jadrolinija ferry from
Split to Stari Grad (23 nautical miles) and then catch a local bus across
the island.

EXPLORING

Hvar is both the name of the island and the name of the capital, near
the island's western tip. Little **Hvar Town** rises like an amphitheater from
its harbor, backed by a hilltop fortress and protected from the open
sea by a scattering of small islands known as Pakleni Otoci. Along the
palm-lined quay, a string of cafés and restaurants is shaded by colorful awnings and umbrellas. A few steps away, the magnificent main
square, **Trg Sveti Stjepan,** the largest piazza in Dalmatia, is backed by
the 16th-century **Katedrala Sveti Stjepan** (Cathedral of St. Stephen).
Other notable sights include the kazalište (a theater) and the Franjevački
Samostan (Franciscan Monastery). Hvar Town is currently a very "in"
spot, so expect it to be crowded and expensive through peak season.
Visitors have included King Abdullah of Jordan and his wife, Queen
Rania, Italian clothing entrepreneur Luciano Benetton, Prince Harry of
England, and Beyonce and her husband Jay Z.

Franjevački samostan (*Franciscan monastery*). East of town, along the
quay past the Arsenal, lies the Franjevački samostan. Within its walls,
a pretty 15th-century Renaissance cloister leads to the former refectory,
now housing a small museum with several notable artworks. ⊠ *Križa
BB, Hvar* 🖂 *25 Kn* ☉ *May–Oct., daily 9–1 and 5–7.*

Jelsa. On Jelsa it feels like island life as it should be. Hvar's third main
town is often overlooked except for the catamaran service it offers direct
to Bol. On the northern coast of the island, you will see many structures
from the Renaissance and baroque periods, though **St. Mary's Church**
dates back to the early 1300s. A **tower** built by the ancient Greeks
overlooks the harbor; it dates to the 3rd or 4th century BC. About
1 km (0.6 mile) east of the modern town is the older **Grad,** with the
original fortified area that was protected by the fortress called **Galešnik,**
and now stands in ruins. This small town is surrounded by swimmable
beaches—including the island's most popular nude beaches—and some
resorts. It is surrounded by a thick forest of pine trees. Jelsa is a great
alternative to Hvar Town which has become an overcrowded tourist
trap in high season. ⊠ *20 km (13 miles) east of Hvar Town, Hvar.*

Fodor's Choice
★

Stari Grad. As its name suggests, Stari Grad, or Old Town, is one of the
oldest towns in Europe, founded in 384 BC. The site of the original
Greek settlement on Hvar, called Pharos by the Greeks, it is a conglomeration of smaller communities. While the theme of many of the main

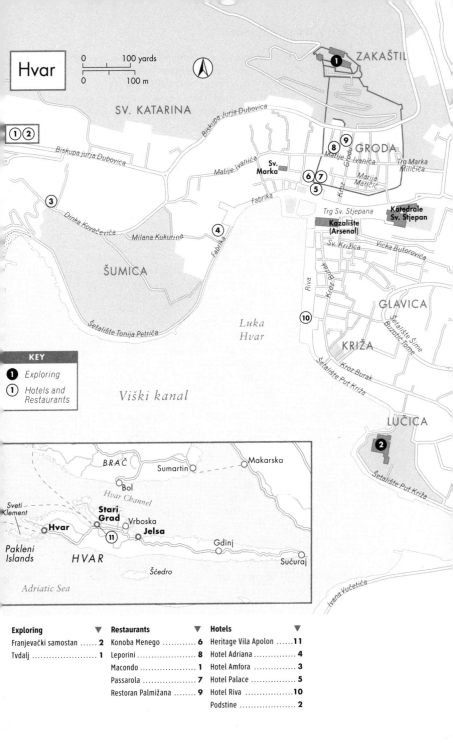

Hvar

0	100 yards
0	100 m

ZAKAŠTIL

SV. KATARINA

Biskupa Jurja Dubovica

GRODA

Biskupa jurja Dubovica

Matije Ivanića

Sv.
Marka

Trg Marka
Miličića

Kroz Grodu

Marija
Maričić

Dinka Kovačevića

Fabrika

Trg Sv. Stjepana

Katedrale
Sv. Stjepan

Milana Kukurina

Kazalište
(Arsenal)

ŠUMICA

Fabrika

Sv. Križića

Vicka Butorovića

Šetalište Tonija Petriča

Luka
Hvar

Riva

GLAVICA

Kroz Burak

Šetalište Šime
Buzatić Tome

KRIŽA

KEY

● Exploring

① Hotels and
Restaurants

Viški kanal

Kroz Burak

Šetalište Put Križa

LUČICA

Šetalište Put Križa

BRAČ

Makarska

Sumartin

Bol

Hvar Channel

Sveti
Klement

Stari
Grad

Vrboska

Jelsa

Hvar

Gdinj

Pakleni
Islands

HVAR

Šćedro

Sućuraj

Adriatic Sea

Ivana Vučetića

Exploring ▼	**Restaurants** ▼	**Hotels** ▼
Franjevački samostan **2**	Konoba Menego **6**	Heritage Vila Apolon **11**
Tvdalj **1**	Leporini **8**	Hotel Adriana **4**
	Macondo **1**	Hotel Amfora **3**
	Passarola **7**	Hotel Palace **5**
	Restoran Palmižana **9**	Hotel Riva **10**
		Podstine **2**

attractions in Stari Grad focus on its ancient history, the city is still very much a living city throughout the whole year and offers a refreshing alternative to Hvar Town. It is also the entry-point to the island for bus transportation from the mainland, as well as the car ferry terminal. The town is 10 km (6 miles) east of Hvar Town. ⊠ *Nova riva 3, Starigrad* ⊕ *www.stari-grad.hr.*

Tvrdalj. This *trvdalj*, or fortress, is the palace of 16th-century poet Petar Hektorović. The villa was first renovated in 18th-century baroque style and a partial restoration was completed in the 19th century. Hektorović attempted to create a "model universe" to be embodied in his home. To that end, a large fish pond is stocked with gray mullet, as they were in the poet's own time, representing the sea; above the fish pond in a tower is a dovecote, representing the air. Ivy was allowed to cover the walls to tie the home to the land. Quotations from his poetry are inscribed on many walls. The home is not open to visitors but the garden is worth a visit and there is also a display of ancient agricultural equipment. ⊠ *8 Ul. Molo Njiva, Stari Grad, Hvar* ☎ *021/765–068* 🕮 *15 Kn* ⊙ *May–June, and Oct., daily 10–1; July–Sept., daily 10–1 and 6–8.*

WHERE TO EAT

$$
MEDITERRANEAN
FAMILY
✕ **Konoba Menego.** On the steps between the main square and the castle, this authentic stone-walled konoba has candlelit tables and whole *pršut* (prosciutto) hanging from the raftered ceiling. Come here to snack on small platters of locally produced, cold Dalmatian specialties such as *kožji sir* (goat cheese), pršut, *salata od hobotnice* (octopus salad) and *masline* (olives), accompanied by a carafe of homemade wine. They also do a special Children's Plate. Before leaving, round off your meal with *pijane smokve* (figs marinated in brandy), and be sure to check out the world atlas where guests sign on the pages of their home towns. $ *Average main: €12* ⊠ *Groda BB, Hvar* ☎ *021/742–036* ⊕ *www.menego. hr* ⊟ *No credit cards* ⊙ *Closed Dec.–Mar.*

$$
MEDITERRANEAN
✕ **Leporini.** A bit off the beaten path, this restaurant sits on a charming cobblestone street going up to the fortress and has cozy outdoor seating with a relaxed atmosphere that is perfect for enjoying classic fresh Dalmatian seafood. Classics like the Hvar *gregada* (fish stew with potatoes and olive oil) or *crni rižot* (black risotto) are highly recommended with the house red wine. More affordable than many other comparable restaurants in Hvar. $ *Average main: €15* ⊠ *Groda, Hvar* ☎ *021/741–387.*

$$$
SEAFOOD
✕ **Macondo.** This superb fish restaurant lies hidden away on a narrow, cobbled street between the main square and the fortress—to find it, follow the signs from Trg Sv Stjepana. The dining room is simply furnished with wooden tables, discreet modern art, and a large open fire. The food and service are practically faultless. Begin with the delicate scampi pâté, followed by a mixed seafood platter, and round off with a glass of homemade *orahovica* (walnut rakija). $ *Average main: €20* ⊠ *2 blocks north of Trg Sv Stjepana, Hvar* ☎ *021/742–850* ⊙ *Closed Dec.–Mar.*

$$$
MEDITERRANEAN
✕ **Passarola.** Tucked away in a picturesque courtyard off the main square, Passarola has quickly risen to the list of top Hvar restaurants over the past few years and has been known to host some famous Hvar

visitors. The food is prepared by an up-and-coming Croatian chef who makes his mark well known with specialties that include steak with truffle sauce and homemade macaroni, the lobster pasta, or the seafood platter with shells and champagne mouse. The wine list is impressive and includes local standouts and a wide international selection. Book a table in advance if you want to choose where you will sit to enjoy the live classical or jazz music in an impressive setting. $ *Average main: €30* ✉ *Dr. Mate Miličića 10, Hvar* ☎ *021/717–374* ⊕ *restaurant-passarola. eu* ⊗ *Closed Nov.–Apr.*

$$$ ✕ **Restoran Palmižana.** On the tiny island of Sveti Klement, a 20-min-
SEAFOOD   ute taxi-boat ride from Hvar Town, this terrace restaurant is backed by a romantic wilderness of Mediterranean flora and offers stunning views over the open sea. The walls are decorated with contemporary Croatian art, and there are classical-music recitals on Sunday morning. Besides fresh seafood, goodies include *kožji sir sa rukolom* (goat cheese with arugula), and *pašticada* (beef stewed in sweet wine and prunes). $ *Average main: 120 Kn* ✉ *Vinogradišće Uvala, Sveti Klement, Hvar* ☎ *021/717–270* ⊗ *Closed Nov.–Mar.*

WHERE TO STAY

$$$ 🏠 **Heritage Vila Apolon.** Located in Hvar Stari Grad, this boutique villa
B&B/INN   offers sophisticated guests a taste of times past in an intimate island set-ting with a fine dining restaurant that is sure to become one of the main dining attractions on the island. **Pros:** top Hvar restaurant; intimate and personal service; reasonable prices in comparison to similar style luxury accommodation on Hvar. **Cons:** still establishing solid clientele base; one room in back has no sea view. $ *Rooms from: €120* ✉ *Šetalište Don Šime Ljubića 7, Starigrad* ☎ *021/778–320* ⊕ *apolon.hr* ⬎ *6 suites/ rooms* ⊗ *Closed Nov.–Apr.* ⚍ *All meals.*

$$$$ 🏠 **Hotel Adriana.** For a top beach-party luxury vacation, Adriana is the
HOTEL   right place. **Pros:** prime location on seafront promenade; beautifully designed interior; luxurious spa. **Cons:** very expensive; most bathrooms have a big shower but no tub; not always up to five-star standards. $ *Rooms from: €385* ✉ *Fabrika BB, Hvar* ☎ *021/750–200* ⊕ *www. suncanihvar.hr* ⬎ *50 rooms, 9 suites* ⚍ *Breakfast.*

$$$$ 🏠 **Hotel Amfora.** This colossal white, modern structure sits in its own bay,
HOTEL   backed by pinewoods, a pleasant 10-minute walk along the coastal path
FAMILY   from the center of town. **Pros:** location in newly landscaped grounds overlooking the sea; chic modern design; private beach cabins. **Cons:** vast 1970s building lacks charm; large and somewhat impersonal; over-priced; inconsistent service. $ *Rooms from: €250* ✉ *Majerovića BB, Hvar* ☎ *021/750–300* ⊕ *www.suncanihvar.hr* ⬎ *246 rooms, 78 suites* ⚍ *Breakfast.*

$$ 🏠 **Hotel Palace.** Commanding a prime site on the edge of the main
HOTEL   square and overlooking the harbor, the Palace remains open most of the year, offering much lower prices during the off-season. **Pros:** centrally located; use of Hotel Amfora pool is free; very reasonable price given the location. **Cons:** rooms are dated; no a/c in rooms. $ *Rooms from: €120* ✉ *Trg Sv Stjepana, Hvar* ☎ *021/741–966* ⊕ *www.suncanihvar. com* ⬎ *62 rooms, 11 suites* ⊗ *Closed Dec.–Mar.* ⚍ *Breakfast.*

$$$$ HOTEL **Hotel Riva.** Located on the palm-lined waterfront, opposite the ferry landing station, Hotel Riva is considered one of Hvar's hippest hotels. **Pros:** prime location on seafront promenade; urban, eclectic atmosphere; excellent bar and restaurant. **Cons:** very expensive; rooms in front are very noisy night and day; small rooms. [$] *Rooms from: €200* ✉ *Obala Riva 27, Hvar* ☎ *021/750–100* 🌐 *www.suncanihvar.hr* 🛏 *46 rooms, 8 suites* 🍴 *Breakfast.*

$$$ HOTEL **Podstine.** This peaceful, family-run hotel lies on the coast, a 20-minute walk west of the town center. **Pros:** peaceful seafront location; beautiful gardens; small beach out front with sun beds and umbrellas. **Cons:** far from Old Town; no nightlife nearby (the hotel's bar shuts at 11 pm even in summer); standard rooms have no views. [$] *Rooms from: €219* ✉ *Podstine BB, Hvar* ☎ *021/740–400* 🌐 *www.podstine.com* 🛏 *40 rooms* 🕘 *Closed Nov.–Mar.* 🍴 *Breakfast.*

NIGHTLIFE AND PERFORMING ARTS

Croatia is generally not a hot spot for nightlife, but the island of Hvar is the exception. Over the past five years the island has initiated a renaissance of sorts by becoming a top party destination of the young and well to-do through "The Yacht Week," Carpe Diem café and bar, and the Hula Hula beach bar. Unfortunately this has more recently led to a less than desirable massive gathering of backpackers in search of the ultimate party and can be off-putting for those looking to enjoy the island's more natural attractions. Several stylish cocktail bars and clubs have opened in the past few years to cater to the annual influx of summer visitors, including the Ultra Music Festival that starts in Split and celebrates its last night with a beach party on Hvar. There are also a growing number of cultured evening events for the more discerning traveler.

BARS

Fodor's Choice ★ **Carpe Diem Bar.** A harborside cocktail bar with a summer terrace decked out with Oriental furniture and potted plants and two burly bouncers at the gate, this is Hvar's (Croatia's!) most talked about nightlife venue. Besides the glamorous see-and-be-seen crowd, it's also popular with twentysomething backpackers looking for a late night party, and has contributed to Hvar's reputation as the next Ibiza. ✉ *Riva, Hvar* ☎ *021/742–369* 🌐 *www.carpe-diem-hvar.com.*

Hula Hula. This wooden beach bar, built into the rocks overlooking the sea, attracts bathers through daytime with its chill music, lounge chairs, VIP tables, and massages. Many stay for the sunset as the beach club transforms into a dance party with DJ music and cocktails. For celebrity-seekers, Beyoncé has been spotted here. ✉ *Coastal path, west of town, Hvar* 🌐 *www.hulahulahvar.com.*

Kiva. Kiva, in total contrast to most of the newer hot spots, is a down-to-earth cocktail bar popular with locals and visitors in search of a friendly, laid-back, late-night drinking den, playing classic rock. You'll find it hidden away in a narrow side street off the harbor, behind Nautica bar. ✉ *Fabrika BB, Hvar* 🌐 *www.kivabarhvar.com.*

FESTIVALS

Hvar Summer Festival. Classical-music recitals in the cloisters of the Franciscan monastery have long been the highlight of the Hvar Summer Festival. Also look out for theater, folklore, and jazz at various open-air locations around town. The annual festival runs for a month sometime between June and September. ⊠ *Hvar.*

SPORTS AND THE OUTDOORS

BEACHES

Although there are several decent beaches within walking distance of town—the best-equipped being the Hotel Amfora's pebble beach, 10 minutes west of the main square—sun worshippers in the know head for the nearby Pakleni Otoci (Pakleni Islands), which can be reached by taxi boats that depart regularly (in peak season, every hour, from 8 to 8) from in front of the Arsenal in the town harbor. The best known and best served are Sveti Jerolim (on the island of the same name, predominantly a nudist beach), Stipanska (on the island of Marinkovac, a clothing-optional beach), and Palmižana (on the island of Sveti Klement, also clothing-optional).

Fodor's Choice ★ **Carpe Diem Beach.** Doubling as a daytime beach club and an after-dark party venue, Carpe Diem Beach lies on the tiny pine-scented island of Stipanska, a 10-minute taxi boat ride from Hvar Town's harbor. It has two pebble beaches complete with wooden sun-beds and big parasols, an outdoor pool and an open-air massage pavilion. There's also a lounge-bar and restaurant, and from mid-July to mid-August it hosts international DJs, playing until sunrise. **Amenities:** food and drink; showers; toilets. **Best for:** partiers; swimming. ⊠ *Stipanska, Hvar* ⊕ *www.carpe-diem-beach.com.*

DIVING

Diving Center Viking. Those with a taste for underwater adventure might have a go at scuba diving. The seabed is scattered with pieces of broken Greek amphorae, while the area's biggest underwater attraction is the Stambedar seawall, home to red and violet gorgonians (a type of coral), which is close to the Pakleni Islands. For courses at all levels, try Diving Center Viking. ⊠ *Hotel Podstine, Podstine BB, Hvar* ☎ *021/742–529* ⊕ *www.viking-diving.com.*

SAILING

Hvar Town is a popular port of call for those sailing on the Adriatic; the town harbor is packed with flashy yachts through peak season.

ACI Marina. ACI Marina in Palmižana Bay on the island of Sveti Klement, one of the Pakleni Otoci, lies 2.4 nautical miles from Hvar Town. This 211-berth marina is open from April through October, and is served by regular taxi boats from Hvar Town through peak season. ⊠ *Palmižana Bay, Sveti Klement, Hvar* ☎ *021/744–995* ⊕ *www.sea-seek.com.*

Hvar Adventure. Hvar Adventure arranges sea kayaking tours from Hvar Town to the Pakleni islets, as well as one-day sailing trips, hiking, cycling and rock climbing. ⊠ *Jurja Matijevića 20, Hvar* ⊕ *www.hvar-adventure.com.*

Sunburst Sailing. A 42-foot sailing yacht called Nera based in Split that is available for fully catered day charters and evening cruises. ☒ *Hrvatske mornarice 1, Hvar* ⊕ *www.sunburstsailing.com.*

YOGA

Trendy Hvar even offers yoga.

Suncokret. Suncokret was founded by a New Yorker and her Dalmatian-born partner. Their holistic wellness retreats combine yoga, nature walks, Reiki, life path workshops, and painting. Guests are accommodated in private cottages in the village, and typical Dalmatian meals are provided. Most courses last one week, but visitors are also welcome to drop in for a session. Dol lies 6 km (4 miles) from Starigrad and 26 km (16 miles) from Hvar Town. ☒ *Dol BB, Postira* ☎ *091/739–2526* ⊕ *www.suncokretdream.net.*

VIS

34 nautical miles southwest of Split by ferry.

Closed to foreigners until 1989, the distant island of Vis is relatively wild and unexploited. Built around a wide harbor, the town is popular among yachters, who appreciate its rugged nature, unpretentious fish restaurants, and excellent locally produced wine.

The pretty fishing village of Komiža is 11 km (7 miles) from Vis Town. Here you're just a 40-minute boat ride away from the Modra Spilja (Blue Cave), often compared to the Blue Grotto on Italy's Capri.

GETTING HERE AND AROUND

To get here from Split, you can either take the SEM Marina fast catamaran service, or a 2½-hour Jadrolinija ferry ride to arrive in Vis Town.

EXPLORING

Modra Spilja (*Blue Cave*). Throughout the summer, local fishermen will take tourists (some coming from Split and Hvar by speedboat) into the Modra Spilja by boat. Hidden away on the small island of Biševo (5 nautical miles southwest of Komiža), the cave is 78 feet long and 39 feet wide. Sunlight enters through the water, reflects off the seabed, and casts the interior in a fantastic shade of blue. If you're lucky, you'll have time for a quick swim, although tourists are now being discouraged from swimming, it depends on who brings you and when you go. It costs 50 Kn just for the cave and it can be a long wait in summer when there are many tourists queuing in small boats to have a look. Ask at the marina or at the tourist-information office to see who is offering trips. ☒ *Biševo island.*

WHERE TO EAT

$ ✕ **Fabrika.** This recently opened tapas bar in Komiža uses the slogan
ECLECTIC *pomalo*, or "take it easy" as its leitmotif to describe the food, the atmosphere, and the owners—a brother and sister team who are also a well-known Croatian singer and fashion blogger. The service may be a little

slow but the cool atmosphere, like the tree painted on the inside wall and the bohemian furniture and original jewelry that are for sale, adds up to a funky little place to hang out over a burger and a drink. Try the Fabburger, a hamburger with parsley, pancetta, and garlic or the shrimp burrito. They also serve a good breakfast, which is available all day. [$] *Average main: €5* ✉ *Riva Sv. Mikule 12, Komiža* ☎ *021/713–155* 💳 *No credit cards* ⏲ *Closed Oct.–Apr.*

$$$$ SEAFOOD 🍴 **Jastožera.** The former lobster house, built in 1883, was cleverly converted to make an impressive restaurant in 2002. Tables are set on wooden platforms above the water, which make things a little wobbly anytime someone walks around. It's even possible to enter the central dining area in a small boat. The house specialty is *jastog sa spagetima* (lobster with spaghetti). [$] *Average main: €25* ✉ *Gundulićeva 6, Komiža* ☎ *021/713–859* ⏲ *Closed Nov.–Mar.*

$$$$ SEAFOOD 🍴 **Konoba Bako.** Popular with locals and visitors alike, this excellent fish restaurant overlooks a tiny bay in Komiža. Outdoors, tables are set right up to the water's edge, and inside there's a small pool with lobsters and amphorae. The *salata od hobotnice* (octopus salad), *škampi rižot* (scampi risotto), and barbecued fish are all delicious, and they will insist you try the lobster soup. [$] *Average main: €25* ✉ *Gundulićeva 1, Komiža* ☎ *021/713–742* ⏲ *No lunch; winter working hrs 5–midnight.*

$$ MEDITERRANEAN 🍴 **Lola Konoba and Beer Garden.** A new garden restaurant, Konoba Lola offers something refreshingly different on the island of Vis. The atmosphere is relaxed, the food is fresh, and most of the vegetables come from Lola's own garden on the mainland. The steak is highly recommended, as are the chocolate truffles for dessert. They also have great cocktails. [$] *Average main: €20* ✉ *Matije Gupca 12, Vis Town* ☎ *095/849–7932* 🌐 *www.lolavisisland.com* ⏲ *Closed Nov.–Mar.*

$$$ SEAFOOD 🍴 **Pojoda.** A modern glass-and-wood conservatory looks onto a courtyard garden planted with orange and lemon trees, accessed through an archway off a narrow side street. Pojoda dishes are named in local dialect: check out the *manistra na brudet* (bean and pasta soup) and *luc u verudi* (tuna stewed with vegetables) or try the *pojorski bronzinić*, a thick brodetto of squid with lentils and barley. [$] *Average main: €25* ✉ *Don Cvjetka Marasovića 8, Vis Town* ☎ *021/711–575* ⏲ *Winter hrs: 4–11 pm.*

$$$$ SEAFOOD 🍴 **Villa Kaliopa.** With tables set under the trees in the romantic walled garden of a 16th-century villa, dinner at this restaurant in Vis Town is an unforgettable experience. The menu changes daily depending on what fresh fish and shellfish are available. Your server will bring a platter to the table so you can choose your own fish before it's cooked. Fish is priced by the weight so be careful what you order, and ask the waiter to clarify because there is no menu with clear prices. [$] *Average main: 100 Kn* ✉ *V Nazora 32, Vis Town* ☎ *091/271–1755* 💳 *No credit cards* ⏲ *Closed Nov.–Mar.*

7

WHERE TO STAY

$$ ⊡ **Hotel San Giorgio.** In Vis Town, east of the ferry quay, this chic little
HOTEL   hotel is hidden away between stone cottages in a quiet, cobbled side
street. **Pros:** traditional stone building in Old Town; modern and com-
fortable rooms; good restaurant. **Cons:** a couple of blocks in from the
seafront (only the top-floor suite has a sea view); often fully booked;
20-minute walk from ferry landing can be difficult for visitors with
heavy luggage. Ⓢ *Rooms from: €152* ⊠ *Petra Hektorovića 2, Vis Town*
☎ *021/711–362* ⊕ *www.hotelsangiorgiovis.com* ↩ *4 rooms, 6 suites*
⦿ *Breakfast.*

$$ ⊡ **Tamaris.** Overlooking the harbor and seafront promenade in Vis
HOTEL   Town, Tamaris occupies a late-19th-century building. **Pros:** on sea-
front promenade in center of town; most rooms have sea views; cheerful
café terrace out front. **Cons:** rooms very basic; service rather indiffer-
ent. Ⓢ *Rooms from: €116* ⊠ *Šetalište Apolonija Zanelle 5, Vis Town*
☎ *021/711–350* ↩ *25 rooms* ⦿ *Breakfast.*

SPORTS AND THE OUTDOORS

DIVING

Issa Diving Centre. Scuba-diving enthusiasts will find underwater attractions including several underwater caves, at least half a dozen shipwrecks, and some spectacular coral reefs. Beginners and those with
previous experience should contact Issa Diving Centre for organized
diving trips and training at all levels. They have four dive instructors and three dive masters, a very experienced team. ⊠ *Ribarska 91,*
Komiža ☎ *021/713–651* ⊕ *www.scubadiving.hr* ☉ *Dec.–Mar.*

MAKARSKA

67 km (42 miles) southeast of Split.

The seafront promenade, lined with palm trees and cheerful open-air
cafés, looks onto a protected bay dotted with wooden fishing boats.
From here one enters the Old Town, a warren of stone buildings and
cobbled streets surrounding the main square, which is backed by the
parish church and a small open-air market off to one side. The atmosphere is relaxed and easygoing. The only drama you'll likely see is
created by the limestone heights of Biokovo Mountain, which seems
to alternate between protecting and threatening the town, depending
on the color of the sky and the cloud formations that ride over its rugged peaks.

Makarska has developed an unpretentious, affordable brand of tourism
that is popular with East Europeans.

GETTING HERE AND AROUND

The cobblestone streets of this small bayside town are most-easily
accessed on foot.

EXPLORING

Park Prirode Biokovo (*Biokovo Nature Park*). Behind Makarska, a large area of the rocky heights that form the majestic Biokovo Mountain have been designated as a nature park. Part of the Dinaric Alps, which run from Slovenia down to Montenegro, Biokovo abounds in rare indigenous plant species, and is primarily limestone with little green coverage. It's possible to reach the highest peak, Sveti Jure (5,781 feet) in 5½ hours from Makarska. However, this is a strenuous hike, especially in summer, for which you will need good boots and plenty of water. It is not recommended to hike it alone. It is best to organize an excursion through Biokovo Active Holidays, a company that offers organized trips up the mountain, traveling part of the way by jeep. ✉ *Marineta, Mala Obala 16, Makarska* ☎ *021/616–924* 🌐 *www.biokovo.com.*

WHERE TO EAT

$$ MODERN EUROPEAN Fodor's Choice ★ 🍴 **Jeny.** At Jeny, one of the only serious fine dining restaurants on the Makarska Riviera, the food alone speaks for itself. The time and care that has gone into creating the wine pairing menu is hard to ignore, but the expertise of the food preparation stands head and shoulders above anything else for miles. The scallops are tenderly cooked, the spinach croustillant is grilled and the filet mignon has a garlic crust that leaves you wanting more. Located 3 km (2 miles) above Makarska in Tucepi on the road to Biokovo, it has a nice view overlooking the Makarska riviera. ■ **TIP→ The management is happy to organize a trusted taxi to bring you to the restaurant.** [$] *Average main: €25* ✉ *Čovići 1, Tucepi* ☎ *021/623–704* 🌐 *www.restaurant-jeny.hr.*

$$ MEDITERRANEAN FAMILY 🍴 **Konoba Ranc.** Surrounded on all four sides by the shade of an olive grove, this restaurant is the perfect place to wind down a day of sun and sightseeing. Come to Konoba Ranc if you are craving a good steak or lamb from the *peka* (covered iron pot over an open fire), or fish prepared on the grill. There is an area for kids to play and they also have apartments to rent. As the name suggests, the fare here is primarily meat and fish. [$] *Average main: €20* ✉ *Kamena 62, Tucepi* ☎ *021/623–563* 🌐 *www.ranc-tucepi.hr.*

$$$ SEAFOOD 🍴 **Stari Mlin.** Ethnic music, incense, and colorful canvases set the mood inside this old stone building, and the internal garden is draped with vines and decorated with pots of herbs and cherry tomatoes. Barbecued seafood tops the menu, but there is an extra surprise here, a select choice of authentic Thai dishes. The owner worked for several years aboard a cruise ship before returning home to run the family restaurant. A bit overpriced, and service can be assertive by suggesting more expensive options. It stays open all year. [$] *Average main: €25* ✉ *Prvosvibanska 43, Makarska* ☎ *021/611–509.*

WHERE TO STAY

$$
B&B/INN
Fodor's Choice
★
🏨 **Boutique Hotel Marco Polo.** Boutique Hotel Marco Polo is more than just a hotel, it is an entire experience. **Pros:** excellent restaurant that serves specific menu each night; pool/spa and beach chairs; rooftop terrace to escape the beachfront crowds; snacks provided for late-night arrivals. **Cons:** Gradac is a popular destination for Eastern Europeans; not a quiet beachfront destination. 💲 *Rooms from: €155* ✉ *Obala 15, Gradac* ☎ *021/695–060* ⊕ *www.hotel-marcopolo.com* ⤳ *25 rooms* ☾ *Closed Nov.–Mar.*

$
HOTEL
🏨 **Hotel Biokovo.** In the center of Makarska, on the palm-lined seafront promenade, this old-fashioned hotel was renovated in 2004. **Pros:** centrally located; handicap access; friendly and helpful staff; pleasant café and decent restaurant. **Cons:** limited facilities; parking can be a problem. 💲 *Rooms from: €57* ✉ *Obala Kralja Tomislava, Makarska* ☎ *021/615–244* ⊕ *www.hotelbiokovo.hr* ⦿| *Breakfast.*

$$$
HOTEL
🏨 **Hotel Porin.** This 19th-century building stands on the seafront promenade and was refurbished to form a small hotel, which opened in 2002. **Pros:** location on seafront promenade in the Old Town; front rooms have lovely views onto the bay; small (so guests receive individual attention from the staff), parking available if you make reservation. **Cons:** often fully booked; limited facilities. 💲 *Rooms from: €160* ✉ *Marineta 2, Makarska* ☎ *021/613–688* ⊕ *www.hotel-porin.hr* ⤳ *55 rooms, 1 suite* ⦿| *Breakfast.*

SPORTS AND THE OUTDOORS

BEACHES

The main town beach, a 1½-km (1-mile) stretch of pebbles backed by pine woods, lies northwest of the center and close to a string of big modern hotels. Alternatively, walk along the narrow coastal path southeast of town to find rocks and a series of secluded coves. Farther afield, the so-called Makarska Rivjera is a 40-km (25-mile) stretch of coast running from Brela to Gradac. And although the Makarska Riviera is not the French Riviera, it offers the stunningly beautiful backdrop of the Biokovo Mountain, several easily accessed islands at its doorstep, and an assortment of small coved private beaches and villages that are each islands unto themselves. Be sure to check out the free app from iTunes, "Makarska Riviera," which, once downloaded, will help you find all the secluded private beaches along the riviera.

DIVING

Local underwater attractions include a nearby reef, known as Kraljev Gaj, which is populated by sponges, coral, octopi, and scorpion fish, while farther out from the coast you can visit the *Dubrovnik,* an old steam boat that sank in 1917.

More Sub. Scuba-diving enthusiasts, as well as complete beginners, can try More Sub for organized diving trips and training at all levels. ✉ *Krešimira 43, Makarska* ☎ *021/611–727* ⊕ *www.more-sub-makarska.hr.*

LASTOVO

Lastovo Island is 80 km (50 nautical miles) west of Dubrovnik (no direct ferry) and 80 km (50 nautical miles) southeast of Split (daily direct ferry connection).

Very few Croatians have visited Lastovo, though they will all tell you that it's beautiful. Like Vis, Lastovo was a Yugoslav military naval base during the Tito years, and was therefore closed to foreigners, so commercial tourism never developed. Today there is still just one hotel.

Lying far out to sea, Lastovo is an island of green, fertile valleys and is practically self-sufficient: locally caught seafood, not least the delicious lobster, and homegrown vegetables are the staple diet. The main settlement, Lastovo Town, is made up of stone houses built amphitheater-style into a hillside, crisscrossed by cobbled alleys and flights of steps; they're renowned for tall chimneys resembling minarets. The only other settlement on the island is the small port of Ubli, which is 10 km (6 miles) from Lastovo Town.

GETTING HERE AND AROUND

Although it is officially in Southern Dalmatia, locals chose to have direct transport links with Split in Central Dalmatia rather than Dubrovnik. To get there, take the Jadrolinija daily ferry service from Split to Ubli, stopping at Hvar Town and Vela Luka en route. Jadrolinija also runs a daily catamaran from Split covering the same route; it's faster but a little more expensive.

WHERE TO EAT

$$$$ ✕ **Konoba Triton.** Triton is widely acknowledged to be the best restau-
SEAFOOD rant on the island, and it's particularly popular with those traveling by sailboat, who can moor up on a small quay out front. The owner catches and cooks the fish himself; he also produces the wine, olive oil, and vegetables. You'll find it in Zaklopatica, a north-facing bay 3 km (2 miles) west of Lastovo Town. There are several apartments to rent upstairs. $ *Average main: 250 Kn* ⊠ *Zaklopatica, Lastovo* ☎ *020/801–161* ⊕ *www.triton.hr* ⊟ *No credit cards* ☉ *Closed Nov.–Mar.*

WHERE TO STAY

$$ ⛺ **Hotel Solitudo.** The only hotel on the island, Hotel Solitudo (confus-
HOTEL ingly sometimes referred to as Hotel Ladesta) is a modern white building on a peaceful bay backed by pines, 3 km (2 miles) north of Ubli. **Pros:** recently renovated; peaceful off-the-beaten-path island; on-site dive shop. **Cons:** basic breakfast; spotty service. $ *Rooms from: €103* ⊠ *Pasadur, 3 km (2 miles) from Ubli, Lastovo* ☎ *020/802–100* ⇘ *60 rooms, 12 suites* ⎮⊙⎮ *Breakfast.*

7

SPORTS AND THE OUTDOORS

BEACHES

The best beaches lie on **Saplun,** one of the tiny, unpopulated **Lastovnjaci Islands,** which are a short distance northeast of Lastovo and are served by taxi-boats through high season.

DIVING

Paradise Diving Center. Paradise Diving Center is a scuba-diving center based in the Hotel Solitudo. Just a five-minute boat ride from the diving center and at a depth of 49 feet lies a reef of red, yellow, and violet gorgonias. Farther afield, experienced divers can expect to explore sea caves and sunken ships. ⊠ *Pasadur, 3 km (2 miles) from Ubli, Lastovo* ☎ *020/802–100* ⊕ *www.diving-lastovo.com.*

SAILING

Marina Lastovo. Marina Lastovo is a 50-berth marina attached to Hotel Solitudo. ⊠ *Pasadur, 3 km (2 miles) from Ubli, Lastovo* ☎ *020/802–100* ⊕ *www.marina-lastovo.com.*

DUBROVNIK AND SOUTHERN DALMATIA

By Andrea
MacDonald

A region would be lucky to have just one sight as majestic as Dubrovnik. In Southern Dalmatia, the walled city is only the beginning. Head south to pine-scented hiking trails in Cavtat, or up the coast to a garden full of exotic trees in Trsteno. Tour an ancient salt factory, feast on world-class oysters and superb red wine from the Pelješac Peninsula, then head out to sea to explore Marco Polo's birthplace on Korčula and Odysseus' mythical cave on Mljet. Along the way you'll find some of the best windsurfing and sailing in Europe, kayak trips to citrus and sage-covered islands, centuries-old houses, millennia-old caves, fresh seafood, and always, everywhere, that big blue sea.

The highlight of Southern Dalmatia is undoubtedly the majestic walled city of Dubrovnik, from 1358 to 1808 a rich and powerful independent republic, which exerted its economic and cultural influence over almost the entire region. Jutting out to sea and backed by rugged mountains, it's an unforgettable sight and now Croatia's most upmarket and glamorous destination.

From Dubrovnik a ferry runs all the way up the coast to Rijeka in the Kvarner region, making several stops along the way, and occasionally extending its itinerary to include an overnight lap from Dubrovnik to Bari, Italy. There are also regular local ferry and catamaran services from Dubrovnik to outlying islands. The nearest and most accessible of these are the tiny Elafitis, ideal as a day trip for someone on a short stay who still wants a brief taste of island life.

Moving down the mainland coast, Cavtat was founded by the ancient Greeks. Today a sleepy fishing town through winter, it turns into a cheerful holiday resort come summer, with a palm-lined seaside promenade, several sights of cultural note, and a handful of reasonably priced hotels.

Back up the coast, northwest of Dubrovnik, lies the village of Trsteno, with its delightful Renaissance arboretum stepping down toward the sea in a series of terraces. Proceeding northwest one arrives at Ston, known for its oysters and salt pans, and its 14th-century walls forming the gateway to Pelješac Peninsula. Pelješac is of particular note for its excellent red wines: several families open their vineyards and cellars to the public for wine tastings. The main destination here is Orebić, a low-key resort with a good beach and water-sports facilities, backed by a majestic hillside monastery. From Orebić there are regular ferry crossings to Korčula Town, on the island of Korčula, one of the most sophisticated settlements on the Croatian islands, with its fine Gothic

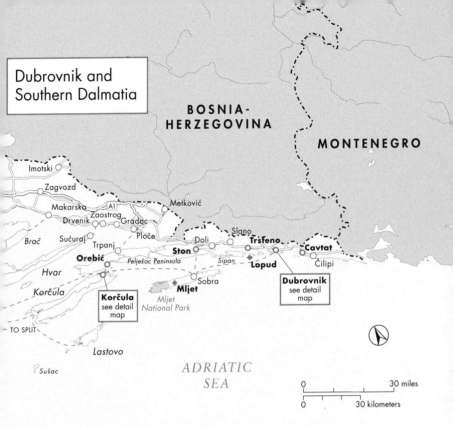

and Renaissance stone buildings bearing witness to almost 800 years of Venetian rule. Nearby Lumbarda provides a good stretch of sand beach, plus a delicate white wine known as Grk. In contrast to Korčula, the sparsely populated island of Mljet offers little in the way of architectural beauty but has preserved its indigenous coniferous forests, which rim the shores of two emerald-green saltwater lakes. They are contained within the borders of Mljet National Park, a haven for hiking, mountain biking, swimming, and kayaking.

ORIENTATION AND PLANNING

GETTING ORIENTED
Occupying the tail end of Croatia before it trails off into Montenegro and the Gulf of Kotor, Southern Dalmatia is bordered to the east by Bosnia-Herzegovina and to the west by the Adriatic Sea. Heading out across the water you will hit Korčula, Mljet and the Elafiti Islands. On the other side is Italy.

WHEN TO GO
Dubrovnik receives visitors all year. Some stay in town for several nights, while many others (locals will say too many) arrive by cruise ship. You might consider scheduling your day trips for the hours when

the cruise crowds arrive and fill up the old town. Fortunately, they disappear come afternoon and by sunset the city is yours again. The city is at its liveliest during the Summer Festival (mid-July to late-August), with everyone from international performers to backpackers scrambling to find a room in the Old Town. Some hotels offer Easter and New Year packages, so you can expect Dubrovnik to be surprisingly busy at these times, too.

The rest of the region is more easygoing. The July and August high season brings an influx of foreign visitors, mainly from Europe. Prices rise significantly during this period, as do temperatures; as compensation, the long summer evenings offer cultural performances and late-night drinking under the stars.

Low season runs from November through April, a period when many hotels and restaurants close completely. That said, through winter you may be lucky enough to find bargain-priced accommodation and blissful days of sunshine and deep blue sky, albeit with a bracing chill in the air. For most people the best time to visit is the shoulder season, May through June and September through October. You'll find no crowds, decent weather, and a chance to tune into the local way of life.

GETTING HERE AND AROUND
AIR TRAVEL
Dubrovnik is served by Dubrovnik Airport (DBV) at Čilipi, 18 km (11 miles) southeast of the city.

The national carrier, Croatia Airlines, operates internal flights between Dubrovnik, Zagreb, Rijeka, Osijek, and Split. Through summer, it also flies regularly between Dubrovnik and Athens, Amsterdam, Barcelona, Berlin, Brussels, Copenhagen, Dusseldorf, Frankfurt, Istanbul, Lisbon, London, Lyon, Munich, Oslo, Paris, Rome, Stockholm, Tel Aviv, Venice, Vienna, and Zurich.

Austrian Airways, British Airways, and Lufthansa all operate scheduled flights to Dubrovnik. Through summer, many other European carriers offer seasonal or charter service to Dubrovnik, including EasyJet, Condor, German Wings, Vueling, and Aer Lingus.

Atlas organizes a shuttle bus that leaves from the bus stop near the cable car or from Dubrovnik Bus Station 90 minutes before each flight. The shuttle bus also meets all incoming flights, and will drop off at the bus stop near Pile Gate or the main bus station. A one-way ticket costs 35 Kn and can be purchased from the Atlas counter in the airport or from the driver. Journey time is approximately 30 minutes.

Airline Contacts Croatia Airlines ✉ *Dubrovnik Airport, Čilipi, Dubrovnik* ☎ *020/773–232* ⊕ *www.croatiaairlines.com.* **EasyJet** ⊕ *www.easyjet.com.* **Jet2. com** ⊕ *www.jet2.com.*

Airport Contacts Dubrovnik Airport ✉ *Čilipi, Dubrovnik* ☎ *020/773–100 general information* ⊕ *www.airport-dubrovnik.hr.*

Airport Transfer Contacts Atlas Shuttle Bus ✉ *Dubrovnik* ☎ *012/415–611* ⊕ *www.atlas-croatia.com.*

GREAT ITINERARIES

Southern Dalmatia is more than just Dubrovnik. The itineraries below aim to give you some idea of what to see in a limited time.

IF YOU HAVE 3 DAYS

Devote Day 1 to **Dubrovnik,** walking a full circuit of the city walls, exploring the historic monuments in the Old Town or riding the cable car to the top of Mt. Srđ, and attending an open-air concert or theatrical performance if the Dubrovnik Summer Festival is in progress. On Day 2 make an early start to visit the arboretum at **Trsteno,** a green wilderness of exotic plant on the grounds of a Renaissance villa. Return to Dubrovnik for a sunset kayaking trip to Lokrum, or take the midday ferry to **Lopud,** one of the car-free Elafiti Islands. If Lopud's romantic escapism appeals, stay overnight; otherwise, return to Dubrovnik for the bright lights. Next morning, splash out on a taxi-boat ride along the coast from Dubrovnik's old harbor to **Cavtat.** Return either by taxi-boat or local bus to Dubrovnik for your final night.

IF YOU HAVE 5 DAYS

Spend your first day in Dubrovnik, as outlined above. Next morning, take a taxi-boat to Cavtat as outlined in the previous itinerary, returning to Dubrovnik in time for the early evening bus to **Korčula Town,** where you should sleep. Next day check out Korčula's Venetian-style architecture in the morning, then spend the afternoon either on the beach at Lumbarda or rent a motorboat and visit the tiny scattered islets of the Korčula archipelago. Stay a second night in Korčula; if you're lucky you might catch an evening performance of the Moreška sword dance. On the next

morning take a ferry to **Orebić** on the Pelješac Peninsula. First walk up to the Franciscan monastery, then devote the afternoon to exploring the local vineyards and wine cellars. Stay the night in Orebić. The following day catch the early morning bus for Dubrovnik. En route you could jump off at **Ston** to explore the 15th-century defensive walls and walk over to Mali Ston to sample the local oysters. **Trsteno** is another possible stop en route. Return to Dubrovnik in the afternoon to prepare for your final night.

IF YOU HAVE 7 DAYS

Spend your first four days as on the itinerary above. On Day 5, wake up in Orebić, then travel southeast along the Pelješac Peninsula to Trstenik to catch the morning ferry to Polače on the island of **Mljet.** Proceed to Pomena, where you will stay the night. Now you are already within the confines of **Mljet National Park,** a paradise of dense pinewoods centering on two interconnected saltwater lakes. Here you can either hike or rent a mountain bike to cycle the perimeter of the lakes, or take time out to swim or dive. In the evening take a national park boat to St. Mary's Islet on Veliko Jezero, occupied by a former monastery, which now hosts a restaurant, making a romantic venue for dinner. On the next morning, drive the length of Mljet to spend a few hours on the sand beach of Saplunara. Leave the island via the port of Sobra aboard the midafternoon ferry for Dubrovnik, where you should spend your final evening.

8

BOAT AND FERRY TRAVEL

Jadrolinija runs a regular ferry service between Dubrovnik and Bari (Italy). Ferries depart from Bari late in the evening, arriving in Dubrovnik early the next morning, with a similar schedule from Dubrovnik to Bari and some traveling in the afternoon (journey time approximately eight hours either direction). The same Jadrolinija vessel covers the coastal route, departing from Rijeka twice weekly in the evening to arrive in Dubrovnik the following day. From Dubrovnik the ferries depart mid-morning to arrive in Rijeka early the following morning (journey time approximately 23 hours in either direction). The ferry calls at Korčula, Stari Grad (island of Hvar), Sobra (on Mljet), and Split along the way. From Dubrovnik, Jadrolinija also runs daily ferries to the Elafiti Islands (Koločep, Lopud, and Šipan), Sobra (island of Mljet), and Split. There are two ways to get to Mljet; a slow ferry which takes around three hours, or the faster (but more expensive) *Nona Ana*, a high-speed catamaran operated by G&V Line, running daily from Gruž Harbor in Dubrovnik to Sobra and Polače, with a journey time of approximately 90 minutes. *Nona Ana* also travels to Korčula and Lastovo in July and August. Through summer (June–September), water taxis run regularly between Cavtat waterfront and Dubrovnik's Old Harbour; you can show up and buy a ticket, which costs around 70 Kn one-way (there is usually some space to bargain). Last, but not least, the island of Korčula is connected to the Pelješac Peninsula by a Jadrolinija car-ferry service (you can jump on even without a car) operating several times a day between Orebić and Domince (2 km [1 mile] from Korčula Town) or a Mediteranska Plovidba passenger ferry between Orebić and Korčula Town. Ticket price is around 15 Kn one-way.

The best place for information about transport, or to buy tickets, is Avansa Travel. They have a very comprehensive website and an office located in Travel Corner across the street from the ferry terminal in Gruž. The staff is very friendly and will simplify everything for you.

Contacts Avansa Travel ⊠ *Obala Stjepana Radića 40, Gruž, Dubrovnik* ☎ *020/492–313* ⊕ *www.avansa-travel.com.* **G&V Line (Nona Ana)** ⊠ *Vukovarska 34, Gruž, Dubrovnik* ☎ *020/313–119* ⊕ *www.gv-line.hr.* **Jadrolinija** ⊠ *Stjepana Radića 40, Dubrovnik* ☎ *020/418–000* ⊕ *www.jadrolinija.hr.* **Mediteranska Plovidba** ⊠ *Trg Kralja Tomislava 2, Korčula* ☎ *020/711–156* ⊕ *www.medplov.hr.*

BUS TRAVEL

There are daily bus services from Dubrovnik to Ljubljana (Slovenia); Medjugorje, Mostar, and Sarajevo (Bosnia-Herzegovina); and Trieste (Italy); plus a thrice-weekly service to Frankfurt, There are regular bus routes between Dubrovnik and destinations all over mainland Croatia, with hourly buses to Split (Central Dalmatia), 14 daily to Zagreb, and four to Rijeka (Kvarner). Within the Southern Dalmatia region, there are four buses daily to Ston and three to Orebić on Peljesac Peninsula, which continue to Korčula. Regular local buses run up the coast to Trstenik, and down the coast to Cavtat (you can also catch the bus to Cavtat at the bus stop near the cable car). Timetable information is available from Dubrovnik Bus Station, near the ferry terminal in Gruž. Remember that if you're traveling between Central and Southern Dalmatia by road, you'll pass through a narrow coastal strip called Neum, which belongs to Bosnia-Herzegovina, so have your passport at hand for the border checkpoint. Most Croatian buses have a 20-minute stop here so people can jump off and shop, since many things are much cheaper in Bosnia.

Contacts Dubrovnik Bus Station ✉ *Obala Pape Ivana Pavla II 44A, Gruž, Dubrovnik* ☎ *060/305–070* ⊕ *libertasdubrovnik.hr.*

CAR TRAVEL

While visiting Dubrovnik and the nearby islands of Mljet and Korčula, you are certainly better off without a car. However, as the city is not linked to the rest of Croatia by train, you may wish to rent a car if you are traveling up the coast to Ston or Orebić, or onward to Split or Zagreb. A car can also be handy if you wish to drive to Međugorje, Mostar, or Sarajevo, in Bosnia-Herzegovina, or to explore further south to the Konavle Region or Montenegro.

Car Rental Contacts Hertz ✉ *Frana Supila 9, Ploče, Dubrovnik* ☎ *020/425–000* ⊕ *www.hertz.hr* ✉ *Dubrovnik Airport, Čilipi* ☎ *020/771–568* ⊕ *www.hertz.hr.* **Thrifty** ✉ *Dubrovnik Airport, Čilipi* ☎ *020/773–588* ⊕ *www.thrifty.com.*

TAXI TRAVEL

In Dubrovnik there are taxi ranks just outside the city walls at Pile Gate and Ploče Gate, in front of Gruž harbor, and in Lapad. Call +385 0800/09–70 to arrange a pickup.

TOUR OPTIONS

Atlas. Atlas organizes one-day excursions from Dubrovnik to neighboring countries (passports required). In Bosnia-Herzegovina, you can visit the pilgrimage site of Medjugorje, where the Virgin Mary is said to have appeared in 1981, or Mostar with its Turkish-inspired Old Town and reconstructed bridge. Or take a day trip to Budva and the Bay of Kotor in Montenegro. Tours can be booked directly with Atlas, at the main tourist information center near Pile Gate, or at Travel Corner in Gruž. ☎ *012/415–611* ⊕ *www.atlas-croatia.com.*

RESTAURANTS

Seafood-lovers rejoice: fresh catch predominates throughout Southern Dalmatia. Squid, prawn, salmon, everything from tuna steaks to drunken octopus to the popular mussels *buzara* (tomato and white wine sauce). Restaurants in Dubrovnik are the most expensive, but also the most sophisticated, where excellent produce is accentuated by sophisticated new flavors, herbs, and recipes still unheard-of in many other towns. The region's top venue for shellfish is the village of Mali Ston on the Pelješac Peninsula, where locally grown *ostrige* (oysters, at their best from February through May) and *dagnje* (mussels, at their best from May through September) attract diners from far and wide. Similarly, the island of Mljet is noted for its *jastog* (lobster), a culinary luxury highly appreciated by the sailing crowd. If you find a restaurant that serves food prepared *ispod peke ("under the bell"),* be sure to try it. A terra-cotta casserole dish, usually containing either lamb or octopus, is buried in white embers over which the *peka* (a metal dome) is placed to ensure a long, slow cooking process. Such dishes often need to be ordered one day in advance. For dessert, the region's specialty is *rožata,* an egg-based pudding similar to French crème caramel. Of course, all

8

meals should be accompanied by a glass of excellent local wine; Plavac Mali, Grk, and Dingač are names you'll get familiar with.

HOTELS

Southern Dalmatia's (and indeed Croatia's) most luxurious hotels are in Dubrovnik; you can stay in renovated palaces, restored summer villas, even a former nunnery! Prices are higher in Dubrovnik than elsewhere, but it is possible to find accommodation to suit lower budgets, particularly in private apartments in the Old Town. Outside Dubrovnik, prices drop and standards generally remain high. There are a number of large, 1970s socialist-era hotels scattered around the area; many are disappointingly impersonal, full of tour groups, and in desperate need of sprucing up. Opt for boutique hotels or apartments wherever possible, where the service is more personal and you have a great chance to live as the locals do. Where once the owners would wait at the bus station with faded photos of their rooms, most are now bookable online. For most of the region, the season runs from Easter through late October, peaking during July and August, when prices rise significantly and it may be difficult to find a place to sleep if you have not booked in advance. *Hotel reviews have been shortened. For full information, visit Fodors.com.*

WHAT IT COSTS IN EUROS (€) AND CROATIAN KUNA (KN)			
$	**$$**	**$$$**	**$$$$**
Restaurants			
under 35 Kn	35 Kn–60 Kn	61 Kn–80 Kn	over 80 Kn
under €5	€5–€8	€9–€10	over €10
Hotels			
under 925 Kn	925 Kn–1,300 Kn	1,301 Kn–1,650 Kn	over 1,650 Kn
under €121	€121–€170	€171–€216	over €216

Restaurant prices are the average cost of a main course at dinner or, if dinner is not served, at lunch. Hotel prices are the lowest cost of a standard double room in high season.

VISITOR INFORMATION

Contacts Cavtat Tourist Office ✉ *Zidine 6, Cavtat* ☎ *020/479–025* ⊕ *visit. cavtat-konavle.com.* **Dubrovnik Tourist Office** ✉ *Brsalje 5, Stari Grad, Dubrovnik* ☎ *020/312–011* ⊕ *www.tzdubrovnik.hr* ✉ *Obala Ivana Pavla II, Gruž, Dubrovnik* ☎ *020/417–983* ⊕ *www.tzdubrovnik.hr.* **Korčula Tourist Office** ✉ *Obala Dr Franje Tuđmana 4, Korčula* ☎ *020/715–867* ⊕ *www.visitkorcula. eu.* **Lopud Tourist Office** ✉ *Obala Iva Kuljevana 12, Lopud* ☎ *020/759–086.* **Mljet Tourist Office** ✉ *Zaglavac BB, Sobra, Mljet* ☎ *020/746–025* ⊕ *www. mljet.hr.* **Orebić Tourist Office** ✉ *Trg Mimbelli, Orebić* ☎ *020/713–718* ⊕ *www. visitorebic-croatia.hr.* **Ston Tourist Office** ✉ *Pelješki put 1, Ston* ☎ *020/754–452* ⊕ *www.ston.hr.*

DUBROVNIK

Nothing can prepare you for your first sight of Dubrovnik. Lying 216 km (135 miles) southeast of Split and commanding a jaw-dropping coastal location, it is one of the world's most beautiful fortified cities.

TOP REASONS TO GO

■ Walk the entire circuit of Dubrovnik's medieval city walls—which date back to the 13th century—for splendid views. Then take the cable car up Mt. Srđ for the postcard-perfect views of the walls, the city and the sea together in all their glory.

■ Eat fresh mussels at a waterside restaurant in the Pelješac peninsula's Mali Ston. They're justifiably famous and served year-round. The best-known restaurant in the area is Kapitanova Kuća, and Vila Koruna serves up a delicious platter, too.

■ Attend a tasting in an old-fashioned stone konoba at a vineyard on Pelješac Peninsula. Either Bartulović Vina or Matuško Vina is a good choice.

■ Swim in Mljet's pristine Veliko Jezero surrounded by dense pine forests; you can also take a boat to the Benedictine monastery on an island in Veliko Jezero.

■ Head out from Dubrovnik in a sea kayak to the scattered Elafiti islands.

Its massive stone ramparts and fortress towers curve around a tiny harbor, enclosing graduated ridges of sun-bleached orange-tiled roofs, copper domes, and elegant bell towers. Your imagination will run wild picturing what it looked like seven centuries ago when the walls were built, without any suburbs or highways around it, just this magnificent stone city rising out of the sea.

In the 7th century AD, residents of the Roman city Epidaurum (now Cavtat) fled the Avars and Slavs of the north and founded a new settlement on a small rocky island, which they named Laus, and later Ragusa. On the mainland hillside opposite the island, the Slav settlement called Dubrovnik grew up. In the 12th century the narrow channel separating the two settlements was filled in (now the main street through the Old Town, called Stradun), and Ragusa and Dubrovnik became one. The city was surrounded by defensive walls during the 13th century, and these were reinforced with towers and bastions in the late 15th century.

From 1358 to 1808 the city thrived as a powerful and remarkably sophisticated independent republic, reaching its golden age during the 16th century. In 1667 many of its splendid Gothic and Renaissance buildings were destroyed by an earthquake. The defensive walls survived the disaster, and the city was rebuilt in baroque style.

Dubrovnik lost its independence to Napoléon in 1808, and in 1815 passed to Austria-Hungary. During the 20th century, as part of Yugoslavia, the city became a popular tourist destination, and in 1979 it was listed as a UNESCO World Heritage Site. During the war for independence, it came under heavy siege. Thanks to careful restoration, few traces of damage remain; however, there are maps inside the Pile and Ploče Gates illustrating the points around the city where damage was done. It's only when you experience Dubrovnik yourself that you can understand what a treasure the world nearly lost

GETTING HERE AND AROUND

There are daily bus services from Dubrovnik to Ljubljana, Medjugorje, Mostar, and Sarajevo (Bosnia-Herzegovina); and Trieste (Italy). There are regular bus routes between Dubrovnik and destinations all over mainland Croatia. It is easier to see Dubrovnik on foot; however, as the city is not linked to the rest of Croatia by train, you may wish to rent a car if you are also planning on traveling up the coast.

EXPLORING

All of the main sites lie in Stari Grad (Old Town) within the city walls, an area which is compact and car-free.

TOP ATTRACTIONS

FAMILY
Fodor's Choice
★

Dubrovnik Cable Car. Reopened in July 2010 after being destroyed in the siege of Dubrovnik, the ultramodern cable car has two light and airy carriages with a capacity of 30 persons each. It's a scenic three-minute ride to the top of Mt. Srdj (405 meters), for spectacular views down onto the Old Town and the islands. You can visit a small museum dedicated to Dubrovnik in the Homeland War 1991–95, plus a memorial with the names of those who died defending the town. Facilities at the top include two viewing terraces with binoculars, Panorama Restaurant where you can have a drink and enjoy an incredible sunset, a snack bar, and souvenir shop. ■TIP→ You can buy a ticket for two return trips for only 150 Kn, which gives you the opportunity to check out both the daytime and nighttime views. ✉ *Lower station, Petra Krešimira 4, Dubrovnik* ☎ *020/325–393* ⊕ *www.dubrovnikcablecar.com* ⚏ *60 Kn one-way; 100 Kn return* ☉ *June–Aug., 9 am–midnight; Sept., 9 am–10 pm; Oct., Apr., and May, 9 am–8 pm; Nov., Feb., and Mar., 9 am–5 pm; Dec. and Jan., 9 am–4 pm.*

Fodor's Choice
★

Gradske Zidine (*City Walls*). Dubrovnik's city walls define the Old Town and are one of the world's most stunning architectural achievements. The walls circle the town, and are part of the fortification system, which also included four gates, including the Pile and Ploče Gates, as well as four towers, including the freestanding Lovrijenac Tower to the west. A popular tourist attraction and lookout point, a walk along the top of the walls is a must-do, offering excellent views of the Adriatic beyond and the town below. Most of the original construction took place during the 13th century, though the walls were further reinforced with towers and bastions over the following 400 years. On average they are 80 feet high and up to 10 feet thick on the seaward side, 20 feet thick on the inland side. They may look familiar to fans of *Game of Thrones;* they are regularly featured as the walls of King's Landing. ■TIP→ The wall walk takes at least an hour if you stop for photos. Plan your walk for the morning or late-afternoon, to avoid the afternoon heat and the cruise-ship crowds. ✉ *Placa, Stari Grad, Dubrovnik* ☎ *020/638–800* ⊕ *www. citywallsdubrovnik.hr* ⚏ *100 Kn (or 150 Kn for Dubrovnik Card)* ☉ *May–Sept., 8–7:30; Nov.–Apr., 9–3.*

Fodor's Choice
★

Knežev Dvor (*Rector's Palace*). Originally created in the 15th century but reconstructed several times through the following years, this exquisite Gothic/Renaissance building with an arcaded loggia and an internal courtyard is one of the most significant buildings along the Croatian Coast. On the ground floor there are large rooms where, in the days of the republic, the Great Council and Senate held their meetings. Over the entrance to the meeting halls a plaque reads: "obliti privatorum publica curate" (Forget private affairs, and get on with public matters). Upstairs, the rector's living quarters now accommodate the Cultural History Museum, containing exhibits that give a picture of life in Dubrovnik from early days until the fall of the republic. ⊠ *Pred Dvorom 3, Stari Grad, Dubrovnik* ☎ *020/321–497* ⊕ *www.dumus.hr* ⊟ *70 Kn (or 150 Kn for Dubrovnik Card)* ⊙ *Daily 9–6.*

Placa (*Stradun*). This was once the shallow sea channel separating the island of Laus from the mainland. Although it was filled in during the 12th century, it continued to divide the city socially for several centuries, the nobility living in the area south of Placa and the commoners living on the hillside to the north. The Placa, commonly known as Stradun, is 300 meters long and cuts straight through the Old Town from the Pile to the Ploče Gate; it is the best people-watching promenade in town. It is paved with limestone and is polished by use; in the middle of summer, when the street is being walked upon by thousands of people, it shines like glass, particularly impressive at night when it reflects the light from the street lamps. ⊠ *Stari Grad, Dubrovnik.*

Fodor'sChoice ★ **Pomorski Muzej** (*Maritime Museum*). Above the aquarium, located on the first and second floor of St. John's Fortress, this museum's exhibits illustrate how rich and powerful Dubrovnik became one of the world's most important seafaring nations. On display are intricately detailed models of ships as well as engine-room equipment, sailors' uniforms, paintings, and maps. Visitors buy a combination ticket, which is valid for four museums, which also include the Bishop's Palace. ⊠ *Damjana Jude 2, Stari Grad, Dubrovnik* ☎ *020/323–904* ⊟ *100 Kn (or 150 Kn for Dubrovnik Card)* ⊙ *May–Oct., 9–6; Nov.–Apr., 9–4 (closed Mon.).*

Vrata od Pila (*Pile Gate*). Built in 1537 and combining a Renaissance arch with a wooden drawbridge on chains, this has always been the main entrance to the city walls. A niche above the portal contains a statue of Sveti Vlaho (St. Blaise), the city's patron saint, holding a replica of Dubrovnik in his left hand. From May to October, guards in deep-red period-costume uniforms stand vigilant by the gate through daylight hours, just as they would have done when the city was a republic. ⊠ *Pile, Stari Grad, Dubrovnik.*

Vrata od Ploča (*Ploče Gate*). One of two gates in the town walls, Ploče comprises a stone bridge and wooden drawbridge plus a 15th-century stone arch bearing a statue of Sveti Vlaho (St. Blaise). As at Pile Gate, guards in period costume stand vigilant here through the summer season. ⊠ *Ploče, Stari Grad, Dubrovnik.*

Fodor'sChoice ★ **War Photo Limited.** Shocking and impressive, this modern gallery devotes two entire floors to war photojournalism. The permanent exhibition showcases photos and video from former Yugoslavia, while recent exhibitions have included images from conflicts in Syria, Afghanistan, and Iraq. Refreshingly impartial, the message—that war is physically and emotionally destructive whichever side you are on—comes through

8

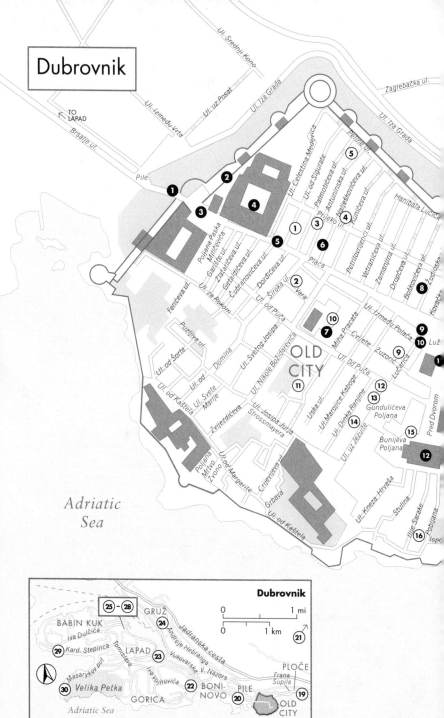

Dubrovnik

TO
LAPAD

Adriatic
Sea

OLD
CITY

Adriatic Sea

Dubrovnik

GRUŽ
BABIN KUK
LAPAD
Velika Petka
GORICA
BONI-
NOVO
PLOČE
PILE
OLD
CITY

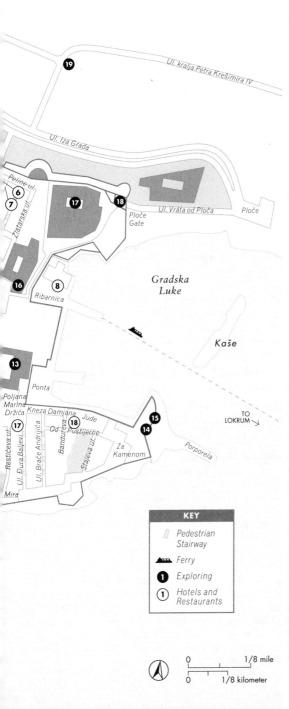

Exploring ▼

Akvarij	15
Bell Tower	16
Crkva Svetog Vlaha	11
Dominikanski samostan	17
Dubrovnik Cable Car	19
Franjevačka samostan	4
Gradske Zidine	2
Katedrala Velika Gospa	12
Knežev Dvor	13
Muzej Pravoslavne Crkve	7
Onofrio Fountain	3
Orlando's Column	9
Placa	5
Pomorski Muzej	14
Sinagoga	8
Sponza Palace	10
Vrata od Pila	1
Vrata od Ploča	18
War Photo Limited	6

Restaurants ▼

Amfora	21
Azur	16
Bota Šare Oyster & Sushi Bar	17
Dalmatino	10
Kamenica	13
Lady Pi-Pi	5
Lokanda Peškarija	8
Nishta	3
Olivia Gourmet	9
Orsan	26
Proto	2
Pupo Tavern	11
Taverna Otto	23
Tovjerna Sesame	20

Hotels ▼

Amoret Apartments	14
Apartments Paviša	7
Dubrovnik Palace	30
Fresh Sheets Bed and Breakfast	15
Hotel Bellevue	22
Hotel Berkeley	24
Hotel Excelsior	19
Hotel Kazbek	28
Hotel Lapad	25
Hotel More	29
Hotel Stari Grad	1
Hotel Zagreb	27
Karmen Apartments	18
Prijeko Palace	4
Pučié Palace	12
Villa Ragusa	6

KEY

| Pedestrian Stairway |
| Ferry |
| Exploring |
| Hotels and Restaurants |

0 — 1/8 mile
0 — 1/8 kilometer

loud and clear. ⊠ *Antuninska 6, Stari Grad, Dubrovnik* ☎ *020/322–166* ⊕ *www.warphotoltd.com* 🖃 *40 Kn* ☉ *May and Oct., 10–4, closed Tues.; June–Sept., daily 10–10.*

WORTH NOTING

Akvarij (*Aquarium*). This dark, cavernous space houses several small pools and 27 well-lit tanks containing a variety of fish from rays to small sharks, as well as other underwater denizens such as sponges and sea urchins. Children will find the octopus in his glass tank either very amusing or horribly scary. ⊠ *Damjana Jude 2, Stari Grad, Dubrovnik* ☎ *020/323–125* 🖃 *40 Kn* ☉ *Year-round 9–6.*

Bell Tower. All walks down the Stradun lead to one point: the bell tower, the centerpiece of Luža Square. It was erected in 1444, but growing instability led to its closure at the start of the 20th century. After nearly 30 years, it was reopened in 1929, using the original designs. The bright white structure, one of the main symbols of the city, reaches 31 meters high and features a moon dial and the original bell from 1506. Look a little closer to see Dubrovnik's two favorite mascots tolling the hours on either side of the bell; known as Maro and Baro, the current figures are made of bronze, while the original wooden men now live in the Rector's Palace. ⊠ *Luža, Stari Grad, Dubrovnik.*

Crkva Svetog Vlaha (*Church of St. Blaise*). This 18th-century baroque church replaced an earlier one destroyed by fire. Of particular note is the silver statue on the high altar of St. Blaise holding a model of Dubrovnik, which is paraded around town each year on February 3, the Day of St. Blaise. ⊠ *Luža 3, Stari Grad, Dubrovnik* 🖃 *Free* ☉ *Mon.–Sat. 7–noon and 4–8, Sun. 7–1.*

NEED A BREAK?

Gradska Kavana. Gradska Kavana occupies the ornate Arsenal building and remains Dubrovnik's favorite meeting place for morning coffee with cakes or an evening aperitif. It has an ample summer terrace for when the weather is nice. ⊠ *Pred Dvorom 1, Stari Grad, Dubrovnik* ⊕ *www.mea-culpa.hr.*

Dominikanski samostan (*Dominican monastery*). With a splendid, late-15th-century floral Gothic cloister as its centerpiece, the monastery is best known for its museum, which houses a rich collection of religious paintings by the Dubrovnik School from the 15th and 16th centuries. Look out for works by Božidarević, Hamzić, and Dobričević, as well as gold and silver ecclesiastical artifacts crafted by local goldsmiths. ⊠ *Sv Dominika 4, Stari Grad, Dubrovnik* ☎ *020/321–423* ⊕ *www.dominikanci.hr/dominikanski-samostan-dubrovnik-samostan-sv.-dominika.html* 🖃 *20 Kn* ☉ *Year-round 9–6.*

Franjevačka samostan (*Franciscan monastery*). The monastery's chief claim to fame is its pharmacy, which was founded in 1318 and is still in existence today; it's said to be the oldest in Europe. There's also a delightful cloistered garden, framed by Romanesque arcades supported by double columns, each crowned with a set of grotesque figures. In the Treasury a painting shows what Dubrovnik looked like before the disastrous earthquake of 1667. ⊠ *Placa 2, Stari Grad, Dubrovnik* ☎ *020/321–410* 🖃 *30 Kn* ⊙ *May–Oct., daily 9–5; Nov.–Apr., daily 9–2.*

Katedrala Velika Gospa (*Assumption of the Virgin Mary Cathedral*). The present structure was completed in 1713 in baroque style after the original was destroyed in the 1667 earthquake. Legend says that Richard the Lionheart was shipwrecked on Lokrum Island, and vowed to show his thanks to God for saving his life by building a cathedral on the spot; locals convinced him to move his plans to Dubrovnik instead. The interior contains a number of notable paintings, including a large polyptych above the main altar depicting the *Assumption of Our Lady,* attributed to Titian. The Treasury displays 138 gold and silver reliquaries, including the skull of St. Blaise in the form of a bejeweled Byzantine crown and also an arm and leg of the saint, likewise encased in decorated gold plating. ⊠ *Držićeva Poljana, Stari Grad, Dubrovnik* 🖃 *Cathedral free, Treasury 15 Kn* ⊙ *Daily 10–noon and 3–5, closed Sun.*

Muzej Pravoslavne Crkve (*Orthodox Church Museum*). Next door to the Orthodox church, this small museum displays religious icons from the Balkan region and Russia, as well as several portraits of early-20th-century Dubrovnik personalities by local artist Vlaho Bukovac. ⊠ *Od Puča 8, Stari Grad, Dubrovnik* ☎ *020/323–887* 🖃 *10 Kn* ⊙ *Weekdays 9–2; closed weekends.*

Onofrio Fountain. Built from 1438 to 1440, the Big Onofrio Fountain is the first sight you see upon entering the Pile Gate. The 16-sided stone fountain, which was even more ornate before the 1667 earthquake, is topped by a large dome and was designed by architect Onofrio Giordano della Cava. Along with the Small Onofrio Fountain at the other end of the Stradun, it was part of a complex water-supply system designed to bring water into the Old Town from a well 12 km (7½ miles) away. The water is still cold and drinkable, and it's a nice place to rest and refuel. ⊠ *Pred Dvorom, Stari Grad, Dubrovnik.*

Orlando's Column. Dating back to 1418, Orlando's Column, located at the end of the Stradun and serving as a popular meeting point, is dedicated to legendary 8th-century knight Roland, who is said to have saved Dubrovnik from a Saracen attack near Lokrum. The white stone column has become a symbol of freedom for the city, and the white Libertas flag is traditionally flown from the top during important events, such as the opening ceremony of the Dubrovnik Summer Festival. ⊠ *Luža, Stari Grad, Dubrovnik.*

NEED A BREAK?

Buža. Walk through an 800-year-old wall to find a secret swimming spot across the sea from a cursed island. Sounds like a fairy tale, but in Dubrovnik such places actually exist, and there are two of them. One of the *Buža* (hole in the wall) bars is marked by a wooden sign pointing toward "cold drinks." The other has no signage at all, you just walk through a doorway in the City Walls and it's there. With tables arranged on a series of terraces built into the rocks and jazzy soundtracks to go along with stunning vistas to Lokrum, both bars make a great place to stop for a drink or a

swim; you can jump right off the rocks in front of the bar into the sea. ✉ ***Od Margarita, Stari Grad, Dubrovnik.***

Sinagoga (*Synagogue*). This tiny 15th-century synagogue, the second-oldest in Europe (after Prague) bears testament to Dubrovnik's once thriving Jewish community, made up largely of Jews who were expelled from Spain and Italy during the medieval period. ✉ *Žudioska 5, Stari Grad, Dubrovnik* 🎫 *20 Kn* ⏲ *Weekdays 10–8.*

Sponza Palace. Originally the location where all trade goods coming into Dubrovnik went to be taxed, this 16th-century Gothic Renaissance palace served as the mint, an arsenal, and eventually a place for the most educated citizens, called the "Academy of the Learned," to discuss cultural matters. It now contains the archives from the Republic, some of the most important documents in the city's history. There's not much to see inside except the occasional art exhibition, but the shady, arcaded interior is a lovely spot to escape the heat and crowds. Turn left as you enter to find the "Memorial Room for the Defenders of Dubrovnik," a small gallery with photographs of those who died defending the city, as well as the harbor under attack, and remnants of the flag that once flew atop Mount Srdj. Even if you're not interested in the palace itself, this heart-wrenching little gallery is worthwhile. ✉ *Stari Grad, Dubrovnik* ☎ *020/321–032* 🎫 *25 Kn* ⏲ *10–7 daily.*

WHERE TO EAT

These are exciting times for foodies in Dubrovnik. As elsewhere along the coast, seafood dominates restaurant menus but here it is being turned into sophisticated sushi, sashimi, and steaks. Yes, restaurants in Dubrovnik are far more expensive than elsewhere in Croatia. But go to the right places, where the quality matches the prices, and you won't mind paying a little extra. The narrow, cobbled street Prijeko, nicknamed "restaurant street," which runs parallel to Placa, is packed with touristy restaurants and waiters touting for customers. Venture further afield to find less commercial and infinitely more agreeable eateries.

$$$$ SEAFOOD Fodor's Choice ★

🍴 **Amfora.** Located on a noisy road near the port, and nothing special from the outside, Amfora could easily be overlooked. But it is the best restaurant in the up-and-coming neighborhood of Gruž, and just might be one of the best restaurants you visit in Croatia. Owner Kristian studied medicine before opening the restaurant, and has transferred his love of research and interest in fresh and healthy eating to his menu. Dishes burst with flavor from herbs grown right on the premises, the Croatian beef is grass-fed, and best yet, the chocolate cake is deliciously gluten-free. Try the sesame-encrusted bluefin tuna steak; it will change your life. [$] *Average main: 120 Kn* ✉ *Obala Stjepana Radica 26, Gruž, Dubrovnik* ☎ *020/419–419.*

$$$ ASIAN FUSION Fodor's Choice ★

🍴 **Azur.** Run by local brothers who own a Mediterranean-inspired restaurant of the same name in China, Azur is an Asian-inspired restaurant right under the city walls, near one of the Buža Bars. Spread over two shady terraces with fresh green linens, it has a hip soundtrack, friendly staff, and fantastic prices for food that you don't find elsewhere in Dubrovnik, such as cashew nut prawns, salmon ceviche, and baba ghanoush. It's fun, laid-back, and cool. Ⓢ *Average main: 110 Kn* ✉ *Pobijana 10, Stari Grad, Dubrovnik* ☎ *020/324–806* ⊕ *www.azurvision.com/#!dubrovnik/crrl.*

$$$
SUSHI
✕ **Bota Šare Oyster & Sushi Bar.** For a change from standard Croatian fare, this chic eatery, which also has branches in Mali Ston and Zagreb offers friendly professional service and beautifully presented sushi, served at tall white tables on a small terrace with views onto Dubrovnik's cathedral. They do a delightful shrimp tempura and a fine tuna tartare, as well as platters of mixed sushi, including salmon maki and amberjack nigiri. Alternatively opt for fresh or tempura oysters (from nearby Ston) and champagne. Ⓢ *Average main: 80 Kn* ✉ *Od Pustijerne BB, Stari Grad, Dubrovnik* ☎ *020/324–034* ⊕ *www.bota-sare.hr* ⊗ *Closed Jan. and Feb.*

$$$$
SEAFOOD
Fodor'sChoice
★
✕ **Dalmatino.** One of the new stars on the restaurant scene, Dalmatino has a cozy, candlelit interior, with original stone walls, coffee-stained for effect, featuring faded photos of old Dubrovnik. Located on a side street off the Stradun, it's a romantic place to settle in for the evening. Try their mussels in cream wine sauce, exquisite John Dory with stir-fried vegetables, slow-roasted meat, and melt-in-your-mouth chocolate fondant for dessert. Ⓢ *Average main: 120 Kn* ✉ *Miha Pracata 6, Stari Grad, Dubrovnik* ☎ *020/323–070* ⊕ *dalmatino-dubrovnik.com.*

$$
SEAFOOD
✕ **Kamenica.** Overlooking the morning market in the Old Town, Kamenica remains popular for its fresh oysters and generous platters of *girice* (small fried fish) and *pržene ligne* (fried squid). It's cheap and cheerful, offers unbeatable value for the location, and is much-loved by locals and tourists alike. Ⓢ *Average main: 80 Kn* ✉ *Gundulićeva Poljana 8, Stari Grad, Dubrovnik* ☎ *020/323–682* ⊗ *No dinner Nov.–Mar.*

$$$
SEAFOOD
✕ **Lady Pi-Pi.** Yep, you read that name correctly. This tiny, family-run konoba set high up in the old town, with a shady terrace and impressive views, was named after the unusual stone statue at the entrance, built years ago by their father. Today the statue, once a horrible embarrassment for the kids but which they have since come to love, plus the cozy atmosphere and simple but delicious menu, draws a nightly crowd. ■ **TIP→ Come here for breakfast or lunch; there will be no line, and you'll have the konoba, plus the views, to yourself.** Ⓢ *Average main: 100 Kn* ✉ *Antuninska 23, Stari Grad, Dubrovnik* ⊜ *Reservations not accepted* ⊗ *Closed Oct.–May.*

$$
SEAFOOD
✕ **Lokanda Peškarija.** Just outside the town walls—and affording unforgettable views over the old harbor—this seafood restaurant is a particularly good value. The seafood on offer is guaranteed fresh each day, not least because the restaurant stands next door to Dubrovnik's covered fish market. It has a beautifully designed, split-level interior with exposed stone walls and wooden beams, plus romantic outdoor candlelit tables by the water. Service can be slow when it is crowded. ■ **TIP→ Definitely not only for tourists, locals love eating here as well, so reservations are recommended, especially for dinner.** Ⓢ *Average main: 90 Kn* ✉ *Na Ponti, Stari Grad, Dubrovnik* ☎ *020/324–750* ⊕ *www.mea-culpa.hr* ⊗ *Closed Jan.–Mar.*

8

$$ VEGETARIAN FAMILY 🍴 **Nishta.** Specializing in vegetarian and vegan fare, this playful eatery on Prijeko Street has just a dozen tables and is deservedly popular; for years it was the only option in town for vegetarians. Though mainly Indian-inspired, their menu features everything from homemade gnocchi with pesto, to pho, to falafel, plus a salad bar and a limited choice of indulgent desserts. ■ **TIP➔ Reservations recommended, especially for dinner.** [$] *Average main: 70 Kn* ✉ *Prijeko BB, Dubrovnik* ☎ *020/322–088* 🌐 *www.nishtarestaurant.com* 🕒 *Closed Sun.*

$$ MEDITERRANEAN 🍴 **Oliva Gourmet.** This simple, modern eatery features fresh and innovative Mediterranean dishes made from locally sourced ingredients, plus an excellent range of wines. The interior has exposed stone walls and modern decor with a vintage flair, plus a handful of outdoor tables for people-watching. Oliva Pizzeria—a takeaway counter built into the side of the building—is a good option for a quick slice. [$] *Average main: 90 Kn* ✉ *Cvijete Zuzorić 2, Stari Grad, Dubrovnik* ☎ *020/324–594* 🌐 *olivadubrovnik.com/gourmet/index.html.*

$$$ SEAFOOD 🍴 **Orsan.** This long-standing restaurant has a pretty, leafy terrace overlooking the Yacht Club Orsan marina, opposite Gruž Harbor, on the edge of the Lapad Peninsula. One of the better restaurants in Lapad, it serves excellent fresh seafood with a smart ambiance and lovely view. Firm favorites include *salata od hobotnice* (octopus salad), *svježa morska riba* (fresh fish) and *rožata* (a Dubrovnik dessert similar to crème caramel). [$] *Average main: 120 Kn* ✉ *Ivana Zajca 2, Lapad, Dubrovnik* ☎ *020/436–822* 🌐 *www.restaurant-orsan-dubrovnik.com.*

$$$$ SEAFOOD 🍴 **Proto.** A reliable choice for dinner, Proto is on a side street off Stradun, with tables arranged on an upper-level, open-air terrace. The menu features an excellent selection of traditional Dalmatian seafood dishes—including oysters from nearby Ston—and notably succulent steaks. The restaurant dates back to 1886 and most locals will respectfully acknowledge that it is still one of the best in town. ■ **TIP➔ Reservations are recommended.** [$] *Average main: 150 Kn* ✉ *Široka 1, Stari Grad, Dubrovnik* ☎ *020/323–234* 🌐 *www.esculaprestaurants.com.*

$$$ SEAFOOD 🍴 **Pupo Tavern.** Before you even know what its name means, Pupo Tavern will make you smile. The waiters are eager, the owner, who moonlights as a singer in a traditional folk band, is young and a little wacky, and the food is surprisingly good. The menu features produce from all around Croatia, from Istrian truffle sauce to goat cheese from Zadar. If you want to try something special, order the fish baked in salt; it takes 45 minutes to prepare, it's a real production when it arrives, and it tastes exactly how you wish fish was always cooked. They have a nice wine list, too; try their sweet teranino liqueur. [$] *Average main: 100 Kn* ✉ *Miha Pracata 8, Stari Grad, Dubrovnik* ☎ *020/323–555* 🌐 *pupodubrovnik.com.*

$$$ MEDITERRANEAN Fodor's Choice ★ 🍴 **Taverna Otto.** Like most of Europe's great neighborhoods, Gruž Harbor started off a little dodgy, just your typical port area. But in the past few years a renaissance has begun, and Otto's Tavern was at the forefront. Located in a cavernous 450-year-old stone building, once used as a boathouse, Otto's has a short, Mediterranean-inspired menu that changes often, ensuring all dishes are consistently fresh. The vibe is cool, the service laid-back and friendly, and it's worth venturing out of the

old town to check it out. $ *Average main: 110 Kn* ⊠ *Nikole Tesle 8, Gruž, Dubrovnik* ☎ *020/358–633* ⊕ *www.tavernaotto.com.*

$$$ ✕ **Tovjerna Sesame.** Just a short

MEDITERRANEAN distance outside of the Pile Gate,

Fodor's Choice this romantic restaurant occupies

★ a vaulted, candlelit space as well as a breezy, vine-covered terrace. Its jazzy soundtrack and bohemian decor from bygone ages (including a custom-made Dubrovnik Monopoly board) are second only to the exquisite menu, prepared by the owner's wife, a Cordon-Bleu-trained chef. Favorites include homemade lobster ravioli, slow-baked lamb, and a chocolate mousse like no dessert you've ever had before (ask about the two secret ingredients). $ *Average main: 110 Kn* ⊠ *Dante Alighierija BB, Pile, Dubrovnik* ☎ *020/412–910* ⊕ *www.sesame.hr.*

> **ST. BLAISE**
>
> The bearded figure of St. Blaise, Dubrovnik's patron saint, was featured on the Republic's coins and flags. The former Bishop of Sebaste in Turkey, Blaise lost his life in AD 316 during a Roman-led anti-Christian campaign. Also a doctor, he once miraculously saved a child who was choking on a fish bone, and still today, those ailing from throat problems pray to him for healing. He was made Dubrovnik's protector in 972, having appeared to the rector in a dream warning of an imminent Venetian attack and thus saving the city.

WHERE TO STAY

There are only three small but extremely desirable hotels within the city walls. The most exclusive establishments line the coastal road east of the center, offering stunning views of the Old Town and the sea, whereas modern hotels with cheaper rooms can be found in Lapad, 3 km (2 miles) west of the center. The most affordable, and often the most unique accommodation is to be found in private apartments; the apartments listed below are located within the Old Town, in narrow streets and historical buildings where hotels only dream of building, and they present a great opportunity to live like a local.

$ 🏠 **Amoret Apartments.** In the heart of the Old Town, these delightful stu-

RENTAL dio apartments occupy four carefully restored 16th-century stone build-

Fodor's Choice ings. **Pros:** located in Old Town; homey and atmospheric rooms with

★ antique furniture; inexpensive by Dubrovnik standards. **Cons:** rooms can be noisy at night (nearby restaurants and neighbors). $ *Rooms from: €100* ⊠ *Restićeva 2, Stari Grad, Dubrovnik* ☎ *020/324–005* ⊕ *www.dubrovnik-amoret.com* ➥ *15 apartments* ▭ *No credit cards* ⦾ *No meals.*

$ 🏠 **Apartments Paviša.** These five apartments represent some of the best

RENTAL value you'll find in Dubrovnik. **Pros:** spacious apartments; excellent value for the money; friendly service. **Cons:** a far walk from the Old Town; no breakfast. $ *Rooms from: €100* ⊠ *Zudioska 19, Stari Grad, Dubrovnik* ☎ *098/427–399* ⊕ *www.apartmentspavisa.com* ➥ *5 apartments* ⦾ *No meals.*

8

$$$$ HOTEL **Dubrovnik Palace.** Located in Lapad, this 10-story design hotel is vast but undeniably chic. **Pros:** chic interior design; excellent sports facilities (including a luxurious spa); seafront location with private beach. **Cons:** expensive; vast with somewhat impersonal service; feels more like a business than a luxury hotel. [$] *Rooms from: €299* ✉ *Masarykov put 20, Lapad, Dubrovnik* ☎ *020/430–000* 🌐 *www.alh.hr* 🛏 *271 rooms, 37 suites* 🍴 *Breakfast.*

$$ B&B/INN **Fresh Sheets Bed and Breakfast.** Jon and Sanja, the Canadian/Croatian couple who run Dubrovnik's popular Fresh Sheets hostel, as well as a retro launderette, have done it again. **Pros:** good location in the Old Town; friendly and personal service; lovely rooms. **Cons:** no elevator; no common areas other than the kitchen. [$] *Rooms from: €148* ✉ *Bunićeva poljana 6, Stari Grad, Dubrovnik* ☎ *091/799–2086* 🌐 *freshsheetsbedandbreakfast.com* 🛏 *6 rooms* 🍴 *Breakfast.*

$$$$ HOTEL **Hotel Bellevue.** Built into a spectacular rocky cliff overlooking the sea, this design hotel is the one you gasp at between the Old Town and Gruž harbor. **Pros:** cliff-top location overlooking the sea; chic interiors; luxurious spa; beach. **Cons:** expensive; not in Old Town; service rather impersonal and sometimes indifferent. [$] *Rooms from: €400* ✉ *Pera Čingrije 7, Dubrovnik* ☎ *020/330–000* 🌐 *www.alh.hr* 🛏 *77 rooms, 14 suites* 🍴 *Breakfast.*

$$ HOTEL **Hotel Berkeley.** One block back from Gruž harbor, this welcoming three-star hotel is run by a Croatian-Australian family. **Pros:** friendly atmosphere; proximity to port; good value for money; outdoor pool; excellent cooked-to-order breakfast. **Cons:** distance from Old Town; no restaurant. [$] *Rooms from: €150* ✉ *Andrije Hebranga 116A, Gruž, Dubrovnik* ☎ *020/494–160* 🌐 *www.berkeleyhotel.hr* 🛏 *29 rooms, 2 apartments* 🍴 *Breakfast.*

$$$$ HOTEL **Hotel Excelsior.** On the coastal road east of the center, this prestigious hotel was the first five-star property in Dubrovnik, dating back to 1913; everyone from Queen Elizabeth II to Francis Ford Coppola has come to stay. **Pros:** seafront location with great views of the Old Town; spacious rooms; luxurious spa. **Cons:** big with somewhat impersonal service; modern but slightly lacking in charm; poor sound insulation between neighboring rooms. [$] *Rooms from: €350* ✉ *Put Frane Supila 12, Ploče, Dubrovnik* ☎ *020/353–300* 🌐 *www.alh.hr* 🛏 *141 rooms, 17 suites* 🍴 *Breakfast.*

$$$$ HOTEL **Hotel Kazbek.** Originally built as a villa for a 16th-century noble family, this property on the Lapad Peninsula, overlooking Gruž Bay, also served as a WWII prison, a schoolhouse, and a storage unit before becoming the gracious, refined Hotel Kazbek. **Pros:** friendly; personal service; richly decorated rooms; excellent à la carte breakfast. **Cons:** distance from old town and bus stop; often fully booked. [$] *Rooms from: €390* ✉ *Lapadska Obala 25, Lapad, Dubrovnik* ☎ *020/362–999* 🌐 *www.kazbekdubrovnik.com* 🛏 *13 rooms* 🕓 *Closed Oct.–Mar.* 🍴 *Breakfast.*

$$$ HOTEL **Hotel Lapad.** Occupying a 19th-century building with a garden and an outdoor pool, Hotel Lapad overlooks Gruž harbor, just a 45-minute walk west of the Old Town. **Pros:** near harbor (ideal for early morning ferries); friendly and helpful staff. **Cons:** distance from Old Town;

big and rather impersonal. $ *Rooms from: €193* ⊠ *Lapadska obala 37, Lapad, Dubrovnik* ☎ *020/455–555* ⊕ *www.hotel-lapad.hr* ⤳ *163 rooms* ⊗ *Closed Nov.–Mar.* ⦿ *Breakfast.*

$$$$ 🏨 **Hotel More.** Rising from a seaside walkway up a forested cliff on
HOTEL Lapad Peninsula, this boutique hotel boasts one of the most spectacu-
Fodor'sChoice lar, peaceful locations in Dubrovnik. **Pros:** friendly service; beautifully
★ decorated rooms and views; excellent restaurant and cave bar. **Cons:** often fully booked, distant from town. $ *Rooms from: €300* ⊠ *Kardinala Stepinca 33, Lapad, Dubrovnik* ☎ *020/494–200* ⊕ *hotel-more.hr* ⤳ *36 rooms, 4 suites* ⦿ *Breakfast.*

$$$$ 🏨 **Hotel Stari Grad.** After a complete renovation in 2013, this boutique
HOTEL hotel has become one of the most talked-about places in town. **Pros:** Old Town location; small and intimate; breakfast served on wonderful roof terrace. **Cons:** no elevator; small rooms; parking difficult. $ *Rooms from: 2100 Kn* ⊠ *Od Sigurate 4, Stari Grad, Dubrovnik* ☎ *020/322–244* ⊕ *www.hotelstarigrad.com* ⤳ *8 rooms* ⊗ *Closed Nov.–Mar.* ⦿ *Breakfast.*

$$ 🏨 **Hotel Zagreb.** Set in a small garden with palms, this red 19th-cen-
HOTEL tury villa is right on the pedestrian-only promenade, leading down to Lapad Bay. **Pros:** located close to transport to Old Town; close to the beach; breakfast served on pleasant open-air terrace. **Cons:** distance from Old Town; food rather disappointing. $ *Rooms from: €130* ⊠ *Šetalište Kralja Zvonimira 27, Lapad, Dubrovnik* ☎ *020/438–930* ⊕ *www.hotelzagreb-dubrovnik.com* ⤳ *24 rooms* ⊗ *Closed Nov.–Mar.* ⦿ *Breakfast.*

$ 🏨 **Karmen Apartments.** An excellent budget choice in the Old Town, these
RENTAL homey, light, and airy apartments look directly onto the fishing boats in the old harbor. **Pros:** location in Old Town; homey and atmospheric rooms with bohemian decor; great views of the old harbor. **Cons:** often fully booked; can be noisy at night (harborside restaurants). $ *Rooms from: €95* ⊠ *Bandureva 1, Stari Grad, Dubrovnik* ☎ *020/323–433* ⊕ *www.karmendu.tk* ⤳ *4 apartments* ▭ *No credit cards.*

$$$ 🏨 **Prijeko Palace.** This is the hotel you'll talk about when you get home.
HOTEL **Pros:** unique design; location in the old town; elevator (one of only a
Fodor'sChoice couple in the Old Town); friendly service. **Cons:** at time of writing, no
★ breakfast was offered; often fully booked. $ *Rooms from: €200* ⊠ *Prijeko 22, Stari Grad, Dubrovnik* ☎ *020/321–145* ⊕ *www.prijekopalace. com* ⤳ *9 rooms, 5 apartments.*

$$$$ 🏨 **Pučić Palace.** In the heart of the Old Town, occupying a beautifully
HOTEL restored 18th-century baroque palace, this small luxury hotel offers the sort of aristocratic delights that its location suggests: rooms with dark wood parquet floors and wood-beam ceilings, antique furnishings, and Italian mosaic-tile bathrooms supplied with Bulgari toiletries. **Pros:** located in Old Town; beautifully furnished interior; small enough that guests receive individual attention from staff. **Cons:** very expensive; lacks many facilities; no parking nearby. $ *Rooms from: €465* ⊠ *Ul od Puča 1, Stari Grad, Dubrovnik* ☎ *020/326–200* ⊕ *www.thepucicpalace. com* ⤳ *19 rooms* ⦿ *Breakfast.*

$ 🏨 **Villa Ragusa.** This is an excellent budget option in the Old Town right
RENTAL next door to one of the Paviša Apartments. **Pros:** location in the Old

8

CLOSE UP

The Republic of Dubrovnik

As an independent republic from 1358 to 1808, Dubrovnik kept its freedom not through military power, but thanks to diplomatic cunning. Would-be aggressors, including Hungary and the Ottoman Turks, were paid an annual fee in return for peaceful relations, and Dubrovnik avoided involvement in international conflicts between Christians and Muslims, preferring to remain neutral.

The republic's economy was based on shipping and trading goods between Europe and the Middle East, and by the 16th century the republic had consulates in some 50 foreign ports, along with a merchant fleet of 200 ships on the Mediterranean. By this time its territory had also extended to include 120 km (75 miles) of mainland coast (from Neum to the Bay of Kotor) plus the islands of Lastovo and Mljet.

The chief citizen was the Rector, who had to be over 50; he was elected for only a month at a time to share management of the republic's business with the Grand Council (composed of members of the local nobility) and the Senate (a consultative body made up of 45 "wise men," all over the age of 40). Most of the military and naval commands were held by members of the nobility, while lower-ranking soldiers were mercenaries from the regions that are now Germany and the Czech Republic. The increasingly prosperous middle class carried on trade. The Archbishop of Dubrovnik had to be a foreigner (usually an Italian), a law intended to keep politics and religion apart.

Outstandingly sophisticated for its time, Dubrovnik was very conscious of social values: the first pharmacy opened in 1317; the first nursing home was founded in 1347; slave trading was abolished in 1418; and the first orphanage opened in 1432.

Town; reasonable prices. **Cons:** no breakfast; located several flights of steps up from the Stradun. **TIP→ If staying at either Pavisa Apartments or Villa Ragusa, you can enter the Old Town via the Buža Gate, near the cable car, to save yourself walking up several flights of steps from the Stradun.** [$] *Rooms from: €80* ✉ *Zudioska 15, Stari Grad, Dubrovnik* ☎ *098/765–634* 🌐 *villaragusadubrovnik.com* 🛏 *5 rooms* 🍴 *No meals.*

NIGHTLIFE AND PERFORMING ARTS

Restrained through winter, aristocratic Dubrovnik wakes up with a vengeance come summer. From wine bars to jazz cafés, dance clubs on the beach, and cocktail bars in caves, Dubrovnik has something for every nocturnal taste. Most nightlife happens under the stars, as bars open their terraces, musicians set up in the squares, and even the cinema is open-air. The world-renowned Dubrovnik Summer Festival offers quality theatrical performances and classical-music concerts with international performers. An after-dinner drink at an outdoor table in the Old Town makes a romantic way to round off the evening. Those in search of more lively pursuits should visit Culture Club Revelin, a nightclub built into one of the towers of the fortified walls.

NIGHTLIFE
BARS

Art Cafe. If you're looking for the student population of Dubrovnik, they're here, drinking coffee in the afternoon and sipping beers and g&t's in the evening, all while sitting in brightly colored bathtubs. Quirky decor, loud music, and lots of locals equal an authentic Dubrovnik experience. ⊠ *Branitelja Dubrovnika 25, Pile, Dubrovnik* ☎ *020/311–097.*

Fodor'sChoice ★ **Cave Bar More.** When the Hotel More was being built, a piece of machinery fell through the ground; it was only then that an 8,000-year old cave was discovered underneath. It has been carefully converted into a three-story bar, with twinkling lights and stalactites, providing an unforgettable setting for a cocktail. ⊠ *Kardinala Stepinca 33, Lapad, Dubrovnik* ☎ *020/494–200* ⊕ *hotel-more.hr/4cave-bar-more.php.*

D'Vino Wine Bar. Tucked away in a narrow side street off Placa, this cozy wine bar has a stone wall interior and mellow candlelight, with a handful of outdoor tables. The owners are friendly, knowledgeable and enthusiastic, and have amassed an impressive selection of international and Croatian wines, served both by the glass and bottle. They offer wine-tastings, so you can try several different types, accompanied by platters of cheese. ⊠ *Palmotićeva 4a, Stari Grad, Dubrovnik* ☎ *020/321–130* ⊕ *www.dvino.net.*

La Bodega. The newest place to see and be seen in Dubrovnik, this four-story wine bar at the east end of the Stradun has bohemian decor, original artwork, and more than 200 wines to accompany their prosciutto and cheese platters. ⊠ *Lučarica 1, Stari Grad, Dubrovnik* ☎ *099/499–1187.*

Soul Caffe. This small, velvet-draped bar with stone walls and a bluesy ambience is where to find the hip locals and other travelers who want to hide from the crowds. They serve excellent coffee in the daytime, dark beers and a wide selection of rakija in the evening, and the service is very friendly. ⊠ *Uska ulica 5, Stari Grad, Dubrovnik* ☎ *091/730–4516.*

Troubadour Hard Jazz Cafe. This is a long-standing Dubrovnik institution with impromptu jazz sessions. Well-worn antiques and memorabilia fill the cozy, candlelit interior, while in summer, tables spill outside onto the piazza for live shows under the stars. ⊠ *Bunićeva Poljana 2, Stari Grad, Dubrovnik* ☎ *020/323–476.*

DANCE CLUBS

Fodor'sChoice ★ **Culture Club Revelin.** Culture Club Revelin, one of the best nightclubs in Dubrovnik, and perhaps all of Croatia, has made a name for itself on the international house music scene, attracting big-name DJs such as Axwell and Fedde Le Grand, to name just a couple. Find it uniquely located in the Revelin Fort, part of the Old Town's fortification system near the Ploče Gate. ⊠ *Svetog Dominika 3, Banje Beach, Dubrovnik* ☎ *020/436–010* ⊕ *clubrevelin.com.*

Eastwest Beach Club. Located on the only sandy beach near the Old Town, Eastwest is a reliably chic establishment. It has a chilled-out lounge atmosphere by day, and VIP vibe by night. It could do with fewer lounge chairs cluttering up the sand, but you can't beat its sunset

8

views over the city walls. You'll find it a five-minute walk east of the Ploče Gate, on Banje Beach. ⊠ *Frana Supila 4, Banje Beach, Dubrovnik* ☎ *020/412–220* ⊕ *www.ew-dubrovnik.com.*

PERFORMING ARTS

FESTIVALS

Fodor's Choice
★

Dubrovnik Summer Festival. The city's cultural highlight is the annual Dubrovnik Summer Festival, which runs from mid-July to late August and attracts thousands of artists from around the world. A variety of open-air classical concerts, ballet, and theatrical performances are held at various venues within the walls, and the city becomes a riot of folklore, traditional dresses, midnight performances, and music. Tickets, ranging from 50 to 500 Kn, can be purchased online or at the festival box office. ⊠ *Od Sigurate 1, Stari Grad, Dubrovnik* ☎ *020/326–100* ⊕ *www.dubrovnik-festival.hr.*

FILM

Kino Slavica. Kino Slavica is an open-air summer cinema in a walled garden between the Old Town and Lapad. Predominantly English-language films are shown in their original versions with subtitles. There is a second open-air cinema right in the Old Town, called Kino Jadran. ⊠ *Branitelja Dubrovnika BB, Pile, Dubrovnik* ☎ *020/417–107.*

SPORTS AND THE OUTDOORS

BEACHES

The more upmarket hotels east of the Ploče Gate such as the Excelsior, have their own beaches exclusively for the use of hotel guests; walk past them along the coast to find your own private spot for a dip. There is the sandy Banje Beach, with lounge chairs provided by Eastwest Club, and a family-friendly beach in Lapad. The most natural and peaceful beaches lie on the tiny island of **Lokrum**, a short distance south of the Old Town. Through high season boats leave half-hourly from the Old Harbor, ferrying visitors back and forth from morning to early evening.

FAMILY
Fodor's Choice
★

Lokrum. Some of Dubrovnik's most natural and peaceful beaches lie on the tiny island of Lokrum, a short distance southeast of the Old Town. Lush and fertile, this tiny island is home to the ruins of an abandoned 11th-century monastery, set in exotic botanical gardens. You can spot peacocks brought over by Hapsburg Emperor Maximillian, who turned the monastery into his summer residence. At the top of the island is a star-shape fortress built by Napoleon's troops during French occupation, later used by the Austrian army. Lokrum swirls with legends and mystery; the story goes that when the Benedictine Monks were expelled from the island to make room for aristocrats, they left behind a curse on any future owners of the land. To this day, it is considered bad luck to stay overnight on the island, though many a pair of romantics has tried; as Lokrum is also nicknamed Lovers Island. A network of footpaths lead down to the rocky shoreline, past the "dead sea" lake, where it's possible to swim. There are cliffs to jump from, coves to bathe in, and a small stretch of coast reserved for nudists. It's a wonderful place to spend a day. To reach Lokrum, take a taxi-boat from the old harbor; they run every half hour during the summer. Round-trip tickets cost 70

Kn. **Amenities:** food and drink. **Best for:** walking; nudists. ⊠ *15-min boat ride from Dubrovnik's old harbor, Island of Lokrum, Dubrovnik* ⊕ *www.lokrum.hr.*

SAILING

ACI marina. The 425-berth ACI marina is 2 nautical miles from Gruž harbor and 6 km (3½ miles) from the city walls. The marina is open year-round, and a number of charter companies are based there. ⊠ *Mokošica* ☏ *020/455–020* ⊕ *marina-base.com/marina/dubrovnik-croatia.*

SEA KAYAKING

Fodor's Choice **Adriatic Kayak Tours.** Is there any better way to spend a summer day than ★ paddling a bright orange kayak through the sparkling blue sea? There are literally a sea full of kayaking companies in Dubrovnik, but the best is Adriatic Kayak Tours. Besides introductory half-day sea-kayaking tours around Zaton bay (with transfer from Dubrovnik included), they run day trips to Lopud, Koločep, and Šipan, and even further to the Konavle Region and Montenegro. They also offer one-week island-hopping trips to the Elafitis and beyond. ⊠ *Zrinsko Frankopanska 6, Ploče, Dubrovnik* ☏ *020/312–770* ⊕ *www.adriatickayaktours.com.*

SHOPPING

The Stradun is lined with shops selling olive oil, Dalmatian wine and *rakija*. Pick up some fun souvenirs, grab an ice cream, then head to the side streets for more unique gifts, galleries, and independent boutiques.

Croata. In the 17th century, Croatian military uniforms featured patterned scarves knotted around the neck. French soldiers appreciated the style, introduced them to Parisian society with the name "cravat," a play on the word Croat, and the rest is sartorial history. You can pick up an "original Croatian tie" from this chain boutique near the Rector's Palace. ⊠ *Pred dvorom 2, Stari Grad, Dubrovnik* ☏ *020/638–330* ⊕ *www.croata.hr.*

Dubrovačka Kuća. A tastefully decorated shop near the Ploče Gate stocks a fine selection of regional Croatian wines and sweets, *rakija*, olive oil, and handmade jewelry, plus works of art by contemporary local artists on the upper two levels. ⊠ *Svetog Dominika BB, Stari Grad, Dubrovnik* ☏ *020/322–092.*

Dubrovnik Treasures. You'll find this lovely oasis of a shop steps away from the bustling Pile Gate. The jewelry is all handmade by the friendly owners of the shop; just try to walk out without a gorgeous piece to call your own. ⊠ *Celestina Medovića 2, Stari Grad, Dubrovnik* ☏ *020/321–098.*

Magnolika. In this tiny, bohemian boutique just off the Placa, you'll find artwork, home decor, jewelry, clothing, and ecological cosmetics made by indie artists from all around Croatia. A good place to find a unique gift that you won't find in a typical souvenir shop. ⊠ *Getaldićeva 7, Stari Grad, Dubrovnik* ☏ *098/195–4040* ⊕ *www.magnolika.com.*

LOPUD

Lopud is 7 nautical miles northwest of Dubrovnik by ferry.

Sometimes you need a break from the city crowds, and the lush, laid-back Elafiti Islands are happy to provide a retreat. Historically, the 13 tiny islets have always been under Dubrovnik's control, first when monks from the Franciscan monastery used to visit the islands to gather herbs for use in their pharmacy; later, the local aristocracy kept summer villas here. Today only the three larger ones—Koločep, Lopud, and Šipan—are inhabited, with a total population of around 1,000, and only Šipan has cars. Any of the three can be comfortably visited as a day trip from Dubrovnik by ferry or, much more fun, by kayak. If you intend to stay a night, Lopud is best equipped to deal with visitors. With a year-round population of approximately 300, it has only one settlement, Lopud Town, made up of old stone houses built around a sheltered bay. The main sights are a semiderelict 15th-century Franciscan Monastery, and the remains of 30 churches built around the tiny island during the golden age of the Republic. There are a handful of seasonal eateries, several small family-run hotels occupying restored villas, and a tourist office, open only from May through October—like most everything else on the island. From town, a footpath leads through pinewoods and herb-scented olive groves: follow the signs, and in 15 minutes you will have crossed the island to arrive at family-friendly Šunj, one of the region's rare sandy beaches.

GETTING HERE AND AROUND

Lopud is accessible from Dubrovnik by ferry. Because only the island of Šipan has cars, these islets are best explored on foot.

WHERE TO EAT

$$$
SEAFOOD
×**Konoba Peggy.** You'll find this family-run konoba on a narrow side street above the ferry landing. Guests sit at wooden tables on a pretty terrace with lemon trees and a wonderful view over the bay and Lopud's elegant church bell tower. The menu features typical Dalmatian fare, including fresh fish cooked over an open fire in front of you, plus succulent steaks. Ⓢ *Average main: 85 Kn* ⊠ *Narikla 22, Lopud* ☎ *098/301–389* ⊘ *Closed Nov.–Apr.*

$$$
SEAFOOD
×**Restoran Obala.** This surprisingly smart eatery offers fine dining on the seafront promenade, with idyllic sunset views across the bay and waiters dressed in traditional Dalmatian waistcoats. The house specialty is *školjke na buzaru* (mixed shellfish cooked in wine and garlic), and if you're lucky you'll also be treated to live music. Ⓢ *Average main: 100 Kn* ⊠ *Obala Iva Kuljevana 18, Lopud* ☎ *020/759–170* ⊘ *Closed Nov.–Apr.*

$$$
EASTERN
EUROPEAN
FAMILY
Fodor's Choice
★
×**RobiNzooN.** It takes a special place to attract visitors away from the shore on an island, to dine inland in a restaurant that specializes in meat dishes rather than seafood. But RobiNzooN is just such a restaurant. Located in a big garden, it exudes local charm, with all members of the family pitching in to serve, cook, and prepare your meal. The bar stools are made of donkey saddles, you can see original olive presses and old

gaslights, they grow garlic in the garden alongside cactus and vineyards, and you can smell the traditional *peka* (lamb under the bell) cooking as soon as you walk in (order in advance if you want to try). There's no view of the sea, but you won't mind. $ *Average main: 100 Kn* ⊠ *Od polja 7, Lopud* ☎ *099/757–4057* ⊗ *Closed Oct.–June.*

WHERE TO STAY

$ | **Hotel Glavović.** With a prime location on the seafront promenade,
HOTEL | this was Lopud's first hotel when it opened in 1927. **Pros:** short walk to ferry terminal; location overlooking the harbor. **Cons:** rooms very basic; no elevator. $ *Rooms from: 890 Kn* ⊠ *Obala Iva Kuljevana, Lopud* ☎ *020/759–359* ⊕ *www.hotel-glavovic.hr* ⤲ *12 rooms* ▭ *No credit cards* ⊗ *Closed Nov.–Apr.* ⦿ *Breakfast.*

$$$ | **Hotel Villa Vilina.** This old stone villa, with palms out front overlook-
HOTEL | ing the sea, has been carefully restored as a boutique hotel with a small pool. **Pros:** traffic-free island with regular ferries to Dubrovnik; location in a raised garden overlooking the harbor; breakfast and dinner served on lovely outdoor terrace. **Cons:** often fully booked; far from urban glamour (no nightlife, shopping). $ *Rooms from: 1406 Kn* ⊠ *Obala Iva Kuljevana 5, Lopud* ☎ *020/759–333* ⊕ *www.villa-vilina.hr* ⤲ *12 rooms, 3 suites* ⊗ *Closed Nov.–May* ⦿ *Breakfast.*

$$ | **Lafodia Sea Resort.** The only luxury hotel in Lopud, this massive prop-
HOTEL | erty rises up a hillside overlooking the harbor and bay. **Pros:** seafront location with views over the bay; new and modern amenities; best swimming pool in Lopud. **Cons:** big and rather impersonal; distance from the ferry terminal. $ *Rooms from: 1150 Kn* ⊠ *Obala Iva Kuljevana 35, Lopud* ☎ *020/450–300* ⊕ *www.lafodiahotel.com* ⤲ *152 rooms, 30 suites* ⊗ *Closed Oct.–Apr.* ⦿ *Breakfast.*

$ | **La Villa.** In a 16th-century villa overlooking Lopud Bay, this boutique
HOTEL | hotel is run by a friendly young Croatian couple. **Pros:** traffic-free island with regular ferries to Dubrovnik; energetic and helpful management; simple but tasteful modern decor. **Cons:** often fully booked; far from urban glamour. $ *Rooms from: 765 Kn* ⊠ *Obala Iva Kuljevana 33, Lopud* ☎ *091/322–0126* ⊕ *www.lavilla.com.hr* ⤲ *8 rooms* ⊗ *Closed Dec.–Mar.* ⦿ *Breakfast.*

CAVTAT

17 km (10½ miles) southeast of Dubrovnik.

While Dubrovnik's streets are being polished under the shoes of thousands of visitors per day, Cavtat's pine-covered trails seem comparatively tourist-free. Just 17 km (10½ miles) south of Dubrovnik, but seemingly a world away, you can find secluded swimming spots, quiet walking paths, and park benches waiting for you to sit and enjoy the beauty and tranquility that you came to Croatia to find.

Founded by the ancient Greeks as Epidauros, then taken by the Romans and renamed Epidaurum, the original settlement on the site of Cavtat was subsequently destroyed by tribes of Avars and Slavs in the early

7th century. It was the Romans who fled Epidaurum who founded Dubrovnik.

Today's Cavtat, which developed during the 15th century under the Republic of Dubrovnik, is an easygoing fishing town and small-scale seaside resort. The medieval stone buildings of the Old Town occupy a small peninsula with a natural bay to each side. A palm-lined seaside promenade with open-air cafés and restaurants curves around the main bay, while the second bay is overlooked by a beach backed by several socialist-era hotels.

GETTING HERE AND AROUND

Cavtat can be visited as a half-day trip from Dubrovnik. The easiest way to get to Cavtat is by bus. Much more fun, but slightly more expensive, is a taxi-boat ride along the coast from Dubrovnik's Old Harbor (7 nautical miles); the journey time is approximately one hour.

EXPLORING

Kuća Bukovac (*Vlaho Bukovac House*). The former home of local son Vlaho Bukovac (1855–1922), perhaps Croatia's greatest artist, has been beautifully converted into a gallery of his life and work. The two floors feature self- and family-portraits and oil paintings from the periods he spent in Paris, Zagreb, Prague, and Cavtat. The house, with walls covered in murals Bukovac painted as a young man, period furniture, and personal items, plus the gardens surrounding it, is a lovely place to spend a quiet afternoon. ✉ *Bukovćeva 5, Cavtat* ☎ *020/478–646* 🌐 *www.kuca-bukovac.hr* 🎟 *20 Kn* 🕒 *May–Oct., Tues.–Sun. 9–1 and 4–8; Nov.–Apr., Tues.–Sat. 9–5, Sun. 2–5.*

Mauzolej Obitelji Račić (*Račić Mausoleum*). In the cemetery, on the highest point of a pine-scented peninsula, Mauzolej Obitelji Račić was created by beloved Croatian sculptor Ivan Meštrović for the Račić family in 1921. Made from white marble and capped with a cupola, it is octagonal in plan, and the main entrance is guarded by two art nouveau caryatids. It is a peaceful site, and the views from the top are fantastic. ✉ *Rat, Cavtat* ☎ *020/478–646* 🎟 *10 Kn* 🕒 *May–Oct., 10–6.*

WHERE TO EAT

$$$$ SEAFOOD Fodor's Choice ★

🍴 **Bugenvila.** One of several restaurants squeezed together along the promenade in Cavtat's old port, Bugenvila stands out from the rest with its vibrant colors, flowers climbing the sides of the terrace, and happy patrons tucking into refreshing caviar, bluefin tuna sashimi, butter-poached lobster, or mojito sorbet. The menu changes regularly, and care is put into making sure it is as fresh and current as possible. It is proof that the exciting, experimental restaurant trends that have ignited Dubrovnik are headed south. [$] *Average main: 110 Kn* ✉ *Obala A. Starcevica 9, Cavtat* ☎ *020/479–949* 🌐 *bugenvila.eu.*

$$ SEAFOOD

🍴 **Konoba Kolona.** Located one street behind Tiha Bay, Konoba Kolona is a firm favorite among locals for its reliably fresh seafood and friendly service. It has two large covered terraces plus indoor seating, and reasonable prices, serving lobster by the kilo, *mussels buzara* (tomato and white wine sauce), and particularly delicious octopus and tuna carpaccio. When the owner is the same person who catches the fish during the day and serves it to you at night, you can't go wrong. $ *Average main: 80 Kn* ⊠ *Put Tihe 2, Cavtat* ☎ *020/478–787.*

$$$$ ✕**Leut.** One of the region's best-known restaurants, Leut is the place
SEAFOOD where politicians, sportsmen, and celebrities come to dine with the Bobić family, who have run it since it opened in 1971 (check out the photos inside). Its spacious, open-air terrace right on the Cavtat quay is a lovely place to spend the evening and treat yourself to fresh lobster or the chef's "seafood selection." $ *Average main: 110 Kn* ⊠ *Trumbićev put 11, Cavtat* ☎ *020/478–477* ⊕ *restaurant-leut.com* ⊙ *Closed Dec.–Mar.*

$$$ ✕**Taverna Galija.** Barbecued fish tops the bill here, along with seafood
SEAFOOD risotto and pasta dishes, colorful salads, and a welcome but limited choice of vegetarian platters. You'll find the kitchen and dining room in a narrow alleyway near the Franciscian Monastery, plus a large outdoor terrace on the seafront. $ *Average main: 100 Kn* ⊠ *Vuličevićeva 1, Cavtat* ☎ *020/478–566* ⊙ *Closed Dec.–Mar.*

WHERE TO STAY

$ ⌂**Castelletto.** There are not many places where you can sit on a lounge
HOTEL chair, admire the bright lights of Dubrovnik on the horizon, and star-
Fodor's Choice gaze all at the same time. **Pros:** lovely staff; excellent buffet breakfast;
★ plenty of outdoor seats. **Cons:** distance from town; often fully booked.
■ **TIP→** If arriving by bus, get off one stop before Cavtat center to avoid the walk back uphill; the bus stops just outside the hotel. $ *Rooms from: €95* ⊠ *Frana Laureana 22, Cavtat* ☎ *020/479–547* ⊕ *dubrovnikexperience. com* ⊅ *13 rooms* ⦿ *Breakfast.*

$$ ⌂**Hotel Cavtat.** Hotel Cavtat represents a nice middle ground between
HOTEL the big resorts in Cavtat and the smaller villas. **Pros:** beachfront location; modern facilities; good restaurant and spa options; beautiful infinity pool. **Cons:** slightly impersonal service; rooms in older building slightly outdated with no view. $ *Rooms from: 140 Kn* ⊠ *Tiha 8, Cavtat* ☎ *020/202–000* ⊕ *www.hotel-cavtat.hr* ⊅ *91 rooms, 1 suite* ⊙ *Closed Nov.–Apr.* ⦿ *Breakfast.*

$$$ ⌂**Hotel Croatia.** Sprawling across its own rocky, pine-studded penin-
HOTEL sula, with quiet walking trails through the property, this vast hotel offers guests the chance to find their own place in the sun or shade, seemingly miles away from the rest of the world. **Pros:** good sports facilities including private beaches; some (but not all) rooms have sea views. **Cons:** modern building slightly lacking in atmosphere; large with somewhat impersonal service. $ *Rooms from: €190* ⊠ *Frankopanska 10, Cavtat* ☎ *020/475–555* ⊕ *www.hoteli-croatia.hr* ⊅ *480 rooms, 7 suites* ⊙ *Closed Nov.–Mar.* ⦿ *Breakfast.*

$$$ ⌂**Villa Pattiera.** This family-run boutique hotel on the seafront prom-
HOTEL enade in the center of Cavtat is a little gem. **Pros:** location on the seafront promenade; friendly and helpful staff; excellent breakfast served on pleasant terrace. **Cons:** often fully booked; front rooms can be noisy. $ *Rooms from: 1407 Kn* ⊠ *Trumbićev put 9, Cavtat* ☎ *020/478–800* ⊕ *www.villa-pattiera.hr* ⊅ *12 rooms* ⊙ *Closed Nov.–Mar.* ⦿ *Breakfast.*

8

SPORTS AND THE OUTDOORS

The beaches east of the center, near **Uvala Tiha** (Tiha Bay), are where you'll find the large modern hotels, complete with volleyball games and aqua aerobics. Walk around the peninsula to find smaller beaches and a more peaceful spot to swim.

DIVING

Epidaurum Diving and Water Sports Center. There are some excellent underwater sights to see around Cavtat, including shipwrecks and amforas. Epidaurum Diving and Water Center organizes certification and dive trips, as well as jet-skiing, parasailing, and other types of water fun. ⊠ *Šetalište Žal, Cavtat* ☎ *020/471–386* ⊕ *www.epidaurum.com.*

HIKING

Ronald Brown Pathway. The Konavle Region and Cavtat are full of excellent hiking trails; one of the most challenging and rewarding is the Ronald Brown Pathway, which leads up to the peak of Stražišce mountain. It is named in memory of a U.S. Secretary of Commerce who was killed here along with 34 others in a 1996 plane crash; the crash site is marked with a cross at the peak. The hike takes several hours and can get very hot, but the views over the coastline all the way to Dubrovnik, as well as the butterflies, plants, and lizards you spot along the way, are worth it. Ask for a map at your hotel; like most hiking paths in Croatia, the way is usually marked only by red and white circles painted on trees and stones. ⊠ *Gornji Obod, Cavtat.*

TRSTENO

24 km (15 miles) northwest of Dubrovnik.

A small village on the coastal road between Split and Dubrovnik (E65), Trsteno has been put on the map by its arboretum.

Fodor's Choice ★ **Trsteno Arboretum.** The area around Dubrovnik has many fine examples of summer villas built by noble families, but the one in Trsteno is something special. Within the grounds of a small Renaissance villa, the arboretum was set up during the 16th century by the Gučetić family. Laid out on a geometric plan, the garden is filled with hundreds of exotic species of trees and shrubs, most of which were brought home from distant voyages by local sailors. There is an original aqueduct still in use, and a baroque fountain of Neptune and two nymphs that dates from 1736. The site has been continuously developed for five centuries, acquiring Renaissance, Baroque, and Romantic forms along the way. The surroundings are breathtaking, with the grounds running down toward a cliff overlooking the sea. Buses run regularly to Trsteno from Dubrovnik. ■TIP→ **The best time to visit is spring or fall, when the leaves are changing color.** ⊠ *Potok 20, Magistrala Trsteno, Trsteno* ☎ *020/751–019* 🎫 *40 Kn* ⊗ *May–Oct., daily 7–7; Nov.–Apr., daily 8–4.*

STON

54 km (34 miles) northwest of Dubrovnik; 67 km (42 miles) plus 2 nautical miles from Korčula.

On the surface, they are sleepy little fishing villages. But Ston (on the main Dubrovnik-Orebić road) and Mali Ston ("little Ston," just off the main road) have three unique properties that make them an excellent stopover between Dubrovnik and Korčula: walls, salt, and oysters. Historically, the town dates back to 1333, when it was founded by the Republic of Dubrovnik, The Republic's chief interest in Ston was its ancient salt pans, which became a major source of revenue. You can take a tour of the massive salt pans to learn about the old processes, many of which are still used today, and see the warehouses where mountains of salt are stored (if you're lucky, you might be allowed to climb one!). In order to protect the settlement, a fortified wall was built, connecting the two villages and effectively controlling land access onto the peninsula. The fortified wall stretches 5½ km (3 miles) long, and is one of the best preserved walls in the world. Locals will tell you it's second in length only to the Great Wall of China; a disputable claim, but nevertheless it is an impressive sight. Begin your visit in Ston, then walk atop the wall to Mali Ston, where you can settle in and spend the rest of the day feasting on famous (and well-priced!) oysters and mussels grown right there in the channel.

GETTING HERE AND AROUND

Located on the main Dubrovnik-Orebić road, Ston is a perfect stop between Dubrovnik and Korčula. The best way to see Ston and Mali Stone, a 15-minute walk from the main village, is on foot.

8

WHERE TO EAT

$$$ ✕ **Bota.** Occupying a 14th-century salt warehouse, Bota is known for its
SEAFOOD menu of outstanding, locally caught seafood. If raw oysters make you squeamish, try the *pohane oštrige* (oysters deep-fried in bread crumbs). Also look out for the extraordinary *stonski makaruli*, a cake made from pasta, nuts, sugar, and cinnamon, unique to Ston. $ *Average main: 140 Kn* ⊠ *Mali Ston, Ston* ☎ *020/754–482* ⊕ *www.bota-sare.hr.*

$$$ ✕ **Kapetanova Kuća.** Known throughout Croatia, the name of this restau-
SEAFOOD rant is synonymous with Ston and fresh oysters. Most people come here exclusively to eat shellfish grown in Mali Ston Channel, but you'll also find a limited choice of meat dishes. The owner and cook, Lidija Kralj, has been presented a cooking award by Croatian national television. The Kralj family also runs the nearby Hotel Ostrea. $ *Average main: 140 Kn* ⊠ *Mali Ston, Ston* ☎ *020/754–555* ⊕ *www.ostrea.hr.*

WHERE TO STAY

$$ 🏨 **Hotel Ostrea.** A former mill, this old stone building has been renovated
HOTEL into a small upscale hotel complete with wood floors and antique furniture. **Pros:** location overlooking the sea in the Old Town; atmospheric homey rooms; excellent seafood restaurants nearby. **Cons:** no elevator (some guests might have problems with the stairs). $ *Rooms from: 850*

*Kn ✉ Mali Ston, Ston ☎ 020/754–555 ⊕ www.ostrea.hr ⇱ 13 rooms,
1 suite ⧆ Breakfast.*

$ 🏠 **Vila Koruna.** Consider this your home base for all things Mali Ston.
HOTEL   **Pros:** close to beach, road to Ston, and bus stop for Dubrovnik; friendly
staff; good restaurant. **Cons:** rooms can get very hot in summer; some
beds are slightly uncomfortable. $ *Rooms from: 660 Kn ✉ Mali Ston,
Ston ☎ 020/754–999 ⊕ www.vila-koruna.hr ⇱ 12 rooms ⊙ Closed
Dec.–Mar. ⧆ Breakfast.*

SPORTS AND THE OUTDOORS

The best beach for swimming lies in **Prapratna Uvala** (Prapratna Bay), 3
km (2 miles) south of Ston.

OREBIĆ

*Orebić is 110 km (69 miles) northwest of Dubrovnik and 2 nautical
miles northeast of Korčula.*

Backed by the rocky heights of Sveti Ilija (3,153 feet), Orebić strag-
gles along the coast, facing across a narrow sea channel to the island
of Korčula. Historically, the town spent several centuries under the
Republic of Dubrovnik, supplying many able seamen to the republic's
merchant navy. From 1865 to 1887 the town even had its own shipping
company: today you can see a string of villas and their gardens overlooking the coastal promenade, built by wealthy local sea captains. You
can learn more about the seafaring history at the charming Maritime
Museum on Orebić's main street, complete with naval instruments,
maps, old documents, and photos. Today Orebić is best known for its
sandy beach, delightful hillside monastery, and as the gateway to the
Pelješac Peninsula and its highly-esteemed red wines.

GETTING HERE AND AROUND

Hourly car and passenger ferries link Orebić to Korčulathrough peak
season; journey time is 20 minutes.

EXPLORING

Several family-run vineyards and wine cellars around Pelješac are open
to the public for wine tasting and purchases. Tasting sessions usually
include a selection of three or four different wines and maybe some
rakija, and are accompanied by bread and cheese. Sessions last between
30 minutes and one hour. You need private transport to reach the vineyards, and it is best to call one day in advance, as vineyards are often
busy with large tour groups.

Franjevački samostan (*Franciscan Monastery*). A 20-minute walk along
a pleasant country road that winds its way up through pine woods
brings you to the 15th-century Franciscan Monastery, perched 492
feet above sea level. The view across the sea channel to the island of
Korčula is spectacular; the view, in fact, explains the monastery's prime
location. During the days of the Republic of Dubrovnik, Pelješac was
under Dubrovnik's control, while Korčula was ruled by her archrival,

Venice. From this privileged vantage point, the Franciscan monks would spy on their island neighbors, under strict orders to send a messenger to Dubrovnik if trouble looked likely. In its heyday, the monastery was home to 20-some monks; now only two remain. It is a most welcoming retreat, with a lovely cloister and a fascinating museum, displaying scale models of the ships that local sea captains sailed across the oceans, and an array of votive pictures dedicated to the Virgin, commissioned and donated by sailors who had been saved from trouble on the high seas. Before leaving, check out the cemetery, where gray marble tombstones shaded by cypress trees mark the final resting places of many a local seafarer. ■ TIP➔ After your visit, continue along the road past the monastery to find Panorama Restaurant. Feast on preordered octopus and wine with the best view in town. ⊠ *Orebić* ☎ *020/713–075* 🖃 *20 Kn* ☉ *Closed Oct.–May.*

Korta Katarina Winery. Located in the former Rivijera Hotel, perched on a hill overlooking Trstenica Beach, the award-winning Korta Katarina winery is a beautiful place to try beautiful Pelješac wines. *Korta* is the name for the typical courtyards outside sea captain's homes around Orebić, while *Katarina* is a family name of the American couple who came to Croatia on a rebuilding mission, fell in love with it, and opened the winery. Call ahead to arrange a visit, which typically includes a one-hour tour of the state-of-the-art winery plus three tastings, or just show up and enjoy a glass of *pošip*, a Dalmatian white wine, or *plavac mali*, a red, on the sweeping terrace. ⊠ *Bana J. Jelacica 3, Orebić* ☎ *020/713–817* ⊕ *www.kortakatarinawinery.com.*

Matuško Vina. Matuško Vina has a vaulted brick cellar, open to visitors for wine tasting through summer. A typical tasting session consists of two red wines, Plavac Mali and Dingać, plus prošek (a sweet wine), loza (rakija made from grapes), and višnjevača (rakija made from cherries), accompanied by bread and cheese. ⊠ *Potomje 5A, Potomje* ✛ *15 km (9 miles) southeast of Orebić* ☎ *020/742–399* ⊕ *www.matusko-vina.hr.*

Vinarija Bartulović. The Bartulović family has been making wine on Pelješac for some 480 years. As everywhere on Pelješac, red predominates, but this vineyard also produces small quantities of rosé. Vinarija Bartulović is especially popular with visitors thanks to its authentic Dalmatian konoba, located in the former wine cellar, with exposed stone walls and rustic wooden tables. It's the best choice if you want to combine wine tasting with a full-blown meal, as the proprietors will prepare lunch or dinner if you call one day in advance. They also organize guided bicycle tours, which include a visit to three different wineries, plus lunch, and can be combined with a stay in the family estate. ⊠ *Prizdrina* ✛ *13 km (8 miles) southeast of Orebić* ☎ *020/742–506* ⊕ *www.vinarijabartulovic.hr.*

WHERE TO EAT

$$$
SEAFOOD

✕ **Karako.** When a restaurant has views this great and a location this prime, it could be forgiven if the food wasn't the best. Such is not the case with Karako; located steps away from the sea, it offers up some of the tastiest seafood around (try their tuna steak), perfectly cooked at a large outdoor grill by an enthusiastic young chef, with friendly service to boot. **$** *Average main: 90 Kn* ⊠ *Šetalište kneza Domagoja 32, Orebić* ☎ *098/976–8371* ▭ *No credit cards* ☾ *Closed Oct.–May.*

$$$ ✕ **Stari Kapetan.** Taking the seafaring theme of the Hotel Adriatic one
SEAFOOD step further, the Mikulić family designed this restaurant to look like an actual ship, with a life-size captain at the helm! At first glance it might seem like a tourist trap, but it is one of the best restaurants in town. Try the seafood platter for two, with tuna steak, grilled squid, mussels, scampi and extraordinary sea bream, plus a glass of homemade plavac, and give a salute to the old captain for me. **$** *Average main: 80 Kn* ⊠ *Šetalište Kneza Domagoja 8, Orebić* ☎ *020/714–488* ⊕ *www. hoteladriaticorebic.com/gourmet-and-wines.html* ☾ *Open year-round.*

WHERE TO STAY

$$ 🏨 **Hotel Adriatic.** Locals are proud of their sea history in Orebić, but the
HOTEL Mikulić family has gone the extra mile; they have turned their hotel
Fodor's Choice into an unofficial seafaring museum. **Pros:** beautifully decorated rooms;
★ friendly service; close to center and beach; excellent restaurant. **Cons:** often fully booked; no elevator. **$** *Rooms from: €170* ⊠ *Šetalište Kneza Domagoja 8, Orebić* ☎ *020/714–488* ⊕ *www.hoteladriaticorebic.com/* ➷ *6 rooms* ☾ *Open year-round* ☉ *Breakfast.*

$$$ 🏨 **Hotel Indijan.** This contemporary hotel, located just in front of a peb-
HOTEL ble beach, has a beautiful lounge bar and terrace with panoramic views of Korčula straight ahead. **Pros:** friendly staff; excellent views; sports facilities. **Cons:** interior could use some refurbishment; hotel can seem a little lifeless. **$** *Rooms from: €189* ⊠ *Skvar 2, Orebić* ☎ *020/714– 555* ⊕ *www.hotelindijan.hr* ➷ *17 rooms, 2 suites* ☾ *Closed Oct.–Apr.* ☉ *Breakfast.*

$ 🏨 **Hotel Mimbelli.** A sweet little gem of a hotel directly across the road
HOTEL from the Maritime Museum and steps away from the sea that has five rooms, each with a different theme. **Pros:** friendly service; individually decorated rooms; central location. **Cons:** hotel and rooms are small; no elevator. **$** *Rooms from: €120* ⊠ *Trg Mimbelli 6, Orebić* ☎ *020/713– 636* ⊕ *www.hotel-mimbelli.com* ➷ *5 rooms* ☉ *Breakfast.*

SPORTS AND THE OUTDOORS

BEACHES
Orebić's best beach, **Trstenica** is a 1½-km (1-mile) stretch of sand and pebble lying on the east side of the island. Through summer it is equipped with showers, sun beds, and umbrellas for hire, plus a snack bar and a section for those who prefer their swims au natural.

DIVING
Adriatic. Diving instruction and dive trips are available from Adriatic, which is a 15-minute drive east of Orebić. It's open from early May through late October. ⊠ *Mokalo 6, Orebić* ☎ *020/713–420* ⊕ *www. adriatic-mikulic.com.*

Exploring ▼
Gradski Muzej
Karčula 4
Katedrala 1
Kopnena Vrata .. 5
Kuća
Marca Pola 2
Marco Polo
Museum 6
Opatska Riznica 3

Restaurants ▼
Aterina 9
KIWI 10
Konoba Belin ... 2
Konoba Mate ... 1
Maksimilijan
Garden 3
Zure 5

Hotels ▼
Hotel Korsal 7
Korcula Waterfront
Accommodation .4
Lešić Dimitri
Palace 8
Pension Lovrié .. 6

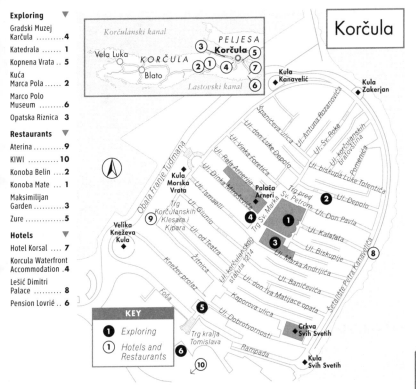

WINDSURFING

Water Donkey Windsurfing and Kitesurfing Center. Just a few kilometers up the road from Orebić, Viganj is regarded as one of the top windsurfing locations in Croatia and beyond. It hosts the Croatian surfing championship annually, and has held both the European and World Championships as well. You can rent equipment and take lessons from the friendly staff at Water Donkey Windsurfing and Kitesurfing Center. They also rent kayaks, bikes, and stand-up paddles. ⊠ *Ponta, Viganj* ☎ *091/152–0258* ⊕ *www.windsurfing-kitesurfing-viganj.com.*

KORČULA

Korčula island is 49 nautical miles northwest of Dubrovnik and 57 nautical miles southeast of Split by ferry.

Southern Dalmatia's largest, most sophisticated, and most visited island, Korčula was named *Kerkyra Melaina* by the ancient Greeks, or "Black Corfu." Between the 10th and 18th centuries it spent several periods under Venetian rule, much to the frustration of Dubrovnik, which considered the Italian city-state its archrival. Today it's known for its traditional sword dances, excellent white wines, and its main, though disputed, claim to fame as the birthplace of Marco Polo. **Korčula** is also the name of the capital near the island's eastern tip, which at first sight seems like a smaller version of Dubrovnik: the same high walls, the circular corner fortresses, and the church tower projecting from within an expanse of red roofs. The main difference lies in the town plan, as narrow side streets run off the main thoroughfare at odd angles to form a herring-bone pattern, preventing cold winter winds from whistling unimpeded through town. Eight centuries under Venetian rule bequeathed the town a treasure trove of Gothic and Renaissance churches, palaces, and piazzas, all built from fine local stone, on which the island's early wealth was based. The center is small and compact and can be explored in an hour.

GETTING HERE AND AROUND

The most impressive way to arrive in Korčula Town is by Jadrolinija coastal ferry from Dubrovnik, which stops here en route to Rijeka. Faster, and also affording incredible views, is the daily bus service connecting Dubrovnik and Korčula Town, which follows the regional road along Pelješac Peninsula, then boards a ferry at Orebić for a short crossing to Korčula. The island is also served by the port of Vela Luka, close to its western tip, with daily ferry and catamaran services running between Split (Central Dalmatia) and the island of Lastovo, stopping at Vela Luka en route. From Vela Luka, a bus runs the length of the island to Korčula Town.

EXPLORING

Gradski Muzej Korčula (*Town Museum*). Located in the 16th-century stone palace of the Gabrielis family on the main square, this museum contains items from all eras of the island's history, from Neolithic stone knives to vessels excavated from Greek and Roman shipwrecks to models of wooden ships built in the 1960s. The palace itself is charming; check out the quirky objects in the original kitchen in the attic, such as gadgets for making macaroni or kneading bread. ⊠ *Trg Sv. Marka, Korčula* ☎ *020/715–786* ⊕ *www.gm-korcula.com* 🎟 *20 Kn* ⊙ *July–Sept.*

Katedrala (*Cathedral*). On the main square, the splendid Gothic-Renaissance cathedral is built from a wheat-color stone that turns pale gold in sunlight, amber at sunset. Enter through the beautifully carved Romanesque main portal, which is guarded by Adam and Eve standing underneath twin lions. Inside, check out the elegant 15th-century ciborium; within, two paintings are attributed to the Venetian master Tintoretto. ⊠ *Trg Sv Marka, Korčula* 🎟 *10 Kn* ⊙ *May–Oct., 9–6:30; Nov.–Apr., by appointment.*

Kopnena Vrata (*Land Gate*). The main entrance into the Old Town is topped by the 15th-century Revelin Tower, housing an exhibition connected with the *Moreška* sword dance, and offering panoramic views over the Old Town. ⊠ *Kopnena Vrata, Korčula* 🎟 *20 Kn* ⊙ *July and Aug., daily 9–9; May, June, and Sept., daily 10–2 and 4–8; Nov.–Apr., by appointment only.*

Kuća Marca Pola (*Marco Polo House*). A couple of blocks east of the main square is the place where the legendary 13th-century discoverer is said to have been born, when Korčula was part of the Venetian Empire. The house itself is nearly in ruins but the tower next door is open, with a very modest exhibition about Polo's life on the first floor and a belvedere up top offering panoramic views. ✉ *Ul. Depolo, Korčula* ☎ *020/716–529* 🎟 *20 Kn* ⏲ *Apr.–June, Sept., and Oct., daily 9–3; July and Aug., daily 9–9* ⏲ *Closed Nov.–Mar.*

Marco Polo Museum. Meticulously researched, a little cheesy but undeniably charming, this multimedia, multistory exhibition, complete with life-size figures in medieval costumes, leads visitors through five stages of the explorer's life, from setting sail from Korcula for the first time, through serving the Kublai Khan, and back home again. The kids will love it, and you will learn a thing or two as well. ✉ *Plokata 19, travnja 33, Korčula* ☎ *098/970–5334* 🎟 *60 Kn* ⏲ *May–Oct., 9:30 am–10 pm.*

Opatska Riznica (*Abbot's Treasury*). Next to the cathedral, the treasury museum occupies the 17th-century Renaissance bishop's palace. This collection of sacred art includes Italian and Croatian Renaissance paintings, the most precious being a 15th-centruy triptych, *Our Lady with Saints,* by the Dalmatian master Blaž Jurjev Trogiranin, plus gold and silver ecclesiastical artifacts and ceremonial vestments. ✉ *Trg Sv. Marka, Korčula* 🎟 *25 Kn* ⏲ *May.–Sept., Mon.–Sat. 9 am–7 pm; Nov.–Apr., by appointment.*

WHERE TO EAT

$$$ MEDITERRANEAN Fodor's Choice ★

🍴 **Aterina.** Follow the scent of fresh basil—Chef Maja's favorite herb—to Aterina, the second incarnation of her locally-beloved restaurant. Occupying a square on the periphery of the old town, with views to the palm-lined promenade and sea below, Aterina offers a refreshing change from typically heavy Dalmatian dishes. Chickpeas, aubergines, homemade pasta, and ginger grace the short menu, along with a seemingly impossible accomplishment: desserts that sound like they could be healthy. Do not leave Korčula without trying the basil cheesecake! [$] *Average main: 90 Kn* ✉ *Trg Korčulanskih Klesara i Kipare 2, Korčula* ☎ *091/799–5549* ⏲ *Closed Oct.–June.*

$ BAKERY FAMILY Fodor's Choice ★

🍴 **KIWI.** European Food Rule number one: If you see locals queuing up for ice cream, get into that queue! Such is the case with KIWI, the island's oldest, and favorite ice-cream shop. Grab a table outside to try traditional pastries such as *klašuni* and *cukarini*, as well as muffins, strudels, and homemade ice cream that does Korčula's Italian heritage proud. [$] *Average main: 10 Kn* ✉ *Biline 16, Korčula* ☎ *020/715–781* 💳 *No credit cards.*

$$$ EASTERN EUROPEAN

🍴 **Konoba Belin.** On the road high above Korčula Town lies Žrnovo, a village full of centuries-old stone houses and the folks whose families built them. Konoba Belin is one such house, and a visit there will give you a glimpse into the local way of life. Call ahead to arrange a short walking tour of the village with the father and a lesson on how to roll traditional Žrnovo macaroni from the mother, or just pop in for dinner and try their homemade macaroni and meat dishes, homemade fritters for dessert, and a glass of Plavac Mali wine. Open from May through September. $ *Average main: 80 Kn* ⊠ *Žrnovo 50, Korčula* ☎ *091/503–9258.*

$$$ ✕ **Konoba Mate.** In the courtyard of an old stone cottage in the village
MEDITERRANEAN of Pupnat (34 km [21 miles] west of Korčula Town, so you'll need to
hire a car or take a taxi), this welcoming eatery serves gourmet fare
prepared from the family's own farm. The menu changes with the sea-
sons, but look out for the house specialty: a platter of homemade *pršut*
(prosciutto), goat's cheese, olives, and eggplant pâté, followed by their
creamy *rožata* for dessert. There's also an excellent wine list, though the
house wine, served by the carafe, is a better value and is extremely palat-
able. $ *Average main: 110 Kn* ⊠ *Pupnat 28, Korčula* ☎ *020/717–109.*

$$$ ✕ **Maksimilijan Garden.** With comfy seats scattered around the shady gar-
BARBECUE den of Croatian/American Maxo Vanka's memorial art gallery, a jazzy
Fodor's Choice soundtrack, and an unrivaled view of Korčula Town ahead, Maksimili-
★ jan Garden is a lovely place to relax at the end of a hot afternoon. The
menu features grilled meats, homemade burgers, and fish dishes such as
vodka-cured salmon and grilled sea bass with a Nordic touch. Maksimilijan Garden is a welcome new addition to the island, and the best
place to watch the sunset over the medieval Old Town. $ *Average main:
100 Kn* ⊠ *Sv. Nikola, Korčula* ☎ *091/170–2567* ▭ *No credit cards.*

$$$ ✕ **Zure.** In the village of Lumbarda, this friendly, family-run eatery offers
SEAFOOD a delicious selection of authentic Dalmatian dishes served at wooden
tables in a walled garden. Everything served here, from the olive oil to
the pomegranate rakija, is grown, caught, or raised by the family and
local cooperatives. What's on offer varies depending on the day's catch,
which father and sons will proudly bring to your table before you order.
Expect goodies such as salted fish and lobster *buzara*. $ *Average main:
100 Kn* ⊠ *Lumbarda, Korčula* ☎ *020/712–334* ⊘ *No lunch. Closed
Jan.–Mar., but may open on request.*

WHERE TO STAY

$ ⚏ **Hotel Korsal.** This friendly, family-run hotel lies on the coast, a
HOTEL 10-minute walk from Korčula's fortified Old Town. **Pros:** proximity to
the Old Town; friendly staff. **Cons:** no pool but there's a small beach
nearby. $ *Rooms from: €90* ⊠ *Šetalište Frana Kršinića 80, Korčula*
☎ *020/715–722* ⊕ *www.hotel-korsal.com* ➷ *18 rooms* ⊘ *Closed Nov.–
May* ⦿| *Breakfast.*

$ ⚏ **Korčula Waterfront Accommodation.** Located in a quiet bay a 10-minute
RENTAL walk from Korčula Town, on a large private dock perfect for sunbathing
Fodor's Choice and impromptu barbecues, these breezy apartments are run by Aus-
★ sie/Croatian Paulina and Antonio, the most helpful couple you could
hope to meet on holiday. **Pros:** helpful and friendly hosts; quiet location
beside the sea. **Cons:** distance from Korčula Town; not many restau-
rants or shops nearby. $ *Rooms from: €70* ⊠ *Šetalište Tina Ujevića 33,
Korčula* ☎ *098/937–0463 Ext. 9* ⊕ *korcula-waterfront-accomodation.
com* ➷ *3 rooms, 2 apartments* ▭ *No credit cards* ⊘ *Open year-round*
⦿| *No meals.*

$$$$ HOTEL Fodor's Choice ★ **Lešić Dimitri Palace.** Lešić Dimitri Palace is more than a hotel. **Pros:** location in the Old Town; stunning interior design; personalized service from friendly staff. **Cons:** very expensive; no pool; no extra facilities for children. [$] *Rooms from: €480* ✉ *Don Pavla Poše 1-6, Korčula* ☎ *020/715–560* 🌐 *www.lesic-dimitri.com* 🛏 *5 apartments* ⏲ *Closed Nov.–Apr.* 🍴 *Breakfast.*

$ RENTAL FAMILY **Pansion Lovrić.** Around the bay and up a hill from the center of Lumbarda, just up the road from a quiet pebble beach, you'll find Pansion Lovrić. **Pros:** incredible views; very friendly service; spacious rooms. **Cons:** distant from center of Lumbarda; short walk uphill. [$] *Rooms from: €80* ✉ *Lumbarda 1, Lumbarda* ☎ *020/712–052* 🌐 *www.lovric.info* 🛏 *4 rooms, 9 apartments, 1 cottage* 💳 *No credit cards* 🍴 *Breakfast.*

NIGHTLIFE AND PERFORMING ARTS

BARS

Fodor's Choice ★ **Cocktail Bar Massimo.** Surely among the world's most impressive venues, Cocktail Bar Massimo is inside one of the turrets of the fortified town walls and offers wonderful sunset views over the peninsula. Drinks are raised to the top of the turret on a pulley, and you have to climb a steep ladder to get to the top (ladies wearing dresses, you have been warned!). ✉ *Šetalište Petra Kanavelića, Korčula* ☎ *020/715–073* ⏲ *Closed Oct.–May.*

DANCE

The Moreška is traditionally performed each year on July 29 (the feast day of Korčula's protector, St. Theodore). The word *Moreška* means "Moorish" and is said to celebrate the victory of the Christians over the Moors in Spain. The dance itself is not native to Croatia and was performed in many different Mediterranean countries, including Spain, Italy, and Malta. The story of the dance is a clash between the Black (Moorish) King and the White (Christian) King over a young maiden. The dance is done with real swords.

Fodor's Choice ★ **Moreška.** The Moreška is a colorful medieval sword dance performed in the evenings, several times weekly through summer, just outside the city walls next to the Kopnena Vrata (Land Gate). Tickets are available at hotel reception desks and travel agencies throughout town. ✉ *Kopnena Vrata, Korčula* 🌐 *www.moreska.hr* 🎟 *100 Kn.*

SPORTS AND THE OUTDOORS

BEACHES

The closest spot for a quick swim is **Banje,** a small pebble beach about 10 minutes on foot east of the town walls, close to Hotel Liburna. For more leisurely bathing, the best beaches lie near the village of **Lumbarda,** which is 6 km (4 miles) southeast of Korčula Town. There are two family-friendly beaches: sandy **Przina,** 2 km (1 mile) south of Lumbarda, and smooth-white-stoned **Bili Žal** a short distance east.

Cro-Rent. A great way to spend an afternoon is to rent a speedboat from Cro-Rent and take to the open sea to explore the tiny scattered islets

8

of the nearby Korčula archipelago, which has many secluded bays for swimming. ⊠ *Ulica 29, Korčula* ☎ *020/711–908* ⊕ *cro-rent.com.*

DIVING

Dupin Dive Centre. This highly recommended center organizes a diving school, plus excursions to a variety of reefs, caverns, and wrecks around the island. ⊠ *PP101, Korčula* ☎ *020/711–342* ⊕ *croatiadiving.com.*

SAILING

ACI marina. The 159-berth ACI marina remains open all year. ⊠ *Korčula* ☎ *020/711–661* ⊕ *www.aci.hr.*

SHOPPING

Cukarin. This family-run store is renowned for its five different types of delicious handmade biscuits, as well as roasted almonds and homemade *rakija* flavored with local herbs. ⊠ *Hrvatska Bratske Zajednice, Korčula* ☎ *020/711–055* ⊕ *www.cukarin.hr.*

Galerija Vapor. Funky jewelry, colorful sculptures, and paintings with pop-art twists adorn the walls of this cavernous gallery inside the Sea Gate that features work by contemporary Croatian artists. ⊠ *Kula morska vrata, Korčula* ☎ *020/715–909.*

MLJET

Polače is 18 nautical miles west of Dubrovnik by ferry.

Mljet is a long, thin island of steep, rocky slopes and dense pine forests, more than a third of which is contained within Mljet National Park. The Kings of Bosnia, who ruled the island during medieval times, gave it to Benedictine monks from Puglia in Italy during the 12th century, who in turn passed it on to the Republic of Dubrovnik in 1410. No great towns ever grew up here, and today it is home to half a dozen small villages, with a total population of about 1,100 people. Lovers of ancient Greek literature will be interested to know that Mljet has been identified as Homer's lost island Ogygia, where Ulysses met the nymph Calypso.

GETTING HERE AND AROUND

Mljet is accessible through Polače by ferry.

EXPLORING

Fodor's Choice ★   **Nacionalni Park Mljeta** (*Mljet National Park*). Within the densely forested park lie two interconnected saltwater lakes, Malo Jezero (Little Lake) and Veliko Jezero (Big Lake), ideal for swimming from spring to autumn. Boats run to the charming 12th-century Benedictine monastery on Otočić Svete Marije (St. Mary's Islet), in the middle of Veliko Jezero, or you can rent a little blue kayak from Mali Most, the bridge between the two lakes, and paddle out there (before you head out, make time to float under the bridge with the lazy current). A series of footpaths and bike paths traverse the park; mountain bikes are also available for hire at Mali Most and at Hotel Odisej in Pomena. A local bus runs from the port of Sobra to the national park at the west end of the island. If you arrive on Mljet through Polače, you are within walking distance of the park. Upon arrival, pay the entrance fee at one of several wooden kiosks (if you stay overnight, this fee is included in the price of your accommodation). ⊠ *Pristanište 2, Govedjari* ☎ *020/744–041* ⊕ *www. np-mljet.hr* ⊠ *July and Aug. 100 Kn; Sept.–June 90 Kn.*

Odysseus Cave. There are wonderful swimming spots all around Mljet, but the village of Babino Polje, in the center of the island, might be home to the most magical spot of all. Greek legend has it that when the hero Odysseus was shipwrecked off the island, he swam into a cave where he was met by a nymph called Calypso; he was so bewitched by her that he stayed for the next seven years. Adventurers can take a car to Babino Polje, the largest settlement on the island with just more than 300 residents, where the cave in question is located; whether you believe the story, it's a great place for a swim, particularly at noon when the sun is high and the water looks aquamarine. There are a few cafés along the way to stop for refreshments. ⊠ *Babino Polje.*

Saplunara. One of Croatia's few sandy beaches, Saplunara lies at the southeastern tip of the island, outside the confines of the national park. Happily, it remains relatively wild and untended, and you will find several seasonal eateries in the tiny nearby settlement of the same name. ⊠ *Saplunara* ✛ *15 km (10 miles) southeast of Sobra.*

WHERE TO EAT

$$$
SEAFOOD
✕ **Restoran Melita.** On St. Mary's Islet, in Veliko Jezero, dining tables are arranged on the waterside terrace in front of the monastery. The setting is definitely beautiful; in fact, that's what you'll be paying for, as the quality of the food is rather disappointing. But it's still worth the trip. The menu includes a range of meat and fish dishes aimed at tourists. 💲 *Average main: 130 Kn* ⊠ *Otok Sv.Marije, Mljet* ☎ *020/744–145* ⊕ *www.mljet-restoranmelita.com.*

$$$$
SEAFOOD
✕ **Stermasi.** In the small settlement of Saplunara lies one of the region's few sandy beaches and one of its top restaurants. Stermasi is pricey, but the views are incredible and the food is excellent quality. Try octopus or goat under the bell, wild boar with homemade gnocchi, or Mljet-style fish stew. Most of the dishes take time to prepare, but with such pleasant service, delicious wines to choose from, and an overall wonderful service, you won't mind the wait. The Stermasi family also has seven apartments for rent. 💲 *Average main: 120 Kn* ⊠ *Maranovici, Saplunara 2, Mljet* ☎ *098/939–0362* ⊕ *www.stermasi.hr.*

$$$
SEAFOOD
✕ **Villa Mirosa.** Overlooking the sea near Saplunara beach, on the east end of the island, this informal, family-run eatery serves barbecued meat and fish dishes on a lovely terrace lined with potted geraniums. The olive oil, wine, and rakija are all homemade, and the seafood on offer is caught by the owners (you can join them on a fishing trip if so inclined). They also have eight rooms to rent. 💲 *Average main: 85 Kn* ⊠ *Saplunara 26, Maranovici, Mljet* ☎ *099/199–6270* ⊕ *www.villa-mirosa.com/* ▭ *No credit cards.*

8

WHERE TO STAY

$$ Hotel Odisej. Although there are plenty of pensions and private accom-
HOTEL   modations on the island, the Odisej is the only hotel. **Pros:** seafront
location in the national park; friendly staff. **Cons:** slightly lacking in
charm; large and rather impersonal; food disappointing. $ *Rooms
from: €108* ✉ *Pomena* ☎ *020/362–111* ⊕ *www.hotelodisej.hr* ⇥ *155
rooms, 2 suites* ⊘ *Closed Nov.–Mar.* ❙❉❙ *Breakfast.*

SPORTS AND THE OUTDOORS

BEACHES

The best beach, **Saplunara,** is sandy and backed by pinewoods. It lies on
the southeastern tip of the island, outside of the national park. Within
the park, the water in Malo Jezero (Little Lake) and Veliko Jezero (Big
Lake) tends to be several degrees warmer than that in the sea, so the
swimming season is somewhat extended.

MONTENEGRO

Visit Fodors.com for advice, updates, and bookings

By Elizabeth
Gowing

An independent country since 2006, tiny Montenegro (about the size of Connecticut) lies on the Adriatic coast and is bordered by Croatia, Bosnia-Herzegovina, Serbia, Kosovo, and Albania. The 650,000 people who live here call it Crna Gora, which, like "Montenegro," means "black mountain"—a reminder of the pine-forested alpine terrain of most of the country.

Montenegro's main draw is its beautiful coastline, dotted with delightful Venetian-era fortified towns, home to excellent seafood restaurants and set against the dramatic mountains of the interior.

Montenegro's first known inhabitants were the Illyrians, who were farmers and hunters, and also worked iron and traded with the ancient Greeks. Urbanization began in the 4th century BC when the Greeks founded Budva, on the coast. In AD 9, the Romans annexed the region into the province of Illyricum (which ran down the Adriatic coast from the Istrian peninsula to Albania), calling it Doclea after the dominant local Illyrian tribe. When the Roman Empire was divided between east and west in AD 395, the fault line passed right through Montenegro. Later, this was to be the dividing line between Eastern Orthodox and Roman Catholic lands.

In the 7th century, the Slavs arrived from the region that is now Poland. They mixed with the descendants of the Romanized Illyrians and lived in the mountains, in clans, each ruled by a Župan (chieftain). Originally pagan, they soon adopted Christianity. In 1077, their independent state of Duklja (the Slavicized version of the Roman name, Doclea) was recognized as a kingdom by the pope. Later, Duklja became known as Zeta (derived from the old Slavic word for "harvest") and kept its freedom through paying off the Byzantine Empire, and fighting off the Ottoman Turks. Because of the constant threat of Ottoman invasion and fear of rival clans, courage in combat was emphasized as a major virtue in Zeta.

Meanwhile, most of the Montenegrin coast was under Venetian rule from 1420 to 1797 though independent Montenegro had its capital at Cetinje, home of the first printing press in southern Europe in 1494.

Due to ties with Italy, Roman Catholicism was the dominant faith here, whereas the Eastern Orthodox Church prevailed in Zeta. In fact, politics and religion became so intertwined in Zeta that from 1550 to 1696 it was governed by bishops. In 1697, the Petrović-Njegoš family took the helm as prince-bishops. The greatest of their rulers, still loved and revered in Montenegro today, was Petar II Petrović-Njegoš who organized a 32-man band of traveling magistrates as well as a police force, paid for from a system of taxation which he organized. He was also an epic poet and his work, *The Mountain Wreath* is considered Montenegro's national poem.

King Nikola Petrović who ruled from 1860 was another notable ruler, and father; six of his nine daughters married royal or aristocratic Europeans, (including a Grand Duke of Russia and King Victor Emmanuel of Italy) which earned him the nickname, "the father-in-law of Europe." King Nikola introduced free elementary education, an agricultural college, post and telegraph offices, and freedom of the press.

During both world wars, Montenegro sided with the Allies. In 1945, it became one of the six constituent republics that made up Yugoslavia, governed along communist lines by President Tito. Yugoslavia was not part of the Soviet Bloc, however, as Tito broke off relations with Stalin in 1948. The country was ruled under Tito's own form of communism—far more liberal than that in the former USSR.

During the breakup of Yugoslavia in the 1990s, no fighting took place on Montenegrin soil though the region did suffer economic hardship and a degree of political isolation. When Croatia and Slovenia claimed independence from Yugoslavia in 1991, Montenegro remained loyal to Belgrade. However, by May 2006, when all that was left of Yugoslavia was the so-called Union of Serbia and Montenegro, Montenegro held a referendum and voted for independence (though it was close run, with only 55.5% of the votes in favor) and became its own democratic republic. Today, tourism is the main force behind the economy, and foreign investors (particularly Russian and British) keen to be in on the potential boom are buying up properties fast.

ORIENTATION AND PLANNING

GETTING ORIENTED
Of the small diamond-shape stretch of mountainous terrain which makes up Montenegro, only the southwestern face is usually visited by tourists as this is the coastal strip. The most charming sites of this stretch of 100 km (60 miles)—as the crow flies—are at the northern end, though because of the short distances involved, more adventurous visitors can use any of the towns along the coast as a base to visit the inland towns and mountains. The coastline borders Croatia at its northern end, and Albania to the south. Onward travel to the better-known towns and island of Croatia is easily arranged by public transport or hired car, and the less-discovered beaches and ancient sites of Albania are also accessible by regular buses across Montenegro's southern border. The UNESCO World Heritage Sites and legendary hospitality of Kosovo and Serbia are also only a bus journey away.

WHEN TO GO
May is a lovely time to visit coastal Montenegro, with temperatures between 14° and 22° Celsius (56° and 72° Fahrenheit) but before the busiest crowds of summer. After that temperatures rise to reach a peak in August with an average daily maximum of 29°C (84°F). These are fine days for sun worshippers or anyone willing and able to laze under sunshades and admire the sparkle on the water, but if you are wanting to explore the towns where sun glare bounces off the white stone, you may prefer to choose a different time of year (or at least plan your

9

Montenegro

BOSNIA-HERZEGOVINA

SERBIA

KOSOVO

ALBANIA

CROATIA

Šula

Pljevlja

Durmitor National Park

Žabljak

Grab

Bijelo Polje

Plužine

Tara

Sinjajevina

Šavnik

Mojkovac

Biogradska Gora National Park

Budimlja

Njegoš

Golija

18

Nikšić

Kolašin

Berane

Rožaje

Vilusi

6

Morača

Andrijevica

9

Grahovo

Cuce

E762

Danilovgrad

Zijova

Gusinje

Plav

Risan

Kosić

Prokletije National Park

Morinj

Perast

Dobrota

Bijela

Prčanj

Podgorica

Herceg Novi

Tivat

Lovćen National Park

Kotor
see detail map

Tuzi

Bay of Kotor

Sveti Stefan

Golubovci

Budva Riviera
see inset

Petrovac

Lake Skadar National Park

Lake Skadar

TO ANCONA

Sutomore

Šušanj

Bar

Rashtish

E851

TO BARI

Ulcinj

ADRIATIC SEA

0   30 miles

0   30 kilometers

Budva Riviera (inset)

E80

2-3

Slovenska Plaža

Bečići

Rafailovici

Trsteno

Jaz

Budva

Sveti Stefan

Mogren Plaža 1 & 2

Budva Gradska Plaža

Ostrvo Sv Nikola

E65

Petrovac

ADRIATIC SEA

Budva Riviera

TOP REASONS TO GO TO MONTENEGRO

In Kotor, climb to St. John's Fortress, following the medieval walls for postcard views.

Indulge in a night (or if you can't afford it, a meal or a day spa pass) at the luxurious **Sveti Stefan Aman** resort. Once a village of old stone cottages, it's now a private island.

Charter a yacht for a private sailing trip round the Bay of Kotor.

Visit Gospa od Skrjelo (Our Lady of the Rock), a lovely church perched on a tiny islet, opposite Perast, just outside Kotor.

Zigzag down the mountain road above Kotor to get a full view of the bay including Kotor, Perast, and the other villages clustered round the sapphire water of the Mediterranean's only fjord.

sightseeing for early in the days). By September temperatures are cooling (average daily minimum and maximum 17° and 26°C, or 62° and 78°F)—and the crowds in the most popular sites (notably Kotor) are thinning—while the sea is still as warm as in June or July (24°C or 75°F) so this is also a great time to visit. After this the season is properly over, and winter on the coast is a little bleak (temperatures in January are an average daily minimum and maximum of 5° to 12°C, or 40° to 53°F) and many businesses shut.

GETTING HERE AND AROUND

AIR TRAVEL
Montenegro Airlines has service from both Tivat and Podgorica Airports to London and various other European capitals. Well served by international airlines, Dubrovnik Airport, in Croatia, is a popular alternative gateway to Montenegro, but it's important to note that car rental agencies may charge extra for taking the vehicle across borders.

Airline Contacts Montenegro Airlines ⊠ *Beogradska 10, Podgorica* ☎ *020/228–187* ⊕ *www.montenegroairlines.com.*

Airport Contacts Podgorica Airport ⊠ *Podgorica Airport, Podgorica, Montenegro* ☎ *020/444–222* ⊕ *www.montenegroairports.com.* **Tivat Airport** ⊠ *Tivat Airport, Montenegro* ☎ *032/670–960* ⊕ *www.montenegroairports.com.*

BOAT TRAVEL
Montenegro Lines operates regular overnight car ferries year-round to the Montenegrin port of Bar, 38 km (24 miles) south of Budva, from Bari in Italy. The crossing takes 10 hours and costs about €88 per person one-way (in a two-berth cabin with bathroom).

BUS TRAVEL
Buses are cheap (e.g., €7.50 for the two-hour journey from Kotor to Podgorica) and cover practically the entire country. They are generally clean and reliable. Numerous small bus lines operate regularly along the coast between Herzeg Novi (in the north) and Ulcinj (in the south),

stopping at most towns along the way. For other routes, inquire at the bus station of departure.

Contacts Kotor Bus Station ✉ *Ul. Put prvoboraca BB, Kotor, Montenegro* ☎ *032/325–809* ⊕ *www.autobuskastanicakotor.me.*

CAR TRAVEL

Although Montenegro's buses have good service along the coast and can get you to most points in the country, renting a car gives you much more flexibility and makes life easier especially when visiting the mountains.

Since the Old Town is compact and pedestrian-friendly, you do not need to rent a car in Kotor. It's easy to reach nearby Perast by bus or taxi.

Contacts Europcar ✉ *Podgorica Airport, Podgorica, Montenegro* ☎ *020/653–141* ⊕ *www.europcar.com.*

CRUISE SHIP TRAVEL

Arriving at Kotor from the water is an impressive experience in itself, so be sure to be up on the deck in advance. Your ship will sail up a 28-km-long (18-mile-long) bay (often referred to as a fjord), with rugged mountains rising in the background. Cruise ships dock on the quay, immediately in front of Kotor's medieval walled Old Town.

TOUR OPTIONS

Many private travel agencies offer tours, including hiking in the mountains, rafting on the Tara River and visits to the towns of the interior, including the "toytown" former capital, Cetinje and nearby Lovćen, and the other national parks, including Lake Skadar (good for birdwatching), Biogradska Gora, and Durmitor. Other companies will offer tours from Montenegro to other countries in the region, including through the Prokletije national park into Kosovo and Albania, or to Dubrovnik or other destinations in Croatia.

ESSENTIALS

BUSINESS HOURS

Offices are open weekdays from 8 to 4. Shops are generally open weekdays from 9 to 9, Saturday from 8 to 1, though some shut for lunch around 2 and may close for as long as three hours. Large supermarkets will have longer working hours and won't close for lunch. Banks stay open weekdays from 9 to 6, Saturday from 9 to 1.

CURRENCY

The official currency has been the euro since 2002, despite the fact that Montenegro has not yet entered the European Union; negotiations are under way for its EU membership.

Kotor post office ✉ *Stari Grad BB, Kotor, Montenegro* ☎ *032/301–038.*

TELEPHONES

The country code for Montenegro is 382.

RESTAURANTS

Along the Montenegrin coast, seafood predominates, with starters including *salata od hobotnice* (octopus salad) and *riblja čorba* (fish soup), followed by risotto dishes—most notably *crni rižot* (black risotto prepared with cuttlefish)—*lignje* (squid), or fresh fish from the Adriatic prepared on a barbecue. The quality is generally excellent, and the prices are slightly lower than in neighboring Croatia. Note that on restaurant menus, fresh fish is priced by the kilogram. Inland, cheeses and meat dishes are more common. Cheeses to try include *sir iz ulje* (cheese preserved in olive oil) and *kožji sir* (goat's cheese), which are generally eaten at the beginning of the meal rather than at the end. Popular meat specialties are *pršut* (prosciutto), *Njeguški stek* (steak stuffed with prosciutto and cheese), and *jagnjece pečenje sa ražnja* (whole lamb roasted on a spit).

Montenegrins are also fond of the ubiquitous Balkan *Šopska salata* (a chopped salad of tomato, green peppers, cucumber, onion, olives, and strong white cheese grated over the top). When it comes to local wines, Vranac is the most highly esteemed red, and Krstac a reliable white.

HOTELS

The main delight of Montenegro's accommodation are the small, family-run establishments, many of which are centuries-old stone villas that have been converted into delightful little boutique hotels full of character, and with great hospitality. However, many visitors still prefer to rent a private room or apartment, which can be arranged through local tourist information offices and travel agencies. The tourist season runs from Easter to late October and peaks in July and August, when prices rise significantly and it may be difficult to find a place to sleep if you have not booked in advance. *Hotel reviews have been shortened. For full information, visit Fodors.com.*

WHAT IT COSTS IN EUROS (€)				
	$	$$	$$$	$$$$
Restaurants	under €10	€10–€16	€17–€20	over €20
Hotels	under €85	€85–€150	€151–€200	over €200

Restaurant prices are the average cost of a main course at dinner or, if dinner is not served, at lunch. Hotel prices are the lowest cost of a standard double room in high season.

VISITOR INFORMATION

Contacts National Tourism Organization of Montenegro ⊠ *Bulevar Sv. Petra Cetinjskog 130, Podgorica, Montenegro* ☎ *077/100–001* ⊕ *www.montenegro. travel.*

KOTOR

44 km (28 miles) from the border crossing between Croatia and Montenegro.

Backed by imposing mountains, tiny Kotor lies hidden from the open sea, tucked into the deepest channel of the Bokor Kotorska (Kotor Bay), which is Europe's most southerly fjord. To many, this town is more charming than its sister UNESCO World Heritage Site, Dubrovnik, retaining more authenticity, but with fewer tourists and spared the war damage and subsequent rebuilding which has given Dubrovnik something of a Disney feel.

Kotor's medieval Stari Grad (Old Town) is enclosed within well-preserved defensive walls built between the 9th and 18th centuries and is presided over by a proud hilltop fortress. Within the walls, a labyrinth of winding cobbled streets leads through a series of splendid paved piazzas, rimmed by centuries-old stone buildings. The squares are now haunted by strains from buskers but although many now house trendy cafés and chic boutiques, directions are still given medieval-style by reference to the town's landmark churches.

In the Middle Ages, as Serbia's chief port, Kotor was an important economic and cultural center with its own highly regarded schools of stonemasonry and iconography. From 1391 to 1420 it was an independent city-republic and later, it spent periods under Venetian, Austrian, and French rule, though it was undoubtedly the Venetians who left the strongest impression on the city's architecture. Since the breakup of Yugoslavia, some 70% of the stone buildings in the romantic Old Town have been snapped up by foreigners, mostly Brits and Russians. Porto Montenegro, a new marina designed to accommodate some of the world's largest super yachts, opened in nearby Tivat in 2011, and along the bay are other charming seaside villages, all with better views of the bay than the vista from Kotor itself where the waterside is congested with cruise ships and yachts. Try sleepy Muo or the settlement of Prčanj in one direction around the bay, or Perast and the Roman mosaics of Risan in the other direction.

GETTING HERE AND AROUND

AIR TRAVEL

Tivat Airport is 8 km (5 miles) from Kotor. Less convenient is the capital's Podgorica Airport, 90 km (56 miles) inland. Alternatively, some visitors fly in to Dubrovnik (Croatia) and drive 60 km (38 miles) down the coast to Kotor.

AIRPORTS AND TRANSFERS Buses run regularly between Tivat Airport and Kotor; inquire at the airport information desks for schedule and fare information. There are frequent buses from Podgorica to Kotor, but you will need to take a taxi from Podgorica airport to the bus station (approximately €8). You can catch a taxi year-round from both Tivat and Podgorica airports.

BOAT TRAVEL

During the summer, private taxi boats operate from Kotor's harbor, taking passengers up the coast to the village of Perast.

BUS TRAVEL

Regular buses run along the coast, stopping in Kotor en route. There's also a special service between Kotor and Budva.

CAR TRAVEL

Having a car in Kotor is not recommended, as the Old Town is pedestrian-only and parking spots can be hard to find, especially in high season.

VISITOR INFORMATION

Kotor's tourist information office gives out free maps and information and can help find private accommodation. You'll find the office in a kiosk just outside the Main Town Gate.

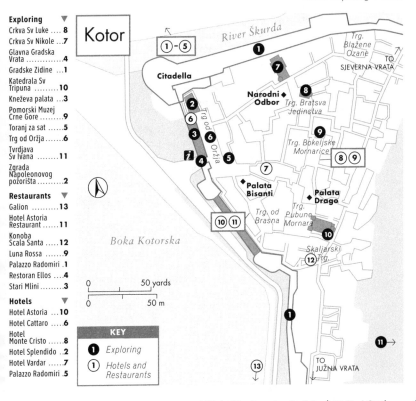

Exploring ▼
Crkva Sv Luke **8**
Crkva Sv Nikole ...**7**
Glavna Gradska
Vrata **4**
Gradske Zidine ...**1**
Katedrala Sv
Tripuna **10**
Kneževa palata ...**3**
Pomorski Muzej
Crne Gore **9**
Toranj za sat **5**
Trg od Oržja **6**
Tvrdjava
Sv Ivana **11**
Zgrada
Napoleonovog
pozorišta **2**

Restaurants ▼
Galion **13**
Hotel Astoria
Restaurant **11**
Konoba
Scala Santa **12**
Luna Rossa **9**
Palazzo Radomiri .**1**
Restoran Ellos **4**
Stari Mlini **3**

Hotels ▼
Hotel Astoria ...**10**
Hotel Cattaro **6**
Hotel
Monte Cristo **8**
Hotel Splendido ..**2**
Hotel Vardar **7**
Palazzo Radomiri .**5**

Contacts **Kotor Tourist Board** (*Turistička Organizacija Kotora*). ✉ *Stari Grad 315* ☎ *032/322-886* ⊕ *www.tokotor.me.* **Tourist Info Biro–Kotor** ✉ *Stari Grad* ☎ *032/325-950* ⊕ *www.tokotor.com.*

EXPLORING

Kotor's Old Town takes approximately half a day to explore. Plan your visit for the morning, when the main sights are open to the public and the afternoon sun has yet to reach peak force.

TOP ATTRACTIONS

Crkva Sv Luke (*St. Luke's Church*). Built in 1195, this delightful Romanesque church is the only building in the Old Town to have withstood all five major earthquakes that affected Kotor. Originally a Catholic church, the building later became an Orthodox place of worship. The church is open every day from 9 am to 9 pm ✉ *Trg bratstvo i jedinstva* ⊙ *9–9.*

Crkva Sv Nikole (*St. Nicholas' Church*). Designed by a Russian architect and built in pseudo-Byzantine style between 1902 and 1909, this is Kotor's most important Orthodox church (the Cathedral, by definition, is Catholic). The gold used to gild the spires was a gift from Russia. ✉ *Trg bratstvo i jedinstva* ⊙ *Daily 8–1 and 5–10.*

Glavna Gradska Vrata. The Main Town Gate (also known as the Sea Gate because of its position on the coast), which accesses the Stari Grad (Old Town) via the western facade of the city walls, dates back to the 16th century, and comprises Renaissance and baroque details. Originally, the outer gate bore a relief of the Venetian Lion, but in Tito's time this was replaced by the socialist star and dates recording the liberation of Kotor on November 21, 1944, at the end of WWII. There are two other entrances to the Stari Grad: the Južna Vrata (South Gate) and the Sjeverna Vrata (North Gate). ⊠ *Jadranski put.*

> ### BEST BETS FOR CRUISE PASSENGERS
>
> **Kotor Old Town.** Roam the car-free streets of this centuries-old fortified town, now an UNESCO World Heritage Site.
>
> **St. John's Fortress.** Follow Kotor's medieval walls uphill to arrive at this small fort, affording magnificent views of the Old Town and the bay below.
>
> **Our Lady of the Rock.** Take a boat ride across the bay from Perast to visit a tiny islet, capped by a church.

Gradske Zidine (*Town Walls*). Especially beautiful at night when they are illuminated, the well-preserved town walls were built between the 9th and 18th centuries. They measure almost 5 km (3 miles) in length, and reach up to 66 feet in height and 52 feet in width. They form a triangular defense system around the Old Town, then rise up the hill behind it to Tvrdjava Sv. Ivana (St. John's Fortress), 853 feet above sea level. You can walk up to the fortress along the walls, but allow at least one hour to get up and back down. Wear good hiking shoes—and don't forget to bring some water. ⊠ *Old Town, Stari Grad.*

Katedrala Sv Tripuna (*St. Tryphon's Cathedral*). Undoubtedly Kotor's finest building, the Romanesque cathedral dates back to 1166, though excavation work shows that there was already a smaller church here in the 9th century. Due to damage caused by a succession of disastrous earthquakes, the cathedral has been rebuilt several times—the twin baroque bell towers were added in the late 17th century. Inside, the most important feature is the 14th-century Romanesque Gothic ciborium above the main altar. Also look out for fragments of 14th-century frescoes, which would once have covered the entire interior. A collection of gold and silver reliquaries, encasing body parts of various saints and crafted by local masters between the 14th and 18th century, is on display in the treasury. ⊠ *Trg Ustanka Mornara* 🕿 *032/322–315* 💶 *€2.50 for combined ticket to cathedral and treasury* ⊗ *Apr.–Oct., daily 9–8; Nov.–Mar., daily 9–4. Mass is held on Sun. at 10 am.*

WORTH NOTING

Kneževa palata (*Duke's Palace*). Built in the 18th century, the Duke's Palace comprises almost the entire west side of the Old Town. Originally it was the official seat of the Venetian governor. Like the Napoléon Theatre, it is now part of the Cattaro Hotel & Casino. ⊠ *Old Town, Stari Grad.*

Pomorski Muzej Crne Gore (*Montenegrin Naval Museum*). Housed within the 18th-century baroque Grgurina Palace, this museum traces Montenegro's cultural and economic ties to the sea. In the 18th century, tiny Kotor had some 400 ships sailing the world's oceans. The exhibition extends over three floors, and includes model ships; paintings of ships, ship owners, and local naval commanders; navigation equipment; and uniforms worn by Montenegrin admirals and captains. ⊠ *Trg Grgurina, Stari Grad* ☎ *032/304–720* ⊕ *www.museummaritimum.com* 🖹 *€4* ⊙ *Aug.–Oct.: Mon.–Sat. 8–8, Sun. 10–4; Nov.–Apr.: Mon.–Sat. 10–3, Sun. 10–4; May–July: 8–6 every day.*

Toranj za sat (*Clock Tower*). Built in the 17th century and considered a symbol of Kotor, the Clock Tower stands directly opposite the Main City Gate. In front of the Clock Tower, the "Pillar of Shame" was used to subject local criminals to public humiliation. ⊠ *Trg od Oržja, Stari Grad.*

Trg od Oržja (*Square of Arms*). The Main Town Gate leads directly into the Square of Arms, Kotor's main square, today a large paved space animated by popular open-air cafés. Under Venice, arms were repaired and stored here, hence the name. Notable buildings on the square include the 17th-century **Toranj za Sat** (Clock Tower), the 19th-century **Napoleonovog Pozorišta** (Napoléon Theatre), and the 18th-century **Kneževa Palata** (Duke's Palace), the latter two now forming part of the upmarket Hotel Cattaro. ⊠ *Trg od Oržja, Stari Grad.*

Tvrdjava Sv Ivana (*St. John's Fortress*). On the hill behind Kotor, 853 feet above sea level, this fortress is approached via a series of bends and some 1,300 steps. The fantastic view from the top makes the climb worthwhile: the terra-cotta-tile rooftops of the Old Town, the meandering fjord, and the pine-clad mountains beyond. On the way up, you will pass the tiny Crkva Gospe od Zdravlja (Church of Our Lady of Health), built in the 16th century to protect Kotor against the plague. Be sure to wear good walking shoes and take plenty of water. The route up starts from behind the east side of the city walls. ⊠ *Above Old Town.*

Zgrada Napoleonovog pozorišta (*Napoléon Theatre Building*). Standing in the north corner of the Square of Arms, this building was turned into a public theater, one of the first of its kind in the Balkans, by the French in 1810. Today, following extensive renovation work, it is part of the upmarket Cattaro Hotel & Casino. ⊠ *Trg od Oržja, Stari Grad.*

WHERE TO EAT

$$$
SEAFOOD
✕**Galion.** A five-minute walk along the coast from the Old Town, this sophisticated seafood restaurant occupies an old stone building with a glass-and-steel "winter terrace" extension overlooking the bay, which, like the outdoor summer terrace, offers views of Kotor's medieval walls. Expect funky modern furniture and chill-out music, and a menu featuring favorites such as octopus salad, homemade gnocchi, and barbecued fresh fish. Ⓢ *Average main: €18* ⊠ *Šuranj BB* ☎ *032/325–054* ⊕ *www.hotelvardar.com.*

$$
ECLECTIC
✕**Hotel Astoria Restaurant.** The restaurant and bar housed in this 13th-century town house fuses ancient and modern, Montenegrin and

international, in a setting dominated by a tree set within the main room, its branches spreading out across the ceiling. Rather inexplicably, around the walls is the mythological account of the origins of the Greek alphabet, but the exuberant mixture of influences continues successfully into the light menu, which offers both Mediterranean and Asian dishes, and—a welcome opportunity for diners in Kotor who don't eat fish—some vegetarian and meat dishes. Try the popular chocolate soufflé from the dessert menu! $ *Average main: €14* ⊠ *322, Stari Grad* ⊕ *www.astoriamontenegro.com.*

$$
SEAFOOD

✕ **Konoba Scala Santa.** The look at this Old Town eatery is rustic but this is one of the best places in town for lobster, excellent mussels, and fresh fish, such as simple barbecued *zubatac* (dentex) drizzled with olive oil and served with a wedge of lemon. The candle-lit dining room has exposed stone walls, a wooden beamed ceiling hung with fishing equipment, and a big open fireplace. In summer, extra tables are set outside on the piazza. $ *Average main: €12* ⊠ *Škaljarska Pijaca BB* ☎ *069/295–833.*

$$$
MEDITERRANEAN

✕ **Luna Rossa.** Choosing one of the alfresco dining opportunities in Kotor's charming squares is tricky, but the Luna Rossa restaurant, housed in an attractive 13th-century stone building, offers a welcoming atmosphere, good food, and a great location. Choose from the rooftop café offering a bird's-eye view, or seating in the square. Its list of local wines is particularly strong, and among the local specialties on offer it's known for fresh fish and particularly excellent squid. $ *Average main: €18* ⊠ *423, Stari Grad* ⊕ *www.hotelmontecristo.me.*

$$$
ECLECTIC

✕ **Palazzo Radomiri.** In the menu offered on the terrace of this 18th-century stone building overlooking the Bay of Kotor, local delicacies are brought together in a fusion with influences from around the world. There is probably no other restaurant on earth where you can choose between Montenegrin cheeses (bought in the local market) and falafel, and have the chance to sample the traditional local *brodeto* fish soup but also vegetarian options. The dessert menu is just as enticing, with homemade cherry pie vying with the extraordinary caramelized olive ice-cream sauce. The Palazzo Radomiri is in the village of Dobrota, about 3 km (2 miles) from Kotor. $ *Average main: €18* ⊠ *Dobrota 221* ☎ *032/333–172* ⊕ *www.palazzoradomiri.com.*

$$
MEDITERRANEAN

✕ **Restoran Ellas.** Ellas serves local meat and fish specialties on a vine-covered terrace lined with wooden tables and benches offering a stunning view of the bay. Inside, the cozy stone-walled dining room has an open fireplace, a tile floor and ceiling hung with nets. The dessert menu is particularly tempting, offering treats such as dried fruit in honey, or pancakes in white wine sauce ⚠ **Ellas is in the village of Dobrota, 3 km (2 miles) from Kotor.** $ *Average main: €16* ⊠ *Dobrota 85* ☎ *032/335–115* ⊕ *www.restoranelas.com.*

$$
MEDITERRANEAN
Fodor's Choice
★

✕ **Stari Mlini.** This old mill on the Ljuta River dates back to 1670 and has been run by the current family of friendly owners for 40 years. It is in the neighboring village of Ljuta, 7 km (4 miles) down the coastal road from Perast. It has been authentically restored and made into a rustic but rather expensive restaurant offering excellent food with an emphasis on fish (you can visit the restaurant's own trout ponds set in the grounds). Try the *crni rižot* or the local cheese stored the traditional way in oil within stone jars that are 200 years old. In summer, outdoor tables are set up along the river (which is more of a stream these days). Mooring available for those arriving by boat. [$] *Average main: €16* ✉ *Ljuta BB* ☎ *032/333–555* 🌐 *www.starimlini.com.*

WHERE TO STAY

$$$$ HOTEL 🏨 **Hotel Astoria.** In the heart of the Old Town the quirky Hotel Astoria and its restaurant, housed in a 13th-century town house, are a breath of fresh air amid the blander options available elsewhere in the center of Kotor. **Pros:** creative design; central location. **Cons:** expensive for its category; the huge fleshy murals of Adam and Eve in the public restaurant may not be to everyone's taste. [$] *Rooms from: €230* ✉ *Kotor 322, Stari Grad* 🌐 *www.astoriamontenegro.com* 🛏 *9 rooms* 🍴 *Breakfast.*

$$ HOTEL 🏨 **Hotel Cattaro.** This solid old hotel is as magically central as it gets, occupying the 19th-century Napoléon Theatre, the 18th-century Duke's Palace, and other historic buildings on the Old Town's main square. **Pros:** located in Old Town; historic building. **Cons:** expensive; slightly lacking in charm; tends to book up. [$] *Rooms from: €129* ✉ *Trg od oružja BB, Stari Grad* ☎ *032/311–000* 🌐 *www.cattarohotel.com* 🛏 *17 rooms, 3 suites* 🍴 *Breakfast.*

$$ HOTEL 🏨 **Hotel Monte Cristo.** The family-run Hotel Monte Cristo, housed in a 13th-century building once the home of the first Bishop of Kotor, offers reasonably priced accommodation in the heart of the Old Town. **Pros:** location; friendly staff. **Cons:** its position in the midst of Old Town café life can make it noisy at night; no elevator or step-free access [$] *Rooms from: €120* ✉ *423-424, Stari Grad* 🌐 *www.montecristo.co.me* 🛏 *8 rooms, 4 suites* 🍴 *Multiple meal plans.*

$$ HOTEL 🏨 **Hotel Splendido.** With splendid views indeed over the fjord, this hotel in a stone villa of white stone set amid oleander stands on the waterfront in Prčanj, 3 km (2 miles) from Kotor. **Pros:** lovely old building; tastefully furnished; good sports facilities. **Cons:** outside Kotor; rather stark decor; private beach is small. [$] *Rooms from: €139* ✉ *Glavati BB, Prcanj* ☎ *032/301–700* 📠 *032/336–246* 🌐 *www.splendido-hotel.com* 🛏 *40 rooms, 3 suites* 🍴 *Breakfast.*

$$$ HOTEL 🏨 **Hotel Vardar.** Described as "the only soundproofed place to stay in the Old Town," the Hotel Vardar is centrally located, some rooms having a view of the lovely main square where the hotel's restaurant offers a chance for people-watching in the shade of sun umbrellas. **Pros:** Old Town location; soundproofing; stylish bathrooms. **Cons:** room decor and public areas lacking in character; no twin rooms; breakfast area is in a dark separate restaurant from the terrace. [$] *Rooms from: €185* ✉ *Trg od oružja, Stari Grad* 🌐 *www.hotelvardar.com* 🛏 *24 rooms, 1 suite* 🍴 *Breakfast.*

$$$ HOTEL Fodor's Choice ★ 🏨 **Palazzo Radomiri.** The owners of this family-run boutique hotel say that they are inspired by local sea captains bringing back diverse treasures from around the world. **Pros:** lovely old building; tastefully furnished; good sports facilities. **Cons:** outside Kotor; stairs and steps throughout make access difficult; often full in summer. [$] *Rooms from: €170* ✉ *Dobrota 221* ✣ *3 km (2 miles) from Kotor* ☎ *032/333–172*

9

⊕ *www.palazzoradomiri.com* ↩ *4 rooms, 6 suites* ⊙ *Closed Oct.–Mar.* ✧| *Breakfast.*

SHOPPING

all nut. You will feel healthier just for stepping inside this charming shop where the stylishly packaged products are made from cold-pressed oils from plum kernels and hazelnut. The shop sells its own brand of face and hand creams, serums, lotions, soaps, and massage oils, and you should try their shampoo made with nettle tincture. For fair-skinned summer visitors this is the place to look after yourself with unique plum, soy, and hazelnut natural sun protection. The oils are also available in food-safe versions: plum kernel oil for sprinkling over grilled meat, or apricot kernel oil as the basis for deliciously unusual dressings. ⊠ *Behind St. Luka Church* ⊕ *www.facebook.com/allnutkotor.*

Market. This market that sells fruit and vegetables is just outside the city walls, on the main coastal road, and is filled with colorful, local, seasonal produce laid out on marble slabs: artichokes, asparagus, and cherries in spring; tomatoes, eggplants, and peaches in summer, alongside pots of the tiny local mountain strawberries. It's also a great place to buy the local dried porcini mushrooms. It takes place every day. ⊠ *E65 runs all the way down coast. The market is on roadside, immediately outside old town walls.*

SPORTS AND THE OUTDOORS

BEACHES

The small pebble Gradska Plaža (Town Beach), just outside the town walls, is fine for a quick dip after a hot day of sightseeing.

SAILING

Several charter companies are based in the protected waters of Kotor Bay. For a one-week trip in August, expect to pay €2,500 for a 40-foot sailboat sleeping six, plus €130 per day for a skipper; prices do not include food, fuel, or mooring fees. Early booking (e.g., by February for the summer) will offer worthwhile discounts. Montenegro Charter Company offers one-day sailing trips (with skipper) on a private yacht around Kotor Bay.

The former military shipyard in Tivat, 5 km (3 miles) away, has been totally renovated and reopened as Porto Montenegro, a luxury marina, able to accommodate some of the world's largest super-yachts.

Montenegro Charter Company ⊠ *Bulevar Sv. Petra Cetinjskog 92, Podgorica* ☎ *067/201–655 mobile phone* ⊕ *www.montenegrocharter.com.*

PERAST

15 km (9 miles) from Kotor.

Tiny Perast is a peaceful bay-front village of stone villas set in gardens filled with fig trees and oleander. It was built by wealthy local sea captains during the 17th and 18th centuries, at a time when it was prosperous enough to have some 100 merchant ships navigating the oceans. In fact, Perast's naval skills were so respected that in the early 18th century, the Russian czar, Peter the Great, sent his young officers to study at the Perast Maritime Academy.

In the bay in front of Perast lie its main attractions: Sveti Djordje (St. George) and Gospa od Skrpjela (Our Lady of the Rock), a pair of tiny, charming islets, each topped with a church. Perast has no beach to speak of, though swimming and sunbathing are possible from the jetties along the waterfront.

Each year on July 22, Perast celebrates the *fasinada,* a local festival honoring the folkloric origins of Our Lady of the Rock, with a ritual procession of boats carrying stones out to the island at sunset. The stones are dropped into the water around the island, protecting it from erosion by the sea for the coming year. The Fasinada Cup sailing regatta is held on the same day.

GETTING HERE AND AROUND

Perast can be reached by car or bus, and can also be visited on an organized half-day boat trip from Kotor's harbor. ■ TIP➜ There are no ATMs in Perast so get cash out in Kotor or elsewhere before you arrive.

EXPLORING

Begin your exploration with a look in the Perast Town Museum, then take a taxi boat from the quayside to visit the island church, Our Lady of the Rock. Head back to town for lunch at one of the area's charming rustic eateries.

Gospa od Škrpjela (*Our Lady of the Rock*). Unlike its sibling island, St. George, this island is man-made. Folklore has it that in 1452, local sailors found an icon depicting the Virgin and Child cast on a rock jutting up from the water. Taking this as a sign from God, they began placing stones on and around the rock, slowly building an island over it. By 1630 they had erected a church on the new island. The original icon (which has been attributed to the 15th-century local artist Lovro Dobričević) is displayed on the altar. Over the centuries, locals have paid their respects to it by donating silver votive offerings, some 2,500 of which are now on display. To get there, hop a boat taxi from the waterfront (a five-minute trip that costs €5 return). Boats run 9–5 out of season and 9–7 in the season. (☎ 069/045–262 ⊕ *www.shiptravel-dado.co.me*). ✉ *Kotor Bay, Perast* ☎ 032/373–753 *for Kotor tourist office information* ⊕ *www.gospa-od-skrpjela.me.*

Muzej Grad Perasta. In the 17th-century Renaissance-baroque Bujović Palace, on the water's edge, Muzej Grad Perasta (Perast Town Museum) displays paintings of local sea captains and their ships, plus a horde of objects connected to Perast's maritime past. ✉ *Obala Marka Martinovića BB* ☎ 032/373–519 ⊕ *www.muzejperast.me* 💷 *€2.50* ⊗ *July–Sept.: 9–8; Oct. and Nov.: 9–5 weekdays; Dec.–Feb.: 9–3 weekdays; Mar.: 9–5 weekdays; Apr.–June: Daily 9–7.*

Roman Mosaics at Risan. These beautiful mosaics (one still under excavation) are from a second-century house in a small excavation site that is worth a brief stop if you are in the area. Particularly charming is the mosaic depicting Hypnos, the Roman god of sleep. Audio guide or tour guide available. ✉ *Risan BB, Risan, Kotor* ☎ *032/322–886* 🌐 *www.risanmosaics.me* 🎫 *€2* 🕒 *May, Daily 9–5; June–Oct., Daily 8–8. In winter by reservation only.*

Sveti Djordje (*St. George*). This natural islet is one of Perast's famous pair of islands. It's ringed by a dozen elegant cypress trees and crowned by the Monastery of St. George, dating back to the 12th century and still inhabited by monks. In the 18th century the island became a favorite burial place for local sea captains, whose crypts remain today. **■TIP→ The island is closed to the public, but you can snap photos from shore or neighboring Our Lady of the Rock to your heart's content.** ✉ *Kotor Bay, Perast.*

WHERE TO EAT

$$$ MEDITERRANEAN FAMILY Fodor's Choice ★

🍴 **Ćatovića Mlini.** In the tiny village of Morinj, 10 km (6 miles) from Perast on the road to Herzeg Novi, this charming family-run and child-friendly restaurant has for 20 years occupied a former water-driven flour mill. Children enjoy the space and the layout with miniature bridges over the water. With the millstream and greenery, this is the perfect place to cool off on hot days; you can choose a table either in the stone vaulted dining room or in the large lush garden next to the stream (in the evening, go for the open garden and avoid the muzak playing in the covered areas), and will be in the company of Montenegrin families enjoying excellent local cuisine. Seafood dishes include *salata od hobotnice, crni rižot,* and *dagnje na buzaru* (mussels cooked in a rich garlic, tomato, wine, and parsley sauce), but the menu is wider than that, offering three kinds of local chicory dish and a very sweet, zingy traditional local dessert, *Bokeški kolač,* made with almonds, maraschino, and lemon. [$] *Average main: €20* ✉ *Morinj BB* ☎ *032/373–030* 🌐 *www.catovicamlini.me.*

WHERE TO STAY

$$ HOTEL

🏨 **Hotel Admiral.** This family-run hotel in an 18th-century stone building on Perast's seafront has eight guest rooms with wooden parquet flooring and tasteful wooden furniture. **Pros:** lovely old building; seafront location; good restaurant. **Cons:** tends to fill up. [$] *Rooms from: €100* ✉ *Obala Kapetana Marka Martinovića BB* ☎ *032/373–556* 🌐 *www.hoteladmiralperast.com* 🛏 *8 rooms* 🕒 *Closed Nov.–Mar.*

$$ HOTEL

🏨 **Restaurant and Hotel Conte.** These four stone buildings dating from the 15th and 16th centuries have been tastefully converted to provide well-equipped apartments, some with kitchens and one with a hot tub. **Pros:** lovely old building; tastefully furnished; good restaurant. **Cons:** Muzak in the restaurant slightly spoils the atmosphere. [$] *Rooms from: €120* ✉ *Obala Kapitana Martka Martinovica* ☎ *067/257–387* 🌐 *www.hotel-conte.com* 🛏 *15 rooms, 3 apartments.*

SVETI STEFAN

Often referred to as the "jewel of the Montenegrin coast," Sveti Stefan is a tiny island protected by 600-year-old defensive walls inside of which nestle several dozen limestone cottages and a small church. The island is actually joined to the mainland by a causeway, with a gravel beach on each side. Originally a fishing village, it was fortified with sturdy walls in the 15th century to protect it from the Turks and marauding pirates. By the late 19th century, however, many residents had emigrated abroad, due to the poor local economy. In 1955, the few remaining inhabitants were relocated so that the entire village could be renovated and turned into a unique luxury hotel. The resort opened with a splash in 1960, attracting over the years international jet-setters and celebrities, from Richard Burton and Elizabeth Taylor, to Claudia Schiffer and Sylvester Stallone. But when the war hit in the 1990s, tourists stopped coming and the economy took a nosedive, leading Sveti Stefan to fall into total disrepair. Now, after years of exhaustive renovation, it has reopened as the Sveti Stefan Aman, an exclusive resort of luxury suites.

GETTING HERE AND AROUND

Sveti Stefan is only about 9 km (5 miles) from Budva so accessible by taxi if Budva is your base. Buses between Petrovac and Budva run along the main road above the resort. A scramble down the steps which lead past the houses and private land owned by families in the village takes you—more directly than the winding road for cars—to the public beach with the picture postcard view of the island.

WHERE TO EAT

$

MEDITERRANEAN

✕ Restaurant Drago. You come to Sveti Stefan either to stay in the fairy-tale island hotel, or to stare at it. If your budget does not permit the former, then the Restaurant Drago is a great place to do the latter. This small family-run and well-established (since 1967) restaurant is on the mainland hillside overlooking the sea and has a large terrace out front. The staff is friendly and multilingual, and the menu includes both seafood specialties from along the coast and heartier roast meats from the mountains. $ *Average main: €10* ⊠ *Slobode 32, Sveti Stefan* ☎ *033/468–777* ⊗ *Closed Nov.–Mar.*

WHERE TO STAY

$$$$

HOTEL

Fodor'sChoice

★

Aman Sveti Stefan. Familiar from the remade *Casino Royale* James Bond movie, and beloved of real-life celebrities (world number-one tennis player Novak Djokovic recently hired the entire island for his wedding), Sveti Stefan is a fairy-tale island hotel, connected to the mainland by a causeway. **Pros:** historic buildings; stunning island location; modern interior design. **Cons:** some rooms have small windows and can be rather dark; very expensive; beaches are gravel. $ *Rooms from: €950* ⊠ *Sveti Stefan Island* ☎ *033/420–000* ⊕ *www.amanresorts.com* ⟿ *50 rooms, 8 suites, 36 cottages* ⟋⊙⟍ *Multiple meal plans.*

9

$ HOTEL **Vila Drago.** You stay at the Drago for the view: all but two rooms at the Drago have the iconic view of the magical island of Sveti Stefan island, and the other two look out at lovely gardens and olive groves (and are compensated by having kitchen and balcony, too). **Pros:** location; welcoming. **Cons:** beaches here are gravel; the Aman Sveti Stefan complex dominates the settlement and those staying elsewhere can feel like also-rans [$] *Rooms from: €82* ✉ *Slobode 32, Sveti Stefan* ☎ *+382 68/514–874* 🌐 *www.viladrago.com* 🛏 *8 rooms, 2 suites* 🍴 *Breakfast.*

UNDERSTANDING CROATIA

**A SHORT HISTORY
OF CROATIA**

CROATIAN VOCABULARY

A SHORT HISTORY OF CROATIA

The Early History of the Croatian Lands

The three main regions that form Croatia today are known as Slavonia, Dalmatia, and Croatia proper (the inland region also known as Civil Croatia). These have also been called the "Triune Kingdom." In addition, the ethnically mixed Istrian peninsula is now considered Croatian territory. Bosnia-Herzegovina has a mixed population and once had a pronounced regional identity, but some Croat nationalists consider it their territory.

Even before the influx of the Slavs between AD 500 and 800, the region of Croatia had a long history. The Illyrians and Thracians were originally at home there, and traces of Hellenistic and Celtic influences can also be seen. From the 3rd century BC to the 1st century AD, Rome controlled the Balkans; indeed, at times Croatian history was closely tied to Roman politics, even though it was hardly a central province of the far-flung empire. For instance, the well-known Emperor Diocletian (AD 284–305) was from Dalmatia, as were four other emperors. After his reign, Diocletian returned to his native Split, where he built a large palace. The city of Pula also contains many important Roman sites dating from this time.

Rome's influence on the Croatian lands has been far-reaching. The Romans developed the region's basic infrastructure and industries related to mining and metallurgy. The Croatian coast was established as an outpost of European high culture; this connection was soon strengthened by the Croats' conversion to Christianity and later by ties to the Renaissance city-states of Italy, especially Venice. The Italian influence can be felt even today, particularly in the Istrian peninsula and on some of the islands.

As the Empire was divided into its eastern and western halves, the internal frontier came to symbolize for many the "fault line" between Latin culture and Roman Catholicism, on the one hand, and Greek culture and Orthodox Christianity, on the other. The division was actually always quite porous and inexact, but its nature changed during the Ottoman Turkish invasions starting in the 14th century. Islam again became one of the major religions of Europe, and new ethnic groups arrived or were created in the former Byzantine lands.

Despite the fact that the Croatian lands clearly belonged to Rome's sphere of influence, the Croatian culture went through some complicated developments after the fall of the western portion of the Roman Empire in AD 476. First, many Croats—like their neighbors, the Slovenes—had been converted to Christianity by Frankish (or "German") missionaries from Charlemagne's Holy Roman Empire. Second, Croatian monks working in Dalmatia developed a unique alphabet, known as Glagolitic, from contact with Orthodox missionaries. Croatia remained Catholic after the official religious break between Rome and Constantinople in 1054, but the Glagolitic alphabet was used in some places into the 19th century, serving to reinforce Croatian identity amidst various political and ethnic rivalries. Finally, the Ottoman occupation of the Balkans made much of Croatia into a contested region of population flux and the new cultural norms associated with being a "bulwark of Christendom."

The first independent Croatian state was formed by the leader Tomislav. In 924 he was crowned king of Croatia and recognized by the pope. Although historians disagree over the exact extent of his territory, Tomislav did set another important precedent as well: he united many regions of the former Roman provinces of Dalmatia and Pannonia (central Croatia and Slavonia). The national symbols of the kuna (currency denomination) and šahovnica (red-and-white checkerboard coat of arms) originated at this time.

Croatia in the High Middle Ages

By 1102 the royal line had died out, and the Sabor (assembly of nobles) accepted Hungarian rule. Croatia preserved its own laws and customs through the Pacta Conventa, which seems to have been essentially a personal union between the countries, not an annexation. Medieval Croatia also achieved considerable cultural heights. The first known writing in Croatian dates from around 1100, on a stone tablet from the island of Krk, known as the Bašćanska Ploča. In the 16th century, Dubrovnik dramatist and poet Ivan Gundulić (1555–1638) wrote *Osman* in the Croatian language to inspire resistance to the Turks. Croatia's unique literary history had begun. Dubrovnik also boasted major scientists and composers. Soon there were three major outside forces contending for Croatian territory: the Ottoman Empire, the Kingdom of Hungary, and the Venetian Republic. The Venetians quickly displaced rivals such as the Byzantine Empire and the kingdoms of Serbia and Bosnia. A major blow came in 1202, when Venice directed the Fourth Crusade to sack the important port of Zadar.

The Ottoman expansion into Europe reached Hungary in 1526; Sultan Suleiman defeated Hungary's King Lajos at Mohacs. The Croatian nobles had already been defeated at Udbina in 1493. Ottoman rule would last for 150 years, but the Hungarian and Croatian nobility quickly opted for personal union with the royal Habsburg family in Vienna. In 1593 the Croats stemmed the tide of Turkish invasion by the successful defense of the fortress-city of Sisak, but intense fighting in the area continued until the Treaty of Karlowitz in 1699. That momentous agreement removed most of Croatia and Hungary from Ottoman sovereignty, and Habsburg rule continued.

The wealthy city-state of Dubrovnik retained its independence until Napoléon's invasion of 1797. Bosnia-Herzegovina, home to many Croats and other groups, would remain under Ottoman rule until 1878. As central Croatia was liberated by the crusading Habsburgs, they created a military frontier zone that is often known by its Croatian (and Serbian) name of Vojna Krajina. The frontier included the Lika region south of Zagreb and stretched all along the southern periphery of the Empire from Italy to Romania. The Austrians recruited Serbs and other groups into the area, adding new minority groups to the Croatian lands.

The nobility, or landowning class, of Croatia played the key role in developments over the next several centuries. Croatia's basic feudal structure was preserved by the Habsburgs, although some nobles from the Zrinski and Frankapan families were executed for plotting against Vienna. The country also remained overwhelmingly Catholic; Catholic scholars working in Venice and Rome also produced the earliest dictionaries and grammars of the Croatian language. These trends stand in sharp contrast to the neighboring Serb lands, where Ottoman rule removed nearly all traces of the traditional elites. The Croat nobles resented Vienna for its attempts at centralization and its territorial compromises with the Ottomans. At times the Croats gravitated, culturally and politically, toward outside powers that could provide leverage in their struggle against Vienna: Russia, France, and even at times their own erstwhile foes the Venetians and the Ottomans.

The Croatian National Revival

The remaining Croatian nobility was revived as a political "nation" by the enlightened despotism of one of the most iconoclastic of the Habsburg emperors, Joseph II (r. 1780–90). Joseph's modernizing vision involved centralization of power in Vienna and, to some extent, Germanization. Both of these processes elicited strong negative reactions around the Empire, where traditional autonomy existed in many areas. In Croatia it was the nobility who responded with alarm both to Joseph and to the excesses of the French Revolution. Many in the Croatian elite chose to strengthen ties with Hungary, forming a political party known as the Unionists, or Magyarones, a term corresponding basically to "Hungarophiles."

In 1809 the invading Napoléon created a short-lived satellite state out of conquered Habsburg lands called the Illyrian Provinces. This state abolished feudalism and turned local administration, including language policy, over to the Croats and Slovenes. These actions increased popular awareness of Croatian nationality. It was from these two starting points—both of them reactions to external events—that the tortured development of modern, mass nationalism in Croatia began.

The Magyarone solution soon became problematic as Hungary gradually increased its control over the Croatian lands decade by decade. Croats, now alienated from both Vienna and Budapest, began to react in various new ways. Of considerable importance was the Illyrian Movement, which was at once a Croatian national movement and a kind of supra-national forerunner of Yugoslavism. Its chief exponent was the writer and editor Ljudevit Gaj, who helped establish the basis for the modern Croatian language. The Illyrians espoused political cooperation among the Slovenes, Serbs, and Croats within the framework of the Habsburg Empire; they were basically federalists and did not seek an independent nation-state just for Croats. The National Party, led by Bishop Josip Strossmayer, revived Illyrianism in the form of Yugoslavism and also greatly enriched Croatian cultural life by founding the Yugoslav Academy of Sciences and the modern University of Zagreb.

In 1848, nationalism and liberalism brought major insurrections across Europe. Although Hungary rebelled, the Croats remained loyal to Vienna. In the middle of the 19th century, the Croatian political scene was dominated by an important figure named Josip Jelačić (1801–59), an Austrian military officer and a convinced Illyrianist. In 1848 the Habsburgs turned to him to help defeat the nationalist uprising in Hungary. He succeeded and managed to unite nearly all Croatian territory under Austrian rule. He also abolished feudalism and promoted Croatian interests on major cultural issues. Although Jelačić is a Croatian hero today, he also propounded a progressive version of nationality based on regional rather than ethnic identity. The long-reigning Emperor Franz Josef tried to placate the Hungarians by issuing the Ausgleich (Compromise) in 1867, breaking the empire in two and renaming it "Austria-Hungary." The Croats wisely negotiated their own version of the Ausgleich, known as the Nagodba, in 1868.

Into the Great War: From Habsburgs to Yugoslavs

This arrangement gave the Croats, at last, a considerable degree of internal autonomy, and Croatia even had representatives in the Hungarian parliament and cabinet and also in Vienna. But it also provided for the Croatian territories to be split up again, with control over Dalmatia and Istria going to Vienna while Slavonia and central Croatia were under the Hungarian crown. In addition, the major port of Rijeka was run as a separate entity by Budapest.

These final Habsburg decades were turbulent. Territorial divisions wounded Croatian pride and hindered economic development. Hungarian manipulation of the political scene and attempts at Magyarization continued. Count Károly Khuen-Héderváry ruled from 1883 to 1903 and became notorious for setting Croatia's Serbian and ethnic Croatian populations against each other. Despite his tactics and the turmoil of World War I, the Serbs and Croats of Croatia actually achieved a considerable level of political cooperation. They succeeded in forming coalitions to push for reunification of the Croatian lands and to oppose misrule from both Budapest and Vienna.

In 1918, with the Habsburg Empire vanquished, a combination of factors induced Croatian politicians to lead their country into the new Kingdom of Serbs, Croats, and Slovenes (called Yugoslavia after 1929). By 1921 many Croats grew suspicious of the new state, run from Belgrade by the Serbian king. Many political parties, as well as the ban (viceroys) and the Sabor, were suppressed. Royal legitimacy was shaky: Serbs dominated the police, military, and economy; agriculture, the mainstay of the economy, languished; and Italy retained possession of large amounts of Croatian territory in Istria and Dalmatia. Stjepan Radić, the leader of the powerful Croatian Peasant Party, alternately boycotted and negotiated with the central government; his murder in 1928 fueled radicalism in Croatia.

As World War II approached, Belgrade grew more willing to compromise with Croatia. A 1939 arrangement known as the Sporazum restored the ban and Sabor and combined many Croatian lands into one autonomous unit. But war broke out just weeks later.

World War II and the Second Yugoslavia

The darkest chapter in Croatian history took place amidst the chaos of World War II. An interwar political agitator on the fascist right, Ante Pavelić (1889–1959) rose to power and ruled the "Independent State of Croatia" for 49 bloody months. Pavelić, who founded the Ustaša (insurrectionist) movement in 1929, originally developed his ideas within the tradition of the Croatian Party of Right. This group, founded by Ante Starčević (1823–96) in 1861, advocated the creation of a greater Croatia, including Bosnia-Herzegovina. They believed that Bosnian Muslims (today's Bosniaks) and Serbs were ethnic Croats who had been forced to adopt other faiths. Pavelić developed ties with similar movements in Nazi Germany, Bulgaria, Hungary, and especially Mussolini's Italy. The Ustaša helped assassinate King Aleksandar in 1934. The most revolutionary aspects of the Ustaša movement were their willingness to use terror and genocide against minorities in order to form an ethnically "pure" Croatian state and their desire to create a mass political movement that displaced the established elites in the country. Mussolini's army installed Pavelić's government in Zagreb after the Axis invasion of 1941, and the Nazis agreed to let Pavelić rule. Croatia was immediately split into two spheres of influence. The Ustaša were unpopular, but they ruled by terror over a population that included vast numbers of non-Croatians, especially Serbs. The Germans were increasingly disconcerted by the Ustaša's murderous policies, which spawned significant resistance movements. The main German goal in the region was simply the extraction of mineral and agricultural wealth. In all, the Ustaša government killed more than 300,000 Serbs, along with tens of thousands of Jews and Roma (Gypsies). In addition to a number of concentration camps like the notorious Jasenovac east of Zagreb—where about 85,000 people, mostly Serbs, were killed—many horrific rural massacres occurred. Pavelić's state was a failure; the communist Partisans and the Chetniks (Serbian royalists) actually controlled much of its territory. Yugoslavia was reconstituted after World War II, this time under the rule of Josip Broz Tito (1892–1980), a communist born in Croatia. The trauma of World War II was the main reason for decades of "Croatian silence" in Yugoslavia. In 1967, leading cultural and academic figures broke ranks with the party and publicly asserted the distinctiveness and legitimacy of the Croatian language. This was divisive, because it ran counter to the official embrace of a common "Croato-Serbian" or "Serbo-Croatian" language and culture.

A period of dissent and crackdown known as the "Croatian Spring" followed. There were demonstrations, strikes, and many debates in print about Yugoslavia's political discrimination and economic exploitation. This lasted until 1972, and resulted in Tito's sidelining numerous prominent Croatian communists, including many who could have provided cosmopolitan, intelligent alternatives to both communism and what came after. The repression belies the fact that Tito's regime became, after 1952, the most liberal socialist state in Eastern Europe; in addition, the LCY (League of Communists of Yugoslavia) was not averse to using the nationalism of some Yugoslav peoples (such as the Bosnians, the Macedonians, and the Albanians of Kosovo) to further its agenda—just not Croatian nationalism.

Famous political figures in Croatia in the postwar period included Tito, of course, but also his close ally Vladimir Bakarić, who held a number of important governmental posts. Franjo Tuđman, a communist Partisan officer during World War II and then a historian, was jailed several times for questioning centralist orthodoxy on national issues. The poet Vlado Gotovac, who again became a pro-democracy dissident under President Tuđman in the 1990s, was purged in the Croatian Spring, and the philosophers Milan Kangrga and Rudi Supek of the countrywide Praxis movement attracted attention and official disfavor with their alternative analyses of Marx.

Despite significant grievances, Croatia underwent considerable modernization under communist rule. There were increases in industrialization, urbanization, life expectancy, standard of living, and literacy. New universities were founded in Split, Rijeka, and Osijek. Croatia's beaches became famous across Europe. The economy was also helped by the large numbers of Croats who worked abroad as *Gastarbeiter* (guest workers), but heavy immigration and low birth rates left many worried about the country's demographic future.

Both Serbia and Croatia felt the heavy hand of Tito's rule; as the most powerful traditional nations in Yugoslavia, Tito neutralized their ability to rock the federal boat. The LCY encouraged nation-building, however, in Bosnia, Macedonia, Montenegro, and among the Albanians of Kosovo both as a counterweight to Croatian and Serbian ambitions and as a developmental strategy.

From Tito to Tuđman and Beyond: Sovereign Croatia

Historians disagree over when Yugoslavia passed the point of no return. At some point in the decade between Tito's death in 1980 and the momentous political changes in Slovenia and Croatia by 1991, the breakup actually began. In 1990, Slovenia and Croatia held free, multiparty elections, declared their sovereignty, and held referenda in which they overwhelmingly approved the idea of independence. But even then the eventual violence was not inevitable. Two highly regarded Croatian reformist politicians, Ante Marković and Stjepan Mesić, were stymied in their efforts to place the Yugoslav federation on a new foundation. What soon exploded were not the so-called ancient ethnic hatreds but rather the aggressive and conflicting aims of various political factions competing in a superheated environment. This violence was furthered by the egoism of conniving politicians, sensationalism in the media, and mixed signals from Western Europe and the United States.

The 1980s had been extremely tense across the country. Serbs and Albanians clashed in Kosovo; hyperinflation, unemployment, public debt, and strikes characterized a ruined economy; and the fall of the Berlin Wall marked the end of other European socialist states. The rise of the dictator Slobodan Milošević in Serbia brought new levels of confrontation to politics and revealed gross Serbian manipulation of the economy. Croats and Slovenes gradually realized that Yugoslavia was unworkable as a country. The Serbian population, incited by ambitious politicians, lashed out at Croat police in the spring of 1991. Thus, even before Croatia's declaration of independence on June 25, 1991, the villages of Pakrac and Borovo Selo became scenes of bitter bloodshed, as did the famed Plitvice Lakes National Park and other areas in central Croatia. There were about 600,000 Serbs living in Croatia, comprising over 12% of the population. The new Croatian government, led by the now-nationalist Tuđman, was brash in its treatment of minorities and irresponsible in its handling of the legacy of World War II, and these approaches greatly increased Serbs' anxiety.

After secession, full-scale fighting broke out. The autumn of 1991 saw two shocking sieges: the bloody street-fighting and massacres at Vukovar in Slavonia and the weeks-long shelling of venerable Dubrovnik for no legitimate military purpose. The contemporary Croatian poet Slavko Mihalić described this era as one in which the Serbian leader—"the one who sends the bombs"—grimly and accurately promised to turn Croatia into a "national park of death." In fact Milošević was willing to let Croatia secede but without its Serb-inhabited regions; later, he and Tuđman agreed on how to partition Bosnia-Herzegovina as well. In May 1992 the war spread to independence-minded Bosnia, where 200,000 people died, many of them civilians, and 2 million were made homeless. In Croatia, 10,000 people were killed and over a fourth of the country fell to the Serbs. Large numbers of Croats and Bosnians were driven from their homes with terror campaigns of "ethnic cleansing." With American aid, Croatian forces rallied in the summer of 1995 and recaptured Slavonia and the Krajina region. Many thousands of Serbs fled and property issues remain unresolved. Croatian forces also committed atrocities in Bosnia-Herzegovina, but most of the international community finally recognized that the lion's share of guilt for the wars themselves belonged to the Serbian government. The Dayton peace accords of late 1995, backed by NATO's military might, paved the way for Serbian withdrawal from Croatia and Bosnia.

President Tuđman was roundly criticized internationally for his authoritarian tendencies and over-zealous nationalism. Internal opposition grew as well, especially over his censorship and policies in Bosnia. Tuđman allowed political parties other than the HDZ (Croatian Democratic Union), but they were weak until his death in December 1999. Since then, Mesić has been president, and the prime ministership has been held by both the Social Democrats of Ivica Račan and the revived HDZ of Ivo Šanader. Since Tuđman's death, Croatia has begun serious cooperation with The Hague war-crimes tribunal. Many other reforms have also succeeded, but open questions include the quest for autonomy by the ethnically and historically distinct region of Istria and Croatia's ability to cooperate on a variety of issues with its neighbors. Most Croats still look forward to joining the European Union in the next several years. —*John K. Cox, Associate Professor of History, Wheeling Jesuit University*

CROATIAN VOCABULARY

	ENGLISH	CROATIAN	PRONUNCIATION
BASICS			
	Yes/no	Da/ne	dah/neh
	Please	Molim (vas)	**moh**-leem (vahs)
	Thank you (very much)	Hvala (lijepo)	**hvah**-lah (lyeh-poh)
	Excuse me	Oprostite	oh-proh-stee-teh
	Hello	Zdravo	**zdrah**-voh
	I'm sorry.	Žao mi je.	**zhah**-oh mee yeh
	Do you speak English?	Da li govorite engleski?	Dah lee **goh**-voh-ree-teh **ehn**-glehs-kee?
	I don't understand.	Ne razumijem.	neh rah-**zoo**-myehm
	Please show me . . .	Molim vas pokažite mi . . .	moh-leem vahs **poh**-kah-zhee-teh mee
	I am American (m/f).	Ja sam yah sahm Amerikanac/ Amerikanka	**ah**-meh-ree-kah-nahts/ **ah**-meh-ree-kahn-kah
	My name is . . .	Zovem se . . .	**zoh**-vehm seh
	Right/left	Desno/Lijevo	**dehs**-noh/**lyeh**-voh
	Open/closed	Otvoreno/zatvoreno	**oh**-tvoh-reh-noh/ **zah**-tvoh-reh-noh
	Where is . . . ?	Gdje je . . . ?	gdyeh yeh
	. . . the train station?	. . . železnička?	**zheh**-lehz-neech-kah
	. . . the bus stop?	. . . autobusna?	**ahoo**-toh-boos-nah
	. . . the airport?	. . . aerodrom?	**ah**-eh-roh-drohm
	. . . the post office?	. . . pošta?	**posh**-tah
	. . . the bank?	. . . banka?	**bahn**-kah
	Here/there	Ovdje/tamo	**ohv**-dyeh/**tah**-moh
	I would like. . .(m/f)	Molim (vas) htio/ htjela bih. . .	hteeoh/htyeh-lah beeh
	How much does it cost?	Koliko košta?	**koh**-lee-koh **kosh**-tah
	Postcard	Razglednica	**rahz**-gleh-dnee-tsah
	Help!	Upomoć!	**oo**-poh-moch

	ENGLISH	CROATIAN	PRONUNCIATION
NUMBERS			
	One	Jedan	**yeh**-dahn
	Two	Dvad	vah
	Three	Tri	tree
	Four	Četiri	**cheh**-tee-ree
	Five	Pet	peht
	Six	Šest	shest
	Seven	Sedam	**seh**-dahm
	Eight	Osam	**oh**-sahm
	Nine	Devet	**deh**-veht
	Ten	Deset	**deh**-seht
	One hundred	Sto	stoh
	One thousand	Tisuća	**tee**-soo-chah
DAYS OF THE WEEK			
	Sunday	Nedjelja	**neh**-dyeh-lyah
	Monday	Ponedjeljak	**poh**-neh-dyeh-lyahk
	Tuesday	Utorak	**oo**-toh-rahk
	Wednesday	Srijeda	**sryeh**-dah
	Thursday	Četvrtak	**cheht**-vruh-tahk
	Friday	Petak	**peh**-tahk
	Saturday	Subota	**soo**-boh-tah
WHERE TO SLEEP			
	A room	Soba	**soh**-bah
	The key	Ključ	klyooch
	With bath/shower	S kupaonicom/ tušem	suh koo-pah- **oh**-nee-tsohm/ **too**-shehm
FOOD			
	A restaurant	Restoran	rehs-**toh**-rahn
	The menu	Jelovnik	yeh-**lohv**-neek
	The check, please.	Molim, račun.	**moh**-leem, **rah**-choon

ENGLISH	CROATIAN	PRONUNCIATION
Can I order, please?	Mogu li naručiti, molim vas?	**moh**-goo lee nah-**roo**-chee tee, **moh**-leem vahs
Breakfast	Doručak	**doh**-roo-chahk
Lunch	Ručak	**roo**-chahk
Dinner	Večera	**veh**-cheh-rah
Bread	Kruh	krooh
Butter	Putar/maslac	**poo**-tahr/mahs-lahts
Salt/pepper	Sol/papar	sohl/**pah**-pahr
Wine	Vino	**vee**-noh
Beer	Pivo	**pee**-voh
Water/mineral water	Voda/mineralna voda	**voh**-dah/**mee**-neh-rahl-nah **voh**-dah
Milk	Mlijeko	**mlyeh**-koh
Coffee	Kava	**kah**-vah
Tea	Čaj	chay

TRAVEL SMART
CROATIA

GETTING HERE AND AROUND

▌ AIR TRAVEL

Flying time from London to Zagreb is 2 hours 30 minutes, from Prague to Zagreb it is 90 minutes, and from Warsaw it is 1 hour 40 minutes.

Flying time from Bratislava to Dubrovnik is 85 minutes, from Budapest to Dubrovnik is 75 minutes, from London to Venice is 2 hours 10 minutes.

Domestic air tickets in Croatia are best purchased online. Airports in both countries have offices for the national airlines (Croatian Airlines in Croatia) but their opening hours are unreliable, and attempting to purchase a ticket at the airport may backfire. The national airline also has a usable website where e-tickets can be purchased.

Airlines and Airports Airline and Airport Links.com. Airline and Airport Links.com has links to many of the world's airlines and airports. ⊕ *www.airlineandairportlinks.com.*

Airline Security Issues Transportation Security Administration. Transportation Security Administration has answers for almost every question that might come up. ⊕ *www.tsa.gov.*

AIRPORTS

In Croatia most international flights arrive at Zagreb (ZAG); however, there are also many connecting flights from various European airports to Split (SPU) and Dubrovnik (DBV), and even a few to Pula (PUY), Rijeka (RJK), and Zadar (ZAD). Trieste, Italy (TRS), or even Venice (VCE) make good alternate destinations for Croatia (particularly Istria and Kvarner).

Information Dubrovnik Airport ☎ *020/773–377* ⊕ *www.airport-dubrovnik.hr.* **Pula Airport** ☎ *052/530–105* ⊕ *www.airport-pula.hr.* **Rijeka Airport** ☎ *051/842–132* ⊕ *www.rijeka-airport.hr.* **Split Airport** ☎ *021/203–171* ⊕ *www.split-airport.hr.* **Zadar Airport** ☎ *023/313–311* ⊕ *www.zadar-airport.hr.* **Zagreb Airport** ☎ *01/626–5222* ⊕ *www.zagreb-airport.hr.*

GROUND TRANSPORTATION

Ground transportation to major cities from airports in Croatia is well organized and reasonably user-friendly. Both shuttle buses and metered taxis operate at most airports all year long.

FLIGHTS

There are no direct air connections between the United States and Croatia, though some U.S.-based airlines offer code-share flights through their European travel partners. Travelers from the United States must fly into a major European hub such as Amsterdam, London, Frankfurt, Budapest, Prague, Vienna, or Warsaw and then transfer to a flight to Zagreb, Split, or Dubrovnik. Several European airlines, in addition to the national carrier, offer connections to Croatia.

Traveling to Croatia using a combination of a major airline and a low-cost European airline is a good idea. If you are traveling to Istria or Kvarner, a budget flight to nearby Venice (2½ hours by car) or Trieste (1½ hours to Rijeka by car) is a sound option. Most of these discount airlines sell tickets only on the Internet. Just be aware that so-called London-based discount airlines rarely fly from Heathrow (more often it's Gatwick or Stansted). All these airlines have stringent baggage limits, and offer few free in-flight services, if any. And if you transfer from a major airline to a discounter, you will have to reclaim your bags and recheck them, so make sure you leave plenty of time between your flights.

EasyJet flies from London to Ljubljana, Split, Rijeka, and Venice. German Wings flies to Split and Zagreb from Cologne-Bonn and Stuttgart, and to Zagreb from Hamburg. Ryanair flies from London to Zadar and Pula in Croatia, and Trieste and Venice in Italy. Sky Europe flies to Dubrovnik, Split, and Zadar from Bratislava or Budapest. Wizzair flies from London to Split and Zagreb, and from Brussels to Ljubljana.

Airline Contacts Adria Airways
☎ 020/7734–4630 in U.K., 01/369–1010
in Slovenia ⊕ www.adria-airways.com. **Aer
Lingus** ☎ 800/474–7424 ⊕ www.flyaerlingus.
com. **Air France** ☎ 800/237–2747 ⊕ www.
airfrance.com. **Alitalia** ☎ 800/223–5730
⊕ www.alitaliausa.com. **American Airlines**
☎ 800/433–7300 ⊕ www.aa.com. **Austrian
Airlines** ☎ 800/843–0002 ⊕ www.austrian.
com. **British Airways** ☎ 800/247–9297
⊕ www.britishairways.com. **Continental
Airlines** ☎ 800/231–0856 ⊕ www.continental.
com. **Croatia Airlines** ☎ 020/8563–0022
in U.K., 01/66–76–555 in Croatia ⊕ www.
croatiaairlines.hr. **Czech Airlines** (CSA).
☎ 212/223–2365 ⊕ www.csa.cz. **Delta
Airlines** ☎ 800/241–4141 ⊕ www.delta.
com. **KLM Royal Dutch Airlines** ☎ 800/225–
2525 ⊕ www.klm.com. **LOT Polish Airlines**
☎ 800/223–0593 ⊕ www.lot.com. **Lufthansa**
☎ 800/645–3880 ⊕ www.lufthansa.com.
United Airlines ☎ 800/538–2929 ⊕ www.
united.com. **USAirways** ☎ 800/622–1015
⊕ www.usairways.com.

EUROPE-BASED DISCOUNT AIRLINES
Information EasyJet ⊕ www.easyjet.com.
German Wings ☎ 870/252–1250 ⊕ www.
germanwings.com. **Ryanair** ☎ 090/6270–5656
in U.K., 353/1–249–7791 worldwide ⊕ www.
ryanair.com. **Wizzair** ☎ 48/22351–9499 in
Poland ⊕ www.wizzair.com.

■ BOAT AND FERRY TRAVEL

Several companies run ferries from Italy to
Croatia. The most popular route, which is
offered by all ferry services, is Ancona to
Split. Jadrolinija also runs services from
Bari to Dubrovnik and from Ancona to
Zadar. From June to September, SNAV
runs a daily high-speed catamaran service
between Ancona and Split. Jadrolinija and
SEM are based in Rijeka and Split, respec-
tively. SNAV is based in Ancona.

From early March to late October the
Prince of Venice hydrofoil makes regularly scheduled trips between Venice
and the western coast of Istria, including
Poreč, Rovinj, and Pula.

Information Jadrolinija. The Croatian
national passenger boat carrier. Runs most
ferries and lines. ☎ 051/211–444 ⊕ www.
jadrolinija.hr. *Prince of Venice* ✉ Obala M. Tita
4, Poreč, Croatia ☎ +385 52/451–200 ⊕ www.
adriatic-lines.com. **SNAV.** Italian Croatia-bound
operator. ☎ 071/207–6116 in Ancona, Italy
⊕ www.snav.it.

■ BUS TRAVEL

Bus travel in Croatia is inexpensive and
efficient. During the high season the worst
you'll have to put up with is crowded
buses. Most buses heading out to tourist sites like Plitvice National Park will be
air-conditioned, but ask before you buy
your ticket, especially if it's a blistering
hot day. Buses from Zagreb to the coast
get booked up quickly in the summer,
so once you know your travel dates you
should purchase your ticket. The bus is
the best option if you are traveling from
Zagreb to Slavonia and you don't like the
train times. Croatian timetables can be
found online, but the websites are mostly
in Croatian.

**Bus Information Autobusni kolodvor
Zagreb** ⊕ www.akz.hr.

■ CAR TRAVEL

In Croatia having a car certainly gives
you greater mobility in rural areas on the
mainland but causes endless complica-
tions if you plan to go island-hopping.
In high season cars can wait for hours to
board ferries even if you have made reservations. In addition, parking in coastal
resorts is very restricted, and there are
tolls on all highways in the country.
Depending on where you plan to go, it
might be a better idea to rent a car only
on those days when you need one.

GASOLINE

In Croatia, most gas stations are open
daily from 6 to 8; from June through
September, many stations are open until
10. In the bigger cities and on main international roads, stations offer 24-hour

service. All pumps sell Eurosuper 95, Eurosuper 98, and Eurodiesel.

PARKING

In Croatia the historic centers of walled medieval towns along the coast (Split, Trogir, Hvar, Korčula, and Dubrovnik) are completely closed to traffic, putting heavy pressure on the number of parking spaces outside the fortifications. Most towns mark parking spaces with a blue line and a sign denoting time restrictions. Buy a ticket at the closest parking machine and leave it in the front window. Make sure to have change on you because not all parking machines takes bills or cards.

ROAD CONDITIONS

In Croatia the coastal route from Rijeka to Dubrovnik is scenic but tiring; it can be notoriously slippery when wet. The new E6 highway that links Zagreb with Rijeka, Zadar, and Split is fast and has frequent, well-maintained rest stops. During winter, driving through the inland regions of Gorski Kotar and Lika is occasionally made hazardous by heavy snow. It's advisable not to take a car to the islands, but if you do decide to drive, remember that the roads are narrow, twisty, and unevenly maintained.

ROADSIDE EMERGENCIES

In case of a breakdown, your best friend is the telephone. Try contacting your rental agency or the appropriate national breakdown service.

Emergency Services Croatia. The Croatian Automobile Club offers 24/7 road assistance. ☏ 987 ⊕ www.hak.hr.

RULES OF THE ROAD

Croatians drive on the right and follow rules similar to those in other European countries. Speed limits are 50 kph (30 mph) in urban areas, 80 kph (50 mph) on main roads, and 130 kph (80 mph) on motorways. Seatbelts are compulsory. The permitted blood-alcohol limit is 0.05%; drunken driving is punishable and can lead to severe fines.

DRIVING TIMES

If your goal is to spend time in Zagreb and then head to the coast, traveling by car is the most efficient way to travel in Croatia. However, if your coastal city of choice is Split, Pula, Zadar or Dubrovnik, then a flight to the local airport will save time. The new E65 highway connecting Zagreb to Rijeka, Zadar, and Split is the fastest route to Kvarner and Central Dalmatia. Zagreb is not yet fully linked with Dubrovnik by highway, so part of that drive will be on the single-lane *Magistrala,* which can be quite busy in high season. The bus system is the second-best option, as there is bus service to just about every seaside town (and remote village) in the Croatia. Train travel to the coast is the poorest option, because there is very little service to southern Dalmatia at all; however, if your trip to Croatia is mostly inland, then train travel is a reasonably good option.

TRAVEL TIMES FROM ZAGREB BY CAR		
Zadar	3 hours	285 km (177 miles)
Pula	3.5 hours	264 km (164 miles)
Rijeka	2 hours	160 km (99 miles)
Split	4 hours	408 km (253 miles)
Dubrovnik	7.5 hours	550 km (341 miles)
Ljubljana	1.75 hours	140 km (87 miles)
Maribor	1.75 hours	115 km (71 miles)

Ask the local tourist board about hotel and local transportation packages that include tickets to major museum exhibits or other special events.

CAR RENTAL

When you reserve a car, ask about cancellation penalties, taxes, drop-off charges (if you're planning to pick up the car in one city and leave it in another), and surcharges (for being under or over a certain age, for additional drivers, or for driving across state or country borders or beyond a specific distance from your point of rental). All these things can add substantially to your costs. Request car seats and extras such as GPS when you book.

As a general rule, rates are better if you book in advance or reserve through a rental agency's website. There are other reasons to book ahead, though: for popular destinations, during busy times of the year, or to ensure that you get certain types of cars (vans, SUVs, exotic sports cars).

Make sure that a confirmed reservation guarantees you a car. Agencies sometimes overbook, particularly for busy weekends and holiday periods.

Traveling by car is a good way to see Croatia, giving you the freedom to flee a crowded seaside beach and take refuge in the relatively unpopulated interior if the mood strikes you. Excursions to the national parks are best done by car so that you can take in all the sites, not just the ones the tour bus shows you. Highways are well maintained, and you can avoid the lines at toll booths by going to the card-only booths.

Croatia uses the kuna. Toll roads in Croatia will accept both euros and kuna but not U.S. dollars, so make sure you have local cash or any major credit card on hand before you get on the highway. Tolls on Croatia's new highways can add up. If driving on local roads to avoid tolls and take in the scenery, make sure you have a map or a navigator because signs sometimes can be ambiguous. The main artery along the Croatian coast—the Magistrala—can come to a standstill on summer weekends, so traveling between popular coastal destinations is best done on weekdays when there's less turnover in package vacations. A new highway from Zagreb to Zadar and Split was completed in 2005; it will also take you halfway down toward Dubrovnik.

Unfortunately, rental cars in Croatia are expensive. Even if you rent locally, companies charge a daily and weekly rate that is generally higher than in most American cities. For an economy car (Opel Corsa or Renault Twingo) you're likely to pay upward of $50 per day even more if you need an automatic transmission. Most companies are represented in the main tourist areas and airports, but you'll do best to look at options online before the trip. The easiest way to book a rental car from abroad is on the Internet.

In Croatia an International Driver's Permit is not necessary to rent a car from a major agency; a valid driver's license is all you'll need. If you intend to drive across a border (as you must do if you drive from Dubrovnik to southern Dalmatia, crossing briefly through Bosnia-Herzegovina) ask about restrictions on driving into other countries. The minimum age required for renting is usually 21 or older, and some companies also have maximum ages; be sure to inquire when making your arrangements.

CAR-RENTAL INSURANCE

Everyone who rents a car wonders whether the insurance that the rental companies offer is worth the expense. No one—including us—has a simple answer. It all depends on how much regular insurance you have, how comfortable you are with risk, and whether money is an issue.

If you own a car, your personal auto insurance may cover a rental to some degree, though not all policies protect you abroad; always read your policy's fine print. If you don't have auto insurance, then seriously consider buying the collision- or loss-damage waiver (CDW or LDW) from the car-rental company, which eliminates your liability for damage to the car. Some credit cards offer CDW coverage, but it's usually supplemental to your own insurance and rarely covers SUVs, minivans, luxury models, and the like. If your coverage is secondary, you may still be liable for loss-of-use costs from the car-rental company. But no credit-card insurance is valid unless you use that card for *all* transactions, from reserving to paying the final bill. All companies exclude car rental in some countries, so be sure to find out about the destination to which you are traveling.

Some rental agencies require you to purchase CDW coverage (known as KASKO insurance locally); many will even include it in quoted rates. All will strongly encourage you to buy CDW—possibly implying that it's required—so be sure to ask about such things before renting. In most cases it's cheaper to add a supplemental CDW plan to your comprehensive travel-insurance policy (⇨ *Trip Insurance under Essentials*) than to purchase it from a rental company. That said, you don't want to pay for a supplement if you're required to buy insurance from the rental company.

In Croatia, quotes include CDW and theft insurance, but expect prices to be on the steep side during the high season. A compact car with both CDW and theft insurance costs about €100 for 24 hours in Croatia if you rent in July or August. Car-rental agencies can be found at airports and major tourist destinations, but make sure to check prices online first as this is where the best deals are found.

You can decline the insurance from the rental company and purchase it through a third-party provider such as Travel Guard (⊕ *www.travelguard.com*)—$9 per day for $35,000 of coverage. That's sometimes just under half the price of the CDW offered by some car-rental companies.

∎ CRUISE TRAVEL

Several Croatian ports, including Dubrovnik, Split, Hvar, and Korčula are common port calls for Eastern Mediterranean cruises. Small ships cruise up and down the country's coastline. ⇨ *For more information on cruising in Croatia, see "Sailing and Cruising in Croatia" in Chapter 1, Experience Croatia.*

∎ TRAIN TRAVEL

In Croatia, Zagreb is connected to Rijeka and Split by rail, but there is no line south of Split to Dubrovnik. International services run from Zagreb to the European cities of Ljubljana, Budapest, Belgrade, Vienna, Munich, Berlin, and Venice.

The "Zone D" Interail pass is valid for Croatia for EU residents, but Eurail is not.

ESSENTIALS

▌ ACCOMMODATIONS

If your experience of Croatia is limited to Zagreb, you may be pleasantly surprised by hotel standards, which in most cases are as high as those in Western Europe. Many properties are new or recently renovated, so most rooms are equipped with modern amenities like Wi-Fi and cable TV.

Outside major cities, hotels and inns are a bit more hit or miss. Sometimes countryside hotels can be rustic but chic, sometimes they can be downright grim, with 30-year-old bathroom fixtures. Checking out a property's website will usually give you some idea. Sadly, you'll still find huge, impersonal Yugoslavia-era concrete boxes, although most have been renovated thoroughly on the inside. In Croatia a room in a private home will almost always be the cheapest option; acceptable rooms are fairly easy to find.

In Zagreb, expect to pay higher prices for hotels, on par with those of Western Europe. Reservations are vital if you plan to visit the capitals, Istria, Dalmatia, or Plitvice National Park during the summer season. Elsewhere in the Croatian countryside, reservations can be made a day or two in advance.

The lodgings we list are the cream of the crop in each price category. We always list the facilities that are available, but we don't specify whether they cost extra; when pricing accommodations, always ask what's included and what costs extra. Properties are assigned price categories based on the range from their least-expensive standard double room at high season (excluding holidays) to the most expensive.

Most hotels and other lodgings require you to give your credit-card details before they will confirm your reservation. If you don't feel comfortable emailing this information, ask if you can fax it (some places even prefer faxes). However you book, get confirmation in writing and have a copy of it handy when you check in.

CATEGORY	COST IN KUNA	COST IN EUROS
$$$$	over 1,650 Kn	over €225
$$$	1,301 Kn–1,650 Kn	€176–€225
$$	925 Kn–1,300 Kn	€125–€175
$	under 925 Kn	under €125

Hotel prices are for two people in a double room in high season, excluding taxes and service charges.

Be sure you understand the hotel's cancellation policy. Some places allow you to cancel without any kind of penalty—even if you prepaid to secure a discounted rate—if you cancel at least 24 hours in advance. Others require you to cancel a week in advance or penalize you the cost of one night. Small inns and B&Bs are most likely to require you to cancel far in advance. Most hotels allow children under a certain age to stay in their parents' room at no extra charge, but others charge for them as extra adults; find out the cutoff age for discounts.

APARTMENT AND HOUSE RENTALS

In Croatia, villa rentals are becoming more popular, particularly in Istria, where some pretty medieval stone houses have been converted into high-end rental properties. Apartment rentals of mixed quality are common all over the coast. Croatia has a well-organized network of independent apartment owners who rent their properties. Often the owners live in a nearby dwelling, so are on hand to get involved if a problem arises. Apartments can be found both in popular destinations like Dubrovnik and Hvar as well as remote islands such as Vis. It's always best to see photos before renting a property for a week or longer.

Croatia Specialists Adriatica.net. Adriatica. net, a Web-based agent, rents villas as well as fully functional lighthouses in Croatia. ☎ *01/241–5611* ⊕ *www.adriatica.net.* **Vintage Travel.** Vintage Travel, a U.K.-based company, specializes in Croatian villa rentals, particularly in Istria. ⊕ *www.vintagetravel.co.uk.*

▌ COMMUNICATIONS

INTERNET

Wi-Fi service has become indispensable in Croatia and you will have to be on an island pretty far out or way in the hinterlands of Lika or Slavonia not to find some signal. Most of the bigger cities (Zagreb, Rijeka, Split, Dubrovnik) even offer free Wi-Fi in the busiest city zones, but most coffee shops, restaurants, and hotels will offer complimentary reception to their guests and patrons.

PHONES

The good news is that you can now make a direct-dial telephone call from virtually any point on earth. The bad news? You can't always do so cheaply. Calling from a hotel is almost always the most expensive option; hotels usually add huge surcharges to all calls, particularly international ones. In some countries you can phone from call centers or even the post office. Of course, the cheapest and easiest way to talk internationally is via smartphones: download an app like Skype or Viber and talk away for free wherever there is Wi-Fi coverage. If using your data plan, make sure to check international roaming charges with your operator as these can be very steep.

Area and country codes are as follows: Croatia (385), Dubrovnik (20), Split (21), Zagreb (1), Rijeka (51), Pula and Istria (52).

CALLING WITHIN CROATIA

To make a local call in Croatia, dial the area code (if you are not already in that area) followed by the number you wish to reach.

Contacts Local Directory Assistance ☎ *988.*

CALLING OUTSIDE CROATIA

To make an international call out of Croatia, dial "00," then the appropriate country code (Australia 61; Canada 1; United States 1; and United Kingdom 44).

The country code for the United States is 1.

Contacts Croatia International Directory Assistance ☎ *902.*

Access Codes MCI WorldPhone ☎ *0800/220–112 in Croatia* ⊕ *www.mci.com.* **Sprint International Access** ☎ *0800/220– 113 in Croatia* ⊕ *www.sprint.com.*

MOBILE PHONES

If you have a multiband phone (some countries use different frequencies than what's used in the United States) and your service provider uses the world-standard GSM network (as do T-Mobile, AT&T, and Verizon), you can probably use your phone abroad. Roaming fees can be steep, however: 99¢ a minute is considered reasonable. And overseas you normally pay the toll charges for incoming calls. It's almost always cheaper to send a text message than to make a call, since text messages have a very low set fee (often less than 5¢).

If you just want to make local calls, consider buying a new SIM card (note that your provider may have to unlock your phone for you to use a different SIM card) and a prepaid service plan in the destination. You'll then have a local number and can make local calls at local rates. If your trip is extensive, you could also simply buy a new cell phone in your destination, as the initial cost will be offset over time.

If you travel internationally frequently, save one of your old mobile phones or buy a cheap one on the Internet; ask your cell phone company to unlock it for you, and take it with you as a travel phone, buying a new SIM card with pay-as-you-go service in each destination.

Contacts Cellular Abroad. Cellular Abroad rents and sells GSM phones and sells SIM cards that work in many countries. ☎ *800/287–5072* ⊕ *www.cellularabroad.com.* **Mobal.** Mobal rents mobiles and sells GSM phones (starting at $29) that will operate in 170 countries. Per-call rates vary throughout the world. ☎ *888/888–9162* ⊕ *www.mobal.com.* **Planet Fone.** Planet Fone rents cell phones, but the per-minute rates are expensive. ☎ *888/988–4777* ⊕ *www.planetfone.com.*

▌CUSTOMS AND DUTIES

You're always allowed to bring goods of a certain value back home without having to pay any duty or import tax. But there's a limit on the amount of tobacco and liquor you can bring back duty-free, and some countries have separate limits for perfumes; for exact figures, check with your customs department. The values of so-called "duty-free" goods are included in these amounts. When you shop abroad, save all your receipts, as customs inspectors may ask to see them as well as the items you purchased. If the total value of your goods is more than the duty-free limit, you'll have to pay a tax (most often a flat percentage) on the value of everything beyond that limit.

As with most European countries, you can import duty-free 200 cigarettes, 1 liter of spirits, and 2 liters of wine into Croatia. Foreign citizens can bring personal items into the country without paying customs taxes.

LOCAL DO'S & TABOOS

GREETINGS
Greetings are an important way to begin any conversation with a local. *Dobar dan/ Dobro večer* (Good day/evening in Croatian) will ease any tensions there might be when you need to complain about a service or make an unusual request. Locals greet each other frequently throughout the day, in the elevator, upon entering a shop, and when asking for directions among other times.

OUT ON THE TOWN
Smoking is still popular in Croatia, but allowed only in outdoor spaces and establishments with special ventilation systems installed.

LANGUAGE
Try to learn a little of the local language. Even just mastering a few basic words is bound to make chatting with the locals more rewarding. Croatia's official language is Croatian, a Slavic language that uses the Latin alphabet. In Istria signs are posted in both Croatian and Italian, and many towns and villages have two names (one Croatian, one Italian). Throughout the country, English is widely spoken by people working in tourism, as are German and Italian.

U.S. Information **U.S. Customs and Border Protection** ⊕ *www.cbp.gov.*

▌ EATING OUT

Food in Croatia varies by region. You'll find some very good restaurants in Zagreb and the coast and some mediocre ones in the interior. Fish is always a good bet here, local calamari and sea bass being real treats for the visitor. Truffle season in Istria is in late October, and that delicacy can be found on virtually every Istrian menu then.

Pizza in Croatia is available in just about every city, town, or village. This is most often served at a sit-down restaurant, making it a good choice for both families and vegetarians. It's usually served one pie per person, not by the slice. In general, pizza in Croatia is freshly baked, thin-crusted, and delicious. They come with toppings like local ham and mushrooms, but expect more exotic things like pineapple, tuna, and frozen peas as well. The classic *margherita* (plain cheese) is always available. *For information on food-related health issues, see Health below.*

MEALS AND MEALTIMES

As the working day begins early here (with some offices opening as early as 7:30 am on weekdays), you'll find cafés open early as well. Lunch is usually served between noon and 3 in restaurants, and dinner is most often served after 7 or so. In the height of the tourist season at the coast, restaurants may stay open later (after 10) to handle the volume. *Bifes* (stand-up take-out places) are open most of the day and serve both hot and cold food. Around 4 pm in Zagreb you'll notice people filling up coffee shops for an afternoon fix of caffeine and perhaps some cake.

Even most basic lodgings in Croatia include some kind of breakfast (*doručak* in Croatian) in the room rate. Savor it; breakfast outside your hotel may be limited to a small melted ham and cheese sandwich (known as a *toast*) in a café. Later in the morning, you can wander into

a cake shop (*slastičarna* in Croatian) for a coffee and slice of cake. You may also find a *burek* (savory meat- or cheese-filled pastry) for breakfast at one of the streetside vendors near high traffic areas. Also be on a lookout for *marendas,* a light pre-made lunch typically served from 10:30 until 12:30 for people on their lunch break. These can be local and affordable meals. Lunch (*ručak* in Croatian) is the main meal for many locals; it usually includes hot food and perhaps a soup. In major cities there are now such lighter offerings as salads and pastas; you can sometimes find a few sandwich shops. On the coast you find grilled meats available throughout the day at snack bars near the beaches. Dinner (*večera* in Croatian) is usually taken in a restaurant (*restoran* in Croatian) and tends to be a bit more formal than in the United States. Meals often begin with soup, followed by grilled meat or fish, and dessert. The exception is at the coast, where lively, outdoor casual restaurants are the norm.

Unless otherwise noted, the restaurants listed in this guide are open daily for lunch and dinner.

CATEGORY	COST IN KUNA	COST IN EUROS
$$$$	over 80 Kn	over €10
$$$	61 Kn–80 Kn	€9–€10
$$	35 Kn–60 Kn	€5–€8
$	under 35 Kn	under €5

Restaurant prices are for a main course at dinner.

PAYING

Credit cards are becoming more and more accepted, but it's a good idea to ask before you order, just in case. ATM machines are found in abundance on the Croatian coast, as well as in Zagreb, so you can usually ensure that dinner goes on as planned. Tips should not be included in the bill, so scrutinize any bill that appears to add one. If service has been good, a

10% to 15% gratuity will be appreciated by the waitstaff.

RESERVATIONS AND DRESS

Regardless of where you are, it's a good idea to make a reservation if you can. We only mention them specifically when reservations are essential (there's no other way you'll ever get a table) or when they are not accepted. For popular restaurants, book as far ahead as you can (often 30 days), and reconfirm as soon as you arrive. (Large parties should always call ahead to check the reservations policy.) We mention dress only when men are required to wear a jacket or a jacket and tie.

WINES, BEER, AND SPIRITS

Wine is produced in Croatia and enjoyed regularly with meals. Croatia consumes more than they produce, so tasting some vintages here is a good idea since you're unlikely to find them at home. Croatia produces wine in Istria, some parts of Slavonia, and most of the Dalmatian coast, especially the Pelješac peninsula.

Cocktails are becoming popular as an aperitif but only in trendy places catering to a stylish and perhaps foreign crowd. The traditional aperitif in this part of the world is *rakija*, a fruit or herbal spirit made in abundance. It's fairly cheap to buy and varies greatly in quality. The fruit varieties (pear, blueberry, plum) are drinkable enough as an aperitif; the herbals are a bit rough going down. Many establishments brew their own with great pride. If you're staying in a family-run pension, trying some of the home brew is an instant icebreaker.

█ ELECTRICITY

Electricity in Croatia is 220 volts; the country uses standard European plugs with two round prongs.

Consider making a small investment in a universal adapter, which has several types of plugs in one lightweight, compact unit. Most laptops and mobile phone chargers are dual voltage (i.e., they operate equally

well on 110 and 220 volts), so require only an adapter. These days the same is true of small appliances such as hair dryers. Always check labels and manufacturer instructions to be sure. Don't use 110-volt outlets marked "for shavers only" for high-wattage appliances such as hair dryers.

Contacts Steve Kropla's Help for World Traveler's. Steve Kropla's Help for World Traveler's has information on electrical and telephone plugs around the world. ⊕ *www.kropla. com.* **Walkabout Travel Gear.** Walkabout Travel Gear has a good coverage of electricity under "adapters." ⊕ *www.walkabouttravel gear.com.*

█ EMERGENCIES

Embassy in Croatia U.S. Embassy ✉ *Ulica Thomasa Jeffersona 2, Zagreb, Croatia* ☎ *01/661–2300* ⊕ *www.usembassy.hr.*

█ HEALTH

Water is safe for drinking throughout Croatia. EU countries have reciprocal health-care agreements with Croatia, entitling those nationals to medical consultation for a basic minimum fee. Citizens from outside the EU have to pay in accordance with listed prices. Most doctors speak some English.

OVER-THE-COUNTER REMEDIES

In Croatia, over-the-counter medications are sold in pharmacies, which are open until 6 or 7 pm on weekdays and 1 or 2 pm on Saturday. In each town there is usually a 24-hour pharmacy for emergencies. Most European pharmacists speak a word or two of English or German, but you're better off asking for a remedy by its medical name (ibuprofen) than its brand name (Advil). Pharmacies don't have a lot of open shelf space for goods, so you will have to ask the pharmacist for what you want. In both countries paracetemol (and its brand name Panadol) is more recognized than acetaminophen (and the brand name Tylenol) for basic pain relief. Claritin, the allergy relief medication, is sold in Croatia at the pharmacy by that name. Many products that Americans would normally find in their local drugstore—cough syrup, diaper cream, cough drops, muscle cream, and vitamins, to name a few—must be bought in the pharmacy in Croatia. While this system is inconvenient if you get an allergy attack in the middle of the night, the upside is that prices are kept down by the government, so many things will be a fraction of the cost at home. The word for pharmacy in Croatia is *ljekarna,* but stick to the equally understood *apoteka.*

SHOTS AND MEDICATIONS

If you travel a lot internationally—particularly to developing nations—refer to the CDC's *Health Information for International Travel* (aka Traveler's Health Yellow Book). Info from it is posted on the CDC website (⊕ *www.cdc.gov/travel/yb*), or you can buy a copy from your local bookstore for $24.95.

Health Warnings National Centers for Disease Control & Prevention (*CDC*) ☎ *877/394–8747 international travelers' health line* ⊕ *www.cdc.gov/travel.* **World Health Organization** (*WHO*) ⊕ *www.who.int.*

▌ HOURS OF OPERATION

In Croatia business hours are from 8:30 to 4. Banks are open in all the main cities weekdays from 8 to 7, and on Saturday from 8 am to noon; in smaller towns banks have shorter hours and are often closed during lunchtime. Post offices are open weekdays 7 to 7, and on Saturday from 7 to noon; in smaller towns post offices are open shorter hours, sometimes only in the morning. During the high tourist season (June through September), post offices are generally open until 8 pm, including Saturday. In Zagreb shops and department stores are open weekdays 8 to 8, and on Saturday from 8 to 1. Malls and shopping centers are typically open 9 to 8, seven days a week. Along the coast most shops are open weekdays from 8 to 1 and 5 to 8, Saturday from 8 to 1. On the islands hours vary greatly from place to place, but usually at least one general store will be open Monday through Saturday for essentials.

HOLIDAYS

In Croatia, national holidays include the following: January 1 (New Year's Day); January 6 (Epiphany); Easter Sunday and Monday; May 1 (May Day); Corpus Christi (40 days after Easter); June 22 (Anti-fascist Day); August 5 (National Thanksgiving Day); August 15 (Assumption), October 8 (Independence Day), November 1 (All Saints' Day), December 25 and 26 (Christmas).

▌ MAIL

From Croatia, airmail letters and postcards take about five days to reach other European countries and two weeks to get to Australia, Canada, and the United States. To send a post card costs 3.50 Kn to Europe, 5 Kn to the United States. A letter costs 5 Kn to Europe, 7.30 Kn to the United States.

▌ MONEY

Costs for goods and services are slightly cheaper than those of Western Europe, mostly because Croatia is not on the euro. Notable exceptions are public transportation, alcohol, and cigarettes, all of which are considerably cheaper in Croatia than elsewhere in Western Europe. Groceries can be expensive at shops on the islands, so if you've rented an apartment for a week or more, consider buying some staples at one of the hypermarkets in a bigger city.

ITEM	AVERAGE COST
Cup of Coffee	$1.50
Glass of Wine	$4.00
Glass of Beer	$2.25
Sandwich	$3.00
1-Mile Taxi Ride in Capital City	$4.00
Museum Admission	$2–$4

Based on an exchange rate of 5.4 Kn to US$1, effective at the time of writing.

Prices throughout this guide are given for adults. Substantially reduced fees are almost always available for children, students, and senior citizens.

U.S. banks seldom have Croatian currency on hand, and it may take as long as a week to order. If you're planning to exchange funds before leaving home, don't wait till the last minute.

ATMS AND BANKS

Your own bank will probably charge a fee for using ATMs abroad; the foreign bank you use may also charge a fee. Nevertheless, you'll usually get a better rate of exchange at an ATM than you will at a currency-exchange office or even when changing money in a bank. And extracting funds as you need them is a safer option than carrying around a large amount of cash.

PIN numbers with more than four digits are not recognized at ATMs in many countries. If yours has five or more, remember to change it before you leave. In Croatia ATMs are now found throughout the country, islands included.

CREDIT CARDS

Throughout this guide, the following abbreviations are used: **AE**, American Express; **DC**, Diners Club; **MC**, MasterCard; and **V**, Visa.

It's a good idea to inform your credit-card company before you travel, especially if you're going abroad and don't travel internationally very often. Otherwise, the credit-card company might put a hold on your card owing to unusual activity—not a good thing halfway through your trip. Record all your credit-card numbers—as well as the phone numbers to call if your cards are lost or stolen—in a safe place, so you're prepared should something go wrong. Both MasterCard and Visa have general numbers you can call (collect if you're abroad) if your card is lost, but you're better off calling the number of your issuing bank, because MasterCard and Visa usually just transfer you to your bank; your bank's number is usually printed on your card.

If you plan to use your credit card for cash advances, you'll need to apply for a PIN at least two weeks before your trip. Although it's usually cheaper (and safer) to use a credit card abroad for large purchases (so you can cancel payments or be reimbursed if there's a problem), note that some credit-card companies *and* the banks that issue them add substantial percentages to all foreign transactions, whether they're in a foreign currency or not. Check on these fees before leaving home, so there won't be any surprises when you get the bill.

Before you charge something, ask the merchant whether he or she plans to do a dynamic currency conversion (DCC). In such a transaction the credit-card *processor* (shop, restaurant, or hotel, not Visa or MasterCard) converts the currency and charges you in dollars. In most cases you'll pay the merchant a 3% fee for this service in addition to any credit-card company and issuing-bank foreign-transaction surcharges.

Dynamic currency conversion programs are becoming increasingly widespread. Merchants who participate in them are supposed to ask whether you want to be charged in dollars or the local currency, but they don't always do so. And even if they do offer you a choice, they may well avoid mentioning the additional surcharges. The good news is that you *do* have a choice. And if this practice really gets your goat, you can avoid it entirely thanks to American Express; with its cards, DCC simply isn't an option.

Major credit cards are accepted in most hotels, and a reassuring portion of shops and restaurants.

Reporting Lost Cards American Express ☎ 800/528-4800 in U.S., 336/393-1111 collect from abroad ⊕ www.americanexpress. com. **Diners Club** ☎ 800/234-6377 in U.S., 303/799-1504 collect from abroad ⊕ www. dinersclub.com. **MasterCard** ☎ 800/627-8372 in U.S., 636/722-7111 collect from abroad ⊕ www.mastercard.com. **Visa** ☎ 800/847-2911 in U.S., 410/581-9994 collect from abroad ⊕ www.visa.com.

CURRENCY AND EXCHANGE

The Croatian currency is called the kuna (Kn), which is made up of 100 lipa. The kuna is not yet fully convertible, so you cannot expect to readily buy the currency outside of Croatia or exchange it once outside the country.

Most hotels in Croatia are already priced in euros, but they can only legally accept kuna as payment. You can pay in euros if they also run an exchange service.

For the most favorable rates, change money through banks. Although ATM transaction fees may be higher abroad than at home, ATM rates are excellent because they are based on wholesale rates offered only by major banks. You won't

do as well at exchange booths in airports or rail and bus stations, in hotels, in restaurants, or in stores.

Even if a currency-exchange booth has a sign promising no commission, rest assured that there's some kind of huge, hidden fee. (Oh...that's right. The sign didn't say no *fee*.). And as for rates, you're almost always better off getting foreign currency at an ATM or exchanging money at a bank.

▎PASSPORTS AND VISAS

U.S. citizens do not need visas to enter either Croatia or Slovenia for a typical vacation visit.

No special visas are necessary to travel through Slovenia or Croatia.

U.S. Passport Information U.S. Department of State ☎ 877/487-2778 ⊕ travel.state.gov/ passport.

U.S. Passport and Visa Expediters Ameri- can Passport Express ☎ 800/455-5166, 800/841-6778 ⊕ www.americanpassport.com.

▎RESTROOMS

Public restrooms can be found in most cities in Croatia, usually near high traffic areas like markets or beaches. Where there are permanent facilities, a price is usually posted outside, and an attendant is on hand to accept payment. At some places by the seaside, coin-operated portable toilets are common, especially in the busy summer season. Make sure you have small coins handy on the beach, as most restrooms are operated automatically.

▎SAFETY

Croatia is relatively safe by Western standards, and there are no particular local scams that visitors should be aware of. Violent crime is rare. Be on guard for pickpockets in crowded markets, and don't wander alone down dark streets at night.

Distribute your cash, credit cards, IDs, and other valuables between a deep front pocket, an inside jacket or vest pocket, and a hidden money pouch. Don't reach for the money pouch once you're in public.

TAXES

In Croatia foreigners who spend over 500 Kn in one store on a single day can reclaim PDV (value added tax) return upon leaving the country. To do this, you need to present the receipts and the goods bought at the *carina* (customs) desk at the airport, ferry port, or border crossing on your way out of the country.

When making a purchase, ask for a V.A.T. refund form and find out whether the merchant gives refunds—not all stores do, nor are they required to. Have the form stamped like any customs form by customs officials when you leave the country or, if you're visiting several European Union countries, when you leave the EU. After you're through passport control, take the form to a refund-service counter for an on-the-spot refund (which is usually the quickest and easiest option), or mail it to the address on the form (or the envelope with it) after you arrive home. You receive the total refund stated on the form, but the processing time can be long, especially if you request a credit-card adjustment.

Global Blue is a Europe-wide service with 225,000 affiliated stores and more than 700 refund counters at major airports and border crossings. Its refund form, called a Tax Free Check, is the most common across the European continent. The service issues refunds in the form of cash, check, or credit-card adjustment.

V.A.T. Refunds Global Blue ☎ *1–866/7066– 090* ⊕ *www.globalblue.com.*

TIME

Croatia is on Central European Time (CET), one hour ahead of Greenwich Mean Time and six hours ahead of the Eastern time zone of the United States.

TIPPING

When eating out in Croatia, if you have enjoyed your meal and are satisfied with the service, it is customary to leave a 10% to 15% tip. It is not usual to tip in cafés or bars. Maids and taxi drivers are not usually tipped. Tour guides do receive a tip, especially if they are particularly good. For porters on trains and bellhops at hotels, 5–10 Kn per bag will be appreciated.

TOURS

Guided tours are a good option when you don't want to do it all yourself. You travel along with a group (sometimes large, sometimes small), stay in prebooked hotels, eat with your fellow travelers (the cost of meals sometimes included in the price of your tour, sometimes not), and follow a schedule.

But not all guided tours are an if-it's-Tuesday-this-must-be-Belgium experience. A knowledgeable guide can take you places that you might never discover on your own, and you may be pushed to see more than you would have otherwise. Tours aren't for everyone, but they can be just the thing for trips to places where making travel arrangements is difficult or time-consuming (particularly when you don't speak the language).

Whenever you book a guided tour, find out what's included and what isn't. A "land-only" tour includes all your travel (by bus, in most cases) in the destination, but not necessarily your flights to and from or even within it. Also, in most cases prices in tour brochures don't include fees and taxes. And remember that you'll be expected to tip your guide (in cash) at the end of the tour.

Deluxe Brendan Vacations ☎ *800/421–8446* ⊕ *www.brendanvacations.com.* **Overseas Adventure Travel** ☎ *800/493–6824* ⊕ *www. oattravel.com.*

Super-Deluxe Abercrombie & Kent ☎ *800/554–7016* ⊕ *www.abercrombiekent. com.*

SPECIAL-INTEREST TOURS

BICYCLING AND HIKING

Most airlines accommodate bikes as luggage, provided they're dismantled and boxed.

Contacts Backroads ☎ *800/462–2848* ⊕ *www.backroads.com.* **Butterfield & Robinson** ☎ *800/678–1147* ⊕ *www.butterfield.com.*

FOOD AND WINE TOURS

Contacts Arblaster & Clarke Wine Tours Ltd. ☎ *0173/026–3111 in U.K.* ⊕ *www. winetours.co.uk.*

HISTORY AND ART

Contacts Smithsonian Study Tours and Seminars ☎ *202/357–4700* ⊕ *www. smithsonianjourneys.org.*

YACHTING AND SAILING

Contacts Adriatic Holidays ☎ *+44 01865– 339–481 in U.K.* ⊕ *www.adriaticholidays.co.uk.* **Sail Croatia** ☎ *+44 0/800–193–8289 in U.K.* ⊕ *www.sail-croatia.com.* **Sunsail** ⊕ *www. sunsail.com.*

▮ TRIP INSURANCE

What kind of coverage do you honestly need? Do you even need trip insurance at all? Take a deep breath and read on.

We believe that comprehensive trip insurance is especially valuable if you're booking a very expensive or complicated trip (particularly to an isolated region) or if you're booking far in advance. Who knows what could happen six months down the road? But whether you get insurance has more to do with how comfortable you are assuming all that risk yourself.

Comprehensive travel policies typically cover trip-cancellation and interruption,

letting you cancel or cut your trip short because of a personal emergency, illness, or, in some cases, acts of terrorism in your destination. Such policies also cover evacuation and medical care. Some also cover you for trip delays because of bad weather or mechanical problems as well as for lost or delayed baggage. Another type of coverage to look for is financial default—that is, when your trip is disrupted because a tour operator, airline, or cruise line goes out of business. Generally you must buy this when you book your trip or shortly thereafter, and it's only available to you if your operator isn't on a list of excluded companies.

If you're going abroad, consider buying medical-only coverage at the very least. Neither Medicare nor some private insurers cover medical expenses anywhere outside of the United States (including time aboard a cruise ship, even if it leaves from a U.S. port). Medical-only policies typically reimburse you for medical care (excluding that related to preexisting conditions) and hospitalization abroad, and provide for evacuation. You still have to pay the bills and await reimbursement from the insurer, though.

Expect comprehensive travel insurance policies to cost about 4% to 7% or 8% of the total price of your trip (it's more like 8%–12% if you're over age 70). A medical-only policy may or may not be cheaper than a comprehensive policy. Always read the fine print of your policy to make sure that you are covered for the risks that are of most concern to you. Compare several policies to make sure you're getting the best price and range of coverage available.

▌ VISITOR INFORMATION

In Croatia **Croatian Tourist Board**
☎ *01/455–6455.*

ONLINE RESOURCES

The first place to start to plan a trip to Croatia is the Croatian National Tourist Board's website. In addition to a general overview of the culture and history of the country, it has lots of practical information on accommodations, travel agencies, and events all listed with phone numbers. Then consult Regional Tourist Board sites (for Kvarner, Istria, and Dalmatia) to narrow the focus even further. Plitvice National Park has a comprehensive website with local accommodations links.

Contacts **Croatia National Tourist Board.** An excellent starting place for a broader overview of Croatia. ⊕ *www.croatia.hr.* **Dalmatia Region.** The website for Central Dalmatia. For Southern Dalmatia see *visitdubrovnik.hr* and for Northern Dalmatia: *zadar.hr* ⊕ *www.dalmatia. hr.* **Istria Region** ⊕ *www.istra.hr.* **Kvarner Region** ⊕ *www.kvarner.hr.* **Plitvice National Park** ⊕ *www.np-plitvicka-jezera.hr.*

INDEX

A

Ada, *108–109*
Adventure tours, *269*
Air travel, *354–355*
  Dubrovnik and Southern Dalmatia, 286
  Istria, 121
  Kvarner, 163
  Montenegro, 329
  Split and Central Dalmatia, 236–238
  Zadar and Northern Dalmatia, 203
  Zagreb and environs, 43–45
Akvarij (Dubrovnik), *296*
Akvarij (Rovinj), *139*
Aman Sveti Stefan 🏨 , *341*
Amélie ✕ , *59*
Amfora ✕ , *298*
Amoret Apartments 🏨 , *301*
Apartment and house rentals, *359–360*
Aquarium Poreč, *146*
Aquarium Pula, *130*
Aquarium Umag, *153–154*
Archaeological Museum, *211–212*
Arena, *129*
Arheološki muzej (Nin), *219*
Arheološki Muzej (Slavonia), *98*
Arheološki muzej (Zagreb), *56*
Arsenal (shop), *218*
Art galleries. ⇨ *See* **Museums and galleries**
Art Hotel Kalelarga 🏨 , *216*
Art tours, *368*
Artatore ✕ , *187*
Arts. ⇨ *See* **Nightlife and performing arts**
Aterina ✕ , *319*
ATMs, *365*
Azur ✕ , *298–299*

B

Balbi Arch, *141*
Banks, *365*
Baranja region, *107*
Bars and nightclubs
  Dubrovnik and Southern Dalmatia, 305–306, 321
  Istria, 133
  Kvarner, 174–175
  Split and Central Dalmatia, 253–254, 274
  Zadar and Northern Dalmatia, 216
  Zagreb and environs, 65
Baška, *189*
Batelina ✕ , *132*
Beaches
  Dubrovnik and Southern Dalmatia, 306–307, 312, 314, 316, 321–322, 323, 324
  Istria, 134, 140, 150
  Kvarner, 176, 182, 185, 189
  Montenegro, 338
  Slavonia, 108–109
  Split and Central Dalmatia, 255, 269, 275, 280, 282
  Zadar and Northern Dalmatia, 217, 220, 232
Bell Tower (Dubrovnik), *296*
Bicycling
  Kvarner, 184, 189, 194
  tours, 368
  Zadar and Northern Dalmatia, 217
Bloody Easter, *85*
Boat and ferry travel, *355*
  Dubrovnik and Southern Dalmatia, 288
  Istria, 121
  Kvarner, 163–164
  Montenegro, 329
  Split and Central Dalmatia, 238–239
  Zadar and Northern Dalmatia, 203–204
Boating, *184, 200*
Boškinac ✕ , *231*
Botanički vrt, *56*
Boutique Hotel Marco Polo 🏨 , *280*
Boutique MAR&VAL, *218*
Brač, *265–269*
Bus travel, *355*
  Dubrovnik and Southern Dalmatia, 288–289
  Istria, 121, 123
  Kvarner, 165
  Montenegro, 329–330
  Slavonia, 91
  Split and Central Dalmatia, 239
  Zadar and Northern Dalmatia, 205–206
  Zagreb and environs, 45
Business hours, *330, 364*

C

Cable cars, *292*
Caffe Galerija Lav ✕ , *59*
Čakovec and the Međimurje, *78–81*
Canoeing, *196*
Car travel and rental, *355–358*
  Dubrovnik and Southern Dalmatia, 289
  Istria, 123–124
  Kvarner, 165
  Montenegro, 330
  Slavonia, 91–92
  Split and Central Dalmatia, 239–240
  Zadar and Northern Dalmatia, 206
  Zagreb and environs, 46
Carpe Diem Bar, *274*
Carpe Diem Beach, *275*
Casinos, *80*
Castelletto 🏨 , *311*
Castles, *75, 79–80, 171*
Čatovića Mlini ✕ , *340*
Cave Bar More, *305*
Caves
  Dubrovnik and Southern Dalmatia, 323
  Istria, 147
  Kvarner, 192
  Split and Central Dalmatia, 276
  Zadar and Northern Dalmatia, 226
Cavtat, *309–312*
Cemeteries, *54, 75*
Central Dalmatia. ⇨ *See* **Split and Central Dalmatia**
Cetina Valley, *263–265*
Cheese, *229*
Chiavalon Olive Oil Tasting Room, *135*
Children, activities for, *30*
Church of Our Lady Mount Carmel, *137*
Church of St. Anthony the Hermit, *186*
Church of St. Roche, *153*
Church of Saints Kosmos and Damian, *137*
Church of the Assumption of the Virgin Mary & St. Pelegrin, *153*
Churches and cathedrals
  Dubrovnik and Southern Dalmatia, 296, 297

Istria, 131, 135–136, 137,
    139–140, 146–147, 151,
    153, 158
Kvarner, 171, 186, 189, 191,
    198
Montenegro, 333, 334
Slavonia, 96, 98, 99, 109, 112,
    113, 116
Split and Central Dalmatia,
    245–246, 256, 261, 270
Zadar and Northern Dalmatia,
    209, 211, 212, 219–220,
    221, 229
Zagreb and environs, 50, 51,
    55–56, 70–71, 74, 76, 79, 80
Čigoć, 87–88
Čikat Bay, 185
Citadel (Krk), 191
Climate, 20
Climbing, 176
City Market (Rijeka), 169
Cocktail Bar Massimo, 321
Communications, 360–361
Cookie Factory Café, The
    ✕, 60
Credit cards, 11, 365–366
Cres, 181–184
Cres Town, 182
Crkva Rođenja Blažene Djevice
    Marije, 159
Crkva sv. Anselma, 219
Crkva sv. Donata, 209, 211
Crkva Sv Eufemije, 139–140
Crkva sv. Križa, 219–220
Crkva Sv. Lovre, 116
Crkva Sv. Lucije, 189, 191
Crkva Sv Luke, 333
Crkva sv. Marije, 212
Crkva Sv Nikole, 333
Crkva sv. Šimuna, 212
Crkva Sveta Marija, 229
Crkva svetag Blaža, 135–136
Crkva svetag Marka, 50
Crkva svetag Vida i Modesta,
    158
Crkva svete Katarine, 51
Crkva svetog Pelagija, 151
Crkva Svetog Vlaha, 296
Croatian Museum of Tourism,
    179
Cruising, 37–40, 330, 334, 358
Cuisine, 31–32, 54, 229
Cuj Winery, 154
Culinary and wine tours, 368
Culture Club Revelin, 305
Currency and exchange, 330,
    366
Customs and duties, 361–362

D
Đakovačka Katedrala, 113
Đakovo, 112–114
Dalmatia. ⇨ See Dubrovnik
    and Southern Dalmatia; Split
    and Central Dalmatia; Zadar
    and Northern Dalmatia
Dalmatino ✕, 299
Damir e Ornella ✕, 151
Dance, 321
Daruvar, 117–118
Daruvarske Toplice, 117–118
Dining. ⇨ See Restaurants
Diocletian, 247
Dioklecijanova Palača, 243
Discounts and deals, 66
Diving
    Dubrovnik and Southern Dal-
        matia, 312, 316, 322
    Istria, 145, 150
    Kvarner, 184, 189, 200
    Split and Central Dalmatia,
        275, 278, 280, 282
    Zadar and Northern Dalmatia,
        217, 220, 223, 225
Dolac open-air market, 51, 66
Dominikanski Samostan (Brač),
    265–266
Dominikanski samostan
    (Dubrovnik), 296
Donji grad (Lower Town;
    Zagreb), 50, 56–58
Dubravkin put ✕, 60
Dubrovnik and Southern Dal-
    matia, 15, 284–324
    climate, 20
    festivals and seasonal events,
        306, 321
    hotels, 290, 301–304, 309, 311,
        313–314, 316, 320–321, 324
    itineraries, 287
    nightlife and the performing
        arts, 304–306, 321
    outdoor activities and sports,
        306–307, 312, 314, 316–317,
        321–322, 324
    price categories, 290
    restaurants, 289–290, 296,
        297–301, 308–309, 310–311,
        313, 315–316, 319–320, 323
    shopping, 307, 322
    timing the visit, 285–286
    tours, 289, 307
    transportation, 286, 288–289
    visitor information, 290
Dubrovnik Cable Car, 292
Dubrovnik Summer Festival,
    306
Duties, 361–362

Dvigrad, 141
Dvor Trakošćan, 73
Dvorac Bežanec ☜, 72

E
Eastern Istria, 158–160
Electricity, 363
Emergencies, 356, 363
Entomološka zbirka, 76
Erdutski Vinogradi, 96
Esplanade Zagreb ☜, 63
Etiquette, 361
Etnografski Muzej, 245
Eufrazijeva Basilica, 146–147

F
Festivals and seasonal events,
    28–29
    Dubrovnik and Southern Dal-
        matia, 306, 321
    Istria, 133–134, 144, 149, 155
    Kvarner, 175, 179
    Slavonia, 100, 107
    Split and Central Dalmatia,
        254, 264, 269, 275
    Zadar and Northern Dalmatia,
        217, 221, 225, 231
    Zagreb and environs, 65–66,
        78, 82, 87
Film
    Dubrovnik and Southern Dal-
        matia, 306
    festivals, 78, 134, 155
    Istria, 134, 155
    Split and Central Dalmatia, 255
    Zagreb and environs, 66, 78
Flightseeing, 189
Floor mosaic, 130–131
Fodor, Eugene, 11
Food tours, 368
Fortica, 159
Fortresses
    Istria, 130, 159
    Kvarner, 191
    Montenegro, 334, 335
    Split and Central Dalmatia, 270
    Zadar and Northern Dalmatia,
        222
    Zagreb and environs, 70, 71, 87
Forum (Pula), 130
Forum (Zadar), 212–213
Franjevačka crkva, 74
Franjevački samostan
    (Dubrovnik), 296–297
Franjevački samostan (Hvar),
    270
Franjevački samostan (Orebić),
    314–315

Franjevački Samostan i Crkva Duha Svetoga, 116
Franjevački Samostan i Crkva sv. Franje Asiškog, 211
Franjevački Samostan i Župa sv Filipa i Jakova, 109
Funicular travel, 56

G

Galerija Branislav Dešković, 266
Galerija Meštrović, 243
Galerija starih i novih majstora, 76
Galerija sv. Toma, 140
Galerija Vidović, 245
Galešnik, 270
Galevac, 222
Gardens
Dubrovnik and Southern Dalmatia, 312
Kvarner, 185–186
Slavonia, 98
Zagreb and environs, 56
Glavna Gradska Vrata, 334
Golf, 67–68
Goli Otok, 191–192
Gornji grad (Upper Town; Osijek), 94
Gornji grad (Upper Town; Zagreb), 50–51, 54–56
Gospa od Škpjela, 339
Gradska groblje, 75
Gradska vijećnica, 74–75
Gradske Zidine (Dubrovnik), 292
Gradske Zidine (Kotor), 334
Gradski muzej (Požega), 115
Gradski Muzej (Split), 245
Gradski Muzej Korčula, 318
Gradski Muzej Vukovar, 107–108
Greeting to the Sun, 213
Grožnjan, 157–158
Guesthouse Maksimilian ⊡, 101
Guvernerova palača, 169, 171

H

Health issues, 363–364
Hiking and walking
Dubrovnik and Southern Dalmatia, 312
Kvarner, 176, 194, 196
tours, 368
History, 85, 304, 344–349
tours, 368

Hodočasnička Crkva Majke Božje Bistričke, 70–71
Hotel Adriatic ⊡, 316
Hotel Bastion ⊡, 216
Hotel More ⊡, 303
Hotel Vestibul Palace ⊡, 252
Hotel Waldinger ⊡, 101–102
Hotels, 359–360
Dubrovnik and Southern Dalmatia, 290, 301–304, 309, 311, 313–314, 316, 320–321, 324
Istria, 126–127, 132–133, 138, 143–144, 149, 152–153, 157, 160
Kvarner, 166–167, 173–174, 180, 183–184, 188, 193, 195, 199
Montenegro, 331, 337–338, 340, 341–342
price categories, 11, 93, 127, 167, 207, 241, 290, 331, 359
Slavonia, 93, 101–102, 105, 110, 112, 114, 117
Split and Central Dalmatia, 240–241, 251–253, 257, 258, 260, 262–263, 264, 268–269, 273–274, 278, 280, 281
Zadar and Northern Dalmatia, 207, 215–216, 220, 223, 225, 227–228, 231
Zagreb and environs, 48, 63–64, 72, 77, 81, 83, 84, 86–87
House rentals, 359–360
Hrvatski muzej naivne umjetnosti, 54
Hrvatsko narodno kazalište, 57
Hrvatsko narodno kazalište Ivan pl. Zajc, 171–172
Hvar, 269–276
Hvar Town, 270

I

Ilok, 110–112
Ilovik, 187
Insurance, 357–358, 368
Internet, 125, 360
Istria, 14, 120–160
festivals and seasonal events, 133–134, 144, 149, 155
hotels, 126–127, 132–133, 138, 143–144, 149, 152–153, 157, 160
internet, 125
itineraries, 122
nightlife and the performing arts, 133–134, 144, 149

outdoor activities and sports, 134, 140, 144–145, 150
price categories, 127
restaurants, 126, 130, 131–132, 136, 139, 141–143, 147, 148–149, 151–152, 154–155, 157, 158, 160
shopping, 134, 145
timing the visit, 121
tours, 125, 156
transportation, 121, 123–134
travel agencies, 125
visitor information, 127
Istralandia, 151
Itineraries, 24–27
Dubrovnik and Southern Dalmatia, 287
Istria, 122
Kvarner, 164
Slavonia, 96
Split and Central Dalmatia, 238
Zadar and Northern Dalmatia, 204
Zagreb and environs, 43

J

Jama Baredine, 147
Jasenovac, 88
Jazz in Lap Festival, 149
Jelsa, 270
Jeny ✕, 279
Josić, 96
Jupiterov Hram, 245

K

Kabola Winery, 154
Kaldanac, 196
Kamenita vrata, 54
Karlovac, 83–84
Kaštel, 130
Kaštelet, 243
Kastav, 173
Katedrala (Korčula), 318
Katedrala Sv Jakova, 256
Katedrala Sv. Stošije, 211
Katedrala Sv. Terezije Avilske, 116
Katedrala Sv Tripuna, 334
Katedrala sv. Vida, 171
Katedrala Sveti Dujam, 245–246
Katedrala Sveti Lovrijenac, 261
Katedrala Sveti Stjepan, 270
Katedrala uznesenja Blazene Djevice Marije, 131
Katedrala Velika Gospa, 297
Kayaking, 307
KIWI ✕, 319

Klapa, *264*
Knežev dvor (Dubrovnik), *292–293*
Knežev dvor (Pag Island), *229*
Kneževa palata, *334, 335*
Knightly Tournament, *87*
Kod Ruže ✕ , *100*
Kompa ✕ , *100–101*
Komrčar Park, *196, 198*
Konkatedrala Sv. Petra i Pavla, *96, 98*
Konoba Bukaleta ✕ , *183*
Konoba Ranjak ✕ , *267–268*
Kopački Rit Nature Park, *103, 105*
Kopnena Vrata (Korčula), *318*
Kopnena Vrata (Zadar), *213*
Korčula, *317–322*
Korčula Waterfront Accommodation 🖫 , *320*
Kornat, *224*
Kornati Islands, *223–225*
Kornati National Park, *223–224*
Korta Katarina Winery, *315*
Kotor, *331–338*
Kotor Old Town, *334*
Kozlović Winery, *154*
Kraneamus Krapina Neanderthal Museum, *72*
Krapina, *72*
Krauthaker, *116*
Krk, *189–195*
Krk Town, *191*
Krka National Park, *258–260*
Kuča Bukovac, *310*
Kuča Marco Pola, *318–319*
Kuča o Batani, *140*
Kula, *186*
Kula Lotrščak, *54–55*
Kumrovec, *71*
Kumrovec Staro selo, *71*
Kutjevačko Vinogorje, *115–116*
Kutjevo, *115*
Kvarner, *14–15, 162–200*
festivals and seasonal events, 175, 179
hotels, 166–167, 173–174, 180, 183–184, 188, 193, 195, 199
itineraries, 164
nightlife and the performing arts, 174–175, 181, 184, 188, 194, 199
outdoor activities and sports, 176, 181, 184, 189, 194–195, 196, 200
price categories, 167

restaurants, 166, 173, 179–180, 183, 187–188, 192–193, 195, 198
shopping, 169, 175–176, 191
timing the visit, 163
transportation, 163–166
visitor information, 167

L

Labin, *158–160*
Lace making, *230*
Language, *350–352, 361*
Lastovo, *281–282*
Lešić Dimitri Palace 🖫 , *321*
Limski kanal, *147–148*
Lipizzan State Stud Farm, *113*
Lisakova kula, *76*
Lodging. ⇨ *See* **Hotels**
Lokrum, *306–307*
Lonjsko Polje, *87–88*
Lonjsko polje Nature Park, *88*
Lopud, *308–309*
Lošinj, *184–189*
Lošinj Marine Education Centre, *186*
Lovran, *179*
Lubenice, *182*
Lungomare, *178*

M

Mail and shipping, *364*
Makarska, *278–280*
Maksimilijan Garden ✕ , *320*
Maksimir Park, *57–58*
Mali Lošinj, *185*
Manita Peć, *226*
Maraschino cherry liqueur, *214*
Marasovići, *226–227*
Marco Polo Museum, *319*
Marija Bistrica, *70–71*
Maritime & Historical Museum of the Croatian Littoral, *171*
Marjan, *246*
Markets
Kvarner, 169
Montenegro, 338
Slavonia, 103
Zagreb and environs, 51, 66, 76
Martin Pescador ✕ , *160*
Marunada (festival), *179*
Matuško Vina, *315*
Mauzolej Obitelji Račić, *310*
Meal times, *362*
Međimurje, the, *78–81*
Medvedgrad, *70*
Memorial Museum Jasenovac, *88*
Meštrovič Atelier, *55*
Miomirisni otoćki vrt, *185–186*

Mirogoj Cemetery, *54*
Mjesto Sjećanja - Vukovar Bolnica, *108*
Mljet, *322–324*
Modra Spilja, *276*
Monasteries
Dubrovnik and Southern Dalmatia, 296–297, 314–315
Montenegro, 340
Slavonia, 109, 116
Split and Central Dalmatia, 265–266, 270
Money matters, *11, 330, 365–366*
Monte ✕ , *142*
Montenegro, *15, 326–342*
business hours, 330
currency, 330
hotels, 331, 337–338, 340, 341–342
outdoor activities and sports, 338
price categories, 331
restaurants, 330–331, 335–337, 340, 341
shopping, 338
telephones, 330
timing the visit, 327, 329
tours, 330
transportation, 329–330
visitor information, 331
Moreška, *321*
Motovun, *155–157*
Motovun Film Festival, *155*
Mount Učka Nature Park, *178–179*
Murter, *223–225*
Museum Marton, *82*
Museum of Ancient Glass, *213*
Museum of Broken Relationships, *51*
Museum of Contemporary Art, *51*
Museums and galleries
Dubrovnik and Southern Dalmatia, 293, 296, 297, 310, 318–319
Istria, 131, 137
Kvarner, 171, 172, 182, 186, 191
Montenegro, 335, 339
Slavonia, 98–99, 107–108, 111, 113, 115
Split and Central Dalmatia, 243, 245, 246, 266
Zadar and Northern Dalmatia, 211–212, 213, 219

Zagreb and environs, 51, 54, 55, 56–57, 72, 76, 79–80, 82, 88
Music
Dubrovnik and Southern Dalmatia, 306
festivals, 78, 144, 149, 175, 225, 231, 254, 275, 306
Istria, 144, 149
Kvarner, 175
Split and Central Dalmatia, 254, 275
Zadar and Northern Dalmatia, 225, 231
Zagreb and environs, 78
Muzej Grad Perasta, *339*
Muzej Grada Iloka, *111*
Muzej grada Rijeke, *172*
Muzej grada Zagreba, *51*
Muzej Hrvatskih Arheološki Spomenika, *246*
Muzej Likovnih Umjetnosti, *98*
Muzej Međimurja, *79–80*
Muzej Mimara, *57*
Muzej Pravoslavne Crkve, *297*
Muzej Slavonije, *98–99*
Muzej za umjetnost i obrt, *57*

N

Nacionalni Park Brijuni, *136–138*
Nacionalni Park Krka, *258–260*
Nacionalni Park Mljeta, *322–323*
Nacionalni Park Plitvička Jezera, *84–87*
Napoleonovog Pozorišta, *335*
Narodni trg (Split), *246–247*
Narodni trg (Zadar), *213*
Našice, *99–100*
Nightlife and performing arts
Dubrovnik and Southern Dalmatia, 304–306, 321
Istria, 133–134, 144, 149
Kvarner, 174–175, 181, 184, 188, 194, 199
Slavonia, 102
Split and Central Dalmatia, 253–255, 264, 274–275
Zadar and Northern Dalmatia, 216–217, 225, 231
Zagreb and environs, 64–66, 78
Niko ✕, *214–215*
Nin, *218–220*
Nin Saltworks, *220*
Northern Dalmatia. ⇨ *See* **Zadar and Northern Dalmatia**
Novigrad, *150–155*

O

Odysseus Cave, *323*
Old town hall (Krk), *191*
Olive oil, *135*
Omiš and the Cetina Valley, *263–265*
Onofrio Fountain, *297*
Opatija, *177–181*
Opatska Riznica, *319*
Orebić, *314–317*
Orlando's Column, *297*
Osijek, *94–103*
Osijek Antiques Market, *103*
Osor, *182*
Osor Archaeological Collection, *182*
Our Lady of the Rock, *334*
Outdoor activities and sports, *37–40*
Dubrovnik and Southern Dalmatia, 306–307, 312, 314, 316–317, 321–322, 324
Istria, 134, 140, 144–145, 150
Kvarner, 176, 181, 184, 189, 194–195, 196, 200
Montenegro, 338
Split and Central Dalmatia, 255, 258, 260, 263, 264–265, 269, 275–276, 278, 280, 282
Zadar and Northern Dalmatia, 217, 220, 223, 228, 232
Zagreb and environs, 67–68

P

Padovec, Ivan, *74*
Pag Island, *228–232*
Pag lace, *230*
Paklenica, *226–228*
Palača Varaždinske županije, *75*
Palaces
Dubrovnik and Southern Dalmatia, 292–293, 298
Kvarner, 169, 171
Montenegro, 334, 335
Split and Central Dalmatia, 243
Zadar and Northern Dalmatia, 229
Palazzo Radomiri ▦ , *337–338*
Paradox ✕, *250*
Park Angiolina, *179*
Park Prirode Biokovo, *279*
Parks
Dubrovnik and Southern Dalmatia, 322–323
Istria, 136–138

Kvarner, *177, 178–179, 196, 198*
Slavonia, 103, 105
Split and Central Dalmatia, 258–260, 279
Zadar and Northern Dalmatia, 221–224, 226–228
Zagreb and environs, 57–58, 84–88
Pašman, *222*
Passports and visas, *366*
Peek + Poke Muzej Djetinjstva, *172*
Pelegrini ✕, *257*
Perast, *338–340*
Performing arts. ⇨ *See* **Nightlife and the performing arts**
Peristil, *247*
Perivoj Krajla Tomislava, *98*
Permanent Exhibition of Religious Art, *212*
Pet Bunara ✕, *215*
Placa, *293*
Plane travel. ⇨ *See* **Air travel**
Plava Laguna, *223–224*
Pod gričkim topom ✕, *59*
Pomorski Muzej, *293*
Pomorski Muzej Crne Gore, *335*
Poreč, *145–150*
Požega, *114–118*
Preko, *222*
Price categories, *11, 365*
hotels, 48, 93, 127, 167, 207, 241, 290, 331, 359
Istria, 127
Kvarner, 167
Montenegro, 331
restaurants, 48, 93, 127, 167, 207, 241, 290, 331, 362
Slavonia, 93
Split and Central Dalmatia, 241
Zadar and Northern Dalmatia, 207
Zagreb and environs, 48
Prijeko Palace ▦ , *303*
Prirodoslovni muzej, *172*
Proskurnjak, Šimunov, *74*
Prvić, *257–258*
Pula, *128–134*
Pustinja Blaca, *266*

R

Rab, *196–200*
Rabac, *158–160*
Rafting, *196*
Restaurants, *362–363*
Dubrovnik and Southern Dalmatia, 289–290, 296,

297–301, 308–309, 310–311,
313, 315–316, 319–320, 323
Istria, 126, 130, 131–132, 136,
139, 141–143, 147, 148–149,
151–152, 154–155, 157,
158, 160
Kvarner, 166, 173, 179–180,
183, 187–188, 192–193,
195, 198
Montenegro, 330–331, 335–
337, 340, 341
price categories, 11, 93, 127,
167, 207, 241, 290, 331, 362
Slavonia, 92–93, 99, 100–101,
105, 109, 114, 117
Split and Central Dalmatia,
240, 246, 247–251, 257,
258, 259–260, 261–262, 264,
267–268, 272–273, 276–277,
279, 281
Zadar and Northern Dalmatia,
207, 214–215, 220, 222–223,
224–225, 227, 230–231
Zagreb and environs, 47–48,
56, 58–62, 70, 72, 77, 81,
82–83, 84, 86
Restrooms, 366
Riječka ulica, 153
Rijeka, 168–176
Risnjak National Park, 177
Rivica ✕, 193
RobiNzooN ✕, 308–309
Roman Mosaics at Risan,
339–340
Roman ruins
Istria, 129–131
Kvarner, 172
Montenegro, 339–340
Split and Central Dalmatia,
245, 247
Zadar and Northern Dalmatia,
212–213, 220
Roman Theater, 131
Rovinj, 138–145

S

Safari Park, 137
Safety issues, 366–367
Sailing, 37–40
Dubrovnik and Southern Dal-
matia, 307, 322
Montenegro, 338
Split and Central Dalmatia,
255, 260, 263, 275–276, 282
tours, 368
St. Blaise, 301
St. John's Fortress, 334
St. Mary's church (Hvar), 270
St. Mary's church (Sali), 221

St. Quirinius, 191
Sali, 221–223
Saljske užance (Donkey Festi-
val), 221
Saltworks, 220
Samobor, 81–83
Samobor Museum, 82
Samoborski fašnik, 82
San Tommaso Winery,
140–141
Saplunara, 323
Sea kayaking, 307
Sea Organ, 211
Shopping
Dubrovnik and Southern Dal-
matia, 307, 322
Istria, 134, 145
Kvarner, 169, 175–176, 191
Montenegro, 338
Slavonia, 103
Split and Central Dalmatia,
255–256, 260
Zadar and Northern Dalmatia,
217–218, 231–232
Zagreb and environs, 66–67, 76
Šibenik, 256–257
Sinagoga, 298
Sisak, 87
Sisak Fortress, 87
Slama festival, 100
Slavoluk Sergijevaca, 130
Slavonia, 14, 90–118
festivals and seasonal events,
100, 107
hotels, 93, 101–102, 105, 110,
112, 114, 117
itineraries, 96
nightlife and the performing
arts, 102
price categories, 93
restaurants, 92–93, 99, 100–
101, 105, 109, 114, 117
shopping, 103
timing the visit, 91
transportation, 91–92
visitor information, 93–94
Sljeme, 68, 70
Smoking, 361
Sokak ✕, 114
Southern Dalmatia. ⇨ See
Dubrovnik and Southern
Dalmatia
Spas, 70, 117–118
Špilja Biserujka, 192
Split and Central Dalmatia, 15,
234–282
climate, 20
festivals and seasonal events,
254, 264, 269, 275

hotels, 240–241, 251–253, 257,
258, 260, 262–263, 264,
268–269, 273–274, 278,
280, 281
itineraries, 238
nightlife and the performing
arts, 253–255, 264, 274–275
outdoor activities and sports,
255, 258, 260, 263, 264–265,
269, 275–276, 278, 280, 282
price categories, 241
restaurants, 240, 246, 247–251,
257, 258, 259–260, 261–262,
264, 267–268, 272–273,
276–277, 279, 281
shopping, 255–256, 260
timing the visit, 235–236
tours, 241, 269
transportation, 236–240
visitor information, 241–242
Spomen Dom Ovčara, 108
Spomen-muzej Biskupa Josipa
Jura Strossmayera, 113
Sponza Palace, 298
Sports. ⇨ See Outdoor activi-
ties and sports
Sports outfitters, 176
Square of the Five Wells,
213–214
Stara Baška, 191
Stara Vrata, 172
Stari grad (Hvar), 270, 272
Stari grad (Pag Island),
229–230
Stari grad (Varaždin), 75
Stari grad Zrinskih, 79–80
Stari Mlini ✕, 336–337
Stari Podrum, 111–112
Statue of Grgur Ninski, 243,
245
Štrigova, 80
Ston, 313–314
Stubičke Toplice, 70
Summer on Stross -
Strossmartre (festival), 65–66
Sušak, 187
Sutivan Sports Rehabilitation
Center, 266
Sveta Marija, 171
Sveta Marija Velika, 198
Sveta Srca Gallery, 131
Sveti Djordje, 340
Sveti Stefan, 341–342
Sveučilišna knjižnica Rijeka,
172
Swimming, 140, 258
Symbols, 11
Synagogues, 298

T

Tavern Tončić ✕, *155, 157*
Taverna Otto ✕, *300–301*
Taxes, *367*
Taxi travel
Dubrovnik and Southern Dalmatia, 289
Split and Central Dalmatia, 240
Zagreb and environs, 46
Tehnički muzej, *56–57*
Telašcica Nature Park, *221–223*
Telephones, *330, 360–361*
Temple of Diana, *220*
Theater buildings, *57, 171–172, 335*
Time zones, *367*
Timing the visit, *20*
Dubrovnik and Southern Dalmatia, 285–286
Istria, 121
Kvarner, 163
Montenegro, 327, 329
Slavonia, 91
Split and Central Dalmatia, 235–236
Zadar and Northern Dalmatia, 203
Zagreb and environs, 43
Tipping, *367*
Titov trg, *159*
Tkalčićeva Street (Zagreb), *55*
Toranj za sat, *335*
Tours, *367–368*
Dubrovnik and Southern Dalmatia, 289, 307
Istria, 125, 156
Montenegro, 330
Split and Central Dalmatia, 241, 269
Zadar and Northern Dalmatia, 209, 228
Zagreb and environs, 47
Tovjerna Sesame ✕, *301*
Train travel, *358*
Istria, 124
Kvarner, 166
Slavonia, 92
Split and Central Dalmatia, 240
Zadar and Northern Dalmatia, 206–207
Zagreb and environs, 46–47
Tram travel, *45*
Tramerka ✕, *180*
Transportation
Dubrovnik and Southern Dalmatia, 286, 288–289
Istria, 121, 123–134

Kvarner, *163–166*
Montenegro, 329–330
Slavonia, 91–92
Split and Central Dalmatia, 236–240
Zadar and Northern Dalmatia, 203–207
Zagreb and environs, 43–47, 56
Trash Film Festival, *78*
Travel agencies, *125*
Trip insurance, *368*
Trg bana Jelačića, *55*
Trg bana Josipa Jelačića, *83*
Trg Kralja Petra Krešimira IV, *229*
Trg kralja Tomislava, *82*
Trg M. Tita, *141*
Trg Marafor, *147*
Trg od Oržja, *335*
Trg Rijecke rezolucije, *171*
Trg Slobode, *153*
Trg Sv. Trojstva (Osijek), *98*
Trg Sv. Trojstva (Požega), *116–117*
Trg Sveti Stjepan, *270*
Trgovački Kasino, *80*
Trica, *102*
Trogir, *261–263*
Trsat, *171*
Trsteno, *312*
Trsteno Arboretum, *312*
Truffles, *156*
Tvrđa, *94*
Tvrdalj, *272*
Tvrđava sv. Mihovila, *222*
Tvrdjava Sv Ivana, *335*

U

Ugljan, *222*
Umag, *153*
Unije, *187*
Uršulinska crkva Rođenja Isusovog, *76*
Uvala Bačvica, *255*

V

Valun, *182*
Varaždin, *73, 75–78*
Varaždin Baroque Evenings, *78*
Vela Placa, *191*
Veli Lošinj, *186*
Veli Zvonik, *198*
Velika Paklenica Canyon, *226*
Veliki Tabor, *71*
Vestibul, *243*
Vidova Gora, *266*
Villa rentals, *126–127*
Vina Dešković, *158*

Vinarija Bartulović, *315*
Vinarija Zdjelarevič ▥, *114*
Vinodol ✕, *62*
Vinoteka Bornstein, *67*
Vis, *276–278*
Visas, *366*
Visitor information, *369*
Dubrovnik and Southern Dalmatia, 290
Istria, 127
Kvarner, 167
Montenegro, 331
Slavonia, 93–94
Split and Central Dalmatia, 241–242
Zadar and Northern Dalmatia, 207
Zagreb and environs, 48–49
Vocabulary, *350–352, 361*
Vodena Vrata, *99*
Vodnjan, *135–136*
Vodnjanka ✕, *136*
Vrata od Pila, *293*
Vrata od Ploča, *293*
Vrbnik, *192*
Vrsar, *148*
Vukovar, *106–110*

W

War Photo Limited, *293, 296*
Watchtower, *141*
Water parks, *151*
Water sports, *269*
Water Tower, *109*
Waterskiing, *195*
Weather, *20*
Westin Zagreb, The ▥, *64*
Windsurfing, *317*
Wine and wineries, *32–36, 363*
Dubrovnik and Southern Dalmatia, 315
Istria, 140–141, 145, 154, 158
Slavonia, 96, 104, 111–112, 115–116
Split and Central Dalmatia, 269
tours, 368
Wine Cellar Krunčići, *145*

Y

Yachting tours, *368*
Yoga, *276*

Z

Zadar and Northern Dalmatia, *15, 202–232*
festivals and seasonal events, 217, 221, 225, 231

hotels, 207, 215–216, 220, 223,
    225, 227–228, 231
itineraries, 204
nightlife and the performing
    arts, 216–217, 225, 231
outdoor activities and sports,
    217, 220, 223, 228, 232
price categories, 207
restaurants, 207, 214–215, 220,
    222–223, 224–225, 227,
    230–231
shopping, 217–218, 231–232
timing the visit, 203
tours, 209, 228
transportation, 203–207
visitor information, 207
Zadar archipelago, 222
Zagreb and environs, 14,
    42–88

climate, 20
excursions from, 68–88
exploring, 50–58
festivals and seasonal events,
    65–66, 78, 82, 87
hotels, 48, 63–64, 72, 77, 81,
    83, 84, 86–87
itineraries, 43
nightlife and the performing
    arts, 64–66, 78
outdoor activities and sports,
    67–68
price categories, 48
restaurants, 47–48, 56, 58–62,
    70, 72, 77, 81, 82–83, 84, 86
shopping, 66–67, 76
timing the visit, 43
tours, 47
transportation, 43–47, 56

visitor information, 48–49
Zagreb Card, 66
Zagrebačka katedrala, 55–56
Zelena Žaba ✕, 105
**Zgrada Napoleonovog
    pozorišta,** 335
Zigante Tartufi, 158
Zlatna Vrata, 243, 245
Zlatni Rat, 269
Zoološki vrt Zagreb, 58
Zoos and animal parks, 58,
    266
Župa Sv. Ivana Kapistrana, 112
Župna crkva sv. Nikole, 76
**Župna crkva sv. Nikole
    Biskupa i franjevački samo-
    stan,** 79
**Župna Crkva Sveta
    Mihovila,** 99

Fodor's CROATIA

Publisher: Amanda D'Acierno, *Senior Vice President*

Editorial: Arabella Bowen, *Editor in Chief*; Linda Cabasin, *Editorial Director*

Design: Tina Malaney, *Associate Art Director*; Chie Ushio, *Senior Designer*; Ann McBride, *Production Designer*

Photography: Jennifer Arnow, *Senior Photo Editor*; Jennifer Romains, *Photo Researcher*

Production: Linda Schmidt, *Managing Editor*; Evangelos Vasilakis, *Associate Managing Editor*; Angela L. McLean, *Senior Production Manager*

Maps: Rebecca Baer, *Senior Map Editor*; David Lindroth, Andrew Murphy, *Cartographers*

Sales: Jacqueline Lebow, *Sales Director*

Marketing & Publicity: Heather Dalton, *Marketing Director*; Katherine Punia, *Publicity Director*

Business & Operations: Susan Livingston, *Vice President, Strategic Business Planning*; Sue Daulton, *Vice President, Operations*

Fodors.com: Megan Bell, *Executive Director, Revenue & Business Development*; Yasmin Marinaro, *Senior Director, Marketing & Partnerships*

Copyright © 2015 by Fodor's Travel, a division of Random House LLC

Writers: Vera Brljevic, Frank Galparsoro, Elizabeth Gowing, Elizabeth Hughes, Robert Komljen, Andrea MacDonald, Armando Chapin Rodríguez, Jadranka Vuković Rodríguez, Ivan Verunica, Sierra Verunica

Editor: Perrie Hartz

Production Editor: Elyse Rozelle

1st edition

ISBN 978–1–101–87803–3

ISSN 2375-2734

SPECIAL SALES

This book is available at special discounts for bulk purchases for sales promotions or premiums. For more information, e-mail specialmarkets@penguinrandomhouse.com

PRINTED IN THE UNITED STATES OF AMERICA

10 9 8 7 6 5 4 3 2 1

ABOUT OUR WRITERS

 Frank Galparsoro & Vera Brljevic are founders of the FrankAboutCroatia Blog, a leading Croatian travel blog. Navigation officer by vocation, and travel writer by profession, Frank traveled to all corners of the world before settling down in Croatia. After she graduated from the University, Vera sailed the high seas, and lived in Canada before returning to her native Croatia where she now works in a hotel industry. They are travelers, writers, trilingual, avid cyclists, coffee addicts, and food and wine enthusiasts.

 Elizabeth Gowing worked as a teacher in inner-city London before moving to Kosovo in 2006, and from there to Albania in 2013. She is co-founder of the Kosovan charity The Ideas Partnership which harnesses the power of volunteers to tackle challenges in the environment, the promotion of cultural heritage and support to Roma communities. She is the translator of three books from Albanian to English and author of *Travels in Blood and Honey; becoming a beekeeper in Kosovo* and *Edith and I; on the trail of an Edwardian traveller in Kosovo*, about inspiring Balkan traveler, Edith Durham.

 After meeting in Bosnia in the aftermath of the Yugoslav wars, **Elizabeth Hughes and Robert Komljen** eventually decided to make their home in Croatia. Born and raised in central Bosnia, Robert is a metallurgic engineer. He finds it ironic that he is the one in the family whose bags are most often packed as he traverses the desserts of the Middle East and the hills of Europe visiting aluminum factories. And although Elizabeth long ago retired her army combat boots, she often draws on her military experience to raise two boys while living in a former communist country that challenges her independent spirit.

 Within ten minutes of her first arrival in Croatia, **Andrea MacDonald**, mesmerized by the stunning old architecture and gorgeous locals, decided to rip up her return ticket and stay. She has since worked at a hostel in Istria learning the proper way to fold bed sheets, spent two summers guiding boat tours around the Dalmatian islands, and wrote a Master's Thesis about her travels around this wonderfully surprising country. These days, she divides her time between her native Canada, leading tour groups around Europe, and searching the rest of the world for a sea as beautiful as the Adriatic.

 Jadranka and Armando Rodríguez have lived in several countries in North America, Asia and Europe, and they are convinced there's no place quite like Croatia. Both scientists by training, Jadranka works at the University of Zagreb as a professor of pharmacy, while Armando provides consulting services to researchers. They run an educational nonprofit foundation for young people that sponsors an annual competition in English communication.

 Sierra and Ivan Verunica are a Seattlite-Croatian couple who met, as passionate travel professionals would, at the border of Chile and Bolivia. They have lived in Western Croatia since 2010, latching onto an opportunity to help develop Croatia and Slovenia as international travel destinations while raising a family on the Adriatic coast. Between their writing and the agency they run, they helped thousands of travelers tune into the eclectic cultural and climatic environment of Western Croatia and Slovenia, and are looking forward to the thousands still to come.